MORAL AWARENESS IN GREEK TRAGEDY

09

DATE DUE FOR RETURN

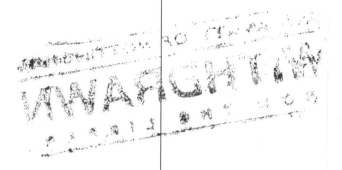

This book may be recalled before the above date.

Moral Awareness in Greek Tragedy

STUART LAWRENCE

OXFORD
UNIVERSITY PRESS

OXFORD

UNIVERSITY PRESS

Great Clarendon Street, Oxford, OX2 6DP,
United Kingdom

Oxford University Press is a department of the University of Oxford.
It furthers the University's objective of excellence in research, scholarship,
and education by publishing worldwide. Oxford is a registered trade mark of
Oxford University Press in the UK and in certain other countries

First Edition published in 2013

Impression: 1

British Library Cataloguing in Publication Data
Data available
Library of Congress Cataloging in Publication Data
Data available
ISBN 978-0-19-965975-3 (Hbk.)
ISBN 978-0-19-965976-0 (Pbk.)

Printed in Great Britain by
MPG Books Group, Bodmin and King's Lynn

I O O68II6B I

Preface

Although one can scarcely attempt the most general discussion of Greek tragedies without some reference to the moral awareness of the principal characters, the subject deserves to be studied in its own right. But before we can do this we need to ponder the implications of analysing the moral consciousness of fictional characters and, more particularly, of doing so in the context of a highly stylized genre and an alien culture. This is the purpose of the two introductory chapters which consider these implications and examine such matters as concepts of the self and the problem of autonomy in the context of the divine intervention that is such a feature of the genre. The succeeding chapters are devoted to individual plays. The focus in each case is a crisis (or crises) faced by a major character. The background to the crisis is examined and in particular any divine involvement or personal responsibility on the part of the character. Moral response is then considered with reference to some key issues which are formulated at the end of the first introductory chapter and brought together in the Conclusion that briefly surveys and compares the performance of the characters under the following headings: moral autonomy and divine intervention; self-definition as individual, type, or in terms of a role; self-redefinition (when provoked by the crisis); intuitive or deliberative moral response; integration of emotions; the influence of others; the agent's morality and the implicit morality of the play; and, finally, moral awareness. The book is addressed primarily to scholars and graduate students, though I hope that undergraduates will find the analyses of specific plays useful.

I turn now to the agreeable task of thanking those who provided help and encouragement. Two Heads of the School of History, Philosophy, and Classics at Massey University, James Watson and Kerry Taylor, strongly urged me to complete a project with which I had been engaged for some considerable time. Graham Zanker, Neil Sewell-Rutter, Sophie Mills, and David Carter all read a number of chapters and offered helpful advice. My thanks also to Hilary O'Shea for her enthusiastic support of the book and to the team at OUP. Finally, my special thanks to Douglas Cairns whose incisive criticism has done much to expand the scope and improve the quality of the book. I am particularly grateful for his unfailing support and encouragement. For the final product, with all its failings, though, I am, of course, wholly responsible—παναίτιος rather than merely μεταίτιος.

The book is dedicated to my dear wife, Susan.

Contents

1

Introduction

The focus of this book is the moral awareness of significant agents in Greek tragedy. By 'moral awareness' I refer to their recognition of moral issues, their ability to reflect on them, and, in some cases, their consciousness of so doing. I shall identify morally charged crises or predicaments and ask a series of morally relevant questions about the way agents respond to these crises. I shall specify and elaborate on these questions near the end of this Introduction; they will inform the detailed discussion of selected plays that makes up the following chapters. Inevitably, some of them have been asked before in the course of interpreting particular plays, but we need a more comprehensive and systematic approach that takes some account of more recent developments in moral philosophy and that will prove interesting and illuminating, not least through an examination of parallels and contrasts ranging over a wide number of plays and taken from all three dramatists. No such study at present exists.

MORALITY: ANCIENT AND MODERN

According to Bernard Gert, 'Morality is an informal public system applying to all rational persons, governing behavior that affects others, and includes what are commonly known as the moral rules, ideals, and virtues and has the lessening of evil or harm as its goal.'[1] Gert argues that '[s]ince moral judgments can be made about all rational persons, it follows that morality is universal and what seem to be different moral systems are simply specifications or variations of a universal morality or moral system.'[2] Gert agrees with Hobbes that 'morality is primarily concerned with the behavior of people insofar as that behavior affects others; it prohibits the kind of conduct that harms others and encourages the kind of conduct that helps them'.[3] Moreover, morality 'is best conceived as a guide to behavior that rational persons put forward to guide the behavior of others, whether or not they plan to follow the guide themselves'.[4] Here we may recall Glaucon's argument in the *Republic* that our chief motive for entering into an agreement with others to act morally or justly (i.e. in accordance with *dikaiosunē*) is our fear that otherwise they will act immorally towards us.[5]

---

[1] Gert (1998) 13.   [2] Ibid. 4.   [3] Ibid. 9.
[4] Ibid.   [5] Plato, *Rep.* 358e–359b.

Now although 'morality applies primarily to behavior that affects the amount of harm suffered by others', it includes also 'behavior that affects only oneself'.[6] In other words, one can have moral obligations to oneself, and this is indeed the primary focus of many of the 'heroic' moral agents of epic and tragedy to the point where they tend to forget that, even in the terms of their own heroic morality, they have obligations to others and in particular to their dependants. This focus on the self is characteristic of the eudaimonistic ethical tradition of Greek philosophy, though it figures also in earlier thought. Since the implicit basis of much Greek ethical thinking is the question 'How can I attain *eudaimonia*?', even if, as is almost invariably the case, part of the answer is to act morally, acting morally is often seen as a kind of responsibility to oneself—a responsibility to act and indeed to be seen to act virtuously. So when the Iliadic Hector regards himself as morally compromised because his failure to heed excellent advice has resulted in the death of many Trojan soldiers, his moral response is not directed away from the self or towards consequences in the form of a resolution to act in order to avoid such an outcome in the future. Instead it is directed towards saving face through an act of courage, even though his courage has in no way been called into question. Moreover, the act of courage he chooses to perform might seem more quixotic than brave since its probable consequence is an even greater number of Trojan casualties. This is because he resolves to face what even to him seems almost certain death at the hands of Achilles, thereby depriving his people of his protection upon which the fate of Troy largely depends.[7] If this face-saving is a moral position, it must be conceived as a moral responsibility to gain or recover honour for oneself; and that is how Hector does conceive it, as can be seen by his rejection of what are obviously competing moral claims. Similarly, the hero of Sophocles' *Ajax* is focused at first entirely on the recovery of his honour, so that the mother of his child has to remind him that he has responsibilities to her, to his son, and to his other dependants—responsibilities he continues largely to ignore. A major moral weakness in tragic agents then is likely to take the form of attributing insufficient weight to the claims of others. The virtues, including heroic courage, are altruistic in that in principle at least they reflect the interests of society rather than those of the virtuous agents themselves. But since virtue is honourable, its practice can easily become a matter of self-interest.

To return to Gert's point about morality being 'a guide to behavior that rational persons put forward to guide the behavior of others, whether or not they plan to follow the guide themselves', we might observe that, while the epic or tragic hero would expect his peers to observe his moral code, he would not expect this of people of lower status or indeed of women. (The moral responsibility which Electra takes upon herself in Sophocles' play many would have considered inappropriate for a woman.) So we have to distinguish here between a commitment to morality as such and adherence to a code on the part of a restricted group.

Since what the Greeks conceived as a moral issue is not in all cases identical to what we would consider one, the question arises as to how to determine what is in fact a moral issue for them. Here we need to be on our guard about Greek words whose English equivalents are such terms as 'good', 'right', and 'ought', the

---

[6] Gert (1998) 12.   [7] Hom. *Il.* 22. 99–110.

application of which is not necessarily moral. (We can say, for example, that if Sophocles' Electra wanted to play it safe and act in a way which she would consider immoral, she 'ought' not to have provoked Aegisthus.) As Gert puts it, 'All linguistic analyses of moral judgments fail because moral judgments are not distinguished from other judgments by their form, or by their function, but by their content.'[8] So 'morally right', for example, is not a redundant expression, but a specification of the sense in which something is right.[9]

We shall identify what the Greeks considered moral issues by observing what thoughts, feelings, words, or actions in the tragedies are 'prohibited, required, allowed or encouraged' by the characters (divine or human) and the chorus.[10] Naturally, we may encounter dispute about these matters, but by the end of the performance the audience will be left with the playwright's implicit overall moral position on the dramatic events, in so far, of course, as this is embodied in the play. (Sophocles' *Electra* may leave us with the view that the matricide was justified, but that does not entail that the dramatist approved of matricide in any circumstances outside the dramatic context.) It is also important to note that the dramatist's implicit overall moral position may be interrogatory; he may wish to leave his audience in a state of moral uncertainty in order to stimulate further thought. Whatever the case, the implicit moral position is as close as we come to a moral authority. Granted there are no such objective authorities in real life (though some individuals may claim to be moral authorities), a play is the deliberate construction of the playwright who will, presumably, wish to give some more or less specific moral coloration to it.[11]

But how does this implicit moral position emerge? This is no simple matter to determine, but, roughly speaking, it emerges from the interplay of the views of the characters (and in some cases psychological elements of the characters), none of whom (and this includes the gods) can be assumed to be morally authoritative, combined with the emotional manipulation of the audience by the dramatist. The views of the sympathetic characters *tend* to reflect the moral views of the society of the play and indeed, admittedly with some refraction, those of the society in which the play is produced, and thus make contact with the views of the audience (views sometimes reinforced by divine sanctions, for example the obligations of *xenia* so horrifically violated by Polymestor in Euripides' *Hecuba*). As Christopher Gill argues, the characters do not tend to espouse idiosyncratic moralities.[12]

To illustrate the above point about the interplay of characters' views, in Sophocles' *Electra*, no character disputes Electra's morality as such: Chrysothemis' objections are entirely prudential (she even says she agrees in principle with Electra's moral position); on the other hand, Clytemnestra disputes her daughter's moral interpretation of the murder of Agamemnon, but in doing so she nevertheless subscribes to the same (retributive) morality as Electra. However, Clytemnestra's moral position and indeed her moral sincerity and seriousness are undermined both by Electra's specific arguments in the agon and by

---

[8] Gert (1998) 20.   [9] Ibid. 21.   [10] Ibid. 4.
[11] I do not wish to suggest here that the overall point, meaning, or focus of a play is invariably some moral argument, position, or attitude. On the problematical subjectivism of ethical judgements in tragedy and the difficulty of determining the author's moral position see Gibert (1995) 39.
[12] Gill (1996) 15–16.

Clytemnestra's overall characterization. Since the characters do not then effectively refute or undermine Electra's moral position, this could only happen through the dramatist's manipulation of the audience's emotions. Here some modern scholars think that the ugliness of Electra's campaign and of the matricide in particular raises moral doubts, or worse. Whether or not this is so, the manipulation of the audience's emotions, though sometimes a complex matter to resolve, is nonetheless an important contributor to the implicit moral position of the play.

As to the moral role of psychological elements of characters, one thinks of Medea's *thumos* with which she is more or less identified until the Great Monologue, though by the end of the speech she has detached herself from it enough to see herself as driven by it. In this case the *thumos* seems to take a moral view (the requirement to punish enemies), but it is also an emotional position (a sense of humiliation and righteous indignation, in the manner of Plato's *thumoeides*), as is its temporary opponent, Medea's maternal feelings (which are also potentially aligned with a moral position, though not actually in Medea's case, as we shall see). But the implicit view of the play, it will be argued, is that Medea's morality is a pseudo-morality. She claims to subscribe to the familiar ancient moral precept 'help *philoi* and harm enemies', though, when it comes down to it, she only harms enemies, so that her 'morality' turns out to be a rationalization of her vengefulness.

LITERARY CRITICISM OR MORAL PHILOSOPHY?

An examination of the moral responses of literary characters straddles the domains of literary criticism and moral philosophy, and in the last two decades or so there has been among some moral philosophers at least a sense of the intellectual and emotional poverty of schematized cases invented for the exemplification of moral problems. These philosophers have therefore turned to literature which appears to afford a rich vein of case studies because the characters whose moral deliberations or dilemmas are narrated or dramatized therein are embedded in a wider and meaningful context rather than being abstract, bloodless figures conjured into a fleeting existence in order to illustrate a moral argument.[13] Moreover,

---

[13] The point is well made by Goldberg (1993) 49: '[S]ome moral philosophy seems a relaxing, if charming, kind of light fiction. It enables us to enjoy the niceties of moral discrimination and argument, and with none of the distracting bewilderments and strains of our ordinary moral lives. It transports us to a world where all the relevant circumstances of a moral problem can be laid out quite definitively; where the moral issues can be pinpointed unmistakably, and the range of choices fully specified; where people's feelings, motives, desires and intentions (including the agent's) can be accurately known, named, and so evaluated with assurance; where people's characters, human virtues, even human dispositions, present themselves with the correct labels already attached to them; and where the agent's thoughts can remain undisturbed even by the possibility of far-reaching, perhaps dismaying, implications in the issue for his whole sense of the world, of other people, of himself, or of the relationships between these.' In respect of Greek tragedy Foley (2001) 118 observes: 'Unlike philosophy, which aims at establishing standards for virtuous behavior, tragedy remains fascinated with flawed, mistaken, and partially appropriate ethical behavior, and with the issues that the cultural system and the dominant morality sacrifice or devalue.' Tragic decisions 'tend to be made in unpredictable, highly specific, and extreme contexts. Emotion, principle, and perception nearly always play

there is the additional advantage of an opportunity for greater moral profundity, because in our immediate reception of a literary work (and by 'our' here I mean the spectator's or reader's, ancient or modern) we have to suspend not only disbelief but also our habitual moral prejudices and commitments and allow ourselves to enter, if only at this primary level of response, the moral world which we encounter.[14] On further reflection, of course, we may reject this world, but the exercise in detaching ourselves for a time from our own moral world will be useful for the shift in perspective and openmindedness which it requires. This effort of detachment is required of all spectators or readers, though the moral world encountered will stand at varying distances from their own.

The fictional world we encounter may be morally cut and dried or it may be indefinite, open, and interrogatory, and therefore without moral closure. Literary characters, moreover, are not usually created solely to illustrate moral arguments; rather they have extended fictional lives and a moral history and may be more or less opaque. The reader or spectator must also respect the genre and its conventions—in the case of Greek tragedy, for example, we have to make allowances for the different moral ambience we find in lyric passages as distinct from a sophistic agon. Furthermore, our response to literature needs to be at once cognitive and affective in a subtly interactive way and thus imaginatively engaged rather than resolutely detached.[15] 'Whereas the impersonal investigator stands apart and in command, analysing an object, the inquirer who responds with creative imagination is thus not wholly separate, aloof and in full control, but mixed up in the subject of inquiry, immersed, implicated, participating in it and imaginatively becoming one with it.'[16]

The philosopher's purpose in drawing examples from literature is thus to enrich moral philosophy, but the enterprise is more problematical than it might appear. Peter Johnson, for example, poses an important question: 'Within any particular genre we look to the criteria of judgement that are appropriate, but in

important roles in tragic choice, and response to the suffering of others is critical. The choices taken by one character strongly affect the lives of others, even to the point of destroying another's capacity for humanity' (ibid. 121). For Nussbaum (1986) 14, 'a whole tragic drama, unlike a schematic philosophical example making use of a similar story, is capable of tracing the history of a complex pattern of deliberation, showing its roots in a way of life and looking forward to its consequences in that life. As it does all of this, it lays open to view the complexity, the indeterminacy, the sheer difficulty of actual human deliberation.' For an early philosopher's discomfort with the conflicted tragic character see Gellrich (1984) 157 on Aristotle: 'the *spoudaios* or *epieikēs*, whom Aristotle makes his tragic agent, is conceived as one by nature resistant to, if not completely removed from, conflict in thought and action... Aristotle's importation of *spoudaiotēs* into his discussion discourages a view of the tragic action as a representation of internal battles of the soul, of intense social rivalries between individuals with competing ethical claims, or of clashes between men and gods.' Moreover, '[i]f the *Poetics* had engaged the issue of ethical and social strife in fifth-century drama, it would have met with material that challenged a view of the unity and coherence of moral values. Aristotle's ethical world, bound by the safety of laws that are rationally ascertainable and consistent, is not the world dramatized by the classical tragedians': ibid.161.

[14] I say 'primary' since, as Cairns (forthcoming) points out, 'we modify, but do not wholly override, our intuitions as to how the world works when we enter the imaginative worlds of fiction.'

[15] 'Our cognitive activity, as we explore the ethical conception embodied in the text, centrally involves emotional response. We discover what we think about these events partly by noticing how we feel': Nussbaum (1986) 15.

[16] Adamson, Freadman, and Parker (1998) 106.

passage between texts what criteria could there be?'[17] It would seem to me that, once philosophers have co-opted literary texts for the elucidation of philosophical problems, the rules of engagement appropriate to literature must apply because it is a task of literary criticism to make sense of the character, who remains a fictional creation even when employed for an analysis that is in principle philosophical.

What I am undertaking in this book is essentially literary criticism, though I draw on philosophy when it can illuminate an issue. Criticism has always been eclectic; it has always ransacked whatever discipline it felt could enrich its inter-pretations, and we have become relatively comfortable with that. So we find Freudian critics, Marxist critics, feminist critics, and so on. But even the most vaguely humanistic critics with no (conscious or at least confessed) ideological axe to grind who discuss, for example, Aeschylean dilemmas, will find themselves interrogating the text in at least a rudimentarily philosophical manner.

THE ANCIENT SPECTATOR AND THE MODERN READER

Literary interpretation can hardly avoid postulating or at least implying some kind of representative reader or spectator without whom the work is not fully intelligi-ble or indeed complete. We could hardly claim to be offering even a basic interpretation of a Greek tragedy, for example, if we chose to ignore its effect on the ancient audience or its very existence as a play. The ancient tragedian wrote from his cultural perspective with a particular sort of audience in mind. It is perfectly legitimate for us in the twenty-first century to engage with the plays as directly as we can and to be moved by them (otherwise we should have to frown upon modern performances intended for the general public), but our situation is somewhat like overhearing discourse in a foreign language in which we are not entirely fluent addressed to another person over the telephone. We may well be able to make reasonable sense of it and even find it in some way illuminating, but we have always to bear in mind that what we hear is not addressed to us, so that we need to construct, at any rate subliminally or intuitively, the responses of the person to whom the words are in fact addressed.

We shall need then to try to construct the response of 'the ancient spectator'. But then *what* ancient spectator? Here we could choose to limit our interest to a more specifically defined group. Hermann Rohdich (1968), for example, in his study of Euripides postulates sophistically educated spectators confronted with a challenge to their (alleged) notion that the human condition is not, in the final analysis, tragic, and part of the value of this approach is to throw the dramatist's tragic world view into sharper relief. It is possible too, of course, to postulate a spectator or reader armed with very specific knowledge, perhaps of one other particular work of literature, which is the assumption underlying a critical comparison of two literary works.

[17] Johnson (2004) 17.

But whatever the nature of the spectators we postulate, we will want to credit them with a degree of intellect and dramatic sensitivity sufficient to make our interpretation interesting and illuminating, and so we shall be sorely tempted to endow them with exaggerated powers of intellect, sensitivity, and memory. In this way they become less representative than ideal. But more problematically even than that, we may find ourselves unconsciously projecting onto these now idealized people a modern style of reading or reception which may coincide only imperfectly with ancient practice. Malcolm Heath has sought to avoid these pitfalls. He argues that tragedy was primarily emotive and intended to produce pleasure, and so his conception of analysis tends towards reconstructing the emotional rhythms and dialectics of the plays.[18] Heath argues too that when the Greeks spoke of their poets as moral teachers they were referring to the provision of 'moral exemplars, cautionary tales and formulations in gnomic utterance of moral, and indeed of technical wisdom'.[19] This is miles away from a modern style of reading, and I reluctantly suspect that there is much truth in it, though the precise nature of the reception of the intelligent and attentive ancient spectator is largely inaccessible to us. Perhaps our best course will be to postulate an ancient spectator who responds attentively, engages intellect and feeling, and holds some of the views and attitudes which, as far as we know, the ancients held.

But does the present investigation founder then on the alleged irrelevance of modern approaches and ideas? Not at all, provided that we are clear about what kind of interpreting we are doing. Heath himself suggests a way around the difficulty: 'It is one thing to ask what the text is saying, another to explore the implications of what it says, its significance or value in the light of the interests which we have brought with us.'[20] Clearly Heath means what the text is saying to the ancient audience to whom the dramatist addressed it. But in so far as a text, like an overheard conversation, is available to anyone who might choose to read or hear it, we may legitimately come to meet it equipped with our own understanding and sensibilities ('the interests we have brought with us'). For this reason I apply our understanding to ancient situations which the ancients themselves understood rather differently. What is necessary in this encounter is to do all one can to understand the ancient position, but then to discover what it can say to us through the filter of an ancient reading.[21] Moreover, what it can say to us may emerge from the kind of analysis which we must frankly admit is impossible for the spectator, ancient or modern, the nature of whose responses is determined (among other things) by the time for reflection that the continuous unfolding of the play allows. To take a striking example, the Aeschylean Agamemnon's dilemma at Aulis is briefly recounted by the chorus in lyric metre so that the time devoted to the episode and the mode of its narration militate against the kind of reflection available to readers who can pause as long as they like in order to analyse it. Scholars and students of the plays can reflect in this way, and to do so is to enrich our understanding, but it is misleading to attribute this enriched understanding to any kind of possible spectator.

---

[18] Heath (1987) 5–16.   [19] Ibid. 47.   [20] Ibid. 72.

[21] 'To understand Greek morality it is certainly necessary to become capable of looking at morality through Greek eyes, but it is necessary also to switch off and become ourselves again whenever we want to know what, if anything, they thought about issues which are important to us': Dover (1974) 2.

To limit the enquiry to the responses of an ancient audience then is to hold Greek tragedy at a distance from us, as an alien and culture-bound artefact rather than a 'possession for eternity'.[22] On the other hand, we must be careful not to violate the ancient text by reading into it implications that are not to be found there, that is by removing what I referred to above as 'the filter of an ancient reading'. The Freudian interpretation of Oedipus is an obvious case in point. What this caveat means in detail will emerge during the analysis of particular texts. When I speak of what 'we' think or feel about a passage, or 'our' response to it, I shall be attempting to take the position of the ancient spectator, which is what the 'primary' level of interpretation requires. When I move outside this context I shall make it clear that I am doing so. Thus to return to the case of Agamemnon at Aulis, we shall have to accept the intended reaction of the ancient audience (as far as we can recover it) as part of the text's immediate implication, and that means that our own reflections will be constrained by, for example, the audience's feelings about the options Agamemnon faces and the importance of heroic morality. But, having integrated this component, we can move on to reflect more deeply and in our own terms on the nature of the dilemma—that is, we can place it in the context of, for example, recent philosophical discussion of dilemmas.

CULTURAL DIFFERENCES

Bernard Williams has warned us against measuring 'the ideas and the experience of the ancient Greeks against modern conceptions of freedom, autonomy, inner responsibility, moral obligation, and so forth' and assuming 'that we have an entirely adequate control of these conceptions ourselves'.[23] He is referring here to what he terms a 'progressivist' account of what we might call Western psycho-ethical history which claims that 'the Greeks had primitive ideas of action, responsibility, ethical motivation, and justice, which in the course of history have been replaced by a more complex and refined set of conceptions that define a more mature form of ethical experience'.[24] Three alleged major inadequacies in ancient conceptions are: (1) an underdeveloped sense of a unified self; (2) a focus on shame rather than guilt (the modern mind associates the latter with freedom and autonomy) and (3) the absence of a concept of the will.[25]

(1) The idea of the underdeveloped self is associated particularly with Bruno Snell who argued that Homeric man was a disjointed collection of psychic functions.[26] This absurd idea is mercifully no longer current, but it relates to the serious issue of the interference of the gods in the thoughts and emotions (the 'mental events') of human agents. Snell wanted to suggest that such agents were actually unable to make decisions without divine intervention, but, as Williams

---

[22] 'The impulse to recognize ourselves in tragedy's words is very strong. I do not want to do away with it. Tragedy is there for whoever wants to read or perform it. It is right and necessary, I believe, to interpret tragedy for whatever you want to get out of it': Padel (1992) 10.
[23] Williams (1993) 5–6.   [24] Ibid. 5.
[25] Ibid.   [26] Snell (1953) 1–22.

points out, there are plenty of examples in the *Iliad* of such decisions.[27] Moreover, even the gods themselves make decisions according to similar patterns and without the contribution of some still higher being. (An infinite regress is clearly in the offing here.) Divine psychological intervention is nevertheless an important feature of Greek tragedy which does indeed raise questions about the boundaries of the self. The next chapter is devoted to a detailed discussion of it.

(2) Williams has done much to put to rest the idea that 'shame cultures' and 'guilt cultures' are mutually exclusive, that the former necessarily evolve into the latter, and that this is a mark of moral maturity. His discussion of the relation between shame and guilt reinstates shame as a respectable moral feeling. There is a regrettable tendency to caricature shame as a mindless concern for what other people will think, as if what they will think will be completely arbitrary. But, as Williams points out, what people will think is grounded in their beliefs concerning the intrinsic value of certain kinds of action: 'some kinds of behaviour are admired, others accepted, others despised, and it is those attitudes that are internalised, not simply the prospect of hostile reactions. If that were not so, there would be . . . no shame *culture*, no shared ethical attitudes at all.'[28]

(3) As to the role of the will in putting decisions into effect, Williams remarks, 'All that Homer seems to have left out is the idea of another mental action that is supposed necessarily to lie between coming to a conclusion and acting on it: and he did well in leaving it out, since there is no such action.'[29] Certainly no such action tends to be reported in ancient or modern narratives of deliberation. At a certain point in the deliberative process one view comes to predominate and the agent proceeds to act on it. The so-called 'will' can appear, at least to the modern mind, to be a factor when agents encounter mental resistance to performing an act upon which they have resolved, in which case we may speak, colloquially, of the need for 'will power'. But another way of looking at such cases is to say that the opposing reasons and feelings have not been put finally to rest, so that summoning the will to act is really the effort of directing the imagination away from the interfering thoughts and feelings. Conversely, in the carpet scene of *Agamemnon*, Clytemnestra directs her husband's imagination away from the relevant issue with a resulting loss of 'will power' on his part.

A more specific cultural difference that is relevant to a good number of Greek tragedies relates to the Greek attitude to the complex of ideas that might be summarized conveniently in the terms retaliation, revenge, and retributive justice. I think it is fair to say that human beings in general have at least a subconscious and perhaps instinctive desire to requite injury with injury. This desire arises from a sense of righteous indignation at the enemy or perpetrator of the injury which, in civilized societies, provides a basis for moral and legal theories of retributive justice. Since these feelings are primitive and instinctual, they need to be carefully regulated. Civic justice eventually evolved in Greek societies, thus alienating the victim from the actual performance of the retributive act. But society not only retained the legitimacy of harming enemies but continued to urge it as morally

---

[27] Williams (1993) 29–32.

[28] Ibid. 83–4: Williams' emphasis. On shame and guilt and their corresponding cultures see the detailed discussion of Cairns (1993) 14–47.

[29] Williams (1993) 36.

acceptable or even required. Negative obligations in respect of enemies were on a par with positive obligations to relatives and friends (*philoi*), as implied in Polemarchus' definition of moral behaviour (*dikaiosunē*) as helping friends and harming enemies.[30] Christianity, on the other hand, enjoins loving one's enemies, so that in our modern culture the urge to retaliate has become more than a little suspect.

A frequent situation in tragedy involves revenge on an enemy who was once a *philos*. This is more poignant and morally problematical for an ancient Greek than it would be for us, because we would not be allowed (by Christian morality, at any rate) to harm that person, whereas a Greek would be positively enjoined to do so. Such harm might be effected through the legal system, but Orestes, in a society without civic justice, is obliged to kill the mother who has become his enemy, and the obligation is overwhelmingly supported by divine and social sanctions. But morally more problematical cases arise when the balance between the moral and the emotional components of the desire to retaliate is disturbed in favour of the emotional. Euripides' Medea, for example, correctly recognizes that Jason deserves punishment for betrayal and perjury, but she does not consider dispassionately what kind or degree of punishment would be appropriate. Instead, in her passion for revenge, she looks for the most devastating form of retaliation possible regardless of the moral implications not only for Jason, but especially for four innocent people, including her own two children.

This failure to consider the appropriateness of the retaliation afflicts also Euripides' Electra in the eponymous play, as well as Electra, Pylades, and the protagonist in *Orestes*. In that play the villain of the piece is Menelaus who has betrayed Orestes by failing to rescue him from the Argive *dēmos*, and once Orestes and Electra have been condemned to death they hatch a plot to punish him. The chosen method reflects Medea's psychology in her retaliation against Jason—the murder of a close relative, in this case Helen. The choice of victim here, however, is partly a function of availability. Helen is easy to capture and kill (or so it would seem). While Medea makes no attempt to justify killing any of her innocent victims, but apparently regards their deaths as what is now euphemistically described as collateral damage, the conspirators tell themselves that Helen deserves to die for causing the Trojan War. But when they contemplate killing the innocent Hermione as well it is all too clear that morality has given way entirely to passionate vindictiveness and the desire to survive at any cost.

GENERIC CONSTRAINTS

Because Greek tragedy is a literary genre, and not a slice of real life, the investigation of the moral performance of the characters must proceed on rather different lines than if they were real people. Authors constitute, so to speak, a much greater threat to the autonomy of their characters than real people experience in their dealings with the real world. Ibsen may have begun with his characters and

---

[30] Plato, *Rep.* 332d.

allowed them once fully conceived to determine the course of his plots, but characterization may be in varying degrees subordinated to plot, motif, or theme. This is unproblematic so long as psychology remains inviolate, but it is possible to argue that in Euripides' *Iphigenia at Aulis*, for example, the sheer motif of change of mind is employed primarily as a means of effecting dramatic surprise as an end in itself.[31] If this is so, we may have to accept the absence of realistic psychological motivation of the various changes of mind, as Aristotle found in the case of Iphigenia. (That the philosopher objected to this alleged implausibility reflects his concern that character, though clearly secondary to plot in his dramatic theory, should still harmonize with it.)[32] Nevertheless, since the tangible stage presence of the characters encourages audiences to focus on them as centres of motivation, let us take psychological consistency of characterization as the rule, though a rule we must be prepared to see broken in particular cases.

Now when we examine the moral responses of a real person we have to do our best to garner all the relevant facts, both material and psychological. Then, in the face of the obviously problematical epistemology of such an enterprise, we apply to the case our own almost certainly muddled, unsystematic, and subjective moral standards. Mercifully, literature is in some ways simpler to negotiate than the real world. A fictional world tends to be more circumscribed (Lady Macbeth's children, for instance, are off limits), though never completely so because the author will inevitably leave loose ends.[33] For example, Apollo's reality and involvement in the action of *Oedipus Tyrannus* are indisputable in a way that a god's involvement could never be in real life, but his purpose therein remains notoriously inscrutable.[34] Moreover, we may know more about literary characters than we know about real people, and particularly more about their motives, which are those and only those of which the dramatist informs us or allows us reasonably to infer. (This means that we can be quite certain that Oedipus' parricide was not the product of unconscious filial hostility.) Moreover, the factual pronouncements of literary characters have to be taken as true unless specifically undermined by other information. Thus Oedipus' account of the murder of Laius is true except for his mistake about the survivor, but Agamemnon's, in *Iphigenia at Aulis*, of the circumstances leading up to his decision to sacrifice is probably unreliable both because of what we know of his character and because when Menelaus denies its

---

[31] For motif-driven characterization in Greek tragedy see Gibert (1995) *passim*.

[32] Aristotle, *Poetics* 1454[a]32.

[33] For this reason we must be wary of the view that 'the language of dramatic persons does not give clues to or "express" their personality, their inward and spiritual being: it *is* their personality, and their being': Gould (2001) 79. Gould (ibid. 80) goes on to remark: 'Garton [(1972) 15] is right in saying that "the attributes of a [dramatic person] differ from those of a person [in the everyday sense] in that the sum of them is totally accessible", whereas "our acquaintance with a person is always less than complete, and there is practically no limit to the theoretically answerable questions we might ask about him."' The latter assertion, about real people, is obviously correct, and it is true that dramatic characters are totally accessible, but this is not equivalent to saying that their language is their personality and their being. To be sure, the language is all we have, but from this (perhaps ambiguous) language we imaginatively (and subliminally) construct a person.

[34] In this Introduction I have on the whole refrained from supporting my generalizations with references when the point is argued, with support from footnotes, in the relevant chapter.

truth his brother makes no attempt to validate his own version. Official messengers are, of course, regularly reliable, though Lichas lies to Deianeira in *Trachiniae*.

Relevance then in general is restricted to what we are told and what we can deduce or intuit from what we are told, and the moral perspective we bring to the fictional data is circumscribed by the culture and the genre. We cannot, for example, dismiss the Sophoclean Electra's concern with retribution as morally irrelevant and judge her from the point of view of Sartrean existentialism. This is to respect the cultural context. Nor can we criticize her for not choosing an option which was not in fact culturally available to her. We can of course defy the more radical postmodernists and offer moral judgements on her cultural context from our privileged position outside of it, but that is to engage in a different kind of interpretative exercise.

The above considerations are general and apply pretty much to any genre of fiction. But there are constraints more characteristic of Greek tragedy to be considered. I am thinking here of such elements of tragedy as the choral ode, interior monologue, dialogue, and the more formal agon. These are tragedy's vehicles of moral reflection. In the odes such reflection tends to be of a more conventional and indeed often platitudinous nature (though the odes of *Bacchae* afford important insight into the moral implications of the Dionysiac way of life, and Aeschylus uses his chorus to articulate the terms of Agamemnon's decision). One might have expected the medium of moral deliberation to have been the interior monologue or the soliloquy—an expectation perhaps conditioned by our experience of Shakespearean tragedy—but the use of this device is comparatively rare, so that we often get the impression that deliberation has already occurred or has been replaced by immediate moral intuitions. One wonders therefore whether deliberative passages are rare because generic conventions tend to discourage them, or if the tragedians in any case tended to favour characters who act on moral intuitions. There are exceptions such as Ajax's deliberations when he recovers from his madness or Medea's during the Great Monologue, but otherwise an interlocutor is introduced as a sounding board. Even so, discussion with others tends to do no more than air moral resolutions which will remain unchanged.

THE TRAGIC WORLD

Greek tragedies are set in what might be termed eclectic or syncretic fictional worlds derived in part from the epic tradition. This has obvious and important implications for causation and thus for moral judgements which are closely linked to causal explanations. The relevant moral context here is not only the fifth-century Athenian culture of the dramatists and their original audience but also the refraction through the plays of that and earlier Greek cultures (and in particular Homeric culture). The epic tradition supplies many of the major heroes of tragedy and their moral world. Although the moral imperatives of such characters as Aeschylus' Eteocles or Agamemnon, of Sophocles' Ajax or Heracles, and even of Euripides' Medea are fully meaningful only against the background of heroic society, they remained intelligible, though at some distance, to the fifth-century audiences whose society retained in modified form a number of significant institutions and attitudes from the heroic moral world.[35] (Alcibiades, one would imagine, would have found little difficulty in understanding Ajax's privileging of his ego over the collective interest.) The conventions of hospitality and supplication, for example, and the injunction to help friends and harm enemies, survived, albeit in a modified form, down to the audience's own day.[36] These inherited beliefs in general were overwhelmingly aristocratic, and thus an obvious source of tension with the growth of democracy.[37] On the other hand, commitment to them was tempered by intellectual and notably political debate, a feature of Athenian life reflected pervasively in tragedy.[38]

Tragedy brings with it certain metaphysical, religious, social, political, and indeed moral presuppositions of a general nature, and these relate closely to causation, and thus to moral responses. But there is no single tragic world, and the spectators must get their bearings as the particular play proceeds. Sometimes the specific difference, as it were, is reasonably subtle, a function of theme or emphasis. For example, Sophocles' *Trachiniae* focuses on the theme of the impossibility of anticipating outcomes, a pessimistic idea which is neither unique to this play nor incompatible with the conventional tragic universe as broadly conceived. But the special focus on that theme structures our interpretation of Deianeira's deliberations with the chorus over the use of the salve which she mistakenly hopes will restore her husband's love to her. Because the very texture of the language of the play so clearly impresses upon us both the dangers of acting in the dark and the unavoidability of so doing, we are particularly sensitive to Deianeira's moral and practical uncertainties about the salve and alarmed by the chorus' advice that she should make trial of it because that is the only way certainty about the outcome can be attained. Of course, what they say is true enough, but hardly a warrant for acting impulsively. The epistemologically problematic world of this play invites us to contemplate what constitutes appropriate deliberation, decision, and action.[39]

The religious world of *Trachiniae* is conventional enough. Euripides' *Heracles* begins in such a world, but presently, through the medium of the characters, proceeds to question, quite insistently, the moral reliability of the traditional gods of tragedy. Although the Olympians' unreliability by no means entails

[35] For the relationship between the world of tragedy and that of the audience see Easterling's (1997) excellent article and in particular her comments on the tragic idiom (22–3).

[36] Blundell (1989) explores moral choice in five Sophoclean plays through a focus on this notorious moral injunction and the 'closely allied' conception of 'justice as retaliation': ibid. 1. See also McHardy (2008) 1: 'A close examination of the circumstances in which revenge is taken or avoided suggests that reactions vary substantially according to the situation, the individuals involved, the literary genre or author and the particular offence depicted.... Tragedy in particular delights in exceptional and problematic revenge acts among *philoi*...'

[37] 'Fifth-century Athens was a society experiencing particularly acute—and exciting—growth pains, and along with the relatively new (or newly dominant) structure of democratic and egalitarian values and political principles, we can see an older and deeply entrenched aristocratic and elitist ideology still more or less openly asserting itself': M. Griffith (2005) 336.

[38] See Cairns (2005) 306. *Oresteia* is only the most familiar example of this, and, as Cairns (ibid.) points out, the final play of the trilogy embodies rather than resolves the debate, as the hung jury demonstrates.

[39] For the play's exploration of epistemological issues in properly dramatic terms see Lawrence (1978) *passim*.

their non-existence, their authority is nevertheless undermined by it and by an emphasis on fortune or *tuchē*. Finally the hero rejects them, and this has important implications for his moral reorientation after the devastation of the madness.

Still the conventions of divine involvement in human affairs are of paramount importance for tragedy in general, and that applies equally to *Heracles*, for all its radical features. These conventions originate (for us at any rate) largely in epic, though modified by elements of Archaic and contemporary religious thought.[40] The gods often intervene, usually immanently and mysteriously, in the physical and psychological world of the characters and, although contemporary audiences certainly believed that the gods intervened in human life, they may not have been accustomed to thinking that they did so in quite so intimate or structured a manner.[41]

The socio-political context of moral response is as important as the religious or metaphysical. Greek tragedies are usually set in states (in particular, Athens, Argos, or Thebes) with many features of the fifth-century polis, but *Ajax*, *Hecuba*, *Troades*, and *Iphigenia at Aulis* are set in military camps, *Philoctetes* on a desert island, and *Trachiniae* apparently in an almost pre-political world that reflects the moral nature of the hero himself. In three of the Orestes plays the matricide is committed in an Argos that predates civic justice. (Euripides' *Orestes* is, as remarked above, problematical.) Certainly the political world of Sophocles' *Electra* appears, like that of *Oresteia*, to predate civic justice. There are no references to judicial institutions, but in any case the tyrants, Aegisthus and Clytemnestra, are beyond the law. This political context provides *prima facie* legitimation for the *talio* justice of the play, but leaves it open to the dramatist to demonstrate its inadequacy or, alternatively, to explore the moral psychology of a person who is, because of the socio-political context, morally obliged to punish a mother in order to avenge a father.

We have been considering the features of the tragic genre, noting that each play has its own specific world; but it is important to recognize that there are sub-genres within Greek tragedy to which the ancients gave no official recognition, so to speak, but which are relevant to our investigation. It is inappropriate, for example, to apply the same moral standards to the murderous Creusa of Euripides' *Ion* and to the murderous protagonist of his *Medea*. The difference is in part at least a function of the sub-genre. The *Ion* is 'tragi-comedy' or 'romantic tragedy'; the rules of the game are altogether different.[42]

The above reflections on our differing moral responses to Medea and Creusa raise the question of implicit moral context. I have discussed above the matter of the play's implicit morality, but here I have in mind a more generalized set of moral assumptions and indeed expectations that the spectator is accustomed to

---

[40] With reference to Archaic beliefs, one thinks especially of pollution. We shall want to know if this is, in the words of R. C. T. Parker (1983) 1, 'a literary mechanism or a living preoccupation'. On the relation of tragic conventions to historical reality see ibid. 14–16, 308–9. As for contemporary religious thought, one thinks of the sort of philosophizing of the divine that produced 'the god who is truly god' of Euripides' *Her.* 1340–5.

[41] On the relation between civic and tragic theology see the finely nuanced discussion of R. C. T. Parker (1997).

[42] Kitto (1961) 311–29, Wolff (1965) 169, Mastronarde (1999–2000) *passim*.

bring to tragedy. For example, the spectator might reasonably expect the chorus or a formal messenger to utter a number of familiar moral platitudes on such matters as thinking thoughts inappropriate for human beings or the impossibility of *eudaimonia*. These platitudes do much to set a kind of general moral tone, but the dramatist may decide to juxtapose them with a morally more sophisticated vision. The chorus of the *Tyrannus* famously discourse on hubris and tyranny, but Oedipus himself strangely fails to fit the pattern. Even more disturbingly, the *Bacchae* chorus voice conventional moral ideas in a religious and psychological context that is anything but conventional.

CHARACTERIZATION AND CONCEPTIONS OF THE SELF

Since we are focusing here on the characters' moral awareness, we shall need to pay close attention to characterization. There are three principal and obviously linked issues here, all of which relate to broader generic conventions: the boundaries of the self; the degree of sophistication with which the characters are conceived; and the techniques which characterize them. Included among these techniques are the devices the dramatist employs to enlist sympathy or the reverse for his characters. In a useful distinction between what he calls the 'character' and the 'personality' viewpoints, Christopher Gill relates the former to detached assessment of characters as 'psychological and moral agents' in a 'determinate ethical framework', and the latter, the 'personality-viewpoint',[43] to 'empathetic' involvement with a 'unique' individual.[44] Gill suggests that the character viewpoint tends to affirm the conventional moral culture (which supplies the criteria of moral judgement), whereas the personality viewpoint tends to be 'ethically nonstandard or interrogatory in its impact, questioning rather than validating existing cultural assumptions'.[45] And for Gill, 'our sympathetic involvement with the hero is a reflection of our engagement with the reasons and reasoning, and with the mixture of psychological pressures and agency, that motivate the violent or (seemingly) unreasonable act on which the tragedy turns'.[46] The tension between sympathy and moral judgement is explored briefly (with relation to Aristotle's *Poetics*) in the next section and at greater length in the chapters on individual plays.

The issue of the boundaries of the self relates to the controversial question of personal autonomy in Greek tragedy, and especially moral autonomy. The term is controversial because it is taken from a modern secular context and applied in very different worlds in which the involvement of the gods renders it problematical. Nevertheless, we shall see that it remains a useful term provided care is taken to observe the ways in which it is 'refracted', so to speak, when it enters the alien environments of ancient tragedy.

Stephen Halliwell sees the Greek notion of character as emerging from a struggle to affirm and maintain (what I shall call) autonomy (though he speaks

---

[43] Gill (1990a) 1.   [44] Ibid. 2.   [45] Ibid. 6–7.   [46] Gill (1996) 105.

of the authenticity and integrity of human agency) against alien forces working against it:

Much of the traditional Greek understanding of character lies in the attempt to find ways of affirming the authentic force and integrity of human agency and responsibility, the components of character, at the point where many different potencies—internal and external; psychological, social, natural, and divine—intersect and become entangled. Against this background, the conception of character, the sense of a person as potentially the source of his own motivation and ethical agency, has to be won and maintained in the face of the competing possibility that people are at the mercy of powers and causes larger than themselves.[47]

Thus in Aeschylus divine intervention on the one hand and the *oikos* on the other encroach on the integrity of the self from opposite directions, as it were, while social forces work through both these factors.[48] As for the distinction between conception and technique, Aeschylus' Agamemnon, Clytemnestra, and Orestes are characterized by rather different techniques, or at least by a significantly different deployment of techniques, but they are conceived with essentially the same degree of sophistication. The protagonist of the *Agamemnon* does not appear in person until nearly halfway through the play, but by then his deliberations at Aulis have been recounted in a schematized form and the choral odes have generalized and discoursed in symbolic terms about successful generals and members of an accursed house. Clytemnestra in *Agamemnon* and Orestes in *Choephori*, by contrast, appear in person earlier and are thus directly characterized much more than is Agamemnon. But it does not follow that a character who appears before us on the stage is conceived in a more sophisticated fashion. For all that Clytemnestra is a powerful and unforgettable figure in the *Agamemnon*, her psychology is as simple as her husband's and her motives as simply conceived. (She is primarily the mother intent on avenging her daughter and secondarily the betrayed wife.) To be sure, she steps right out of her socially appointed role. But this is not presented as the consequence of a process of agonized reflection on the part of a highly individuated person; she simply repels us as a woman in a role strongly condemned by society. (If we want examples of women who reflect more on their unconventional stances we must look to Sophocles' Electra or Euripides' Medea.)

An important question for our investigation is whether specific characters are individually conceived, that is whether they can transcend their roles and the moralities that attach to them. Christopher Pelling suggests that when we speak of individuality we

may ... be concerned with self-consciousness, a clear awareness of one's own or others' identity as something which will involve definitions of social role, status, and responsibilities, but ... will not be *exhausted* by those definitions: already in Homer, we can ask whether Agamemnon has the qualities to live up to his position, and the question makes sense. But we may mean something a little different, more clearly introspective: a person's capacity to describe or analyse psychic events, or simply his awareness of himself as a locus

---

[47] Halliwell (1990) 59.

[48] 'Cut off from his family, civic and religious roots, the individual was nothing; he did not find himself alone, he ceased to exist': Vernant and Vidal-Naquet (1981) 58.

for decision-making; and this consciousness of the self as a rational agent will often imply a readiness to accept some sort of 'responsibility' for those decisions, and a normal obligation to bear their consequences.[49]

This is a useful unpacking of the implications of the term, and it is heartening to find as early as Aeschylus' Eteocles a character who satisfies all these criteria; nevertheless, we should sound a note of caution here. Malcolm Heath rightly warns us against reading too much into the individuality we do find: 'Such Sophoclean characters as Electra or Philoctetes carry great dramatic conviction, because their individuality has been worked out in the details of the text; but the individuality that is thus worked out is not in itself detailed or subtly nuanced: it consists rather of a few basic traits, clearly and consistently delineated.'[50] Similarly, Joel Kupperman, a moral philosopher, in a discussion of character, not in the sense of 'dramatis persona', but with reference to a real person's 'normal pattern of thought and action',[51] observes that drama 'lends itself to characters of a few lines strongly etched rather than to characters that are far more intricate and less strongly etched . . . To be like a character in a play . . . is usually to have a small number of distinctive and readily noticeable characteristics.'[52] The word 'character' has moral overtones.[53]

It is significant, I think, that Pelling places the term 'responsibility' in inverted commas in the above passage, for it is important to feel the same uneasiness about it as we feel about 'autonomy', and for much the same reasons since the terms appear correlative. On the other hand, it is worth noting, with Douglas Cairns, that

it is a basic fact that the belief in humans' responsibility for their actions is deeply engrained in language and thought. Such beliefs survive even when held in conjunction with other, incompatible beliefs. In no literary genre at any period does a belief in effective divine causation entirely remove the sense that human beings are, at least to some extent, answerable for what they do.[54]

There is then a popular feeling that agents are responsible. Is it then unreasonable to suggest that there is a correlative popular belief or assumption that the actions for which they are held responsible proceed from a self which is intuitively felt to be in some way independent or able to initiate actions?

If characters are no more than types or an amalgam of types or roles, then their moral attitudes will reflect this, but they will be unable to reflect on them beyond meditating on the duties attached to the roles. Such roles may of course conflict; the Aeschylean Agamemnon at Aulis is aware of his conflicting roles of general and father and he chooses the general's role over the father's. The 'he' that chooses must be distinct from the general and the father, so that conflict of roles entails a measure of detachment from each of the roles in question. The Euripidean Agamemnon is torn by unresolvable uncertainty at Aulis partly because he distinguishes himself so clearly from all his roles. He is a man who is a general but who sometimes wishes he were not. A character may identify with a role and be quite self-conscious about the obligations and responsibilities it entails. Thus

---

[49] Pelling (1990) p. v.   [50] Heath (1987) 119.   [51] Kupperman (1991) 13
[52] Ibid. 6.   [53] Ibid. 7.   [54] Cairns forthcoming 18.

the Aeschylean Agamemnon qua general feels a responsibility to his peers and to his own honour in that role. In his case this feeling is no more than implicit, but the Eteocles of the *Seven* actually states what his role entails and all but declares that he intends to fulfil it. Most notoriously, the Creon of Sophocles' *Antigone* issues a kind of programmatic statement on the qualities required in a ruler, with the implication, of course, that he himself displays them.[55]

Characters, notably in Sophocles, will sometimes define themselves in relation to the moral claims of their noble ancestry (*eugeneia*) so that their deliberations in a crisis centre on how rather than whether to act morally. The situations in which they find themselves, moreover, narrow their moral choices. Ajax is a humiliated warrior, therefore there will be strong moral pressure on him to vindicate his honour. The (very Iliadic) moral conflict here comes from the other, potentially incompatible obligation of a warrior to protect his dependants.

The caveat against exaggerating the individuality of Greek tragic characters and thereby diverting the focus of attention from the moral choices they make may serve to remind us of the particular pressures exerted on the individual by family and state, which make up the context of their moral activity. (Indeed, Aeschylean characters are particularly obviously incomplete in isolation from their family.) So we shall be concerned (where applicable) with a character's sense of moral obligation to self, to family, to peers, to the state—and indeed to the gods.

MORAL EVALUATION, EMOTIONAL ENGAGEMENT, AND ARISTOTLE'S *POETICS*

The objectivity of our moral judgements about real people is often compromised by emotional involvement. The same is true for fictional characters, but our feelings, positive or negative, will be to a large extent the product of authors' deliberate manipulation, provided they do not misjudge the range of our feelings. A Greek tragedian is free to manipulate the 'facts' (material and psychological) of his fiction. It is a psychological fact of *Oresteia* that Clytemnestra's murder of her husband is motivated by anger at the sacrifice of their daughter, but that motive, established in the first play, is ignored in the second. When Clytemnestra pleads for her life before Orestes, she fails to mention this mitigating motive and effectively reinforces her son's emphasis on her adultery. This is clearly a factor in Aeschylus' strategy for presenting the matricide in a particular light. It is not exactly that the earlier motive is no longer valid or that Clytemnestra has unaccountably forgotten to mention it; it is just that the audience is invited not to focus on it or at least to give it less weight than they might otherwise have done. Most notoriously, perhaps, in ancient literature, the poet of the *Odyssey* tells us that Orestes murdered Aegisthus and ordered a grave for his mother (3. 306–10). By the almost ludicrous omission of the matricide Homer is signalling its thematic irrelevance to his audience. To take a contrasting case, Euripides' Hippolytus displays negative qualities that severely compromise his *sōphrosunē,* but at the end

---

[55] Aesch. *Sept.* 1–3, Soph. *Ant.* 175–91.

of the play through the medium of Artemis the dramatist leaves us with a narrowly adulatory view of the young man that at least works against the more balanced judgement that the facts of the play itself should have brought us to entertain.

As Gill's analysis makes admirably clear, this tension between sympathy and moral judgement is essential to a proper engagement with the moral thinking and individuality of the character. However, as he points out, it runs counter to Aristotle's view that 'we apply similar types of ethical standards to figures in poetry and in real life', and 'our emotional responses to them (those of pity and fear, for instance) are graduated precisely in accordance with our ethical judgements on them'.[56] For Aristotle the essential tragic emotions of pity and fear, far from being a function of arbitrary subjectivity, are, to put it somewhat paradoxically, rational responses to objectively pitiable people in objectively pitiable situations which have arisen out of a causal sequence that reflects what is objectively necessary or probable.[57] This leaves the tragedian no scope for the deliberate creation of disharmony between feeling and judgement. Indeed, such disharmony would presumably constitute for Aristotle evidence of dramatic incompetence.

Let us briefly consider the implications of Aristotle's theory in the *Poetics* for characterization in general and moral deliberation in particular. We begin with his notion of character (*ēthos*) in the dramatic context of tragedy. For the philosopher,

character . . . is a specific moral factor in relation to action, not a vague or pervasive notion equivalent to modern ideas of personality or individuality—least of all to individuality, since *ēthos* is a matter of generic qualities (virtues and vices). . . . [Dramatic characterization] must involve the *manifestation* of moral choice in word or action . . . [and] . . . if character is to play a part in tragedy, as it is ideally required to do, there must be no uncertainty or ambiguity about it; we must be able to identify it as a specific dimension of the action, embodied in clear evidence for the ethical dispositions of the agents.[58]

Dramatically significant *ēthos* then for Aristotle has nothing to do with highly individuated characters, unconscious motives, or even settled and pervasive moral attitudes or orientation, but is 'that which reveals moral choice (*prohairesis*)—that is, when otherwise unclear, what kinds of things an agent chooses or rejects' (*Poetics* 1450^{b}9) in specific situations.[59] As Aristotle observes in an earlier passage, character does not feature for its own sake, but for the sake of the actions that spring from it and which it thus characterizes (1450^{a}20). 'Thought' (*dianoia*), which is closely associated with character as its verbal expression, is the term employed 'to cover the parts in which, through speech, they [the agents]

---

[56] Gill (1996) 100. Thus for Aristotle, 'tragedy, at its best, can offer an experience in which judgement and emotion are in harmony, as the complementary elements of a response to the pattern of action portrayed by the poet': Halliwell (1986) 26.

[57] Necessity is included with probability because of the generalizing quality of poetry as compared with history. 'Poetry should in some sense rise above mundane life (though not with a necessarily optimistic import) and elevate human action to a higher level of intelligibility, so that it acquires something that even the philosopher might recognise as significant': Halliwell (1986) 106.

[58] Halliwell (1986) 151–2: Halliwell's emphasis.

[59] The translations of the *Poetics* throughout are those of Halliwell (1995).

demonstrate something or declare their views' (1450ᵃ6; cf. 1450ᵇ10). It is, moreover, 'the capacity to say what is pertinent or apt' (1450ᵇ5).

Moral deliberations therefore will manifest both *ēthos* and *dianoia* and will be
of central revelatory importance, though, generally speaking, there is no need to
probe beneath the surface of characters' morally significant statements which are
taken unproblematically (by the Aristotelian) to reflect their true moral nature
(unless of course the character is obviously deceitful). Now our sympathy for
dramatic characters depends on our ability to identify with them, to recognize
them as 'like us' (1454ᵃ23). For Aristotle this is not a subjective consideration or
dependent on the dramatist's ability to manipulate our feelings independently of
our moral judgement, but is inseparable from our (ideally objective) moral
appraisal. As Halliwell observes, 'Aristotle's conception of the emotions, pity
and fear, itself rests on a cognitive basis: properly educated, at any rate, these
emotions are not arbitrary or irrationally impulsive, but are aligned with the
recognition and understanding of certain types and patterns of suffering and
misfortune.'[60]

We will object of course that Aristotle does not allow for the fact that a moral
reaction to a situation or person, real or fictional, is only one kind of reaction, and
that moral reactions themselves require further investigation in order to tease
them apart from other reactions that accompany and perhaps taint them. For
example, as we shall see, it would be simplistic to examine Agamemnon's deliberations at Aulis as if only moral considerations were at issue either for him or for
us in our complex reaction to him. Sympathy can be powerfully enlisted for
characters simply by presenting situations through their consciousness. We see
this in Ajax's reflections and deliberations (and notably in his deception speech),
in Medea's Great Monologue, and even more strikingly in Shakespeare's Macbeth,
even after he has deliberately embraced evil. However, our sympathetic identification with the thinking of morally dubious and even evil characters needs to be
based on an initial respect for them. For this reason there will be little sympathetic
identification on the part of the audience with the thinking of King Claudius in the
scene in which Hamlet catches him attempting to pray.

Strictly speaking, from the Aristotelian point of view, pity and fear, tragedy's
defining emotions, respond to a pitiable *situation* which is a probable or necessary
outcome of a logically coherent chain of events (for example, a reversal from
prosperity to misery) (1451ᵃ12–15), though a morally upright character who is
'like us' (1453ᵃ5) is required to feature in the situation in order to ensure that such
a reversal will indeed be properly pitiable. Although for Aristotle tragedy is an
emotional experience defined by the evocation of pity and fear, there is a moral
element in it, since these emotions are precisely conditioned or regulated by the
moral status of the character to whom they are directed. The 'soul, as it were' (οἷον
ψυχή, 1450ᵃ38) of tragedy for Aristotle is the logical arrangement of the incidents
(the plot) which have the universality of poetry (οἷα ἂν γένοιτο, 1451ᵇ5) rather
than the specific and often arbitrary quality of historical events (τὰ γενόμενα,
1451ᵇ4). The plot then represents not so much an arbitrary fiction as a philosoph-
ically generalized and 'more elevated' (σπουδαιότερον, 1451ᵇ6) vision of reality.

---

[60] Halliwell (1986) 76–7.

This vision is purely secular, but it excludes not only the Greek gods but also arbitrary fortune, and in doing so it operates with a superficial conception of the self alien to Greek tragedy, while it minimizes the tragic exposure of the characters and especially the morally challenging sense of the absurd with which they can be confronted. Within this artificially restricted world-view Aristotle has to allow for *hamartia* (1453ª9), the error of judgement which is a function of an all but unavoidable ignorance on the part of the character.

The characterization of Oedipus' sons in the *Seven* provides a good example of un-Aristotelian practice. Right up to his departure to meet Polyneices, Eteocles is the principal focus of the play. We follow his arguments, identify with his point of view, and infer his character (*ēthos*) from his expressed thought (*dianoia*), right through the shield scene in the conviction that we are being authoritatively led— until he opts for fratricide. At that point our horror and outrage are reinforced by the reaction of the chorus, so that Eteocles' defence of his resolve to meet his brother conflicts with conventional morality. But here we need to switch to Gill's 'personality viewpoint'. If we stay with Aristotle the play will have little more to say to us.

Controversy thus arises over whether we are to accept Eteocles' reasoning or go with the chorus. Polyneices, on the other hand, is presented only indirectly through the views of Amphiaraus (who seems reliable) and of the formal messenger who describes the emblem on his shield and his actual behaviour which is discrepant with the emblem. Eteocles emerges as the upright defender of Thebes, while Polyneices has come to attack and perhaps destroy his own native city. If we appeal to the tradition and object that Polyneices is in the right because Eteocles had agreed to surrender the throne to him at the end of the year, we shall receive no support from Aeschylus who tells us nothing. In real life we would insist on exploring the matter of the agreement as essential to the moral evaluation of the situation, but in drama we have to follow the dramatist.

But far and away the most interesting case of the tension between moral evaluation and psychological identification in Greek tragedy is Medea. From Gill's 'character viewpoint' (which, as we have seen, is Aristotle's exclusive viewpoint), Medea's behaviour is morally indefensible: she connived at the murder of two innocent people, her brother and Pelias, before she arrived in Corinth, and during the course of the play she murders four more—the king and his daughter and her own two sons. Medea herself presents these crimes as appropriate retribution directed at Jason for his infidelity and desertion, but no audience could accept this. From Gill's 'personality viewpoint', however, we are invited to empathize with Medea in her exile, in her desertion, in her social disabilities as a woman, and in her agonizing battle with her *thumos* in the Great Monologue; and we do so despite the fact that these perspectives can contribute no more than mitigation. But the personality viewpoint does more than this; it prevents us from dismissing Medea as 'the other', as totally alien to ourselves, and that keeps the play intensely relevant to us. In this way, the emotional engagement of the spectator emerges not as a distraction from but as integral to a balanced moral judgement.[61] A similar

---

[61] 'Whereas the impersonal investigator stands apart and in command, analysing an object, the inquirer who responds with creative imagination is thus not wholly separate, aloof and in full control,

paradox applies to real life: to have no empathy with (or, indeed, aversion from) the people we judge actually impoverishes our moral understanding.

MORAL CRISES

In a stimulating investigation of the moral dimension of modern fiction, S. L. Goldberg distinguishes 'conduct morality'—moral responses to specific crises—from 'life morality'—broadly the whole texture of the characters' moral lives, which is inextricable from all the other aspects of their lives and provides the proper explanatory context for their conduct morality.[62] Life morality though can be applied more rewardingly to the novels of Henry James than to Greek tragedy where character can be quite schematically conceived, especially in Aeschylus. The dramatic focus in each of a number of Aeschylus' tragedies is a moral crisis and the character's deliberative response to it. Such crises, in the sense of critical climactic *moments*, are less a feature of Sophocles' and Euripides' plays where we tend to find a more extended crisis, like the plague in the *Tyrannus* or Phaedra's passion for her stepson in *Hippolytus*. (I shall use the term 'crisis' to refer to both the short and the long variety since it is not the duration of the situation which is crucial here, but, as the term 'crisis' suggests, its 'critical' nature.)

In the case of Sophocles, this crisis may be generated partly by the hero himself, in the sense that it takes a particular sort of person, the Sophoclean hero, to recognize fully the moral implications of a crisis and to rise to its challenge, whereas in Aeschylus the character is, dramaturgically speaking, generated by the crisis—that is, more a function of the abstract requirements of the crisis itself. This means that the foci of interpretation of *Agamemnon* are the decision at Aulis and the carpet scene, because it is in these scenes that the qualities that the choral odes attach to Agamemnon as a military commander are dynamically exemplified. While Agamemnon *is confronted* by divine contrivance with a crisis which he has to solve before he can continue with the campaign against Troy and later by bold human contrivance with a second and analogous crisis before he can resume possession of his palace, Sophocles' Electra *finds herself in what she and she alone (rightly) interprets* as a crisis, a morally untenable and outrageous situation, and we come to understand her unconventional response to it from a number of scenes that reveal her thinking while contrasting her attitude with those of other people. Euripides' characters also find themselves in prolonged moral crises (such as Phaedra's passion or Medea's desertion by her husband), but they tend to lack

---

but mixed up in the subject of inquiry, immersed, implicated, participating in it and imaginatively becoming one with it': Adamson, Freadman, and Parker (1998) 106. The notion of the 'not wholly separate' enquirer, at times the 'objective' assessor, at others sympathetically and indeed empathetically engaged, chimes with Martha Nussbaum's (1986: 15) insistence on emotional knowledge that originates in a response which combines the cognitive with the affective. On the emotional power of identification with the characters and Plato's strictures thereon see Blundell (1989) 14–15. Sometimes the audience will be induced to sympathize simultaneously with characters that hold conflicting moral views: ibid. 16.

[62] Goldberg (1993) 42.

the moral endurance or perhaps integrity to respond adequately. Phaedra is already all but defeated by her passion, a crisis that comes upon her (from one perspective at least) from within her own mind; and Medea, though initially proceeding with confidence against an external evil, ends up a morally deluded and partly pathetic victim of a morally destructive force, her *thumos*, that, like Phaedra's passion, assails her from within and which would remedy one evil with a far greater one.

ELEMENTS OF MORAL RESPONSE

I turn now to the elements of moral response with particular reference to the deliberative process, that is the causal sequence of mental events that constitutes deliberation and regularly culminates in decision and action. Of course not all moral attitudes or resolutions in tragedy result from such a process. In some cases no moral deliberation is deemed necessary, as the agent has an immediate intuition (correct or incorrect) as to what is required. In other cases moral intuition gives rise to sheerly practical deliberations as to the best *means* of acting on such an intuition. Or again moral deliberation may be inferred to have already occurred. In any case, the elements of the deliberative process are relevant to any moral response, for even if an agent is happy to circumvent deliberation altogether and form an instantaneous resolve based on moral intuition, it is no less important for an observer to ask if the questions that should have arisen in the corresponding deliberation have been adequately settled in the immediate response.

In the section above on 'The Ancient Spectator and the Modern Reader', I argued for the legitimacy of applying modern perspectives to ancient tragedy, provided we do so 'through the filter of an ancient reading'. Accordingly, the questions I ask are modern and adapted, in the light of the character of tragedy, from a modern philosophical analysis of the deliberative process. On the other hand, since it makes obvious sense to enlist ancient philosophical sources when these can illuminate the investigation, in the detailed discussions of particular plays I have alluded to the views of Aristotle where applicable and, in the case of Medea, employed the familiar Platonic paradigm of the tripartite *psyche*. For my modern source I have turned to the admirably lucid analysis of Walter Glannon, partly because his is an approach in terms of 'event-causation' as opposed to 'agent-causation' and partly because his understanding of the controversial notion of autonomy, for all that it is thoroughly modern and secular, sits well with certain cases of divine psychological intervention in the tragedies.[63] As for an event-centred approach to deliberation, it has the advantage of being more inclusive since, as David Velleman argues, the agent 'can still lay claim to these functions [i.e. those associated with mental events] even if they are performed, strictly speaking, by some proper subset of him'.[64] And if the functions—the mental

---

[63] Glannon (2002).   [64] Velleman (1992) 475.

events that constitute deliberation—belong to agents, then they can be held
responsible for them.

But what it means to 'belong to the agent' needs further examination. While
Kupperman would link responsibility more to character, an 'event-causation'
approach goes directly to the mental events, bypassing, though not denying, the
link between character and these events. This will emerge from the following
summary of the 'component conditions of causal control' of the deliberative
process, as identified by Glannon. The summary highlights and in some cases
implicitly defines the key concepts (which I have italicized) for our investigation.

> The evaluative notion of *moral responsibility* is grounded in the descriptive notion of *causal
> responsibility*, which in turn is grounded in *causal control*. There are seven component
> conditions of causal control: (1) the cognitive capacity to respond to practical reason for
> action and to form intentions to act; (2) the cognitive capacity to respond to theoretical
> reason about the circumstances of action and the consequences of what we do or fail to do;
> (3) the affective capacity to have and to respond appropriately to emotions, which influence
> both practical and theoretical reasoning; (4) the capacity for *reflective self-control* over and
> to identify with the emotional states (desires, beliefs, reasons, and intentions) that issue in
> actions; (5) the volitional capacity to execute intentions in choices and choices in actions;
> (6) the physical capacity to perform actions, identified with voluntary bodily movements;
> and (7) the causal sensitivity of events in the world to one's beliefs and actions. All of the
> motivational states that I have mentioned must be *autonomous*. If these states have been
> generated by coercion, compulsion, or various types of external manipulation, then one
> must have the *capacity for reflective self-control*. One must be able to eliminate or else
> modify or reinforce these states and come to identify with them as one's own. This capacity
> is both cognitive, involving practical and theoretical reason, and affective, involving
> emotions.[65]

Moral awareness is of course a necessary condition of these cognitive and affective
capacities to respond.

It should be noted here that Glannon rejects '[t]he traditional conception of
freedom [which] says that a person chooses and acts freely and responsibly if and
only if he can choose and act other than the way he in fact does. But autonomy
and responsibility do not require alternative possibilities of any sort in the causal
pathway leading to action.'[66]

This exclusive focus on the 'causal pathway' has implications for agents whose
freedom to opt for alternative courses of action is cancelled by divine intervention,
in that it does not for that reason excuse them from moral responsibility. This
harmonizes nicely with the ancient view of the matter.

Of these component conditions only the first four will be of significant concern
to us, as none of our agents have any trouble physically executing their intentions,
moving their bodies accordingly, or existing in a world that allows these things to
happen. The fifth condition concerns the (problematical) application of the will,
discussed above ('cultural differences', at (3)). But to return to the omission of
character from the process, Glannon's analysis does not concern itself with the
source of the mental events (thoughts, feelings, and so on). What is important for
him is that, whatever their source, the agent is able to exert reflective self-control
over them. On character he remarks: 'particular actions and not the more general

---

[65] Glannon (2002) 25–6: my emphases.   [66] Ibid. 14.

concept of character should be the *primary* concern of responsibility. Although many actions are expressive of one's character, one's actions are neither logically nor causally entailed by one's character.'[67]

This may well be true of real people, but not of a dramatis persona whose character is schematically defined by a few characteristic actions, to the point that there is no room for any other kind of action. The whole character-centred approach to moral deliberation which is such a feature of the tragedies means that we shall have to supplement Glannon's components with some investigation of the agents' moral self-definition. This is of course crucial to the present project, the focus of which is moral awareness rather than moral responsibility.

Even if character is not 'the primary concern of responsibility', agents' aware-ness of their own characters will enable them to be on the lookout for patterns of thought or feeling which may be associated as much with weakness as with strength. One thinks here of the propensity for Sophoclean heroes in particular to respond in the light of what they conceive their characters to be, or indeed, to require. As Kupperman remarks, a strong character 'is strongly resistant to pressures, temptations, difficulties, and to the insistent expectations of others'.[68]

Finally, it should be made clear that because the above conception of delibera-tion is thoroughly modern it is not intended as a Procrustean bed, but will be applied in an exploratory spirit with proper respect for the ancient conceptual context.

METHODOLOGY

I turn now to the methodology of the analyses of individual plays that follow. A major task will be to identify in each case the moral crisis and its causation. I shall be concerned with the agent's contribution (if any) to the production of the crisis in the context of threats to his/her autonomy of thought or feeling, such as divine intervention or inherited character or guilt. In considering the crises themselves and the agents' deliberations where applicable, I shall not attempt to apply a checklist of questions in a set order to each character; that would detract from the flexibility of approach required when dealing with a very diverse collection of plays and would tend to disrupt the flow of the argument. The Conclusion at the end of each chapter will, however, review these questions more succinctly and the general Conclusion will offer comparisons between dramatists, characters, and plays. However, a range of what will become familiar issues will emerge at the appropriate time as we proceed through the plays. Some of these issues relate to the deliberative process and to Glannon's 'component conditions'.

Now because Greek tragic agents tend to relate moral issues primarily to their own characters or roles rather than simply, like a modern consequentialist, to the

---

[67] Glannon (2002) 68: my emphasis. Kupperman (1991) 58 concedes this point: 'Character only produces a propensity to act in certain ways.'
[68] Ibid. 14.

supposedly intrinsic moral demands of the situation, we need to begin with self-definition.

Is the agent self-defined? If so, in moral terms? As an individual or as a type? If as a type, is this self-definition in terms of a role or roles that carry conventional moral obligations?

The self-definition of the agent may be more explicit, as in the case of the Eteocles of the *Seven* or the Creon of *Antigone*, each of whom declares what a person with his role and in his position is required to do; or more implicit, as in the case of the Aeschylean Agamemnon who at Aulis clearly sees himself as a father, but more significantly as the commander in chief of the Greek expedition to Troy. In *Philoctetes*, Neoptolemus defines himself as a rather limited type, as the son of Achilles who, having inherited his qualities, is obliged to emulate them.

The first of Glannon's conditions requires the agent to recognize a morally charged situation for what it is. So let us formulate our next question thus:

Is the agent aware of the specifically moral implications of the crisis?

Even if ethics is restricted to explicit use of a decision-procedure . . . a crucial step before we can implement a decision-procedure is that we notice that a situation is problematic and then reflect on it. Thus, priority must be given to the moral agent's sensitivity, to her or his awareness that a case is morally problematic. Second priority goes to the agent's conscientiousness, as reflected in the willingness to reflect seriously on what seems morally problematic.[69]

However, agents may be morally aware in their crises and yet still fail to give appropriate weight to competing moral claims or fall under the influence of non-moral considerations. Hence our next question:

Does the agent act in harmony with his or her morality?

The agent's morality may differ from the implicit morality of the play, a problematical issue discussed above. This suggests our next question:

Is the agent's morality appropriate in the play's terms?

Returning now to Glannon, from his second component ('the cognitive capacity to respond to theoretical reason about the circumstances of action and the consequences of what we do or fail to do') we may formulate the question:

---

[69] Kupperman (1991) 72.

Does the moral agent understand the facts of the situation and the probable consequences of available courses of action?

Misunderstandings in this regard corrupt or distort moral deliberations, as with Deianeira's misplaced optimism about the salve or Oedipus' erroneous assumptions about his own identity and that of Laius' killer. The facts here, however, include the agents' characters, as our moral judgements are affected not only by 'circumstantial luck' (the situations we find ourselves in) but also by 'constitutive luck' (who we are by heredity and environment). Indeed, the Archaic Greek idea of our *daimōn* or destiny combines these two types of luck. This early concept of the *daimōn* is, in my view, actually a subtler notion than the later perhaps morally motivated Heraclitean identification of *daimōn* with *ēthos* (character), which effectively merges these two kinds of luck and exaggerates the extent to which our characters create our fortunes. (Oedipus' *daimōn* is more than his character combined with the circumstances it produces or moulds; it includes the uncanny 'coincidences' in his life.[70])

That the facts of the situation include the agent's character means that moral awareness entails a degree of self-knowledge in the modern individualized sense of the term. The degree of reflection that this self-knowledge implies lends support to Glannon's statement that our combined cognitive and affective capacity to reflect on our mental states is not '*determined*' by heredity and environment; we [real people, that is] are not mere 'social constructs'.[71] On the other hand, some literary characters may be defined in quite limited or schematic terms so that their reflective capacity relates entirely to a few simple roles and the notions characteristic of those roles. One might want to claim, for example, that Aeschylus' Orestes is defined as the representative son in a given social context, and that his ability to reflect on his deliberations concerning the matricide does not transcend that simple definition.

Glannon's third and fourth components, as we have seen, relate to emotions— the third to 'the affective capacity to have and to respond appropriately to emotions, which influence both practical and theoretical reasoning', and the fourth to 'the capacity for reflective self-control over and to identify with the emotional states (desires, beliefs, reasons, and intentions) that issue in actions'. This suggests our next set of questions:

Do agents integrate their emotions appropriately into the deliberations? To what extent are the agents' views of their moral obligations rationally thought out, and to what extent conventional or based on emotion?

Emotions that are neither arbitrary nor merely idiosyncratic will make an important contribution to moral deliberations if they are related to social norms

---

[70] According to Mikalson (1983) 66, 'most often gods and daimons [in popular thought] were distinguished in the sense that the gods were given credit for successes while the daimons were held responsible for failures'.

[71] Glannon (2002) 20: my emphasis.

(emotions such as shame or righteous indignation). We cannot control the sheer emergence of our emotions into consciousness, but we can, in principle, reflect on them once they have emerged and thereby control how or whether they are realized in action. Emotions in general, though, will be based on the cognitive understanding of a situation. 'Emotions are essential to moral agency. They enhance social cooperation by enabling us to recognize the needs and interests of other persons. Norms about how people are expected to behave toward others develop at least partly from these emotions.'[72]

Our next question relates to Glannon's threats to autonomy, that is 'coercion, compulsion, or various types of external manipulation':

> **Does the agent deliberate freely or is he or she subject to human or divine manipulation? If there is divine manipulation is the agent's deliberation corrupted or harmlessly overdetermined?**

Freedom of *action* is not the issue here—the ability to activate or realize a moral decision—but rather the freedom of the deliberative process that precedes the action and the agent's owning the process.

If a hypnotist induces the desire to stop smoking in a person who already has the desire to stop smoking, then that desire remains the person's own. The hypnotist's action is a superfluous sufficient condition for the desire and therefore plays no causal role in the way the smoker acquires and retains that desire. Manipulation alone does not undermine autonomy.[73]

However, more than *sheer* overdetermination is involved when the god inspires some feeling, like the bloodlust with which the Fury inspires Aeschylus' Eteocles, and a further stage is reached if that feeling alters the agent's otherwise autonomous deliberation.

CRITERIA OF SELECTION

A brief word about the selection of plays for examination. I have chosen those plays which I believe will yield the most illuminating answers to the questions which our investigation raises. The reader may wonder why I have omitted Antigone. I have done so partly because I have little to add to existing analyses of her character, while I find Electra, who is sometimes compared with her, morally much more interesting. Briefly though, Antigone's moral principles lend support to her emotionally based commitments to her family, but she fails to give the polis its due. Creon begins by rationalizing the policies that stem from his autocratic personality in his famous programmatic speech about the need to govern fearlessly and put the state before friends and relatives. This creates an

---

[72] Glannon (2002) 35.   [73] Ibid. 71.

impression of moral commitment, but that it is no more than rationalization becomes clear as he grows more and more irrational and insecure.

Another play whose absence might be regretted is *Orestes*. We saw that the moral universe of that play is problematical because of the uneasy amalgam of conflicting worlds. For this reason it is hard to gauge the validity of Tyndareus' attack on Orestes for the matricide and the latter's reply to that attack. While it would be an agreeable challenge to try to sort out these inconsistencies and settle on an appropriate moral perspective (or indeed perspectives), Orestes himself is an inadequate moral agent. His consuming desire throughout the play is to free himself from the oppression of his supernatural and human adversaries (the Furies and the hostile Argive *dēmos*), and, although in doing so he deploys moral arguments in defence of the matricide, his arguments and, later, actions do not proceed from moral commitment but from a sheer desire to survive. Moreover, as the three *philoi*—Orestes, Electra, and Pylades—conspire to kill Helen and kidnap Hermione, they self-deludingly rationalize their unlovely scheme as a heroic enterprise.

2

Moral Autonomy and Divine Intervention

INTRODUCTION

As we saw, following Glannon and looking at the matter from a modern perspective, the critical factor in moral responsibility is the autonomy of the deliberative process.

All of the motivational states that I have mentioned must be *autonomous*. If these states have been generated by coercion, compulsion, or various types of external manipulation, then one must have the capacity for reflective self-control. One must be able to eliminate or else modify or reinforce these states and come to identify with them as one's own. This capacity is both cognitive, involving practical and theoretical reason, and affective, involving emotions.[1]

Similarly, for Aristotle, an act is compulsory (βίαιον) 'when its origin is from without, being of such a nature that the agent (πράττων) or person compelled (πάσχων), contributes nothing to it (*NE* 1110ᵃ1–3).

The threats to moral autonomy specified above are all external. External, presumably, to the conscious deliberating mind, so we shall need to include unconscious mental events in the category of 'external manipulation'. This will be a useful strategy, because divine overdetermination and such factors as one's *daimōn* (discussed below) which fail to coincide with or cut across modern (and indeed Aristotelian) psychological categories tend to operate within this zone of unconscious events, so that a twofold division emerges which is open and general enough to apply to both cultures, ours and that of Greek tragedy. We have then: (1) the conscious mind characterized by deliberation and regulation of mental events; and (2) all mental events that fall outside it, whether we want to include these in the self or attribute them to a divine being.

We like to think of ourselves as conscious agents constantly deciding on courses of action, but much of our mental life simply presents itself to consciousness. These spontaneously emerging psychological events are no more under our control than are external pressures in the sense that we cannot prevent them impinging on our consciousness, though we may be able to regulate their effect

---

[1] Above, Ch. 1, under 'Elements of moral response'; Glannon (2002) 26: see ibid. 40 on Aristotle and involuntary actions.

once they have emerged.[2] They may, like obsessive thoughts, belong to a pattern of mental events characteristic of us as individuals. Other spontaneously emerging thoughts may strike us, rightly or wrongly, as anomalous or out of character. On such occasions we may remark, 'I don't know what got into me.' Our basic psychological model then is likely to be that there is an unconscious region of the mind from which such thoughts emerge, sometimes under the stimulus of external events. For the Greeks this unconscious region is the domain in which divine intervention operates.[3] Autonomy cannot apply to this spontaneous emergence of mental events in consciousness, whether the source is conceived as some god or 'the unconscious'. Autonomy can only begin to apply when consciousness reacts to these mental events. Therefore what we need to consider in assessing the examples from tragedy is the autonomy or otherwise of the agent's conscious reflection on these spontaneously emerging mental events; and I am arguing that 'autonomy' is a perfectly reasonable term to apply to this reflection when there is no interference from any entity distinct from the conscious self.

Divine intervention is clearly a case of 'external manipulation' in the sense that it forces its way unbidden into consciousness. According then to Glannon's model, autonomy is intact so long as agents remain in control of their thoughts and feelings, or at least those thoughts and feelings that contribute to the decision. Of course, writing for our era, Glannon has in mind manipulation of the secular sort more easily recognized by the agent. If I know that someone is strongly pressuring me to reach a particular decision, I nevertheless retain my autonomy provided that I can resist the pressure and decide independently. I may of course decide that the pressure is exactly in the direction of the decision I had already intended to make, like the hypothetical case of the hypnotized agent cited in Ch. 1. On the other hand, I may unselfdeceivingly come to believe that, whatever the motive of the pressuring agent, the decision which that agent wants me to make is after all the right one, though not the one I had intended to make. Whatever the specific scenario, the key issue is whether I, the agent, remain in control.

Now it may be objected that this modern secular model of external interference in the thought processes of an otherwise autonomous individual is too sharply antithetical to apply to ancient tragedy where the boundaries between an inchoately conceived self and the 'interfering' deity are murky or, more charitably, paradoxical. Consider the following, which goes to the heart of J.-P. Vernant's view of Greek tragedy:

---

[2] Seneca devotes a considerable part of the second book of his *De Ira* to an interesting discussion of this issue in respect to controlling emerging anger at the stage at which it is scarcely more than subliminal.

[3] 'When the gods give someone a reason . . . the space for their intervention is left by the fact that there is no explanation of why that reason should have occurred to the agent or should have prevailed if it occurred. Such spaces still exist in our world. People act for reasons, and those reasons often explain what they do; but why one reason should prevail rather than another, or take over someone's attention, can remain hidden. Homer's gods, in such cases as these, operate in the place of those hidden causes': Williams (1993) 32. This said, I do not wish to suggest that the Greeks explained *all* such thoughts as god-inspired.

The tragic consciousness of responsibility appears when the human and divine levels are sufficiently distinct for them to be opposed while still appearing to be inseparable. The tragic sense of responsibility emerges when human action becomes the object of reflection and debate while still not being regarded as sufficiently autonomous to be self-sufficient. The particular domain of tragedy lies in this border zone where human actions hinge on divine powers and where their true meaning, unsuspected by even those who initiated them and take responsibility for them, is only revealed when it becomes a part of an order that is beyond man and escapes him.[4]

This alleged inseparability of the human and divine levels is an idea that derives a certain *prima facie* plausibility from the striking, but by no means routine occasions in tragedy when a deity inspires a human agent with a thought or feeling, particularly when the human is unaware of this happening. It receives some support also from more prolonged causal sequences characterized by immanent divine activity. But there are long stretches in tragedy (and of course in Homer) during which the divine interest, though perhaps never entirely absent, is, to say the least, latent. During such periods human agents appear to operate quite freely and to be held responsible for their actions. To take a strong case, most, if not all, of the action of Euripides' *Hecuba* falls into this category; and all the Orestes characters of the matricide plays deliberate without Apollo encroaching directly on their psychological processes, although they are influenced in varying degrees by his oracle (as indeed were real people in fifth-century Athens). Moreover, it is quite clear in both Homer and tragedy that characters can make decisions without divine involvement, though on some occasions the gods are indeed participants. No doubt in some cases the difference is to be explained in literary rather than psychological or religious terms, while other cases involve genuine epiphanies. Psychologically, it would have been entirely possible for Sophocles to have motivated Oedipus' self-blinding without recourse to divine involvement, but to have done so would have deprived the hero of an insight central to the play. Literal epiphanies may be occasions for their Joycean counterparts.

CATEGORIES OF DIVINE INTERVENTION

It is perfectly valid then to employ as a working model a conception of the self that is distinct from the divine forces that sometimes intervene in psychological activity.

Divine intervention may be 'psychological' or more remotely 'panoramic'. The former involves putting thoughts directly into the agent's mind. Agents will in all probability be unaware of such thoughts as alien intrusions, either because (1.1) the thoughts are completely in harmony with their character or (1.2) because the interfering deity has induced some delusional state in them. If the thoughts are characteristic of the agent, an obvious question arises as to the point of the divine contribution. Is it a 'superfluous sufficient condition', a fifth wheel to the coach? In that case, autonomy remains unthreatened. If, on the other hand, the agent is

---

[4] Vernant and Vidal-Naquet (1981) 4–5.

deluded, then deliberative autonomy has obviously been lost. When (1.3) agents are aware of the alien thoughts, it may still be in their power to regulate them. They may be aware of the presence of a deity, as Ajax is aware of Athena and converses with her, or they may be aware simply of an alien emotion, as Eteocles seems to be at the climax of the shield scene of the *Seven*.

What I am calling 'panoramic intervention' occurs when the gods broadly shape the destiny of the characters or exercise a general control over a sequence of events without being represented as directly intervening in human mental states. This is typical of religious thinking because if a god is to be of any use to his worshippers he must, unlike the gods of Epicurus, intervene in some way in their affairs. Popular religious thought, naturally enough, is innocent of the causal difficulties that arise from this kind of thinking. As Mikalson observes: 'Although the Athenians had rather specific beliefs about the areas of human life in which the gods intervened, they seem to have been content, on the popular level, with only the vaguest notions about the nature and mechanical operation of this intervention.'[5]

This kind of pervasive intervention became much more problematical with the development of Christian theology with its god intervening in history and the cardinal importance it attributes to free will. Christian theology has traditionally distinguished God as primary cause from the secondary human or natural cause. Aquinas, for example, thought that 'there is ... nothing against one and the same action issuing from a primary and secondary agent',[6] an idea that was to have a long theological history, though it seems to raise the problem of free will in an acute form, while with the development of scientific determinism the door seemed more tightly shut on divine intervention. The only way out of the impasse is to attack scientific determinism and offer a new causal model.[7] Naturally in Greek tragedy we cannot expect to discover causal clarity at the point of intersection of the divine and the human. We can only ask what the Greeks thought the gods contributed by their involvement.

Divine participation may be apparent, for example, (2.1) through some power-ful pressure, or *anankē*, such as Agamemnon confronts at Aulis, or (2.2) through a number of 'coincidences', as in the ironical plot of *Oedipus Tyrannus*. There may be (2.3) little intimation of divine participation in the narrative of the events themselves, though we may be told that a divine plan is being worked out, as in the case of Aphrodite's intervention in *Hippolytus*. Coincidences are a most plausible way of slipping the divine into the sequence, because they do not violate the natural order—they are causally, rationally, naturally explicable—but they suggest the numinous. They defy probability but do not, strictly speaking, violate secular

---

[5] Mikalson (1983) 53.   [6] Thomas (1983) 2.

[7] e.g., according to the philosopher Alfred North Whitehead, the inspiration for Charles Hart-shorne's influential 'process theology', 'God is in the environment of every non-divine event. As such, each event receives data from God as well as from non-divine causes. Accordingly, to give a sufficient explanation of any event, reference must be made to God as well as to the influence of previous non-divine events and to the self-determination of the event in question': D. R. Griffin (1983) 125. Another possibility is to focus on agents and actions rather than on events, which facilitates the claim that 'the acts of human agents cannot be exhaustively explained in categories which reduce them to causally necessary happenings': Kirkpatrick (1983) 172. And, by extension, this applies to God's acts if one sees God as an agent alongside other agents.

causation and so they seem to undermine it without really doing so. The natural-istically improbable must be distinguished from the naturalistically impossible.

The wider panoramic intervention may incorporate a psychological interven-tion, as in the case of Oedipus' self-blinding. The potential infringement of autonomy in the 'psychological' cases is easy to see, but a similar threat operates at a more metaphysical level even in the 'panoramic' cases.

Although these types of divine involvement may pose only a temporary threat to the autonomy of the characters, this is enough to compromise particular sequences of deliberation. Of course, a much more radical threat would be posed by causal determinism, one of the bugbears of modern ethical theory, which, briefly, is 'the thesis that, for any given time, a complete statement of the facts about that time, together with a complete statement of the laws of nature, entails every truth as to what happens after that time.'[8] Causal determinism, however, is not a feature of Greek tragedy. What we find, on occasion, however, is rather an unphilosophical and rather incoherent notion that we may perhaps describe as 'popular' or 'very soft' determinism which entails that only certain landmark events are preordained.

PSYCHOLOGICAL INTERVENTION

(1.1) Intervention in harmony with character

After Agamemnon's murder, Clytemnestra first proudly represents the deed as an act of justice and as the work of her hand (Aesch. *Ag.* 1405–6). But as the chorus drive her on to the defensive she claims first that she, Agamemnon's wife, did not perform the act she has just so enthusiastically embraced as her own (1497), and then, inconsistently, that she did indeed do it, but that she is not Clytemnestra but the *alastōr* of the house 'impersonating' Clytemnestra (1497–504). The chorus will concede only that she and the *alastōr* may have collaborated (1505–8), so that she cannot be innocent (*anaitios*, 1505)—and that collaboration presumably took the form of divine possession.[9] Here then is a case for moral autonomy, with the agent implausibly denying responsibility and another party strongly insisting on it, and this in the problematical context of divine overdetermination.[10] Moreover, the idea of Clytemnestra's autonomy is supported by the overwhelming impression that she is very much her own woman with her own strong motivation for killing her husband.[11] If this collaboration scenario is accepted, we have a case of psychological intervention, and indeed of overdetermination in its pure form, as it were, that is as a superfluous sufficient condition of an event, in that the *alastōr* appears to make no material contribution, and the murder seems sufficiently explained without its agency. But we are given no account of Clytemnestra's

---

[8] Fischer and Ravizza (1993) 14.

[9] For a discussion of *aitios* and its compounds in *Oresteia* see Hammond (1965) 53.

[10] For a brief discussion of autonomy and divine collaboration with Greek and NT examples see ibid. 44.

[11] On the question of Clytemnestra's responsibility see the excellent discussion ibid. 43–4.

deliberations prior to the killing, so there is no opportunity for us to observe the intervention of a collaborating *alastōr* at that point. The activity of such a being can only be reasonably inferred from the fact that Agamemnon was cursed and that he is now dead in a vengeance killing connected with the family curse. The *alastōr* then is an agent in a larger divine plan.

Similarly, with reference to *Persae*, as E. R. Dodds observes, the messenger 'attributes Xerxes' unwise tactics at Salamis to the cunning Greek who deceived him, and simultaneously to the *phthonos* of the gods working through an *alastōr* or evil daemon; the event is doubly determined, on the natural and on the supernatural plane'.[12] I would say that the *alastōr* here is the apparently superfluous immediate determinant of Xerxes' tactics (psychological intervention), but behind the *alastōr* are the gods motivated by *phthonos* (panoramic intervention).[13] This *alastōr* remains, to our way of thinking, causally superfluous, but the divine *phthonos* confers a higher meaning on the event when we take a broader view of it. Moreover, the divine 'plane' may have the additional function of universalizing the human events.

What (H. D. F. Kitto asks with reference to *Oresteia*) 'is the dramatist's idea of the relationship between what the gods do and what the human agents do? . . . [T]he human agents are absolutely autonomous; when the same action is attributed to both gods and men, the effect is to make us contemplate it as an individual action which has the nature of a universal.'[14] Now this is essentially a literary rather than a causal or a metaphysical interpretation. The divine involvement helps us to see the individual actions in a different light. This is doubtless true, but there is a danger that the gods will be denied not only causal effect but also metaphysical significance, so that, while literally accepted, they will be effectively rationalized out of the plays, reduced to *mere* literary devices. This produces serious distortions when Kitto, writing of the *Seven*, tells us that 'Eteocles, being what he is, no other outcome was possible . . . the inherited doom is but the projection of inherited situation and inherited character.'[15] Fortunately, however, Kitto does not consistently apply this reductive principle, for, commenting on the scene in *Agamemnon* in which Cassandra divests herself of her priestly regalia, he rightly states that we are made to feel that 'it is none other than the god himself who, in his anger, is driving her to die'[16]—a reading that takes us beyond the natural motivation of the human agent.

Clytemnestra's murder of Agamemnon is overdetermined by the activity of an avenging spirit, an *alastōr*, but we are not told whether the spirit intervened in her deliberations or simply in the execution of the deed. We know too little for a deeper understanding of the process, nor can we reasonably expect tragedy— which is not, after all, philosophy—to enlighten us. We know a good deal more, however, about the *daimōn* in *Oedipus Tyrannus* that assisted the hero in the events leading up to and including the self-blinding. First of all, the messenger insists, significantly in the light of what follows, that what Oedipus has done he did uncompelled (ἑκόντα κοὐκ ἄκοντα . . . αὐθαίρετοι, *OT* 1230–1). As the collaboration of a spirit did not exonerate Clytemnestra, so what Oedipus will do in

[12] Dodds (1950) 31.   [13] One thinks of Iris and Lyssa, the agents of Hera in *Heracles*.
[14] Kitto (1961) 70.   [15] Ibid. 48.   [16] Ibid. 76.

collaboration with another spirit will be done without compulsion or in accordance with his desire. The messenger goes on to describe Jocasta's frantic reaction to the revelation, interrupted by Oedipus who broke in, 'raving' (φοιτᾷ, 1255), calling for a sword and asking where he could find Jocasta. But in his 'mad state' (λυσσῶντι, 1258) it was, in the opinion of the messenger, a deity (δαιμόνων ... τις, 1258) that showed him the way and certainly not one of the human bystanders. Oedipus here is not mad in the sense of deluded; he is frantic and overwrought. The intervention of a *daimōn* is inferred from the fact that Oedipus' uncertainty seemed immediately resolved without human help and from his calling out 'as if there were a guide' (ὡς ὑφ' ἡγητοῦ τινος, 1260); no such *daimōn* was of course visible. There are no further references in the narrative to such a spirit, but Oedipus' vehement and overwrought state of mind continues until the completion of the self-blinding.

It would seem from the above that the *daimōn* (Apollo, perhaps, in Oedipus' case) attaches himself in a manner familiar from Aeschylus to a pre-existing attitude of mind. In *Persae* we are told that if the mortal is enthusiastically committed the god 'attaches himself' (συνάπτεται, *Pers.* 742). Whereas, in *Ajax*, Athena actually intensifies the hero's madness (*Aj.* 59–60), the *daimōn* here seems to clear the way for the fulfilment of Oedipus' purpose; and Oedipus, like Eteocles with respect to the Fury in the *Seven*, recognizes the objectification of his destiny in the form of the deity (*OT* 1311). Eteocles, as we shall see, fatalistically acquiesces in the Fury's purpose while he perceives within himself an alien mental state. But Oedipus is in accord with the *daimōn* as he seeks out an appropriate response to the indescribable horror that has descended upon him, and it is clear that the blinding is unpremeditated, as Oedipus sees the brooches on his mother-wife's body and knows at once what he must do. Once the messenger has introduced the idea of the guiding *daimōn*, we naturally infer that this being may have inspired Oedipus to perform the self-blinding, but in doing so it has only facilitated a response that he himself considers appropriate and strongly defends after the event. Far from wishing to evade responsibility, Oedipus insists on it.

So does the *daimōn* interfere with Oedipus' 'deliberations'? Oedipus' mental state is such of course that 'deliberations' are hardly at issue; nevertheless, he is searching for a response. (His first impulse seems to have been to kill Jocasta.) In such an unprecedented and (one is tempted to say) absurd situation, any kind of normal rational response must be doomed to irrelevance. We saw that the messenger insisted on the voluntary nature of Oedipus' acts, and Oedipus himself tells the chorus that Apollo inspired the blinding but that the act was the work of his own hand (1329–31). We can say then that Oedipus acted autonomously, and that, far from perverting his judgement, the *daimōn*, paradoxically enough, clarified for him the 'right' course of action for which he was groping in the strange circumstances.

(1.2) Intervention producing delusion

After recounting verbatim Agamemnon's deliberations at Aulis (which will be discussed in detail in Ch. 4), the chorus tell us that when he had put on the yokestrap of necessity (*anankē*), his mental wind veering in a direction that was impious, impure, unholy, from that point (*tothen*) he turned to a mindset that would stop at nothing; for men are emboldened by miserable infatuation (*parakopa*), whose shameful schemes are the beginning of their sufferings. In short, he brought himself to become the sacrificer of his daughter . . . (Aesch. *Ag.* 218–25: tr. Sommerstein).

This would seem to imply that the unholy thoughts to which his mind had turned accompanied and presumably motivated the putting on of the yoke of *anankē*. It was then a short step from there to an utterly reckless state of mind, but this progression was determined or perhaps overdetermined by *parakopa* which, as *tothen* (220) suggests, arose after the veering of his mental wind.

But what exactly is this *anankē* and whence the *parakopa*? For Albin Lesky the *anankē* is 'the overwhelming force of the situation'. He speaks of

the king's personal decision springing from his will, but the freedom of will is overshadowed by the overwhelming force of the situation which clearly influences the decision. Thus it is correct to speak of a free choice up to a point; as for the final decision, however . . . *acte voluntaire, necessité*, and *perturbation* are united in it. . . . The sacrifice of Iphigeneia is not only a horrible necessity imposed upon him; it is at the same time his personal and passionately desired deed, for which he is responsible and for which he has to atone.[17]

It is notable that the divine intervention implied in this view does not involve direct psychic invasion, but takes the form of manipulation of outward circumstances—the creation of an *anankē*—in such a manner as to induce a particular state of mind in the human agent. Lesky's references to 'his will' and 'the freedom of will' are taken up by J.-P. Vernant who, like Williams, reminds us that the will is 'a complex construction whose history appears to be as difficult, multiple and incomplete as that of the self, of which it is to a great extent an integral part'.[18] Vernant prefers the view that the decision is generated not by the will but by 'an *anankē* imposed by the gods'.[19] Since the hero 'appropriates' the necessity that faces him, 'the margin of free choice, without which it would seem that the subject cannot be held responsible for his actions, is reintroduced at the heart of the "necessary" decision'.[20] Therefore

the problem is to determine whether the *anankē* . . . always . . . takes the form of an external pressure exerted upon man by the gods. May it not also be presented as being immanent in the hero's own character or appear in both these aspects at the same time so that, from the tragic point of view, the power which engenders the actions appears in two opposed but inseparable guises?[21]

Carefully negotiating his way around the anachronistic concept of 'the will', Vernant proceeds to argue that 'when Agamemnon was carried away by his desire he was acting if not in a willed manner (*voluntairement*) at least voluntarily (*volontiers*), of his own volition (*hekōn*) and that, in this sense, he does appear to be *aitios*, the responsible cause of his own actions'.[22] Thus the application of 'the will' as a kind of faculty is replaced by the more passive *hekōn*, that is, acting

---

[17] Lesky (1966*a*) 81–2. Similarly Snell (1928) 125.
[18] Vernant and Vidal-Naquet (1981) 29.
[19] Ibid. 30.   [20] Ibid. 31.   [21] Ibid. 47.   [22] Ibid. 51.

in a way that is at least not contrary to one's desires. In this paradoxical formulation irresistible divine pressure is supposedly reconciled with the autonomy of the human agent. But even if we are prepared to accept that acting out of a psychological *anankē* is compatible with acting *hekōn*—since the compulsion is endogenous—in what sense can the same *anankē* be conceived as expressing itself at once in external events and psychologically?

Surely there are simpler solutions. If we take *anankē* to refer to a metaphysically unavoidable action, the sacrifice of Iphigenia, then it is perfectly possible that Agamemnon only thinks that he is free, unlike Eteocles who embraces such a necessity recognizing it for what it is. But in neither case do we have to duplicate the necessity in the psychology of the agent. Another option is to deny that *anankē* refers to necessity in the strict sense. As Dover points out, the term 'is applicable to any physical, legal or moral force to which resistance is shameful, painful, perilous or for any other reason difficult'.[23] We must also dispute the phrase 'immanent in the hero's own character'. What seems to happen is that the character, Agamemnon in this case, responds to a sense of powerful *anankē* by embracing it, and, as we have seen, the chorus describe his state of mind at the time as *parakopa*—which, far from suggesting a mental process 'immanent in the hero's own character', registers precisely a departure from it. In fact, it looks very much as if the gods have deluded Agamemnon or at least inspired in him an undesirable and extreme mental state. Admittedly, there is nothing explicit to this effect in the text, but Eteocles' strange and divinely induced mental state at the climax of the shield scene of the *Seven* is described by the chorus of that play in very similar terms, though—as we shall see—Eteocles is not essentially deluded. When he learns of the allocation of the seventh gate to his brother, he becomes at once (rightly) convinced that his father's curse has now been activated by the Fury and he describes the family as 'god-maddened' and 'god-hated' (Aesch. *Sept.* 653–5). Indeed, he recognizes this madness (σὺν φοίτῳ φρενῶν, 661) not in himself but in Polyneices whose mental attitude he describes, in terms similar to those applied to Agamemnon in this passage, as 'utterly reckless' (παντόλμῳ φρένας, 671; cf. *Ag.* 221: παντότολμον). His own state of mind, though, is undeniably strange, and the chorus urge him to be unlike Polyneices in temper (ὀργήν, 678), accuse him of madness (τί μέμονας; 686), and refer to his 'warrior's mad infatuation that fills the heart' (θυμοπληθὴς δορίμαργος ἄτα, 686–7). We know that the Erinys is working through him, as it is presumably working also through Polyneices, and that, despite what is, paradoxically enough, a rationally defensible accommodation to the inevitable divine will, he seems less horrified than he should be at the prospect of the miasma consequent upon the shedding of kindred blood. This seems equally true of Agamemnon in this passage, although he lacks Eteocles' insight into the divine will. Nor is there any reference to an Erinys, though with a bit of encouragement from Aeschylus one might have called to mind the Erinyes of the house of Atreus. But, as it is, these Furies have not yet entered the play.[24]

---

[23] Dover (1973) 65.
[24] Lloyd-Jones (1962) 192; Hammond (1965) 42–3. 'The crime of Atreus . . . is introduced only after Agamemnon has already left the stage': Gagarin (1976) 63.

Perhaps we are to feel that certain types of situation have an almost supernatural power to tempt people. In any case, it would be reckless to assert that Agamemnon is acting autonomously by Glannon's criteria while he is subject to *parakopa*, a 'knocking sideways', as it were, of his mental processes. Clearly at Aulis there is an overarching 'panoramic' intervention which at the point of the decision itself at least borders on 'psychological' intervention. But it is possible that Agamemnon's actual decision proceeds from his character, or at least from his self-identification with the role of commander-in-chief. In other words, the divine intervention in the form of *parakopa* (if this is what is happening) corrupts perhaps only the mood in which Agamemnon decides, but not the integrity of the deliberations themselves. Is Agamemnon then deluded, after all? Certainly he lacks Eteocles' comprehensive understanding of the implications of his situation. He does not realize that his decision has sealed his fate.

But there is a further problem. The precise application of the *anankē* here is a contentious issue. We are told that Agamemnon 'put on' ($\check{\epsilon}\delta v$, 218) the yoke of *anankē*. This could mean either that he actively chose, even embraced, what was in any case either literally irresistible (substantially Lesky's position) or all but so (Dover's position), or that in making his decision he created an *anankē*—that of his murder at the hands of his avenging wife. Luckily, however, nothing of great causal significance hangs on the choice of interpretations, since there is in any case strong constraint operating both before and after the decision.

(1.3) Awareness despite intervention

When Eteocles learns that his brother is stationed at the seventh gate he correctly realizes that the curse is about to be fulfilled. He forbids himself tears for fear of inflaming further a highly emotional situation (*Sept.* 656–7) and proceeds to argue, as far as we can tell from the text, apparently as calmly as before, that Polyneices has no claim to justice and that he (Eteocles) will appropriately face him himself. The chorus on the other hand perceive anger or rage in him ($\dot{o}\rho\gamma\acute{\eta}\nu$, 678), and then madness (686), and 'spear-mad delusion' ($\delta o\rho\acute{\iota}\mu a\rho\gamma os$ $\check{a}\tau a$) when Eteocles insists on his resolve. Eteocles rejoins that he is only contemplating what 'the god' is hastening on (689) and then he mentions Apollo's hatred of the family (691). The chorus accuse him of 'a savage-biting desire' ($\dot{\omega}\mu\omega\delta a\kappa\grave{\eta}s$ $\check{\iota}\mu\epsilon\rho os$) to shed kindred blood. He agrees ($\gamma\acute{a}\rho$, 695), explaining it as the product of his father's curse. We have then here something like Agamemnon's recognition of an *anankē*, except that this is undeniably an inescapable *anankē*. His own highly emotional state, his powerful desire, Eteocles attributes pretty clearly to supernatural inspiration, whether we see it as a personified curse (*Ara*), or as the Erinys, or as Apollo, or all together. Agamemnon was, as far as we can tell, unaware of his *parakopa*, nor was that state unequivocally the work of a divine power. But in Eteocles' case there is awareness and a stronger sense of a divine intervention. All this said, it by no means follows, as we shall see in the next chapter, that Eteocles is deluded or his judgement warped by this strong desire.

PANORAMIC INTERVENTION

Let us now consider three cases of panoramic intervention: the wider divine involvement in the Aeschylean Agamemnon's activities, Apollo's involvement in the destiny of Oedipus in Sophocles' *Oedipus Tyrannus*, and Aphrodite's manipulation of Phaedra and her stepson in Euripides' *Hippolytus*.

(2.1) In *Agamemnon*, several divine forces operate, though not always in concert. There is the *alastōr* (*Ag.* 1501) of the House of Atreus, an entity that seems to duplicate the chorus of Furies to which Cassandra refers (*Ag.* 1190), and there are many references to vague powers that suggest an impersonal fate and to personified agents such as Dike (Justice), Ate (Delusion), and Menis (Wrath).[25] But it is Zeus who is *panaitios* (the cause of everything) and *panergetēs* (the doer of everything) (*Ag.* 1486), which perhaps need not be taken in the strong sense to mean that he is immanent throughout the entire causation but can be understood in a weaker sense to mean that everything is eventually brought under his control—an idea reflected in the resolution of the *Eumenides*.[26] For this to happen Zeus would not need to interfere directly in all human events, both psychological and physical, but he *would* need to anticipate them, or at least counteract undesired developments, and incorporate them into his plan. In this way he could anticipate Agamemnon's decision without intervening in his deliberations. The Trojan War proceeds under Zeus's auspices. The chorus inform us that he 'sends' (πέμπει, *Ag.* 61) the Atreidae against Paris, but since there is no suggestion of a specific command perhaps we should translate 'escorts' or 'speeds on his way'. Zeus as *panaitios* is active (in some mysterious way) through his human agent Agamemnon in casting his symbolic net over Troy (*Ag.* 361), and Agamemnon acknowledges the contribution of the gods in general when he describes them as 'joint causes' (*metaitious*, 811) with him of the sack of Troy. This type of intervention then is 'panoramic', and we can see that this can take the stronger form of ongoing immanent intervention in events or the weaker form of factoring autonomous events into a broader plan.

Agamemnon then *is* an agent of the will of Zeus. We know that Zeus sent the portent of the pregnant hare. The text is silent on the precise nature of the supreme god's intervention, but Zeus may perhaps be imagined as having designed the portent in such a way as to provoke Artemis' reaction and thus create Agamemnon's dilemma (although this is perhaps to peer illegitimately into the dramaturgical machinery of the play in a futile search for metaphysical coherence). At any rate, it is consistent with Zeus's designation as *panaitios* to have anticipated (but not necessarily directly caused) both Artemis' reaction and Agamemnon's decision. But Agamemnon is also subject to the family curse. The curse might appear to predetermine his death and therefore its prerequisite, the sacrifice of Iphigenia, and thus his deliberations. This is the view of

---

[25] e.g., *to peprōmenon* (68, 685), *moira* (130, 1330–1, 1535–6), *daimōn* (1342, 1468, 1660), *menis* (702), Ate (735, 1192, 1433), Erinys (749, 1433), *alastōr* (1501, 1508), Dike (1607).

[26] Hammond (1965) 45 denies Zeus's omnipotence in *Oresteia* (and elsewhere) on the grounds that he has to employ Athena to persuade the Furies in *Eumenides*. Absolutes such as omnipotent and omniscient are admittedly a bit hard to reconcile with the mechanics of anthropomorphic religion, but with the epithets *panaitios* and *panergetes* Zeus comes pretty close to the former.

Lloyd-Jones,[27] but it is ably refuted by Hammond in one of the best articles on this play. Lloyd-Jones would have it that the Atreid curse renders unfree all parties who are subject to it. Agamemnon's death is a product of the curse and his decision at Aulis is a prerequisite of that death, *ergo* Agamemnon's decision was unfree, and Zeus took away his wits. Hammond objects that the curse does not appear until Aegisthus introduces it late in the play and argues that Agamemnon's murder is overdetermined—the work of Clytemnestra, Zeus, and the *alastōr*.[28] Hammond considers Agamemnon's deliberations at Aulis to be autonomous, though overdetermined,[29] but Lesky, as we have seen, adopts a more paradoxical position.

(2.2) Now let us take another example of panoramic involvement, this time from Sophocles' *Oedipus Tyrannus*. Some claim that Apollo only predicts and so the humans are free, at least as concerns the onstage action.

According to Bernard Knox, Oedipus

is absolutely free and he is fully responsible for the catastrophe. Sophocles has very carefully arranged the material of the myth in such a way as to exclude the external factor in the life of Oedipus from the action of the tragedy. This action is not Oedipus' fulfillment of the prophecy, but his discovery that he has already fulfilled it.[30]

Again in his much later introduction to the Fagles translation of the play:

There is not one supernatural event in it [the play], no gods . . . nothing that is not, given the mythical situation, inexorably logical and human. So far as the action is concerned, it is the most relentlessly secular of the Sophoclean tragedies. Destiny, fate and the will of the gods do indeed loom ominously behind the human action, but that action, far from suggesting primeval rituals and satanic divinities, reflects, at every point, contemporary realities familiar to the audience that first saw the play.[31]

Leaving aside the fact that the above seems to assume that fifth-century Greeks thought pretty much as we do (logically and secularly!) and that Apolline intervention must be 'satanic', can the divinely predicted events that form the basis for the action really be so easily dissociated from it? Knox himself concedes that they cannot:

This presentation of the hero's freedom and responsibility in the context of the dreadful prophecy already unwittingly and unwillingly fulfilled is an artistic juxtaposition, a momentary illusion of full reconciliation between the two mighty opposites, freedom and destiny. It is an illusion because of course the question of responsibility for what happened *before* the play, of Oedipus' freedom in the context of divine prophecies fulfilled, is evaded.[32]

But even in the play itself there are some features that are resistant to this theory. Teiresias, for example, predicts the self-blinding. Knox replies that, since Oedipus does not believe the seer, the prophecy has no causal effect.[33] But this is to ignore the irony that Jocasta's reference to the triple crossroads, which is an essential link in the causal chain leading to the revelation, is inspired by Oedipus' reference to Teiresias' prophecies. Another problem is the plague, which Knox denies was caused by Apollo because he is not blamed for it but asked to cure it.[34] But a god

---

[27] Lloyd-Jones (1962) *passim*.   [28] Hammond (1965) 42–4.
[29] Ibid. 50.   [30] Knox (1957) 5–6.   [31] Knox (1984) 134.
[32] Ibid. 150.   [33] Knox (1957) 6–7.   [34] Ibid. 9.

may well correct something that he has himself caused once humans have rectified the situation that induced him to cause it. (One thinks of the plague in *Iliad* 1.) Moreover, Apollo notoriously both instils and remedies sickness. Prophecy, according to Knox, relies on free human action for its fulfilment.[35] This is often so, but, as we saw in the case of Aeschylus' Agamemnon, since the free action is foreseen it can be incorporated into a preordained result through the manipulation of outward circumstances. We may perhaps legitimately assume that Apollo knows what circumstances to invent in order to produce the required outcome; and these circumstances provide a dramatic arena for a man of Oedipus' character. Here therefore we have a case of panoramic intervention.

Knox's basic view is echoed in an influential article by Dodds who effectively distinguishes philosophical determinism from the flabbier popular variety which allows the agent to act freely within the restrictions of certain preordained events. Like Knox, he insists that the gods know the future but do not order it.[36] Similarly, for George Gellie:

The Apollo of the play is not cruel, only omniscient. The processes of the play are very cruel indeed, and the part played by coincidence in Oedipus' career is frightening. But it is not the murder and the marriage that destroy Oedipus; it is the discovery. He is destroyed by the truth, and Apollo cannot be blamed for knowing, or being, the truth.[37]

Kitto takes much the same position about the relationship between the divine and the human causation as he adopted for Aeschylus.

What happens is the natural result of the weaknesses and the virtues of his [Oedipus'] character, in combination with other people's. It is a tragic chapter from life, complete in itself, except for the original oracle and its repetition. Sophocles is not trying to make us feel that an inexorable destiny or a malignant god is guiding the events. But we are made to feel . . . that the action is moving, at the same time, on a parallel and higher plane.[38]

This idea that the circumstances of the action are produced entirely by the interaction of the characters ignores the many 'coincidences' of the play. The theory of parallel rather than intersecting planes of operation effectively banishes the gods from the action by its implication that events in the human world are correlated with events in a separate divine world. However, the gods of the *Iliad*, always more transparent than the gods of tragedy, live their own separate lives apart from specific acts of intervention where the 'planes' of action intersect. But Kitto himself has no desire to exclude the gods from the significant action of the play; and he rightly observes, with reference to events such as the timing of the arrival of the Corinthian shepherd, that '[t]he presence of some power or some design in the background is already suggested by the continuous dramatic irony.'[39]

According to G. M. Kirkwood too, Apollo's agency is confined to prediction,[40] while the remarkable coincidences of the play are not of divine origin.[41] But then Kirkwood introduces the idea of Oedipus' *daimōn*, which he characterizes (rightly, in my view) as partly a projection and objectification of the hero's character and partly an independent external power. 'The daimonic gives no moral or

---

[35] Ibid. 39.   [36] Dodds (1988) 42.   [37] Gellie (1972) 105.   [38] Kitto (1961) 139.
[39] Ibid.   [40] Kirkwood (1958) 276.   [41] Ibid. 280.

theological explanation of suffering or the cruelty of circumstances. It means . . . the inclusion in oneself of something foreign to oneself, a drive against oneself from within, an inner fate that is personalized and to some degree externalized.'[42]

Lesky, on the other hand, while seeing the hero as fighting against 'dark powers', specifically denies that the Aeschylean notion of a *daimōn* 'as partner (*syllēptōr*)' applies to the Sophoclean hero: 'Whatever he [the hero] does is prompted entirely by his own will, although the outcome is outside his control.'[43] But Oedipus himself, faced with the prospect of being Laius' killer, calls himself *echthrodaimōn* (beset by a hostile *daimōn*) (*OT* 816) and imputes the calamity to a cruel *daimōn* (828); and later, when the self-blinded hero returns to the stage, the chorus ask him what madness came on him and what *daimōn* leapt upon his *moira* (destiny) 'that was already beset by a negative *daimōn*' (*dysdaimoni*, 1302), and Oedipus himself remarks on how far his *daimōn* has sprung (ἵν᾽ ἐξήλου, 1311) (i.e. to the extent of the self-blinding).[44] It would seem then that Oedipus' destiny has been further extended, in a sense through an external supernatural agent, but also through his own character, since after the blinding he informs the chorus that, while Apollo brought to pass 'these sufferings of mine' (1330),[45] he (Oedipus) struck his eyes with his own hand because there was nothing pleasurable for him to see.

Peter Euben characterizes Oedipus as 'the unwitting [presumably before the self-blinding] but full partner of the god in his own destiny, neither autonomous nor a puppet.'[46]

In the end, Oedipus realizes that mortals cannot control their fate in the sense of taking it in their own hands and making it anything they wish. This does not mean that his fate is simply given or passively received, still less that he is morally exonerated from the consequences of deeds done in ignorance. It does mean that his fate becomes real only through the action of his character, that he is made by the destiny he helps fashion. . . . The idea that mortals are, despite their prowess, victims of barely discernible forces, which they nevertheless precipitate and constitute, is hard for an exceptional man like Oedipus to bear.[47]

While it is true that Oedipus is not explicitly 'morally exonerated', neither is he morally condemned, either by himself or by others. In so far as he sees himself as in some sense 'bad', the cause is his pollution rather than any sense of moral delinquency. Oedipus can perhaps be said to be (in part) the victim of forces he 'precipitates', but the claim that he also 'constitutes' such forces is more problematical. How we see the matter will depend on where we draw the boundaries of the self. Perhaps it would be better to say that his *daimōn* rather than his 'self' constitutes these forces. As we have seen, *daimōn* is a wider concept than

---

[42] Kirkwood (1958) 285. On the various meanings of *daimōn* see Cairns (forthcoming): 'the divine power which is envisaged as the dispenser of good and bad fortune becomes a metonymy for that good or bad fortune itself.'

[43] Lesky (1965) 117.

[44] Winnington-Ingram (1980) 173–8.

[45] 'The main reason why "it was Apollo" for Oedipus is simply that, as no one could deny, what Apollo had decreed had come to pass': R. C. T. Parker (1983) 17. It is reasonable (to the Archaic mind) to think that a god who predicts a destiny also brings it about.

[46] Euben (1986) 117.   [47] Ibid. 105.

character, though it includes it, or at least significant aspects of it. Character is an aspect or function of self, and aspects of the *daimōn* lie outside both character and self, as will be clear from my analysis of the self-blinding above.

J. D. Schwartz terms the participation of god and man 'dual or merged agency' and refers to Oedipus' 'responsible and voluntary acts'.[48] A man's *daimōn*

> has attended him from birth and has from the beginning shared in constituting his personality: it does not 'frustrate' his intentions because from childhood it has been active in shaping the entire range of characteristic responses from which his intentional acts derive.... The god and the mortal, joined since Oedipus's fateful birth, are doubles: both detest reticence and both are consumed with a passion for knowledge, driven to push the action through to its conclusion.[49]

But this view identifies the *daimōn* too closely with character; it makes insufficient allowance for (in Kirkwood's words cited above) 'the inclusion in oneself of something foreign to oneself, a drive against oneself from within', the element in fact that makes for tragedy. This element is also mysteriously externalized, ultimately in the person of Apollo whose purposes may indeed overlap with those of Oedipus but are not identical with them. Apollo works through Oedipus, but is hardly immanent in every event of his mental life. Oedipus' autonomy (or otherwise) will depend then, among other things, on the degree and extent of this immanence.

(2.3) In Euripides' plays the gods can be as conspicuously involved in the action as the Furies in Aeschylus' *Eumenides* or Athena in Sophocles' *Ajax*, and yet this involvement is often accompanied by such an emphasis on naturalistic causation and 'realistic' psychology that their agency can seem superfluous. A particularly striking case is that of Aphrodite in the *Hippolytus* who declares both her intention to punish the hero with death and the means she is employing to bring this about—primarily the inspiration of Phaedra with an irresistible passion for him. But when the details of the passion emerge, hereditary and environmental explanations are offered for it. Are these sophisticated explanations hints for us not to take the goddess literally, or is this just another case of overdetermination (but with the natural component 'updated'), which regularly entails one human (or naturalistic) as well as one divine cause?

Much will depend on dramatic focus and emphasis. It will be clear from our examination of Aeschylus and Sophocles that in both categories of intervention, the 'panoramic' and the 'psychological', it helps if there is some evidence of disturbance of the natural course of events; and we saw how in the *Tyrannus* Apollo's broader panoramic involvement is manifest in the coincidences and ironies of the plot, while in the self-blinding scene Oedipus seems to be in some mysterious communication with his *daimōn*. In the case of Euripides' *Hippolytus* then we shall be looking for intimations of some disturbance of the natural causation. Without such disturbance, we may feel that the two explanations, the divine and the naturalistic, are merely juxtaposed.[50]

---

[48] Schwartz (1986) 188, 194.   [49] Ibid. 202–3.

[50] Such an effect is not confined to Euripides, as we saw when considering Clytemnestra's collaboration with the *alastōr* in *Agamemnon*.

The interesting critical history of this problem of divine intervention in Euripidean drama begins, rather eccentrically, just before the turn of the twentieth century, with the so-called Rationalists,[51] and in particular A. W. Verrall who, denying that Euripides could have believed in the traditional Greek gods, went so far as to 'rationalize' these gods out of his plays altogether—that is, to deny their presence even on the literal level of the action. This theory led to the idea of two plays in one—one for ordinary dullards and another radically different one for those in the know.[52]

A generation later E. R. Dodds, while strongly concurring with Verrall that Euripides did not believe in the gods of myth, insisted that the tragedian thought that the 'inhuman and non-rational forces' which afflict characters such as Phaedra were indeed divine. Aphrodite, on the other hand, as she appears in human form in the prologue of *Hippolytus*, he considered more a 'petty fiend' than a goddess. In short, the gods as literally presented are satirically conceived, but they nevertheless symbolize 'eternal cosmic powers.' The point of the satire is 'to show that they must be interpreted as principles, not as persons.'[53]

The satirical explanation of the goddesses re-emerges nearly half a century later with G. J. Fitzgerald who finds the literal goddesses inadequate, since 'Euripides traces the connections between character or personality and action with a precision that renders the divine account both redundant and simplistic.'[54] Their function then is to facilitate an attack on the traditional world-view.[55]

The interpretation of the gods (or some of them at least) as symbols of impersonal forces of nature became the orthodox position in Euripidean scholarship. Here, for example, is the view of Lesky:

> Here [in *Hippolytus*] there is no question, as in the beginning of the *Ajax* or the end of *The Eumenides*, of a devout poet revealing his deepest thoughts on the relation between god and man. Aphrodite and Artemis are for Euripides not the real great powers which give the action its essential significance, they are for him the means, borrowed from popular religion, of crystallising inner experiences. What really matters throughout are those experiences themselves, the motive forces in the actual drama as it develops between the prologue and the epilogue in which Aphrodite and Artemis appear.[56]

Again, for Kitto, Aphrodite

> is not a mythical being whose existence Euripides is trying to disprove, not a cult whose observance he is trying to discredit; she is one of the elemental powers in nature, to Euripides as to Aeschylus. To both poets she and Artemis are complementary forces which have to be reverenced... To Aeschylus the law of Zeus does not tolerate partial adherence; Euripides puts the same idea into psychological rather than moral terms and will show us that there are laws of nature that demand obedience as well as laws of morality.[57]

---

[51] 'Rationalist' in the nineteenth-century sense of 'anticlerical': Dodds (1929) 97.

[52] e.g. in his discussion of *Alcestis* Verrall argues that the shocking and frivolous treatment (by late Victorian standards?) of a resurrection and of the characterization of the principals proves that Euripides' purpose is to 'kill the legend': Verrall (1895) 102. Alcestis, according to Verrall, does not die at all; the perceptive spectator will realize that she merely faints at the prospect of dying and has to be resuscitated (ibid. 94).

[53] Dodds (1929) 101–2.   [54] Fitzgerald (1973) 21.   [55] Ibid. 34–5.

[56] Lesky (1965) 150.   [57] Kitto (1961) 204.

Thus Kitto, while in agreement with Dodds in regarding Aphrodite as a symbol of an impersonal force of nature, does not see in her a secondary function of discrediting the state religion. Her secondary function is, in his view, rather to provide a 'tragic frame' for the fates of Phaedra and Hippolytus and to show that those fates are not 'in their hands'. Kitto accepts Phaedra's hereditary explanation of her passion but sees it as simultaneously, 'on a different plane', the work of Aphrodite[58]—'a potentially disastrous element in our nature'.[59]

D. J. Conacher returns to Dodds's satirical view of the goddesses of *Hippolytus*, but, in his view, the purpose of the satire is not to attack the state religion but 'to weaken our literal acceptance' of the goddesses so that we shall see them as symbols of elemental and impersonal forces—though Conacher has it that the Greeks (including in all probability Euripides himself) would have attributed Phaedra's passion to 'a divine power which was real enough, even if one could not grasp it with understanding'.[60]

For Winnington-Ingram, the goddesses of the *Hippolytus* symbolize 'real', 'powerful', and 'superhuman' forces that work through the complex human causation of the play—causation that includes hereditary and environmental influences.[61] He speaks, for example, of Aphrodite working through Theseus' characteristically passionate nature 'to further her purposes'.[62] But '[t]here is a depth and solidity in this tragedy upon the human plane that cannot adequately be expressed by two angry and sexually preoccupied goddesses', therefore '[i]t is by the tragedy that we understand the gods, not by the gods that we understand the tragedy.'[63] The idea of divine inspiration of the characters in harmony with natural causation appears also in Kovacs: 'In Phaedra's sudden delirium we are meant to see the direct action of Aphrodite, the fulfilment of her promise . . . to bring Phaedra's secret to light.'[64]

But once we reduce the humanized, personal deities to the level of still external but now unconscious forces, we narrow the gap between them and similar forces originating within the psyche, and the difference that remains relates to different conceptions of the self and its contents. To return to our two categories of overdetermination, the panoramic and the psychological, while a god can feel anger or *phthonos* and devise a plan to destroy a mortal, an external unconscious force can do no more than its intrapsychic equivalent. Similarly, to recur to Oedipus' self-blinding, if in that scene for the *daimōn* to which Oedipus calls out and by which he is led we substituted an unconscious, external power exactly equivalent to a psychologically generated impulse, we would be left, effectively, with nothing more than a naturalistically conceived sequence of events.

One of the finest articles on *Hippolytus* remains that of Bernard Knox, written nearly sixty years ago, though his deterministic view of the action has, quite rightly, been rejected. Discussing a major theme, Knox comments: 'The choice between silence and speech is more than a unifying factor in the play, it is a situation with universal implications; a metaphor for the operation of human free will in all its complicated aspects. And the context in which it is set demonstrates

---

[58] Ibid. 205.   [59] Ibid. 206.   [60] Conacher (1967) 28, 273.
[61] Winnington-Ingram (1960) 175–6, 184.   [62] Ibid. 187.   [63] Ibid. 183, 189.
[64] Kovacs (1987) 41. See also Dimock (1977) 250–6, Gregory (1991) 61.

the non-existence of the human free will, the futility of the moral choice.'[65] That context is Aphrodite's declared plan which (it is alleged) leaves no room for the characters to manoeuvre. But the free/determined polarity is anachronistic. On the alleged determinism Conacher rightly argues:

> the fact that all of the characters achieve by their combined actions a result which none of them (at least with the wisdom of hindsight) would want, proves not the lack of free will nor the futility of moral choice, but rather the *limitations* imposed on both, first, by the circumstances in which these characters are placed, and secondly, by the operation of the 'free will and moral choice' of the other characters.[66]

What then are we to make of Aphrodite as a meaningful agent in the action of the *Hippolytus*? Let us take a closer look at the prologue, but less from a metaphysical than from a dramaturgical perspective. The goddess informs us of Hippolytus' rejection of her and of her plan to destroy him through Phaedra's infatuation. Phaedra herself is not divulging her passion; none of the household knows of it (40), but Aphrodite will reveal 'the matter' (πρᾶγμα, 42) to Theseus and it will be made public (42). Theseus will then kill his son with curses (44).[67] Phaedra is being destroyed (ἀπόλλυται, 47) through the goddess' contrivances, despite retaining her good reputation.

Whether or not the audience had prior knowledge of the myth, they must have found this account perplexingly elliptical. What exactly is 'the matter' that Aphrodite will reveal? Phaedra's infatuation? If so, why should that induce Theseus to curse Hippolytus? And how will Aphrodite reveal this matter? In person? By manipulating the human characters? And how will Phaedra retain her reputation if her infatuation is revealed? If, on the other hand, the audience expected an immoral Phaedra, on the basis of some previous version of this myth or a similar myth, they might well wonder how anything like the traditional story could unfold.[68] A noble Phaedra might well seem fatal to the tale. By means of Aphrodite then the dramatist has stirred a great deal of curiosity in the audience.[69] This must be one of her major functions.

But she serves a more important function as well. Traditionally, the young man in this 'Potiphar's wife' story rejects the errant wife's advances out of a properly righteous indignation and horror. But Hippolytus, no ordinarily decent young man but fanatically chaste, is to be destroyed by the sexually incontinent Phaedra. This irony suggests the two antithetical goddesses: Aphrodite who inspires Phaedra's lust and Artemis who provides a devotional focus for Hippolytus' chastity.

---

[65] Knox (1979*b*), 207.   [66] Conacher (1967) 49.

[67] Or, as it turns out, with one of three curses.

[68] Gibert (1997) undermines the common assumption that the lost *Hippolytos Kalyptomenos* was necessarily an earlier play whose offensive elements our play was written to 'correct'. McDermott (2000), however, whose study proceeds 'from the standard assumption that the existing play was a revision' (239, n. 3), argues that a number of passages in the extant play provide evidence of metatheatrical comment on the lost play. In particular she argues that Euripides 'conceptualized his modifications in plot and characterization as a change of mind and at several key points during the play invested his characters' words with a double meaning reflective of the authorial "second thoughts" by which he had revamped his plot' (ibid. 257).

[69] Euripides 'is not concerned to give an exact synopsis of his plot, but rather . . . to mislead and mystify without outright misstatement': Barrett (1964) ad 42.

The actual stage appearance of neither goddess was essential to the causation, even if the dramatist had wanted to suggest divine inspiration of the passion,[70] but Euripides needed a divine figure in the prologue to foreshadow the outcome—though, as we have seen, somewhat misleadingly—and Aphrodite was the obvious choice. But Aphrodite had to be motivated to appear, and the obvious motivation was the desire to respond to Hippolytus' contempt. And then an affronted Olympian would naturally not only predict but actively *cause* events, which would entail a plan to destroy Hippolytus. All of this changes the focus of the myth radically, from the injustice of the innocent Hippolytus' destruction by the contrivances of an evil woman to the divine punishment of human impiety, a story pattern of great tragic power (as it is in *Bacchae*).[71] Of course, Aphrodite is petty and crudely vindictive, and that enlists sympathy for the human characters.[72] On the other hand, she is more than a personal deity, so that Hippolytus' tragedy can seem to stem more significantly from his neglect of a necessary reality of nature. I say 'seem' because there are problems with interpreting his death as the consequence of his fanatical virginity once the focus moves away from the offended personal deity.

Aphrodite is, naturally enough, quite unforgiving, but this is wholly unremarkable in a Greek god who is, so obviously in this case, also an impersonal force of nature. We are not invited here to think that such a conception of divinity, being unworthy, necessarily self-destructs. A similar conclusion has often been drawn from the nurse's later remark to the effect that Aphrodite must be a power 'still greater than a god' (361) if such a power exists.[73] But the nurse's comment is based on the idea that the goddess 'has brought destruction on this woman and me and the whole house' (362), which is hardly a sensational achievement for a vindictive Greek divinity. In a sense, for a Greek there *is* nothing greater than a *theos*. The term was never limited to any traditional conception; indeed the philosophers retained it (and sometimes the names of individual gods) when they were developing their more abstract and exalted metaphysics.

After the prologue the focus shifts to Phaedra who is carried on to the stage in a delirious state which has resulted from three days of self-inflicted starvation, though the chorus speculate as to a divine source, which reinforces the audience's idea that Aphrodite is responsible. The first clue to the nature of Phaedra's illness emerges when she incomprehensibly overreacts to the Nurse's accidental mention of Hippolytus (309–12). Now in the *Tyrannus* a vital clue emerges in parallel circumstances when Jocasta in an attempt to reassure Oedipus about the unreliability of prophecy *casually mentions* the triple crossroads (*OT* 716, 726–30), though 'chance' events in a world pervaded by Apolline prophecy are probably to

---

[70] According to Blomqvist (1982) 403, the specific purpose of Aphrodite is not part of these myths or of Euripides' earlier play. Conacher (1967) 47–8 believes that the two goddesses were involved in some earlier version.

[71] Köhnken (1972) 189, e.g., points to the tragic irony in the discrepancy between the knowledge imparted to the audience in this prologue and the characters' limited understanding before the epilogue.

[72] 'Does Aphrodite complain that this [Hippolytus' chastity] threatens the propagation of the species? No. She merely takes Hippolytus' refusal as a personal affront.' Dimock (1977) 242–3. Aphrodite also removes some guilt from Phaedra.

[73] Conacher (1967) 29.

be attributed ultimately to Apolline immanence. Here too, in the light of the prologue, there is some justification for feeling that Aphrodite is somehow behind this mention of Hippolytus' name. It is, after all, the first link in the causation leading to the fulfilment of her purpose.

The nurse works away at her mistress until the truth comes out, and then she disobeys her specific instructions to approach Hippolytus with a proposal that he and Phaedra should sleep together. Hippolytus is naturally horrified, though it is important to see that anyone, except a libertine, would have been. The young man, having previously sworn not to divulge what the nurse would tell him, now revokes his oath (612). Phaedra, overhearing this much of their conversation, decides that she must calumniate Hippolytus in order to forestall his divulging the matter to Theseus and thus destroying her reputation and, in consequence, that of her children. She adds a secondary motive—punishing Hippolytus for his insensitive and self-satisfied condemnation of her in the form of a misogynistic tirade (688 ff.). But not only a prudish person would be capable of such an outburst. Prudery is not a prerequisite for misogyny. Hippolytus then reaffirms his oath (656–8), but Phaedra is now, it would seem, out of earshot. She writes the incriminating letter which Theseus reads after her suicide, Theseus curses Hippolytus and Poseidon engineers the young man's agonizing death.

The critics are right to maintain that all of this is a bit too complicated to explain as the work of an interfering deity, and the inconsistencies in Aphrodite's monologue suggest that her primary function is not to provide a metaphysical dimension to Phaedra's passion. Nor is there any suggestion that she intervenes during the action, unless we regard the statement of her intentions in the prologue to be sufficient to make us think throughout of her overdetermination of the action. Of course, if we want to respond to the play as a tragedy of divine punishment, we have to take that line, but, as we shall see in Ch. 13, much more interesting things happen on the purely human level so that our attention is naturally there.

3

Aeschylus: *Seven against Thebes*

INHERITED DIVINE HOSTILITY

The great crisis of the *Seven* comes in the play's recognition scene when Eteocles accepts the inevitability of mutual fratricide. What then are the divine and human origins of this crisis? Eteocles is inextricably enmeshed in the fortunes of his *oikos*, and in these fortunes the gods take a personal interest.Thus Eteocles in his deliberations as king and general has not only to take account of the gods' general governance of the world (as he does in appointing opponents for the invading Seven) but also to respond to their particular involvement with his family. Eteocles' grandfather Laius made an enemy of Apollo by disregarding an oracle, and the god's hostility has plagued the house ever since. Moreover, his father Oedipus cursed him and his brother,[1] and we shall need to know why in order to assess his guilt or innocence.

Since the first two plays of the trilogy are lost, reconstruction of the family's tragic history must remain provisional. However, the second stasimon of the *Seven* (720–91) summarizes that history, though none too transparently. Laius, commanded by Apollo to die without issue if he would save the city (743–9), disobeyed the god, 'mastered by his own bad counsels' (κρατηθεὶς ἐκ φιλᾶν ἀβουλιᾶν, 750),[2] begetting Oedipus who killed him and married Jocasta, mother and son alike subject to 'delusion' (*paranoia*, 756).[3] The discovery of the parricide and incest so unhinged Oedipus that 'with a mad heart he perpetrated twin evils': he blinded himself 'with father-slaying hand' and cursed his sons because he was angry about a wretched *trophē* (ἀθλίας ... ἐπίκοτος τροφᾶς)' (778–90). If this is a

---

[1] As Sewell-Rutter (2007) 59–67 contends, we should not speak of the Labdacid house here as accursed. The curse begins with Oedipus and intensifies the atmosphere of doom that already hangs over the house. R. C. T. Parker (1983) 201, citing *Iliad* 4. 160–2, argues that inherited guilt (or at least collective guilt) is not exclusively post-Homeric, and (ibid. 200–1) tends to involve inherent family corruption, apart from specific external causes such as invoked curses. Even when one of the agents is in fact, like Orestes, innocent, it is a compulsion created by past crimes that drives him to his terrible act': ibid. (Aeschylus' Eteocles we shall discover shares Orestes' innocence.)

[2] Hutchinson (1985) 167 suggests that Laius was motivated by desire for children rather than sexual pleasure. Likewise Sommerstein (2008) i. 230 n. 109.

[3] Hutchinson (1985) 168: Oedipus and Jocasta are meant, not Laius and Jocasta. 'It does not seem incredible that παράνοια should be ascribed to Oedipus: ἔτλα has just been used of the act, as if it were conscious, and ἀρτίφρων is used at its discovery (778). Homer's use of νήπιος is not wholly dissimilar (e.g. *Iliad* 16. 46).'

reference to a traditional act of filial contempt or neglect on the part of the sons,[4] then we must take 'angry about a wretched *trophē*' to mean 'angry about the wretched manner in which his sons repayed or indeed failed to repay their *trophē*'. Roisman, however, interprets the phrase rather differently:

There can be no dispute that Oedipus' self-blinding reflects his rage against himself as perpetrator of the most awful of all deeds, mating with his mother. His cursing of his sons should be viewed similarly. His sons are to suffer not for their own fault, but because they are an extension of an accursed father. By their very existence the sons symbolize to Oedipus his incest, pollution and degradation. Oedipus punishes himself by preventing the perpetuation of his line.[5]

This is inherently plausible and fits better with the implication of the lines that the discovery and the curse took place on the same occasion.

The important theme of madness is prominent in these verses. The 'bad counsels' of Laius recall the bad counsel of Xerxes (οὐκ εὐβουλία, *Pers.* 749), further characterized by Darius as a 'sickness of the mind' (νόσος φρενῶν, 750), or madness, in respect of which Xerxes believed, though only a mortal, that he could overcome Poseidon by chaining the Hellespont, an attitude apparently divinely overdetermined (742). Though we are not told that Laius was suffering from a similar divinely inspired state of delusion, the parallel is suggestive, and Oedipus and Jocasta were, as we have seen, the victims of *paranoia*, presumably 'delusion' in the sense of a tragic ignorance of the nature of their relationship rather than in the sense of a distortion of their mental functioning. (At *Agamemnon* 1455, Helen is described by the related term *paranous*, where there is a similar implication of unawareness of the wider implications of one's actions rather than of madness in the modern sense.) Eteocles, too, will be accused, by the chorus, of a kind of madness, and the charge will be reiterated with reference to both brothers after the mutual fratricide. Madness in various forms and its antithesis, *sōphrosunē* (soundness of mind), are a major theme of the play.

THE QUARREL OVER THE KINGSHIP AND THE MORAL AUTHORITY OF ETEOCLES

But even if it is most uncertain that Eteocles wronged his father, must he not be convicted of wronging his brother over the kingship? Traditionally, the brothers sought to avoid the fulfilment of the curse by an agreement to rule in alternate years, but when Eteocles refused to surrender the throne at the end of his year of tenure Polyneices gathered a force from Argos and attacked his native city. All this is explicit in Euripides' much later *Phoenissae*, but Aeschylus never mentions it, at least in the surviving *Seven*, which would seem to be a much more suitable place to

---

[4] See Sommerstein (2008) i. 234 n. 116.
[5] Roisman (1988) 82. See Hutchinson (1985) p. xxv. For the contrary view see Gantz (1982) 17–23 and Sommerstein (1989) 123.

air it than in the previous play since it is of crucial importance to our moral assessment of the brothers.[6]

However, not only does Aeschylus avoid specific reference to the quarrel, but he actually engages the audience's sympathy strongly for Eteocles while presenting Polyneices as the unjust invader. This engagement of sympathy is effected pervasively and perhaps primarily by the dramatization of the events through the dual perspective of a city under attack and of Eteocles himself who dominates the stage at least as much as do Sophoclean heroes such as Oedipus or Electra.[7] But Eteocles' domination of the play is more than a function of his personal presence and the number of lines he speaks; more significantly, his moral interpretations during the shield scene are overwhelmingly authoritative until his climactic conflict with the chorus over the fratricide, at which point they naturally become problematical. We know that they are authoritative because no one disputes them, the consequences are positive (the city is saved), and the morality itself (in this case piety) is conventional. Polyneices, in contrast, never appears in person, and our assessment of him is based on the messenger's account of his words, his behaviour, the significant emblem on his shield (631–48), and the negative comments of Amphiaraus (576–86). Moreover, moral evaluation of this second-hand information is influenced by Eteocles' own powerful assessment (658–71). Furthermore, since we strongly identify with Thebes as well as with its leader, we naturally detest Polyneices as one of the dreaded Seven.

With Eteocles' response to his brother's presence at the seventh gate, however, the moral balance of the drama shifts together with the focus, which moves from the state to the family. A horrified chorus challenge their king's judgement, and, the quality of his case aside, it is hard for us not to share their horror. But then, after the report of the fratricide, there is a further shift of moral balance as the brothers are regarded as morally indistinguishable. This new position, however, is presented without argument, amid the shrill emotionalism of tragic lamentation.

But let us turn to the consideration of the relevant passages. Six champions into the shield scene, the presumably objective Amphiaraus condemns the expedition, inveighing against Tydeus for advising Adrastus, the Argive king, to embark on the war, thereby summoning the Erinys associated with Oedipus' curse (571–5). He proceeds to rebuke Polyneices for invading his own country (580–6), conceding neither that Eteocles has wronged his brother, nor that the invasion would

---

[6] Sophocles in *Antigone* also ignores Polyneices' case, focusing instead, like Aeschylus, on his intention to destroy his native city. His purpose is presumably to set up the sharpest possible moral antithesis between the brothers (110–26, 192–210, 514–25). Not even Antigone tries to maintain the (for her) irrelevant position that Polyneices had some justification. Other cases of ignoring tradition include the motivation for Artemis' anger in the *Agamemnon* and, most instructively, Homer's treatment of Orestes' matricide in the *Odyssey* (3. 306–10), where Orestes kills Aegisthus but apparently merely *buries* his mother. Similarly, the Aeschylean Eteocles and Polyneices clearly have a quarrel over their inheritance (as implied in the dramatically relevant curse), but the audience is all but instructed to ignore the details and to assume that Eteocles is in the right, just as Homer wants us to assume that Clytemnestra has been killed but not to associate the killing with Orestes (or with anyone else!).

[7] At least as much, because in Sophocles, unlike in Aeschylus, conflicts between the protagonist and secondary characters are a central technique of dramatic exposition.

have been justified on the basis of any 'legal claim' (*dikē*, 584).[8] The only inference we can safely draw from this is that Polyneices conceives himself, rightly or wrongly, to have been unjustly exiled by his brother, but for what reason we are not informed. This inference is confirmed shortly afterwards in the reported words of Polyneices himself.

In the speech reported by the soldier messenger, Polyneices claims to have justice on his side and that the purpose of his invasion is to possess his native city and to range freely in his home (648), but he refers only to an unjust exile without mentioning any violation of an agreement (637–8), which leaves us free to imagine that his brother might have exiled him for some other and perhaps justified reason. Most significantly, however, there is a glaring discrepancy between Polyneices' behaviour and the blazon on his shield which claims sponsorship by the goddess of justice (642–8). For not only does he wish to defeat his brother, if necessary, in mutual fratricide, but he hurls curses down on the city too and shouts in premature triumph over it (631–8). It is clear enough then that, whatever claim to justice Polyneices might have, the cure is worse than the disease, but his attitude also suggests that he may be possessed by the Erinys so that his claim to moral authority is invalidated by his mad state.

Despite a dearth of positive evidence against Eteocles' legitimacy, we find some perverse inventiveness among his modern detractors. For example, he is alleged to be oppressed by a guilty or accursed man's sense of isolation, and too much is made of his statement that his name would be execrated in the city if he failed to defend it properly (4–8). This is no more than a comment about the invidiousness of rule, but it is squeezed to mean that the Thebans already blame the invasion on his failure to vacate the throne.[9] Even the fierce, tearful determination of the Seven (42–53) has been adduced as evidence of some crime on Eteocles' part.[10] The point is rather the terror they inspire in the Thebans and an audience sympathetic to the latter.[11]

If Eteocles is in the wrong, it is strange that there is not a single comment to that effect anywhere in the play. At Euripides' *Phoenissae* 154–5 the paedagogus at least is worried that the justice of Polyneices' case might adversely affect the city's defence, but in Aeschylus' play the decisive factors in the city's salvation and the family's destruction are the morally upright characters of Eteocles' chosen seven

---

[8] For *dikē* in this sense see Hutchinson (1985) 136 who cites *Eu.* 491 and *Ch.* 461. Sommerstein (1989) 111 thinks that Amphiaraus implies here that Polyneices has justice on his side and would have condemned him outright, as he condemns Tydeus, if he had thought otherwise. But neither of these seem to me to be safe inferences.

[9] On the irrational nature of much of the criticism levelled at leaders see R. C. T. Parker (1983) 267.

[10] Vellacott (1979–80) 215 sees their mood as 'deep and desperate rage'. They seek 'the redress of some wrong which they cannot let pass'. Their 'deep indignation' is 'the natural consequence of some act of Eteocles . . . an act which this bloody ritual now tells us has indeed been committed and has brought its necessary effect in this implacable anger'.

[11] See Hutchinson (1985) 48–9: 'The Seven must act thus because they believe that they will die. Only so would such fierce men weep, and only so would their abstention from lament appear heroic (52–2). It cannot be coincidence that they place the *mnemeia* for their parents on the chariot of Adrastus, who alone will escape from Thebes. . . . In the central scene most of them display only unbounded confidence; here their awareness of doom corresponds to that of Eteocles.'

(including himself), Apollo's hatred of both brothers inherited from Laius, and the curse enforced by the Erinys.[12]

Having established that there is neither filial nor fraternal impiety for Eteocles to acknowledge, we must conclude that the divine hostility towards him is morally unjustified. This will come as no surprise in the Greek religious universe.

THE CURSE AND ETEOCLES' MENTAL STATE

But what of Eteocles' mental state in the early scenes of the play, in particular in respect to the curse and its accompanying Erinys and to his harsh treatment of the female chorus? This enquiry is necessary because it has been argued that Eteocles is actively possessed by the Erinys throughout the play and not merely at the climax of the shield scene, and that his treatment of the women is influenced by memories of Jocasta and the incestuous union.

We begin with the curse. The arrival of the spy with news of the seven Argive champions and of the invading army's approach (39–68) prompts Eteocles to pray to the gods to preserve the city (69–77). During this brief invocation he appeals to the personified Curse (*Ara*) and powerful Erinys of his father, asking that the city 'at least' (γε) should not be destroyed (70–2). This suggests that Eteocles realizes what the curse means for his own destiny but is ignoring it for the time being in order to focus on the fate of the city which he apparently regards as a separate issue.[13] This interpretation is later supported by his mention of his nightly dream about the curse's fulfilment (710–11) and by his bleak fatalism.[14] And in the event Apollo and the Fury keep their hatred of the brothers separate from their (and the other gods') good will towards the city. Moreover, Eteocles' reference to the curse prepares the audience for its later irruption into the play.

Now at the beginning of the play, Eteocles remarks that the gods will receive the credit for a successful outcome and he the blame for a disaster (4–8). To my mind, this is no more than cynical realism, but Winnington-Ingram detects an 'attitude

---

[12] We might wonder why, rather than avoiding specific discussion of the quarrel, Aeschylus does not actively substantiate Amphiaraus' and Eteocles' claims concerning Polyneices' injustice by altering the tradition to make Eteocles the elder brother and therefore entitled to rule in perpetuity. Perhaps he was confident that any sympathy the audience might be inclined to feel for Polyneices could easily be stifled if sufficient emphasis were placed on the horrors and the impiety of the invasion (as e.g. in Jocasta's arguments at Eur. *Phoen.* 568–83). On such a basis he might avoid a more cumbersome reinterpretation.

[13] Lesky (1961) 12 rightly argues that Eteocles does not misinterpret the curse in this passage, but fails to interpret it at all, being merely conscious of a 'dark cloud over his head'.

[14] There is no need to argue, with Otis (1960) 158, that Eteocles 'does not grasp either its [the curse's] direct, personal meaning of fratricidal duel or its ominous application to the burial earth which the brothers at death will divide between them (732–3)'. Nor need we take the antithetical view, criticized by Otis (1960) 157, that Eteocles here consciously 'accepts his *own death* as the price of the city's safety' (Otis's emphasis), a view at odds, as ibid. 158–9 observes, with the fact that 'he expects to conduct the sacrificial *tropaia* of victory and himself to bedeck the temples with the enemy spoils (271–78)' and with his horror at what he at once sees as the implication of Polyneices' presence at the seventh gate. His acceptance of his destiny comes only at that point.

of mistrust, a sense of isolation, not only from other men but also from the gods',[15] and considers this to be evidence that Eteocles is already possessed by the Erinys, especially because the ancient audience, fresh from *Oedipus*, and therefore mindful that the hero is a man accursed, might well expect such a condition to be mirrored in an abnormal mental state.[16] This is flimsy 'evidence' indeed, and in any case there are counter-examples: Phoenix in the *Iliad* (9. 453–7) and Hippolytus in Euripides' play (*Hipp.* 887–90), though accursed, display no consequent abnormality of behaviour.

In any case, this is not how ancient madness works. In a discussion distinguishing temporary from long-term madness in Greek thought, Ruth Padel argues that a man under a curse suffers from the latter type of insanity, pointing out that Aeschylus presents the house of Oedipus as θεομανές (653), which she interprets to mean 'permanently "maddened by gods"'.[17] However, '[t]his possibility of the long-*term* does not necessarily involve, as it began to do in the nineteenth century and still does for us, the quite separate idea of the long *hidden*. What the fifth- and fourth-century examples imply is chronic susceptibility to obvious, temporary mad fits.'[18]

If this is so, and ancient conceptions of madness are certainly radically different from our own, we should expect Eteocles' madness to show itself not continuously but in episodes of spectacularly deranged consciousness at critical junctures, and that is precisely what the chorus claim to see when he announces his intention to meet his brother. If then a curse is to be fulfilled through an act resulting from a morally significant decision on the part of the victim, as in the case of Eteocles deciding to meet his brother, then it seems very likely that the victim's moral judgement will be distorted as he deliberates, and we shall investigate presently whether this happens in Eteocles' case. But there is no reason to expect Eteocles to display *continuous* mental derangement and therefore continuous corruption of judgement. It is better to assume the integrity of his judgement at least until he learns of his brother's presence at the seventh gate.

As to his harsh treatment of the women, he deplores their panic which threatens to spread throughout the city (181–6, 191–4) and urges good counsel instead (223–5); he envisages *men* consulting the gods in the usual way through sacrifice and divination, though he has no objection to the chorus worshipping the gods (230–1, 236–8).[19] In interpreting this passage some readers have been inexplicably bent on ignoring the distinction that Eteocles makes between the

---

[15] Winnington-Ingram (1983) 26.   [16] Ibid. 25.
[17] Padel (1995) 34.   [18] Ibid. (Padel's emphases).
[19] Hutchinson (1985) 73–4 rightly disagrees with Brown (1977) 305, who contrasts the chorus' trust in the gods with Eteocles' pragmatism. Eteocles trusts the gods to destroy hubrists and the chorus are not sure of the help they implore. Eteocles deplores the chorus' manner of praying. Supplication should be left for more desperate situations. 'The chorus's action would suggest, to Greeks, a premature terror and despair. This view is strongly supported by 266. Eteocles' anger becomes much more natural, and we see that the contrasting approaches to ritual draw with them contrasting approaches to the danger of Thebes ... However, it is in relation to the peril of the city that this scene confronts the ethos of male and female ... The area of the confrontation is obviously no less fundamental to the play than the elements confronted.'

right and wrong way to involve the gods.[20] From a modern point of view he can of course be criticized for his misogyny, and although misogyny is a depressingly familiar ancient topos, the dramatist must have had some purpose in introducing it. That purpose, however, can hardly have been psychoanalytical, and, as Brown observes,

Some have supposed that Eteocles is influenced by memories of Jocasta and knowledge of his incestuous origin, but this notion can at once be ruled out on the simple grounds that Aeschylus does not say so, and that such a surprising degree of psychological realism would need to be made very clear if an audience was to take it in.[21]

Indeed, the lamentable propensity of ancient males to think the worst of women is sufficient to make the episode psychologically plausible; its dramatic purpose, on the other hand, is to stress that the attitudes and behaviour of king and chorus are divided on gender lines, and that women do not behave well in circumstances requiring typically 'masculine' courage.[22] Moreover, the chorus do not actually disagree with Eteocles; in fact they are too frightened to think straight (203–7). All they could think to do was to run to the images of the gods for refuge (211–15). All of this of course vindicates Eteocles, and their prolonged exchange with him prepares the audience for a similar division by gender at the climax of the shield scene, where masculine overconcentration on martial courage is balanced by female sensitivity to the claims of kin. (*Oresteia* amply demonstrates that Aeschylus liked to associate moral dilemmas with incompatible priorities inspired by or at least related to gender differences.) What is emphasized then is the contrast between Eteocles' appropriate attitude in the earlier scene and his shocking readiness to violate kin ties later.

THE SHIELD SCENE

Eteocles now turns to the selection, in the so-called shield scene, of the seven Theban opponents to meet the opposition at the gates of Thebes. His approach to this selection impinges on his own destiny because he chooses himself as one of the champions. The selection process requires a high sensitivity to the likely reactions of the gods, that is a particular kind of moral awareness, and Eteocles displays this in abundance. Both the scout and Eteocles convey a strong

---

[20] Podlecki (1964) *passim.* Brown (1977) 300 rightly dismisses Podlecki's criticisms as 'special pleading', referring to Eteocles' sensible pragmatism.

[21] Brown (1977) 303.

[22] As Brown (1977) 305 remarks, 'The Chorus exemplifies womankind for Eteocles because it must do so in some degree for us; we are to see its timidity and its intuitive religious feeling as essentially feminine qualities in antithesis to his masculine courage and practicality.' Jackson (1988) 289 would elevate the chorus' attitude here into a theoretical position: 'The Chorus' assertion of the gods as the only real power entails a denial of the value of human endeavour.' But the chorus are not opposed to what Eteocles is doing; they are merely incapable, through hysteria, of acting rationally, though they naturally seek to defend their behaviour on the grounds of piety. They do not e.g. answer Eteocles' claim that they are fomenting panic in the citizens (191–4, 254), but are clearly overwhelmed by their own panic generated by the sounds of the approaching enemy.

impression that the outcome of the battle hinges on the issue of each of these single-combat encounters and thus on Eteocles' selections, each of which is a response to the moral character of the enemy warrior at the particular gate.[23] As the messenger describes each warrior in ethico-religious terms—and most of them are characterized by impious arrogance—Eteocles chooses a suitably modest and pious opponent whose moral qualities will win divine approval and allow the opposition to self-destruct by offending the gods. In this way the audience are discouraged from applying secular, realistic criteria of the kind that are insisted on in the equivalent scene of Euripides' *Phoenissae* (697–755). The hubris of five at any rate of the Seven is repeatedly described in terms of their boastful attitude. To this is added the idea that they are not thinking like human beings, that they are unholy and even mad.[24] The grand exception, Amphiaraus, on the other hand, is characterized in strongly positive terms, first by the messenger as 'most sound of mind' ($\sigma\omega\phi\rho\sigma\nu\epsilon\sigma\tau\alpha\tau\sigma\nu$, 568) and then by Eteocles himself as (again) 'sound of mind' ($\sigma\omega\phi\rho\omega\nu$) 'righteous' ($\delta\iota\kappa\alpha\iota\sigma\varsigma$), 'brave' ($\dot{\alpha}\gamma\alpha\theta\delta\varsigma$), and 'reverent' ($\epsilon\dot{\nu}\sigma\epsilon\beta\eta\varsigma$)— all in a single striking verse made up entirely of these four adjectives and their noun (610)—and one who wants not just to seem but to be the best/bravest ($\dot{\alpha}\rho\iota\sigma\tau\sigma\varsigma$, 592). These qualities, which Eteocles clearly admires, may be used as touchstones of his own performance at the climax of the scene. Thus the moral domain of the play is sketched out: the arrogant, impious, and mad against the sound-minded, righteous, and reverent. The moral focus moreover is on the appropriate attitude to the gods, but in the context of the interests of the state.

When Eteocles appoints a moderate-minded warrior to confront a hubrist, the result is virtually foregone. His moral awareness of the implications of the attitudes of the arrogant champions seems to put control of events in his hands, but sensitive though he is to the likely divine reaction to the arrogant Argives, his understanding remains incomplete until the messenger announces Polyneices' presence at the seventh gate. Up to that point Eteocles is rightly confident that the gods will nullify the efforts of the hubristic Argives,[25] but he does not yet see that Apollo and the Erinys are working immanently through the choices he makes (and thus, ironically, through his moral and religious insightfulness) in order to bring about the salvation of the city and the destruction of his family.[26] This immanent intervention is at least 'panoramic', as the gods are naturally involved in the fate of Thebes, having been invoked earlier in the play, while Apollo and the Erinys, of course, have a particular interest in the fate of the brothers. There is no

---

[23] I take the view that the postings have not already been made. See the discussion of Winnington-Ingram (1983) 23–5 and his n. 21.

[24] e.g. 387, 391, 404, 406, 425, 436–8, 480, 484, 500, 502, 551, 566.

[25] The sixth champion, Amphiaraus, however, is problematical in his modesty, though he disapproves of Polyneices' expedition on the grounds that no legal claim (*dikē*, 584) could possibly justify attacking one's own country. Eteocles can do no more than match him with another modest opponent, but since Amphiaraus foresees his own doom (587–8) there seems little cause for concern. What distresses Eteocles though is that here is a moral man who will be dragged down by his bad company (597–614).

[26] Presumably the Erinys is concerned only with the fulfilment of the curse; Apollo is similarly intent on the destruction of the family, but it is by no means clear that he is opposed to the salvation of the city. At any rate, it seems reasonable to infer from the arrogance of the champions that the other gods invoked in the course of the drama strongly support Thebes.

impression, however, that these deities have thus far been intervening in Eteocles' mental processes, though, logically, they would need to anticipate his postponement of his self-selection to the end. A similar kind of immanent involvement applies, as we shall see, in the *Tyrannus*, wherein Apollo at least anticipates Oedipus' reactions to the events which the god partially arranges and wholly superintends.

Although Eteocles suddenly realizes that the gods are intent on his destruction, he continues to believe (again rightly) that they will support him as a general and a soldier (though not as a son of Oedipus). He has to die, but the seventh gate holds with the rest.

There is no suggestion that Eteocles erred in deferring his own appointment to the end. Nor is his original decision to include himself among the seven a concession to the hysterical chorus.[27] In his moral and religious awareness here, Eteocles is outstanding among Greek tragic characters. Aeschylus' Agamemnon, as we shall see in the next chapter, is unaware, except in the most general sense, of the implications of sacrificing Iphigenia and inclined to suppress his uneasiness about it and about treading on the fabrics, while Sophocles' Oedipus (at Thebes) is completely unaware of Apollo's immanent activity until the revelation.[28] In *Agamemnon*, the principal lines of the play's causation are effectively sketched out in the choral odes, enabling the audience to judge Agamemnon's attitudes and behaviour within a context of which he is apparently completely unaware,[29] while in the *Tyrannus* Oedipus and all the characters are deluded for most of the play, though the audience is constantly aware, through the dramatic irony, of the folly of human pretensions to understanding and control.

ETEOCLES AND THE SEVENTH GATE

We turn now to Eteocles' response to the crisis that has irrupted into the play. With the announcement of Polyneices' posting to the seventh gate he is at once rightly convinced that the gods are bent on the immediate fulfilment of the curse (653–5); and although it did not enter into his deliberations in the course of allotting the first six antagonists, his reference to what appears to be a recurrent dream (710–11) indicates that the curse has never been far from his consciousness. Up to this point, in his selection of champions, he has been actively shaping the human conflicts through his insight into the likely divine reaction to arrogance or modesty, and his motive has been to save the city. This means that the heroic ethic to which he subscribes functions, as it should, in the interest of the polis.

---

[27] Kitto (1961) 49.

[28] Otis (1960) 159 is more impressed with Eteocles' 'wholly misplaced self-confidence.' But as Eteocles is confronted with the threat of each of the first six Argive warriors, he responds correctly with an entirely appropriate moral confidence. He does not realize, of course, until it is announced, that Polyneices is waiting at the seventh gate, but he never boasts or implies that he will be able to deal with all the champions or avoid the fulfilment of the curse.

[29] The chorus inform us e.g. of the nature and attitudes of Zeus and the other gods, placing Agamemnon's dilemma in its broadest context; they criticize Agamemnon's decision (*Ag.* 218–27) and tell us that *polyktonoi* and city-sackers are exposed to divine wrath (*Ag.* 461–70).

Eteocles now realizes—and the realization is completely rational in the play's terms—that he must shape his own behaviour, fatally, in harmony with the unrelenting divine hostility towards his family. As Jackson puts it, '[h]e has performed his role as commander of the defence of Thebes, and it has led him straight into a fratricidal duel with Polyneices. How can he take this otherwise than as the will of the gods?'.[30] Indeed, this paradox is one of the most striking aspects of the episode, for fatalism is deplored in modern Western cultures that believe either that there is no predetermined course of events or that if there is we cannot know it. A fatalistic attitude therefore seems like premature hopelessness on the basis of inadequate evidence.[31] But in the ancient context no other course is possible. No deliberation is necessary; the insight is immediate and all that remains is to expound the implications, which Eteocles proceeds to do, and to reassert them when the chorus protest. There is no question then of shared deliberations or of a change of view. The chorus' objections are understandable but miss the mark, so that their dialogue with Eteocles serves only to allow him to explain his position. That at any rate is its intellectual dimension. Of course, it serves also to engage our sympathy, as the chorus themselves display an undeniable affection for their king. The fulfilment of the curse is what Eteocles always feared and always expected. This acknowledgement of reality—a reality which in this case takes the form of an inflexible divine purpose—is, as we have seen, a precondition of moral action. It remains now for Eteocles to enact the divine will with as much moral integrity as the situation allows. But does even this limited freedom remain to him? The answer to this question will depend on the contribution of Apollo and the Erinys to his mental processes.

APOLLO, THE ERINYS, AND ETEOCLES' MORAL AUTONOMY

The gods hate his family, Eteocles declares, and have driven them mad (653–4), though he clearly believes in the sanity and soundness of his own present analysis. (Moreover, we must also ask in what sense they are mad, since the Greek terms can imply anything from an unavoidable misconception to raving madness from divine possession.) But, as I argued earlier, this is precisely the sort of situation in which an Erinys proceeding to activate a curse might be expected to corrupt the judgement of her victim. But *is* Eteocles' judgement corrupt? He rejects as mad nonsense Polyneices' claim to having justice on his side, on the grounds that at no time in his life, from birth itself to maturity, did his brother behave justly (661, 664–7), and this pattern of habitual injustice is now clearly confirmed in his destructive attack on the city (668–9). Accusations of madness in tragedy may mean no more than we mean when we say 'You must be mad to think that!', though in this case the madness Eteocles attributes to his brother he probably

---

[30] Jackson (1988) 295.

[31] This is the view e.g. of North (1966) 40 who speaks of Eteocles 'leaping to the conclusion that he must meet his brother there' [i.e. at the seventh gate].

believes is inspired by the family Fury. The play provides no evidence in support of Eteocles' general claim here about his brother's character, though the claim that Polyneices was unjust *in his infancy* must be a rhetorical exaggeration. We are on safe ground only in accepting what was also the view of Amphiaraus (580–6): that Polyneices' present course of action is unjustifiable even if he has been unjustly exiled by his brother. On the other hand, in a literary context, at least, the absence of a contrary view testifies, perhaps, to the accuracy of the view expressed.[32]

In any case, relying on this view (672), Eteocles will face Polyneices, standing 'leader to leader, brother to brother, enemy to enemy', for who could do so with more justice (τίς ἄλλος μᾶλλον ἐνδικώτερος; 673–5). Eteocles is here applying the same principles of selection as he applied to the first six pairings and thus ranging himself with the just and the sound-minded. He is also showing a continuing concern for the city. This was also an opportunity for Aeschylus to challenge Eteocles' claim to justice with reference to the tradition of his robbing his brother of his share of the kingdom. It is notable also that Eteocles refrains from boasting of his own just nature, so he does not, as it were, defect to the side of the city's boastful adversaries. We are left to infer his righteousness from his strong sympathy for Amphiaraus, another man confronting an ineluctable destiny, who, as we have seen, is characterized in the most strongly positive terms. Eteocles can claim to be brave, like Amphiaraus, in confronting his doom, but does he evince that seer's other noble qualities? Is he not instead overtaken by the family madness?[33]

The threatening power of Polyneices, like that of his comrades, is defused by rhetoric and moral argument (658–71). Eteocles takes the moral high ground— presumably in his role as the defender of a city unjustly and even impiously attacked. As Kirkwood puts it, Eteocles' choice of himself 'is a deliberate and rational choice, not a piece of possessed madness, and . . . it is a reasonable *ad hominem* selection'.[34] So to that extent his judgement is uncorrupted.[35] Eteocles' judgement therefore qua city-defender turns out to be correct to the extent that his public and private roles can be separated.[36] The seventh gate does hold, as the messenger will report (792–802), and that may suggest that the gods did indeed agree that it was Eteocles rather than Polyneices who had justice on his side,

---

[32] Thus the Sophoclean Oedipus' account of his road-rage incident must be taken as correct in the absence of a conflicting view. Occasionally a conflicting version will be offered; Menelaus contradicts Agamemnon's account of the circumstances surrounding the sacrifice of Iphigenia in *IA*.

[33] Helm (2004) 36 claims (wrongly, I think) that, since Amphiaraus joins the Seven 'against his better judgment', he is subject to 'temporary folly' in doing so, but Amphiaraus is rather a tragic figure caught up in an expedition of which he consistently disapproves.

[34] Kirkwood (1969) 1.

[35] According to Brown (1977) 311, Eteocles is not sacrificing himself for the good of the city or he would have said so in justifying himself. Certainly the city is no longer his primary concern, but it is still a secondary concern in harmony with his primary concern. See Hutchinson (1985) 150, Kirkwood (1969) 13–14, and Winnington-Ingram (1983) 52–4.

[36] As McHardy (2008) 33 points out, while personal revenge was acceptable and even admired in Homeric warfare, it was largely incompatible with hoplite war, which we are to presume generally applies in this play. But Eteocles' single combat with his brother recalls that mode of fighting in the *Iliad*, while it combines the interests of the state with those of personal hostility.

at least in the matter of the attack on Thebes.[37] Or it may simply mean that the gods wished to spare the city since their quarrel was with the Labdacids. Be that as it may, Eteocles' performance as the defender of Thebes can do nothing to mitigate the divine hostility to his house.[38]

Eteocles then is right to face Polyneices, 'leader to leader' and 'enemy to enemy'—but surely *not* 'brother to brother'; and it is to this aspect of the situation that the chorus now respond when they beg him not to become like his brother in 'temper' or 'anger' (ὀργήν, 678) in his readiness to shed kindred blood. (In their outrage they refer to their leader's emotional state rather than to the immorality of the fratricide he contemplates, but they must consider it immoral.) Now although the audience presumably sympathized with Eteocles against the chorus in their earlier exchange, in this case the women have behind them all the weight of the natural abhorrence of shedding kindred blood, so that the spectators' moral judgement (though not, presumably, their sympathy) is in danger of deserting the protagonist who may seem to have lost his mind. But it will be remembered that Gill suggests that 'our sympathetic involvement with the hero is a reflection of our engagement with the reasons and reasoning, and with the mixture of psychological pressures and agency, that motivate the violent or (seemingly) unreasonable act on which the tragedy turns'.[39] Gill's analysis is strikingly applicable here as we listen to and are won over by the hero's interpretation of his predicament in terms of his own morality and of the external psychological and supernatural pressures which he rightly discerns to be acting upon him.

Eteocles' reply to the chorus ignores the enormity of fratricide since the deed is in any case inevitable and focuses exclusively on the obligation of the warrior to shun the shame (αἰσχύνης, 683) of cowardice and win glory (εὐκλείαν, 685),[40] an idea implicit at this point (683–5), but made more prominent at 717 where Eteocles applies to himself the anachronistic term 'hoplite'—a reminder, perhaps, that his devotion to his reputation for courage remains appropriate in his post-Homeric political context. This reminder is helpful, because Eteocles' natural obsession with the family curse to some extent diverts his attention from the saving of the city to the fulfilment of the divine will in the narrower context of the family. Normally, one would expect martial courage to be the most valued of the virtues among the population of a city whose very existence hangs in the balance and for its warriors to subordinate all other considerations to the need of

---

[37] The messenger (793–801) makes a general statement about the gates holding. He does not say in as many words that the seventh gate held, but that is surely implied. Solmsen (1937) 206 is therefore wrong to say that 'there is not the slightest evidence in the play that the king's combat or death has any effect upon the fate of Thebes.'

[38] Solmsen (1937) 208 suggests that there is a compromise between the chthonic powers who want the blood guilt paid for and the Olympian deities who protect Thebes 'because they stand for political and moral justice'. But, apart from the dubiousness of the latter claim, Apollo, as well as the Erinys, is bent on the destruction of the family, and the city is saved through the logic of the appointments in the shield scene. In the view of Otis (1960) 166, Eteocles has rightly seen that 'his death is decreed by the gods . . . as the very condition of the city's safety'. But, surely, specifically his *death* is necessitated purely by the hostility of Apollo and the Erinys, whereas the salvation of the city requires him merely to play the role of righteous adversary in the manner of his Theban comrades at the other gates.

[39] See p. 15.

[40] Agamemnon at Aulis similarly rates the warrior's role above that of the family member, but he believes that he has a choice.

the moment. As the Creon of Sophocles'*Antigone* rightly observes (at 182–90), friends and family are less important than the survival of the state which makes such relations possible. (Creon's mistake, of course, was his failure to realize that Polyneices' burial was very much in the interest of the state.) But subordinating the interests of the family is one thing; kin murder is quite another, especially if it is not clearly presented as the necessary condition of the city's salvation, as is, for example, the sacrifice of Menoeceus which Teiresias presents as his father's duty in Euripides' *Phoenissae* (at 911–16). The 'feminine' privileging of the family in the extraordinary situation of the *Seven* thus seems to carry some weight, and for the chorus Eteocles is less brave than mad, irrationally motivated, as they see it, by a kind of insane lust for battle (θυμοπληθὴς δορίμαργος ἄτα, 686–8). For them what would normally be a display of the highest moral virtue is converted into its antithesis, an act so heinous as to be inexplicable as that of a sane person. The term ἄτα ('delusion') which they use to describe this infatuation one naturally connects with divinely induced derangement and thus in this case with the curse.[41] Perhaps then it is through this alleged battle-lust that the Erinys and Apollo intervene to pervert Eteocles' judgement. If so, then his limited freedom to enact the divine will with moral integrity may be fatally compromised.[42]

It is important to notice here that the chorus do not accuse Eteocles of being motivated by personal hatred for his brother, unless we are to understand them to be responding to his designation of Polyneices as his *echthros* (675), which may mean no more than 'public enemy'. They seem instead to be responding to the perceived insanity of believing that failure to attempt to kill one's own brother in battle will be construed as cowardice.[43] Eteocles appears to ignore the charge of insanity but actually replies obliquely to it in expressing a wish that the curse be fulfilled, since 'the god is urging the matter (τὸ πρᾶγμα) along' (689–91). Now, in Hutchinson's view, 'Eteocles sees the hand of divinity, not in the impulse within him, but in the allotment of the seventh gate to Polyneices,' so that it is the latter that the god is allegedly urging on.[44] But Eteocles may indeed be acknowledging here that 'the matter', the course of events, the fulfilment of the curse) can be urged on through divine manipulation of both material and psychological events (the material event of Polyneices' appearance at the seventh gate informs him that the fulfilment of the curse is imminent) while asserting that in a sense his own feelings and impulses, and their possibly divine origins, are irrelevant (this is his oblique response to the charge of madness). All that matters here is the divine will, and he *must* be right to yield to it. Therefore it is futile to deliberate as if there were an option not to commit fratricide. Eteocles can only ask, absurdly, how he can act virtuously or honourably in the process of committing fratricide. Since this is impossible, the best he can do is to act as a warrior and ignore the fraternal role.

[41] Brown (1977) 310–11 says *ata* merely describes Eteocles' state without implying a divine source, but it would be natural here to assume that the curse will be fulfilled by the Erinys working in part through the mind of her victims. On ἄτα as 'delusion' see Sommerstein (forthcoming).

[42] In reply to the chorus' reference to his alleged *ate*, Eteocles refers to the 'god' (*theos*, 689) and then to specifically Apollo's hatred of the whole race of Laius (690). But Oedipus' curse is an overdetermining factor here, through the activity of the Erinys.

[43] One thinks here of the Euripidean Electra accusing her brother of cowardice for his reluctance to commit matricide (Eur. *El.* 982).

[44] Hutchinson (1985) 155.

For Eteocles then there can be no conflict between the interests of the state or those of the family and his own. He has two options only: brave fratricide or cowardly fratricide. That of course concerns his moral responsibility to himself.

The chorus can only reiterate their claim that he is motivated by a 'sharp-biting lust' (ὠμοδακής...ἵμερος, 692) to shed kindred blood;[45] and at last Eteocles implicitly agrees (γάρ, 695), but without accepting the alleged irrationality of his intended action. But what exactly is the nature of this desire? Is it a hate-inspired urge to kill his brother, or simply a kind of *amor fati*, a longing to get the inevitable over and done with through an act that *incidentally* entails fratricide? (695–7). That Eteocles hates his brother is a natural and morally unproblematical response in the Greek cultural context, given the grave implications of their disagreement, but there is no strong evidence that this hatred is swollen to the point at which the culture would consider it insane or even extraordinarily vehement. Vellacott believes, without evidence, that Eteocles has been waiting for an excuse to indulge his hatred for Polyneices,[46] and Vernant would have it that Eteocles 'abandons himself to a hatred for his brother that altogether "possesses him"'.[47] But Eteocles' statements about his brother (at 658–71) are morally critical rather than mere outpourings of hate and to be understood in terms of the pattern of the defusing of the pretensions of the Seven which we find throughout the shield scene. In his exchanges with the chorus it is clear that, if he is obsessed, it is not with a murderous and fratricidal madness but with the inevitability of his destiny (see 683–5, 689–91, 695–7, 703–5, 709–11), and no case can be made for dismissing his constant references to that inevitability as mere rationalizations of fratricidal lust, because there is no independent evidence of such lust to support such a view.

We can conclude then that Eteocles experiences a strong desire to yield to his destiny, accompanied by battle lust, a desire which only incidentally entails the impiety of fratricide, an act which he does in fact regard as 'inherently bad (718–19)'.[48] The desire to get it over and done with is paramount, and that desire is fully rational in the play's terms. The divine will must be fulfilled. The desire then might seem to be sufficiently motivated by Eteocles' sheer understanding of his predicament, and Jackson would have it that the curse works through him only in the sense that he must respond to it: 'He can scarcely determine to fight his brother . . . without calling up in himself the necessary attitudes of emotion and will. This necessity is what justifies the Chorus' charges. Eteocles has summoned the resolution to break one of the strongest taboos. . . . Once having made his choice, he cannot but transform himself into the character the Chorus envisage.'[49] But the evidence is against this view. Far from trying to talk himself into an

---

[45] The desire is conventionally impious in so far as it is a desire to commit fratricide, but it is not, paradoxically, a desire contrary to divine will.

[46] The curse 'sanctioned the act which Eteocles lusted to commit; . . . the attack of the Seven brought a welcome opportunity, and the women's panic a reasonable excuse for taking part personally in the battle': Vellacott (1979–80) 216. Jackson (1988) 296 says the speech is not 'a one-dimensional expression of lust for fratricide' as Kitto (1961) 51 and Herington (1986) 89 read it.

[47] Vernant and Vidal-Naquet (1981) 11. Sewell-Rutter (2007) speaks of the 'willingly fratricidal Eteocles' (30) and of his 'insanely destructive and polluting desire' (33).

[48] Gill (1990a) 25.

[49] Jackson (1988) 297.

impious frame of mind, Eteocles seems emotionally numb to the implications of
fratricide and generally anxious to avoid emotionalism (656–7).

Now we would expect the Erinys to derange her victim, which is indeed how the
chorus seem to see it (I have remarked upon their use of the term ἄτα). But the
notion of derangement sits uneasily with the rationality of Eteocles' resolve. That
resolve, nevertheless, is to commit an impiety—though in this case to do so is,
paradoxically (and tragically), the only rational course.[50] Eteocles' derangement,
however, while it does not lead to a wrong decision, is nevertheless evident in his
failure properly to register the enormity of fratricide—a failure perhaps partly a
product of his commitment to salvaging a warrior's honour from a situation
which precludes fraternal piety. No doubt he could reply that to allow himself
to become upset by dwelling on such a horrific act would serve no useful purpose;
still it might seem that the Erinys has deprived him of any decent man's abhorrence of a terrible pollution. Certainly his first reaction is one of horror and
perhaps pity for his family as he suddenly realizes the imminence of the mutual
fratricide (653–5), but he seems to do his best to suppress any sense of a tragic
dilemma with his realization that there is in fact no freedom of choice. For the
audience the tragedy perhaps consists in the existence of such a predicament—the
inescapability of fratricide and what it entails, the impossibility of morally pure
action. We cannot criticize Eteocles for his devotion to the warrior ethic, for it is
his performance as a warrior that contributes to the defeat of the Seven and the
salvation of Thebes. Nor can we find fault with his readiness to kill his brother, for
there is no alternative. Nor again can we say that 'he makes his compulsions for
himself in a process of appropriation' as though a deeply fratricidal nature
resulting from an ancestral taint produced the necessity he objectifies.[51] The
phenomenon of overdetermination allows a focus on either or both of the causal
agencies (human and divine). In this case the human agent's *very recognition* of
divine hostility to some degree projects the divine agency outside his psyche for all
that it operates also within it. Eteocles could hardly say, 'The gods have predetermined my death, but since they are counting on my hatred of my brother to
bring this about, I shall thwart them by deciding not to meet him.' His prior
knowledge of his destiny makes attempts to thwart it absurd, in the way that it is
logically absurd to blame Oedipus for not making more concerted attempts to
avoid parricide and incest. Thus all that is left to criticize in Eteocles is perhaps
an insufficient sensitivity about fratricide, but then such sensitivity could only
disable him.

As a case of ἄτα, then, Eteocles' possession by the gods is unusual, but not only
because the battle-lust it inspires seems, in the perverse and tragic circumstances,
not entirely inappropriate. It is also unusual in that divine derangement generally
occurs in circumstances in which agents have no idea that it is happening, and the
decision that they make is wholly wrong because their judgement is corrupted
by a god. Eteocles is unusual in being aware both of the gods' impending
fulfilment of his evil destiny and even of what the chorus term his 'evil desire'

---

[50] Though Sewell-Rutter (2007) 33 thinks that 'the witlessness of the grandfather is carried through
into the "madness"' of Oedipus and of the brothers. (See also ibid. 34–5, 48.)
[51] Ibid. 161.

(κακοῦ... ἔρωτος, 687–8) which the gods have presumably inspired in him (γάρ, 695), a desire which, as we have seen, harmonizes with his rational decision to face his destiny as soon as possible. (For a modern parallel, we might imagine the case of an inebriated person made more emotional by alcohol, but not to the point at which rational judgement is corrupted.) For this reason it is not quite true that Eteocles is 'experiencing a nightmarish loss of will (in the ordinary sense) and surrendering to (what he sees as) irrational forces at work within himself'.[52] There is no loss of will; though he experiences an appalling sense of inevitable doom, he actively and resolutely accommodates himself to that doom.

Indeed, his awareness of the divine will seems to be such an overwhelming factor in his choosing to commit fratricide that it is by no means obvious that he would have chosen to do so without it. An audience could have approved of Agamemnon's decision at Aulis had he appealed to the will of Zeus Xenios that Troy be sacked, just as approval of Orestes' decision to kill his mother depends overwhelmingly on the fact that Apollo has commanded the deed. We condemn Agamemnon at Aulis because his decision seems motivated at best by a sense of responsibility to his warlike peers and at worst by a desire for personal glory while it ignores the divine will altogether (*Ag.* 205–17). But, as was observed above, Agamemnon is almost totally unaware of the wider divine context, while the audience are informed of it (and of its implications for Agamemnon himself) through the choral odes. Clytemnestra's strategy in the carpet scene resembles that of Eteocles in the shield scene inasmuch as she attempts to contrive a situation which she believes will enlist divine support. The gods will surely punish Agamemnon for the arrogance he makes so strikingly manifest by treading on the embroideries. But Clytemnestra, though later disposed to see herself as an agent of a divine *alastōr* (*Ag.* 1497–504), deludes herself into believing that a pact might be made with it which will protect her from retribution in her turn (*Ag.* 1568–77). Eteocles is never thus deceived about his family's curse.

IS ETEOCLES A FREE AGENT?

Granted the divine influence then—albeit influence in harmony with the victim's rational judgement—is Eteocles to be regarded as in any sense a free agent? Certainly Eteocles himself and the chorus assume that he has the power to influence his thoughts and emotions and to make rational decisions. On becoming aware of the activation of the curse with the stationing of Polyneices at the seventh gate, Eteocles is seized apparently by a desire to 'lament and weep', but he decides to resist it (656–7). The chorus, as we have seen, urge him not to become like his brother in temper (678) and not to be swept away by battle-lust and to cast out the evil desire at its onset (687–8); thus they too assume that he can resist his own powerful impulses. Eteocles acknowledges the desire but argues that it is better to fulfil the curse now (695–7). Clearly then it is not a matter of being unable to resist the desire, but rather of choosing not to do so and on rational grounds. Again the

---

[52] Gill (1990a) 25.

chorus bid him not to encourage this feeling (698), and again Eteocles argues that there is no point in delaying the inevitable (702–4). Moreover, the final sticho-mythia of the scene strongly reinforces the idea that both parties, Eteocles and the chorus, believe that Eteocles is free to decide; and this provides the moral context for the judgements of the audience. Eteocles denies that he can be deflected from his resolve, appeals again to the warrior ethic of courage, and answers the objection that he will be shedding a brother's blood not by saying that he cannot control a mad desire to do just that but by reiterating that that is what the gods have made inevitable, sooner or later. Eteocles thus denies that the curse can remain unfulfilled, but he obviously deliberates and acts on something akin to what we might term an implicit assumption that he is free (somewhat in the manner of the later Stoic sage) to accommodate himself to the divine will. To be sure, in the ensuing great ode there is an overwhelming sense of ineluctable fate, but that has never been in doubt. The curse must be fulfilled, but Apollo and the Erinys work by confronting Eteocles with their purpose and factoring in his reaction to it. The only specifically moral comment that the chorus offer after the event is that the brothers perished through their 'impious attitude(s)' (ἀσεβεῖ διανοίᾳ, 831), that is through a frame of mind that made them prepared to commit fratricide.[53] But this adds nothing to the view which they expressed to Eteocles in the previous scene when they failed to grasp that really no other course of action was possible.

ETEOCLES' MORAL AWARENESS

Eteocles fulfils all Pelling's criteria of individuality.[54] He is clearly aware of his own and others' social roles and responsibilities, but his characterization transcends those categories inasmuch as we can ask (and indeed he asks himself) whether he is living up to his position. He has also a capacity to describe and analyse psychic events, to decide rationally, and to accept responsibility and the consequences of his decisions and actions. He is not, however, an idiosyncratically conceived individual, but the sum of his attitudes associated with his roles of king, general, and brother and an ability to reflect thereon.

Eteocles begins the play innocent, as far as we can tell, of all guilt in respect of his father and his brother. He is fully aware of the curse at that stage of the drama, but relegates it to the back of his mind during the shield scene up to the announcement of Polyneices' presence at the seventh gate. There is no question of his mind being permanently corrupted by the Fury and thus of his judgement being flawed when he makes his selections of defending champions. On the contrary, his ethico-religious awareness ensures appropriate and successful choices. But while in making these selections he is at least in theory aware also

---

[53] As Sewell-Rutter (2007) 33–4 observes, the 'opposition between Eteocles and Polyneices that reaches its height at the end of the *Redepaare* now collapses utterly, and nothing more is said of the relative justice or piety of the two opposed causes. They are so closely joined in their terrible fate that they are barely distinguishable, barely individuated.'

[54] See pp. 16–17.

of the inevitability of the curse's fulfilment, he does not realize how this will come about until confronted with Polyneices' appointment, at which point he is at once fully aware of his impending doom. This realization is not ethico-religious, but simply religious: the purpose of the Fury and the hatred of Apollo are amoral.

Confronted with Polyneices' presence at the seventh gate, Eteocles correctly realizes that it is his inescapable destiny to meet him in combat. In choosing to do what is fated he chooses to act bravely in order to retain his honour as a warrior and morally in terms of his obligation as the city's principal defender (for he is in fact the right opponent to defeat his brother, and the gate does hold). Amphiaraus similarly realized that he faced an unavoidable doom, and he was ready to meet it with dignity, showing himself to be indeed σώφρων, δίκαιος, ἀγαθός, εὐσεβής. But Amphiaraus was not doomed to fratricide, and the difference makes Eteocles' predicament infinitely more tragic. Amphiaraus was, of course, caught up with an impious crew, and the parallel with Eteocles is reinforced by the latter's membership of the Labdacid family. Laius, we remember, disobeyed an oracle and consciously (it would seem) jeopardized the city's preservation, and the rot set in from there. Eteocles, like Amphiaraus, is indisputably *agathos*, though the positive connotation of the term is rendered problematical by the circumstances in which the quality is displayed. As for the other qualities, perhaps we should say that at least he does not evince their opposites, since no other course was open to him. How can one be moderate, just, and pious in committing fratricide? This kind of paradox is piquantly tragic; Sophocles' Electra finds herself violating certain virtues as conventionally understood in her attempt to exemplify those very virtues in a higher form.

An old, but unfortunately persistent, view (revived more recently by Vernant) that Eteocles is really two different and incompatible men—the defender of the polis and the 'Labdacid of legend' caught up in a family curse—will not sustain critical inspection. (In Vernant's case it arises from a structuralist theory which in its quest for polarities considerably exaggerates the tensions in tragedy while failing to do justice to the extent to which potential anachronisms are successfully integrated.[55]) Eteocles the statesman does not suddenly evaporate, though the impact of his realization inevitably shifts the focus of his thinking. In fact, Eteocles does much to redeem his grandfather's transgression. He does not share the female chorus' belief that honour is cancelled by the accompanying fratricide, though he does concede that he is inspired by a battle-lust (which, as we saw, is not to be construed as frenzied hatred for his brother). This battle-lust perhaps obliterates a natural horror at the prospect of fratricide, but Eteocles is also clearly anxious to repress unrestrained lamentation. Although considerations of free will are here, strictly speaking, anachronistic, we found substantial evidence that both the chorus and Eteocles himself assume that he possesses the power to decide and act, and that this power is never questioned in the play.

Eteocles' moral awareness is remarkable in both its recognition of the Fury-inspired delusion referred to by the chorus and its ability to survive it. His decision to accept and enact his fated destiny is obviously rational and correct, while a normal horror at the prospect of fratricide could serve no useful purpose in

---

[55] Vernant and Vidal-Naquet (1981) 11.

a situation where a warrior's courage is the most useful mental state. The negative aspect of the tragedy of Eteocles (as of Sophocles' Oedipus) consists in a destiny which dooms him to offend against kin; the positive aspect (as for Oedipus) is the courage and clear-sightedness with which he accepts that destiny. And as a god, it would seem, latches onto Eteocles' battle-lust, so does Apollo induce Oedipus to blind himself. There is a terrible appropriateness, nevertheless, to both the battle-lust and the appalling mental state that brought on the self-blinding, and both men embrace and defend the resulting acts.

CONCLUSION

Throughout the shield scene Eteocles effortlessly chooses appropriate opponents for the first six Argive champions on the basis of a clear moral and religious awareness of the sort of opponent required. At the end of the scene he at once realizes that the fulfilment of the curse is inevitable, that the moral issue concerns only the manner of his death and that he must die bravely. No deliberation is required. He defines himself as a Labdacid subject to the curse and as a warrior, king, and leader with the moral obligations conventionally attached to those roles (hence his determination to die bravely). His moral awareness is outstanding throughout the shield scene. His evaluation of his brother is largely correct and he rightly insists that there is no alternative to fratricide. He acts in harmony with his morality. This morality is appropriate in the play's terms because his only options are a brave or a cowardly death. He fully understands the facts of his predicament and that his only choice is in how to die. The emotional component of his resolve is a strong desire which the chorus characterize as evil, a desire inspired or at least intensified by the Fury. This desire is appropriate to his resolve in that it strengthens it without compromising his rationality.

4

Aeschylus: *Agamemnon*

THE PORTENT OF THE EAGLES AND THE HARE

Aeschylus' Agamemnon faces two closely related crises: first a moral dilemma (whether to sacrifice his daughter, Iphigenia, in order to secure favourable winds for sailing to Troy) and later the temptation to enter his palace on blood-red fabrics, an act likely to inspire divine *phthonos*. In the previous chapter we began our investigation of Eteocles' moral awareness by considering the wider divine and human context of his crisis at the seventh gate. We saw that he was defined in part as a member of an *oikos* in which gods took a special and hostile interest. Agamemnon's crisis at Aulis appears very near the beginning of the trilogy, whereas that of Eteocles came as the final climax of the last play, by which stage Aeschylus had established the entire religious and moral world of the drama.[1] Some such context begins to emerge in *Oresteia*—though never of course with systematic clarity—as the circumstances of the decision at Aulis are recounted by the chorus in the parodos. Other relevant factors such as the gods' attitude to city-sackers, the Atreid curse and Atreid heredity are introduced only later, though before the second crisis of the carpet treading so that that event at least can be seen in the context they provide. The dramatic order of introduction is important because the presence or absence of a moral and religious background will affect the audience's appraisal of events.

Before the Trojan expedition could sail from the assembly point at Aulis, a portent appeared—two eagles killing a pregnant hare—which symbolized the sack of Troy (107–30), since the eagles represented the Atreidae and the hare (implicitly) Troy. But built into this omen is a negative implication. According to the seer Calchas, Artemis, as the protectress of the unborn, objects not to the eagles killing a hare as such, but to their killing of a *pregnant* hare, and in requital she demands the sacrifice of Agamemnon's daughter Iphigenia if the fleet is to proceed to Troy. Thus the sack of the city would appear to hang on the pregnancy of the eagles' victim. Calchas, however, does not assume that Artemis objects to the expedition, as he carefully distinguishes the 'blameworthy' (κατάμομφα, 145) content of the portent from its 'auspicious' (δεξιά, 145) analogue, that is the sack of Troy. While the goddess may well consent to the sack of Troy as symbolized by the 'sacrifice' of the hare (as presumably she would have consented to the death of an *un*pregnant

---

[1] I am avoiding the term 'theological' for fear of implying that Aeschylus was a systematic religious or philosophical thinker or that the religious ideas of the chorus are authoritative or necessarily consistent.

hare), she will demand in return for the slaughter of the foetus 'another' (implic-itly, Iphigenia's) sacrifice (150), that will entail the murder of Agamemnon by Clytemnestra.

It is clear enough that the hare and her unborn young represent the general cost of the war in human suffering, whether or not Artemis is angry solely on account of the hare or also on behalf of the Trojan young.[2] Aeschylus presents the war ambivalently as at once the triumph of Zeus Xenios and a waste of lives (presumably on both sides, and affecting combatant and civilian alike) for the sake of a promiscuous woman (62, 447–8). It is entirely appropriate then that the portent should encapsulate this moral ambivalence, and that its ultimate conse-quence in the play—the murder of Agamemnon—should thus appear in part a punishment or at least a price paid for the waste of lives.[3]

Artemis' anger is a necessary dramaturgical and symbolic device to create a dilemma for Agamemnon in respect of which he is not entirely the innocent victim.[4] For it is not quite true to say that he simply finds himself confronted with a morally intractable situation, a war he is obliged by Zeus Xenios to prosecute even at the cost of his own daughter's life, in which case the divine command would simply overrule all other considerations, as it does for Orestes. Agamem-non, however, unlike Eteocles or Orestes who are aware of the divine will, shows no awareness of any explicit divine command to sack Troy (and indeed no such command appears to exist) and so he forfeits (or is denied) the consequent mitigation of responsibility for his decision.[5] Nussbaum is wrong here to speak of Agamemnon 'piously executing Zeus's command'. She defends his decision to sacrifice 'both because of consequences and because of the impiety involved in the other choice. Indeed, it is hard to imagine that Agamemnon could rationally have chosen any other way. But both courses involve him in guilt.' It will not do here to read in a command from Zeus. No one at any point refers to a specific command. Calchas might easily have done so, and Agamemnon omits it from his delibera-tions. This makes his situation crucially different from that of Orestes who receives an unequivocal command which is decisive for his deliberations. If we take the liberty of reading in a similar command in Agamemnon's case we obliterate this important distinction.

The dilemma in which Agamemnon finds himself therefore is conditional upon the portent (and thus on Zeus) which makes the sacrifice of Iphigenia a prerequi-site for the war, but it is also conditional upon Agamemnon's own powerful desire for the war. The divine contribution here does not stem from a god's punishment; Agamemnon has done nothing wrong, unlike in the traditional version of the story in which he angered Artemis by killing a stag in a sacred domain, boasting

---

[2] 'It is not as an arbitrary partisan of Troy, but as patroness of innocent youth and fertility that Artemis recoils from the indiscriminate predation which she knows a war under the Atreidae will be': Peradotto (1969) 247. See also Kitto (1956) 3 and (1961) 68. Lebeck (1971) 35 thinks that Artemis' anger is caused by the *cena Thyestea*. See also Ewans (1975) 22, 28.

[3] If Agamemnon 'must shed so much innocent blood "for an unchaste woman", let him first shed his own daughter's innocent blood—and take the consequences': Kitto (1961) 69.

[4] On the role of Artemis see Lawrence (1976) *passim* and the reply of Sommerstein (1980).

[5] See Kitto (1961) 71. Nussbaum (1986) 34.

that he was a superior hunter to the goddess.[6] But, viewed from another perspective, the dilemma is not entirely unfair in that it places Agamemnon in a situation similar to that in which he will find himself if he chooses to prosecute the war, and which symbolically foreshadows that situation. For in order to conquer Troy Agamemnon must be prepared to preside over massive loss of innocent life, and his decision to sacrifice his own daughter anticipates his willingness to do that. Iphigenia is the war's first victim.

The background to Agamemnon's deliberations over the sacrifice is presented in the parodos. Because the episode at Aulis occurs ten years before the action of the play, the actual deliberations are not directly dramatized, but they are quoted verbatim by the chorus. The king appears first as one of a pair with his brother Menelaus, and initially undistinguished from him: 'the Atreidae, a pair firmly yoked in the honour of their twin thrones and twin sceptres given by Zeus' (43–4: tr. Sommerstein). Together they launched a thousand ships, 'shouting "War!" (the cry for a mighty war) from an angry heart, like vultures' wheeling around their robbed nest until a pitying deity sent an avenger (48–58).[7] In like manner, Zeus Xenios 'sends' ($\pi\acute{\epsilon}\mu\pi\epsilon\iota$) the sons of Atreus against Paris for the sake of Helen, a woman of many men (60–2). The vulture simile may strike us as somewhat inappropriate, since what has been lost is a wife, not children, and, more significantly, vultures are naturally predators or scavengers rather than prey. However, Aeschylus' point is more subtle: Agamemnon, though a victim, will become a sort of predator and he will 'prey' on the young, beginning with his own. The simile is proleptically ironical.[8]

The imagery of birds wheeling about a nest conveys to the audience no sense of the man in his physical (or indeed moral) immediacy; instead it subtly categorizes him in an abstract way as caught between the roles of victim and predator, looking back to the theft of Helen and forward to his murder at the hands of Clytemnestra (in the role of victim or prey), and forward also to the sacrifice of his daughter (in the role of predator). This role-changing is taken up in the portent of the eagles and the hare in which the Atreidae become the aggressors and Troy the victim. The characterization of Agamemnon is thus linked to the wider patterns and themes of the trilogy, but he himself remains, at least for the moment, the shadowy site of abstract concepts and qualities. This is important in considering his role as a moral agent. Eteocles, it will be remembered, defines himself as a general obliged to behave in a certain way and he is standing there in flesh and blood before us, morally active throughout the play. Agamemnon does not explicitly define himself in moral terms, although we shall see when we examine his deliberations that he implicitly defines himself as a father, though even more as a military commander with responsibilities to his peers.

---

[6] As Jones (1962) 76–7 argues, the traditional cause of the goddess's anger is irrelevant here and should not be read in. Kitto (1956) 4–5 thinks that Artemis is angry with Agamemnon for what he is going to do (destroy innocent life at Troy).

[7] I have adapted Fraenkel's (1950) translation here to bring out the full sense; for which see his note ad 48 ff.

[8] On the imagery of simile and portent see Lebeck (1971) 8–16.

AGAMEMNON'S DELIBERATIONS AT AULIS

It is important that Agamemnon's deliberations are embedded in choral lyric, a mode that tends to distance the audience from the event (and thus from the agent himself) and to work more by association and emotion than by inviting the logical or rational response prompted by narrative or dialogue. It is remarkable then that this passage (Agamemnon's deliberations) should be of such cardinal importance for understanding the trilogy. The impact of the decision-making is much less than, for example, in the *Supplices* where Pelasgus' deliberations under the pressure of the chorus are considerably prolonged and are presented on stage in such a way that we can feel his mental anguish as he casts about for an escape from a course of action to which he keeps returning as morally inescapable. Similarly, Eteocles' resolve is dynamically dramatized in his mutually agonizing exchanges with the chorus. One has to wonder then just what impact Agamemnon's reported deliberations will have on an audience, considering that he is absent from the stage, has not yet made an appearance on it, and will not do so for some five hundred lines. On the other hand, the 'lyric utterances of a chorus ... often carry a special authority of their own, by reason of the traditional function of choruses as performers of communal wisdom and memorialization.'[9]

Let us turn now to the deliberations themselves.

... and the older king spoke, saying this:

'It is a heavy doom not to be persuaded (τὸ μὴ πιθέσθαι), and heavy if I am to kill my child, the adornment of my house, polluting a father's hands with streams of a slaughtered maiden's blood near the altar. Which of these [courses of action] is without *kaka* [bad/undesirable/unpleasant consequences?] (τί τῶνδ' ἄνευ κακῶν;) How can I prove a deserter of the fleet (λιπόναυς γένωμαι), losing my alliance (ξυμμαχίας ἁμαρτών)? [I cannot,] because (γὰρ) it is only right/natural[10] [θέμις] that they [his peers] [or she = Artemis?] should desire with the most extreme passion [ὀργᾷ περιόργως] a sacrifice of a maiden's blood to stop [the unfavourable winds]. May it be well.' (205–17)

Agamemnon's quoted speech, compared with what a real person would say, is a simplified, even partially rationalized, unindividualized, and certainly abbreviated summary of a train of thought and feeling, incorporating simple, brief arguments for and against the sacrifice, and an implicit decision to proceed. There is no impression of the way agonizing dilemmas are confronted in real life, with arguments repeatedly and sometimes obsessively reviewed before a final decision is made. Here Euripides' Agamemnon in his *Iphigenia at Aulis* offers an instructive contrast. Instead of a purely verbal and quite schematized deliberation process in which an agent determines upon a course of action after a brisk and rational review of options, Agamemnon is present on the stage in dialogue with his old servant, and his confused state of mind (ἀπορῶν, *IA* 40) is conveyed, not by words (he is silent at the time), but by his bodily gestures which are described by the servant. (He is constantly rewriting a letter which we presently learn is addressed to Clytemnestra and concerns instructions to send Iphigenia to Aulis ostensibly to be married to Achilles. His bodily gestures convey his intense vacillation and

[9] M. Griffith (2005) 347.
[10] For the translation 'natural' see Sommerstein (2008) ii. 26–7 n. 48.

frustration, and it transpires that he is torn by irresolvable uncertainty about whether or not to proceed with the sacrifice of his daughter.) Indeed, to the old man his master seems mad with confusion (Eur. *IA* 42), and Agamemnon himself will presently say that he ceased to think rationally when he decided on the sacrifice and is now falling into 'delusion' or 'disaster' (ἄταν, *IA* 138). Aeschylus, on the other hand, is unconcerned with individual idiosyncrasy or realism. His account of the deliberations is designed less to represent them in their concrete immediacy than to schematize the process of making a decision and to indicate the alternatives.[11] In this, curiously enough, he is closer to modern philosophy which is more likely to be interested in the rational arguments deployed than in the irrational impulses which in actual human situations punctuate or disrupt them. (That said, what we have here are not the bloodless intellectualized alternatives of a philosophical example.) Neither is there any sense of a physical place in which the deliberations occurred, nor another person to oppose him, as the chorus opposed Eteocles. Nor again is there any questioning of Calchas and thus of the reality of the dilemma.[12]

Agamemnon is faced with two options, though his deliberations do not suggest that he has any clear sense of facing a specifically moral dilemma, that is 'a situation in which compelling moral considerations favor each of the courses of action open to him.'[13] First he states that it would be a 'heavy doom' (βαρεῖα... κήρ)(that is, a terrible consequence, but not necessarily a moral evil) not to be persuaded (that is, not to kill his daughter). I have avoided translating τὸ μὴ πιθέσθαι as 'disobey', since Artemis has not issued an outright command to sacrifice Iphigenia but has merely made the sacrifice a condition of the sack of Troy. Presumably Agamemnon means 'being persuaded to go to Troy on that condition'. On the other hand, it would be an equally 'heavy doom' to kill his child, and he imagines briefly but vividly enough what this would entail (209–11), a reaction which, as the term 'pollute' implies, is both moral and religious, but we may see in the words an emotional revulsion as well. (Of course, there is nothing here about the intrinsic worth of a human being or human rights, both thoroughly anachronistic notions.) Agamemnon then would appear to be moved partly at least by a sense of moral obligation to gods and family. At this point the balance seems inclined against the sacrifice, inasmuch as the negative consequences only of the sacrificing option have been imagined, although the term 'heavy doom' has been applied to both options and the idea of equal negativity reinforced by the summarizing 'Which of these courses is without *kaka*, that is without unpleasant or nasty (and perhaps, but not necessarily, morally evil) consequences?'.[14] The emphasis then is on consequences and emotional reactions rather than the intrinsic immorality of the act itself. Moreover, although each course involves consequences that are *kaka*, it by no means follows that Agamemnon is, or sees himself, as facing an *irresolvable* moral dilemma, as he would have been had there

---

[11] On the loss of immediacy see Rosenmeyer (1982) 224.

[12] Dover (1973) 62 argues that we should look at Agamemnon's predicament more realistically. How could he be sure that Calchas was right?

[13] Mason (1996) 3.

[14] '[I]n ordinary Greek usage *agatha*, "good things", and *kaka*, "bad things", often denote respectively material comforts and discomforts': Dover (1974) 52.

been 'no morally relevant difference between the alternatives'[15]—if, for example, he had been unconditionally required to sacrifice a daughter but allowed to choose between Iphigenia and (say) Electra.

But now Agamemnon briefly imagines the consequences of failing to sacrifice: 'How can I prove[16] a deserter of the fleet, losing[17] my alliance?' (212–13). What is entailed for him in 'losing the alliance'? Is he reluctant to let his peers down (indicating a moral concern for the wider 'society' of military alliances and guest friendships), or is he afraid of missing out on glory? Or both? And is the glory motive (if it applies) to be construed morally as an obligation to himself (as it is for Eteocles and indeed for Hector at *Il.* 6. 442–6) or amorally as a sheer desire? In making this distinction we are allowing the possibility that the man exists apart from his roles as father and general. Jones disagrees,[18] but we can allow a range of 'personal' desires that naturally but not inevitably attach to a role, such as the general's desire for glory, and, as we have seen, if there is a conflict of roles there must be some third factor which decides between them.[19] Fraenkel opts for the altruistic interpretation when he translates 'fail *in my duty to* the alliance'. Hammond, on the other hand, thinks that Agamemnon 'prefers the pomp and ceremony of the ships and the confederation' (the selfish motive).[20] Conacher fairly observes that the text is unclear on this point.[21] Certainly the reluctance to be or be shown as a deserter might be read as nicely conveying the tension between a natural enough moral desire to do what is right and an equally natural but self-interested concern with the shame attendant upon failing to do so and, conversely, with the glory of the war. Thus Agamemnon's horror at the option of desertion may just as plausibly be interpreted as proceeding from mixed motives (moral and non-moral) as may his revulsion against killing his daughter, and there is nothing to suggest which option will prevail. It would seem reasonable then to interpret his words to imply that he is, up to this point at any rate, sensitive to competing moral claims and that there is no straightforward conflict between morality and self-interest since both motives can plausibly be said to perch on both horns of the dilemma.

Agamemnon clearly finds abandoning the expedition inconceivable and so with the very enunciation of the idea he decides against it. In the ensuing lines (214–17) he offers no reason for his decision, though he is clearly anxious to assert that it is justified and to put to rest his residual doubts. In a famous passage in the *Iliad*

---

[15] Sinnott-Armstrong (1996) 50.

[16] For this sense of γίγνομαι (i.e. 'become and be seen to be') see Thuc. 1. 90. 1 (γενομένην).

[17] For 'lose' here see Sommerstein (2008) ii. 25 n. 47: 'The phrase ξυμμαχίας ἁμαρτών could also probably mean "failing in my obligations to my allies"; but nothing in this play, or even in the *Iliad* suggests that Agamemnon is under any relevant obligation to any of his allies except Menelaus—and Menelaus, we know, (cf. 202–4 above), was as distressed by Calchas' declaration as Agamemnon was. The rendering adopted here, which is easier grammatically, will refer to the possible loss of Agamemnon's hegemonic position after the blow to his prestige that would result from the abandonment of a great undertaking to which he had set his hand.'

[18] Jones (1962) 114–15.

[19] See p. 17.

[20] Hammond (1965) 47. See also Sommerstein (1989) 365.

[21] Conacher (1987) 13.

(ll. 401–10) Odysseus deliberates whether to run away or stand and fight.[22] The point at which the decision is made is signposted by a formulaic dismissal of the need for deliberation (ll. 407) and this is followed by a moral justification: only cowards run away. Agamemnon, on the other hand, appeals to no moral code—presumably because the dilemma involves competing claims of both morality and self-interest which he has not in fact rationally resolved, whereas Odysseus was confronted by a conflict which was quite clearly between the claims of heroic morality and sheer self-interest.

Agamemnon would seem to become aware then during the course of his deliberations that he faces what we would more formally describe as a moral dilemma, or at least that there are important moral issues involved, though his response is only partly moral, and he is moved by other considerations. He recognizes both a moral requirement not to kill his daughter and what he considers to be an overriding moral requirement not to desert his peers. But we might fairly object that he should have formulated the latter as a requirement to do the implicit will of Zeus Xenios and to punish the moral wrong committed by Paris for which the Trojans are held collectively responsible—surely a much stronger moral requirement.[23] Indeed, he might have argued that, since Zeus required the sack of Troy, not only was he (Agamemnon) logically required to sacrifice Iphigenia, but even that Zeus would somehow ensure that he did. This would put him in a position not unlike that of Eteocles. Agamemnon's limited awareness then compromises his very formulation of the dilemma, while his overrating of the claims of his peers compromises his weighing of the competing moral claims.[24]

AGAMEMNON'S AUTONOMY

Now there is no indication in the passages that relate the decision and its implementation that Agamemnon's decision is overdetermined by Zeus or indeed any other god, nor that he has received any oracle or specific command from Zeus relayed by Calchas. We have been told that Zeus 'sends' ($\pi\acute{\epsilon}\mu\pi\epsilon\iota$, 61) the Atreidae, but since no specific command is either referred to or present in the mythological tradition, $\pi\acute{\epsilon}\mu\pi\epsilon\iota$ is better translated 'escorts', 'conveys', or perhaps 'speeds' in the sense of 'expedites' or 'urges on'.[25] Moreover, we shall presently be told that 'the raging bird' (the eagle portent) $\pi\acute{\epsilon}\mu\pi\epsilon\iota$ (111) the Atreidae to Troy (an idea reiterated in $\pi o\mu\pi o\acute{v}s$ τ' $\dot{\alpha}\rho\chi\acute{\alpha}s$ at 125). Since a portent cannot literally 'send'

[22] On Odysseus' deliberations and moral deliberations generally in Homer see Lawrence (2003).
[23] Agamemnon 'is indeed the agent of Zeus, and the Chorus sees him as such, but he himself does not': Helm (2004) 42.
[24] '[G]enuine moral dilemmas are ontological, not merely epistemic; the truth of the conflicting ought-statements is independent of the agent's beliefs': McConnell (1996) 36.
[25] 'The statement "Zeus sent the Atreidae…" is a religious interpretation of the chorus, not an empirical description. It does no more than indicate their belief in the right or legal claim under which the war might be justified': Peradotto (1969) 251. See also Gantz (1982) 12, Winnington-Ingram (1983) 86, Conacher (1987) 86. For the sense 'convey' see Soph. *Trach.* 571. For the sense 'speeds' see *Ag.* 853.

them, again the sense must be that it somehow, as an expression of Zeus's will, authorizes or sets the seal of approval on the expedition, while stopping short of an explicit command.

It seems preferable then to think of the expedition as not so much 'required'[26] by Zeus as harmonizing with his will as the god of hosts and guests. This is not to say that the war was not morally objectionable to other gods or even to Zeus in other capacities. To do the will of any specific deity is no guarantee of acting morally or even with unequivocal piety and still less of protection from harm. But Agamemnon does not expect to be protected by Zeus, nor does he see himself as compelled by the god, for in his dilemma it never occurs to him (unlike his son in the next play) to plead the divine will. Although we are never told that Zeus directly influences (much less predetermines) Agamemnon's decision at Aulis, it later appears that the god worked through the Greek army to cast his figurative net about Troy (355–61). As we saw in Ch. 2, it is not inappropriate to imagine that Zeus Xenios 'works through' Agamemnon in some mysterious way, if not actually influencing his deliberations at Aulis, then at least foreseeing their outcome and factoring it into his plans for Troy (which are by no means recent: see 362–6) and (perhaps) for the House of Atreus. But there is nothing of this nature presented to us with dramatic immediacy (unlike in *Seven* when the Fury seems to enter into Eteocles and directly influence his 'decision') and divine intervention is no more than implied in the subsequent odes.

Agamemnon appears to experience neither remorse nor regret for his violation of the (overridden) moral requirement not to kill his daughter. Remorse is appropriate only if one believes one has acted wrongly, and Agamemnon seems to believe that he has behaved rightly in assenting to the overriding moral requirement. Regret, on the other hand, is appropriate even when the agent feels that he has acted rightly, and we may want to censure Agamemnon for not expressing regret, as Sophocles' Electra expresses regret (but not remorse) for her morally necessary persecution of her mother.[27] Agamemnon's revulsion against the idea of sacrificing his daughter may strike us as short-lived and even perfunctory, but that is at least partly a function of Aeschylus' economy. It is also, however, necessary in order to preserve the force of the carpet scene which (among other things) symbolically re-enacts the sacrifice. Such a re-enactment would be incoherent if Agamemnon had subsequently changed his mind about the sacrifice.

There was no room in Aeschylus' drama for an individualized Agamemnon obsessed with the sacrifice and constantly recurring to it, such as we find in Euripides' *IA*. Once Aeschylus' Agamemnon has made the decision and acted upon it, he forgets the anguish that attended it—or, more to the point, the drama forgets it, obviously unconcerned to focus on the agent's consciousness, even if some minimal consciousness must be presupposed.[28] Still, in the final analysis, we are left with a specific person who makes a choice out of perfectly intelligible

---

[26] Jones (1962) 75–6.

[27] On remorse and regret see McConnell (1996) 38.

[28] A similar dramaturgically motivated phenomenon appears, though in reverse order, in *Choephori* wherein Orestes entertains no qualms about the matricide or awareness of the likelihood of pursuit by his mother's Furies until immediately before the deed.

motives, and that is sufficient for us to form a moral judgement, even if that judgement is attached as much to an abstract point of view (the perspective of a military commander) as to the dramatic character with whom it is associated. In this case, clearly, Gill's 'personality viewpoint' is in a number of ways attenuated.[29]

Apart from the possible involvement of Zeus in the decision, there is another feature of the situation which, to the modern mind at least, casts some doubt on Agamemnon's deliberative autonomy. Once his decision has effectively been made, he states that it is *themis* (right? natural?) for them (his peers [σφ'] or Artemis? (216) to desire it 'with the most extreme passion' (215–16),[30] an emotional state as bizarre as that of Eteocles in his eagerness to shed his brother's blood, and one which, it would appear, Agamemnon is here projecting onto others.

The chorus tell us that Agamemnon changed to an 'unholy' state of mind (219–20) at the time when he put on the yoke of *anankē* (218). This is not a case of rigid determinism (which would be, as we have seen, anachronistic), but rather of very strong, but in principle resistible pressure. The constraint presumably is the sum of all the factors in the situation which pressured Agamemnon to sacrifice his daughter, and in making his decision he has chosen to heed these factors.[31] The chorus might appear to regard the decision as voluntary, if that can be inferred from their criticizing it, though it must be admitted that they later apparently approve of the destruction of Troy by the action of Zeus Xenios for which the sacrifice is a prerequisite. As Jones rightly observes, the chorus are inconsistent in condemning the sacrifice while never suggesting that Agamemnon could or should have acted otherwise.[32] They are perhaps merely registering their horror at the deed.

There is certainly an impression that Agamemnon has been reviewing genuine options.[33] At the moment when he put on the yoke of strong compulsion, that is, presumably, when he had just irrevocably decided and was on the point of implementing his decision, his mind was already altered[34] (from his initial horror at the thought of sacrificing his daughter) to an unholy state, and from that point (τόθεν) he became 'completely reckless' (τὸ παντότολμον φρονεῖν) because (γάρ)

---

[29] See p. 15.

[30] On the referent of σφ' see Ewans (1975) 27–8 and Winnington-Ingram (1983) 84–5 and his n. 16.

[31] Or one may identify the *anankē* with the consequences of the decision, including Clytemnestra's revenge—see e.g. Lattimore (1964) 40, Hammond (1965) 48, Peradotto (1969) 253, Conacher (1987) 14. Lebeck (1971) 36 sees Agamemnon's decision as 'predictable', given his antecedents, but not 'predestined'. Lesky (1965) 74, on the other hand, implies that the yoke is synonymous with the dilemma itself.

[32] Jones (1962) 78–9.

[33] 'The sacrifice of Iphigenia is not only a horrible necessity imposed upon him, it is at the same time his personal and passionately desired deed, for which he is responsible and for which he has to atone': Lesky (1966a) 82. Contrast Denniston and Page pp. xxiii–iv (their emphasis): 'Agamemnon is *compelled, for no fault of his own,* to sacrifice his daughter. Zeus has approved, indeed he has dispatched, the expedition to Troy: it is his will that Troy should fall; it is nowhere suggested that Agamemnon might have disbanded his army; indeed it is said that the army will think it "right and proper" that Iphigenia should be sacrificed. Iphigenia is clearly doomed, whatever Agamemnon may do.'

[34] The present participle *pneōn* implies the simultaneity of the 'unholy change of mind' with the putting on of the yoke.

he had been emboldened by 'shameful contriving *parakopa* or infatuation' (αἰσχρόμητις ... παρακοπά), that is the state that accompanied the second and final stage of his deliberation (his sense that desertion was out of the question) (218–22). One might be tempted to see *parakopa* as synonymous with *ate* (delusion)[35] which is often associated with divine intervention, but (as we saw in Ch. 2) there is no reference to any such intervention in the passage. Even so, the chorus clearly condemn the decision and the state of mind in which it was made. They would certainly deny that Agamemnon is morally aware at this point.

    Here we must distinguish the rightness or wrongness of the decision itself from the state of mind in which it was made. If, in the final analysis, we are to approve of the sack of Troy and of the purpose of Zeus Xenios (and how can we not?) then Agamemnon decided correctly. But, as we have seen, he does not decide for that reason. It seems more likely that Zeus is using Agamemnon's deluded state, his *parakopa*, whatever its source, to effect his purpose, as he will later use Clytemnestra. The chorus's position then would seem to be that when Agamemnon recognized the force of *anankē* (a very powerful compulsion, at least) he succumbed to a strange emotional state. But what is this *anankē*, and did Agamemnon assess it correctly? It was not, as we have seen, direct pressure from the gods— or not at least as Agamemnon formulates it. We might say that Zeus required the war and therefore the sacrifice, which is a very strong *anankē* indeed, but Agamemnon sees only the overwhelming pressure of the ignominy of desertion. Otherwise stated, he identified with his role as a general. It would seem then that this complete identification with one role to the exclusion of the other (paternal) role is an unbalanced and extreme reaction the subjective correlative of which is Agamemnon's deluded mental state, his *parakopa*. Moreover, such extreme, even deluded reactions could be seen as, in a sense, natural reactions to extreme dilemmas which cannot be resolved without a residual sense of committing a heinous wrong.

THE WIDER CONTEXT OF THE DECISION AT AULIS

Although it is important to consider Agamemnon's decision in its immediate context, that is on the basis of what the audience has been told at that point, we should also consider the broader context established through the rest of the play, particularly because the carpet scene introduces another decision that is thematically connected with the earlier one, and at that later point in the play we have learned more about Agamemnon from the chorus and from his onstage speech. The information is conveyed obliquely. The first stasimon begins with a celebration of the sack of Troy, 'netted' by Zeus Xenios and Night (355–61). The chorus go on to observe that 'Some used to say that the gods did not deign to concern themselves with such mortals as trampled underfoot the grace of the sacrosanct' (... ὅσοις ἀθίκτων χάρις πατοῖθ᾽) (369–72: tr. Sommerstein), but dismiss the view as impious, linking such acts with bloated arrogance and excessive wealth (376–8)

---

[35] Fraenkel (1950) ad loc.; Hammond (1965) 48 n. 17.

and observing that 'there is no defence against excess of wealth for a man who has kicked (λακτίσαντι) the great altar of Justice (Dike) into oblivion' (381–4: tr. Sommerstein). Temptation (Peitho) opens the way to this impious act. Thus in this passage we are afforded a kind of symbolic preview of Agamemnon's fabric trampling in its context (excess of wealth), psychology (arrogance bred by wealth and vulnerable to temptation), and moral significance (impiety for which punishment will be inescapable).

The context relates the generalization to the Trojans, but the trampling imagery will be enacted physically in the carpet scene by Agamemnon himself, while the references to wealth and impiety apply as much to him and his family as to Troy. Agamemnon's physical act of treading the 'carpet' (strictly, 'fabrics') thus takes on symbolic resonance. Moreover, the trampling imagery reappears after the carpet scene in Cassandra's reference to Thyestes' adultery conceived as 'trampling' (πατοῦντι, 1193) on a brother's bed. Agamemnon's specific act is thus generalized both before and after the event. Among other things he is the type of the impious trampler in which the metaphorical trampling is more significant than the literal.[36] The symbolic nature of the carpet scene is important in assessing Agamemnon's moral performance in that scene.

Towards the end of this long ode, the emphasis shifts from the punishment of the Trojans to the resentment of the Argives (Greeks) for the loss of life on their side (437–57). This human resentment is apparently supported by divine anger at *polyktonoi*, 'those who kill *en masse*' (461). The Furies punish such men (462–7), as Zeus casts a thunderbolt upon those whose reputation is too high (468–70). This condition is specifically instantiated in the sacker of cities (471–4). So Agamemnon is in danger, not from his character per se but from his roles with which he is in this play so closely identified. What is conveyed here is not personal information about Agamemnon or his character but a sort of theory about him as defined by external considerations of roles (general, king, man of wealth) which in themselves are deemed sufficient to produce a certain attitude. Agamemnon's 'character' is thus reduced to such roles or functions. Again there is a strong contrast with the Agamemnon of *IA* who experiences a conflict between his roles and his personal inclinations.

But Agamemnon is not only a sacker of cities, he is also a son of Atreus.[37] Do his family legacy and in particular the notorious curse affect his moral deliberations at Aulis or in the carpet scene? Agamemnon is doomed by the curse and it may be that the Erinyes that bring the curse to fulfilment work partly by perverting the judgement of the victim when he is at the point of making a crucial decision. As we saw, it is just possible that Aeschylus wished to suggest by the chorus's reference to Agamemnon's *parakopa* that the avenging Furies of the

---

[36] On trampling in the trilogy see Lebeck (1971) 38–40, 68, 74–9.

[37] For Jones (1962) 93 Agamemnon scarcely exists as a morally significant individual. 'The vagaries, contradictions and obscurities which . . . frustrate the search for an intelligible, and not merely for an acceptable, morality or rationale of guilt and innocence, are not there for Aeschylus because Agamemnon himself—the Agamemnon of the critics, the autonomous, self-sustaining modern man—is not there. Aeschylus's Agamemnon draws his life, and with his life his guilts and innocences, from the *oikos*.' This goes too far; Agamemnon is only in part defined as a member of the House. The sense of individual guilt is diluted by the extent to which he falls short of individuation, and 'his' guilt tends to attach to his roles. Aegisthus finds him guilty qua Atreid: ibid. 74.

house had perverted his judgement, thus providing the decisive element in the victory of the general over the father. However, as argued above, there is no clear suggestion of such divine intervention in the parodos, and it is a dubious critical procedure to imagine the audience reading it in retrospectively.[38]

Related to the idea of the family curse as a determinant of Agamemnon's behaviour is the notion of inherited character. In the second stasimon the chorus expound a parable featuring a lion cub (717–36) which has been raised in a civilized environment but which nevertheless matures to display the savage 'character' (*ēthos*, 727–8) it has inherited from its parents. Then, immediately following this parable, we find the related idea of behaviour 'inherited' from previous behaviour (758–71): 'it is the impious deed that breeds more to follow, resembling their progenitors. . . . An old act of outrage (*hubris*, 763) is wont to give birth to a new young outrage [766] . . . the unholy arrogance of Ruin, black for the house, in the likeness of her parents' (tr. Sommerstein).[39]

The primary referent of the lion cub is Paris, as Nappa has convincingly shown, though other critics have identified it with Helen, whose name is mentioned immediately before the parable.[40] But, in any event, Agamemnon has a claim to be considered as a secondary referent, since the chorus's moral and religious generalities are at this point more relevantly applied to the Atreids than to the Trojans or to Helen. However, if we take the parable in isolation, it does not after all apply very well to Agamemnon (except that both he and the cub are *polyktonoi*: 461, 734). It would seem to suggest rather a person brought up away from their natural home in a more civilized or humane environment (like Orestes),[41] but manifesting in spite of that their fundamentally destructive nature. When, however, the related idea of ancient hubris begetting a younger hubris is taken in conjunction with the parable, one might detect a suggestion at least that Agamemnon's character and actions are 'inherited' from his father Atreus.

Since all we really know about Atreus is that he did not baulk at killing young kin as the most effective way of achieving a purpose, it is, in the play's terms, only that trait which Agamemnon could have conceivably inherited from him.[42] (Though Orestes inherits no such tendency.) This would mean that Agamemnon's inherited character helped to tip the balance in favour of the sacrifice at Aulis, and it is just conceivable that we are to imagine the curse as working

---

[38] On the curse Kitto (1961) 66 observes 'that the first play is two-thirds finished before ever the Curse is mentioned, and that the trilogy does not end with the lifting of the Curse but with a reconciliation between the Erinyes and the Olympian deities, brought about by Athena, and not in Argos but in Athens, with the prosperity of Attica as the important issue'. Sewell-Rutter (2007) 75–6 rightly argues that the curse is only one causal factor among many accorded varying importance throughout the Trilogy.

[39] See Helm (2004) for an excellent discussion of the 'genealogical' relationship between impiety, *hubris*, *ate*, and related terms in Aeschylus in the context of earlier Greek thinking.

[40] Nappa (1994) *passim*.

[41] See Vellacott (1984) 147. The cub suggests destruction from within the house and it 'creates a sense of foreboding by rendering symbolically not only what has happened at Troy, but what will happen at Argos': Nappa (1994) 85. Thus the cub might also be seen as Clytemnestra who fawns and who is an 'alien' in the house.

[42] Peradotto (1969) 256 refers to a 'teknophonous' *ēthos*, but this should not be seen, anachronistically, as a kind of psychopathology.

through this *ēthos*, though it must be emphasized that there is no supporting textual evidence.

THE CARPET SCENE

At last Agamemnon enters the play in person. The technique is diametrically opposite to that of Euripides in his *IA* half a century later. That play begins with the appearance on stage of Agamemnon agonizing over the writing of a letter he is holding in his hand. The audience's first impressions are thus of the physical person. They do not know why Agamemnon is so distressed, nor are they privy to the contents of the letter. The abstract and conceptual dimension is developed only after this initial arresting physical impression. But Aeschylus' figure appears before us overlaid with many preconceptions: Agamemnon the 'king, sacker of Troy, son of Atreus' (as the chorus address him at 782–3), vulture, eagle, lion and lion cub, trampler. His characterization appears the sum of this typology. We await confirmation, the enactment of the predictable.

Agamemnon enters by chariot. The commander-in-chief is satisfied with his work. The moral ambiguities and the precariousness of his position as a city-sacker elude him: '[W]e have punished that arrogant abduction, and on account of a woman a city has been ground into dust by the Argive beast, the offspring of the Horse, the shield-bearing host . . . a lion, eater of raw flesh, leaped over the walls and licked its fill of royal blood' (822–5, 827–8: tr. Sommerstein). (The lion image, recalling the cub of the parable, is unconsciously ironic.) Moreover, his guilt (at least in his wife's eyes) is partly visible in the person of Cassandra. He is, however, aware of the envy he will have aroused (832–44).

All through his first speech of forty-four verses Agamemnon has remained upon his chariot. He continues there through the fifty-eight verses of Clytemnestra's reply. Towards the end of that speech his wife urges him to descend from the chariot, focusing attention specifically on the instrument of trampling and the surface to be trampled:

. . . but do not set your foot on the earth, my lord, the foot that sacked Troy! Servants, why are you waiting, when you have been assigned the duty of spreading fine fabrics over the ground in his path? Let his way forthwith be spread with crimson, so that Justice may lead him into a home he never hoped to see. (906–11: tr. Sommerstein)

Agamemnon at first refuses to tread the fabrics, partly out of fear of the impiety of walking on material designed to honour gods[43] and partly out of a reluctance to waste the substance of the house, but Clytemnestra in a short stichomythia overcomes his resistance, whereupon he says:

Well, if that's what you want, let someone quickly take off my shoes, which serve like slaves for my feet to tread on; and as I walk on these purple-dyed [robes], may no jealous eye (ὄμματος . . . φθόνος, 947) strike me from afar. For I feel a great sense of impropriety (*aidōs*,

---

[43] Taplin (1978) 80 argues that impiety as such is not the main point of the scene: 'The impiety which we witness here may be seen to stand for the other factors which condemn Agamemnon.'

948) about despoiling this house under my feet, ruining its wealth and the woven work bought with its silver. . . . Now, since I have been subjugated into obeying you in this, I will go, treading on purple, to the halls of my house.   (944–9, 956–7: tr. Sommerstein)

Agamemnon's treading upon the fabrics is not a prerequisite of his murder. It is a symbolic statement, a re-enactment of the decision at Aulis and of its implications at Troy, neither of which can be dramatized directly.[44] Indeed the connection with Troy is made as Agamemnon's foot that figuratively trampled the real Troy now literally tramples a figurative Troy. Agamemnon thus renews his guilt before our eyes.[45]

The psychology of the stichomythia has long been a matter of critical dispute.[46] Rosenmeyer strikes the right balance here: 'Agamemnon falls because the temptations offered are meaningful in terms of the type he is, no matter whether such arguments might have sufficed for a more complex flesh-and-blood personality.'[47] (It will not do to sever all meaningful connection between the carpet trampling and Agamemnon's character, however conceived.) Essentially, Clytemnestra distracts her husband from his anxiety about divine envy (which he knows he must on all accounts avoid) by conjuring up the prospect of human envy which can seem even positively desirable.[48] Although Agamemnon is not individually characterized, there is (as Easterling maintains) psychology in the way Clytemnestra

---

[44] Heath (1987) 21–2; Winnington-Ingram (1983) 90; Conacher (1987) 38–9; Lebeck (1971) 40: 'In reality there is but one moment of choice; all further action arises from it. The decision to tread upon purples is a necessary consequence of the decision reached at Aulis.'

[45] Simpson (1971) *passim* wrongly denies that Agamemnon is guilty of *hubris*, and attributes the trampling to Clytemnestra's manipulative powers alone. There is also the matter of the wasting of the house's substance, emphasized by Jones (1962) 87–8. The red carpet symbolizes the blood of Agamemnon's victims: see e.g. Lebeck (1971) 80–6. Agamemnon's body then for a moment springs into a rich thematic, imagistic, and dramatic life in the carpet scene with the focus on the trampling foot. As we look inside the man, as it were, we discover no individual psychology expressed through this action, but as we look out to the Aeschylean world we connect the action to wider moral and spiritual realities. Character here is a means of articulating themes. The point that Goldhill (1990) 108 makes about Orestes in *Choephori* is relevant here: 'What is recognized here . . . is not merely a bounded, unique, and autonomous individual. Rather, the language in and through which the figure of Orestes is formulated is part of the (figural) language of the trilogy, part of its specific textual dynamics, part of its *narrative*. The language does not merely express (his) "character", nor does it merely offer access to an individual "character". The representation of a fictional figure is (over)determined by the fictional narrative in which the figure plays a part.'

[46] For plausible psychological readings of the stichomythia see Winnington-Ingram (1983) 91–3, 106–7 and Cairns (1993) 194–200. Taplin (1978) 82 stresses the theme of the contest between male and female, while Lebeck (1971) 76 emphasizes the power of Persuasion. Similarly Buxton (1982) 106–8, cited with approval by Gibert (1995) 78, who denies that Aeschylus dramatizes the '"mechanics" of Peitho' (107), while suggesting, with (in my view) inadequate textual support, that Agamemnon is a victim of Ate working through Persuasion (108). Goldhill (1986) 12–14 emphasizes Clytemnestra's 'undercutting arguments' rather than Agamemnon's psychology.

[47] Rosenmeyer (1982) 222.

[48] Clytemnestra suggests that to walk on the fabrics is 'not intrinsically wrong, and makes Agamemnon admit that in other circumstances . . . and for another agent . . . the act might take on a different aspect. The point of this startling exploitation of the sophistic commonplace that the character of an action may vary according to agent and circumstance is the failure of Agamemnon to grasp what is only too apparent to the audience—that the character of the action does in fact *change* with the circumstances': Cairns (1993) 195–6.

manipulates her husband.[49] Agamemnon craves human envy but would avoid divine; this is just the natural attitude of any Greek general in the heroic mould.[50]

Thus Agamemnon yields because he is a warrior general who would enjoy his glory. We have been warned in the odes that the gods destroy the mass-killers and city-sackers because of such glory, and here Agamemnon instantiates the generalization. He would die in any case, but Clytemnestra lures him into incriminating himself before the gods. Morally, he baulks at spoiling the material substance of the house, as he baulked at killing its human substance in the shape of his daughter,[51] but the issue is more obviously religious than moral. Though piety, a moral virtue, is involved, the emphasis is as much prudential, as it will be for Orestes. It is *dangerous* to offend the gods. Agamemnon does wrong, but, more significantly, he symbolically re-enacts the wrongs he has already committed, wrongs typical of the successful warrior general.

There is no report of *parakopa* in the carpet scene,[52] but Agamemnon chooses dangerous glory as he chose it at Aulis. There, as we saw, while he spoke of losing the alliance, he was perhaps as much concerned with glory, and certainly he is concerned with it now. It is as if the amoral, egotistical motive at Aulis has come to the fore under the pressure of military success at Troy. He treads upon the substance of the house (as he killed his own daughter) and on the blood of all his victims. This is not consciously done, but these victims are the unacknowledged corollary of choosing glory.[53] There are then important and illuminating analogies with Aulis. There is a similar contest between the values of the *oikos* (symbolized in the fabrics) and the attraction of military glory, but instead of a clash of values each side of which contained a moral component we now have more of a clash between (1) sheer egotistical pride and (2) moral values associated with the family and religious values concerned with divine envy.

THE CARPET AND AKRASIA

Does Agamemnon then act against his rational judgement which at the beginning of the scene is clearly in tune with the moral and religious implications of the situation? Is he unable to control his desires? In other words, does he succumb to what Aristotle and the philosophers call akrasia?

---

[49] Easterling (1973) 21–3.

[50] 'When we see Agamemnon persuaded to walk on the fabrics, we need not infer any motives peculiar to him, but rather ones which we find intelligible in wider human terms: we are content to be convinced that "someone of such-and-such a type would naturally react like this." ... [B]ut we can still ask how differentiated the concept of "such-and-such a type" really is': Pelling (1990) 254. The answer is that Agamemnon has a general's desire for glory.

[51] The symbolic association of the fabrics with Iphigenia is important. That Agamemnon's guilt in this scene should involve nothing more than possible soiling of fabrics seems inadequate *pace* Jones (1962) 86–8.

[52] *Pace* Lloyd-Jones (1962) 197 who thinks Zeus has inspired Agamemnon with *atē* or *parakopa* in order to fulfil the curse. The curse 'comes first, and determines everything that follows' (ibid. 199).

[53] On Iphigenia's death as symbolic of the deaths at Troy see Kitto (1956) 5.

Akrasia occurs when the rational mind has decided on a course of action but a contrary (irrational) desire blocks its implementation. That is the clear-cut case. Suppose, however, that the rational mind is less than fully committed, being plagued by residual doubts which combine with the irrational emotional resistance (which is routinely the sole antagonist in akrasia) to overturn the decision ('Perhaps the gods won't see me do it or perhaps they won't care'). Immediately after deciding to sacrifice Iphigenia (214–17) Agamemnon seems to betray some such residual uncertainty in his expressed hope that all will turn out well (217), but in that case there is no akrasia because he does abide by his decision. In the carpet scene, on the other hand, his original decision is to refrain from treading, but by the end of the scene he has revoked it. How does this come about?

Clytemnestra orders the spreading of the fabrics (910). Agamemnon rejoins: Don't honour me like a barbarian in a manner suited to gods alone! (922). I am afraid to walk on the fabrics, being a mortal. Honour me like a man, not a god (924–5). So he is quite clear about the reasons not to tread. He does, however, undertake to reply to a hypothetical question, provided that it is understood that he has no intention of changing his mind. Thus it emerges that he would walk on the fabrics if so advised by an expert in specified circumstances. Priam would have walked on them, so why should *he* fear men's censure? (931–9). Agamemnon is now distracted from the real issue, and once his wife has found him a way of yielding to a woman without losing face he can yield to her will (940–1). He still goes in fear, however, of divine envy (*phthonos*) and is reluctant to waste the house's substance (944–9).

With some help from his wife, then, Agamemnon's desire to tread has won out over his better judgement, but something not unlike akrasia seems to be operating both because he continues to be aware, even if that awareness has been attenuated to a persistent unease, a worry in the back of his mind, and because his change of mind is really no more than a rationalization of the 'incontinence' which undermined his original resolve. Whereas in deciding to sacrifice Iphigenia the case against the deed was deliberately rejected, in the present scene he decides not to tread the fabrics, and even reiterates that decision, but then he changes his mind. This he does against his rational judgement from which he has been distracted enough for his desire to gain the ascendancy. In sum, this is no textbook case of akrasia in which the rational judgement remains unchanged while its irrational antagonist prevents it from being converted into effective action. Instead, the rational judgement is assailed by irrational pressure masquerading as valid argument, so that it is abandoned. The conflict between that judgement and the pressure is, however, similar to the dynamics of akrasia in that the desires associated with the pressure predominate.

Interestingly, this fits Aristotle's idea that in cases of incontinence reason fails to operate because the knowledge upon which it is based is not fully present to consciousness:

But the word 'know' is used in two senses. A man who has (ἔχων) knowledge but is not exercising (χρώμενος) it is said to know, and so is a man who is actually exercising his knowledge. It will make a difference whether a man does wrong having the knowledge that it is wrong but not consciously thinking of (θεωροῦντα) his knowledge, or with the knowledge consciously present to his mind. The latter would be felt to be surprising; but it is not surprising that a man should do what he knows to be wrong if he is not conscious of the knowledge at the time. (*NE* 1146^{b}32–6: tr. Rackham)[54]

In sum, Aristotle thinks of non-rational desires and emotions 'as obscuring the reasoning that would lead to correct action, rather than as opposing the desire (*orexis*) that advocates that action.'[55] So the *akratēs* or incontinent person is not directly the victim of a bad desire but rather of faulty reasoning. The agent may not be 'consciously thinking of' (1146^{b}34) his knowledge at the relevant time, that is it may be latent for some reason. When we are asleep, drunk, mad, or in a passion, knowledge we otherwise possess ceases to be available to us (*NE* 1147^{a}14–18); or knowledge may be superficial or inadequately assimilated, as when we can repeat the proof of a theorem in geometry but without really having understood it or 'absorbed' (συμφυῆναι) it into our minds (*NE* 1147^{a}22). Certainly in this scene Agamemnon ceases to 'use' or 'have regard to' his justified fear of divine envy which constituted his rational awareness.[56] While he is neither drunk nor mad nor in a passion, he is certainly distracted from full rational consciousness by a strong desire supported by the spurious rationality of his wife's arguments.

AGAMEMNON AND MORAL AWARENESS

Unlike Eteocles facing his brother, Agamemnon is unaware of the broader implications of his decision at Aulis. He has no sense of the will of Zeus, nor does he realize that he acts with *parakopa*. Nor is he aware of the influence of the curse or of the family heredity (factors whose contribution remains uncertain to the audience as well). Although, unlike Eteocles, he does not explicitly define himself as a military commander, his rather schematized decision is narrowly based on that role, both its responsibilities and its temptations—a role which entails much innocent human suffering as a corollary of the conquest approved by Zeus Xenios.

Although the conceptions of character applied to Eteocles and Agamemnon have much in common (it does not matter in this regard that the former is highly aware and the latter scarcely at all), what chiefly distinguishes them is a function of dramatic technique. We come to Eteocles as a character of flesh and blood before us on the stage and our sympathy is clearly enlisted for him. Agamemnon, on the other hand, appears only after he has been presented in a very schematized, largely negative way, so that our sympathy is never really very strongly engaged for him. The decision at Aulis has important consequences. The carpet scene is more symbolic; it does, however, help to draw out some of the implications of the

---

[54] Broadie and Rowe (2002) ad *NE* 1146^{b}33–4: using came to be equated with *theorein*, 'reflecting on or operating intellectually with something one has learned'.

[55] Bostock (2000) 139.

[56] In the *Protagoras* (356–7b) Plato offers a model of akrasia whereby a smaller but immediate pleasure which seems more important because of its temporal proximity is chosen instead of a greater but deferred pleasure. Using that model, one might interpret Agamemnon as failing to realize that the long-term consequences of incurring divine *phthonos* should weigh more than the short-term pleasures of human adulation.

earlier deliberations, clarifying Agamemnon's motives. But, most interestingly, Agamemnon's deliberations are met with significant opposition from another character. The hitherto internal conflict is externalized. This is to some extent reminiscent of Eteocles' conflict with the chorus of the *Seven*, though they could in no way weaken the protagonist's resolve. Clytemnestra's resistance, by contrast, brings out a hidden motive in Agamemnon. Similarly in *Choephori* the same Clytemnestra will attempt to deflect her son from his matricidal purpose.

CONCLUSION

When Agamemnon deliberates at Aulis he is torn between two conflicting moral requirements: the need to save his daughter and the need to pursue the Trojan War. But ranged on each horn of this dilemma are also emotional commitments: to his daughter and to the expedition and the glory associated with it. Agamemnon thus implicitly defines himself as a father and as a general (each of which roles entails conventional moral responsibilities of which he is aware), but the general triumphs over the father and Agamemnon acts in harmony either with what he sees as the morally more pressing claim or with what he sees as the more attractive option (the one that offers personal glory). In the play's terms the decision is right if the Trojan War is right, and the war is the will of Zeus. But Agamemnon's reasons for deciding as he does are perhaps wrong or at least inadequate reasons. Agamemnon's understanding of the facts of his predicament is clear enough even if he does not understand exactly how the gods are contriving matters behind the scenes. On the other hand, he has no inkling of the longer-term consequence of his decision—namely his own death. The emotional component of Agamemnon's deliberations (his enthusiasm for the glory of the expedition) perhaps has a disproportionate influence over them. Certainly once the decision is made, the strange, perhaps divinely induced state of *parakopa* which comes upon him intensifies his readiness to perform the sacrifice rather than subverting his rationality. Agamemnon's moral values are throughout conventional and, as we have seen, probably corrupted by emotions.

5

Aeschylus: *Choephori* and *Eumenides*

PRESSURES ON ORESTES

At Aulis Agamemnon had received no specific divine command, although the gods had clearly contributed to his dilemma. Artemis, in making the sacrifice a prerequisite for the sack of Troy, was responding to Zeus's portent which was not a command but a prediction of the sack of Troy that encapsulated its moral ambivalence, while catching Agamemnon in that ambivalence in an act that was both a prerequisite for the war and a symbolic statement of the nature of the acts of war over which he as a military commander would inevitably preside. Orestes, on the other hand, is commanded by Apollo to commit matricide. In this the Olympians are backing, though more strongly than Zeus Xenios in Agamemnon's case, the patriarchal society which would independently have required the same response.

Orestes' 'choice' is to obey or not. In either case he faces the wrath of a parent's avenging Furies, but there can be no question of disobeying a direct command of Apollo and one originating, as we later discover, from Zeus himself (*Eum.* 19). It would seem preferable to incur the hostility of the Furies alone rather than alienating *both* the Furies *and* the Olympians. Moroever, if, in avenging his father, Orestes alienates his mother's Furies in the course of obeying Apollo, there is a reasonable expectation that Apollo will protect him; whereas if, in failing to avenge his father, he alienates his father's Furies in the course of obeying no god at all, he can expect no divine support from any quarter. His mother's Furies will not protect him from his father's Furies (so to speak) if he forbears to kill her; the role of Furies (at this stage, at least) is entirely punitive. Thus Orestes' course of action is much clearer than Agamemnon's was for him.

The absolute nature of this situation is, however, a function of myth and tragedy, whereas in the real world, according to McHardy in a recent book, '[a]nthropologists have stressed that individual actors make decisions based on calculations of benefits and risks.'[1] This makes it simplistic to say that revenge was absolutely required in certain (historic as opposed to literary) circumstances.[2] 'The evidence suggests that men often decide to take the largest risks in order to protect valuable possessions and assets, in particular women, livestock and other valuable property. Achieving higher status than others and fighting over power are

---

[1] McHardy (2008) 6.   [2] Ibid. 7.

also important reasons for acting aggressively and hence, revenge is frequently associated with disputes over status and power.'[3] Moreover,

there is little evidence to suggest that blood feuds were rife in ancient Greece; there is instead a tendency in the extant texts to show attempts at settlements and compromises following a homicide. A close examination of the Greek textual evidence suggests that although an ideal of revenge on behalf of kin is frequently expressed, family members might not act without other compelling motivations such as financial or political gains and men are depicted making careful calculations before leaping into action.[4]

Such practical motives do indeed inspire Orestes, though they are overridden by the divine command, thus producing one of those absolute situations characteristic of tragedy.[5]

THE TEMPORARY SUPPRESSION OF THE DILEMMA

Aeschylus unnaturally postpones the crisis by denying Orestes the awareness even of any *potential* dilemma for over nine hundred lines into this short play, until his mother warns him to beware her Furies, to which he replies 'How am I to escape my father's [Furies] if I let this go?' (925). To be sure, before that point Orestes is overwhelmingly aware of the clear command which he has received from Apollo through the Delphic oracle, and he is absolutely clear about one thing: if he fails to kill his mother he will be hounded to death by his father's avenging Furies (269–90). But the divine command did not confront Orestes with an agonizing dilemma because he made the god's will his own, supporting it with his own motives—and he receives, as it were, the backing of the play (notably through the great kommos) at least until the deed is done. The Euripidean Orestes has received, apparently, a similar command, but his emotional and moral dissociation from it creates a brooding sense of imminent crisis that surfaces only when he sees his mother and his sister insists on the matricide.

Therefore, right up until Orestes' hesitation over the deed (899), there is an overwhelming sense of the rightness and virtual inevitability of the talio which entails the slaughter of Aegisthus and Clytemnestra. During that time the whole play is behind Orestes. This is in stark contrast to the first play's apparently ambivalent attitude to the corresponding action, the sacrifice of Iphigenia, and to the highly indirect characterization of Agamemnon. Moreover, Clytemnestra is guilty while Iphigenia was innocent. A slight doubt, it would seem, is registered when Electra enquires of the chorus whether to pray for a 'juror' ($\delta\iota\kappa\alpha\sigma\tau\dot{\eta}\nu$)[6] or for one who brings justice ($\delta\iota\kappa\eta\phi\acute{o}\rho o\nu$) (120), but this is immediately allayed in the chorus's answer, 'Say simply "One who will kill in retaliation"' (121), because it is (obviously) right to requite evil with evil. Clytemnestra's nightmare testifies to the

---

[3] McHardy (2008) 6.

[4] Ibid. 9. See also ibid. 103 and Harris (2001) 135.

[5] McHardy (2008) devotes a chapter (103–20) to Orestes' motives.

[6] Perhaps 'a glimmer of something less crude, though we have to wait long before the glimmer becomes daylight': Kitto (1961) 79.

unappeased wrath of her dead husband (33, 40–1); her belated and hypocritical offerings are futile since nothing can cleanse spilt blood (48, cf. 66–74). Electra invokes the wrath of the dead, already stirred; she appeals for Hermes' mediation with the powers of the dead; and she calls on Agamemnon's spirit to free her from her slavery to the tyrants who killed him and to bring back the exiled Orestes (124–37). She prays too for the modesty and piety her mother lacks (138–41) and for the killers' deaths at the hands of Agamemnon's avenger (142–4), a prayer reinforced by the chorus (152–63).[7] Her prayer seems swiftly answered, as Orestes will presently declare (212–13), for as soon as the earth has drunk the piously redirected offerings, Electra catches sight of the tokens of recognition and everything grows towards the climax of his appearance before her as a plant grows from a seed (204).

Thus Orestes is seen to be caught up in powerful supernatural forces and in his appointed avenger's role. Indeed, he now prays to Zeus as one of the eagle Agamemnon's brood caught in the coils of the terrible viper, Clytemnestra (246–9). This predatory imagery, carried over from the previous play, emphasizes the way in which the individual characters are caught within their roles as defined by the talio, though the imagery here is counterbalanced by flesh and blood characters interacting on the stage. It is noteworthy though that it is the nobility rather than the predatory nature of the eagle that is now emphasized. Agamemnon's moral failings will be ignored in this play. The most prominent representative of the talio in Orestes' case is the god Apollo who instructed him to kill his father's killers in the same way they killed him or suffer terrible agonies of mind and body and eventual death (269–77), involving his father's Furies (283) and his wrath (μῆνιν, 294).[8]

Orestes thus has no doubts about his appointed role or of the consequences of deviating from it. There is, moreover, no question of any such deviation, for, the reliability of the oracle aside, 'the work must be done' (298), as many 'longings' (ἵμεροι, 299) converge: the god's instructions (ἐφετμαί, 300), great grief for his father (300), his own poverty (301), and the oppression of the Argive people by the tyrants (302–4). Such motives are entirely and respectably conventional and role-determined, and they entail obligations to state, family, and self.[9] This virtual identification of Orestes' thinking with conventional expectations, at least before the matricide, puts great emphasis on the 'character viewpoint' at the expense of that of 'personality'. His father could summon no such impressive array of arguments in support of the sacrifice of Iphigenia.[10]

---

[7] McHardy (2008) 13 comments that vengeful women must usually rely on men: 'their power is restricted to the power of speech by which they can persuade or deceive. Women are also depicted using curses.'

[8] Apollo threatens Orestes with Chthonian powers: Winnington-Ingram (1983) 136–7.

[9] 'There is a studiously abstract, official air about these desires. They are, in fact, not desires at all, but formal explanations dragged in to shore up the divine directions with a modicum of personal engagement. Their briefness and lack of conviction makes them pale before the divine threats': Rosenmeyer (1982) 246. In the main this is correct, but the motives are convincing as such so long as we accept that Orestes is all but identified with his role.

[10] 'These new avengers, free of any guilty motives, must yet do what is worse than anything done in the *Agamemnon*; herein lies the tragic power of the play': Kitto (1961) 80.

As the chorus invoke the great Moirai and Zeus and the justice of the talio—hostile speech for hostile speech, and bloody blow for bloody blow, for the doer suffers (306–14)—Orestes' concern is to enlist his dead father's help for the task ahead. Uncertain about making his needs known to the dead, Orestes is reassured by the chorus that the dead do indeed hunt down their killers (324–8) and are even now gathering to give aid (375–9). It is law (*nomos*) that blood of the murder victim shed upon the ground calls for more blood, for a plague summons an Erinys from those who died before, that heaps disaster on disaster (400–4).

Apart from requiring the support of his father's spirit, Orestes will need to feel the appropriate hatred for his intended victim, and so his sister and the chorus proceed to inform him of the indignities to which his father was subjected by his killers (423–55). Thus he can say, 'Let me kill her and die!' (438).[11] There is no baulking at matricide; everything contributes to identifying Orestes with his role. Aeschylus is saving the dilemma for the fatal moment. Orestes feels and has felt no qualms whatever about the matricide, and the purpose of this great kommos is decidedly *not* to help him cope with any reluctance.[12] The kommos brings its purpose to a strong climax with a powerful invocation of Agamemnon to help himself and his avengers (479–509).

Again a prayer seems immediately answered when Orestes turns to the interpretation of Clytemnestra's nightmare (527–50). This reinforces the sense of the merging of his purpose with that of the Olympian gods. Though this event precedes the action of the play and was referred to near the beginning, the attention paid to it here, straight after the invocation, creates the illusion at least of a causal link, rather like that between Jocasta's prayer for deliverance in the *Tyrannus* and the immediate arrival of the Corinthian.

STRIKING A BALANCE

It is hardly surprising that the matricide in *Choephori* is neither described nor directly evoked. (It is *indirectly* evoked through the description of the content of Clytemnestra's dream.) The evocation of both Iphigenia's and Agamemnon's deaths in the previous play naturally emphasized the repulsiveness of the killings, but with the matricide Aeschylus is walking a tightrope.

---

[11] Orestes does not mean that his life will not be worth living once he has killed his mother (otherwise why he is so concerned with recovering his patrimony?); he means that he must achieve the matricide if nothing else in his life. Cf. Eur. *El.* 663 and perhaps Aesch. *Ag.* 539.

[12] *Pace* Winnington-Ingram (1983) 140. Lesky (1965) 80 rightly maintains that it is not 'the description of the outrage upon his father and Electra's anguish which made Orestes decide to kill his mother, for he had already taken that decision when he appeared on the stage. But we should remember that in human acts both divinely ordained destiny and human will participate . . . Apollo's command, however, made the act of Orestes one that was largely forced on him from outside. This will ultimately prove the reason for his acquittal. But to make this act fateful for him initially, it must be entirely integrated with his own will.' He has of course willed the matricide in terms of the 'desires' he enumerated earlier (299–304), but the kommos reinforces this in a strongly emotional way. See also Kitto (1961) 83.

In the *Eumenides* the cases for and against the deed seem evenly balanced to the hung human jury, but the Olympian gods (ultimately Zeus) come out powerfully in favour of the male Orestes, and the audience's sympathies are enlisted strongly for him throughout both plays. So, if Aeschylus, like Euripides in his *Electra*, had gone out of his way to stress the ugliness of the deed, the audience would have dismissed it at once as an unqualified obscenity. But if, on the other hand, he had effectively denied Clytemnestra's maternity, the matricide as an emotional reality at least would have all but evaporated from the play. In sum, the deed must be allowed an appropriate emotional impact, but without precluding a judicious weighing of the arguments on each side.

Clytemnestra's dream is Aeschylus' symbolic account of the matricide, as the carpet scene was his symbolic enactment of Agamemnon's crimes. The content of the dream is utterly repulsive, dehumanizing Orestes in line with the predatory imagery of the trilogy. Clytemnestra dreamt of giving birth to a snake:

> CHORUS. She swaddled it and lulled it to rest like a baby (529). . . . She
>   herself, in her dream, put it to the breast.   (531)
> ORESTES. Her nipple surely was wounded by the monster?   (532)
> CHORUS. Yes; in the milk it drew forth a clot of blood.   (533)

But Orestes himself is not especially repelled; he takes it, rightly, not only as a symbolic statement of his imminent deed, but also as a command to perform it (540–50). (Agamemnon might have interpreted the portent of the pregnant hare in a similar way had it been preceded by a clear instruction from Zeus Xenios.) The child is born, cared for by the mother and turns on that mother in the most horrible way. Orestes is a vicious snake, as his father was a predatory eagle. And yet he is not. The snake image, precisely because of its status as a 'mere' symbol, shields us from the ugly reality of matricide conjured up so repulsively in Euripides' *Electra*. The symbol of the snake refers more to Orestes' objective role than to any personal feelings about the matricide or the physical details of the act itself; moreover, it refers to the wider moral implications of that role of agent in the endless alternation of agent and victim in this primitive, savage world of the talio. On the other hand, it is not entirely irrelevant to Orestes' feelings for, while of course he does not approach the murder of his mother with a sanguinary eagerness, there is nevertheless a sense in which he embraces the act as his own.

This should be remembered by those who would stress his moral innocence in contrast to his father. Both father and son perform morally ambivalent actions, though Orestes does so with superior justification, and both are identified with a role—Agamemnon with that of the military commander, Orestes with that of the avenging son. Agamemnon, like his son, embraced his predatory role (as the lion that licked royal blood: 827), but the negative aspects of the sack of Troy (the sufferings of innocents, Greek and Trojan) make the whole enterprise seem less justifiable than the matricide where there can be no question of Clytemnestra's innocence. In this respect the nurse's speech is relevant. 'Her remarks prevent the sympathy from shifting to the ignorant victims of Orestes' plot, for not only does she invoke the hatred which Aegisthus inspires, but she recalls that Orestes was not a blood-sucking snake but a harmless and defenseless baby.'[13] And if the

---

[13] Rose (1982) 50.

repulsive physical immediacy of this symbolic matricide has tilted the scales somewhat against Orestes, then Aeschylus counteracts our feelings in the ensuing ode that sets Clytemnestra in the company of such notorious women as Althaea, Scylla, and the Lemnians (585–636). Aeschylus is still secure on his tightrope. The interpretation of the dream helps to merge Orestes even more, if that is possible, with his externally imposed role: his mother is to die violently and he is to become a snake and kill her (549). Again, he expresses no reluctance.

MATRICIDE

In the mechanema, the plot to trap the killers unaware, Orestes, again embodying his appointed role, employs treachery in requital for treachery, as Apollo Loxias decreed (555–9). That this is a fitting requital is reinforced by the chorus' ode on treacherous women (593–638). Again, when Clytemnestra answers the door and Orestes catches his first sight of his mother (668), he merges completely with his role and betrays not the slightest unease; though, of course, more realistic psy-chology would have been ruinous here. As the deed approaches, the chorus pray for divine assistance (783–825) and at last raise the issue of possible reluctance, but they insist that when she cries 'Son!', Orestes is to call 'Father!' and then to complete a 'calamitous deed' for which he will nevertheless be 'blameless' (ἀνεπίμομφον ἄταν) (826–31).

Clytemnestra, on being informed that 'the dead are killing the living' (the dead Agamemnon working through the 'dead' Orestes[14]), realizes at once what is meant, that she is to die by treachery as she killed by treachery, and prepares to defend herself by calling for 'an axe to kill a man' (887–9). The axe never arrives, but we have an impression of an aggressive and determined Clytemnestra. The stichomythic debate between mother and son remains appropriately impersonal. Clytemnestra fails to play her strongest card—the brutal sacrifice of her daugh-ter,[15] Orestes' sister—and is defined primarily as Aegisthus' lover and, conse-quently, her own husband's murderer (893–5, 903–7, 909, 916–17, 920, 927).[16] Thus her only defence is her sheer maternity, but when she shows her breast and evokes the sensuous experience of suckling (896–8), the audience will remember that her tears for her son's 'death' were feigned (737–40) and that it was the old nurse who was moved as a mother should be (744–65).[17] Orestes is moved to

---

[14] Kitto (1956) 52.

[15] Iphigenia's death is referred to only briefly in this play en passant by Electra at 242. See Kitto (1956) 44–5 and (1961) 82. As Zeitlin (1965) 491 observes, Clytemnestra's motive of avenging her child fades in Choephori: 'by denying her two remaining children, she has denied her role of mother'. Clytemnestra objects to Agamemnon's prolonged absence at the war (920). 'Agamemnon wrongs Clytemnestra as a mother by killing Iphigeneia, and he wrongs her as a wife by leaving her alone at home to suffer in his absence for ten years. His absence is an offense against marriage from a woman's point of view, committed in order to reaffirm marriage from a man's point of view': Gagarin (1976) 94.

[16] 'Orestes' violent response to Aegisthus and his mother is driven in large part by their adultery and the way in which their affair dishonours his father and himself': McHardy (2008) 103.

[17] Orestes too argues that she is no real mother (912–13), and avoids addressing her as such: Lesky (1965) 81.

aidōs by the appeal (899);[18] otherwise he would appear a monster rather than a representative son in these circumstances and the play would be about a psychopath rather than about a moral and socio-religious dilemma. He puts aside his doubts when Pylades appeals to the risks of alienating Apollo to whom Orestes had perhaps sworn an oath (900–2).[19] There is no appeal to the god's *moral* authority here, nor any suggestion that Orestes believes on balance now that the matricide is wrong. Indeed, he will continue to believe in it in the next play, despite the sufferings inflicted on him by the Furies (*Eum.* 595–6).[20] Orestes then is finally implacable, and Clytemnestra's attempts to exonerate herself by pleading the constraints of destiny merely recoil on her, for Orestes is clearly entangled in the same destined chain of events (910–11, 922–3, 927–30).[21]

In this scene Orestes confronts his dilemma squarely for the first time and makes his decision to proceed with the matricide. When Agamemnon confronted his dilemma he did so in isolation, certainly not in the presence of Iphigenia, and it will be remembered that he did imagine briefly the implications of the projected sacrifice. Once he had decided to proceed, however, he became deaf to his daughter's appeals and even gagged her. In the present scene, Orestes both decides and then quickly proceeds to the act itself. Unlike his father, he listens to his victim's objections and pleas.

We saw how difficult it was to disentangle moral motives from motives of self-interest at Aulis. Orestes' deliberation (even briefer because he has essentially already decided) is occasioned by the sight of his mother's breast with its powerful appeal to maternity. Orestes supplies then the motive against the deed, which corresponds to Agamemnon's reluctance to sacrifice: 'Is *aidōs* to restrain me from killing my mother?' (899). But the immediate motive for proceeding (as distinct from the motives he announced earlier which still presumably apply) comes from an external source, from Pylades representing the god, so that it carries much more weight than Agamemnon's sudden and unexplained embracing of the option to kill reinforced by his mysterious *parakopa*. This does much to mitigate

---

[18] 'Orestes' response is clearly instinctive and involuntary, and it springs automatically from his awareness of the most deeply held traditional beliefs, and the fact that he overcomes it demonstrates the moral ambivalence of his revenge': Cairns (1993) 201.

[19] On the πιστὰ εὐορκώματα (901) see Sommerstein (2008) ii. n. 177.

[20] 'Orestes wills the deed himself, and . . . accepts his personal responsibility for it': Garvie (1986) p. xxxi. '[U]ntil Clytaemnestra bares her breast before him, we nowhere see him arguing over the rights and wrongs of matricide, he is nowhere presented as hesitant or reluctant, and even to suppose that he has constantly to overcome a secret repugnance towards what he has to do goes beyond the evidence of the text. . . . Even after the murder he does not really repent or question the rightness of the deed, though he comes to appreciate its horror': ibid. pp. xxxii–iii. For a strongly opposing, but, I think, untenable view see Zeitlin (1965) 496, also Gagarin (1976) 99. Vellacott (1984) 151 mistakenly believes Orestes 'makes it clear that what he does is against his own judgement and is carried out in obedience to a god who terrifies him'. Accordingly he finds a changed Orestes in the final play (ibid. 156): 'The sense of horror which made him pray for his own death has left him. His mental and physical suffering has not sharpened his moral sense, but has accustomed him to guilt. He is concerned now not with any moral issue but with legal status, with ritual purity, and with regaining his inheritance. He has no qualms about what he did; only about how to escape punishment for it.'

[21] Aeschylus 'seems concerned to show . . . the deed of Orestes as the inevitable balancing of Justice, free of any taint of personal or passionate involvement, such as rendered the function of Clytemnestra as familial *alastōr* more than a shade ambiguous': Conacher (1987) 123.

Orestes' responsibility, since not only is the motive external (the god's overwhelming pressure), but also the pressure (from Pylades) to entertain that motive, as in his deliberations Orestes calls on external support. The externality of the motive means too that Orestes' personal motives (including the recovery of his patrimony) are not decisive, whereas a narrower self-interest almost certainly tainted Agamemnon's reluctance to be branded a deserter. Moreover, that the divine intervention is external rather than taking the form of mental invasion removes Orestes still further from the decision, since when gods work through the mind there is usually some ambiguity about the origin of the resulting decision because there is uncertainty as to where the divine initiative ends and human motivation begins.[22]

The matricide accomplished, its negative implications can no longer be suppressed. In the ekkyklema scene over the corpses, Orestes deflects the usual mourning for the visible victims into an attack upon them and mourning for their own victim, as he spreads out the bathrobe in which his father was entangled preparatory to his murder (980–1006). But the Furies attack, though Orestes proclaims that the matricide was not without Dike (1027), as his mother was a god-hated, father-killing miasma (1028). He pleads Apollo who said he would be 'exempt of blame' (ἐκτὸς αἰτίας κακῆς) if he did the deed but would suffer terrible agonies if he did not (1029–33). Indeed, Orestes never disowns the matricide and therefore does not need to redefine his moral position. More importantly, Aeschylus transfers the interest from Orestes to the abstract issues brought into focus by his dilemma.

ORESTES IN COURT

Just as the negative, 'anti-Apolline' aspects of the matricide appear in *Choephori* only when Orestes confronts his mother just before the deed, so in *Eumenides* Apollo's view of the Furies dominates the first part of that play. The Furies themselves are repulsive to the god and his priestess, though Athena is more conciliatory. Generally the ancient goddesses are angry both on moral principle (they object to those who shed kindred blood like Orestes escaping their punishment) (149–54, 162–7) and because they see the Olympians as seeking to deprive them of their ancient dispensations (παλαιγενεῖς ... μοίρας, 172), for it is their respected office (τιμή) to pursue matricides (208–10).[23] Apollo objects that they have no respect for the marriage bond in their failure to pursue women who murder their husbands (209–24), but they have no wish to be rational (227, cf. 430).

---

[22] For Jones (1962) 101 the question Orestes directs to Pylades 'flows not from inner uncertainty but from the need to achieve full exposure of the Oresteian dilemma', i.e. it is to be interpreted dramaturgically rather than psychologically. While Jones submerges the individual almost entirely in the group (the house of Atreus), I am arguing that we can speak of individual consciousness provided we bear in mind that it is severely circumscribed by role, including that of being an Atreid.

[23] The Furies consider themselves *euthudikaioi* (312). Their *lachos* came to them from the Moirai (333–40, 389–96). Athena says the Furies have a *moira* not easily dismissed (476).

Orestes on the other hand, speaking and acting as Apollo directs (276–9), considers himself cleansed of pollution by the sacrifice of swine and argues that no one has been harmed by contact with him (285, cf. 451–2). As for the ethico-legal aspect of the matricide, Apollo takes full responsibility in that he persuaded Orestes to do it (84, cf. 465, 579–80), and his authority in all things is delegated by Zeus (19)—and in the trial he claims that, being a prophet, he never lies and always says what Zeus bids and that the jury should follow Zeus's will (βουλῇ, 620) which is stronger than an oath. Apollo states that because Agamemnon was more important than a mere woman his death was 'not the same' (625), that is, more serious; that the mother is not the true parent of the child (witness the case of Athena who was born without a mother) (640–66). The god follows up these two ideas with a promise of an Argive alliance (667–73). The votes are even, but Orestes is acquitted by the casting vote of Athena who admits to a preference for the male (734–41). Once acquitted, Orestes thanks Athena for supporting his family and promises Athens an Argive alliance (754–77). He is silent about the justice of the verdict. The Furies are enraged that the ancient *nomoi* have been 'ridden down' and that they are now without honour (778–80 = 808–10). Athena denies that they have suffered dishonour (796): the vote, after all, was even and the trial had the benefit of Zeus's 'clear testimony' (λαμπρὰ μαρτύρια, 797), as conveyed by Apollo. The Furies are unconvinced, so Athena employs persuasion (804–7) and threats (824–36) and gradually they are won over not by rational arguments against their moral position but by the promise of a new dispensation in which they will retain their function of punishing inherited crimes (927–37). Athena commends Persuasion, Zeus Agoraios and 'contention for the good' (ἀγαθῶν ἔρις, 970–5).[24]

The injustice of the pre-Areopagan dispensation arose from the tendency of the talio to breed further crime because every act of punishment is treated not as an end but as a further crime. The transfer of responsibility from the next of kin to the state obviously removed this tendency—though it did not eliminate the revenge motive.[25] So it is the sheer fact of a trial that produces a just *system*. Within the framework of the vendetta, however, Orestes acted justly in performing the matricide, though the act was an outrage against the Furies and against the instinctive *aidōs* of a child for a parent. When we speak of Orestes, though, we are speaking not of an individual but of a representative son in a particular dilemma.

---

[24] 'Aeschylus portrays a cosmic and political order which is neither moral nor just, but rather tyrannical, in the sense that its ultimate foundations are force and fear': Cohen (1993) 45. Zeus's 'justice' is applied to guilty and innocent alike: ibid. 49. '[T]he justice of Zeus does prevail, but it is the arbitrary justice of the right of the stronger: persuasion and compulsion, backed by fear and force. Thus Orestes, the self-confessed matricide, goes free. Agamemnon is honoured as the great king who made the city of Troy no city, the Erinyes are bought off, and Iphigeneia, Cassandra, and the hare and her brood, have the consolation of having learned through suffering that their fate has been ordained by the justice of Zeus': ibid. 55.

[25] Cairns (2005) 307. McHardy (2008) 11–15 has some excellent observations on the engagement of vengeful relatives with the judicial process.

CONCLUSION

Despite the constant physical presence of Orestes on the stage, there is even less emphasis on the individual than in Agamemnon's case because he simply represents the decent man confronted with a morally problematical situation which is the central focus of the drama. The 'purity of intent and moral sensitivity with which Orestes executes his legal claim',[26] which a number of critics have seen in the young man's characterization, are corollaries of this focus and not mysterious deviations from the paternal *ēthos*. It is not then Orestes' decision in the cultural circumstances which is morally problematical, but the cultural circumstances themselves. (Agamemnon, on the other hand, is condemned for his decision.) Orestes naturally espouses patriarchal values and is required to avenge his father, which he also actively wants to do, and Aeschylus would not wish to dissociate him from the role with which he is identified. But his moral responsibility is mitigated by the pressure from Apollo which is not only religious but represents also the ethico-social pressure of the circumstances. It is mitigated but not completely removed, because this divine pressure constitutes one of Orestes' freely embraced motives. (In the final play the god removes all *legal* responsibility from Orestes.) That Orestes has his own motives that coincide with the god's pressure means that he is indeed fused with his role, and that he freely chooses what the god requires. That he hesitates is necessary to keep him decently and representatively human and to stress the dilemma which is in the final analysis a human (rather than merely an abstract) one and to be felt as such. Like Eteocles, he has no choice but to conform to the divine will, and like Eteocles he is damned either way, which is a reflection on the moral universe rather than on his personal morality. But no Fury inspires Orestes' deed by mental invasion (the Atreid curse is no longer explicitly invoked),[27] though supernatural assistance is indubitably present somehow through events. How precisely this supernatural influence works remains mysterious, but it does seem to operate at a greater distance, as it were, than such invasive powers as divine *atē* or a mind-possessing Fury.

That Orestes is faced with a moral dilemma is clear to him only when he finally confronts his mother. Before that, he is sure only that he must obey Apollo, and his own motives coincide with this pressure, so that he experiences no dilemma. The god's command carries moral authority only within the discredited system of the family feud. Orestes is identified with his role as avenging son and true heir to the throne of Argos. He recognizes his obligations to the (Olympian) gods, to Argos, to his dead father, to the family line, and to himself (the need to recover his patrimony). His ethic is entirely conventional, but rendered problematic by the conflicting claims of his two parents. Orestes does little deliberating as such. He

[26] Peradotto (1969) 258. See ibid. 258–61 for examples of the son's moral superiority to the father. For a rebuttal see Vellacott (1984) *passim* who rightly observes, at 148, that, if Orestes were significantly morally superior to his father, the point needed to be emphasized: 'both reason and dramatic logic require that the moment of this revelation, the cause and features of its working, should have been somewhere articulated as the central message of the entire work.'

[27] After *Agamemnon* the curse is 'virtually dropped in favor of another perspective that stresses the culpability of Clytemnestra and Aegisthus': Rosenmeyer (1982) 245. Moreover, the Furies never suggest that Orestes has inherited guilt: Gantz (1982) 15.

starts out with an unswerving devotion to his revenge, and questions it only briefly with the involvement of Pylades which has the effect of the sudden incursion of an outside force into his terms of reference. There is, however, no divine mental invasion. Orestes has no occasion to change his moral attitude to the matricide. Even more than Agamemnon, the moral position he espouses is significantly that of the Olympian gods—a position they assume for the greater end of producing a better system of justice.

APPENDIX: CLYTEMNESTRA

For all the power of Clytemnestra as a stage figure and her dramatic importance as an embodiment of female resistance to the male heroic ethos, Aeschylus refuses to take her seriously as a morally motivated figure, at least in *Choephori*. She is presented as a monster, and not, in the manner of Sophocles' vengeful Electra, as a woman inspired by nobility of moral purpose. The logic of her revenge requires her to practise deceit (which places her in an invidious light, as it receives none of the support or legitimation accorded Orestes' deceit in *Choephori*), and it is not until after the killings that it is possible for her to speak honestly and openly about her motives (*Ag.* 1372–98). Cassandra, one of her intended victims, naturally views her in an entirely negative way (e.g. 1108, 1111, 1125–9) and from the chorus she elicits only horror and revulsion in her exultant *schadenfreude*, for all her claims of having acted with justice (e.g. 1399–1400, 1407–11).

Of course Clytemnestra's implicit criticism of the double standards that subject her to far more opprobrium for killing her husband than he earned for killing his daughter will weigh more heavily with a modern audience. But for Aeschylus and his ancient audience, husband-murder is simply beyond the pale of justification. Nor does her association with the revolting Aegisthus, for all its tactical necessity, help her case. In *Choephori*, as we saw, there is much emphasis on her inhuman evil (e.g. 585–636). She is not permitted the defence of having avenged her daughter, while Agamemnon is 'rehabilitated' with his crimes suppressed. Furthermore, she cannot claim, unlike her husband and son, to have acted under some form of externally announced or imposed divine constraint. Agamemnon found himself facing a dilemma imposed by Artemis, and Orestes was expressly obeying Apollo's instructions. She, on the other hand, decided independently that she would transgress all social expectations to take revenge on her husband— though we are not privy to the course of her deliberations. After the event, it occurs to her to blame the *daimōn* or *alastōr* of the house, but the chorus will (rightly) not permit her to evade personal responsibility in that way, even though they accept that such an avenging spirit may have acted through her.[28] This is substantially Orestes' position when he argues that if destiny acted through her in the murder of her husband, the same destiny will presently work through the perpetrator of matricide (*Cho.* 910–11). Clytemnestra of course knew that she was infringing conventional moral standards, but perhaps we are to take it that she

---

[28] On this passage see Ch. 2, p. 35.

genuinely believed that she was acting in accordance with a superior, gender-neutral morality.

CONCLUSION

There is no indication that Orestes has struggled with the moral dilemma of the matricide before the crisis when his mother shows him her breast. Until then all motives have combined to urge the deed. At that point there is brief deliberation in the form of the question to Pylades occasioned by a sudden access of filial *aidōs.* Similarly, in the *Medea,* an access of (maternal) feeling will render problematic for the protagonist a hitherto uncomplicated moral and emotional commitment to the deed of violation of *philia.* Orestes is implicitly defined by his role as his father's son, with all that that conventionally entails, but he is not self-conscious about it. The morality is conventional, though the situation itself is very unconventional indeed. Orestes himself is aware of his moral obligations to his father, but only belatedly and briefly of his mother's competing claims. After brief hesitation he returns fully to his earlier commitment overwhelmingly endorsed by Apollo. So in the difficult moral world of the play Orestes makes the only possible decision, but he does so, it would seem, with the understanding that he is likely to be pursued by his mother's Furies. There is no disjunction between his moral resolve and his emotions. Apart from the brief access of *aidōs,* he is completely emotionally committed to the deed. Finally, there is no indication of immanent divine involvement in Orestes' decision; the god's pressure is exerted entirely externally through the oracle.

6

Sophocles: *Ajax*

AJAX AND ATHENA

When Ajax recovers from his mad attack on the animals he believed to be his human enemies, he is faced with responding to his humiliation. As a heroic warrior he has obligations to himself (to salvage his honour), to the *philoi* who comprise his family (especially his father Telamon, his son Eurysaces, his half-brother Teucer, and his 'wife' Tecmessa), and to the men he brought with him from Salamis who make up the chorus of the play. There is also the matter of his relations with his now alienated heroic peers and thus the question of his integration into society at large (though the play is set not in the polis but in a military camp). The initial focus, however, is Ajax's relationship with Athena. I have devoted some considerable space to this issue since it is the key to Ajax's character and therefore to his moral awareness.

The prophet Calchas explains the reason for Athena's hostility more than half way into the play.[1]

When men grow to a size too great for them, the prophet said, they are brought down by cruel misfortunes sent by the gods, yes, each one who has a human nature but refuses to think only human thoughts. But he [Ajax] from the moment of his leaving home was found to be foolish (ἄνους, 763) when his father spoke well. 'My son,' his father said to him, 'wish for triumph in battle, but wish to triumph always with a god's aid (σὺν θεῷ, 765)!' And he replied boastfully and stupidly (ὑψικόμπως κἀφρόνως, 766), 'Father, together with the gods even one who amounts to nothing (ὁ μηδὲν ὤν, 767) may win victory; but I am confident that I can grasp this glory even without them.' Such a boast as that he uttered; and a second time, when divine Athena urged him on and told him to direct his bloody hand against the enemy, he made answer with these dreadful and unspeakable words, 'Queen, stand by the other Argives; where I am the enemy shall never break through.' By such words as these he brought on himself the unappeasable anger of the goddess, through his more than mortal pride (οὐ κατ' ἄνθρωπον φρονῶν, 777). (760–77: tr. Lloyd-Jones)[2]

On the face of it, this looks like a conventional case of hubris, reminiscent of five at least of the Seven against Thebes and particularly Capaneus who, like Ajax, 'does not think like a human being' (Aesch. *Sept.* 425), boasting that he will sack Thebes whether the gods wish it or not and expressing his contempt for Zeus's thunder

---

[1] Some scholars would like to minimize the importance of this passage. For a discussion and vindication see Tyler (1974) 26–31, Hester (1979) 253.

[2] For the motif of the father encouraging his son to be pre-eminent while issuing a warning see Zanker (1992) 21.

(*Sept.* 428–31). We saw too that Xerxes was similarly deluded in his attempt to overcome Poseidon by chaining the Hellespont (Aesch. *Pers.* 745–50). Such hubris is often associated with at least metaphorical insanity, as in the case of Xerxes who suffered from a god-inspired 'disease of the mind' (νόσος φρενῶν, Aesch. *Pers.* 750), though the messenger here stops short in characterizing Ajax as 'senseless' (ἄνους). These hubristic mental states are typically described briefly and in conventional, even stereotypical, terms and without exploration of their psychological origins or wider context, as in the messenger's description in the shield scene of the *Seven* and indeed in the above narrative of Ajax's responses to his father and to the goddess herself. But what makes Ajax's case more interesting is the play's extended focus on his mental life, especially from the time when he awakes from the madness through to the end of the deception speech. In fact the particular nature of Ajax's hubris provides the key to a deeper understanding of his character.

Aeschylus' Eteocles inherited divine hostility from his forebears. Athena's anger at Ajax, however, originates entirely in the personal offence described above. Ajax claimed to be able to achieve his purpose without divine help.[3] The heroes of Homeric epic, at any rate, are usually delighted to receive divine assistance, and consider their own achievements enhanced rather than compromised by it.[4] But Ajax wants to take full credit for his deeds. The issue here runs deeper than a personal rejection of an anthropomorphic goddess; it is a radical misunderstanding of a mortal's place in the scheme of things, as Calchas states (760–1). The trite and familiar 'theology' can be interpreted psychologically here, as it illuminates Ajax's whole outlook on life. Modest people are aware that their achievements are the product of a complex variety of factors, most of which are outside their conscious comprehension, let alone control—such factors as heredity, environment, the assistance of others, and good luck; and in our era publicly successful people (athletes, for example) are accustomed to express their gratitude to all those who have helped them attain their success. Acknowledgement of the contribution of factors that lie outside ourselves entails a certain humility about our achievements, but conversely it mitigates the ignominy that attaches to our failures. But for Ajax the world exists to admire his performances, not to contribute to them and thereby overshadow his role, and when the world fails to applaud he wants no part of it. This attitude is a kind of 'metaphorical' madness; it will be punished by raving madness.[5] It is also a kind of pathological obsession with independence which raises a pervasive question for Greek tragedy, that of the integration of extraordinary men into the democratic polis, a question that will recur notably in the case of Euripides' Heracles. In these terms it is easier to understand why Ajax was rendered distraught by the Judgement of Arms and why

---

[3] We might have expected him thus to have angered all the gods, and this is his view at 457–8; but only Athena's hostility is apparent, and Ajax has no qualms about seeking help from other gods in his final speech (824–55). Contrast, however, his earlier view that he owes the gods nothing (589–90).

[4] 'The idea that a hero might boast that he does not need divine aid is foreign to the *Iliad* and belongs more properly to fifth-century tragedy': Zanker (1992) 21–2.

[5] 'Though Ajax is truly mad only when he cannot "see" properly, and kills cattle instead of men, his previous behaviour resembles madness': Padel (1981) 110. 'One type [of madness in tragedy] is foolishness, a misjudgement in which men neglect and dishonour god: a distinct state of mind describable in terms of madness. One possible name for it is "metaphorical madness"': ibid. 112.

he felt that just about everything, sentient or otherwise, had turned into his enemy—for he considers himself 'obviously hated' by the gods, the army, the whole of Troy and even the soil itself (457–9).

Ajax regarded himself as the best warrior once Achilles had died, and rightly so, at least by the criterion of sheer military prowess.[6] (Odysseus himself later agrees: 1336–41.) But the Judgement of Arms appeared an implicit rejection of this claim, perhaps in obliquely intimating that the broader and more adaptive skills of Odysseus are of greater worth to society, and of course specifically democratic society, though the play as a whole vindicates the distinctive contribution of both men. This judgement is potentially a more serious blow to Ajax than the confiscation of Briseis was to Achilles because it would appear to represent the army's considered and even 'official' view of him, even if he tries to evade this truth by dismissing the judicial process as corrupt.[7] Homer's Agamemnon never deliberately relegates Achilles to a lesser rank *as a warrior* (his own claim to superiority is based on the power he enjoys as leader of the expedition and as king of Mycenae);[8] he simply lashes out, foolishly and without peer support, in an attempt to dishonour a man whose supreme prowess is never in doubt.[9]

Defeated in the Judgement of Arms, Ajax decided to kill the Atreidae who, he believes, engineered the verdict together with Odysseus, the recipient of the arms (442–6). This response in itself is extreme enough to be described as mad. Achilles in the first book of the *Iliad* (1. 188–222) briefly contemplates a similar action but withdraws. In his case, two goddesses, Hera and Athena, are motivated, out of affection, to intervene in his interest, and Athena descends to urge him not to kill Agamemnon, assuring him that he will receive ample compensation for the insult. The goddess appears only to Achilles and they actually converse, in a sort of parallel universe apart from the other characters. Athena's intervention may represent Achilles' second thoughts, as Homeric epic likes to dramatize and externalize what we would probably conceive as entirely private deliberations. Ajax, on the other hand, has made himself an enemy of Athena, so that her intervention is naturally malign. Still, Ajax's madness does not so much violate his character as exaggerate already existing tendencies. Now although Achilles is struck by a momentary impulse to kill Agamemnon (*Iliad* 1. 188–92), because, unlike the Sophoclean Ajax, he is aware of his proper place in the scheme of things, he obeys Athena and desists (1. 215–18), resorting to a more restrained way of reminding the expedition of his importance. But not only is the slight to Ajax's honour, as we have seen, much more serious, at least to a man who is determined to be seen as the best, but, unlike Achilles, Ajax is alienated from Athena (who is again the intervening deity), which means also from *sōphrosunē* and indeed a kind of instinctive common sense which would have made him retreat before trying to kill his personal enemies. Unlike Achilles, he cannot back

---

[6] Though 421–6 seems to imply that Ajax is the greatest, *tout court.*

[7] Ajax himself appears to believe that the Atreidae somehow manipulated the vote in Odysseus' favour (441–9), but we are never told why Odysseus won or whether any skulduggery occurred. On the claims of Ajax see especially Teucer at 1266–89 and Odysseus at 1336–41 (which appears to condemn the Judgement!).

[8] *Iliad* 1. 131, 178, 185–7.

[9] See Nestor's view at 1. 275–84.

down. In consequence, extreme 'metaphorical' madness progresses to literal, raving madness.

We have seen that the Greeks did not recognize a settled psychological condition corresponding to our 'mental illness' or 'personality disorder', though an individual might be subject to repeated 'possession' by a deity;[10] but the boundaries of Ajax's madness are hard to define.[11] Certainly, the severe distortion of his cognition and emotions by the goddess has a clear beginning and end, but both his purpose before the madness (the intended slaughter of his personal enemies) and his statements and reactions after it prompt the characters and chorus to continue to speak of him as in some sense not in his right mind.[12]

Athena, in maddening Ajax, distorted his perceptions, 'casting upon his eyes mistaken notions' (δυσφόρους ἐπ' ὄμμασι γνώμας βαλοῦσα, 51–2: tr. Lloyd-Jones), but she also 'urged him on beset by mad disorder' (ἐγὼ δὲ φοιτῶντ' ἄνδρα μανιάσιν νόσοις ὤτρυνον, 59–60), which suggests that his madness consists not merely of a perceptual dysfunction but also of an intensification or aggravation of his 'sane' attitude.[13] This is perhaps a further indication that the madness proper, caused directly by Athena, is a kind of extension of a state which was bordering on madness at least in the modern sense. How else would one describe his intention to kill his enemies? Even the savage torture of the animals he deems to be his human foes, which is probably a function of Athena's inspiration, is a 'logical' extension of the ethic of denying all sympathy to an enemy and doing all one can to enjoy harming him.[14] As Athena reminds Odysseus, the sweetest laughter is at the expense of an enemy, and what is that but culturally sanctioned sadism? With compassion withdrawn and divine sanction implicitly granted, there is no reason to draw the line short of the most appalling savagery.[15]

The goddess's taunting of the mad Ajax finds a parallel in Dionysus' teasing of Pentheus in Euripides' *Bacchae*, where again we find a god aggravating the 'sane' tendencies of a mortal. God and mortal are temporarily in (ironical) accord. Those who previously resisted the god are in their mad state now only too pleased to accept assistance. But while Pentheus loses all self-assertiveness (consider, for example, his admission at *Ba.* 934 and his yielding to a divine imperative at 951–4), Athena pretends to subordinate herself to Ajax, assuming the role of 'ally' (συμμάχου, 90) that Ajax prescribes for all his well-wishers. Ajax treats her as a loyal friend and, ironically enough, promises her an offering in return for her help (91–3). He calls her 'mistress' (105), but that does not prevent him insisting on having his own way when she tells him not to torture the animal he has mistaken for Odysseus (111). (When he rejected her help in battle he still called her 'Queen' (at 774). He actually 'bids' (ἐφίεμαι, 112) her to χαίρειν (formally, a sort of farewell greeting, but the strong verb of ordering strikes a curious note; and

[10] See p. 56.

[11] Simpson (1969) 88, e.g., refers to 'the madness present in his murderous purpose.'

[12] e.g. 337–8, 371, 611. On the uncertain boundaries of Ajax's 'madness' see Biggs (1966) 224.

[13] Athena represents 'the highest intensification' of Ajax's nature: ibid.

[14] Simpson (1969) 92 thinks, without textual support, that the madness was produced by a conflict between Ajax's desire to harm his enemies and his realization that they were (or had been) friends.

[15] 'There is a morbid parallel that can be drawn between Athena and Ajax in their emotionality toward their prey; they exhibit no compunction whatever in the almost sensual delight they receive from toying with a helpless enemy': Nielsen (1978) 22.

we are reminded of a similar instruction indirectly presented to Aphrodite by Hippolytus at Eur. *Hipp.* 113). Athena here allows him his way and, repeating the word ἐφίεμαι he instructs her to be this kind of 'ally' (σύμμαχον) (116–17).

This spurious and ironical accord perhaps suggests that alienated mortals such as Ajax and Pentheus can meet these gods only in madness.[16] Consciously they reject them, but since they represent unavoidable aspects of the conditions of human life, there is no escaping some kind of association with them. Pentheus rejects Dionysus because the god embodies those forces of disorder that appear to him to threaten the polis—represented in particular by women out of control, the Greek male's worst nightmare. Ajax, on the other hand, is a warrior intent on winning first prize for valour. For such a man the supreme threat is anything that might overshadow that egotistically individual achievement.[17]

How far does Athena's influence over Ajax extend and what is her purpose for him? The boundaries of the *literal* madness Athena inspires are (as we have seen) clear enough. As for her declared purpose, she tells Odysseus that she is 'eager to direct you in your hunting' (36–7) and that she is displaying Ajax's 'illness' (νόσον) 'so that, having seen it, you may tell all the Argives' (66–7). It seems implied too that one motive in sending Ajax mad was to protect his intended victims (45)—something that we might reasonably deduce in any case from her affection for Odysseus.[18] Moreover, it seems, as stated above, that Athena wants to share her *schadenfreude* with a 'friend', and, finally, to remind Odysseus (who is to tell the Argives) of the power of the gods and their intolerance of human arrogance towards them—an arrogance whose content is not specified until later. It is important to note these motives, since they provide us with our best insight into the thinking of any Sophoclean god.

But does Athena desire Ajax's death? Certainly there is nothing explicit to that effect.[19] Later we are told that her wrath against him will continue only for the present day (756–7). This appears a weak form of panoramic intervention since its implementation is conditional upon Ajax stirring from his tent. But surely we must presume that Athena knows (by divine foresight or by understanding her victim) that Ajax will indeed leave his tent in order to kill himself.[20] Thus she oversees his actions, but she need not impair the autonomy of his motivation.

The restriction of Athena's anger to a single day makes little sense unless there is a concealed irony.[21] Its dramaturgical purpose is clear enough; Sophocles had to

---

[16] Nielsen (1978) 22 n. 19, citing *Iliad* 5. 125, suggests that Ajax's madness 'may be an intentional and ironic perversion of the *menos* that Athena often grants in battle to heroes who beg her for assistance'.

[17] Indeed, Ajax's character is the link between his offences against Athena and his offences against men. See Tyler (1974) 35.

[18] *Pace* Tyler (1974) 28, but the motive will come in a poor second to avenging an insult.

[19] Ibid. 25. 'It is sufficient to say that Ajax's suicide was an indirect effect of Athena's intervention, precipitated of course by the shame she imposed on him, but nevertheless more immediately due to his own character and choice' (ibid.). See also ibid. n. 4.

[20] Whitman (1951) 70 argues that Ajax cannot endure ignominy for more than a day. Biggs (1966) 227 thinks that Ajax fears relenting if he does not die at once.

[21] '[I]s this a sign of moderation in the goddess, or a cruel joke, a merely apparent choice...?': Mastronarde (2005) 328.

motivate a hurried search for Ajax.[22] But there is no suggestion that Athena continues after the madness to invade Ajax's mind or interfere with external events, or indeed that she is bent on ruining his reputation after his death: 'Athena no longer intervenes; but her very absence, leaving the field clear for Teucer and for her protégé Odysseus, is tantamount to her connivance in the rehabilitation of Ajax.'[23] We may wonder if Apollo's withdrawal from the *Tyrannus* after the self-blinding has a similar implication. Indeed, Athena's observation to Odysseus that all human affairs may suffer decline *or restoration* within a single day (131–2), a notion that is echoed in the deception speech at 646–7, has an optimistic implication and perhaps confirms the idea that Athena's anger will last only a single day.

How does Ajax himself understand Athena's involvement and what attitude does he adopt towards her? Does he, for example, attain self-knowledge in the broad Greek sense of an understanding of the place of human beings in the scheme of things? When he awakes he states that the goddess is 'torturing him to death' (402). Perhaps he remembers his mad conversation with her and so correctly attributes his madness to her inspiration (450–3),[24] but there is no sign of his blaming himself for his arrogance towards her—consider, for example, the unqualified self-approval implied in his advice to his son to be like his father in all respects but without what he regards as his bad luck (550–1). As we have seen, he sees himself as hated not only by Athena but by all the gods—and not only by the gods but by the Greeks, the Trojans, and even the landscape (457–9). (He ignores the affection of his family and dependants represented by the sailor chorus.) Ajax is one of the more deluded heroes (at least before his deception speech), seeing himself as unaccountably victimized by the world. Amid all this hostility, actual or merely supposed, he acknowledges no further obligations to the gods (589–90). (He seems to believe, like Eteocles, that the only thing the gods want from him now is his death, and perhaps he is right.)

In the course of the deception speech,[25] Ajax speaks of accepting change, making his peace with the Atreidae and the gods, and in particular Athena through a ceremony of purification (655–6).[26] But in the event he kills himself and curses the Atreidae and the whole Greek army. In his final speech, in spite of what he said earlier about the gods' universal hatred and his earlier rejection of Athena's support, he nevertheless prays to Zeus to send a messenger to Teucer with the news of his death 'so that he may be the first to handle me when I have fallen upon this sword . . . and I shall not be seen first by some enemy and cast out as prey for dogs and birds' (827–31: tr. Lloyd-Jones). And though it is Tecmessa who discovers the body, Teucer is on the scene before any of Ajax's enemies.

---

[22] Similarly in *Trachiniae* (155–77) the oracle that Heracles will either die or find peace is employed to heighten his wife's anxiety about his return.

[23] Greene (1944) 150.

[24] According to Crane (1990) 97, 'Ajax has spoken directly to Athena and he understands very well what she has done to him.'

[25] There are useful summaries of the critical views in Hester (1979) 247–53 and Garvie (1998) 184–6.

[26] 'By giving ritual acknowledgment and honor to the superiority of Athena as goddess, Aias will repay the debt owed her because of his former lack of respect. He will thus become a friend of the gods once more and thereby secure their future aid in avenging his death and in protecting his dependents after his death': Belfiore (2000) 111.

No god then is hostile to the burial of Ajax or actively works against it. He asks Hermes for a quick and painless death (831–4) and he calls on the Furies in a curse directed at the Atreidae and the whole Greek army (835–44). But there is neither reconciliation with Athena nor mention of her in this final speech. We are made to feel that Ajax has made his decision to die quite independently.[27]

Ajax is then probably right to think that Athena is intent on his humiliation and death, though he does not realize the strangely finite nature of her anger and his own independent role in accomplishing her will. In dying then he is in a sense yielding to implicit divine will (654–6), and in the manner of Aeschylus' Eteocles. For the gods wanted Eteocles dead and they knew (it would appear) that he would come to know it when faced with his brother at the seventh gate and that he would realize that there was no escape. They left it open to him, however, to choose a warrior's death. The same option remains open to Ajax and he makes the same choice. But there is a significant and very Sophoclean difference because, while the necessity which Eteocles recognizes is that of the divine will, Ajax is responding to the inner necessity of his own nature—a nature at odds with the world.

Athena is in a sense one of the conditions of the universe which Ajax sees as generally hostile. This distorted view is not an isolated mistake but, as remarked above, originates in and is a function of his character. He also comes to see, in the deception speech, that if he chose to survive he would have to yield and learn to practise *sōphrosunē*; but he chooses rather to remain out of step with the world. Understanding the conditions of human life as Ajax, to some extent, comes to do, is an aspect of the larger existential self-knowledge that consists of fully understanding the implications of being a man and not a god, but in a sense Ajax chooses to be more than a man, and this leaves him with death as his only option. He achieves the limited self-knowledge of recognizing his own inability, or perhaps refusal, to change (which others might describe more negatively as obstinacy, for he does not censure himself for it).

AJAX'S DELIBERATIONS

So much for Ajax's understanding of his relations with Athena, the gods, and indeed the world in general.[28] But how does he see his obligations to his fellow

---

[27] 'Ajax sees his death as a reconciliation with the gods, and the reconciliation is successful. It is not an atonement, and Ajax is not penitent: his suicide is what he chooses, and it also serves the gods' hostility': Scodel (1984) 20. Meier (1993) 178 goes too far in declaring that Ajax 'sacrifices himself. Only by doing this can he demonstrate the newly learnt prudence that is so pleasing to the gods. He thus heals the great rift that he caused in the order of the world.' Kirkwood (1958) 47 rightly observes that 'Ajax dies bitter, unforgiving, unrepentant.' Garvie (1998) states, ad 646–92, that Ajax, 'while acknowledging the claims of *sōphrosunē*, cannot bring himself emotionally to accept it in his own case.... But we should not underestimate the attractiveness of *sōphrosunē* which Ajax clearly sees. The whole speech shows us Ajax resisting and overcoming what is now his strongest temptation.' But is it a temptation? There seems to be no struggle. The world is thus and some can conform, but he is unable and unwilling to conform. He must be true to himself and to his inflexible standards.

[28] Crane (1990) 96–101 argues that Ajax replaces the gods in general and Athena in particular with *chronos* (v. 646) as the great agent of mutability. 'The deception speech ... shows an Ajax with a vast picture of the world, a world that dwarfs men and gods alike. He no longer sees himself as an

mortals?[29] His view on this matter naturally reflects his distorted view of the world which therefore has serious moral implications. When he returns to sanity, Ajax confronts his crisis. This is not a divinely engineered Aeschylean dilemma that requires him to choose between two clearly defined options. The crisis *is* of course divinely engineered and presumably, as we have seen, with the intention of forcing Ajax to suicide, but Athena does not issue a command to Ajax or communicate her will to him in any way. She merely produces a situation which she knows (we presume) he will find untenable. It is up to the mortal then to formulate the problem, and he decides that the problem is how to vindicate his honour. Some other man might never have created this crisis nor reacted to it in the way that Ajax does. While Aeschylus' characters are created to illuminate an abstract moral crisis, in Sophocles character and situation are more closely interdependent.

But it takes time for Ajax to formulate this problem and more time to solve it. At first he is simply despairing and passive, seeing the men of the chorus as the only ones who can put him out of his misery, and he calls out to them to make an end of him (356–61). This initial unheroic reaction of despair finds a parallel at *Trachiniae* 1010–14 when Heracles calls on those served by his labours to kill him, thus releasing him from his agony.[30]

Ajax laments that his bravery has become a mockery, directed as it was against harmless animals (364–7), and he expects to be killed for his attempted murder of his enemies (406–9). In his own view he has done nothing wrong. He regrets only the failure of the deed and certainly not the intention itself; indeed he would still like to kill his enemies (372–3, 387–91). He marvels at the incomprehensible disjunction between his intrinsic worth and his present ignominy, brought out by the contrast between his own experience and that of his father Telamon whose performance in no way outshone his son's (434–40). Honour, then, mysteriously, does not always accompany virtue. Euripides' Phaedra will make a similar discovery, but both characters are so caught up in conventional morality that they cannot follow their insight through to the Aristotelian idea that honour is only a secondary thing, the natural (but, unfortunately, not inevitable) reward for virtue.[31]

---

immutable and all-powerful entity, but his new perspective does not correspondingly enhance his respect for gods such as Athena. He forgets the gods because he has suddenly perceived larger and more powerful forces. Athena could deceive him, humiliate him before his fellows, but in the end Ajax flees time and its relentless effect upon human life' (ibid. 100–1). A similar personification of time in a context of the denigration of divine power appears at Eur. *Her.* 506. Certainly the hostility of a personal deity retreats in importance before the larger issue of the nature of the world (an aspect of which, I argue, Athena symbolizes) and its incompatibility with Ajax's character.

[29] As Tyler (1974) 32–3 observes, the human characters are uninterested in Ajax's impiety. According to Tyler ibid. 36 this produces a dual plot. One might contrast the activity of Aphrodite in *Hippolytus* in which the goddess's quarrel with the hero makes a decisive impact on the human characters.

[30] It also finds an echo, as R. C. T. Parker (1983) 317 remarks, in the reactions of other, polluted heroes.'[W]e see a convergence between the consequences of pollution and of disgrace. The Sophoclean Ajax in his shame does not react very differently from Oedipus and Heracles in their pollution. He spurns food and drink, feels hated by both gods and men, could not look his father in the eye, and devotes himself to night because he is "unworthy to look with profit on any god or man".'

[31] Aristotle *NE* 1095[b]23–30.

At length Ajax's despair modulates into deliberations (457). Aeschylean characters such as Agamemnon and Orestes are confronted with dilemmas and thus with clear-cut alternatives with competing moral claims, but Ajax is faced with an unbearable state of affairs from which he will naturally want to escape. As he sees it, a central feature of this situation is that he has become the object of universal hatred (457–9). (He forgets of course the love of Tecmessa, of Teucer, and of his Salaminian followers, presumably because they are not the sort of people whose applause one especially craves.) Beset thus by enemies, he first contemplates simply amoral escape: he could go home. But that would be to face his father empty-handed (γυμνόν, 464), which, far from relieving his distress, would only aggravate it to its furthest conceivable limit. What he imagines would be Telamon's response on his return brings home to him his own deeper, moral reaction to his disgrace.[32] Clearly his father would be unimpressed by the fine distinction between reputation and moral reality, and although Ajax himself is aware of it, as an adherent of traditional heroic morality, he cannot—anachronistically as well as uncharacteristically—dismiss reputation as irrelevant.[33]

This first option then is quickly dismissed, though imagining its implications has made one thing clear: whatever he does he must redeem his honour. Therefore the next option is a deed of extreme martial courage: to enter into single combat with one Trojan after another (μόνος μόνοις, 467). It might seem to us morally irrelevant to redeem by an act of courage a disgrace unrelated to a failure in courage, but the Iliadic Hector does likewise.[34] The point presumably is to make it clear that, despite any unrelated shortcomings, one is superb in the area in which one chiefly defines oneself. Unfortunately, however, the brave actions Ajax contemplates would only gratify his enemies (466–70). This is not only an unattractive prospect; by heroic standards it is positively immoral.

So how then is Ajax to show his father that he is not 'gutless' (ἄσπλαγχνος, 472), for it is 'shameful' (αἰσχρόν, 473) for a man whose life is characterized by unvarying misfortune (κακοῖσιν, 474) to go on living. One must live honourably (καλῶς, 479) or die thus. The only heroic act remaining to him then is suicide, since any other demonstration of valour would involve the collateral damage of helping his enemies. That his suicide might leave his family exposed does not

---

[32] When Ajax considers what to do he imagines his father's reaction to his return (462–6): 'Not only is his language full of the most basic images of shame, of sight and nudity, but it expresses directly a reciprocal relation between what he and his father could not bear. But . . . it is not the mere idea of his father's pain that governs the decision, nor the fact that it is, uniquely, his father. Ajax is identified with the standards of excellence represented by his father's honours. . . . He has no way of living that anyone he respects would respect—which means that he cannot live with any self-respect': Williams (1993) 85. Belfiore (2000) 109 argues that Ajax's actions 'are shameful, in large part, because he has acted as an enemy to his *philoi*, whose fortunes depend on him and whose disgrace is entailed by his'. Even so, Ajax himself is uninterested in acknowledging it. Even in the deception speech, when he does acknowledge the impact of Tecmessa's appeal, he is moved only to what he regards as a contemptible feminine pity (650–3) and not to a sense of shame.

[33] Ajax cannot 'live with any disparity between society's view of him and his own self-evaluation': Biggs (1966) 226.

[34] See Ch. 1, 'Morality: Ancient and Modern'.

enter his head—or not at least for the moment. Nor is he concerned for his soldiers left vulnerable by his disgrace.[35]

TECMESSA'S PLEA

The Iliadic Hector similarly places his obligations to himself and to his father above all other considerations, but he at least recognizes potentially conflicting obligations to his family.[36] Ajax, on the other hand, needs to be reminded of the gentler aspects of heroic morality which he has conveniently and self-centredly forgotten (485–524). This is the role of Tecmessa, and she argues that he owes her a favour (*charis*, 522) in return for her favours to him.[37] Like the Homeric Achilles, Ajax tends to forget that the heroic code requires more than demonstrations of martial *aretē*, and, as Graham Zanker puts it, Tecmessa is 'defining the noble man as one who is responsive to kindness and affection'.[38] There is after all then a kind of choice, but no god has formulated it for Ajax; nor has he formulated it himself. Typically in Sophocles, the hero resolves quickly and undividedly on a course of action so that it falls to the other characters to formulate alternatives. Realistically considered, though, Ajax's options after the madness are very limited. He cannot continue as a functioning member of the Greek expeditionary force, and it is hard to imagine that anyone would have accepted him into another army. More than that, his very life is presumably in danger. Although Tecmessa, Teucer, and the Salaminian soldiers all take the view that he should survive to protect them, this is hardly a realistic option, even for a man who is less intent than Ajax on avoiding dishonour. Admittedly, the play seems to leave open the possibility of his surviving; and this may be because otherwise the arguments of his dependants,

[35] The chorus need protection and have nothing to gain from the Trojan expedition. 'The job of the hero is created by these very people, the weak and defenceless, who followed their leader to Troy. Ajax, however, came in search of fame and wealth. When Ajax commits suicide, the sailors lose their protection and become victims of heroic morality': Sorum (1986) 366. Or rather they become the victims of a one-sided, selfish interpretation of heroic morality.

[36] Though Hector's sympathetic awareness of his family's plight is clear from *Iliad* 6. 450–93, he nevertheless exposes himself to what he regards as all but certain death at the hands of Achilles, thereby ensuring Troy's fall.

[37] The passage is often compared and contrasted with Andromache's appeal to Hector at *Iliad* 6. 405–39. For Tecmessa, 'the family is the immediate home and the individuals she loves. Her obligations are to their present and future, not to the past': Sorum (1986) 367.

[38] Zanker (1992) 23. It is important to acknowledge that such virtues are integral to the code. Knox (1979) 126, however, misleadingly argues that the play is enacted in what is effectively a post-heroic age: 'one in which action is replaced by argument, stubbornness by compromise, defiance by acceptance. The heroic self-assertion of an Achilles, an Ajax, will never be seen again; the best this new world has to offer is the humane and compromising temper of Odysseus, the worst the ruthless and cynical cruelty of the Atreidae. But nothing like the greatness of the man who lies there dead.' But as Heath (1987) 204 points out, Agamemnon and Menelaus 'are non-heroic, quite simply as weak and dishonourable men. If there is any ethical polarity to be found in this play, it is to be found here: not in a contrast between old and new, but within the old, between the admirable and the contemptible.' See also Cairns (1993) 240–1.

and of Tecmessa in particular, would be irrelevant and the suicide itself would cease to seem a choice at all.[39]

Ajax's failure even to consider Tecmessa's claims suggests that his morality is of that convenient sort that corresponds in large measure to what one wants to do, and Blundell sees Ajax as 'motivated by pleasure in that he indulges to the full the desires to which his conceptions of justice, honour and *eugeneia* give rise. But he is not willing to acknowledge that other values, or justice, honour and *eugeneia* in a different guise, may conflict with these personal desires.'[40] Blundell's criticism of Ajax's morality of 'higher selfishness' reflects a notorious problem with the self-centred eudaimonism of later ancient ethical theories. In principle, the courage that Ajax would vindicate by his suicide is a valuable virtue in his society, but, like Achilles as long as he remains aloof, Ajax is, in Nestor's words about Achilles, 'the only one to profit from his *aretē*' (*Iliad* 11. 762–3). Paradoxically, the moral nobility he would vindicate is supposed to benefit his society, but Ajax has turned his back on society so that his nobility is now exercised solely for his own benefit.[41]

Ajax is, however, moved by Tecmessa's appeal, although he is reluctant to admit it, even to himself. A degree of concession is already implicit in his instructions about the future of his son who is to repay his (Ajax's) parents for the upbringing (*trophē*) which he received from Ajax (567–71). Thus it is easy to say, with Blundell, that he passes his obligations on to Teucer, rather than face them himself.[42] On the other hand, as Belfiore argues, Ajax 'expresses a great deal of concern for his *philoi*, although this is not always apparent either to them or to modern scholars.'[43] Ajax's suicide will secure Tecmessa a place in Telamon's house, free Eurysaces from vengeance at the hands of the Atreidae, and give Teucer 'a way to prove that he is not plotting to usurp Aias's place'.[44] Nevertheless, it remains puzzling that the play itself makes so little of these likely positive outcomes. Ajax's concern can seem perfunctory. Perhaps this can be attributed to his stern and laconic personality or his preoccupation with his primary focus, the vindication of his own honour. Or, on the other hand, perhaps the play does not invite us to reflect on these possible outcomes, in the same way that it does not invite us to ask what would have happened had Ajax decided to live on.

[39] Moreover, 'we want Ajax to remain true to himself, and suicide seems indeed to be the only solution': Garvie (1998) ad 545–82. Despite Tecmessa's claims, the play itself offers 'no practicable or honourable alternative' to suicide: Heath (1987) 183. Ajax does not have the option to carry on from where he left off before the night raid. No one in the play explicitly explores the implications of his surviving—not even Ajax himself in the deception speech. Winnington-Ingram (1980) 43 n. 96, believes that the question will obviously not arise and that we are not to consider it.

[40] Blundell (1989) 72.

[41] Gill (1996) 21 makes the point that Ajax does not espouse an idiosyncratic morality but is intent on making a statement (an 'exemplary gesture') that vindicates traditional moral standards from the point of view of an alienated member of society. Sorum (1986) 362 well observes: 'Ajax's exclusion from the community negates his potential to function as a hero, and yet his ethic remains Homeric. From this conflict emerges a criticism of the ideal, for, as the principles of heroism are carried to their logical conclusions, the balance is destroyed between the individual and social aspects of the hero's role.'

[42] Blundell (1989) 80.

[43] Belfiore (2000) 112.

[44] Ibid. 113.

THE DECEPTION SPEECH

In the deception speech, Ajax reaches a new understanding of the nature of the world and of society, but he has no wish to act on it.[45] If anything, it confirms his determination to die.[46] In this speech, Ajax is disturbed to find himself softened, indeed 'feminized' by Tecmessa's appeal (648–53). First there is the pity which he cannot quite avoid feeling. We have seen how emotions that arise unbidden into consciousness must be processed during moral deliberations.[47] Here is an excellent case of an entirely appropriate, socially valorized emotional reaction that the agent should recognize as a warning that he has not properly considered the full implications of the situation. But Ajax contemptuously dismisses this inchoate pity as a sign of moral weakening, which he implicitly defines as any modification of his character. After all, for Ajax, character (or at least *his* character) is, in a sense, the source of morality—which is a perfectly reasonable view if far and away the supreme virtue is heroic courage, of which he himself is the supreme exponent.

On the other hand, Tecmessa's brief mention of the vicissitudes of her own life which took her from royalty to slavery (485–90), provides perhaps a catalyst for his own recognition of the universal nature of mutability (646–52, 668–82) which he associates with yielding ($ὑπείκει$, 670). But Ajax cannot acquiesce in, let alone embrace his new state in the manner of Tecmessa (491). Such a world is too unattractive to him. The mutation of his character he perceives as having already begun, but, as is clear from his resolve here and from his final speech, he has no intention of surviving to accept authority or mutability in friendship and enmity (678–83), nor does he believe that he is morally obliged to do so, for he does not approve of such a world. And if Ajax's morality is out of harmony with the world, there is nothing for him to do but leave it.[48]

---

[45] See Barlow (1981) 116–20 on the contrast with the more flexible Euripidean Heracles.

[46] 'Ajax recognizes the principle of mutability in the world and will have none of it': Winnington-Ingram (1980) 54. 'Despite the outwardly stern inflexibility which he displayed in the last scene, Ajax has been moved to pity; and he remarks on the fact that his feelings are not exempt from the universal pattern of change with surprise and some indignation: he refers to his earlier inflexibility with a mocking irony, and to his weakening with contemptuous sarcasm (650–2). But the implications of that contempt show that he rejects the weakening he describes; his feelings have been stirred, but his will is unmoved': Heath (1987) 186. Ajax is affected by Tecmessa, but 'his confession that he has been moved is unwilling and contemptuous': Kirkwood (1958) 103. March (1991–3) 19–21, however, believes that Ajax is deeply affected by Tecmessa's arguments and integrates them into his intended suicide the ground for which has now changed. See also Simpson (1969) 94: 'Tecmessa has compelled him to abandon his earlier reason for suicide and to seek a higher justification for it which he articulates in the speech at 646 ff.' As Ajax 'understands the pattern of change in the universe, it dictates not that he change his nature, but rather that he remove himself': ibid. 98.

[47] See Ch. 1, 'Elements of Moral Response'.

[48] At the end of this analysis of his reflections on his life and his future it is worth noting, with Harris (2001) 352, that Ajax 'is the first hero of a surviving play who is allowed moods'. One is struck by the space devoted to his lucubrations about his future, in contrast with the Aeschylean characters discussed in the previous chapters—and by the more realistic sense of an interior debate. Greek tragedy 'is often about the interior state of its leading characters, and can be supposed to have contributed to the new obsession with such states': ibid.

AJAX IN RETROSPECT

After the hero's death the play does much to remind us of his past greatness, though of course it cannot vindicate his madness or the 'sane' intention that led to it.[49] Tecmessa declares that the Atreidae will miss Ajax's martial prowess (962–3), and the extreme sorrow and desperation of Teucer confirm Ajax's former value to his *philoi* (974–83, 992–1039). The sailor chorus also lament the loss of his protection (1211–15). Of course, both Atreidae speak against him and belittle his achievements. Menelaus reminds us that, if it had not been for the goddess, he, his brother, and Odysseus would now be dead (1052–61). The lesson he draws from this is the need for proper respect for authority in a state or an army (1069–86), but he weakens his case by casting Ajax in the role of a common soldier (δημότην, 1071), a misrepresentation easily refuted by Teucer who points out that Ajax came as no one's subordinate (1097–108). That obedience is required from a common soldier is obviously unobjectionable, but it is irrelevant here. It would have been better to argue simply that allied commanders should not try to kill their peers. But no one is disputing that point. Ajax can be defended only on the basis of his earlier performance.

Agamemnon takes a different tack, claiming that Teucer, a 'nobody' (οὐδὲν ὤν) is defending Ajax, another 'nobody' (τοῦ μηδέν) (1231). Teucer's insignificance, as Agamemnon sees it, is a function of his illegitimate birth, whereas he argues that Ajax is insignificant for two reasons, first because he did nothing outstanding (1236–7) and secondly because he is dead (1257). The first argument is patently false and the second beneath contempt. In the light of this, Agamemnon has the gall to urge Teucer to practise *sōphrosunē* (οὐ σωφρονήσεις; 1259), a quality which, in the deception speech, Ajax had come to see that he would have to display if he intended to survive and which presumably included 'respecting' (σέβειν) the Atreidae! (666–7, 677). It is easy to share Ajax's contempt for a world dominated by such people (Philoctetes is similarly contemptuous of a 'heroic' society represented by the Odysseus of that play). Teucer attacks Agamemnon on the score of ingratitude (χάρις, 1267) for Ajax's former considerable services (itemized at 1269–89), but this sort of argument can count against Ajax when we remember that he was guilty of the same offence against Tecmessa (522–4).[50] Presently Agamemnon will caution Odysseus against bestowing *charis* upon an enemy such as Ajax (1354), but Odysseus will reply that the man's nobility takes precedence over his status as an enemy (1355, 1357). Finally, Agamemnon authorizes the burial as a *charis* to a friend (1371), though Ajax will remain 'most hated' (ἔχθιστος, 1373). Ironically enough, then, Ajax depends for his burial on the granting of a *charis*, a moral requirement which he himself ignored in the case of his loving concubine, and that *charis* in turn depends on the friendship of Agamemnon and Odysseus (1328–31, 1351, 1353), though Ajax disapproved of both men—rightly of the former, though mistakenly of the latter.

---

[49] For a discussion of the post-suicide scenes and a review of the criticism see Davidson (1985) *passim*.
[50] The parallel is reinforced by the use in both passages of a compound of ῥεῖν—ἀπορρεῖ (523), διαρρεῖ (1267)—to describe what might be called the leaching away of χάρις.

ODYSSEUS

Odysseus' view of the matter is influenced by his earlier encounter with Athena who invited him to laugh at Ajax, their mutual enemy (79). After taunting her victim she changed her tone, making an example of him by way of an at once gentle and sinister reminder to her favourite (118–21). But she may not have counted on Odysseus' human pity which began the process of realigning his sympathies. It is ironic that our sympathy for one of the most brutal heroes of Greek tragedy takes its cue from the response of his greatest enemy, and that sympathy, once engaged, is sustained through Ajax's tortured reflections on his future. Odysseus remembers his own and his enemy's human condition and pities him; we are all ghosts or fleeting shadows (125–6).[51] Though it seems unnecessary in Odysseus' case, Athena warns him against arrogance towards the gods or conceit among men on the grounds of superior might or wealth (127–30). The gods are fond of sensible men (τοὺς σώφρονας), that is to say those who respect the boundaries between gods and mortals, and hate evildoers (τοὺς κακούς, 133), who in this context are presumably the opposite of the σώφρονες.[52] Odysseus has little reason to fear alienating the gods by arrogance, but in this earlier scene he is struck by our general human vulnerability.

The pity aroused for Ajax in the earlier scene allows Odysseus to transcend Athena's morality and thus to insist on justice for his former enemy in this final scene of the play. This contrasts with Ajax's refusal to feel this morally constructive emotion which lies at the heart of both the *Iliad* and *Philoctetes*. There were more than intimations in the earlier scene of the familiar Euripidean disjunction between the moral standards of gods and those of human beings. It is easy to be disgusted by Athena's cruel and crude *schadenfreude*, reminiscent of Aphrodite in *Hippolytus* or Hera in *Heracles*, and to find the accompanying moralizing all the more distasteful because of it. Euripides' Heracles is so disgusted with divine cruelty and injustice that he rejects the gods, at least in their anthropomorphic conception, and focuses on humanity (Eur. *Her.* 1340–51). And the theology, as it were, in these cases is less important than the general lesson that the gods (whatever they are) do what they will with us. Athena, a goddess, is naturally incapable of a pity that arises from a shared vulnerability. There is a natural ethical barrier between gods and mortals. Gods have no moral obligations, at least to us, and the obligations we have to them are summarized in the virtues of piety and *sōphrosunē*. But virtues directed at the gods are rendered futile in the face of divine implacability. This means that the victim's moral obligations relate now entirely to human beings. As we saw, the gods' implacable hostility freed Eteocles to focus on his post-mortal reputation among men (Aesch. *Sept.* 683–5).

Odysseus argues that Ajax should be buried in accordance with justice (δίκην, 1335) and divine laws (τοὺς θεῶν νόμους, 1343), even though he was an enemy (1344–5). Despite his hostility, he considers Ajax the best (ἄριστον, 1340) of all the

---

[51] On Odysseus as 'the model of an Aristotelian spectator' see Konstan (1999) 5. Hubbard (2003) 160 observes that Odysseus experiences Aristotelian pity and fear, that he represents the audience, 'and his personal growth in witnessing the events of the tragedy represents theirs as they exit the theater at the end of the day'.

[52] On *kakous* in this sense see Stanford (1963) ad loc.

Greeks who came to Troy apart from Achilles (1336–41). It was right to hate him while he was alive, but no longer (1347). Agamemnon regards this as capriciousness in friendship, but Odysseus reminds him of the fluidity of friendship and enmity (1358–9). Agamemnon, like Ajax, disapproves of such fluidity, but Odysseus deplores obstinacy (1360–1). Soon he will offer friendship to a former enemy, Teucer, who will accept it up to a point but not on Ajax's behalf (1376–80, 1395).

Another major irony of Ajax's burial is that it depends on a flexible view of *philia* which he himself strongly deplored.[53] To that extent the play seems to side with Odysseus' *philia* morality. Unlike Achilles in the *Iliad*, we never see Ajax engaged in close *philia* with a comrade; we only see him as a *philos* in its other sense of family relation, and in that sphere his performance must seem inadequate because of his egotistical absorption with his own honour. While the sort of friendship we see in the play must pale before the passionate devotion of Homer's Achilles for Patroclus, it seems more admirable than any friendship displayed by Ajax, unless—which seems most unlikely—the exploits Teucer describes (1269–89) were motivated by it. The superiority of the Odyssean flexibility clearly consists in its ability to observe the friend/enemy-based morality while being able to transcend it, when required, in order to recognize and reward merit.[54]

In sum, the post-suicide scenes celebrate Ajax's martial *aretē*, but, far from vindicating his morality, they contribute to the implicit critique of it by doing much to recommend 'enlightened self-interest' and a more flexible, Odyssean attitude to human relations.[55] Sophocles thus leaves unresolved the problem of comfortably integrating extraordinary individuals into society—a problem as old as the *Iliad*.[56] Of course, Ajax and other extraordinary figures of myth, such as Heracles and Oedipus, *were* integrated into the community in death through hero cults, but it is apparent from the post-suicide scenes of the *Ajax* that the hero is much easier to assimilate in death than in life. In life he would have remained

---

[53] It depends too on the *sōphrosunē* the hero rejected: Cairns (2005) 318.

[54] 'Odysseus' generosity represents the crowning form of *eugeneia* in the *Ajax*. However grand and awe-inspiring Ajax's devotion to τιμή, however moving the appeal to affection given expression by Tecmessa, it is Odysseus' combination of the sense of justice and the conditioning factor of emotional responses like pity which finally succeeds in resolving the quarrel over Achilles' armour in its last stages': Zanker (1992) 25. 'Ajax lives by the strict reciprocity that demands that you treat others as they have treated you; Odysseus extends this principle into a version of the Golden Rule, that you should treat others as you would like to be treated yourself (123–6, 1365)': Cairns (2005) 319.

[55] According to Goldhill (1986) 160, '[I]t is almost as if this continual retrospective definition of Ajax, the hero, despite his untenable position, grows in stature in comparison with the men who follow him and argue about him.' He sees Ajax as 'an outsider in his greatness' and 'positively dangerous to ordinary society' (ibid.). Ajax obviously appears great in contrast with such moral pygmies as the Atreidae, and Odysseus can seem relatively diminished by his careful and unspectacular morality. On the ways in which Sophocles manipulates our sympathies towards Ajax in the final scenes see Cairns (2005) 318–19: 'The raw material for characterizing Ajax as a hubristic, impious criminal and the Atreidae as defenders of essential civic and military institutions is there in the play, but the poet chooses not to present it in that way': ibid. 319.

[56] See Cairns (2005) 320. Much the same applies to Philoctetes who is at most nominally reintegrated into society. In fact, he and Neoptolemus enter a mutual admiration society of two (or perhaps three, if one includes the deified Heracles).

hostile, uncooperative, and indeed radically antisocial, but once he is dead it is possible to dwell exclusively on his former prowess and to honour him for it.

THE AJAX OF THE PLAY AND AJAX THE CULT HERO

The relationship between these cultic heroes and their counterparts in the plays is one of the puzzles of Greek tragedy. One might think that a critical portrait of a hero, such as we find of Ajax and of Heracles in *Trachiniae*, would undermine respect for that hero. But it seems, on the contrary, that they were secure in their heroic status in the way that respect for Dionysus is secure despite Aristophanes' humiliating portrait of him in *Frogs* or even Euripides' much more serious and morally ambivalent presentation of that god in *Bacchae*—plays produced at a festival in the god's honour. Just as no one seriously believed that the comic Dionysus resembled the real god, perhaps a similar disjunction existed between the divergent and often mutually inconsistent tragic incarnations of the heroes and their perceived reality as 'historical' figures. After all, modern Christian audiences do not (or certainly need not) consider *Jesus Christ Superstar* as a threat to what they regard as the revealed truth of the Gospels or to their conception of the living Christ. The exception to this apparent disjunction is of course the *Coloneus* in the course of which Oedipus seems gradually to assume the character one associates with cultic heroes. Because the Greeks had neither revealed religion nor sacred texts, their conceptions of their gods and heroes were very fluid. They were also morally undemanding. Indeed, some have argued that the heroes' very transgressiveness paradoxically renders them appropriate guardians of the state, though I am less than entirely convinced.[57] Thus attacks on the morality of gods and heroes would not have been perceived as particularly threatening. As is well known, what was not allowed was attacks on the *reality* of the gods—or not at least outside poetic literature.

CONCLUSION

This first of our Sophoclean agents has to formulate for himself the precise nature of his crisis. He begins by simply giving vent to his distress. From there he moves on to consider his options, beginning with the escapist impulse simply to go home. But as he considers that option he realizes its impossibility because of the humiliation it would entail to return empty-handed to his father. Thus he realizes that he owes it to himself to vindicate his honour. He moves from that moral

---

[57] 'Ajax's single-minded pursuit of individual honor issues in violence and pollution, thereby revealing the anarchic threat implicit in his heroic mode, which makes that mode unacceptable within the polis; yet his terrible obsession, his pollution, and his volatile violence endow Ajax with the stature of tragic agonist, as once they must have established him as the hero of cult. Like Oedipus or Orestes, he is a liminal figure who has transgressed the boundaries yet therefore may become the *daimon* 'divinity or hero' who protects boundaries': Bradshaw (1991) 99–100.

realization to a consideration of the means and here it is essential not to help his enemies. Thus suicide turns out to be the only choice. So he does not begin with an assumption that he is embarking on a process of moral deliberation. The basic moral requirement simply emerges as the other option (going home in dishonour) is dismissed.

Ajax defines himself implicitly in terms of his role as a warrior, but also in individual terms as the best man at Troy (in other words, the warrior with the greatest prowess and courage). The warrior role carries, as he sees it, a responsibility to his own honour. He does not, however, accept the wider responsibility of the warrior to protect his family and dependants, at least when this is incompatible with vindicating his honour. So Ajax is only partially aware of the moral implications of his predicament, if we assume (reasonably, I think) that the play as a whole endorses the heroic code in its recognition of broader moral responsibilities to family and friends. Ajax is clear about the facts of the situation; his heroic honour could only be effectively restored by suicide. But he does not integrate his emotions appropriately into his deliberations, for, though moved to pity by Tecmessa's pleas, he deliberately discounts this feeling as morally corrupting since by 'feminizing' him it erodes his self-concept from which his self-centred 'morality' is almost exclusively derived. This self-centred focus of his morality it never occurs to him to question. While he listens to his shame, he will not listen to his pity. Despite Athena's involvement in his life and perhaps indirect contrivance of his suicide, his deliberations are autonomous.

7

Sophocles: *Trachiniae*

IS HERACLES A CREDIBLE MORAL AGENT?

The Sophoclean Heracles, all but identified with his wonderful body, faces a moral crisis with its disintegration, and particularly at the point when he realizes that prophecy apparently confirms his imminent death. Like Ajax in his predicament, he has moral obligations to himself as a warrior, but his relations with peers, family, and society are more problematical, partly because of the superhuman aspects of his nature, but also because of the unusual social milieu of this play. Then there is the divine realm and his special relationship with his Olympian father.

Both the hero and indeed the world of *Trachiniae* have an air of the pre-political and morally primitive. The play is set in the remote era of Heracles' world-civilizing Labours, and his personal history stretches back to embrace even more remote civilizing activities such as the battle of the Giants.[1] Moreover, although this greatest of the Greek heroes was a civilizer of a monstrous and barbarous world, he was as often as not imagined as himself barbarous, monstrous and uncivilized, as exemplified in poorly motivated or gratuitous episodes of violence and even madness, or in an extraordinary capacity for indulgence in food, drink, sex, and general buffoonery.[2] Thus Heracles is naturally at home in the play's world of monstrous and terrifying beings such as multiform river gods and centaurs. However, in this milieu, his wife, Deianeira, a woman of considerable moral sensitivity, is completely out of place. Temporarily resident in Trachis, an area whose very name suggests something rough and uncivilized, she occupies

---

[1] 'Heracles lies on the margins between the human and the divine . . . ; he is a marginal, transitional or, better, *interstitial* figure': Silk (1993) 121: Silk's emphasis. 'In Homeric epic, Heracles is an extravagant figure outside the normal heroic sphere. He is an isolated superman who fights monsters, not a feudal warrior within a social hierarchy who fights with, and against, others like himself': ibid. 121. 'Heracles is like the monsters he fights, but some of these, like Achelous, are gods themselves. . . . Heracles is apparently self-sufficient, *autarkēs*. In the *Politics*, Aristotle notes that the person who through *autarkeia* needs no social organization to support him is either to be classed as an animal—or a god': ibid. 123. On Heracles as *apolis* see also C. Segal (1981) 60 and Foley (1985) 191: Heracles, 'occupying an unstable position between beast and god, order and disorder, is a figure belonging to one of the earliest generations of Greek myth, extraordinarily prone to violence and never quite part of civilized life. . . . The least domestic of heroes, he is never allowed to rule as king and never fully integrated into the political and social life of a Greek city.'

[2] '[M]onstrous violence could only be put down by an answering excess of violence': Winnington-Ingram (1980) 89. 'Heracles fights monsters and takes on their monstrousness': Silk (1993) 124.

the house of an absent *xenos* (39–41).[3] Her little enclave is the housewife's world of gentle and loving civilities, and soon she will retreat into the private sanctuary of the matrimonial bedroom to die, when her brief interaction with the monstrous 'outside' world has destroyed her life.

This monstrous world contains Deianeira's first suitor, the river god Achelous who 'asked her father for her hand in three forms—as a bull, as a dappled or changeable serpent, and in a man's skin but with a bull's face with streams of water flowing round his shaggy chin' (9–14). Such incarnations can doubtless be interpreted as symbolic projections of a maiden's fear of male sexuality, but they are emblems too of the sensual, erotic, not to say Dionysiac world with which Heracles is thoroughly in tune. Deianeira, however, finds her husband human and civilized enough to be welcomed as a saviour from such a monster (21). The contest between the rival suitors Deianeira was herself too terrified to watch (21–5), but the chorus later evoke the occasion in an ode to the universal and invincible power of Cypris who subdued even Poseidon, Hades, and the son of Cronus himself (497–502). We hear of the powerful bodies, the blows, the dust, the outlandish taurine Achelous; of Zeus's son brandishing lance, bow, and club (512), of the clang and clash of the weapons (517–18), and of horns and arms and bodies grappling like wrestlers—with Cypris as umpire (515–16). Whether Deianeira's saviour was really much more human or civilized than his antagonist is unclear.[4] Deianeira herself offers no explanation of her husband's motives in contending for her hand in marriage, but an ode invokes the universal power of sexual attraction which plays such a sinister role in Heracles' liaison with Iole, who, as Segal puts it, 'enters [the play] as a nameless female, without identity, sought only for her sexuality, as a beast would seek a mate'.[5]

We gain a more distinct impression of Heracles from Lichas' admittedly partly mendacious account of his master's exploits in Boeotia.[6] Eurytus, we are told, though a long-standing *xenos* of Heracles, subjected him to crude insults and then, in a drunken state, threw him out of his house (262–9). But Heracles' response was on much the same moral level when he killed the innocent son (Iphitus) in order to punish the guilty father, and did so in an uncharacteristically stealthy and unceremonious manner by hurling him over a cliff (269–73). This world of crude passions and of impulsive reactions and counterreactions is far removed alike from the polis and from the households of the more civilized *xenoi* of the *Odyssey*. Zeus duly punished Heracles for the manner of his murder of Iphitus by enslaving him for a year to the barbarian queen Omphale (275–9), but in requital Heracles sacked Oechalia because, in his morally simplistic way, he regarded Eurytus as 'exclusively responsible' (μεταίτιον μόνον βροτῶν, 260–1). This story, however, though characteristic enough of the hero, is later emended, and Heracles is assigned a different motive for the attack on the city. In the revised version of Lichas' narrative, the motivation is attributed to 'Eros alone among gods'

---

[3] For Ceyx and his house see Kamerbeek (1970) ad loc.

[4] Easterling (1982) ad 497–530: 'there is no attempt to distinguish the glorious Heracles from his monstrous opponent Achelous'.

[5] C. Segal (1981) 63.

[6] As Winnington-Ingram (1980) 82 observes, the untruthful part of the narrative concerns the motive of Heracles for sacking Oechalia.

(354–5).[7] Unable to persuade Eurytus to let him have his daughter as an unofficial sexual partner, Heracles attacked the city on some flimsy pretext (ἔγκλημα μικρὸν αἰτίαν θ᾽ ἑτοιμάσας, 361).

Deianeira's account of the slaying of the centaur Nessus confirms the picture of a reactive rather than reflective hero. As the centaur conveyed Deianeira across the Evenus he laid lustful hands on her, and as soon as Heracles heard her cry out he turned and let fly with an arrow that pierced Nessus through the lungs (562–8). The unreflecting immediacy of this response (εὐθύς, 566) recurs in an even more striking form when Heracles kills Lichas as soon as he learns that he brought the robe on his wife's behalf (772–84). Heracles neither wonders nor cares whether Lichas knew that the robe was poisoned; still less does he enquire into his wife's motives; he simply reacts as the anger rises in him, the impulsive nature of the response underlined by the simultaneous spasm through his lungs (777–8). The sudden and violent brutality of this reaction is further enhanced by the description of Lichas' brains pouring out over the rock (777–82) with the motif of the corrupted sacrifice which it perhaps embodies.[8] Far from being a credible moral agent, then, Heracles seems to live almost entirely in the present, like an animal. All but unendurable agony can be expected to level a man with the beasts, and yet the hero's fundamental nature is less distorted than exaggerated by his pain.[9] His sufferings emphasize his characteristically physical definition, as his tremendous vitality is less diminished than turned against him.

HERACLES' INITIAL SELF-PITY

And yet, as we watch his agony, we begin to feel that Heracles falls into both categories of Aristotle's apolitical animal, the superhuman as well as the subhuman,[10] an important point when considering the vexed question of the apotheosis. His spasms are massive as he is thrown to earth and made to leap into the air (786). He screams and shouts, and the crags, headlands, and mountains of Euboea resound with the din. In his illness his already simplistic thought processes are further attenuated (see 1120–1). As through the smoke of the sacrifice he catches sight of his son weeping (794–6), his immediate thought is for himself and for the humiliation he would avoid even at the cost of his son's life (797–800). And yet, in spite of this, Hyllus describes him as 'the best man of all men on earth' (811). The judgements of all the characters are similarly uncritical[11]—a warning to be wary of judging Heracles by ordinary human standards.[12]

[7] Perhaps it is a question of priorities: the primary motive was erotic, the secondary motive revenge.

[8] 'The shedding of human, not animal, blood is itself a pollution of the sacrifice. But the details of the shattered skull and brain cause a particular shiver of horror. Lichas becomes a second human victim, even more sacrilegiously, for the skull of the sacrificial animal was to be kept intact, and the sight of the brain was a horrible desecration': C. Segal (1981) 72. Biggs (1966) 228 thinks that Heracles is, as it were, trying to get at the pain through Lichas because he is Deianeira's agent and she is the supposed source of the pain.

[9] See Winnington-Ingram (1980) 83.

[10] Aristotle, *Pol.* 1253ª3.

[11] See McCall (1972) 156, 158–9.

[12] Silk (1993) 126 comments: 'In his brutality the Sophoclean Heracles embodies a model of life which, by any human standard, must seem repellent; yet the devotion he inspires in his son and wife,

When the hero is carried onto the stage, he is absorbed in his agony and at first capable of little feeling or thought beyond self-pity (983–99).[13] Then he complains briefly of the injustice that not one of the beneficiaries of his Labours will come to his assistance (1010–14), though the only assistance he wants is in dying (cf. 1031–3, 1040). Humiliatingly, his destruction comes at the hands of a mere woman, when none of the formidable opponents of the Labours was able to achieve as much (1048–63). He thinks naturally of revenge, but is forced to rely on his son to fetch Deianeira to him (1064–70). But even the sweet taste of vengeance is denied him (1133); his wife is already dead.

Here, though, we discover the first trace of the heroic morality we might expect—the warrior's simple devotion to courage—for Heracles despises what he sees as his own cowardly, womanly reaction to his agony, the only pain ever to have forced a groan or tear from him (1070–5).[14] And yet he continues to suffer and impotently lament until he learns of Nessus' part in his fate (1141–2) when he recalls the prophecy that he would be killed by no living creature ($\pi\rho\grave{o}s\ \tau\hat{\omega}\nu$ $\pi\nu\epsilon\acute{o}\nu\tau\omega\nu\ \mu\eta\delta\epsilon\nu\acute{o}s$, 1160), but only by one that had died (1159–63). Clearly he had deemed this impossible, but now he accepts what he sees as the inevitability of his death at the hands of a dead creature (1143–6). But *is* his death inevitable? What of the traditional apotheosis? If he is reporting the oracle's words more or less verbatim, then he is right to expect death rather than teleportation to Olympus. But oracles are tricky, and it is at least possible that we are to take it that Heracles received simply a prediction that he would not die at the hands of a living creature and that he himself wrongly took this to mean that he would be killed, but by a dead creature. Though, in a further ironical twist, it now *appears* that he is indeed dying through the contrivance of at least one dead creature.

A notable theme of Heracles' expostulations thus far has been horror at the disintegration of his body, attacked by an enemy within (987, 1027–30). The personified *nosos* eats his flesh, drains the vessels of his lungs, and drinks his blood, so that his whole body is destroyed (1054–7).[15] With affectionate pathos he apostrophizes his hands, back, chest, and the 'dear' (*philoi*) arms that performed his Labours (1089–102). Now his body is ravaged and mangled (1103–5), so if some significant moral response is imminent, it will need to proceed from substantial self-redefinition.

HERACLES' MORAL RESPONSE

With the mention of Nessus, everything changes. There is a short burst of self-pity as Heracles recognizes (what he conceives to be) the certainty of his death

---

who are the chief victims of his repellent behaviour, seems to place him in some kind of ideal, supra-human plane beyond judgement.'

[13] McCall (1972) 157–8 likens Heracles' entrance to that of Odysseus in *Odyssey* 5: 'the Telemachy has portrayed him as one of the most illustrious of heroes, but he is weeping by the shore'.

[14] Faraone (1994) 115–16 thinks that Heracles has been feminized by the 'love' charm.

[15] 'The disease itself becomes an almost living being: the violence of the bestial Nessus lives again in the body of his slayer and feasts on his flesh and blood' (1053–55)': C. Segal (1981) 69.

(1143–5). He links the 'Nessus' oracle with the play's earlier prophecy that stated that at this time he would find rest from his Labours (1169–71). 'Rest' he had taken to mean happiness (πράξειν καλῶς, 1171), but the reference was apparently to his death, for it is the dead that rest from their labours (1173).

We saw how Ajax moves from self-pity to moral deliberations. Heracles' options, however, are much more restricted. Like Eteocles, he can only consider how he is to die, and for both men the answer is immediately obvious: bravely, as befits a heroic warrior. Heracles now requires his son to swear to carry out his will, which includes constructing a funeral pyre and burning him alive on it. He is to do this without a tear or a groan or else suffer a father's heavy curse (1193–202). Heracles goes on to insist that Hyllus marry Iole (1219–29), a demand motivated explicitly by his desire that no one sleep with her but himself. Since that will be impossible, Hyllus, as his son, will have to stand in for him. The demand is in keeping with the man's grossness and colossal egotism. It also, however, establishes a line of Spartan kings, which might seem to justify it from the perspective of historical hindsight if not in the immediate context. The first demand, the immolation on the pyre, might be similarly justified—as a necessary mythic prerequisite for the apotheosis—though not in terms of Heracles' motivation which remains obscure, thus producing the sense that he is privy to some special knowledge.[16] Indeed, with his understanding of the true import of the two oracles, the fulfilment of which testifies at least to a minimal order in the universe, Heracles' understanding seems to expand mysteriously to embrace some kind of insight into the divine purpose and to suggest that Zeus is 'panoramically' involved.

However, the status of the apotheosis in the play is problematical. Some scholars argue that its literal omission testifies to its irrelevance. George Gellie, for example, opines that 'the apotheosis influences the play by being proposed to our minds and then being left out of the action . . . If apotheosis is hinted at, and then the hint is not made good, we are surely being asked to observe the gap, not to fill it.'[17] The problem of the relation of the play to the myth tradition is particularly acute here. Heracles himself remains convinced until the end that he is going to die. This view is shared by Hyllus who rails at the heartless gods in the play's final words.

[16] 'No explanation is offered for these directions [Heracles' to Hyllus] , but Heracles speaks with confident authority, and it is natural to assume that he is recalling the commands of Zeus (cf. 1149–50.)': Easterling (1982) 9.
[17] Gellie (1972) 77. 'The deification remains outside the play, at an unspecified distance, and has no connection with the human fate represented within it': Reinhardt (1979) 63. See also Seale (1982) 208. '[T]he play's logic need not extend beyond the *nosos* and the presumed subsequent death of Heracles; the pyre on Oeta and the marriage of Hyllus and Iole are not necessary for the conclusion of this story. We can only suppose that they have some importance in their own right for the light they throw on what is happening to Heracles': Easterling (1982) 9. For Silk (1993) 126–7, Heracles seems 'confined to the human sphere which the gods, in a separate existence, manipulate and mock. . . . Situated on the margins between the human and the divine, on the verge of an apotheosis that never comes, Heracles represents *both* those deep, immortal longings which all men feel or repress, and which the Greeks felt to be dangerous to admit, *and* the huge but human sufferings and dislocations that are felt to go with them. Having chosen to dramatize this disturbing anomaly, Sophocles confronts us with its implications right up to the end' (Silk's emphasis).

Deborah Roberts argues, with reference to Sophoclean drama in general, that although allusions to future events in the myth tradition 'are not part of the play's story, they are nonetheless somehow continuous with that story; [and] to this extent they disrupt the play's closure.'[18] By this

we are made to understand . . . that our judgment at the end of the play (which may itself be a complex judgment), though grounded in the play's action, is inevitably provisional, and that we will not be able to remedy that provisional nature. We cannot know the final outcome; and given not only the variability of Greek myth but the variety of ways in which any story may be told, we ourselves, though more informed than the characters, can have only partial knowledge of what is to come.[19]

These observations are particularly applicable to the *Trachiniae,* because they relate so closely to the theme of epistemological uncertainty.[20] The idea of the unknowability of the future is thus maintained until the very end when the audience are included in this ignorance. In this way the extreme pessimism of the characters at the end is questioned in the light of both the epistemological theme and the apotheosis tradition.

How then does this affect our appraisal of Heracles' moral performance? First we need to be clear that apotheosis confers no moral seal of approval on a character. The postmortal fates of mythological characters are not generally based on moral deserts. Otherwise why does the rather second-rate Homeric Menelaus end up in Elysium while Achilles has to make do with Hades?[21] It is clear too that the heroization of Oedipus in the *Coloneus* is not to be conceived as some kind of reward for good behaviour, and if there is any connection with Oedipus' character it is to be found in his increasingly superhuman pitilessness, a quality disparaged by his daughter Antigone.[22] In default of evidence to the contrary, we can take it that if we are to entertain the apotheosis as a possibility (and Sophocles goes no further than that) it is conferred simply because Heracles is the son of Zeus. (Helen's traditional metamorphosis is based on a similar consideration.)

So if Heracles has been vouchsafed some epiphany or mysterious insight to accompany his knowledge of the fulfilment of the oracles, he still believes that he is going to die, and the only comfort that can come from his new understanding is an awareness of the minimal coherence of the universe implied by a fulfilled prophecy.[23] In this respect, Heracles' position is not dissimilar to that of Oedipus at Thebes. The coherence is amoral; it does nothing to explain or justify the hero's agony. As far as morality goes, Heracles, like Ajax and Eteocles before him, must act independently of the gods who seem indifferent to him, if not downright hostile. Naturally, he chooses to be brave, but the only bravery now open to him

---

[18] Roberts (1988) 190.   [19] Ibid. 191.   [20] See Lawrence (1978) *passim.*
[21] Homer *Od.* 4.561–70.   [22] *OC* 1181–203.
[23] '[T]here is a suggestion, however mysterious and obscure, that some significance should be attached to the manner of Heracles' death, and that it fits into a larger scheme of things in which Zeus's will is mysteriously fulfilled. Whether this is leading to a good or bad end is not made clear, and Heracles himself shows no sign of understanding it. But his behaviour after he has interpreted the oracle suggests that he has at last grasped something—the paradox, perhaps, that the most a human being can achieve . . . is an acceptance of the great gulf between human and divine knowledge. And this itself is arrived at only through extremes of suffering': Easterling (1982) 10. See also Scodel (1984) 40–1.

consists of silent, uncomplaining endurance—a quality associated with some of the more humiliating labours of the myth tradition.

HERACLES AND SELF-KNOWLEDGE

Once convinced that he is about to die, all that interests Heracles is to make the appropriate arrangements and adopt the proper attitude of courage. He naturally engages in no deep reflection about his own contribution to his present condition. But there is an irony that should not escape the audience at least, which is that all the hostile forces ranged against him have been empowered by his own lust and violence.[24] The extended crisis in this play is as self-inflicted as was Ajax's predicament. Indeed, as Easterling points out, the 'qualities attributed to Heracles' enemies, their unapproachability, savagery and violence . . . are all characteristic of Heracles himself'.[25] But this is the moment in which sensitive moral agents will realize that the consequences of their own previous errors and transgressions have descended upon them. Heracles is not a sensitive moral agent, but with that kind of realization it might have been possible for him to assert his higher rational and moral self against the beast within, and this is just what Charles Segal claims he achieves.

By confronting this more primitive self with a more developed human self, by suffering and then overcoming the 'ancient gift of the beast of old', as by fitting the old oracles with the new (1165), Heracles wins again his old victories over the beasts and can become the truly civilizing hero, worthy to be Zeus's son and 'best of men.' We witness Heracles' loss and then recovery of his humanity, and, as in the case of Oedipus, the process requires the confrontation with and the integration of the old and the new (cf. *Trach.* 1165 and *OT* 916).[26]

If Heracles' 'primitive self' here is his bestial lust and violence, then the 'more developed human self' is that which is capable of looking to the future and imagining and demanding the ethical ideal of courageous endurance.[27] The

---

[24] 'The Centaur and his gift belong to an earlier, more primitive world that still survives. Nessus lives in buried, remote strata of our being but can still return, symbolically as we would say, with unexpected virulence. Heracles has subdued this archaic world of bestial powers, but he has not entirely subdued the archaic bestiality within himself. The Centaur's poison, acting in concert with the heat of his own lust and his own anarchic impulses, brings it to life again': C. Segal (1981) 98–9. 'What we are witnessing is the terrible manifestation of love's power in the hideous physical form which expresses its true nature, disease. Heracles' fate is to be viewed as the direct outcome of his passion for Iole and Deianeira's passion for him': Seale (1982) 205. 'As the play unfolds, a very close connexion develops between *erōs*, the madness, the sickness of Heracles, the poison, and the violence of the beasts. In the Exodos, where the sickness of Heracles is presented on stage, we are shown the physical realization of an idea first presented as a metaphor: at 445–6 Deianeira describes the passion for Iole as "this *nosos*". And when Heracles repeatedly speaks of the *nosos* as a wild beast (974–5, 979–81, 987, 1026–30) we are reminded both of his encounters with Achelous and Nessus (9–21, 507–21, 565–8) and of his own violence (779–82)': Easterling (1982) 5. See also Biggs (1966) 229.

[25] Easterling (1982) ad 1089–106.

[26] C. Segal (1981) 99.

[27] There is 'a sudden glow of spirit in this hero of physical strength. His address to his *psyche* points to that inner world which is man's most distinctive possession and his sharpest point of differentiation from the beasts': ibid. 105.

'confronting' of these is then simply the re-emergence, from the bestial agony, of the demand for (human) courage; and, as Segal states, this comes from interpreting the oracles, for an animal is incapable of formulating a meaning, whereas the oracles point to some kind of coherence, however minimal and mysterious. But Segal claims too much for Heracles. This most physical of heroes, even in his recovery of his limited humanity, achieves, as we have seen, not a glimmer of awareness of his servitude to his animal self—still less does he renounce its evil. Segal also seems to imagine that Heracles' lustful motivations and spontaneous violence were somehow absent from his earlier labours and represent a falling off. Kane is similarly positive about Heracles' achievement, but in terms of a moral progression or evolution rather than a return to a former superior moral condition:

Heracles comes to his final labors by way of renouncing (or sublimating) the hedonistic motivation that has hitherto reconciled him to a life of struggle. . . . the hero's "laboring", detached from its earthly motive, purged of all but the most elementary self-interest, entails this consequence at last: the same acts which make the hero's immortalization physically possible also guarantee that he deserves it.[28]

But the 'hedonistic motivation' is less actively 'renounced' by Heracles than simply rendered impossible by the disintegration of his body. To be rendered incapable of lust is hardly to transcend it. Indeed, as we have seen, the hero's determination that no one else lie with Iole testifies to a continuing, though frustrated, sexual egotism. Nevertheless, that a moral (or at least brave) Heracles remains certainly provides evidence of a being of more substance and nobility than the Heracles submerged in his bodily desires. Easterling, unlike Segal and Kane, is justifiably chary of conceding Heracles a significant moral dimension, but

his special status has to be taken into account, and even if he is morally quite unlike the typical Sophoclean hero he is surely meant to command the audience's deep interest and at the end even their respect, when he speaks with a new kind of authority about the oracles and prepares to endure unflinchingly the extremes of pain. (1159–73, 1259–63)[29]

Seale, too, is right about Heracles, but he exaggerates the eclipse of the humane in misinterpreting Hyllus' position.

In the end Hyllus becomes a true son, and a divorce between human understanding and brute insensitivity is complete with the latter in the ascendancy at the end of the play. Nothing appears to be learnt from the painful process of revelation and what Heracles hands on to his son is not a new wisdom from suffering but his own heroic ideals.[30]

Certainly Hyllus acquiesces and even swears to obey his father, but he never approves of Heracles' demands or of his insensitivity about Deianeira.[31] On the other hand, that he subscribes to and has always subscribed to heroic ideals is unsurprising. No other ethic was available to him.

---

[28] Kane (1988) 210.
[29] Easterling (1982) 7. Heracles 'is in no position to take morally interesting decisions': ibid. 6.
[30] Seale (1982) 208.
[31] 'The absolute obligation this [i.e. Hyllus' oath] imposes on Hyllus is the only force strong enough to overcome his revulsion at Heracles' commands': Easterling (1982) ad 1181–90.

Heracles could not consistently renounce the evil of his animal self without renouncing with it the performance of the labours made possible by that very animal vitality. Heracles is not a rounded man; and his extraordinary achievements depend on an extraordinarily unbalanced nature.[32] One is reminded of Euripides' Heracles who cannot abandon the bow which is the symbol of his morally ambivalent capacities (*Her.* 1376–85). But Sophocles' hero is incapable of seeing this indisseverability of good and evil, so that, *pace* Segal, he cannot properly reclaim his title of 'truly civilizing hero' in so far as that would entail that the mind that performed the civilizing labours was itself civilized. During his physical agony what was human in Heracles was in partial eclipse. With the realization of the mysterious coherence of his destiny, that limited humanity returns, but it can scarcely be said to advance very far.

HERACLES' MORAL ISOLATION

Heracles' moral response is, like that of Ajax, very much a function of his self-absorption, though he seems less concerned than Ajax with vindicating himself before others. Ajax, we remember, was anxious about what his father would think, though, as we saw, this was in part a projection of what he himself thought. Heracles' moral resolve, in contrast, emerges entirely from his independent self-definition as a brave warrior. His (divine) father can supply no moral exemplar here. Nor does the hero appeal to his supreme *eugeneia*. Heracles is less interested in an audience than was Ajax, even though in his earlier weakness he cried out for his body to be exposed to public pity (1076–80). Indeed he is traditionally conceived as a loner by reason of his transcendent prowess. This does not prevent his depiction as a valued *philos*—one thinks of Theseus, Iolaus, and Philoctetes, and of Euripides' *Alcestis* and *Heracles*, in which Heracles' *philia* is a major theme. Still, the present Heracles is, if anything, even more of a loner than Ajax,[33] and a warrior whose prowess is so prodigious as really to need no assistance. The self-absorption of Sophocles' hero makes him a bad *philos*. Like Ajax, he seems to have no friends, and his treatment of his only available relative, his son Hyllus, is devoid of affection. Heracles and his wife never meet; nor is there any evidence that he has ever reciprocated her devoted love, even in the rather minimal manner required of an ancient Greek husband. Amphitryon is absent too, and the hero is alienated from his divine father who first punishes him (for the murder of Iphitus) (270–80) and then, as far as we can tell, abandons him precisely at the moment his son offers sacrifice to him (763–71). (Whether he redeems this neglect with an apotheosis is, as we have seen, uncertain.) Ironically enough,

---

[32] 'His *aretē* was indeed supreme: it was physical strength, endurance and courage carried to their highest physical point': Winnington-Ingram (1980) 84. 'But monstrous violence could only be put down by an answering excess of violence and by a man of peculiar and astounding quality for whom nothing counted except the cultivation and exercise of his abnormal strength and courage, his narrow traditional *aretē*. Yet it is the very qualities in virtue of which he can perform his function which bring about his undoing (ibid. 89).

[33] Heracles 'seems even more remote from humanity than Ajax': Biggs (1966) 228.

Heracles' closest intimate is the terrible *nosos* itself which he personifies as another monster akin to those he spent his life subduing (987, 1027–30, 1053–6).

Heracles' isolation is naturally reinforced and figuratively expressed by the overwhelming physical and mental pain that absorbs the whole of his consciousness.[34] In an orgy of self-pity, he cries out for others to pity him (1076–82), but he has to supply his own pity and direct it, self-reflexively, to his beloved and personified body parts (1089–100). When with his new understanding he is ready to issue instructions to his family (1143–50), he finds that his mother Alcmene and his other children are far away in Tiryns and Thebes (the physical remoteness again suggesting its psychological counterpart). Like Ajax, he sees his present son Hyllus as an extension of himself, and far from feeling affection or acknowledging *charis* he demands unswerving filial obedience (1175–8) and threatens that disobedience in 'little things' (σμικροῖς) (like marrying Iole) will nullify the *charis* that Hyllus has vowed to confer (1228–9). What he requires of his son is simply outrageous, as Hyllus himself indignantly protests (1233–7) and the ancient audience must have felt. The son is effectively required to kill his own father by burning him alive and to marry the woman who destroyed the lives of both his parents—a thing a man would do only if avenging spirits had driven him out of his mind (1191–237). Both Ajax and Heracles have their lonely confrontations with death. Ajax turns away from his concubine and son to die a solitary death, dramatically reinforced by his isolation on the stage, and Heracles denies himself any effective comfort from his son by reducing him to an instrument of his at once egotistical and yet strangely impersonal will. Both heroes fall back on their lonely heroic *aretē*.

Ajax and Heracles do, however, reach a degree of understanding. Ajax articulates his in the deception speech, but it involves no self-criticism and only confirms his will to die. The only understanding Heracles appears to attain is awareness of what he needs to do in approaching the climax he believes to be his death. Quite apart from the agonizing physical constraints under which Heracles' limited virtue can operate, it must also be exercised in a sort of ethical void. Ajax refuses to accept the conditions of life and in a way both defies Athena and gives her what she wants;[35] Heracles does accept life's conditions but he can take no comfort in accommodating himself to a world that cannot reciprocate his services, a world wherein his divine father, having punished him once, seems now to be abandoning him.[36] To the audience such an abandonment might well seem no more than fair recompense for Heracles' performance as a father and to reflect the logic of his character. He is unaware of any honour from Zeus, though, ironically, the play leaves open the possibility that he is about to receive the ultimate accolade. Though in a later incarnation to become a Stoic sage, this Heracles can take no comfort in accommodating himself to an immanent Logos. He remains, deservedly, alone as he has always been and thrown entirely upon his own resources and his own sense of self-worth. For we may ask, for whose benefit

---

[34] On the way in which the *nosos* isolates him from the world, see Biggs ibid.

[35] He remains unrepentant, but in dying he gratifies Athena's desire to punish him.

[36] 'Zeus, who is held responsible at the end of the play for all the havoc and misery the characters have endured, seems to stand for nothing more than a universe that endowed man with mind and will, only to put these at the mercy of his biological drives': Biggs ibid. 229.

is his new courage exerted? For there is little sense in this play of a heroic *community* (let alone a polis) in which honour can be enjoyed in this life or anticipated in Hades. As Segal observes, this is the only play of Sophocles in which a human community, the polis or the heroic society of warriors, does not exert strong pressure on the protagonists. Trachis is the vaguest of political entities (cf. 39–40). This is a play, not of cities, but of wild landscapes.[37] Cities here are either hopelessly distant, like Heracles' Tiryns, or objects of plunder, like Eurytus' Oechalia. While he is obviously highly honoured by the Greek community (e.g. 1112–13), he never actively enjoys this (significantly impersonal and loveless) honour because he makes no real contact with that community.

Heracles remains the lonely warrior who subscribes to an ideal of heroic courage based ultimately on community needs and values, but, as for Ajax and Homer's Achilles in his withdrawal, that ideal has shrunk to a purely selfish thing. Indeed, his 'morality' is of that most rudimentary kind that hardly extends to obligations to others and which, far from being consciously articulated (let alone rationally conceived), is little more than a felt need to be true to an equally rudimentary self-concept. That self-concept, however, is (rather ironically) based on conformity to a moral ideal.

THE PROBLEM OF AUDIENCE SYMPATHY

The Sophoclean Heracles is without a doubt the most brutal and unsympathetic of Greek tragic heroes. Ajax was brutal enough in his savage response to the Judgement of Arms, but he was mad, which meant that his naturally brutal tendencies were exaggerated. Moreover, Odysseus' pity, as we saw, set his behaviour in a sympathetic context—that of general human vulnerability. Ajax's reaction to Tecmessa's plea was brusque and peremptory, but in the deception speech he did at last admit to feeling some pity for her and for his son, even if he felt obliged to stifle it. Above all, because we saw him working through the implications of his dishonour and deliberating on an appropriate response, and later reflecting further on that response, the sheer engagement with his thinking was enough to hold our sympathy. Similarly, Shakespeare engages our sympathy for Macbeth by presenting him first as a decent and noble man and retains that sympathy by admitting us into his agonized deliberations, so that even when he deliberately invokes evil spirits, although we are morally aghast, we continue to feel for this man whose mind has been brought step by step to embrace evil in this way.

Heracles never embraces what he knows to be evil, but he preserves an unwavering and callous alienation from others that frequently borders on contempt. There is no Odysseus to frame his behaviour sympathetically. As we have seen, Heracles is a complete loner without peers, and though he has performed even greater services than Ajax, the absence of a normal social context for those services leaves us admiring them but without sympathy or affection for the hero

[37] C. Segal (1981) 62.

himself. Our dislike, and even revulsion, must of course be heavily qualified by his indescribable physical agonies, but even those agonies work, through their super-human scale, to set him apart from us. Moreover, there is little moral reflection with which an audience can engage. Heracles' options are so restricted that, as he sees it, like the Aeschylean Eteocles, he can only die bravely or die like a coward.

DEIANEIRA

Deianeira's decision to employ the salve to recover her husband's love produces the fulfilment of the play's two oracles. These oracles merely predict; they do not command. Moreover, they elicit no attempts to evade them, unlike in the *Tyrannus* where the prophecies contribute ironically to their own fulfilment. The oracles of the *Trachiniae* at most imply a mysterious coherence and presumably the working out of the will of Zeus. There is no strong sense of divine immanence (that is to say, nothing like the arrival of the Corinthian in the *Tyrannus*), let alone of divine commands of the kind we found in *Oresteia*. Deianeira faces a problem-atical decision because she finds herself confronted with her husband's infidelity, though combined with what seems to her at first a possible means of ending it forever. That such an apparent means exists is in part a product of Heracles' character. The poisonous salve itself is derived from the blood of the hydra, and is available only because Heracles killed the creature in the course of one of his famous Labours. Then it is another victim of Heracles, the centaur Nessus, who gives the salve to Deianeira in revenge for his fatal shooting at the hero's hands. In a sense then, Heracles' violence is doubly recoiling upon him when he dons the lethally anointed robe. But Deianeira only contemplates using the salve because of Heracles' characteristic lustful promiscuity. The hero's character then contributes in a number of ways to the existence of a situation which invites a decision.

The situation in which Deianeira finds herself is not presented to her as an impasse or a dilemma in which she is compelled to choose between two options where the consequences of both are absolutely clear and undisputed. That is to say, she does not face the sort of dilemma which Aeschylus' Agamemnon and Orestes face. Instead, the situation, more like that of Ajax, merely opens up the possibility of a decision to act rather than to remain passive. Ajax could not endure his humiliation; can Deianeira endure the loss of Heracles' love and her wifely status? Her problem is twofold: there is the practical question as to what will be the physical consequence of employing the salve (though the uncertainty attaching to that question carries moral responsibilities) and there is the moral question as to the rightness of interfering in her husband's life. Similarly for Ajax there was the practical question of how to restore his honour without undesired consequences such as helping his enemies. But the uncertainty about the practical outcome in Deianeira's case reflects also the general epistemological uncertainty which is a major theme of the play. This is reinforced by the language both Deianeira and the chorus use to discuss the issue.[38] Moreover, the inherent

---

[38] See Lawrence (1978) 297–8.

uncertainty of the human condition is, as in *Hamlet*, compounded by a human character plagued by an inability to operate decisively amid such uncertainty and in Deianeira's case intimidated by a strange and monstrous world. For Ajax, by contrast, the practical consequences were easy to foresee.

Deianeira always expects the worst (1–5). In her youth she was confronted with a terrifying suitor, the river-god Achelous, who presented himself in three intimidating forms so that she would have preferred to die rather than marry him (6–17). When Heracles came to save her from Achelous, his contest with the god was too terrifying to watch, and after they married she remained unhappy because of his constant absence on some labour or other. Deianeira is in every way the antitype of Heracles.[39] Neither god nor beast, she is thoroughly human. Her greatest virtue (in our modern eyes, at least) is perhaps compassion, and we see this in her extraordinary empathy with her rival Iole and her tolerance of Heracles' infidelities (436–49). But empathy is a two-edged sword. While it leads to broader understanding (as it might have done for Ajax), it can also vitiate moral judgement. Deianeira, in refusing to blame Heracles for his infatuation with Iole is exercising compassion inappropriately, especially since he appears to be intending to introduce a concubine into the marital home.[40] While one can sympathize with people who find themselves suddenly seized by desire, that is no reason to judge them innocent of the consequences of indulging the desire. Such passions may be attributed to Aphrodite, but the victims of the goddess are expected to resist, as the Euripidean Phaedra expects of herself (at *Hippolytus* 388 ff.) and Hecuba (at *Troades* 988) expects of Helen. In any case, Deianeira's sympathy is here severely strained, as the angry bitterness and jealousy— which she immediately censors as 'dishonourable' (οὐ γὰρ . . . καλόν, 552)—in the next scene show (531–53).[41] Furthermore, she is critical of other vices such as wilful deception from which we can infer that she considers the agent responsible in such cases (449–54). Her compassionate understanding then does not induce her to discount moral responsibility in any theoretical sense. On the contrary, when she catches herself in an act of deception she will hold herself fully responsible for the disastrous consequences. She wants to let her husband off because she loves him.

Though she is unwilling to blame her husband, she is nevertheless anxious to recover not only his erotic fidelity (one hesitates to call it 'love') but also—what is perhaps at least if not more important—her position in the *oikos* (550–1).[42] She could simply accept the situation, but that would empty her life of meaning. So she

---

[39] McCall (1972) 143–55 has a good discussion of her character in the context of Heracles as her antitype.

[40] Deianeira mistakenly believes that Iole reciprocates Heracles' passion (444). On her refusal to be (or at least to admit to being) angry with her husband, Harris (2001) 266 comments that she is contrasted with the negative female stereotype.

[41] Gibert (1995) 97–9 attributes Deianeira's change of attitude to Aphrodite whose power is celebrated in the intervening ode. If so, this is not a personalized Aphrodite with a specific purpose (as in *Hippolytus*), but little more than the personification of sexual love, as Gibert's comment (ibid. 99) about Nessus' harnessing her power implies. One might see Deianeira as torn by a struggle in which compassion is defeated by jealousy

[42] Faraone (1994) 120–1. Carawan (2000) 203–4. *Pace* various critics (e.g. Conacher [1997] 30), line 444 supplies the only evidence in the play that Deianeira feels *eros* rather than just *philia* for Heracles. Otherwise we know that she admires him (176–7) and that she is anxious for his return.

anoints the robe. But she brings her misgivings to the chorus. First of all, she wants nothing to do with 'evil and bold acts' (κακὰς ... τόλμας, 582) and she hates those women who perpetrate them (583), but she has anointed the robe because she wants to win her husband back (584–6). She is obviously afraid then that what she contemplates is indeed a bold and evil act, and she wants the chorus' advice. If they think her contemplated action is 'rash' (μάταιον, 587) she will proceed no further. Since μάταιος can mean 'rash' in either a moral or a purely practical sense, the nature of her uncertainty is less than transparent. The context—her hatred of 'bold and evil acts'—would suggest the moral sense, but the chorus' answer implies the practical. They would see no objection provided 'there are grounds for confidence in what is being done' (πίστις ἐν τοῖς δρωμένοις, 588), that is if she has good reason to think that the salve will work. That the chorus are referring to practical considerations is confirmed by their assertion that the only way to find out is to try it (592–3), for that is hardly the way to test the *morality* of an action. Deianeira's response to this is an implicit acceptance of their position and a decision to go ahead (594–5). The chorus have done nothing to allay her moral uncertainty (though she may wrongly assume that they have done so implicitly), and have in effect foolishly encouraged her to throw caution to the winds. We see here how, in her overwhelming desire for the salve to work, Deianeira has ignored all moral and practical considerations, and, unlike the familiar self-legislating Sophoclean protagonist (and, incidentally, like Agamemnon in the carpet scene), has allowed others to validate a dangerous desire. It was not at all clear that a wife should in principle interfere thus in her husband's life, and it was morally irresponsible not to have thought about the possibility that the salve might have some other, undesirable and perhaps fatal effect. This wilful moral blindness under the pressure of a strong desire is reminiscent of Neoptolemus in the opening scene of *Philoctetes.*

Faraone, on the other hand, contends that Deianeira *is* aware of the basically poisonous nature of the charm, because when she initially describes it she refers to it as clotted blood dyed by poisonous gall (572–4). Faraone infers from this that Deianeira sees no risk if the dosage is low.[43] It is suprising then that she does not explicitly rationalize her employment of the salve in this way, but in any case she disregards this implicit warning. Carawan, like Faraone, insists that Deineira is aware of the poisonous basis of the salve but goes on to claim that '[t]he reason for her apprehensiveness is plainly revealed in the record of erotic magic: such remedies work by causing pain and suffering. . . . The effective agent was usually a known toxin, intended to weaken the victim and thus render him compliant. . . . she clearly realizes that the blood is tainted with the venom . . . and that poison is the essential ingredient.'[44]

Does she, however, make that connection, obvious though it may be to an unengaged observer? Since she never betrays the slightest awareness or concern about such possible suffering, it seems more likely that she is unaware or, as it

---

[43] Faraone (1994) 123.

[44] Carawan (2000) 207. Contrast Gellie (1972) 65: Magic was prohibited by Athenian law, but Deianeira's response contrasts with Clytemnestra's: 'Magic to her is the harmless way . . . The only expedient left for her that stops short of Clytemnestra's axe is magic, which to her knowledge will hurt no one.'

were, 'in denial'. Therefore it is not the case that she 'acts with the knowledge that she will do grievous injury . . . and in this knowledge lies the burden of guilt'.[45] That Deianeira would proceed with such knowledge is completely out of character. The last thing she wants to do is to harm the man she loves. Her apprehensiveness, as her words tell us, concerns her reputation and ultimately her moral integrity.

Deianeira then, like Neoptolemus under the influence of Odysseus in *Philoctetes*, is prepared to fudge the moral issue, allowing the end to justify the means, provided that all's well that ends well.[46] She does not specifically *argue* that what she sees as the probable success of the attempt morally justifies the interference; her emotional commitment to the successful outcome is sufficient. Here the gap is exposed between morality and reputation, as she is prepared to do what is 'shameful' (αἰσχρά) provided she does not suffer the 'shame' (αἰσχύνη) of discovery (596–7). But while it may be relatively easy to forget that we have performed an irresponsible action if the consequences are neutral or positive, when disaster results we are particularly hard on ourselves. So, once Deianeira is convinced that disaster is imminent, she cannot bear to live with the evil reputation she will incur, not because her ultimate concern is reputation but because she is a woman who sets great store by her moral integrity (721–2). The earlier fudging was a temporary moral lapse of which she is now all too painfully aware. (Again Neoptolemus springs to mind.) Thus the gap between virtue and reputation closes again. She does not want to be thought of as a bad woman (κακή, 722) because that will reflect the truth as she now clearly sees it. Once she is convinced of the salve's lethal effects she has no hesitation in resorting to suicide.

CONCLUSION

Heracles has always defined himself implicitly by his unique physical capacities and morally in terms of the values of the heroic warrior. Now that his body is disintegrating around him, only the heroic value of courageous endurance remains available to him, So he resolves to endure his agonies bravely, and in view of his confined situation the play surely implicitly validates this aspect at least of his moral response. We can say therefore that he is intuitively aware of his (conventional) moral obligations to himself, but, as we have seen, his relations with others are more morally problematical. We can say too that his moral awareness is severely limited in that he lacks any understanding of the qualities in his own nature which contributed to his plight. As to the emotional aspect of his moral reflections, his major challenge is to abandon self-pity and to 'screw his courage to the sticking place'.

Deianeira implicitly defines herself in conventional terms as a 'good' aristocratic woman who is morally obliged not to engage in acts such as would endanger or compromise her husband. So, while her morality is appropriate in the play's

---

[45] Carawan (2000) 229.

[46] 'The passage is a masterpiece of half advice, half assent, half decision': Lattimore (1964) 33.

terms, in her desire to recover her husband, she temporarily abandons that morality when she fails to consider the moral implications of her proposed action. At the same time she renders herself wilfully ignorant of both the facts of the situation (the nature of the salve), as far as these can be known, and the probable consequences of available courses of action. As for her emotions, she allows her desire for the salve to work to override serious moral and practical reflection.

8

Sophocles: *Oedipus Tyrannus*

APOLLO AND OEDIPUS' RADICAL IGNORANCE

Oedipus at Thebes faces two major crises: the plague resulting from the pollution caused by Laius' murder and the eventual revelation of his true identity. The plague is, on one level, an intellectual problem, but it presents also a moral challenge to an agent in Oedipus' position whose kingly role requires him to muster the necessary resourcefulness to obtain the knowledge sought. Of course, for a man of Oedipus' temperament this is scarcely a challenge at all. But as the investigation proceeds and the investigator begins to suspect the worst, the moral challenge turns out instead to be summoning the courage to face the truth (though once he suspects what this truth is, Oedipus at once insists on knowing it) and to respond appropriately. Oedipus, like Aeschylus' Eteocles, will have to accept that, despite his basic moral innocence, he is an object of loathing to the gods, although the question of his death will be for him to decide.

Oedipus, for all his confidence in his investigative powers, is more radically ignorant than any other tragic protagonist, in that his whole life is constructed on a monstrous lie. Eteocles at least knew that the gods were out to destroy his family, though he put it from his mind until the climax of the shield scene; so when he was finally forced to face the imminent fulfilment of his destiny he was confronting nothing radically new or unsuspected. Oedipus, on the other hand, in spite of receiving an oracle that declared that he would kill his father and marry his mother, seems unaware at first of the immanent involvement of the god Apollo in his life.[1] He has been able to persuade himself, more or less, in his rationalistic way, that he could avoid and has avoided the prophecy's fulfilment. The divine will ought to be partially manifest to Oedipus both through that oracle and through the direct oracular command to find the murderer at the beginning of the play. But Oedipus has yet to discover the extent to which the divine purpose is thwarting and will continue to thwart his own moral and intellectual purpose while pushing his investigation in directions he neither foresees nor intends.

With the best will in the world moral action is impossible without knowledge of the circumstances in which action is required, but in the world of the *Tyrannus* knowledge is the property of the god Apollo who releases it when and how he pleases. Man is not here the measure, for this is not the philosopher's world in

---

[1] On the god's involvement in the play see Ch. 2, 'Panoramic intervention', and Lawrence (2008) *passim*.

which the knowing human subject is conveniently matched with the object to be known. This is not, that is to say, a world in all respects conformable to reason,[2] though Oedipus investigates it as if it were. What else can a human being do?

Personal morality relates closely to that form of knowledge which is perhaps quintessential for us—knowledge of self. And since the self is part of the world, understanding oneself and understanding the world are interdependent. Self-definition in turn relates to social class and, more specifically, to our place or role within that class. Sophoclean protagonists are characteristically highly self-conscious about their parentage and social background, and their noble birth (*eugeneia*) provides a strong spur to virtuous action.[3] For all of them, save Oedipus, this *eugeneia* is unproblematical. Oedipus, however, grew to manhood with a spurious identity, though with the temporary compensation of being considered 'very great' (μέγιστος, 776) as, it seemed, the natural son and heir of Polybus and Merope, the king and queen of Corinth.

OEDIPUS' SELF-SEARCH BEGINS

This identity, however, was challenged by a drunken guest at a royal party and Oedipus began to brood about it (βαρυνθείς, 781). The next day he interrogated his parents (ἤλεγχον, 783: a Socratic term) and was temporarily reassured by their response—anger at the man who had made the remark (783–5)—a reaction which Oedipus presumably took as a denial of the aspersion. It is interesting to note, however, that Oedipus prefaces his account of this brief but obviously pivotal episode with the observation that it was strange, though not worth the serious attention (σπουδῆς) which he gave it (777–8). Now if he can say *that*, after all the ensuing distress over the oracle's prediction of parricide and incest, he can only mean that he should have taken no notice of the aspersion cast on his birth because it was not true; and indeed when he informs Jocasta of these events he entertains no doubts whatever that Polybus and Merope are his real parents.[4] And yet without the interrogation of the oracle, which was the consequence of his anxious concern, he would never have learned of the supposed need to avoid Corinth. The reassurance he took from his adoptive parents' response, however, was all too brief and he could not get the subject out of his mind (786).

So he travelled to Delphi to enquire of the god, but was denied the honour of a direct reply (ἄτιμον, 789);[5] instead he was informed of his destiny to commit parricide and incest (787–93). His response was natural enough but not, strictly speaking, rational, for his doubts about his parentage evaporated in the horror of what he had heard and he resolved at all costs to avoid contact with Polybus and

---

[2] This lack of conformability to reason is reflected in the riddling and ambiguous language of the play. See e.g. Vernant and Vidal-Naquet (1988) and C. Segal (1988) *passim*.

[3] See e.g. Kirkwood (1958) 177.

[4] When he asks Teiresias who his parents are, is this a plot contrivance or sign of a buried uneasiness?

[5] Oedipus was touchy about his status: for which see Gregory (1995) 143.

Merope (794–7).[6] He then made his way to the triple crossroads, between identities, as it were, but, as we shall see, with a lingering sense of his royal status. There he killed the man who was in fact his father together with (he supposed and continues to suppose) his entire entourage (798–813).

AT THE TRIPLE CROSSROADS

In making moral judgements about his performance at the crossroads we have to assume that Oedipus' account of the actual sequence of events and of the threat Laius' party constituted to his own life is completely unbiased, and dramatic convention does indeed justify that assumption; otherwise Sophocles would need to supply us with a conflicting and more convincing version of what happened, or at least allow Oedipus to provide us with information open to a interpretation less favourable to him.[7] Although the episode occurred before the action of the play, it is relevant to Oedipus' moral history, particularly since the qualities he displayed are displayed again in the course of his investigation and are relevant to our appraisal of his performance.

According to Oedipus then, as he approached Laius' party,

> I was met by a herald and a man riding in a wagon ... and the leader and the old man himself tried to drive me from the road by force. In anger I struck the driver, the man who was trying to turn me back; and when the old man saw it, he waited till I was passing his chariot, and struck me right on the head with his double-pointed goad. Yet he paid the penalty with interest (οὐ μὴν ἴσην γ᾽ ἔτεισεν, 810); in a word, this hand struck him with a stick, and he rolled backwards right out of the wagon, and I killed them all.
>
> (802–13: tr. Lloyd-Jones)

The pattern is clear: Oedipus twice reacts (or overreacts) to provocation.[8]

Now, according to R. D. Griffith, since Laius' rank and age were apparent to Oedipus, he should have given way to the king.[9] He should, moreover, have respected the inviolability of a herald whose function would have been apparent from the staff or *caduceus* which he must surely have been carrying.[10] But by the time Oedipus laid hands on him he (Oedipus) was fighting for his life. Gregory, on

---

[6] Gregory, ibid. 143, argues that in avoiding specifically Corinth (794) Oedipus thought it most likely that his real parents (whoever they were) were to be found there. Kane (1975) relates Oedipus' reaction to his besetting tendency to assume that he knows when he does not: 'The parricide occurred not simply because Oedipus did not know where he stood but because he insisted on acting as if he did know': ibid. 190. 'While the hero himself perceives no connection between the two events juxtaposed in his narrative (the oracle and the fatal meeting at the crossroads), the audience sees that the second event, *qua* parricide, was the consequence of the first, and thus that invisible lines of force extend between them': ibid. 196.

[7] As e.g. Menelaus corrects Agamemnon's account of the dilemma at Aulis and his own reaction to it in Euripides' *IA* (87–103, 337–62).

[8] There is a vagueness about the number of people involved. Are the herald and the leader one and the same? The driver is presumably distinct from the herald against whom Oedipus does not use violence in the first instance. (When he 'kills them all' the situation has changed significantly.)

[9] R. D. Griffith (1992) 197–9.

[10] Ibid. 200.

the other hand, thinks that Oedipus would have had no way of knowing Laius' rank since the king 'was not accompanied by the sizable retinue appropriate to an *aner archegetes*'[11] (contrast Eur. *Phoen.* 40), while Oedipus had been accustomed to think of himself as Corinth's future king. But one might have expected a man distinguished for his high intelligence to have drawn some pertinent inferences, if only from the sheer fact of Laius' riding in a wagon. Oedipus then acted with his usual impulsiveness.[12] Laius naturally retaliated with a blow to Oedipus' head, but Oedipus gave more than he got (810). He was now doubtless in mortal danger and obliged to 'kill them all' (813).

Now in the Attic law of the time of the play's performance (and thus a relevant criterion of judgement in the eyes of the original audience) self-defence 'was a mitigating circumstance in a case of intentional homicide, rather than grounds for lawful homicide...Yet Oedipus does not argue self-defense, claiming, as he would have to do, that Laius was about to kill him, stating in fact that on this occasion Laius wanted only to drive him from the road (805).'[13]

Oedipus' impulsive character then was an obvious contributor to the road rage incident, but his moral responsibility is greatly disproportionate to the consequences since he was acting out of unavoidable ignorance of Laius' identity as his father and in circumstances in which violence had escalated to a point where his life was in danger.[14] And in any case, Oedipus' overwhelming concern in this narrative is not with his moral responsibility for the massacre but with whether he may have killed Laius.[15]

OEDIPUS' INTELLECTUAL, EMOTIONAL, AND MORAL IDENTITY

On arrival in Thebes, Oedipus solved the riddle of the Sphinx. We are told little of the circumstances. We do not know whether he acted out of that compassion which he later displays for the sufferings of the Thebans or merely from the pleasure of applying his intellect to the challenge of solving a riddle.[16] In any case, he was not only adopted by the Thebans but chosen to be their king. When we

---

[11] Gregory (1995) 145.   [12] Griffith (1992) 200–1.   [13] Ibid. 196–7.

[14] Harris (2001) 172 thinks that an ancient audience would have looked unfavourably on Oedipus' angry overreactions. On the conventional irascibility of rulers see ibid. 230. Landfester (1990) 62 thinks that suffering in the play is entirely the result of the abuse of human freedom, but this is to underestimate Apollo's contribution. Similarly, Erbse (1993) 60 blames Oedipus for killing a man who could have been his father and marrying a woman who could have been his mother.

[15] The nature of Oedipus' *hamartia* as I have described it here harmonizes with the view of Rorty (1992*b*) 10. Moreover, the 'cancer that lies at the heart of the tragic protagonist's *hamartia* often involves his not knowing who he is, his ignorance of his real identity. To know who one is is to know how to act: it involves understanding of one's obligations and what is important in one's interactions. The kind of ignorance that literally involves not knowing one's family is particularly dangerous because it affects all of a person's sacred, political and ethical conduct': ibid. 11. See also Sherman (1992) 178. 'Oedipus acts out of an ignorance that is stultifying. There is little he contributed to bring it on, and little he could have done at critical moments to come to an earlier recognition': ibid. 189.

[16] The priest refers to his 'enthusiasm': προθυμίας (48).

meet him at the beginning of the play, he is thoroughly identified with his supposedly adoptive people, having severed, it would seem, all relations with the Corinthians. He is now identified, intellectually, morally, and emotionally, with his role as king of Thebes. His moral allegiance therefore, unlike that of the majority of Sophoclean heroes, is profoundly political. As the play proceeds, though, we become aware of a strong bond with his immediate family, first with Jocasta and later with his daughters, though that family is, as far as he is aware, a comparatively recent creation. Ironically enough, he feels too a kind of bond with the dead Laius as his predecessor as king and husband (245, 258–68). His supposed Corinthian parents, Polybus and Merope, are to be shunned in terror and almost blotted out of memory because of the prophecy.

Thus Oedipus' identity has been a fluid thing, and remains so until the revelation. Indeed, instead of the customary heroic appeal to *eugeneia*, he has forged his own identity himself through those moral and intellectual qualities which, in lieu of a conventional social self-definition, will come to seem his essential self—and a more durable self for the manner in which it is formed.[17] When, later in the play, he comes to entertain the possibility that he may be of ignoble birth, he is unconcerned; if he is the child of Fortune that is nothing to be depressed about.[18]

Oedipus' emotional engagement with his people emerges powerfully in his opening speech and at once appears as the source of his moral motivation. A common feature of Sophoclean heroes is a self-conscious moral commitment (derived from an awareness of their noble birth or *eugeneia*) to be true to their natures as expressed through certain virtues (such as courage or filial piety). This attitude is naturally linked with a concern with honour carried sometimes to the point of obsession. But Oedipus, though proud of his accomplishments, is, for a Greek hero, unusually strong in the 'other-regarding' virtues which are accorded particular emphasis in modern ethical thinking. This other-regarding quality is apparent in Oedipus' 'paternal' role (τέκνα, 1, 6; cf. παῖδες, 58), in his decision to converse with the suppliants in person (6–7), in his desire to help in any way he can (11–12), and in his declared pity (12–13), a feeling of which, unlike Ajax, he is unashamed. Even more striking is his total identification with the problem and with the people's distress, for he suffers individually as they do, though collectively too as the king who represents them (59–64). Characteristically, his distress is accompanied by constructive thought (65 ff.) and, as he will presently display, a moral determination to act ('I would be a knave if I failed to do all that the god reveals,' 76–7). This attitude wins our sympathy and strong moral approval. Oedipus has successfully forged a new identity together with the moral and emotional concern for his people that befits a king.

But Oedipus' pride in his own intelligence and resourcefulness emerges strongly too in this first speech ('I called Oedipus, famous to all': 8). He defines himself unconventionally in terms of his qualities of mind, somewhat like the Homeric Odysseus, though that hero was more distinguished for creative mendacity than

---

[17] 'Oedipus' nobility is broader and less definable than that of any of the others [i.e. Sophoclean protagonists]. He might be said to be his own ideal, inasmuch as his nobility consists of his undeterrable and fearless insistence on knowing himself, even to the last horrifying detail': Kirkwood (1958) 179.

[18] The idea of being a child of fortune 'would have terrified any other man': Knox (1957) 30.

for discovering the truth. But Oedipus' finest quality must surely be his intellectual honesty, a fearless devotion to truth and its moral implications, whatever the cost to his self-concept or honour. Oedipus' intellectual honesty is actually more impressive than his intellect per se, for his deductive powers can be vitiated by the very swiftness of a mind that jumps to not entirely irrational, but still false conclusions (such as his suspicions concerning Teiresias and Creon) on which he is prepared to act without adequate investigation. However, once apprised of error, he fully acknowledges it and takes the consequences.

When Oedipus arrives in person to meet the suppliant delegation led by the priest, he comes with the best will in the world, inspired by compassionate, even paternal, love and supreme self-confidence. He loves his people and suffers with them. He would do everything in his power to relieve them of their affliction, as he, the famous Oedipus, did before when he rid them of the Sphinx (1, 5–13, 58–67). And it would seem he is the only man who can help. His credentials are impeccable, if unusual. He is no doctor, but neither is he a religious expert, or at least not officially, like Teiresias. He did, however, solve the riddle of the Sphinx, apparently by a kind of intelligent intuition involving a degree of divine inspiration, if we can believe the priest who emphasizes that Oedipus 'had nothing to go on' (35–9).[19] And in the Apolline world of the play a mental faculty that connects directly with divinity has much to recommend it. It appears then that the powers attributed (correctly or otherwise) to Oedipus here are intuitive rather than rationally deductive; which is remarkable, considering that his approach to finding the murderer will be more deductive than intuitive. Intuition, associated again with divine inspiration, will re-emerge with the self-blinding. Oedipus' mind is not therefore exclusively secular and rationalistic, though in his angry and arrogant tirade against Teiresias he will contrast his own seemingly autonomous intellectual powers favourably with the inspiration of the seer (398). Rather it would appear that he has forgotten or implicitly denies in that scene the divine contribution (as the priest saw it) to his solution of the riddle. Oedipus is not naturally inclined to irreligion. The whole quest for the killer is based on a pious acceptance of Apollo's existence and will—a fact that should be remembered if we are tempted to see Oedipus as a pure example of the sophistic rationalist. Oedipus feels at times the nearness of his god and their active cooperation, but he is inclined to forget it and he has yet to learn the extent and profundity of their relationship.

THE SEARCH FOR LAIUS' KILLER: OEDIPUS AND APOLLO

With Creon's return from Delphi with 'good news' (87), Oedipus can proceed with his investigation. But he depends entirely upon the god whose instructions he must now carry out. There can be no 'scientific' investigation of the plague itself which is but a kind of spontaneous or 'natural' symptom and therefore sign of the

---

[19] Cf. 34: δαιμόνων συναλλαγαῖς. 'But hidden encounters with divinities everywhere mock that success on which the Priest here congratulates him': Knox (1957) 233.

miasma. Instead Oedipus needs to go beyond the pollution and its purely physical expression to its inner meaning which has a sort of personal dimension—personal because an anthropomorphic, though deeply mysterious, divinity presides over it. Apollo, it turns out, requires the death or exile of Laius' murderers (100–1; αὐτοέντας, 107), which only presents Oedipus with a new problem: the identity of the killers. But at least the solution of this new problem will require empirical evidence, and, whatever may have been the form of intelligence he employed in the solution of the riddle, Oedipus now operates by secular rationality.[20] It seems that the god wishes to present the man with a mystery that naturally invites recourse to the rational powers of which he is proud, with the purpose of demonstrating to him the inherent limitations of those powers.

Oedipus wonders where on earth the killers are and where a trace of the crime committed long ago can be found (108–9). (The information supplied by the oracle would seem dauntingly spare.) Creon, who appears guardedly optimistic (110–11), tells him that the killers are to be found in Thebes and that the murder occurred when Laius was abroad. Oedipus, now warming to the challenge of investigation (120–1),[21] asks about witnesses, but there was only one and in his fright he could give only one piece of information, that Laius was killed by robbers—not one, but many (122–3). Thus the oracle, at least as reported by Creon, and the survivor's information conspire to mislead concerning the number of killers.[22] Oedipus, speaking perhaps generically, though with unconscious irony, responds as though Creon had referred to a single robber (ὁ λῃστής, 124).

Oedipus speculates that no robber would have dared to kill a king unless someone in Thebes had paid him, and he cannot comprehend why no investigation was conducted at the time (124–9). At any rate, he is confident of success now: 'Well, I shall begin again and light up the obscurity. Phoebus is right, and you are right, to show this concern on behalf of the dead man, so that you shall see me also justly fighting for him, and defending the cause of this country and of the god' (132–6: tr. Lloyd-Jones).

This is a declaration utterly characteristic of Oedipus in both its boundless self-confidence and its moral dedication, but he seems to assume that Apollo, having issued his oracle, intends to make no further contribution to the process of discovery, and that now his own wits must complete the job. (This means that from this point on Oedipus assumes a universe conformable to reason as far as concerns his investigations.) But if, like a kind of physician, he is to remedy the city's illness (217), he needs first of all a clue (τι σύμβολον, 221); and, since the investigation will have to proceed by eliciting information from various people, his logical course will be to enquire of those who would be willing to tell and to intimidate those who would not. And so the ensuing proclamation (223–45,

---

[20] On the nature and imagery of Oedipus' investigative process, see the comprehensive exploration, in Knox (1957) 107–58. 'The tightly organized and relentless process by which Oedipus finds his way to the truth is presented by the language of the play as an equivalent of the activity of man's mind in almost all its aspects; it is the investigation by the officer of the law who identifies a criminal, the series of diagnoses by the physician who identifies the disease, and it is also the working out of a mathematical problem which ends with the establishment of a true equation': ibid. 150–1.

[21] Note the recurrence of the term προθυμίας: cf. 48.

[22] Cf. 292: τινων ὁδοιπόρων.

252–68) and the accompanying curse (269–75)[23] that he now brings down unwittingly upon himself are in the circumstances (and of course ironically) a perfectly rational way of eliciting information.[24] Not only that. Oedipus sees proclamation and curse as a powerful statement of ethico-religious commitment, a mark of his 'alliance' with the god and with Laius (as the murdered king's avenger) (244–5). Oedipus is indeed more than a secular rationalist.

We gain a disturbing insight here into the way in which Apolline reality thwarts not only the investigative intelligence but indeed the positive ethico-religious will. Instead of advancing straightforwardly and systematically, as he believes, towards the solution of an intellectual problem (the identity of the killer), Oedipus is only aggravating his own future sufferings. The apparently rational means are absurdly discordant with the actual ends, and yet Oedipus *is* advancing inexorably towards the truth, though by a kind of anti-logic.[25] The situation is, in essence, similar to that faced in the *Seven* by Eteocles who exercises his ethico-religious sensitivity in the shield scene but is unaware of how precisely that sensitivity is being employed by Apollo and the Erinys to fulfil his malign destiny. In the *Tyrannus* it is important to realize that Apollo is active behind the scenes pursuing a purpose; he is decidedly not merely a convenient symbol for the events of the play viewed as 'a natural result of an interaction between character, circumstances in the past, and mere chance combinations in the present.'[26]

For all his confidence in his investigative powers, Oedipus could make little progress with the evidence obtainable from secular human sources. What he does manage to glean is itself uncertain (robbers or travellers?) and misleading (there was in fact only one traveller). Meanwhile he is forced to consult another divine source, Teiresias; and, because he naturally operates on the secular level of rational investigation, the net result is that he is sidetracked from the issue of the killer(s) to the theory of a conspiracy between the seer and Creon and provoked into reopening the question of his parentage ('Wait! Who is my father?': 437). Ironically, Oedipus has by the end of the scene received the answer to his question, but he cannot accept it, in part because of the cryptic way in which the information is conveyed, but more due to the outrageous content of the revelation, which is even harder to accept because it does not emerge in a logical manner as the end-product of an empirical investigation.[27] Oedipus sets great store by knowing, but he is yet to experience knowledge as other than liberating. Teiresias, on the other

---

[23] I am assuming the spuriousness of 246–51.The earlier part of the speech is not strictly a curse but a declaration punctuated by imperative language.

[24] With the curse he unwittingly becomes his father's avenger: McHardy (2008) 101.

[25] 'Human knowledge is actively sought and willed as the achievement of man's intellectual power. The divine knowledge comes, it seems, by chance, on precarious and unpredictable paths': C. Segal (2001) 68.

[26] Ibid. 54. While Apollo certainly does not force or predetermine Oedipus' responses, nor does he passively observe the actions of a free agent, as seems implied by Dodds (1988) 41. Vernant and Vidal-Naquet (1988) 105–6 puts it better: 'at the end of the road that he [Oedipus], despite and against everyone has followed, he finds that even while it was from start to finish he who pulled the strings it is he who from start to finish has been duped'.

[27] Commenting on Oedipus' reaction to the eventual revelation, Knox (1957) 19 observes: 'His understanding of what happened to him must be a complete rational structure before he can give way to the tide of emotion which will carry him to self-mutilation.'

hand, feels the burden of an unprofitable knowledge (316–18), though to Oedipus his refusal to speak is not 'lawful' (ἔννομ') but 'unfriendly to the city which nurtured him' (322–3).

It is characteristic of Oedipus to feel a strong moral obligation where he feels a strong emotional commitment, and so he feels passionate anger towards the seer whom he considers a traitor (330–6). Teiresias' position though is strangely paradoxical through his possession of more than human knowledge. Is it wrong of him to withhold what he knows? There is no reason to think that he is privy in detail to Apollo's purpose and intended action behind the scenes, as it were. He wishes he had never come, but his coming is clearly part of the god's purpose, for without it Jocasta would never make her important reference to the triple cross-roads in her attempt to discredit prophecy. Oedipus considers his refusal to speak cowardly and inexplicable, since (as the prophet himself says) the truth is destined to come out in any case (341–2). Teiresias, however, is referring to Apollo's role in bringing it to light in his own way rather than directly through Oedipus' investigation. It is as if he feels that, in view of the god's close involvement in events, his own actions are finally irrelevant, so he wishes to avoid immediate unpleasantness for himself and for Oedipus (320–33).

Ironically, the truth emerges more readily precisely when Oedipus gets side-tracked from his rational investigation. His angry and irrational outburst (345–9) is not of course intended as a finely calculated ploy for eliciting the truth from Teiresias, but such is its effect, and at this point, precisely when Oedipus unconsciously abandons reason in this way, the identity of the murderer comes to light (350–3). Naturally he is incredulous, hearing only a cryptic statement of a fact that will be credible only when he has finally tracked it down by his own deductive methods.[28] Humanly accessible knowledge requires a context to render it intelligible. Meanwhile it is altogether understandable that Oedipus should fly into a rage, lose faith in Teiresias, contrast his own mental powers favourably with divination, and infer the existence of a conspiracy between the seer and Creon who stands to gain if Oedipus is discredited (354–403). And yet the more obvious flaw in this theory, which otherwise does seem the only rational explanation of Teiresias' accusations, is its highly implausible assessment of the characters of both men.[29]

To this assessment of his character Creon responds in the next scene. He offers the sort of sober and rational defence which should appeal to a man of Oedipus' cast of mind, but Oedipus is too angry to listen; instead he is diverted still further from his investigation into a slanging match with his brother-in-law which appears irrelevant to the investigation while provoking the further diversion of Jocasta's intervention. Then, and in response to Oedipus' misguided

---

[28] 'The kind of knowledge which is involved must be arrived at by detours; the revelation must be piecemeal': Seale (1982) 228. Bain (1993) *passim* defends Oedipus' failure to grasp the truth.

[29] Kane (1975) 191 comments that Oedipus 'substitutes reasoning for perception. Having drawn an intelligent deduction from what he sees, he is quick to treat this deduction as a manifest fact.' At ibid. 192 he cites Teiresias on Oedipus' failure to perceive (413–14, 415–16, 421–2, 424). Ironically, it is Teiresias' reference to Apollo's process of revelation which, through a misunderstanding, provokes Oedipus' conspiracy theory: Seale (1982) 225. Oedipus' suspicions are also plausible on his empirical level of operation. As he asks Creon, why did Teiresias not denounce Oedipus at the time of Laius' death (568)?

condemnation of the seer (and not to any enquiry arising out of his systematic investigation), Jocasta alludes *en passant* to the triple crossroads, the scene of Laius' murder (716), in the course of a story designed to prove the worthlessness of prophecy (at least as communicated by human agents) (707–10, 857–8). Oedipus at once compares his own experience at the crossroads to what Jocasta can tell him about Laius' appearance and entourage (729–54).[30] Could *he* be Laius' killer? (744–5).

The reference to the incident is necessary if Oedipus is to be motivated to summon the Theban survivor, which in turn is essential for the revelation (754–65, 834–62). The whole investigation is in fact a kind of sham instigated by Apollo. Its result, and thus presumably its purpose, is (as was suggested above) to invite Oedipus to use his rational investigative powers. But the truth which Oedipus is required to uncover is humanly inaccessible without the incursion into the investigation of events beyond his contrivance. And Oedipus' rationality, already undermined by anger, is now further undermined by terror. Keyed up by all kinds of distress, he ceases, like a rational (ἔννους, 916) person, to judge the present by the past (911–17). The 'helmsman' (κυβερνήτην, 923) is losing the control which was always in fact illusory. Jocasta too has succumbed to irrationality, for in her insistence that the survivor of the massacre cannot retract his statement she unaccountably hopes that persistence in a falsehood publicly proclaimed can somehow protect them from the unwelcome truth (848–50).

With the information concerning the triple crossroads that has fallen to him, as it would seem, accidentally, Oedipus has been able to continue his enquiries by sending for the survivor. Jocasta, in her concern for the now scarcely rational Oedipus, prays to Apollo for deliverance (911–23) and that comes in the shape of the Corinthian with his 'good' (934) news. This arrival is yet another event quite outside the control of Oedipus' investigation, and, as an ironical reply to the prayer, has rightly been adjudged strong evidence of Apolline activity. Deliverance will indeed come, but for the *city* and not in the form desired.[31] Moreover, with the Corinthian's arrival Oedipus can pick up his investigations again, though this time taking up a different thread.

Oedipus' anxiety about the predicted parricide finds immediate release (974) with the news that Polybus is dead, so the king can now join his wife in discounting divination (946–9, 964–75), that is until he remembers the prophesied marriage with his mother (976–88). As the Corinthian messenger sets about reassuring him on that score too he releases a veritable torrent of essential information: Polybus and Merope were not Oedipus' true parents but received him from the messenger in his earlier role as Corinthian shepherd, who had in turn taken him from a Theban shepherd who was Laius' slave (989–1044). Oedipus soon learns from the chorus that this shepherd is also the sole survivor

---

[30] He might also have compared the fastening of the child's ankles with the fastening of his own as he remembers it. See 1034–6.

[31] On the irony of the Corinthian's entrance see Seale (1982) 237. 'There is a sudden waywardness about the action which contrasts noticeably with the planned appearances of Creon and Teiresias and which actually sets back Oedipus' latest arrangement, the arrival of the herdsman.' Indeed, Seale ibid. 238 (his emphasis) sees in it 'the sense of a *pursuing* doom, of a fiendish game in which appearance actively seeks out its victim'.

of the massacre for whom he has already sent (1045–53). Jocasta, realizing that Oedipus is about to learn the truth (1056–7), tries to deter him from pursuing the enquiry, but Oedipus, determined to know the truth about his birth, orders the man to be brought to him at once (1069).

Laius' murderer is no longer the principal focus of the king's mind. He had been pursuing this question only to be told by Teiresias that *he* was the killer. This he did not believe, but Jocasta in her attempt to discredit prophecy gave him reason to fear that it was in fact true. The resolution of that question depended on interrogating the survivor of the massacre. Meanwhile, with the Corinthian's news, Oedipus thinks he has reason to disbelieve prophecy and even to live, as Jocasta advocates, at random (977–9), until he learns that Polybus and Merope were not after all his parents.[32] Logically, then, at this point Oedipus has every reason to fear the prophecy again, reminded now that he does not, after all, know the identity of his parents, while the question of the murder at the crossroads remains unresolved. But Oedipus is focused narrowly on the sheer identity of his parents rather than on the related question of the fulfilment of the oracle about them (1076–85), and he would appear to have fully embraced Jocasta's (former) philosophy of a random universe (at least from our limited human perspective),[33] for he considers himself the child of Chance (1080), a notion which he celebrates with a kind of hysterical irrationalism, as if chance were an actual deity rather than an abstract principle of indeterminacy, though at the same time he is aware that her maternity might well imply ignoble birth (1077–85).[34] When the chorus join him in his irrational elation (1086–109), we know that Sophocles is building him up for a fall.

On the other hand, as Kane has observed, for Oedipus Chance is 'the kindly giver' (τῆς εὖ διδούσης, 1081), which can only refer to his good fortune in being brought up as a royal son:

Oedipus is a 'child of chance, the kindly giver,' because an unforeseeable accident caused him to be bestowed as a 'gift' on Polybus and Merope. This is the evidence for his judgement that he can afford to summon the shepherd. (How could learning the identity of his true parents affect the kingly legacy which chance had once bequeathed to him?)[35]

Oedipus is optimistic about his identity because he 'knows' he won't be revealed as base (1036).

But when the shepherd arrives, his testimony produces the very result which Oedipus had pronounced impossible[36]... The hero has precipitated this catastrophe by acting on

[32] '[T]he critical rationalism of Protagoras, with his appeal to human intelligence as the criterion of reality, abolishes prophecy as an incidental feature of the abolition of the supernatural as a whole': Knox (1957) 45. See also his longer discussion at ibid. 159–84. So the vindication of prophecy is also that of traditional religion. The alternative to the traditional religious view is Jocasta's 'Live at random'.

[33] Jocasta does not claim that the universe is *essentially* chaotic, only that no reliable foreknowledge of events is available to humans. Indeed, she refers to Apollo revealing the future when he needs to (723–5).

[34] The optimism is less a function of character than of Sophocles' need to build Oedipus up before his fall.

[35] Kane (1975) 203. Oedipus 'makes out of Jocasta's nihilizing chance a goddess who controls the universe and has selected him as her chosen vessel': Knox (1957) 180.

[36] See also 1397. '[T]he revelation of his parentage, far from raising him to the level of the gods, reduces him below the level of all normal humanity': Knox (1957) 181.

'knowledge' that was misconceived, but not illogical. More particularly, he has, like Jocasta, been misled by the ambiguity of *tuchē*, whose role in bestowing him on Polybus and Merope seemed to bespeak a 'kindly' nature.[37]

It is clear enough then from our revue of the course of Oedipus' enquiry that he is entirely dependent on Apollo's gradual release of information for the revelation of the truth, though the god utilizes and indeed actively encourages his determination to investigate at all costs. Oedipus' metaphorical roles, which relate to his investigative persona, associate him with 'the most impressive and revolutionary achievements of the whole human race',[38] but the 'scientific' methods that led to these achievements, when pursued in the play's Apolline universe, end only in tragic absurdity. 'Oedipus the helmsman has steered the ship of state into a storm which threatens to destroy it, and his own destiny into an unspeakable harbor. The hunter has tracked down the prey only to find that it is himself. And the sower is not only the sower but also the seed.'[39] These horrific absurdities are a function of the human condition and its fundamental ignorance. Even so, Oedipus is no ideal exponent of rational investigation, for, though aware of his ignorance, he 'acts not once but repeatedly as though he were privy even to hidden facts, treating the many phantasms of his imagination (124–5, 139–40, 380–9) as though they were manifest revelations (534–5)'.[40]

It is clear, moreover, that the events themselves are divinely shaped as well as divinely disclosed. No secular logic, let alone the notion of Chance, or Tyche (which is no more than a thinly veiled non-explanation, a virtual confession of mortal ignorance), can make sense of Oedipus' life—the prophecies given to his parents and to him, fulfilled through the mortals' very attempts to evade them; his miraculous salvation by the man who was later to be the sole survivor of the incident at the crossroads and by the man who was later to bring the news of his adoptive father's death; the classificatory and 'mathematical' absurdities produced by the incest.[41] Reality here is not some passive material, like Democritus' atoms,

---

[37] Kane (1975) 205. In his general conclusion, Kane ibid. 208 observes: 'In effect, the characters set themselves up as prophets in competition with the professional seers, whose *techne* they scorn. In place of "inspiration" and birdsigns, their predictions are based on *gnome*. The unseen consequences of the present are inferred from the apparent lessons of the past. Calculation from experience, not clairvoyance, becomes the key to predicting the future. Needless to say, the play demonstrates the futility of this method, for every time the characters employ it, their actions bring about the vindication of the oracles they had sought to disprove.'

[38] Knox (1957) 111.

[39] Ibid. 116. Cf. C. Segal (1981) 232. Knox links Oedipus' need to know with the scientific spirit of the age (ibid. 116 ff.). 'Oedipus investigates, examines, questions, infers; he uses intelligence, mind, thought; he knows, finds, reveals, makes clear, demonstrates; he learns and teaches; and his relationship to his fellow men is that of liberator and savior' (ibid. 117). On the play's use of scientific, including medical and mathematical, vocabulary, see ibid. 117–57.

[40] R. D. Griffith (1992) 204. See also Kane (1975) 189–90: 'the circumstance which has the greatest effect on his destiny is not simply that he is ignorant of the facts but that, like people whom Socrates met on the streets, he often acts as if he knew what he does not'. For C. Segal (2001) 66: 'Oedipus uses his human knowledge primarily in conflict with the divine, to block, deny, contradict, or evade it.'

[41] 'Such a fantastic series of coincidences [in Oedipus' life] seems expressly designed to mock the idea that human destiny is predictable; it is a paradigm of the inconsequent anarchy of the universe': Knox (1957) 179. 'Oedipus founds his innocence on a basic law of noncontradiction, the fundamental logic in man's apprehension of reality. Here, however, noncontradiction gives way to a fantastic,

fully conformable to human reason and yielding obligingly to investigation, but the shaping of a personal god who interacts with mortals. Moreover, it is dia-chronic, a mysteriously patterned and unique sequence of events rather than a permanent dynamic of scientifically predictable laws.

Apolline reality here forces discovery, but on its own terms and for its own purposes. It allows humans little scope to shape their own lives and shrinks the boundaries of effective moral activity in a world in which it can be hard to separate the human from the divine. Armed with what ethic can Oedipus respond to his destiny in such a world?

THE SELF-BLINDING

With the revelation of the truth, Oedipus entered the house, crying out (1252) and calling for a sword with the apparent intention of killing his polluted mother-wife (1255–7). In a frenzied state ($\lambda \upsilon \sigma \sigma \hat{\omega} \nu \tau \iota$, 1258), he was led, it would seem, by some divinity to whom he shouted (1260). But, finding the dead Jocasta, he took her brooches and blinded himself, with the declared intention of cutting himself off from the visible results of his misfortunes ($\kappa \alpha \kappa \acute{\alpha}$) (1271–4). Thereupon he returns to the stage, tortured by physical and emotional pain together (1317–20). The chorus, unable to attribute the self-blinding to any explicable human motivation, believe that Oedipus was (temporarily) mad and therefore urged on by a god ($\tau \acute{\iota} s$ σ', $\mathring{\omega}$ $\tau \lambda \hat{\eta} \mu o \nu$, $\pi \rho o \sigma \acute{\epsilon} \beta \eta$ $\mu a \nu \acute{\iota} a$; $\tau \acute{\iota} s$ $\acute{o}$ $\pi \eta \delta \acute{\eta} \sigma a s$ $\mu \epsilon \acute{\iota} \zeta o \nu a$ $\delta a \acute{\iota} \mu \omega \nu$ $\tau \hat{\omega} \nu$ $\mu \eta \kappa \acute{\iota} \sigma \tau \omega \nu$ $\pi \rho \grave{o} s$ $\sigma \hat{\eta}$ $\delta \upsilon \sigma \delta a \acute{\iota} \mu o \nu \iota$ $\mu o \acute{\iota} \rho a$; 1299–302; $\tau \acute{\iota} s$ σ' $\acute{\epsilon} \pi \hat{\eta} \rho \epsilon$ $\delta a \iota \mu \acute{o} \nu \omega \nu$; 1328). Oedipus agrees that it was indeed a god, specifically Apollo, that brought to pass ($\tau \epsilon \lambda \hat{\omega} \nu$) these sufferings ($\pi \acute{a} \theta \epsilon a$, 1330) of his—perhaps his whole evil destiny but certainly the self-blinding—but his own hand struck, the motivation was still his own (1331–2), as the messenger had implied in characterizing the disasters he would report as 'voluntary and not involuntary' ($\acute{\epsilon} \kappa \acute{o} \nu \tau a$ $\kappa o \grave{\upsilon} \kappa$ $\mathring{a} \kappa o \nu \tau a$, 1230).

The self-blinding, impulsive or not, was a deliberate act motivated by a desire to escape the sight (and indeed all sensuous experience) of a world disfigured in so many ways by Oedipus' pollution (1334–9, 1371–90, 1409–12).[42] Oedipus is now filled with self-loathing, describing himself in religious, rather than specifically

---

irrational "logic" of paradoxes in which opposites can in fact be equal and "one" can simultaneously be "many"': C. Segal (1981) 216. In his later book (2001), Segal points to patterns of return in Oedipus' life: the two shepherds came together in his infancy and again at the revelation; Oedipus returns to the furrows of his mother (1403–8); Laius tries to get rid of his son but he comes back to kill him; the oracle to Laius returns, assuming different forms in Oedipus' youth and maturity. 'Sophocles does not use these coincidences as proof of a deterministic universe, but rather as the facts of an uncanny pattern of a life that is thus marked as tragic' (ibid. 62).

[42] Cairns (1993) 217–18 relates the self-blinding to a sense of *aidōs*: 'In a sense, it is in this situation, where Oedipus, the revealer, stands revealed as a sight which affronts gods and men, and where he can bear neither to see nor to be seen, that all the language of seeing and showing which so permeates the play finds its culmination; and both Oedipus' behaviour at this point and the language in which it is described make it inevitable that the audience will characterize his response as *aidōs*, a concept which . . . is closely related to ideas of seeing and visibility, and particularly associated with the eyes.'

moral terms as 'most accursed' (καταρατότατον, 1345), 'the mortal the gods most detest' (θεοῖς ἐχθρότατον βροτῶν, 1345–6), 'abandoned by the gods' (ἄθεος, 1360), and 'the offspring of unholy parents' (ἀνοσίων . . . παῖς, 1360). But there are at least intimations of a more strictly moral dimension to his response when he speaks of his deeds as 'greater than hanging' (κρεῖσσον' ἀγχόνης, 1374)—that is, presumably, deeds that deserve a more severe punishment than death by hanging—and when he rephrases ἀνοσίων παῖς as κακός τ' ὢν κἀκ κακῶν ('evil and the offspring of evil parents': 1397). The blinding is also, as Cairns observes, an act of appropriation, 'a way of recognizing that the parricide and incest are *his* acts, even if he committed them in ignorance and despite his efforts to avoid them'.[43]

Though Oedipus defends the blinding against the option of suicide, which would entail the immediate sight of his parents in Hades (1367–74), he is quite prepared to die if the Thebans decide to annihilate his pollution in that way (1409–12). Thus his concern for the city is unabated. To do this, however, they will need to touch him, and so he reassures them that they cannot contract his pollution by doing so; only he can bear it (1413–15).[44] This notion, alien to the religion of miasma, seems for a moment to anticipate the attitude of Theseus in Euripides' *Heracles* who denies that a pollution (literally an *alastōr*) can pass between friends (Eur. *Her.* 1234). And yet Oedipus is far from abandoning the idea of pollution, and when Creon arrives he begs him to cast him from the land (1436–7). Still, the notion of passing one's guilt, as it were, on to another might well seem alien to a man distinguished for his readiness to take responsibility for his actions. He has now a vague sense of his destiny as some special suffering for which he was saved and he accepts whatever his future *moira* may bring (1455–8).

The self-blinding has a kind of symbolic appropriateness as a statement about Oedipus' earlier ignorance: he had eyes, but could not see, though he believed he could, as is shown by his arrogant taunting of Teiresias about his physical and mental blindness.[45] Similarly, now that Oedipus is blind himself, he is closer to Teiresias in appearance and perhaps in insight (consider his intuition about his destiny),[46] and, like the seer, though in a sinister way, he is closer to Apollo who instigated the self-blinding mysteriously behind the scenes. The blindness then has a kind of strange rightness about it, particularly as it seems sanctioned by divine destiny—and, of course, the myth tradition.

[43] Cairns forthcoming.

[44] 'In his growing strength, Oedipus begins to act out, though he will not complete, the ritual pattern of the scapegoat. . . . Thus the Thebans need not fear pollution from his touch any longer. Oedipus has separated himself from the monstrous, polluted self that has been hidden within him for so long': C. Segal (2001) 114–15.

[45] After being in 'a world of illusionary seeing and hearing', Oedipus wants to block off his organs of sense: ibid. 244. 'The assault on himself is made against the single offending part, his eyes, eyes which have seen what they should not have seen and not seen what they should have seen. He is punishing the eyes which did not in the past perform their due function and also shutting himself off for the future from a light he can no longer endure': Seale (1982) 247.

[46] See ibid. 250.

IS THE SELF-BLINDING A FREE ACT?

Does Oedipus then act 'freely' in blinding himself, if (as the chorus suggests—and Oedipus does not demur), Apollo 'incited' (ἐπῆρε, 1328) the act and 'fulfilled' (τελῶν, 1330) his miserable destiny. For Aristotle, at any rate, an involuntary or compulsory (βίαιον) act is one whose cause is external to the agent who contributes nothing to it. The secular philosopher is thinking here of material or human, rather than metaphysical, constraints. On the other hand, '[a] voluntary (ἑκούσιον) act would seem to be an act of which the origin lies in the agent, who knows the particular circumstances in which he is acting. For it is probably a mistake to say that acts caused by anger or by desire are involuntary (ἀκούσια)' (*NE* 1111ᵃ22–6: tr. Rackham). Moreover, 'we think that the irrational feelings (ἄλογα πάθη) are just as much a part of human nature as the reason, so that the actions done from anger or desire also belong to the human being who does them. It is therefore strange to class these actions as involuntary (*NE* 1111ᵇ1–3: tr. Rackham).

By these criteria the self-blinding is voluntary as proceeding from Oedipus' mind, even though that mind is prey to the 'irrational feelings' to which Aristotle refers. But in the context of the 'panoramic intervention' that operates in this play, the English term 'free' is surely problematical. As Cairns puts it:

Though there is a sense in which Oedipus' actions can be characterized as manifesting one kind of what ordinary English calls 'free will' and at the same time a sense in which the major events of his life are determined, the precise kinds of human action presupposed by the *OT* are not well captured in terms of either pole of the later philosophical antithesis of free will and determinism. Even though Oedipus takes ownership of his actions, the circumstances in which those actions were performed are such that it would be perverse to call them 'free'.[47]

It will be remembered that, in Glannon's view, while the autonomy of the mental states of the deliberating agent is threatened by 'coercion, compulsion, or various types of external manipulation', it can be preserved if there is 'reflective self-control' which allows one 'to eliminate or else modify or reinforce these states and come to identify with them as one's own'.[48] At the same time, as we saw in Ch. 1, Glannon rejects '[t]he traditional conception of freedom [which] says that a person chooses and acts freely and responsibly if and only if he can choose and act other than the way he in fact does. But autonomy and responsibility do not require alternative possibilities of any sort in the causal pathway leading to action.'[49]

Now it is clear enough that neither 'deliberation' nor 'reflective self-control' are terms that apply at all well to the mental circumstances of the self-blinding, but Oedipus experiences no dissonance between Apollo's inspiration and his own endogenous motivation, as we can see from his appropriation of the act. It is not even clear that he is aware of any alien pressure to blind himself, though he concludes after the event that Apollo must indeed have been involved. If then we

---

[47] Cairns forthcoming 21.
[48] See p. 24; Glannon (2002) 26.
[49] See p. 24; Glannon (2002) 14.

join Glannon in rejecting 'the traditional conception of freedom', we need not concern ourselves with the question as to whether Oedipus could have acted otherwise had he so wished. We can say, therefore, that he acted 'autonomously', while acknowledging, with Cairns, that the context confers a 'perverse' quality on the term.[50]

OEDIPUS AND SELF-KNOWLEDGE

Oedipus has attained self-knowledge. This is a wide term, however, that requires more precise definition. In our modern Western culture, self-knowledge refers to understanding one's own character—in particular its moral strengths and, above all, its moral weaknesses. But to the ancients the application was more general: the knowledge that you are human and mortal in the sense of accepting the natural limitations of that condition. Such an understanding has moral implications in so far as it is related to the observance of *sōphrosunē* and *eusebeia* in one's dealings with the gods. But the emphasis may be less moral than existential, as it is here. Oedipus certainly attains that kind of basic and universal self-knowledge which the more confident human beings are in danger of lacking or forgetting, but he never attains self-knowledge in the modern sense. He does not, for example, condemn himself for violent impulsiveness; and for him to have done so would have distracted us from the more central issue of the massive existential ignorance and vulnerability that we share with him. What he does come to know is his own basic, literal individual identity as defined by the literal identity of his parents, and from that he becomes aware of his parricide and incest and its religious implications, but also of the broader existential implications of being human.[51]

Apollo, it would seem, in requiring Oedipus to find Laius' killer, sets him a riddle that fits his nature; he must rise to the challenge and learn. The knowledge he attains is, appropriately, not the purely objective knowledge that emerges from a dispassionate scientific investigation, but is intensely subjective. Oedipus' search for truth leads back to himself and his status vis-à-vis the traditionally personal and yet strangely remote Sophoclean gods. And in so far as we, as spectators, empathize with his experience, our learning too has an affective as well as a cognitive dimension.[52]

Oedipus set his rational mind to the enquiry after Laius' killer (105), but the answer came not at all like 'dead' information, but as a lesson that the universe actually intended Oedipus to learn, for we can infer intention from Apollo's

---

[50] For Schwartz (1986) 202–3, Oedipus is 'free to obey the will of the god. Destiny is man's character. To the sophists it was a man's nature (*phusis*) from whence his deeds sprang. To Plato it was his rational soul. To Sophocles it was the hand of Apollo and the hand of Oedipus. The god and the mortal, joined since Oedipus's fateful birth, are doubles: both detest reticence and both are consumed with a passion for knowledge, driven to push the action through to its conclusion' (ibid. 203).

[51] In the fifth century, 'To know who one is is to know who one's parents are . . . It is also to know what they are, for in Sophocles' world as in Homer's identity and status overlap, and sense of self is inextricably connected with sense of position' so that Oedipus' anxiety is social, not existential': Gregory (1995) 146. This is true so long as he is unsuspecting of his pollution.

[52] See p. 5 and n. 15.

traditional conception as a personal, anthropomorphic god of self-knowledge, for all his Sophoclean remoteness. That Sophocles retains some contact with this personal conception of Apollo is suggested by the comments of Teiresias about Apollo working out Oedipus' destiny, in the ironic response to Jocasta's prayer and in the Delphic injunction to know yourself. The ultimate truth in such a world is not a fact about something 'out there' in the context of which I am free to establish my own identity; it is my actual personal relationship with the divine realm, and that relationship, in a way perhaps characteristic of 'primal' religion, reveals my comparative insignificance.

OEDIPUS THE NOBLE MONSTER

If, however, we define ourselves primarily, at a more differentiated or individuated level, by our moral qualities—as, for example, warriors such as Eteocles, Ajax, or Heracles define themselves by their courage—what threatens identity is above all the possibility of moral failure. None of those heroes can be cowards without ceasing to be themselves; and, to Ajax's mind, to remain alive in a state of permanent dishonour would be to live the life of a coward (*Aj.* 470–80). Oedipus' strictly moral identity, on the other hand, is not under threat. The revelation of the truth brings out no vice (that is, no intended evil) on his part and no profoundly significant moral flaw, but, overwhelmingly, all but unavoidable error.

Moreover, Oedipus has acted rightly by the gods and the polis; his errors of judgement are understandable. He was mistaken to believe, for a moment with Jocasta, in the unreliability of prophecy, but he did not act on that notion. This is not to claim that Oedipus has no faults. An incomplete list would contain impatience, irascibility, impulsiveness leading to violence, and overconfidence. The spectator is aware of these qualities as they find dramatic expression, but that is all. The play is not critical of Oedipus' moral integrity; but it reveals the limitations of moral choice. Oedipus could not escape committing his 'crimes', and now he cannot escape a sort of blame because the negative terminology of religious pollution overlaps with that of moral condemnation—a symptom, per-haps, rather than a cause of a confusion between the moral and the religious spheres.[53]

Oedipus' failure then is more fundamental than personal ignorance. It is a failure in *being*, and for that reason totally beyond his control. For no moral or rational reason, Oedipus is a freak who does not 'deserve' to live. By all rational human standards he is an effective and loving king; and yet neither the polis nor the natural world can readily harbour him, such is the nature of his miasma.[54]

---

[53] There is another overlap—between pollution and an increasingly sophisticated legal system. As R. C. T. Parker (1983) 313 observes: 'Because pollution and guilt can be closely associated, the imagery of pollution may be used to express moral revulsion.'

[54] On Oedipus and Aristotle's 'political animal' see Vernant and Vidal-Naquet (1988) 122: Oedipus 'is above and below human beings, a hero more powerful than man, the equal of the gods [as he appears at the beginning of the play], and at the same time a brutish beast spurned and relegated to the wild solitude of the mountains'. Moreover, 'given that this figure is the model of man, the boundaries that

Oedipus is the individual upon whom this mysterious and unique doom has descended, and yet his destiny is representative, and the chorus draw the obvious moral from his story: human happiness is precarious and fleeting, or, rather, illusory (1186–96); the generations of human life add up to zero. Oedipus' pollution is at once symbol and worst-case scenario of our insignificance in the face of the divine.[55]

After his disastrous madness, Ajax takes stock of his life, redefining its meaning and working out what is now morally required of him—or, rather, what he morally requires of himself. In doing this he salvages much of his previous self-concept, as he takes the view that essentially he is still the greatest of the Greeks at Troy and that his predicament is due to misfortune rather than a failing on his own part. The attack on Oedipus' self-concept is far more radical. Not only is he not a great man, he is not even a man in the sense of a political animal that can be accommodated by a society. Thus he is a kind of monster, but a monster that continues, even after the revelation, to act with the highest of human moral standards, as is shown in his concern for his city and above all for the future care of his daughters.[56] He makes no claims to positive worth, unlike Ajax, because his sense of pollution ensures that he will characterize himself in the most disparaging terms; but his words and actions implicitly convey that morally he is unchanged and indeed vindicated for the courageous endurance which he has never had to display before.

Oedipus was bound then to think and act within the parameters of his own (Archaic) culture as defined in the play and so, at one level, he must be judged in those terms. If we allow ourselves to empathize with the hero and with the sensibilities of his world, we shall have access to a deeper insight than if we dismiss miasma as superstition. Indeed, Sophocles himself deliberately circumscribed his dramatic universe in such a way as to make that insight possible. As we know from the *Coloneus*, he was perfectly capable of raising the question of Oedipus' moral innocence which he so conspicuously excluded from the *Tyrannus*. The society and culture of the play do not accurately mirror Sophocles' view of his own culture, which was, of course, thanks to the sophists, in intellectual ferment. Rather he chose to deny Oedipus the relief of finding refuge in his own

---

contained human life and made it possible to establish its status without ambiguity are obliterated' (ibid. 125). This god/beast status is reminiscent of Sophocles' Heracles, but in his case it is a function of character and environment. Oedipus' predicament is disturbing in its absurdity.

[55] 'The moral import of the *Oedipus Tyrannus* centres more on the fragility of human nature than on Oedipus' virtue or vice; and in such a case it matters that Oedipus is the sort of person he is, but only in the sense that *even so great a man as he* can be vulnerable. We can extract a moral from that for ourselves, but it is not obvious that Oedipus himself *needs* to be conceived in especially normative terms, any more than we need feel that his extraordinary circumstances or fate could recur in our own life': Pelling 258 (his emphasis).

[56] C. Segal (2001) emphasizes Oedipus' concern for his daughters and contrasts the Aeschylean Oedipus who, on his discovery of the incest, curses his sons (ibid. 116). Oedipus is horrified by the incest but relates to his girls compassionately as individuals (ibid. 138). Oedipus 'can ask for pity and try to shelter those he loves from the hard life he knows awaits them. Despite his isolation and the sufferings of his house and his city, he helps reknit the bonds of family and society. Although he is no longer king, his appeals to the elders and to Creon help the curse-driven city to regain its health as a human community' (ibid. 118).

moral innocence. This enables us all to experience the feeling of radical and irrational worthlessness in the face of an inhuman universe, though some readers have felt that the sheer order implied by the existence of the infallible Apolline prophecies makes Oedipus' disastrous life at least minimally bearable.[57] This is perhaps a matter of personal taste, but Oedipus is left in a condition that is worse than that of post-Christian humans faced with an indifferent universe in which they have to forge their own values and believe in their own worth rather than having meaning conferred upon them by a deity. Oedipus' condition is worse because the gods do exist and in their eyes his value is actually less than zero. He has to cope with a universe which is not merely indifferent, but actively and personally hostile, at least to him.

Despite the hero's negative existential value, Sophocles contrives matters so that the audience will naturally feel that Oedipus is far from worthless, that in fact he shows his greatest virtue in his humiliation, for, as Knox observes, he accepts the full consequences of the curse and insists on exile or death in accordance with the oracle.[58] However, Oedipus only 'gradually gains a new strength and a new understanding.'[59] He insists on bringing everything out into the open as he had done before, and even the blinding is shown to be deliberate and not impulsive. His desire for exile shows his continued concern for the city. Oedipus demonstrates his adaptability by taking on his new beggar's role, but at the end of the play he has to be reminded that he is no longer in control.[60] 'Sophocles' tragedy presents us with a terrible affirmation of man's subordinate position in the universe, and at the same time with a heroic vision of man's victory in defeat.'[61] Euripides' Heracles is similarly a good man brought down in an irrational universe, but he (and Euripides) question the validity of the divine perspective, with the aid of the tools of philosophy, for 'the god who is truly god' (Eur. *Her.* 1345) is (as we shall see) incompatible with the gods of the play.

Thus Oedipus' virtues win approval from a human audience even if they are irrelevant from the perspective of the gods. His determination to discover the truth prevails even when he fears the worst, and his responsibility to his people shows in his determination to be revealed for what he is and to be exiled or killed in fulfilment of the oracle.[62] He evinces also a courageous acceptance and indeed an assertiveness which is applied paradoxically to insisting on his worthlessness and thereby discrediting that idea at least from the human perspective. The great man and the terrible monster coexist in an extreme tension that recurs in

---

[57] 'The existence of the prophecy is the only thing that makes the discovery of the truth bearable, not only for us but for Oedipus himself.' Oedipus' one consolation is 'the fact of divine prescience demonstrated by the existence of the original prophecy': Knox (1957) 43. Kirkwood (1958) 287 thinks deity is 'in harmony with ultimate justice'; Kitto (1958) 49 argues that *dikē*, 'the regular order of things', is restored by the revelation. Buxton (1996) 42–3, on the other hand, comments on the peculiar 'opacity' of the 'metaphysical structure' of this play, which makes 'the solace harder to be sure about'.

[58] Knox (1957) 187.

[59] C. Segal (2001) 133. '[T]he hero's understanding of the meaning of his life comes only at the end, in the flickering uncertainties of his struggles with his pain, his blindness, and the successive waves of contradictory emotions': ibid. 135–6.

[60] Knox (1957) 187–93.

[61] Ibid. 196.

[62] 'This is the awesome fulfilment of the public commitment he first made': Seale (1982) 247.

Euripides' *Heracles*, although there, against the background of sophistic religious speculation, the notion of the polluted monster collapses in the face of the hero's obvious moral worth. In the Euripidean play Theseus' dismissal of pollution assists Heracles to take an assertively moral attitude of self-vindication, as he blames his polluted state on Hera (Eur. *Her.* 1303–10). But in Oedipus' world, as we have seen, the negative terms applied to a polluted being overlap with those applied to a morally vicious person, preventing Oedipus from thinking clearly about his own moral status. For this reason we might say, paradoxically, that in the final scene Oedipus lacks moral awareness while evincing the highest moral integrity. (On the other hand, he would doubtless reply that moral awareness is utterly irrelevant when you are a polluted monster.)

A notable feature of Oedipus' response to the worst destiny conceivable is his rejection of suicide. This rejection associates him again with Euripides' Heracles rather than with Ajax. We saw that that hero's suicide could be criticized, for all its spectacular courage, as a selfish gesture. Euripides, however, in his *Heracles* and Sophocles in his later tragedies of heroic endurance (*Electra*, *Philoctetes*, and the *Coloneus*) explore the implications of a less spectacular form of courage. Ajax claimed that a life of dishonour, made up of one meaningless day after another, was not worth living, but such lives as remain to the tragic endurers after their terrible reversals are not mere lives (such as pursued by the protagonist of the *Orestes*), but are accepted as morally significant lives.

Sophocles' *Oedipus Tyrannus* explores the gulf between human and divine knowledge. In most of the crucial actions of his life—the solution of the riddle of the Sphinx and marriage to Jocasta, the hunting down of Laius' killer—Oedipus acts with a good moral will but in disastrous ignorance. This reflects the fundamental insight of the play that truth is never fully revealed to us; we can only seek to lay a part of it bare when a specific situation seems to call for it (as when Oedipus is moved to ask the oracle about his parentage or to seek the cause of the plague), and even then it is at the behest of the deity rather than in our power whether to reveal it as a whole or in part, straightforwardly or cryptically. Otherwise we act always in a large degree of ignorance and we risk acting disastrously. Thus the play is pessimistic about the effectiveness of moral action. Oedipus' world resists rational investigation and fails to reward the moral will; indeed it even cruelly enlists that will as a means of aggravating suffering (as in the case of Oedipus' curse). Apollo withholds information and presents it in his own way and in his own good time to teach Oedipus about investigation and knowledge (which emerges sometimes when not directly sought) and thus about the unbridgeable gulf between humans and gods.[63] No stronger statement could be made against the kind of Aristotelian optimism that thinks that we can attain *eudaimonia* through the cultivation and exercise of intelligence, knowledge, and moral commitment.

---

[63] On the place of gods and mortals in the universe of the play Cairns (forthcoming) 32 comments: 'This is an order based on hierarchy and power; such power may be justly distributed, if we believe that the gods exist and are vastly superior to men, and it may be justly exercised, if we believe that gods have the right to demonstrate how wide the gulf is between them and us; but it is not an order which pays much heed to the rights, claims, or interests of human beings.'

CONCLUSION

Oedipus does not deliberate about either major crisis: whether to find the killer or how to react to the revelation. His resolve to investigate is a spontaneous and immediate expression of his character. This is a feature of Sophoclean agents: their situations tend to fit their characters. In reacting to the revelation, Oedipus, in what is virtually a manic state, acts again without deliberation, but nevertheless, as the messenger indicates, as if with a purpose, though, paradoxically, without being conscious of that purpose until he sees the brooches which inspire the blinding. This paradox results from the psychological intervention of Apollo (or the *daimōn*) who, as we saw in Ch. 2, serves to define and heighten the mortal's at first unconscious purpose. Hence the blinding appears at once impulsive or improvised and at the same time what Oedipus (or the *daimōn*) intended (since it is part of his prophesied destiny).

Oedipus implicitly defines himself as a king with moral obligations to his people as such (that is, in terms of a role), but also as an individual in terms of his qualities of character. These qualities are presented as very much his own rather than inherited and thereby related to *eugeneia*. He is strongly aware of the moral necessity of the investigation. He is also aware of a need to respond to the awful truth, but the terms are as much religious as moral. His moral awareness with respect to his future is confused by the pollution. He acts in accord with his moral principles in respect of both crises. He is right to pursue the investigation, and the play's implicit acceptance of the reality of pollution somehow validates the blinding and even his self-loathing, and yet Sophocles insists on his moral nobility at the end.

In his epistemologically problematical world, Oedipus does not understand the facts beyond the plague and then, after the initial oracle, the need to search for Laius' killer; and of course he lacks the crucial knowledge of his own identity. Still he does know that failure to pursue the investigation is not a moral option. (Nor would he be attracted by it.)

We have seen that there are no moral deliberations as such, but the emotions driving the investigation are appropriately passionate: a keen determination to help and to use his powers. He does not think out his moral obligations in either situation. The blinding is not entirely a response to a sense of moral obligation. The emotion that drives it is a kind of madness, perhaps inspired in part by the *daimōn*, but also by horror and self-disgust.

Although divine immanence is a feature of the play's causation, it is not ubiquitous. Apollo's intervention is both psychological (during the events leading up to the self-blinding) and panoramic, that is he has a plan which involves material intervention (the oracles and the 'coincidences') but also anticipation of Oedipus' responses. This more remote, panoramic involvement applies to Oedipus' autonomous response to the plague. The blinding, on the other hand, is overdetermined, with the *daimōn*/Apollo focusing and intensifying Oedipus' scarcely conceived and at first inchoate purpose.

9

Sophocles: *Electra*

Although in most of the previous plays under discussion more or less hostile gods in various ways created moral predicaments to which the characters were compelled to respond, in this play both Orestes and Electra freely initiate their own moral responses to what they see as a situation that requires such a response. Accordingly, Orestes travels to Delphi and asks Apollo *how* to take revenge (32–7), while his sister independently sets in motion her own limited retribution while awaiting his return. There are indications that Apollo and a number of other gods are involved, as it were, behind the scenes, especially at the climax and in the ironical answer to Clytemnestra's prayer (634–59), but in a supporting rather than a hostile role. Until then, though, Electra comes across unequivocally as an autonomous, self-motivated moral agent.[1]

Apollo presented the Aeschylean Orestes with a moral dilemma of a particularly acute kind, involving a choice between pursuit by his mother's Furies and pursuit by the Furies of his father. But neither the gods nor society impose a moral dilemma or indeed any moral requirements on Sophocles' Electra. She imposes a moral demand on herself: to do all she can to avenge her father. This self-imposed demand does not involve her in a dilemma because she sees a clear and morally unproblematical duty to avenge her father by working towards the execution of both of his killers; and the issue of pursuit by the Furies simply does not arise, either in her mind or in fact. But, although there is no dilemma, she is nevertheless emotionally distressed because her duty as she sees it entails filial impiety towards her mother. It is not that she loves her mother; far from it. It is rather that she hates having a mother who deserves to be and must be treated with contempt and who must be hounded to death, and she dislikes the person she must herself become in order to perform her moral duty as she sees it.

The necessarily nasty Electra is a corollary of the notorious 'harm your enemies' ethic, and it is commonly held that her nastiness, particularly during the killings, constitutes part of the dramatist's case against this ancient ethic. It will be argued here, however, that, whatever Sophocles thought of a morality of harming

---

[1] On the question of the influence of family history and the curse see Sewell-Rutter (2007) 130–5. Sophocles 'works out the woes of the house not through the climactic operation of a pre-existing curse, not through the sudden revelation that an Erinys is at work, but through the desires, concerns and epistemic status of his protagonists' (ibid. 133).

enemies, he accepts it for the purposes of the play because he is more interested in Electra's moral commitment and its emotional toll on her.[2]

ELECTRA'S MORAL POSITION

When we are introduced to the protagonist (86–120) she is mourning her murdered father with the passionate intensity that belongs to recent bereavement (86–95). The chorus sympathetically deplore what they see as her emotional self-indulgence (137–9), but her mourning continues because there is no closure. Agamemnon was murdered and inadequately lamented (94–102), and the resulting moral miasma continues unabated. But, more significantly, Electra considers herself *obliged* to mourn, both in protest against the ongoing immoral state of affairs in the palace and in Argos at large (103–9, 254 ff.) and as a way of reminding the killers of their crime. And she is effective in this, because Clytemnestra will later declare her relief that now Orestes is, as she believes, dead, her daughter will cease to 'drain her life blood' (783–7).[3] Electra's extended mourning thus turns out to be a rationally justifiable moral policy. But it is more than policy. It is a spontaneous expression of her deepest feelings, as we see when her emotions seem so to overwhelm her that she finds their most eloquent articulation through the medium of mythic parallels of endless lamentation (107, 145–52). She is grateful for the chorus' compassion, but she must reject their advice: 'Allow me to wander [in grief] in this way (ὧδ' ἀλύειν), I beg you' (135–6).

Despite her emotionalism, Electra is able to justify her policy. As she will presently declare, all sense of shame (*aidōs*) and reverence (*eusebeia*) will disappear if the killers are not killed in turn (247–50).[4] Now she insists, if she ceased to mourn her father she would be an irresponsible and naive fool (νήπιος, 145). On the other hand, she recognizes that it is passionate wrath (ὀργά, 222) that drives her to render outrage (δείν', 221) in return for the morally outrageous circumstances (δεινοῖς, 221) in which she is obliged to live.[5] But as long as this situation lasts, she will continue with the self-destructive behaviour which the chorus have condemned (ταύτας ἄτας, 224; cf. ἄτας, 215). No right-thinking person (καίρια, 228) would want her to do otherwise. She has to generate 'one mischief after another' (ἄταν ἄταις, 235) because it cannot be right or honourable to neglect the dead (237). That would be contrary to the deepest human instincts (ἐν τίνι τοῦτ ἔβλαστ' ἀνθρώπων; 238). Thus the spring of her morality she recognizes as

---

[2] Similarly, Sophocles adopts different attitudes to Oedipus' guilt and pollution in his two Oedipus plays.

[3] See Minadeo (1967) 123 on Electra's alleged ineffectuality.

[4] North (1966) 64–5 accuses Electra of redefining ethical terms, but she is rather explaining how these terms, with their usual meanings, apply in the strange context in which it is morally necessary to be conventionally unfilial to one's mother.

[5] Harris (2001) 279 thinks that Electra's anger 'is an explicit theme' and that 'she seems to gain credit from attempting to resist it and, ultimately, blame for surrendering to it . . . The Chorus tells her early in the play to turn her *cholos* over to Zeus, and she is aware of her *orge* and what can be said against it [176–7, 222, 331, 369]'. But Electra does not attempt to resist her anger; nor does she finally surrender to it. Rather it provides an emotional driving force for her moral will.

instinctive. On the other hand, it is clear that her moral instincts are grounded in her noble status, and indeed she appeals to this in explaining her motivation (εὐγενής, 257). Presently she will lament that in her situation she cannot practise the conventional self-restraint (σωφρονεῖν, 307) or filial piety (εὐσεβεῖν, 308), but in a nasty (and evil) (κακοῖς, 308) predicament her behaviour must also be nasty (κακά, 309)—but not, as we shall see, evil.

So personal grief and moral principle are interdependent in Electra's motivation. She is emotionally distressed by her father's fate and her own predicament, but equally morally outraged on her own and her father's behalf and, more objectively, on behalf of moral principle itself. Each of these factors contributes to the momentum of her passionate wrath (ὀργά). The moral intuition precedes the wrath and fuels it. But for a tragic agent she is to an unusual degree prepared to discuss and reflect upon her position.

Later in the play, when she thinks of killing Aegisthus, a latent but familiar aristocratic desire to win honour enters the picture, as she proposes that she and her sister kill him not only in order to avenge their father (955) and to recover their patrimony and thereby their marriage prospects (960–2), but also to win a reputation for piety (εὐσέβεια) in the eyes of Agamemnon and the 'dead' Orestes (969). They will, moreover, be free (970) and win glory (εὔκλειαν, 973), affection (φιλεῖν) and respectful adulation (σέβειν) (981) in the eyes of their fellow citizens. It is shameful for the nobly born to live a shameful life (989).[6]

To some extent then Electra is motivated by a desire for honour, but this idea enters the play at this comparatively late stage only after her primary motives have been established. In fact, she has internalized the virtues which are rewarded by the honour she also desires and which remain therefore primary.

Electra, like Ajax, subscribes to an ethic of personal integrity, which raises again the issue of self-centred eudaimonism. Terence Irwin has charged her with disregarding the interests of others.

Electra chooses to think of her obligation to the dead instead of the ties she might form with the living—those she might form by a reconciliation with Clytemnestra and by the marriage she has renounced. Antigone and Electra cannot deny their choices have adverse effects on other people to whom they have obligations; the interests of these others as well as their own interests seem to speak against their choice.[7]

---

[6] Gellie (1972) 120 suspects not only that Electra is deluding herself in believing that she can kill Aegisthus but even the genuineness of the sentiments: 'It is hard to escape the feeling that Electra is riding on a cloud of words again and that the words are generating the sentiments rather than the other way around. The lack of love in her life has made her a pathetic figure. She is the more pathetic now for hoping that by assuming this masculine toughness she will win more love. This comes close to the heart of Electra's tragedy. Her feminine capacity to love and be loved is unbounded, but the need to hate so long and so grimly has distorted her more generous impulses and her thinking about them. . . . On the one hand Electra's competence to act is absurdly inadequate for the task ahead. Her brave words are as unprofitable as ever and now they are foolishly so, but bravery like this is still admirable.' The plan to kill Aegisthus, though perhaps intended to bring her as close as the myth allows to doing the deed herself, does more to emphasize the disjunction between mere word and effective deed, between moral consciousness and moral act. As Burnett (1998) 124 observes, Electra has no interest in the means by which the deed will be done and cares only about 'the inner sense of the project'. See also the detailed discussion of MacLeod (2001) 140–6.

[7] Irwin (1988) 66.

But it would be wrong for Electra to compromise with the killers in the manner of her sister, and in her own moral terms (with which the audience is encouraged to concur) she acts in some degree in Chrysothemis' deeper interests by involving her in a small way in her own defiance of the regime.[8] She certainly does not act in disregard of the interests of those who are not regarded as enemies. Irwin also claims that the Sophoclean hero, unlike the Platonic Socrates, prefers to adhere stubbornly to a position rather than to argue it rationally.[9] This is generally true (though it does not follow that the position in question is rationally indefensible). It is not, however, true of Electra who does discuss her position with others (her mother, her sister, the chorus), though she hears nothing from any of them that can or indeed should induce her to change her mind. Indeed, after their initial criticisms the chorus begin to back down (251–3).

Electra's *moral* position is not fundamentally different from that of the chorus or indeed that of her unheroic sister who condemns it as dangerous and impractical rather than immoral. Electra's attitude is firmly grounded in the values of her society, as we have seen. As Gill observes: 'The ethical life of a human being is, at the most fundamental level, shared rather than private and individuated. . . . Human beings reach their ethical foundations through shared debate . . . rather than by adopting an individual stance or autonomy or self-legislation, or by embarking on a programme of individual self-realization.'[10] The Sophoclean hero is no exception. Electra's moral principles are characteristic of her culture and class; uncharacteristic are the moral problematics of her particular circumstances and, if we are to imagine that the stand she takes in the play has emerged from an interior debate, as we have seen, she is prepared to defend that stand publicly, thereby rehearsing perhaps that earlier debate. Similarly in *Iliad* 9 Achilles presents to the embassy the results of his private reflections on his dishonour at the hands of Agamemnon. Moreover, in so far as we identify with Electra, she becomes, like Achilles, the vehicle by which we think through the moral issues.[11]

DOES THE PLAY IMPLICITLY ENDORSE ELECTRA'S MORAL POSITION?

We must now consider whether Electra's moral certainty is endorsed by the drama as a whole. We need to examine both the moral world of the play and the devices Sophocles uses to guide our feelings and judgements. Now the world of

---

[8] Electra persuades her sister not to convey Clytemnestra's offerings to their father's grave (431–71). Arguing from a different moral perspective than that of Electra, it would of course be possible to see this as a merely 'instrumental' use of another person.

[9] Ajax and Electra close their minds to advice, but Socrates gives Crito a hearing and wants to proceed from 'agreed assumptions': Irwin (1988) 78. 'Socrates is open to argument, and the argument gives him good reasons for doing what Ajax and Electra do without good reason' (ibid. 80). Electra's motivation, though, is her (obviously correct) conviction that the situation in the palace and in Argos is morally evil and for that reason must be resisted.

[10] Gill (1996) 15–16.

[11] Ibid. 16; Kitzinger (1991) *passim.*

a Greek tragedy bears no precise relationship to any real historical world. Ostensibly the plays are set in what might loosely be termed 'the heroic age of myth'. Orestes' vengeance therefore will be justified by the absence of civic justice. But none of the three tragedians fought shy of social, political, or legal anachronisms, so the audience was obliged to construct the world of a specific tragedy progressively and tentatively as the action unfolded.[12] The 'default setting' therefore of Sophocles' *Electra* will be the world of Homeric myth unless the dramatist signals otherwise through the introduction of anachronisms.

Electra naturally invokes the talio against her father's killers, but Segal thinks that this only goes to demonstrate 'the inadequacy of a society whose system of justice rests on blood-vengeance, for here the avengers run the risk of coming to the same level as the criminals'.[13] Admittedly, vendettas arise in a society in which retributive justice is in the hands of families and individuals rather than the state, but this is because the parties involved deny the legitimacy of the punishments meted out by their enemies.[14]

Electra may seem to be thoughtlessly contributing to a counterproductive feud, but she is right to view the proposed matricide as punishment for a crime that cannot be legitimately defended as the punishment of a prior crime.[15] Clytemnestra's attitude and behaviour are universally condemned in the play while Electra's moral position, at least, is endorsed by everyone except her father's killers. As we have observed, even Chrysothemis does not dispute her sister's morality, and if Sophocles wished to question the talio it is strange that he missed the opportunity to do so through her and the chorus or by arousing, as Euripides does, some significant sympathy for Clytemnestra. But the moral problematics of the play do not relate to the talio. In fact the audience is given a totally negative view of Clytemnestra well before she enters the play, and the question of Electra's nasty behaviour towards her is explicitly raised and justified on more than one occasion. Not only are we aware that Clytemnestra sleeps with Aegisthus (which is after all a datum of the myth), and has borne him children while the noble line of Agamemnon's children has been rejected (589–90), none of which can be explained as legitimate revenge for the death of Iphigenia (591–2),[16] but there is the

---

[12] Euripides, in particular, was prepared to introduce anachronisms that could lead to incoherence. Perhaps the most dissonant of these occurs in *Orestes* when Tyndareus argues that Orestes should have tried his mother for murder rather than killing her himself (492–507). At this point it would seem that the audience is required to rethink their natural presupposition that the appropriate court did not yet exist. Nevertheless, the matter is too problematic to be resolved by a simple adjustment, for Orestes continues to function in the 'Homeric' world, and his reply to Tyndareus does not address his objections.

[13] C. Segal (1981) 252.

[14] '[O]ne of the major flaws in the justice of the talio: if wrong may always be returned for wrong, then a further wrong may always be returned for the second, and so on ad infinitum, as long as the second wrong (the first act of revenge) is considered a wrong (rather than a rightful punishment)': Blundell (1989) 171–2.

[15] With reference to feuds in the real world, McHardy (2008) 6 observes: 'Naturally enough... participants do not always agree on the starting point for a dispute and there is also a tendency to recall past grievances or to dredge up long-forgotten disagreements in order to provide justification for an attack.'

[16] A similar argument concerning the ill-treatment of her innocent children by Agamemnon appears in Euripides' *Electra* where Clytemnestra explains her neglect of Orestes as motivated by fear (1114–15).

monthly festival in celebration of the killing (277–85), and Clytemnestra's crudely strident abuse strips her of all dignity.[17] Electra has to watch all this (282), which makes it impossible for her to practise (conventional) *sōphrosunē* or *eusebeia* (307–8), but rather when the situation is nasty she too must behave in a nasty way (308–9). If a conventionally minded Greek had urged the victim of such treatment to turn the other cheek, it would have been on prudential rather than on moral grounds.

In the agon both parties adhere to the talio, so that Clytemnestra must claim that the first crime was committed by Agamemnon while Electra must argue her father's innocence so that the original crime will turn out to be his murder. Accordingly, Clytemnestra claims that her verbal abuse of her daughter is merely in retaliation for abuse unfairly initiated by Electra (523–4). She claims that she killed her husband justly (528) because he was the only Greek who had the audacity to sacrifice Iphigenia, even though he did not suffer the pangs of her childbirth (530–3), an argument that seems to undermine her stronger (because more impersonal) claim to be the agent of justice in that it suggests that the sacrifice was primarily an offence against herself.[18] But, that aside, any argument against the sacrifice founders on Artemis' stipulation of Iphigenia as the victim and on Agamemnon's having absolutely no choice: he could go neither home nor to Troy (573–4). Electra goes even further in her exoneration of Agamemnon by minimizing his offence against the goddess: he killed the stag in an idle moment (παίζων) on impulse, and uttered some boast (568–9), but not apparently the traditional one that he was a better hunter than Artemis, since the goddess demanded the sacrifice in requital for the stag (571–2), rather than for impious arrogance.

Admittedly, Electra is the source of the account of Agamemnon's predicament at Aulis, and some critics are reluctant to believe her, because they think that she allows her emotions to overcome the rational element in her moral commitment to the point of being prepared to cast about, if necessary, for any justification she can find.[19] But there is no warrant in her characterization generally to distrust her in this way. (The contrast with Euripides' Electra is instructive, and there is much more reason to be sceptical about *her* highly subjective criticisms of her mother in the agon of that play.[20]) If Electra were a real person we might be wary of what is admittedly a second-hand account of the events (ὡς ἐγὼ κλύω, 566), but the convention in drama is (as we saw in the case of Oedipus' account of the murder of Laius) that we must believe unless we are offered a contrary and more convincing version.[21] Admittedly, this is an agon in which a healthy scepticism

---

[17] Kells (1973) 7, on the other hand, thinks that Clytemnestra attains tragic stature when she weeps momentarily for the 'death' of Orestes.

[18] 'Her [Clytemnestra's] first argument against Agamemnon asserts her superior claim to Iphigenia based on the pain she had in bearing and raising her, while Agamemnon becomes the destroyer of this property to which he had no right... his outrageous boldness is a direct affront to her rights as a mother': Kitzinger (1991) 313.

[19] e.g. Blundell (1989) 172.

[20] Eur. *El.* 1069–79.

[21] As MacLeod (2001) 85 states, 'no one disputes Elektra's story or suggests that it is false, and no one, not even Klytaimnestra, offers an alternative version'. Ringer (1998) 160, on the other hand, insists that the account is based on hearsay: 'In Sophocles' play, *logos* and appearance seem to carry more

towards both speakers may be appropriate,[22] but our sympathy (and thus the balance of credibility) must be overwhelmingly with Electra. It seems implied too that Clytemnestra was perfectly aware that Agamemnon had no choice, but she chose to justify a killing that was motivated by the persuasions of Aegisthus (560–2).[23] Some readers have found, justifiably, an irony in Electra's comment: 'You say that you killed my father. What could be a more shameful statement than that, whether you killed him justly or not?' (558–60). It might appear that the same objection could be levelled, a fortiori, at the projected matricide. But since Electra is about to show that Agamemnon died *un*justly, she does not need to argue that even if he had died justly his wife would have had no right to kill him. Nevertheless, she is herself prepared to admit that, from a certain conventional perspective, her whole campaign against her mother is shameful. The shame, however, is unavoidable because she is confronted with a moral imperative. Similarly, in *Choephori*, Pylades argues that, in the face of the divine command, Orestes must ignore the shame he feels at the prospect of killing his mother.

There may seem to be an even stronger irony in Electra's warning to Clytemnestra not to establish a talio ethic, lest she become its first victim (577–83). She is not thereby implying, however, that such an ethic is wrong; she is observing rather that it is contrary to Clytemnestra's own interests to support the talio when she is guilty of a particularly atrocious murder. Electra herself, on the other hand, can safely act as the agent of the talio because in killing her father's killers she would be punishing a crime rather than (in principle, at least) fuelling a vendetta in which all the supposed agents of justice would also be guilty of a fresh crime.

Electra can embrace the talio then because she is confident that her mother is in fact guilty of a crime, whereas Clytemnestra cannot be so confident of her husband's guilt. Electra has just explained that her father did not kill Iphigenia as a favour to Menelaus; but supposing he had, that would scarcely authorize Clytemnestra to kill him (577–9). That *nomos* would justify her own death. Electra is arguing here that, even in those circumstances, it would not be clear that Agamemnon had committed a wrong that deserved punishment, let alone death, and that at the hands of his own wife. Thus the killing of Agamemnon would be unjustified (as indeed it was), so that the retributive act of killing Clytemnestra would be an act of justice. Again, the crucial factor with the talio is to distinguish original crime from retributive act. In practice this can be difficult, but in this case the crime is the murder of Agamemnon, and the killing of his murderers is retributive justice. Electra concludes by regretting her verbal

---

significance than truth, and truth itself seems virtually impossible to determine.' The objection of C. Segal (1966) 536 that Agamemnon could have disbanded the army and returned home by land is not valid because that possibility is not raised in the play. Moreover, it would amount to an attempt to circumvent a god by means of trickery, thus inviting merciless requital.

[22] See Lloyd (2005) 86–7.

[23] 'While the rhetoric of Clytaemnestra's speech is speedy and diverting, Elektra's methodically peels away layer after layer of Clytaemnestra's argument to reveal the character behind it': Kitzinger (1991) 314. In general, Electra wins the agon 'because she appeals to and demonstrates a justice that goes beyond the letter of this law [the talio] to include the character and motive of the avenger and her ability to articulate the necessity of her act': ibid. 312. In general, Kitzinger's discussion of the agon is the best I have seen.

abuse of her mother, but claims again that the situation makes it necessary: shameful ($a\grave{\imath}\sigma\chi\rho o\hat{\imath}s$) deeds produce shameful responses ($a\grave{\imath}\sigma\chi\rho\acute{a}$) (621).[24]

Some commentators have argued that the moral similarities between mother and daughter are more significant than the differences. Blundell, for example, maintains that 'like her mother, Electra uses a veneer of dubiously rational argument to justify behaviour prompted by passionate feeling'.[25] That Electra is passionate is not in doubt, but the passion reinforces a valid moral argument supported by evidence about Agamemnon's dilemma (evidence we have to accept).[26] And since Electra's account of her father's dilemma is true, her mother did not act with Dike. Clytemnestra's whole behaviour (as reported) does not suggest a woman of moral integrity; indeed we are strongly influenced against her. But Blundell must argue as she does in order to support her view of the drama as a whole: 'the play explores the nature of revenge by presenting us with characters who believe in their own justice, with their arguments, motives and passions, and demonstrating the rationally insoluble character of their disputes'.[27]

But it is only mother and daughter who engage in moral (as opposed to merely prudential) disagreement, and there is nothing insoluble about it. Clytemnestra is a hypocrite. Blundell continues: 'We see how the talio can be used as an objective mask for the passions that give rise to deeds of irrational brutality—passions of lust, hatred, grief and wrath.'[28] Certainly it can be so used and doubtless often was (and is), but Electra is motivated at once by emotion *and* by moral conviction, which, as we have seen, are interdependent. Since her moral arguments are valid enough in the play's terms, there is no more reason to dismiss them as mere rationalizations of her feelings than to accept a thief's dismissal of his victim's moral indignation as a rationalization of a desire to recover his stolen possessions. Here we might contrast the Euripidean Electra's use of the oracle to sway Orestes. Euripides' virago offers no moral argument here or anywhere else in the play; she simply appeals to divine authority, and we have abundant prior evidence that her own motivation is primarily emotional.

Both Blundell and Winnington-Ingram object and see Sophocles as objecting to the talio in general: 'The principle [of justice to which Electra subscribes] is retaliation . . . founded not upon reason but upon passion.'[29] But retribution is not unreasonable; it is a basic principle of justice. Winnington-Ingram objects to Electra's contention that she is driven to 'evil' by her mother: 'evil in the past sets up a process, compulsive and inevitable, determining evil in the future'.[30] The basic meaning of *kaka*, however, is 'unpleasant' or 'nasty', and though it often means 'morally bad' as well, we need to be guided by the context. Clytemnestra's

---

[24] 'Essentially all Klytaimnestra's crimes have the same *fons et origo*; the rejection and violation of the two closest ties of the *philia* relationship, spousal and blood-kin, the basic ties upon which any human community rests. She cannot claim what she herself has rejected': MacLeod (2001) 68.

[25] Blundell (1989) 172.

[26] Winnington-Ingram (1980) 220 and n. 15 thinks that Sophocles trivializes Agamemnon's dilemma, not wishing us to take it too seriously as an explanation—which would all but destroy Electra's case. Indeed, one might go further and say that he actually removes the dilemma altogether, but with the clear purpose of rendering Agamemnon innocent and Clytemnestra guilty so that the matricide will appear as sheer retribution without being at the same time another crime.

[27] Blundell (1989) 172.   [28] Ibid.

[29] Winnington-Ingram (1980) 222.   [30] Ibid. 224.

behaviour is nasty (and evil), therefore Electra's must be nasty (but not evil because justly retributive).[31] If the murder is not punished there can be no *aidōs*, no *eusebeia* (says Electra) (245–50), and yet, objects Winnington-Ingram, 'the mind—and the actions—of the blood-avenger are such as to exclude *eusebeia*'.[32] But Clytemnestra has forfeited conventional *eusebeia* by the enormity of her actions, and Electra is obliged to practise *eusebeia* as best she can in the circumstances through recognition of her father's superior claim.

But, it may be objected, Electra *herself* admits to having inherited her mother's 'shameless' nature.

In 605–9 . . . Electra suggested that if she was full of *anaideia,* this was due to the *phusis* she inherited from her mother; in 616–21 she accepts the charge of *anaideia,* but explains it in terms of the education she has received at her mother's hands; in terms, then, of both sides of the great fifth-century antithesis between heredity and education, *phusis* and *nomos,* Electra's character, from which springs her conduct, including her eventual participation in matricide, is the counterpart of her mother's in the deepest possible sense.[33]

But Electra rightly considers herself morally (and thus absolutely fundamentally) antithetical to her mother. Her reflections on their similarities are sarcastic and touch only the surface of their natures.[34] The highly moral Electra is disgusted to find herself descending to her mother's level of outward behaviour, but she understands why this is happening and why, morally, it must happen. It is a necessary consequence of the un-Christian ethic of requiting *kaka* with *kaka*. Her mother has 'taught' her shamelessness only in the sense that she is morally compelled to repay Clytemnestra's shameful behaviour in her own coin.[35] Both women are prepared to conduct themselves with a conventional *anaideia* in respect to the bond of *philia* between them, but their reasons for doing so could hardly be more dissimilar, as the play has by this point clearly established.[36]

As to the claim that Electra's retributive morality is founded on passion rather than reason, her commitment to the punishment of her father's killers is passionate indeed, but, as we have seen, this entails in part a genuine devotion to what she believes is morally right. All morality has an emotional ground in that it is concerned with certain basic and irreducible desires which we recognize in ourselves and by empathy attribute to and valorize in others. But there is also a

---

[31] For such shifts in the use of terms see Goldhill (2000) *passim*.

[32] Winnington-Ingram (1980) 225.

[33] Cairns (1991) 26.

[34] Stevens (1978) 119; Szlezak (1981) 12–13.

[35] Electra 'may act shamefully and this behaviour may have as its model Klytaimnestra's behaviour, but it is not her nature (*phusis*) or character, but her schooling which makes her act that way. She has had to learn to be shameful and her mother's shameful deeds have been her teacher': McLeod (2001) 100.

[36] As March (2001) observes ad 608–9, 'there is no suggestion here that Electra has inherited her mother's evil nature, despite, e.g., Segal (1966) 499–500, Winnington-Ingram (1980) 245–6, Cairns (1993) 246; see rather Stinton (1975) 81 and n. 78. Her "bad behaviour" has been imposed on her by her situation: see her own words at 221, 307–9, 616–21 and 624–5.' Kitzinger (1991) 316–17 catches nicely the sense of similarity in difference: 'Paradoxically, Elektra's willingness to acknowledge the nature she shares with her mother marks the difference between the two women. If the task of condemning Clytaemnestra forces Elektra to become a reflection of her mother, that reflection has at the same time made incredible Clytaemnestra's claim to just action.'

rational component in morality. (Aristotelian moral maturity, for example, is characterized by a fusion of cognitive and affective elements.) Electra feels the reasonable desire that killers be punished appropriately. The rational component enters in deciding what precisely constitutes an appropriate punishment, and cultural views will be strongly influential here. Cultures generally impose some sort of restraint on punishment. Electra's desire to requite a death with a death here seems more reasonable than the Euripidean Medea's desire to requite perjury, marital betrayal, and desertion with the deaths of four innocent people including a king, a princess, and her own (and her principal victim's) children. Electra's retribution is measured and in harmony with ancient sentiment; Medea's passionate vindictiveness is out of control.

Clytemnestra has no case; she is clearly an enemy who deserves to suffer and to die for what she has done, but Electra must regret that her own mother is that sort of person and that she cannot therefore love and respect her in harmony with her natural moral instincts. Indeed she admits to her mother that her own behaviour is conventionally wrong in that she might well be described as 'nasty' (κακήν), 'loud-mouthed' (στόμαργον), and full of 'shamelessness' (ἀναιδείας), and in this she resembles Clytemnestra (605-9). However, this sort of behaviour is, she rightly claims, unnatural to her, contrary to her moral instincts we might say, but provoked by similar behaviour on her mother's part (616-25). Indeed the code of harming enemies gives Electra's contempt for her mother a special poignancy since she is required (as she sees it) not only to despise her mother but also to hate her and do all she can to make her life wretched and eventually help to bring about her death. Electra's morality goes against the Aristotelian idea that virtue is pleasurable in that it actually requires the agent's unhappiness. As an ancient Greek, Electra has no trouble hating an enemy, even one who was the closest of *philoi*. So her regret is not personal in the sense that she finds it difficult to hate *this* mother. But she finds it distressing that she has the sort of mother whom one cannot help hating and whom one is morally obliged to hate. None of this is very Christian, I fear, but it is the source of wonderful moral paradox.

DOES ELECTRA'S MORAL STAND DESTROY HER LOVING NATURE?

We have seen that the chorus are worried about Electra. They urge her not to hate too much (177). By indulging in a grief that is ἀμήχανον (140)—that can lead to no productive result (as they see it)—she is effectively destroying herself emotionally (διόλλυσαι) (140-4), producing her own ruin (οἰκείας ... ἄτας) (214-16) by constantly engendering conflicts for (or in?) her inharmonious soul (σᾷ δυσθύμῳ ... ψυχᾷ, 218-19), which cannot be waged with her powerful enemies. But has Electra been brutalized by a morality that advocates harming enemies—and has it encouraged a nasty malice in her that has perverted her essentially loving nature?

Electra's disharmony is partly the sheer internal resonance of external conflict, but partly also (as we have seen) the product of the internal conflict between the instinctive morality of filial *eusebeia* and the calculated morality in this situation of abuse of a mother. Electra herself is clearly aware of this. The situation compels her to behave in a way that is repugnant to her and yet morally right. 'I am quite aware of my temper', she says ($\xi\xi o\iota\delta$', $o\dot{v}$ $\lambda\dot{a}\theta\epsilon\iota$ μ' $\dot{o}\rho\gamma\dot{a}$, 222) with a degree of detachment unique among Sophoclean heroes who normally find little to regret in their own behaviour. Shortly she will express a kind of shame and apologize for her attitude (254–7). Electra's personal tragedy (if we are to think in such terms) thus assumes an extra dimension in that she herself is aware of what has been lost by her decision (for which she cannot nevertheless feel remorseful). In a strong moral paradox she asserts that she must keep up her 'ruinous acts' ($\ddot{a}\tau as$, 224)— ruinous to her own mental state because contrary to moral intuition.

Moral commitment can be bought at a terrible emotional cost, but we may feel that this is nothing compared with maintaining our moral integrity. The danger is that we will not maintain it, that in fighting an evil we might descend to the weapons of our opponents. Does Electra then maintain her moral integrity? We might be inclined to say that she remains true to the spurious morality of the heroic code and that by our standards she is corrupted in enjoying the spectacle of the sufferings of her mother and Aegisthus. This is not the traditional ancient view, though it is possible that Sophocles was uneasy about the malice that generally accompanies acts of revenge. After all, Electra herself, as we have seen, is troubled by her at least outward similarity to her mother.

To help resolve this question of Electra's alleged moral corruption we need to consider in detail the presentation of the revenge killings. First, the dream that prefigures them lacks the nasty and disturbing qualities of the corresponding dream in Aeschylus which symbolizes the matricide as a brutal, inhuman killing involving an unnatural attack on the maternal breast, the source of the nourishment of life. The dream in Sophocles, on the other hand, suggests that the killings are simply a means of clearing the way for the restoration of right rule (417–23).

Moreover, there is in the Sophoclean play no agon immediately before the deed in which the moral issues might have been aired.[37] The issues have been thoroughly canvassed already, particularly in the agon between mother and daughter which, unlike in Aeschylus and Euripides, occurs well before the matricide. Thus the audience have had time to set their minds against Clytemnestra, nor are they asked to disturb their settled opinions and sympathies as the deed approaches.[38]

For this reason I cannot agree with Kitzinger's contention that we accept Electra's moral direction in the play only to the point where she falls under the influence of her brother's deception and believes him to be dead: 'The distance thus created between the audience's knowledge and Elektra's deprives her speech of its power to reflect reality and makes her an object of pity rather than the persuasive interpreter she has been . . . The undermining of Elektra's presence and language continues in each episode that follows until Orestes' entrance.'[39]

---

[37] The agon (516 ff.), as in Euripides, where again the principal focus is Electra, is between mother and daughter.

[38] Clytemnestra's sorrow at Orestes' 'death' is minimal and short-lived. She chooses to see him as an exile rather than a son: MacLeod (2001) 120–1. She 'cannot later claim the status of a mother, having forfeited it by her own repudiation of it; nor, more significantly, does she have the right to ask for pity, for devoid of it herself, she has lost the right to demand that it be shown to her': ibid. 125.

[39] Kitzinger (1991) 319–20.

When Electra learns the truth (Kitzinger contends[40]), she cannot recover her role of interpreter because of the need to repress talk in favour of action. She is then forced to adopt Orestes' deceit.

> The kind of justice that Elektra brings to our attention in the first scenes of the play is abandoned; action is performed finally without *logos*, without a linguistic system of value and comprehension formed around and through it. For an audience whose understanding of justice has been fashioned by the first half of the play, the acts that end it cannot constitute justice—at least not human justice.[41]

But Electra's *moral* authority is in no way compromised by her temporary ignorance of the *factual* situation, and, as we shall see, there is little to surprise or unsettle us in the final section of the play which would call for further moral elucidation.[42] Electra has always intended her own retribution to be an inadequate substitute for the killings which her brother would perform.[43]

Not only Apollo, but the gods in general, including the Furies (merging with Orestes and Pylades at 1388), seem to lend their support to the avengers: Orestes prays (surely successfully) to Apollo for help in vindicating justice (1376–83). The chorus declare that the dead have been avenged (1417–21) and 'live' (ζῶσιν, 1417) (in the sense that Agamemnon lives again in the avenging son).[44] It has been suggested that Orestes' use of deceit makes him unheroic, and it is even explicitly stated in the play that there are no hostile men inside (1369);[45] but Hermes in particular supports the avengers (1396), and that surely helps to vindicate the treachery which Apollo commanded them to employ and which is both practically necessary and traditional. This kind of divine support hardly qualifies as intervention, though logically it must entail some kind of overdetermination. Only Apollo could be seen as 'panoramically' involved, but there is not a single case of psychological intervention in the play.

Sophocles is careful to involve Electra morally but not physically in both killings. Euripides' evocation of the matricide through the words of the tormented killers themselves provides eloquent evidence indeed as to why the Sophoclean Electra could not be physically involved. It was necessary for Sophocles to preserve the sense that the deed was horrible though morally necessary, but Euripides' evocation is so revolting that any attempt to justify the matricide would appear

---

[40] Kitzinger (1991) 324–5.

[41] Ibid. 300. See also Lloyd (2005) 97.

[42] Unlike in Euripides' *Electra* where characters and audience alike are severely shaken up by the details of the matricide.

[43] 'Those who suppose that since the return of Orestes, Elektra has been increasingly marginalized and her voice silenced, fail to acknowledge what an active part she takes in the *dolos* stratagem. Previously, a victim of it herself, she has now become an agent of it, and it is her deceptive behaviour (along with the lie) which causes Aigisthos to reveal his *hybris*': MacLeod (2001) 173.

[44] 'Every power, from Olympian to ghost, is thus [see 1378, 1392, 1413–14, 1419] on the side of the avengers, and so the killings follow rapidly without hindrance or suspense': Burnett (1998) 132. Likewise March (2001) 16–17. But some critics see the emphasis on vengeful gods as a justification of the sense of moral unease which they find: e.g. C. Segal (1966) 526–7: 'The prominence given to the chthonic powers at the end suggests the enveloping atmosphere of darkness and hate which remains despite the victory. As in a nightmare—and this is a play of nightmarish visions—the guilty are struck down, but something almost as terrible rises up in their place (1417–18).'

[45] C. Segal (1981) 253.

obscene. The Sophoclean Electra's off-stage verbal exhortations allow her to bring her programme of revenge through to completion, while restricting her own role to the conceptual and psychological level. It is as if in playing the role of the Aeschylean Pylades she joins her independent moral will with that of the god who overdetermines Orestes' equally autonomous motivation.[46] It was important not to compromise the act's human inspiration by suggesting that Electra's mental processes are passively entangled in the complex machinations of divine powers.[47]

Sophocles could hardly avoid associating Electra closely with the deed because his play's principal focus has been her campaign of protracted vengeance and its psychological and ethical implications. It would have been unsatisfyingly anticlimactic to sever Electra from the very culmination of her revenge, but in linking her closely with matricide Sophocles risked alienating the audience from her. The moral rather than physical participation of Electra is reinforced by the fact that on 'the auditory level the whole scene is enacted between Clytemnestra and Electra along with the chorus'.[48] For Kitzinger, on the other hand, Electra's physical abstention from the matricide creates a very different effect:

> her words mime the action, become, as far as possible, the action . . . yet they are so plainly removed from it that they are shockingly futile and empty. . . . Her words here cannot take the place of the action that we must imagine taking place inside. . . . Elektra's words fill Orestes' silence, but in doing so distract from, rather than complete, our experience of the murder.[49]

Certainly Electra's words substitute for an account of the matricide as actually performed by the male avengers, but the purpose is to link the deed as closely as possible with her, though short of allowing her to do it, and not to produce moral unease over the physical dimension of the retribution which belongs essentially to Orestes and is therefore of only secondary dramatic importance. One must admit though that the matricide remains something of an embarrassment. If it really is a good thing, why is it necessary to dissociate Electra physically from it? One suspects that Sophocles had come up against the limitations of the myth as Homer did at *Odyssey* 306–10 where he plainly wished to dissociate Orestes from the matricide while feeling unable to ignore Clytemnestra's death.

The victim dies off stage with the conventional shriek (1404) the similarity of which to the death cries of Aeschylus' *Agamemnon* suggests an appropriate retributive justice. It has been argued that Electra displays 'sheer malice', a

---

[46] 'The myth requires that Orestes commit the matricide but Electra appears mentally, if not physically, to appropriate the act by the violence of the language by which she wills it': Seale (1982) 75. March (2001) ad 1398–441 demurs: 'Some critics argue that Electra is in effect taking part in the deed of murder itself . . . but this is to read too much into the scene. Electra will in fact play no *direct* part in the vengeance until it is time to deal with Aegisthus. . . . As far as Clytemnestra's death goes, Letters (1953) 259 makes the nice distinction that Electra is her mother's "hanging judge, not her executioner".'

[47] Unless we see her as possessed more than metaphorically by the Furies as their 'victim and agent': Winnington-Ingram (1980) 239.

[48] Seale (1982) 75. See also Woodard (1966) 141: 'what we see and what we hear at the moment of matricide make Electra the dramatic agent of vengeance. It is as though her shouts were swords.' See also the detailed comments of Ringer (1998) 201–2 who thinks that the deed 'is made paradoxically more horrible and more futile by the fact that she merely "seems" to kill her mother' (ibid. 202).

[49] Kitzinger (1991) 326.

'gloating pleasure' or 'fiercely exultant hatred' over the matricide.[50] In the absence
of stage directions, however, we know only the following. When her mother begs
for mercy, Electra declares that she showed none for her husband or indeed for
Orestes (when she thought he was dead) (1410–12),[51] and she urges her brother to
strike a second blow. All that can be safely inferred from these statements is that
Electra, unsurprisingly and uncontroversially, considers mercy inappropriate in
the circumstances and that she insists on strict 'eye for an eye' retribution.
(Clytemnestra is to receive precisely the treatment she meted out to Agamemnon
in Aeschylus at *Ag.* 1343–5: a second blow resulting in much the same death
cry.[52]) The spirit in which these remarks are made can be inferred only from what
we know already about Electra's character and moral commitment. They cannot
be used as evidence of an Electra whose standards have declined since the earlier
scenes. Moreover, the deed is partly a repayment of the ills that Electra received at
her mother's hands.[53] There is no account or evocation, because Sophocles, like
Aeschylus and unlike Euripides, wished to insist on the justice of the deed and not
risk alienating the audience from the avengers. The chorus are allowed to mention
that the killers have bloodstained hands, but they do not blame them (1422–3).

It is clearly significant that reflection on the deed after the event in an 'ekkyklema' scene in which the bodies of the victims are displayed is forestalled by the
use of Clytemnestra's body in the intrigue surrounding Aegisthus' murder which
is still to come. Orestes merely observes that the deed was right if Apollo was right.
The implication is that of course he was—a position assumed by the Euripidean
Electra in her argument with Orestes (Eur. *El.* 967 ff.). The play has already put the
moral issue to rest, and to raise it here in passing without attempting a proper
discussion would be dramatically distracting, to say the least. Some critics, however, have tried to cast doubt on the oracle. Sheppard (*passim*) argued that Orestes
was wrong to ask *how* rather than *if* he should exact vengeance on his father's
killers, but this makes nonsense of the god's injunction to use stealth to kill
them justly (Orestes had not even mentioned killing them) which more naturally
implies that he approves of the deed (32–7).[54] Is it really conceivable that a Greek
god would not approve of righteous vengeance, unless he had a vested interest to
the contrary? Orestes' question about the means rather than the end is intended to
underline his comfortable moral unanimity with the god.

---

[50] Horsley (1980) 26; Seale (1974) 74; C. Segal (1966) 523.

[51] 'Klytaimnestra receives no pity because she has none herself. Elektra shows no pity, not because
she has none, but because her mother has forfeited pity. This does not make the refusal of pity any less
ugly, but it does justify it. What we witness during the matricide is an act that is neither honourable nor
glorious, only just, but is, for all its justice, *aischron*': MacLeod (2001) 171.

[52] Gellie (1972) 127. C. Segal (1966) 501 sees in Electra's cries amid the Aeschylean echoes
'something of the monstrous force and energy of the mother as they appeared at the climax of her
powers, the cutting down of Agamemnon.'

[53] '[I]t is not so much (as in Aeschylus) the fact and the nature of Clytaemnestra's killing of her
husband, but the accumulated wickedness of her behaviour over seven years or more thereafter, that
makes her killing by her son, in this play, the lesser of two evils. It is fitting that after carrying out the
killing, Orestes says not, as we might expect, "Now my father is avenged", but, to Electra, "You need not
fear that your mother's arrogance will ever degrade you again" (1426–7)': Sommerstein (1997) 208–9.

[54] See also Kells (1973) ad 35 ff.

Segal attempts to dig a different escape route from that of Sheppard, claiming desperately that 'the precise details of the oracle are left vague, and nowhere in the play does Apollo give explicit and unambiguous sanction for the matricide'.[55] For Kitzinger too the oracle is no help: the play 'so studiously avoids exploring the nature of this divine command that, if it is to be a justification, it is one that remains incomprehensible'.[56] What I find 'incomprehensible' rather are the critics' difficulties here. The god's instructions as to means are very clear, and while on their own they imply sanction, the term 'just' (*endikou*, 37) is also used to describe the projected killings. If it is suggested that Orestes supplied that adjective as his own moral interpretation, it can be rejoined that the whole prologue is designed to suppress rather than provoke moral doubt. Apollo's ethic is hardly inscrutable; like Electra he supports the talio. The critics' difficulties are created by their refusal to accept that a Sophoclean play could adopt such a moral position.[57]

Blundell, on the other hand, is prepared to accept that the god fully supports the killings, but thinks that the audience need not agree.[58] Now certainly we may reject the morality of some of the gods of Greek tragedy (one thinks of Apollo in Euripides' *Electra*, Athena in the *Ajax*, Hera in *Heracles*, or Aphrodite in *Hippolytus*, to take only four obvious examples), but there is no warrant for doing so here, since Electra has defended the killings and no one, apart from the victims, has seen fit to adopt a Euripidean view and disagree. Nor is there the radical volte-face of Euripides' play, with its remorseful avengers. Blundell's view is offered in support of her (invalid) argument that the play implies the unworkability of the talio. I have argued rather that, whatever Sophocles thought outside the context of this play, his focus here is on Electra's genuine and agonizing moral predicament (though not 'dilemma'), and that therefore he had no desire to cut the Gordian knot by declaring what was obvious since *Oresteia*: namely that, ultimately, her predicament was unnecessary once it was realized that the whole ethic of the personal talio had been superseded by courts of law.

It is important that Aegisthus' impending murder, rather than the matricide, is the climax of the play. This removes the focus from the matricide and further discourages reflection on it.[59] Some critics, however, are offended by the alleged

---

[55] C. Segal (1981) 280.

[56] Kitzinger (1991) 301 n. 12. 'Orestes, in his silence and reliance on Apollo's judgement, may express a recognition of divine justice, but at the same time he fails to satisfy the human need to understand... The god knows at the start of the play, and implies in the oracle that we learn for ourselves in its course, that it is beyond the capacity of human beings to join this act with language that comprehends and justifies it. It can only be performed *doloisi*, with all the hiddenness and obscurity that the word implies. They can serve its necessity, but they cannot make it a fully human act, endowed with an adequate articulation of the feeling and thought that make sense of it': ibid. 326–7. Ringer (1998) 203 thinks that Orestes' statement conveys a 'delicate ambiguity'.

[57] Gellie (1972) 107 relates the passage, appropriately, to the play's dramaturgy: 'the word 'righteous' in Apollo's reply is a moral judgement in itself... It is true that Sophocles is taking us at a run past the god's decision, because this play, unlike Aeschylus's, will relegate moral qualms to the background, but he knows that we will be prepared to run only if the brief statement is made utterly unequivocal.'

[58] Blundell (1989) 182–3.

[59] 'The play focusses primarily on the murder of Clytemnestra qua revenge, not matricide. This is one reason why Aegisthus dies last. We are left with the grim brutality of summary vengeance, without the complicating emotion of horror at matricide': Blundell (1989) 181.

malicious cruelty of the avengers' sport with Aegisthus.[60] But if revenge is righteous it would be silly not to enjoy it, and these executioners are less cruel than Medea or Hecuba. Doubtless the audience savoured the ironies of the scene. The exposure of Aegisthus' corpse, if that is what Electra has in mind, is unpleasantly reminiscent of *Ajax* and *Antigone*, and Segal is right to speak of 'deliberate outrage',[61] even if the motive behind Electra's injunction is no more than sheer indifference to the fate of the body.[62] However, as Burnett and March point out, the corpse is not to be deliberately mutilated or expressly forbidden burial, and it is not altogether clear that the 'appropriate gravediggers' are indeed predatory animals, as is usually assumed.[63] Electra is chiefly concerned to remove Aegisthus from her sight and she will not let him speak (1483 ff.)—not presumably out of fear that he might be able to mount a credible defence or move the avengers to pity, but because she has waited long enough for his death and nothing he could say in his own defence would be relevant.[64]

Aegisthus, however, does manage to refer to the future ills of the house, and this has disturbed the critics. According to Segal, for example, the play moves to an end, a *telos*, but there remains 'a feeling of entrapment in the hatred and evil of the Pelopid house in Aegisthus' last, prophetic speech', and, in the view of Blundell, the lines must refer to 'future punishment for the matricide'. On the other hand, March suggests that Aegisthus may be referring only to the implications of Clytemnestra's death and of his own. In any case the lines cannot refer to the Furies,

for Aegisthus implies that the future evils are dependent on *his own* death (1496), and never in any version of the myth is there a suggestion that *his* murder results in anything other than triumph and just revenge for Orestes and freedom for Electra. Moreover, if this really is meant to be a hint of some future trouble, we must note that it is of events destined to take place under 'this very roof'... which would surely exclude the Furies' pursuit.[65]

[60] '[T]he calculated cruelty of the vengeance, which is reminiscent of Euripides, is also revealing about the avengers themselves': Seale (1982) 77.

[61] C. Segal (1981) 271. 'We feel no pity at all for Aegisthus, but this deliberate outrage of his corpse casts doubt upon the restoration of a fully civilized order in the city' (ibid.). But contrast his earlier view, for which see the following note.

[62] 'Her [Electra's] emphasis in these lines [1485–90] is not upon savoring the vengeance, but finishing it and banishing all sight and memory of it. Thus in 1487–89 she does not openly taunt Aegisthus with threats of dogs or birds, but leaves the reference to his burial (or non-burial) so vague that it is quite possible that she actually means to give his body proper care. Her verb, *prothes*, is the regular expression for the laying out of a corpse': C. Segal (1966) 520–1.

[63] Aegisthus' non-burial is appropriate to a defilement to be removed: 'His corpse will receive no injury, but it will be borne away out of sight (1489) and left where it can no longer infect the community.... This proposal brings a conceptual fulfillment to Orestes' entering wish, which was that he might be a purifier here in Argos': Burnett (1998) 136. Electra just wants him out of her sight. She does not actively prevent his burial as the Atreidae try to do in *Ajax* or Creon in *Antigone*: March (2001) ad 1488. 'Only by full requital of the extreme *kaka* under which she has suffered can she find release; thus she demands the harshest treatment for Aegisthus' body': Woodard (1966) 142.

[64] 'Remembering the words of her brother that superfluous speech would only deprive them of the right time (1292), she counsels her brother to carry out the punishment immediately' [1487–90]: MacLeod (2001) 176.

[65] C. Segal (1981) 264; Blundell (1989) 176–7; March (2001) ad 1498. Critics who approve of Electra's morality and of the talio see no reason for Fury pursuit (e.g. Burnett [1998]139; March [2001] 18). Those who do not approve maintain either that Sophocles leaves the matter open

Indeed, the failure of the Furies to pursue Orestes confirms Electra's notion that the Furies are actually, in un-Aeschylean fashion, angered by Clytemnestra's adultery and murder of her husband, and that their pursuit is embodied in Electra's crusade.

Those critics who argue for Electra's moral degradation tend to find that her malice is accompanied by emotional desolation in the final scene. Blundell points to the absence of the joy which was earlier anticipated, whereas March (who rejects the moral degradation theory) anticipates joy in the immediate future:

> The action is held, poised, at the moment when Aegisthus is about to die, the moment for which Electra has been waiting down all the long years. So the play ends with Electra too, in a sense, held, poised forever, in that transfiguring moment of joy just as she is about to receive her longed-for release after years of pain, her final deliverance.[66]

True, the play has invited us to anticipate such a future, but the grim finale is hardly conducive to our thinking in such terms. For Winnington-Ingram, 'Electra's joy [at her reunion with her brother] has flowered only to wither in the cold wind of a vindictive killing.' Electra's hatred *is* engrained in her and remains uppermost in the closing scene.[67] Electra is certainly a fury to Clytemnestra, drinking her blood, but she has hardly been 'suffering a degradation of which she was herself aware'.[68] She simply remains on course until she attains what she always wanted, the death of her father's killers, and her hatred for her enemies coexists, as it did in most ancient Greeks, with her love for her friends. A Christian sensibility will doubtless find these states incongruous if not incompatible. Would the 'degradation' critics have preferred her to have performed the volte-face of her Euripidean counterpart? But even *that* Electra does not abandon an ethical position, if she could be described as ever having had one. It is her *feelings* that undergo a change when she is confronted with the messy and appalling physical details of matricide. The 'degradation' critics have tended to read in the moral corruption they expect to see, even to the point of imagining an Electra who *looks* desolate.[69] But, as Kirkwood points out, '[m]ost of the end of the play, from the

---

(Winnington-Ingram [1980] 227), or that the Furies are symbolically incarnated in the avengers themselves. In the latter case it is sometimes suggested that these inner Furies prey both on Agamemnon's killers and on his avengers (Electra is 'the victim and the agent of the Furies': ibid. 228). 'The visitation of external Furies . . . would detract from this spectacle of human beings acting as their own Furies from the combination of destructive, self-deceptive passions with a self-defeating conception of justice': Blundell (1989) 180. See also MacLeod (2001) 179 and Sewell-Rutter (2007) 102: 'We are left not with a sense of future links in a continuing chain of disaster, but with a stark and strikingly final closure as Aegisthus goes into the house to his death.' See also ibid. 131–4.

[66] Blundell (1989) 177; March (2001) 20.

[67] Winnington-Ingram (1980) 230. See also Gellie (1972) 122.

[68] Winnington-Ingram (1980) 233.

[69] For Seale (1982) 78 Electra remains on stage, 'a picture of physical and spiritual destruction'. March (2001) ad 1490 rightly observes on Electra's reaction to her release: 'There is no trace here of uncertainty in her words, as Segal (1981, 266–7) claims: he speaks of Electra's "futility . . . uncertainty . . . lonely agony . . . the loneliness of her tragic realization . . . her spiritual and inward isolation", all quite unfounded in the text.' Equally unfounded, not to say wildly speculative, is the textually unsupported and psychologically implausible attempt of Horsley (1980) 25 to relate Electra's alleged psychological undoing to an alleged shock: 'The realization that he [Orestes] is dead, thus dashing all her hope, and then that he is in reality alive, contrary to all she has been led to

recognition on, is caught up in such a rush of excitement and so relentless a flood of action that there is little time for reflection . . . What is lacking is an explicit portrayal of Electra's moral and emotional state at the end.'[70]

CONCLUSION

No moral pressure is placed on Electra by the gods or by society. She faces a moral crisis because she is of sufficient moral sensitivity to recognize one and to believe that she herself must respond. Electra defines herself only partly in terms of conventional identity and roles, as she sees the moral implications of these roles very differently from those around her. Her moral position is partly intuitive and instinctive (her filial piety towards a father). It does not seem to be the product of *protracted* rational reflection in the sense of agonizing over the correct course of action, for she has no doubts as to the rightness of her moral campaign against her mother. She acts in part out of a pure moral impulse in that she loves the good and she recognizes the claims of *philoi* as far as she can (she can accommodate her father's claim but not the incompatible claim of her mother). Her moral conviction is supported by strong emotion. She is true to her own self-conception but her morality is also other-regarding in her devotion to her father. Still Electra must be presumed to have reflected over the need to violate the conventional obligation of filial piety to a mother, a reflection in effect forced upon her by her strong loyalty to her father. She is compelled to weigh the incompatible claims of two different people to receive filial piety. Honour as such does not loom conspicuously large in her thinking and her moral ideals are conventional in an unconventional situation in which they have to be unconventionally applied. Electra is a character whose moral life is depicted with a considerable degree of sophistication. Her self-definition while facing her protracted crisis does not change, nor is it threatened, though she becomes acutely aware of the emotional cost of her campaign.

The talio is universally accepted in the play. If Sophocles had wished to undermine a corresponding acceptance by the audience, he would have had to rely on a clash between their ethical views and the manifest ethic of the play. But no such clash can be demonstrated.[71] It was not sufficient to show that the consequences of pursuing the talio were grim, as that could be taken as read.[72]

---

believe, is a major jolt to her whole being. This is what destroys her. Apollo may thus be seen to be the force behind the ruin of Elektra as a person, and it is in this conjunction that her tragedy lies.'

[70] Kirkwood (1958) 168–9.

[71] Modern criticism of the talio morality in the play is in danger of being self-validating, sometimes in quite subtle ways. Gellie (1972) 121 e.g. wonders: 'Is he [Sophocles] pressing so hard and so obviously against our disposition to take into account Clytemnestra's rights as a mother, in order that our minds will snap back under the pressure and keep up their own running advocacy for her, in counterpoint to the pointing of the play?' In other words, certain moral positions are so obviously illegitimate that any attempt to support them must be self-refuting—and the more uncompromising the case, the stronger the self-refutation!

[72] The play's '"success" does not lie in solving the moral problems of the Orestes-legend. These problems do not lie at the center of the play, but do contribute to the tone of irresolution and the continued presence of "evils" at the end (see 1498)': C. Segal (1966) 540–1.

Electra pays a high emotional price for her justified moral stand, but she is neither morally corrupted in the play's terms nor rendered incapable of love or joy. At worst she has been morally obliged to indulge a capacity to hate which has blighted her life to this point. Sophocles, however, stops short of saying that a morality which requires such a self-sacrifice is thereby suspect. Electra is placed in a situation anachronistic to the audience. Civic justice had rendered her predicament impossible.[73] The interest is in her moral self-legislation when the state does not remove the burden of responsibility for an act as terrible as matricide. Electra gives vent to malice but it is not excessive (contrast Medea or the malice her counterpart at *Orestes* 1302–10 displays at the prospect of murdering Helen), though she shows no regret, but rather a grim determination to exact condign punishment. In Scodel's words: 'The triumph of the end is real. The play does not make vengeance pretty. Electra's nobility is not gentle, and she is driven beyond due limits; Orestes is determined to make Aegisthus suffer as much as he can (1504). But the result is just.'[74]

---

[73] The existence of civic justice does not, however, automatically remove the vindictive feelings of the injured parties. A modern Electra might be equally determined that her mother be punished and at a comparable emotional cost.

[74] Scodel (1984) 88.

10

Sophocles: *Philoctetes*

ARETĒ, TIMĒ, AND PHILIA

The Greek term *aretē* refers to both (amoral) excellence and (moral) virtue. Homeric excellence is a natural (though not an invariable) product of aristocratic birth and is identified with martial prowess of which the specific moral virtue of courage is a major element. This emphasis on courage makes moral sense as warriors are very useful people to societies constantly at war. Their social value, however, is an insufficient spur to the warriors themselves whose more self-centred motivation derives chiefly from the *timē* (honour) they get from their peers and the society in general. Unfortunately, they can become so obsessed with martial prowess as a source of honour that not only do they lose sight of Aristotle's point that it is the *aretē* rather than the honour that validates it that is of central importance,[1] but they tend also to undervalue such non-aretaic virtues as *philophrosunē* ('fellow feeling' or 'friendly cooperation'[2]), related to the institutional and affective bond of *philia* (or to use the Homeric term, *philotēs*), and respect (*aidōs*) for vulnerable people such as suppliants, beggars, and guests.[3] Thus the Iliadic Achilles withdraws and exposes his comrades to the temporarily victorious Trojans, and both Hector and the Sophoclean Ajax go to their deaths to redeem their honour, even though their dying harms family, friends, and society, while the faults for which they would atone are not even failures of martial courage.[4] Thus the pursuit of honour, when taken to extremes, can alienate a warrior from friends, peers, and society.[5] And yet honour would seem rather pointless if one cannot bask in it in the company of one's peers, and so the alienated Achilles is

---

[1] Aristotle *NE* 1095^{b}23–30.

[2] The translation of Adkins (1982) 303.

[3] Although these lesser virtues can be seen as integral to the heroic code (Zanker [1994] 42), as Scott (1979) 1 observes, social values 'were never, in the time of Homer or for a long time after, regarded as cardinal virtues or *aretai*'. On proper respect for these vulnerable people see Gagarin (1987) 290–2 who (ibid. 300) accepts pity as a Homeric virtue, but not loyalty, because of its relation to *philia* which he sees largely as an extension of self-interest. But responsibilities to one's *philoi* are surely in principle morally significant, although the claims of impartiality or justice, e.g., may transcend those of loyalty. Crude self-interest can lead to an immoral neglect of proper affection for and a sense of responsibility towards *philoi*, whereas a 'higher' self-interest is basic to Greek ethical eudaimonism.

[4] Hector's error was tactical (*Iliad* 22. 99–107), inspired by overconfidence. The importance of courage appears also in his reply to Andromache at 6. 404–65 where he would particularly avoid the charge of cowardice which would be fatal to the personal honour that for him at least takes priority over family and state.

[5] On acceptably moderate pursuit of honour through competition see Finkelberg (1998) 14–16.

compelled, in Nestor's words, to 'be the only one to profit from his *aretē*' (*Iliad* 11. 762–3).[6]

The Homeric Achilles is the classic example of the alienation which results from preoccupation with honour derived from martial *aretē*, but the Sophoclean Ajax is an even more extreme case because of the unwavering rigidity of his attitude. (Achilles, unlike Ajax, is, superficially at least, reintegrated into the community.) The Heracles of *Trachiniae* is rather different in not having to respond to a more or less deliberate slight to his honour and the resulting necessity to choose between *philia* and the claims of that honour, but his whole heroic but self-absorbed life alienates him physically and indeed psychologically from friends and family and guarantees him a lonely death despite the presence of his son and his supreme worthiness to be honoured for his labours.[7] *Philoctetes*, on the other hand, begins with extreme alienation, both physical and psychological, and ends with a substantial redefinition of *aretē* that gives active and cooperative *philia* a new and timely prominence.

ACHILLES' SON

Neoptolemus in the *Philoctetes* is of particular interest in connection with this redefined *aretē* because he is a young man whose views are still developing. At the beginning of the play he defines himself as his father's son and in terms of his inherited *phusis* rather than more abstractly with reference to desirable moral qualities, though of course he associates his *phusis* with what he considers such qualities. A typical young person, he is responding to a role model, in this case his famous father whom he has never seen. Thus he defines himself through a particular rather than a generic role; he is not simply a heroic warrior who, like (say) Aeschylus' Eteocles, defines himself as such, but Achilles' son. The moral obligations that flow from this are then closely associated with his father's qualities.

If there is any truth in the story he tells Philoctetes that on his arrival at Troy the army saw him as the very image of his father (356–8), then that experience would have reinforced his mode of self-definition.[8] Neoptolemus' view of his father focuses on two moral qualities recognizable from the *Iliad*—his hatred of hypocrisy and deceit (*Iliad* 9. 312–13) and his formidable *aretē* conceived as martial prowess—although his immature son has reduced and debased the latter to a legitimation of the use of force to achieve one's ends even off the field of battle (90–1). The compassion and outstanding capacity for *philia* of the Homeric

[6] The translation is that of Finkelberg (ibid. 22) who points to the similarity to Patroclus' comment at 16. 29–32. The profit that Achilles alone will derive from his *aretē* is presumably what he would call honour from Zeus (*Iliad* 9. 607–10). Finkelberg (ibid. 24) also compares Aristotle's preference for actualized over merely potential virtue.

[7] The Euripidean Heracles, on the other hand, in a play that celebrates *philia* above all else, actually makes his glory depend on his vindicating *philia* (*Her.* 574–82), and though he involuntarily violates *philia* in the worst conceivable way, it is *philia* again (in the person of Theseus) that rehabilitates him.

[8] On the relationship between truth and falsehood in this speech see Roberts (1989) 170–1.

Achilles are omitted from Neoptolemus' moral self-conception, as if the son were inspired exclusively by the limited and disgruntled Achilles of *Iliad* 9 and of the later aristeia. But if we are to do full justice to the Homeric Achilles, we must take into account the depth of his loving commitment to Patroclus. Homer's Achilles is characterized from the beginning by compassion, as we learn from Andromache, of all people, at *Iliad* 6. 414–19, and incidentally from Achilles himself during his extraordinary encounter with Lycaon (21. 100–5). This quality is in eclipse for most of the poem, though it returns deepened and transfigured by suffering at the end. We shall see that just as the father in the Homeric conception had to learn to incorporate a full and active compassion into his moral world (and that is perhaps the major moral lesson of the greatest of all Greek poems), so must the Sophoclean son.

Neoptolemus is naturally set on winning glory as his father did, so the bait which Odysseus dangles before him is irresistible. He is already aware when he arrives in Lemnos that it is his destiny to take Troy (114), so we can imagine that his heart is set on it, for it would be hard to conceive of a more glorious martial destiny. Therefore when Odysseus now informs him that Philoctetes' bow is a condition of the fulfilment of this destiny, we can see that only the strongest moral scruples could induce him to relinquish the prospect of such fame. Neoptolemus then must secure, or, not to put too fine a point on it, steal Philoctetes' bow (69, 78, 115). What Neoptolemus initially fails to realize, though, is that true glory is impossible without moral integrity.

The idea of morally compromised glory never arises for the other heroes discussed in this book. For Eteocles, for example, reputation depends on courage, so he must face his brother; and Ajax must find a courageous way to redeem his honour. But in Neoptolemus' special circumstances, martial courage is insufficient for the particular glory upon which he has set his sights, and it is not clear how he can attain that glory without deceit, as Odysseus insists. And yet with deceit there can be no true glory.

Presumably because Neoptolemus is a young man and a recent arrival at Troy, the prestigious Odysseus is able to impress upon him the need to obey and be socially responsible to the Greek army. He remarks that his job is to speak and that of Neoptolemus to listen (25), but this cannot be too hard for Neoptolemus when the will of those in power coincides with his own. Furthermore, Odysseus has encouraged him to regard Philoctetes as no more than a means to the end of personal glory, a motive that appears to carry more weight with him than the good of the army, as it did for a while with his Iliadic father.[9]

Odysseus does not attempt the corruption of Neoptolemus by arguing directly that morality will have to be sacrificed to self-interest; rather he suggests the desirability of aspiring to more sophisticated virtues than Homeric *aretē*, at any rate in its crudest form of sheer martial prowess. He tells him he must be 'noble' (γενναῖον, 51)[10] not only in 'body' (σώματι, 51)—which is perhaps a deliberately

---

[9] The emphasis is on Neoptolemus' personal advantage (108–20).

[10] *gennaios* 'is an aristocratic term of approval, rooted in the faith in inherited excellence most clearly enunciated by Pindar, for whom the *gennaios* spirit passes by nature (*phue*) from father to son (*Pyth.* 8. 44).... By using such language, Odysseus is appealing to Neoptolemus' pride in his birth and desire to live up to his *phusis*': Blundell (1988) 137. For Philoctetes' application of the word to

reductive view of Achillean *aretē* designed to hint at its inadequacy by focusing on the element of violence while ignoring the openness and honesty—and urges him to open his mind to some morally novel ideas (52–3). Presumably, he is to prove γενναῖος in some new and sophisticated sense that Odysseus will presently explain. At least, the suggestion is that nobility may extend to qualities which Neoptolemus in his youthful *naïveté* has not yet incorporated into his list of virtues. Odysseus is of course experienced and has learned to respect words as more efficacious than deeds (96–9). The older man acknowledges that it is not in accord with Neoptolemus' *phusis* to use deceit (which he does not try to deny is wrong in principle), but victory is sweet and the end justifies the use of such means (79–82), or, as Odysseus puts it, they will be seen in the long run to have acted rightly (δίκαιοι, 82)—no doubt because only thus can Troy be taken. Only when Odysseus tells Neoptolemus that he must give himself up to shamelessness (ἀναιδές, 83) 'for a brief part of a day' (83), but be called thereafter the most god-fearing (εὐσεβέστατος, 85) of mortals, does he admit that what he is advocating is immoral, at least from a conventional point of view, though how can it really be immoral if it is not so in the long run? (And perhaps there is a kind of *eusebeia* in furthering the designs of the gods, in this case the capture of Troy.)

In reply Neoptolemus claims that it is not in his nature (ἔφυν), nor was it in his father's, to engage in treacherous plotting (88–9). He is happy to use force (βίαν, 90), but not deceit (δόλοισιν, 91), and he shrinks from being called a traitor (προδότης, 94). He would prefer to fail acting nobly (καλῶς) than to win by foul means (κακῶς) (94–5). Rather than answering this directly, Odysseus remarks that age has made him respect words more than deeds (96–9). Otherwise expressed, it is immaterial to consider the morality of actions; the focus should rather be on finding the right words in order to mould situations to one's requirements (as he is now manipulating Neoptolemus). Presently he will say that it is not shameful to lie if it saves the day (109).

Neoptolemus' immediate response is to cut straight through Odysseus' moral sophistries ('You are just telling me to lie, aren't you?', 100), but the older man wears him down by continuing to dangle the bait before him (109). Corruption begins when Achilles' son begins to play with the idea of deceit, wondering now not whether he should but whether he could practise it. Would not an essentially honest man's face give him away? (110). But Neoptolemus goes on to wonder what's in it for him (κέρδος), if Philoctetes comes to Troy (112). He has now sunk therefore to the point of toying with the idea of subordinating his morality to a much desired end. So when Odysseus tells him that the sack of Troy depends on his use of the bow (115), he replies that such an end would be desirable (116). Odysseus now represents the deceit as a positive virtue, as a mark in fact of *sophia*, so that Neoptolemus will win a reputation as *sophos* as well as *agathos* (119).[11] (So it is not a question of departing from morality, but, as Odysseus has already implied, of extending its scope.) These Greek words are highly ambiguous. Is

Neoptolemus and the latter's moral odyssey in terms of it, see 75–6, 799, 801, 1068, 1402, and the discussion of Avery (1965) 289.

[11] Scodel (1984) 92 comments on the inconsistency of Odysseus' moral attitude towards the practice of deceit.

Neoptolemus to be *sophos* in the sense of 'cunning' or in the sense of 'wise', 'prudent', or 'sensible'? Or, again, taking the long-term view, is it wise to be cunning?[12] Is he to be *agathos* in the sense of 'brave' (that is, is he to add *sophia*, however conceived, to his already existing martial prowess?). Or is he to be *agathos* in the sense of generally virtuous (perhaps for obeying Odysseus and helping the army). Odysseus (and Sophocles) has the advantage of the morally less circumscribed world of Greek tragedy wherein anachronisms abound and Homeric and sophistic values can coexist, so that *agathos* cannot be straightfor-wardly confined to its martial, Homeric sense.

This moral obfuscation is enough to win over Neoptolemus, who now agrees to cast off all shame (πᾶσαν αἰσχύνην ἀφείς, 120), that is to ignore the admittedly shameful nature of the means when the end is so desirable, won over as he is now to Odysseus' moral world in which a few hours' shamelessness is apparently perfectly compatible with goodness, bravery, justice, cunning, wisdom, and even piety! So Neoptolemus can feel that the reputation he will win, far from being spurious, will be based on a wider and perfectly legitimate conception of virtue or nobility. Achilles' son, then, it would seem, allows his already limited and some-what inchoate moral awareness to be suppressed by his great desire for glory and by Odysseus' sophistries. For this to happen he has allowed one emotion (the desire for glory) to suppress another (the desire to feel morally comfortable). His emotions are therefore not properly integrated into his moral deliberations. Nor has he engaged intellectually with Odysseus' 'morality'. Instead he has allowed it to supply him with the justification he craves. One thinks of Agamem-non in the carpet scene allowing his wife to rationalize one feeling (a strong desire to trample on the fabrics) while encouraging the suppression of another (the unease attendant on a strong intuition that it would be foolish to trample on them). Similarly, in *Trachiniae*, Deianeira allows bad advice to encourage her to act foolishly. In all three cases, there is a vested interest in not examining a moral issue too closely.

THE INFLUENCE OF PHILOCTETES ON NEOPTOLEMUS

In order to carry out the first part of his mission, actually locating Philoctetes, Neoptolemus has to imagine his quarry's likely lifestyle (162), a piteous one eloquently evoked by a compassionate chorus, thus arousing pity in the audience (169–90). Pity, however, is the wrong attitude for a man engaged on Neoptolemus' mission, so he resists any such feeling by explaining Philoctetes' sufferings imper-sonally as divinely caused (191–200). In this way he begins to compound the wilful moral ignorance he has embraced, for to shut out pity is to cut oneself off from a morally relevant emotion, indeed to brutalize oneself.

But as Neoptolemus becomes acquainted with Philoctetes, he ceases to treat him, in un-Kantian fashion, as no more than a means to an end. At first the

---

[12] A reputation for *sophia* 'need not be scorned by one who has been brought up like Achilles to be a speaker of words as well as a doer of deeds (*Il.* 9.443)': Blundell (1988) 138.

abandoned hero appears a wild and scary monster of a man whose sufferings are no more than the fulfilment of a divine plan, but he soon reveals himself to be thoroughly civilized despite his lifestyle. Philoctetes has suffered a radical spatial alienation from all society, and it was forced upon him rather than freely chosen in reaction to a perceived injustice. Nevertheless, his anger and hatred are directed only towards the individuals responsible rather than to Greeks as a whole with whom he wants to be friends (224), and not even towards the whole of the Greek army,[13] until he learns that almost all the heroes he admires are dead (410–52). He is set against returning to Troy because he identifies the war with his personal enemies, Odysseus and the Atreidae. His settled desire is to leave the island and return to his home and his father (484–99, 662–5), as Achilles contemplated at *Iliad* 9. 356–66.

When Philoctetes begins to speak he addresses the newcomers, Neoptolemus and the chorus, as *xenoi* (219) and solicits pity (οἰκτίσαντες, 227), hoping that they have come as friends (*philoi*, 229).[14] When Neoptolemus reveals his own identity (240–1), Philoctetes calls him 'son of a dearest father' (242) and will frequently henceforth address him as son.[15] Neoptolemus lies to the effect that he has never heard of Philoctetes (249–53), who is distressed by this, seeing himself as god-hated (254) and imagining his enemies mocking him while his sickness 'flourishes' (τέθηλε) and gains strength (257–9). Indeed, his sickness seems to feed on his hatred, if it is not identified with it. He explains how he was abandoned and how he felt when he woke up to find it so (261–316). Philoctetes has entangled Neoptolemus in a web of special relationships (*xenos*, *philos*, and 'son') and sympathetic feeling (chiefly pity). All of these relationships and feelings activate conventionally defined moral obligations which run counter to the dehumanizing and instrumentalizing of Philoctetes that are essential to the success of Odysseus' scheme.

But Neoptolemus presses on in his Odyssean role, apparently ignoring these newly activated moral obligations and embarking on his false tale (343–90), a tale whose fabrication requires him to imagine the likely reactions of his famous father, for, having a similar *phusis*, they would doubtless react in a similar way. When he arrived in Troy (in the false tale), the army recognized a strong resemblance to his father (356–8), and when he was denied Achilles' arms he

---

[13] At *Iliad* 16. 17–18 Achilles conveniently lumps all the Achaeans together with Agamemnon as collectively responsible for his withdrawal. He convicts them of *hyperbasia* (transgression). If this is a rational extension of Agamemnon's guilt, it must refer to their effective condoning of the confiscation (see Zanker [1994] 95).

[14] On the relationship between *philia* and *xenia* rituals, see Belfiore (1993–4) *passim*. 'The two men not only become *philoi* who like and respect one another, they also establish a *xenia* relationship, initiated by definite prescribed acts and sanctioned by the gods, that obligates each of them to carry out certain responsibilities towards the other': ibid. 114. On the development from pity to friendship, see Blundell (1989) 200–1 and Hawkins (1999) 348: 'The emotional forces and motives that make for right decisions are deployed in what seems a hierarchical pattern, beginning with the purely individual and subjective feelings of pity and shame. Shame is directed toward the self; pity is directed toward another: neither emotion in itself produces the action that this play requires to demonstrate *ethos*. Philia— affection, friendship, love—is an emotion like these, but unlike them, it also refers to a relationship, such as friendship. And friendship, as the Greeks conceived it, is characterized by mutual benefits, sharing, and trust: it issues in action, manifesting itself in receiving or giving acts of kindness.'

[15] Avery (1965) 285–9 has a good discussion of this point with comprehensive citations.

flared up in wrath (369), a reaction that obviously recalls the Quarrel of the *Iliad*, especially when Neoptolemus (in the tale) abused Odysseus with every kind of insult (374–6) and sailed off in a huff (382–4).

As Achilles' son throws himself into his deceitful role he unwittingly conjures up that part of his noble moral nature which he has indeed inherited, while Philoctetes' rapport with him grows considerably (405). In this way he paradoxically exerts a benign moral influence contrary to his immoral project.[16] For example, he gives the impression of being at one with Philoctetes in lamenting that the good men in the Greek army are dead while the evil thrive (420),[17] and this attitude is one with which he would naturally concur even though he declares it here in order to further his deceitful scheme. This shared attitude has the positive moral effect of fostering a genuine relationship of *philia* with Philoctetes. By a delightful irony, as the morally false Neoptolemus pretends to be the true son of Achilles, he draws unconsciously on the very qualities that make him Achilles' true son.

Neoptolemus tries to comfort the older man with the unconsciously ironical reflection that clever plans (σοφαὶ γνῶμαι) are sometimes tripped up (431–2) and actually anticipates him with the idea that the gods destroy the good men rather than the villains (437). Moreover, 'where the worse man has more power than the good, what is good perishes, and the coward is in power, the men in that place I will never tolerate' (456–8). Of course, Philoctetes strongly shares this view, and it constitutes another unconscious irony in that both men do in fact return to Troy and thus to the company of the allegedly evil and corrupt. Philoctetes is prepared to go so far as to call the gods 'evil' (κακούς, 452), though he does not hold this view consistently throughout.[18] In any case, the web of new relationships between the two men is reinforced by shared feelings.

PHILOCTETES SUPPLICATES NEOPTOLEMUS

Philoctetes now supplicates Neoptolemus to take him with him, urging him to 'endure' (τλῆθι, 475) the discomfort of the stench, that is to make a special effort, just as Odysseus had urged him to make the special effort to deviate from his normal character in order to tell lies (τόλμα, 82). To employ a useful modern colloquialism, on both occasions Neoptolemus is exhorted to move outside his 'comfort zone'—on the first to embrace a new and sophisticated form of *sophia* that recognizes that the end may well justify the means, and on the second to prove that his newly awakened compassion is more than merely verbal. But the terrible stench is never a problem for Neoptolemus (see, for example, 869–901),

---

[16] As Gellie (1972) 137–8 observes: 'Neoptolemus is asked to lie and agrees to do so, yet almost everything he says is either truth itself, or (where we cannot know) compels our belief in its truth, or—and this is perhaps the most important of all—becomes truth in the course of the play.... This game with truth may be Sophocles' subtle and very difficult way of suggesting that a nature committed to truth cannot, with the worst will in the world, forget itself.'

[17] Like the disease at 259.

[18] Contrast e.g. 1035–9.

which suggests a natural capacity and predisposition to endure for another—a kind of practical pity which is part of the Heraclean ideal enunciated later (1418–22).[19] Thus the encounter with Philoctetes, despite its immoral purpose, is bringing to light moral resources in Neoptolemus of which he has not himself been aware and which, therefore, he has not consciously incorporated into his rather simplistic and crude moral self-definition. It is morally significant too that he finds it much easier to rise to Philoctetes' challenge to endure the stench of the wound than to rise to Odysseus' challenge to practise deceit. But moral maturity comes with meeting such challenges.

In pleading with Neoptolemus to help him, Philoctetes tells his young friend that for the nobly born (γενναίοισι) what is shameful (αἰσχρόν) is hateful (ἐχθρόν), whereas what is good (χρηστόν) is glorious (εὐκλεές) (475–6, cf. 477–8). This lofty deliverance is of course a rather fuzzy platitude with which no one could possibly disagree and which must take its sense from the context, and we remember that Odysseus spoke of the need to extend the sense of the term γενναῖος (51). What is shameful here is not conventional martial cowardice but a kind of heartlessness that issues in the rejection of a suppliant. The moral effort required on Neopto-lemus' part will take less than a full day (480). Odysseus offered a similar reassurance (83).

Moreoever, Philoctetes adds an appeal to a sort of Virgilian *pietas*, for he is worried about his father who might be dead (492–9). Such an appeal should carry a lot of weight with Neoptolemus who is deeply attached to the memory of a father he has never seen, and one thinks of Priam's famous supplication at *Iliad* 24. 485–92, where the only thing that can break down Achilles' resistance is precisely that sort of appeal. And in both passages two fathers are at issue, while Neoptolemus' innate capacity for pity provides the emotional impetus to a noble action.[20]

Just as Neoptolemus consents to take Philoctetes 'out of this land to wherever we may desire to sail' (528–9), the merchant arrives to motivate a swift departure. Neoptolemus tells the merchant that he is hostile to the army and that Philoctetes is his 'very great friend' (φίλος μέγιστος) because he hates the Atreidae, and we may remember that his Iliadic father chastised Phoenix for not sharing his hostility towards Agamemnon, as *philoi* should be united in hatred (585–6; cf. *Iliad* 9. 611–15). According to the merchant, Odysseus and Diomedes are even now sailing to the island to take Philoctetes back to Troy either by persuasion or by force (πείσαντες . . . ἢ πρὸς ἰσχύος κράτος, 594). Helenus said they must persuade Philoctetes to come and take Troy (πείσαντες λόγῳ, 612). Odysseus undertook to fetch him willy nilly (ἑκούσιον or ἄκοντα) and display him before the army, presumably as a kind of demonstration of his own cleverness (614–19). Philoctetes' reaction is that he certainly will not allow himself to be put on display

---

[19] Stephens (1995) 158–68 rightly insists that the wound must not be trivialized as a minor inconvenience.

[20] Blundell (1988) 140 observes that 'it is not reason, but feelings [specifically pity] which alert him [Neoptolemus] to the demands of his *phusis*. Hawkins (1999) 337–40 has a good discussion of the ethical function of feelings in *Philoctetes*: 'The play demonstrates that our emotional responses function as heuristic tools for exploring an ethical dilemma and coming to a decision as to what action seems best' (ibid. 339–40).

in that humiliating way (628–30). The merchant ploy is intended to make him all the more anxious to leave for home since that is the result (635–8). It can certainly only confirm him in his resolve to avoid Troy.

THE BOW

Neoptolemus, however, having previously raised no objections to sailing (cf. 528–9), now claims that the wind is temporarily unfavourable (639–40), but when his new friend insists, he agrees to sail anyway (645–6). We inevitably wonder if he is looking for excuses. Certainly Sophocles teases us for a moment with the possibility of an about-face. However, the young man's attention is now drawn to the famous bow which he asks to be allowed to hold (656–7). He wants to hold and kiss it as if it were a god, but only if it is religiously permissible (*themis*) to do so (654–61). There is a delicious tension here originating in our uncertainty as to the extent, if any, to which Odysseus' influence continues to prevail in the mind of Achilles' son. According to Philoctetes, it is indeed *themis* (662) for Neoptolemus to hold it because of his religiously sensitive (ὅσια, 662) words (his concern for what is *themis*) and because he has consented to take Philoctetes home to see his father and friends (665). He will be able to boast that he has held it because of his *aretē* (669)—that is the characteristically Philoctetean virtues of 475–6. Philoctetes himself secured the bow by kind action (εὐεργετῶν, 670). Neoptolemus says he is pleased to have Philoctetes as a *philos*, 'for whoever knows how to return a kindness is a friend more precious than any possession' (671–3). The kind of friendship involved, though, is grounded in respect and readiness for practical mutual assistance rather than the passionate devotion Achilles felt for Patroclus.

The bow symbolizes the *aretē* of Philoctetes, but in what exactly does that consist? It is not the conventional Iliadic *aretē*, as Philoctetes is an archer. His role is simply to shoot his unerring arrows, so that either no particular skill or valour is required or, much more likely, the arrows are unerring because the skill is the same. But the bow is actually more powerfully symbolic of the cooperative virtues associated with *philia*, and we wonder to what extent Neoptolemus really regards it as a holy object and what symbolism he sees in it at this stage.[21] It is also an emblem of Heraclean endurance. Before they leave, Philoctetes wants to salute his home that is no home (533) 'so you may learn how I eked out my existence and how brave (εὐκάρδιος) I was' (535). No one else, he thinks, could have endured it (536–7), and for a hero no small part of that was enduring the eclipse of his reputation.[22] Philoctetes is another lonely hero forced to maintain his self-esteem

---

[21] The bow 'represents Philoctetes' friend Heracles, and it has the divine qualities of the hero. Later in the play, Philoctetes will personify the bow itself as the friend that pities him . . . (1128–31)': Belfiore (1993–4) 121. 'The bow is clearly a symbol of friendship, of the mutual exchange of favors given and received—first between Heracles and Philoctetes, and now between Philoctetes and Neoptolemus': Hawkins (1999) 350. See also Gill (1980) 138: 'the bow (and heroic achievement) is inseparable from human friendship'.

[22] Beye (1970) 67 sees the bow as a sign of Philoctetes' ineffectuality on Lemnos, but on the island the bow becomes the hero's means of survival and thus a kind of symbol of his Heraclean *aretē* of endurance, a subtler virtue than that which requires display and immediate recognition.

in both physical and moral isolation from his peers, and the danger once again is that an entrenched and bitter hostility will render that moral isolation permanent, especially since the hero's sufferings are so extreme and so undeserved. (The chorus compare his agonies with those of Ixion, the ultimate reprobate [674–85].) On the other hand, unlike Ajax and the Heracles of *Trachiniae*, Philoctetes is naturally affectionate and has before him the inspiration of the very different Heracles of this play and his relationship with him.

Now, surely, they will embark. But suddenly Philoctetes' pain attacks him, the pain that symbolizes his hostility. (Here Sophocles has negatively redefined as an emotional wound that intractable hostility which some heroes at least consider a positive virtue.) Neoptolemus offers assistance (760) and Philoctetes wants him to guard the bow as long as the painful episode lasts (762–73). Neoptolemus consents and receives the bow (774–6), but refers ambiguously again to their destination as 'wherever the god thinks right and our mission lies' (779–81: tr. Lloyd-Jones). Is he deceiving still or hedging his bets? He pledges to stay until Philoctetes recovers (813).

When the chorus urge their master to steal the bow while its owner is unconscious, Neoptolemus declares that Philoctetes must come in person to Troy and that the triumph is to be his as well as Neoptolemus' own (839–41). This is not of course a fresh piece of information which he has mysteriously plucked out of the air, but a moral insight relating to the spiritual inseparability of the hero and the bow.[23] That is, he is well on the way to being converted to the ideal of glory shared by friends, though he is not yet ready for an entirely disinterested exercise of the virtue of compassionate *philia* so long as it threatens to exclude altogether the possibility of a more public and recognized glory.

NEOPTOLEMUS' MORAL CRISIS

When Philoctetes awakes he is impressed that Neoptolemus could endure the stench of the wound and he attributes this to his noble nature and ancestry (ἀλλ' εὐγενὴς γὰρ ἡ φύσις κἀξ εὐγενῶν, 874). He asks the young man for physical support, expecting none from the chorus whose presumably ignoble natures will lack the required stamina to bear the smell (889–92). As Neoptolemus physically supports his suffering friend his moral crisis comes to a head (895). The physical contact here is an important catalyst, for it is a strong emblem of friendship. Similarly the aged chorus of Euripides' *Heracles* support one another, and Heracles himself is supported by his friend Theseus as he leaves the stage 'a helpless

---

[23] On Neoptolemus' increasing awareness of the spiritual dimension of the bow and the divine purpose, see C. Segal (1977) 142–3: 'Neoptolemus' relation to the gods' purposes, his "piety" ... undergoes change and development in the course of the action. Initially limited and self-centered in his understanding of the oracles, Neoptolemus becomes the only human character to grasp their meaning (839–842). He alone expounds a general view of man's obligations to the divine order and to his own destiny (1316 ff.) and he alone recognizes the divine quality in the bow (198; 697) and the benefits of health and glory for Philoctetes himself (1329–1335; 1340–1347).'

wreck'.[24] Neoptolemus believes that he has abandoned his *phusis* (902–3), a moral statement, since he has for some time been tortured by the thought of appearing *aischros* (906) and now he will be found to be *kakos* for concealing what he should not and speaking 'the most shameful of words' (αἴσχιστ᾽ ἐπῶν) (908–9). These moral terms imply that he has reverted to an Achillean morality of scrupulous honesty. Accordingly, he admits that he is taking Philoctetes to Troy to capture the city with him (919–20).

Therefore, unwilling as yet to abandon glory at Troy in order to take Philoctetes home, Neoptolemus defends his deceit, claiming that he is acting in accordance with a 'strong necessity' (πολλὴ... ἀνάγκη, 922) and that both justice and expediency (τό τ᾽ ἔνδικον... καὶ τὸ συμφέρον) require him to obey those in power (926). Now what makes this play particularly morally tantalizing is the problem of what Achilles' son actually believes at any given time. We know that in the first scene he was genuinely motivated not only by the promise of personal glory, but also by the pressure of authority—an authority which at that time he completely respected. By now he has pretty clearly come to accept much of Philoctetes' morality and presumably with it at least to some extent that hero's moral view of the surviving Greek leaders at Troy. He could certainly claim, without hypocrisy, that the will of the gods requires him and Philoctetes to take Troy (the necessity to which he here refers), and that it is for that reason in some sense 'just' (ἔνδικον). But he does not appeal directly to the divine will; he appeals to a now dubious moral authority and with an Odyssean invocation of expediency (συμφέρον) that clearly brings to mind the sophistic antithesis between the just and the expedient with which the audience were only too familiar.

Neoptolemus is here reverting to the Odyssean position that the end justifies the means, while excusing himself by saying that he is only obeying orders. Perhaps we are to see this Odyssean argument as sincere and at the same time as all that remains of the Ithacan's influence. Or perhaps it is a temporary moral regression designed to fill the gap, to supply a justification for a great enterprise the import of which Neoptolemus does not yet fully understand but to which he is nonetheless committed. The pervasive uncertainty about Neoptolemus' moral position at any given time makes it impossible to decide. At any rate, no less a figure than Heracles will be needed to put everything in its appropriate context.

NEOPTOLEMUS' DILEMMA

Philoctetes reviles Neoptolemus for his deceit, but begs him to 'return to his true nature' (ἐν σαυτοῦ γενοῦ, 950). Achilles' son, however, is confused. Like a character from Aeschylus, he faces a moral dilemma. Though he does not himself formulate it in such terms, there is a conflict between (1) divine necessity, or what he seems to intuit as his own and his new friend's rightful destiny, supported by a morally dubious human authority, and (2) his new morality that combines the Achillean

---

[24] *Her.* 106–29, 1424.

standards of sincerity and honesty which he has always embraced with the new
devotion to compassionate *philia* inspired by Philoctetes. But the situation is
complicated since the devotion to *philia* belongs to both sides of the dilemma.
This is because there is a contradiction between Philoctetes' true interests (going
to Troy) and what he conceives his interests to be (going home). Should Neoptolemus ignore Philoctetes' own view of the matter and simply act in his true
interests? If he does so, however, he will be profiting from the earlier deceit
which now enables him to force Philoctetes to do his will. But that violates the
condition of wilful consent. Neoptolemus has got himself into a position in which
morally he can only agree to take Philoctetes home. In that way he fulfils his moral
obligation to him, but he violates their mutual destinies, and those destinies are
not, like that of Eteocles in the *Seven*, highly undesirable; on the contrary they
represent the crowning glory of the relationship of the two men. The problem is
Philoctetes' intractability, but this very quality can seem like a virtue. It is typical
of Sophoclean heroes, and in this case it is related to an accepted heroic standard:
hatred of one's enemies and refusal to benefit them in any way.

Neoptolemus then grasps intuitively that it is in some meaningful sense right
that he and Philoctetes fulfil what has been presented as their destiny, but he
cannot yet properly articulate his intuition. He has, however, as we have seen,
already intuited that there can be no question of his taking Troy with the bow but
without the man, because he has learned to conceive of a shared destiny, a kind of
apotheosis and glorification of the Philoctetean morality which he has come to
embrace. In making this claim for Neoptolemus I am of course aware that I cannot
point, as it were, to chapter and verse. But that is only to recognize again the
innovative subtlety of the play, namely the uncertainty that hangs over the
development of the young man's character. This uncertainty is in the text, or
perhaps rather the subtext, and for this reason interpretation is bound to range
legitimately further than is often permissible.

Neoptolemus' morality is partly a matter of 'gut feeling', as one would expect
when morality is so closely related to *phusis*. He experiences an 'awesome pity'
(οἶκτος δεινός, 965). Philoctetes realizes that the youth is not really *kakos* but has
learned *aischra* (shameful behaviour) from bad men (971–2). Neoptolemus,
completely overwhelmed by his moral dilemma, lamely asks the chorus (of all
people!) what he should do (974). At this point Odysseus himself appears and
demands the bow (974–5). The dialogue is now exclusively between the two older
men, and Neoptolemus says and does nothing for very nearly a hundred verses,
even when Philoctetes, calling him son (παî), orders him to return the bow to him
(981). Odysseus demands that both the bow and its owner come away with him,
by force if need be. He claims to represent the will of Zeus (989–90), but
Philoctetes naturally rejects the idea (992), although he later asserts that the
gods acted justly in prompting Odysseus' mission, though for his (Philoctetes')
sake (1035–9). This is the first hint of any ability on his part to dissociate the idea
of his returning from Troy from the selfish purposes of his personal enemies there.

Neoptolemus, as we have seen, has remained silent through these exchanges,
and now Philoctetes interprets his passivity as compliance with Odysseus' will
(1066–7). Odysseus at once realizes that the slightest pressure from Philoctetes is
likely to sway the young man in the hero's favour, so he orders him to ignore him

lest his nobility (γενναῖός περ ὤν, 1068) sabotage the mission.[25] Neoptolemus'
answer is to evade his dilemma by agreeing to stay until preparations for
sailing are completed and in the hope that Philoctetes will cut the knot by
consenting to leave with them (1074–80). But Philoctetes is completely intransi-
gent (1081–1217).

Neoptolemus himself must resolve the dilemma, and he does so by renouncing
his shameful use of deception which was contrary to *dikē* (1228, 1234, 1246) and
employed in obedience to Odysseus and the entire army (1226). The question of
divine will and destiny is raised here neither by Odysseus nor by Neoptolemus,
nor does Neoptolemus refer to his new morality. The sole issue for him is now, as
it was at the beginning, Achillean sincerity and openness. However, in defying
Odysseus another Achillean quality is required, physical courage, and in this he
shows his lineage (1254–8).

Although Neoptolemus is now committed to returning the bow to Philoctetes,
he still hopes to persuade him to go to Troy. Unfortunately, his earlier deceit has
undermined his credibility (1281–6). Neoptolemus now hands the bow over just
as Odysseus re-enters to forbid it in the name of the Atreidae, the whole army, and
the gods (1293–4). (We remember that the gods were not invoked in the earlier
exchange with Neoptolemus.) Philoctetes puts an arrow to the bow (1299), but
Neoptolemus tries to stop him shooting Odysseus (1300) who now leaves. Philoctetes wanted to kill a hated enemy, but Neoptolemus says that that would not be
'fine' (καλόν) for either of them (1304). Philoctetes tells Neoptolemus that he has
shown his true Achillean nature (1310). Why would it not be fine to shoot
Odysseus? Has Neoptolemus transcended the narrow heroic morality of harming
enemies? Or does he regard murder as an overreaction, as it clearly would have
been in the Iliadic Achilles' case when Athena intervenes in the Quarrel, or in
Ajax's had Athena not intervened in that case too?

Neoptolemus tries again to persuade Philoctetes. He tells him he is no longer
worthy of pity because his sufferings are self-inflicted and he has become savage
and refuses to be counselled (1321). Philoctetes must come of his own free will
(ἑκών) to Troy to be cured by the sons of Asclepius (1332) and take Troy with the
bow and in company with Neoptolemus (1335). The fall of Troy is also fated to
occur this summer according to Helenus (1338). (Presumably this implies that it is
divine will that Philoctetes come to Troy.) As Kitto observes, in this final attempt
to persuade Philoctetes, Neoptolemus ignores the pressure of the divine will
(which the hero could hardly resist), and employs only 'personal and prudential'
arguments. He does not argue that Philoctetes' consent would release the rank
and file of the army from their sufferings.[26] Nor, one presumes, would such an
argument carry much weight with him. Similarly, in the *Iliad*, Achilles' return is
motivated by the death of Patroclus, and not concern for the Greeks in general,
though he does regret his former uselessness in the face of the sufferings of his
comrades.[27]

---

[25] As Kirkwood (1958) 145 observes, Odysseus can now appeal only to his authority as representative of the army. He can no longer subvert Neoptolemus' morality.

[26] Kitto (1961) 308.

[27] *Iliad* 18. 98–104.

PHILOCTETES' DILEMMA

Now it is Philoctetes' turn to face a moral dilemma. 'Alas, what am I to do? How am I to fail to be persuaded (πῶς ἀπιστήσω) by the words of this man who gave me advice out of friendly feeling towards me (εὔνους) (1350–1).'[28] This statement, thus expressed, is somewhat puzzling, as it might seem to imply that one should believe what a person says if they speak from the heart in what they conceive to be one's interest. But perhaps Philoctetes' position is roughly as follows: 'I now have no reason to think that what Neoptolemus says is false, but the essential issue is a moral one. This young man has now proved himself a worthy friend. Am I not then morally obliged to yield to a friend's reasonable request?' In his focus on this moral issue he ignores the tangible benefits he would receive by yielding (return-ing to civilization, being cured of his wound, and winning glory in company with his new friend). The problem of course is his hatred of Odysseus and the Atreidae, a hatred which in heroic terms he might well feel morally required to preserve, and he certainly *wants* to preserve it. How can he return to society to be with and speak to men he detests? (1352–7). He goes on to say that 'it is not the pain of the past that stings me, but the sufferings still in store for me at their [his enemies'] hands that I seem to foresee; for when men's mind has once become the mother of evil deeds, it begets yet more evil' (1358–61: tr. Lloyd-Jones). This worry is precisely that which Achilles voices to the Embassy at *Iliad* 9. 344–5. Agamemnon can offer all the material compensation imaginable, but the leopard's spots will remain unchanged. (We might note too that in both cases Agamemnon is motivated by self-interest and concern for the army, rather than genuine remorse or compassion for his victim.)

It is naturally hard for Philoctetes to understand why Neoptolemus is happy to return to the men who allegedly deprived him of his father's arms (1362–7). Similarly the Iliadic Achilles disapproves of Phoenix for appealing on behalf of a man (Agamemnon) who should be his enemy since he ought to have the same friends and enemies as Achilles (*Iliad* 9. 613–15).[29] The Embassy could not persuade Achilles, but they spoke on behalf of the whole Greek army. Neoptole-mus, on the other hand, speaks in his own and now at last also in Philoctetes' interest, while the Greek army is hopelessly contaminated by its debased repre-sentatives (men such as Odysseus), now that all the good men have died.[30] Philoctetes, it must be remembered, has suffered a greater injustice than the Iliadic Achilles, having been unjustly rejected and forcibly ejected from human society.[31]

---

[28] The translation 'fail to be persuaded' makes more sense here than 'fail to believe', because the issue concerns what Philoctetes is to do, not merely what he is to think.

[29] On the requirement to have the same friends and enemies see Blundell (1989) 47 and her n. 109.

[30] This is an important theme of the play, as the space devoted to it (410–52) testifies. The wound is also a symbol of Philoctetes' incompatibility with the society of the Greeks at Troy (see e.g. Tessitore (2003) 74). Healing the wound means compromising with his enemies (ibid. 76–7). According to C. Segal (1977) 150, 'The only true "cure" is reconciliation with the divine order and reacceptance of human society.'

[31] Achilles, at his most extreme, rejects not only the guilty Agamemnon, but the whole Greek army. Philoctetes, though ultimately more 'venomous' (Beye (1970) 65) because of his forcible expulsion from society, is at first delighted to hear the Greek language (234) and to be reunited with Greeks. As Avery

Philoctetes then, like Achilles, is torn between yielding to a friend and maintaining his hostility to enemies. He decides on the latter and urges Neoptolemus to abide by his oath to take him home (1398–401). Neoptolemus consents and in doing so rejects public glory in favour of *philia* and its moral obligations.[32] After all, the taking of Troy is really to be a celebration of their *philia*, and if this *philia* is to be genuine and complete Neoptolemus must be pushed to the limit. The young man is compelled to abandon his own selfish quest for glory in order to prove himself a true friend to Philoctetes (1402). But that glory is in danger of being meaningless except in partnership with his new friend, since the rest of the army is, we have been encouraged to think, morally worthless. In making this sacrifice, ironically, he proves himself worthy of the glory of Philoctetes' companionship at Troy while Philoctetes gains a companion to make the sack of Troy worthwhile. Neoptolemus redeems the enterprise (if not the other participants); there will be at least one decent person at Troy for Philoctetes to fight in company with.[33] But since a sudden change of mind on Philoctetes' part in consequence of such a realization would be implausible, the play now requires the epiphany of the only *philos* who could influence him.[34]

HERACLES

Heracles tells Philoctetes he will be judged foremost in *aretē* for shooting Paris (1425). The *aretē*, however, is, unconventionally, that of an archer. But martial *aretē* is not really at issue; the glory for taking Troy is a reward for *philia* and for the endurance of suffering on Lemnos.[35] That the spoils are to go to Heracles' pyre (1432) confirms this, as it seems to imply that they are to be seen as a tribute to the Heraclean ideals of endurance and *philia* rather than conventional Homeric *aretē*. The real moral focus of the glory of the two warriors is their shared enterprise. The

(1965) 280 observes, he shows no bitterness until he discovers that his name is unknown, and he temporarily loses his humanity after Neoptolemus betrays him (ibid. 280). However, he rejects the whole Trojan expedition on account of his mistreatment at the hands of Odysseus and the Atreidae. Avery (ibid. 283–4) suggests that this bitterness is more profoundly directed at the immanent evil of the world, and is exacerbated by the hero's ten-year ordeal.

[32] As Gill (1980) 142 well argues, 'Sophocles seems to have framed this final request to Neoptolemus so as to constitute the supreme demand of friendship. Not only is Neoptolemus asked to surrender his own interests to that of his friend, he is also asked to respond to a claim of a kind hardly recognized in the Greek theories of friendship, the claim that he respect his friend's wishes rather than act for what seems to him his friend's good.' (For the latter, with references from Aristotle, see Blundell (1989) 35.) For Knox (1966) 138, Neoptolemus' decision 'adds a new dimension to the nobility of his great father . . . The renunciation of future glory shows a nobility of soul which surpasses even that his father showed when he yielded to old Priam's plea and gave up the body of Hector for burial.'

[33] At least that is the logic of the play. The myth tradition suggests the terrible irony that Neoptolemus will turn out to be the *least* decent Greek at Troy and a disgrace to his father (as Virgil's Priam tells him at *Aeneid* 2. 533–43)—but we cannot be sure that Sophocles wants the ending qualified by such an irony, unless that is the import of 1440–1.

[34] For critical views of Heracles' role as *deus*, see Hawkins (1999) 356 n. 55.

[35] Consider especially ἐκ τῶν πόνων τῶνδ' (1422). All three Sophoclean heroic endurers (Electra, Philoctetes, and the old Oedipus) are in some way rewarded.

bow does not represent an extension of an effective and intelligent killing machine (as in the *Odyssey* or Euripides' *Heracles*), but a creative *philia* bond.

Philoctetes is finally persuaded to return to Troy only by Heracles who significantly promises him shared glory with Neoptolemus (1434–5), perhaps of the kind fondly imagined by Achilles in company with his great friend (at *Iliad* 16. 97–100)—glory that largely ignores those he considers unworthy to honour him. This glory, based as it is on a new valuation of heroic friendship and cooperation, devalues somewhat the whole focus on honour and glory in its individual, competitive form. Companionship, with the gentler virtues that cement it, emerges as an end in itself and no longer merely the social context for the old form of honour. This, as I remarked earlier, is the great lesson of the *Iliad*. But the *philotēs* of Achilles and Patroclus had become unhealthy as Achilles transferred all his affection to him. His hopeless wish that no Greek or Trojan would survive the war so that he and Patroclus might take Troy on their own and enjoy the resulting glory together represents a callous and immature dismissal of worthy comrades. Furthermore, Achilles never consciously adopts pity as an ideal, therefore its expression tends to be temporary and precarious.[36]

In Sophocles' play, on the other hand, the surviving Greek heroes at Troy, as represented by Odysseus and the Atreidae, are indeed unworthy,[37] so that the sack of Troy itself needs to be revalued; and Heracles does not require Philoctetes to accept his personal enemies as comrades.[38] The focus shifts, as in the momentary fantasy of the Homeric Achilles (at *Iliad* 16. 97–100), to a pair of mutually affectionate heroes whose *philia* endows the sack of the city with the required new meaning.[39] Moreover, this revaluation of *aretē* harmonizes with the conception of *aretē* that has emerged from the pre-existing Heraclean ideal which Philoctetes had already to a great extent adopted and from the creative interaction of Philoctetes and Neoptolemus throughout the play. For this reason the *deus* does not require an unnatural wrenching of feeling on the part of Philoctetes, particularly since, as Heracles clearly explains, he will be allied significantly with Achilles' son and not with his enemies.[40] Troy ceases to be an arena for the winning of

---

[36] Blundell (1988) 143–4 has a useful discussion of the contrasts between Neoptolemus and the Iliadic Achilles and the similarities between the latter and Philoctetes.

[37] On the 'complete corruption' of the Greek army see Scodel (1984) 96.

[38] Hawkins (1999) 356. Kirkwood (1994) 425 puts it well: 'For Philoctetes willingly to accept his fated heroic role at the sack of Troy is in some sense a reentry into human society, but the grounds for his acceptance have . . . little to do with any broad reintegration. There is no evidence in the play that Philoctetes will relinquish his hatred of the Greek leadership; the only future that is touched on by Sophocles is what lies in store for Philoctetes and Neoptolemus': On Philoctetes' continuing alienation at Troy see also C. Segal (1977) 158. On the omission of the future of Odysseus and the stratagem of the Wooden Horse, so clearly alien to the redefined *aretē* of this play, see Roberts (1989) 173.

[39] 'The image of the two lions brings together the archaic and the classical: it recalls the conventional epic simile familiar to us from Homer, but it is used in such a way as to emphasize not victory in battle but *philia*, the virtue of collaboration, cooperation, and mutual benefit': Hawkins (1999) 356. '[H]eroic achievement depends on authentic friendship': Gill (1980) 139. Nevertheless, now that the heroic natures of Philoctetes and Neoptolemus are 'realized', 'the only place which offers such natures full scope for their greatness' is 'the battlefield of Troy': C. Segal (1977) 149.

[40] Heracles 'turns the two men back from the road they had started on (the road to Philoctetes' home, 1416); but, in a deeper sense, he confirms the personal "road" they have taken (the establishment of true friendship), and associates the continuation along that road with the fulfilment of the oracle

conventional glory and becomes instead a place where the cooperative ideal of *philia* is celebrated. Philoctetes has been, in his isolation, alienated also from Heracles who has become a remote, divine figure. The new relationship with Neoptolemus reinstates the pattern of the earlier relationship, with Philoctetes assuming Heracles' role, but perhaps the most disturbing aspect of the vision of this play is that the collective remains unredeemed, and the bond between the two men as exclusive as in Achilles' fantasy wish. Tessitore[41] sees Philoctetes' rejection of the army, to which Neoptolemus implicitly subscribes when he agrees to take his new friend home, as representing an unrealistic demand for ideal justice and as a rejection of the necessary moral compromises of politics and of the glory that is only possible within a broadly political context that allows 'involvement in a political good greater than oneself'.[42] This is true and admirable in principle, but I cannot see that the play endorses it. Heracles, it is true, redirects Philoctetes to Troy, but he does not urge reconciliation with the Greek leaders.[43] Scodel suggests that while society (represented by the Greek army at Troy) provides a necessary context for the destinies of Neoptolemus and Philoctetes, 'the two form a better society unto themselves, in which their deeds have their place, and at the same time the gods provide a fuller and eternal context'.[44]

The Homeric Achilles has in his mysteriously profound love for Patroclus a basis for both a wider *philotēs* with his peers and a still wider, though of course more diluted, compassion for human beings in general, including 'enemies' like Priam. The Sophoclean Ajax, on the other hand, is pathologically alienated from everybody, though it must be remembered that his world is characterized by a disconcerting fluidity which does not leave *philia* unaffected. Indeed, in such a world, friendship seems to remain superficial and a matter of temporary alliances, though Odysseus demonstrates that a wider, diluted compassion is possible. The Heracles of the *Trachiniae*, on the other hand, is indissolubly associated with a world of primitive violence in which love (in the person of his wife, Deianeira) appears a sensitive and vulnerable growth. The world of *Philoctetes* is much more promising. There the humanity of the hero reaches out to appeal to that of the still immature Neoptolemus and becomes the instrument of his maturation, forming a new bond in the spirit of the great bond between the hero and Heracles. This is a union based on tangible mutual services, in contrast to the mystical and unexplained union of Achilles and Patroclus. But it serves more to isolate its membership of two from the rest of humanity than to unite them with it. Thus we feel that in *Philoctetes*, while the potential isolation of the heroic outlook has been to a limited degree counteracted by an *egoisme à deux*, the gulf between

---

(1423–4, 1434–7)': Gill (1980) 143. Moreover, 'Philoctetes' reply expresses not simply submission to divine will but a deeply-felt response to a personal friend (1445–7)': ibid. 144.

[41] Tessitore (2003) 77–82.

[42] Ibid. 82. Cf. Reinhardt (1979) 191: 'separation from the course of the world is absurd'.

[43] As Kirkwood (1958) 150 states, when Philoctetes accepts his destiny at the end, 'he rises above the cruelty and unreliability of the Greek leaders; the acceptance of his destiny is a pact between deity and the idealism that he and Neoptolemus both finally represent'. It is of course possible to rise above the moral level of one's peers in some collective enterprise while still being committed to that enterprise; but no such commitment is clearly in evidence here.

[44] Scodel (1984) 102.

genuine heroes on the one hand and failed heroes and ordinary mortals on the other has, if anything, widened. Moreover, it is never clear that Philoctetes enthusiastically embraces the morality of returning to Troy. He goes because his mighty friend tells him to go.

CONCLUSION

Neoptolemus defines himself in terms of what we might call a subset of the warrior, that is in terms of a particular warrior with particular heroic virtues, namely his father. The moral requirements that derive from this self-definition therefore relate to two of his father's conspicuous virtues—his sincerity and his martial prowess. When Odysseus orders him to practise deceit, Neoptolemus is well aware that he is facing a moral crisis, but his overwhelming desire to win the glory of taking Troy leaves him vulnerable to the Ithacan's moral sophistries so that he reluctantly agrees to practise the required deceit. However, acute unease follows, and this unease is severely exacerbated by the moral influence of Philoctetes on the youth's immature, but essentially noble moral nature. While Neoptolemus has a rather basic understanding of the moral implications of his predicament (he knows it is wrong to practise deceit), he does not at first understand the moral nature or anticipate the moral influence of his quarry whom he is trying to treat impersonally as a means to an end. Eventually his moral discomfort becomes unendurable and we encounter a fine example of the salutary contribution of an emotion to moral awareness. (Ajax, we remember, resisted the stirrings of pity.) By the end, Neoptolemus has learned much and his moral outlook has greatly expanded and matured, but almost without his realizing it.

Philoctetes is a heroic warrior and therefore espouses such conventional moral ideas as helping friends and harming enemies and a concern for reputation. This explains the particular form of his psychological torture on Lemnos. But his relationship with Heracles which is based on cooperative *philia* has kept him human and inspired his endurance. It is this positive side of his morality that has such a profound effect on Neoptolemus. Philoctetes' moral crisis revolves around whether or not to go to Troy. His positive morality urges him to yield to Neoptolemus' friendly counsels, but his negative morality insists that he remain implacable towards his enemies. Philoctetes then is the only Sophoclean character we have encountered who is torn between incompatible moral claims, though Ajax stood on the brink of that once he acknowledged his pity. Neoptolemus and Deianeira were torn between the moral and the expedient, but only as long as they wilfully avoided the moral issue. As long as he is left free to decide, Philoctetes chooses the negative option, presumably because his feelings of hatred towards his enemies are so overwhelming. (In his case emotion obstructs moral judgement.) Once Heracles has spoken he changes his mind, presumably on the same grounds as those which made him uncertain whether or not to heed Neoptolemus. That is, finally, the obligation to heed a friend won out, but only because of the overwhelming moral authority of the friend in question.

11

Euripides: *Medea*

SYMPATHY AND MORAL JUDGEMENT

As in life, so in literature, sympathy and judgement are often at odds, and this is strikingly illustrated in Medea's characterization. We speak of 'the audience', but audiences are comprised of a variety of people with a variety of moral beliefs and sympathetic allegiances. Male and female spectators are likely to have reacted rather differently to Medea, and spectators would vary also in the degree to which they would allow themselves to be manipulated by the dramatist into empathizing with those they considered unlike themselves. Manipulation of this kind, however, is a major dramatic strategy of this play, and it has a major impact on our moral assessment of Medea.

We begin with the audience's likely prejudice against this woman from Colchis. As Ruby Blondell observes, the Greeks 'projected their own culturally undesirable qualities onto outsiders. Many such "barbarian" attributes are reflected in Medea: unrestrained emotion (especially extreme displays of grief and anger); lust, sensuality, and transgression of normative Greek gender roles; bestiality; wealth, especially gold ... luxurious clothing (like Medea's gifts to the princess); brutal violence and lawlessness; untrustworthiness, duplicity, and expertise with magic drugs.' But at the same time, Medea 'violates in the most dramatic way the positive ideals and desirable stereotypes of Greek womanhood—sexual restraint, deference first to one's father and then to one's husband, and devotion to one's children'.[1] If the ancient audience entered the theatre with such prejudices, any confirmation of them would only serve to cement negative moral judgements of her.

Our initial impressions of Medea are conveyed through the nurse and tutor who are devoted to her (49–88). Medea, the nurse tells us, under the influence of a violent passion for Jason, left her homeland and persuaded Pelias' daughters to kill their own father (6–10). This nasty episode is passed over quickly as a service to Jason, and the nurse goes on to say that the Corinthians were pleased to have Medea and that husband and wife enjoyed a harmonious relationship (11–15). Although there is a brief reference to Medea's exile (12), it is not at this point presented as an act of desertion of her natal family, nor is there any reference to her infamous murder of her brother.[2] We are not invited to condemn Medea then for her immoral past but to see that past positively as proof of her devotion to a

---

[1] Blondell (1999) 154. See also Page (1938) pp. xviii–xxi.

[2] Medea later refers to her brotherless state (257), but without explaining how it came about.

now faithless husband. But marital harmony is gone, thanks to Jason's desertion. Medea is morally outraged by his perjury and is taking the desertion very hard (27–35). In Medea's special circumstances (an exile who has burned her bridges) the intensity of her suffering is understandable, but it takes a disturbing form: she irrationally 'hates' her children (36, 89–95, 98–118) and is contemplating the murder of Creon and Jason (39–45).

It will now be clear that Medea, though in a sense a pathetic victim, will make no feeble adversary (44–5), and since the audience's emotions have been engaged for her they may well enjoy the prospect of revenge which for the Greeks was at once a pleasure and a duty. But just how far should revenge go? An ancient audience would have appreciated the joys of revenge by litigation and in the pre-Areopagan environment of Greek tragedies such as Sophocles' *Electra* they would have been prepared to countenance a bloodier sort of vengeance so long as they were reassured as to its moral necessity. But the murder of an unfaithful husband is another matter. Nor could there be any question of countenancing the murder of an innocent king and princess. While Sophocles' *Electra*'s plans for her mother are structured and contained within her explanation of her moral commitment, our first impressions at any rate of Medea in her vindictiveness are of an anarchic and irrational woman.

Medea's address to the chorus (214–66) is the first move in her revenge strategy. She requires their silence, although this is not apparent to us until near the end of the speech (260–3). In the meantime she makes a strong bid for understanding in her characterization of marriage from the female perspective. Realizing that people are likely to respond with prejudice to strange behaviour, she feels obliged to clear the air by explaining herself (214–24). The women of the chorus must understand the extremity of her situation. First one needs to realize how a wife feels in her disempowerment in marriage, particularly when her husband treats her badly (230–51).[3] And that applies to all women, but Medea herself is a special case because of her status as a foreign exile (252–8). Therefore another woman will surely understand and support her at least by silence if she tries to level the score with her husband (259–63).

It is impossible to know just what view Euripides' male audience took of Medea's female perspective on marriage. Perhaps they found it as absurd as the antics of Aristophanes' *Lysistrata* or *Ecclesiazousae*, or it may have opened their eyes, for all that it is, on one level, the inversion of a familiar topos. Medea's 'feminism' is, however, disingenuous, conveniently skating over a declaration of intended murder (265–6, especially μιαιφονωτέρα).[4] We may also be struck by

---

[3] On women's lot as a contemporary theme and Sophocles' *Tereus* see Knox (1977) 218–21; McDermott (1989) 46–7. The role reversal extends further—to *male* infidelity: McHardy (2008) 62. 'As a wife who betrays her husband in adultery threatens the offspring of the marriage, so the future of Medea's children is threatened by the sexual infidelity of their father . . . In choosing a lover over her husband the Athenian woman would be rejecting her children and if she were caught and divorced, her relationship with her children would be at an end. Just so in the world of the play Jason's children are threatened with exile and seem to have been abandoned by their father (86–8). By betraying his wife and children Jason makes himself an enemy of his own house': ibid. 63.

[4] A point against the thesis of Rohdich (1968) 48 that Euripides does all he can to associate Medea with the generality of women.

the contrast between the ravings of the previous scene and this controlled and rational speech. This is in part a function of tragic convention with the move from the lyric outburst to speech, but it nevertheless demonstrates a quality we are to see again—Medea's ability to *see* reason even when the basis of her behaviour is more deeply irrational. Indeed, the relationship between reason, represented by *sophia*, and the irrational is a major theme of the play, with, of course, important moral implications. The spectator's empathy and adverse moral judgement are perhaps uneasy bedfellows at this point since, while all that Medea says in this speech is true and such as to encourage us to empathize with her, the underlying motive of the speech is to induce the chorus not to betray her bloody schemes.[5]

In her hypocritical attempt to reassure Creon who has arrived to expel her we see more of Medea's formidable abuse of reason which she employs brilliantly in the service of a morally corrupt end. Creon is afraid of her because she is 'clever' (σοφή, 285)—he is referring to her skill in witchcraft and baneful drugs—and of her hostility towards him and his family. Medea attempts to defuse these fears; first by pretending that Creon was referring to a more theoretical *sophia* (perhaps like that of Euripides' intellectual contemporaries, the sophists) and denying that she possesses it, and then by arguing that she could have no rational motive for hating him (292–315).[6] She intends him to leap, somewhat Socratically, to the conclusion that *therefore* she does not *in fact* hate him.[7] In other words, she exploits the disjunction we frequently find between rational conviction and emotional attitude. While she does not perhaps possess sophistic *sophia*, she does in fact possess *sophia* in drugs and magic, precisely as Creon fears, and a third kind of *sophia*, the skill in manipulating people by adroit abuse of reason and emotion. Ironically, though, her abuse of reason as a means to a barbarous end will finally recoil upon her.

When her disavowal of *sophia* proves unsuccessful, Medea resorts to a more directly emotional appeal as a suppliant (324–48), a conventionally sympathetic role, but since her disingenuousness is clearly manifest to the audience, sympathy is in danger of migrating to Creon.[8] The likelihood of this is increased during Medea's subsequent reflections in the course of which she gloats over the king's folly and the murders it will allow her to commit (364 ff.), but the tide of sympathy flows back to her in the second half of the speech wherein she reappears as the pathetic victim in need of sanctuary (386–94).

---

[5] For the 'uncertainty and duality in the audience's reception of Medea' see Mastronarde (2002) 11–12.

[6] Rohdich (1968) 48 fails to acknowledge that Medea's attempt to normalize her *sophia* is disingenuous.

[7] The Creon of *OT* similarly argues (583 ff.) that it would be irrational of him to conspire against his king, but in his case the argument is supported by his temperament.

[8] On Medea's use of persuasion against enemies in the context of Jason's abuse of language see Boedeker (1991) 95–101. Kovacs (1993) 56, on the other hand, argues that Creon's 'deliberate refusal to show *aidōs* . . . is an offense against Zeus Hikesios, and it gives the lie to his claim (349) that he has too much *aidōs* for his own good.' On conflicting sympathies see Konstan (1999) 12.

MEDEA'S SELF-CONCEPT

We gain now a deeper understanding of Medea's motivation and why it is so compelling and extreme. Her inflexible determination is a product of her self-concept which is stronger than a broadly human self-esteem, for she is the granddaughter of Helios, the sun god, and the daughter of a noble and indeed royal father (406). This noble lineage, being presumably the source of (aristocratic) virtue and of courage in particular, thereby demands courage from her (εὐψυχίας, 403); she must not incur the scorn of her enemies (404–5). Thus her motivation is recognizably heroic, Greek, male, and even Sophoclean,[9] and conceived as moral in so far as the heroic code is moral. (It is, however, also stereotypically female in its uncompromising dedication to revenge.[10]) Like a Homeric warrior, she defines herself by her moral obligations. This implies the inseparability of moral action (at any rate as conceived by the agent) and personal psychological security. Such talk is familiar from the likes of an Ajax but is strange on the lips of a woman and a barbarian, in a non-military context, and involving deceit. It produces a kind of *Verfremdungseffekt* that could well prompt us to ponder the inappropriateness of the heroic revenge code, at least in this context, and perhaps in *any* context, though that is much less certain. We note too the unheroic means she intends to employ, means which involve a woman's traditionally evil wiles. Recent criticism has remarked on the way Greek society has forced female stereotypes on Medea who then can only adopt the male heroic stereotype to recover her self-esteem. This backfires on her because she is, finally, not a male heroic warrior but a woman and most significantly a mother.[11]

JASON

Jason's attempts at self-exculpation put our sympathies firmly back in Medea's court. He claims not to have left his *philoi* in the lurch (459), but in his first

---

[9] On Medea's resemblance to the Sophoclean hero see Knox (1977) *passim*. On her stereotypically male qualities see Blondell (1999) 162.

[10] On the traditionally ruthless and uncompromising nature of female vindictiveness (with some illuminating 'historical' cases from Herodotus) see McHardy (2008) 37–42. Thus 'strong "masculine" revenge for a sexual offence combines with the excessive "feminine" vengeful desires to create one of the most notorious revenges in Greek literature' (ibid. 63).

[11] Barlow (1989) *passim*. See also Blondell (1999) 164–5: 'women's power over men is located within the family. So when the violent, vengeful nature typical of the heroic male is unleashed in the person of a woman, it leads to acts of appalling violence against intimate family members, rather than outsiders, who may be slaughtered with relative impunity . . . As a woman, then, Medea is caught in a double bind: If she is to crush her husband as he has crushed her, she must strike within this female realm. But by doing so, she also destroys her "essential" femininity (herself as mother) in the service of "masculine" revenge, and earns the horrified condemnation of her community.' Rehm (1989) 106 observes that when Medea resolves upon the filicide she 'seems to have abandoned any connection with a new female poetics, falling back instead on the old—destructive—*logos* of male heroics' (cf. ibid. 109). At ibid. 110 he sees the Great Monologue as a debate between heroic values and 'the yet unattained "female" *logos* which Medea and her play struggle towards and ultimately fail to achieve'. One wonders what sort of *logos* this might be: not presumably the acceptance of a Tecmessa, but some sort of victory over Jason which is not at the same time destructive of Medea herself and her remaining *philoi*. Euripides insists, though, it would seem, that Medea's vengefulness is irreducible: a function of female as much as of male human nature.

apologia (446–64) he ignores his desertion of Medea in order to concentrate on the alleged irrationality of her response to the predicament which is the product of his betrayal. When forced to defend himself against the charge of desertion, he argues that he has shown himself both *sophos* and *sōphrōn* (prudent and wise?) and a 'great *philos*' both to Medea herself and to their mutual children (548–9).[12] Living in exile with all the associated difficulties, he naturally sought to secure his family's position, both financially and socially, by marrying the princess. An *oikos* relies on friends (*philoi*), and impoverished exiles have few, if any.[13] His plan was actually to knit the family together by contributing more children via the princess and thus create *eudaimonia* (εὐδαιμονοῖμεν, 565), which he conceives in terms of external goods (559–61). A pity we have to put up with women (573–5), but then Medea is obviously no more to him than a minor irritation. Jason's pursuit of *eudaimonia*, in so far as it is rational and calculated, anticipates later Greek ethical theories, and even seems to caricature them in its self-centred focus on the agent's own happiness. Jason's cold-hearted rationality contrasts unfavourably with Medea's emotionalism, and yet both characters are associated with *sophia*, though in different ways: Jason with cold logic applied selfishly to human relations, Medea with her special skill with magic and drugs and above all with her manipulative planning embodied repeatedly in the play in the form of her *bouleumata* (plans). In both cases *sophia* that should be the principal guide in the conduct of life turns out to be the slave of an inadequate world-view.

HEROIC VALUES AND FILICIDE

In due course possessed of a refuge through Aegeus but still without a means of escape from Corinth, Medea announces the filicide.[14] The motive is as before—to avoid the scorn of her enemies (791–7). No one is to think of her as ignoble, powerless, or acquiescent (φαύλην κἀσθενῆ ... ἡσυχαίαν), but as 'hard on her enemies and well-disposed to her *philoi*' (βαρεῖαν ἐχθροῖς καὶ φίλοισιν εὐμενῆ, 807–9)—apart from the little detail of the filicide, one presumes—for such people enjoy the most glorious lives (810). Medea, like Homeric and Sophoclean heroes, is self-consciously devoted to a moral code. Incredibly, though, she fails to see its

---

[12] '[A]s we read Jason's speech down to line 567 we find it hard to see which elements in his conduct he regards as *sophos* and which as *sōphrōn*; his formulation of a desirable end and perception of the means to it are presumably *sophos*, and perhaps he thinks himself *sōphrōn* in being able to tear himself away from Medeia's bed for the purpose of a marriage more politically advantageous': Dover (1974) 121. On Jason's 'instrumental' approach to *philia* see Schein (1990) 57; on Jason's *sophia* and *sophrosunē* see Rohdich (1968) 57–8.

[13] On the ills of exile cf. Eur. *Phoen.* 387–99.

[14] 'Medea's decision to kill the children but let Jason live on without future hopes is closely paralleled in Euripides' *Hecuba*, where Polymestor is forced to witness the murder of his children before he is symbolically castrated to prevent him siring any replacements': McHardy (2008) 63. Schlesinger (1968) 82, 87 argues that Medea had learned from Creon the importance of children to a man and that that idea has now been confirmed by Aegeus—hence the filicide as the most effective revenge on Jason. See also Rohdich (1968) 49–50, Mastronarde (2002) 20–1. Gibert (1995) 53–4, on the other hand, argues that the filicide motif here, rather than psychology, drives the plot.

incompatibility with filicide. Sophocles' Electra, on the other hand, was fully aware that in doing all she could to further her mother's punishment she was acting in a conventionally unfilial manner. Medea's 'morality' is conveniently (and unsurprisingly) self-centred.

The chorus strongly disapprove (811–13) but do not withdraw their sympathy from Medea.[15] In their ensuing ode (824–65) their disapproval is reinforced by their failure to imagine her, the child-killer, in their idealized conception of a cultured and civilized Athens (846–50). She *cannot* be 'one of us'. And yet the chorus (and thus presumably the audience), though alienated by the almost inconceivable inhumanity of her vindictiveness, continue to sympathize with Medea.

After the spurious reconciliation in which Medea recycles Jason's arguments (skirting dangerously close to overt parody) and claims that she now sees the wisdom of acting as he advocated, the plot against the palace advances and the filicide draws closer. Her appropriation of Jason's 'rationality' and *sophia* underlines the ease with which this intellectual virtue can be subverted to dubious or evil emotional ends. In their ode (976–1001) before the Great Monologue, the chorus divide their sympathies among the children, the princess, Jason, and finally Medea. Such a multiple perspective indicates how we the audience are to apportion our sympathies, and it seems that we are to look upon everyone as a victim.[16] This is appropriate preparation for the ensuing Great Monologue (1021–80)[17] in which Medea, divided between her vengefulness and her maternal feelings, herself appears as both the agent and the victim of her own murderous plans. She displays here her first signs of serious regret about the filicide while initially remaining completely committed to it.

THE GREAT MONOLOGUE

Medea's famous monologue is not structured as a rational review of the arguments for and against the filicide; the decision has already been made, and it has emerged

[15] 'Like the chorus, we find ourselves struggling to be freed of that to which we have already given our allegiance. Seduced into approving Medea's revenge [i.e. the original plan to kill Jason rather than the children], we cannot approve it at all': Buttrey (1958) 16. We have been drawn in with the chorus who have come to regard the murders of Medea's enemies as justified and as vindicating women: we are thus involved 'sympathetically in a kind of morality which cannot stand examination. Medea's murder of her children must strike us as pretty terrible. Yet Euripides has forced us to admit that murder per se is justifiable': ibid. (But Buttrey goes too far in implying that we morally approve of Jason's murder and therefore of murder as such, at least in principle. We have not been drawn into anything so conscious or specific. Rather we feel a general sympathy with the idea of Jason receiving his comeuppance.)

[16] Another case of conflicting sympathies: Konstan (1999) 12.

[17] My interpretation of the Monologue assumes, without argument, the authenticity of the whole while recognizing textual difficulties, such as the abrupt transition after 1055 (excised by Kovacs 1986). I have adopted Diller's (1966) interpretation (accepted e.g. by Stanton (1987) 101) of *kreisson* (1079) to mean 'master of' rather than 'stronger than' since the latter is an impossible reading unless we take *thumos*, with Burnett (1998) 273–87, to refer to Medea's maternal feelings. I share, however, the slight misgivings of Foley (2001) 251 n. 37 in seeing Diller's reading 'as both possible and preferable, and problematic only because it is the more obscure alternative'. On the evidence against this reading see Burnett (1998) 276 and Harris (2001) 169–70.

not from a deliberation but from a sort of intuitive inspiration as to the most effective means of destroying Jason.[18] Medea is superbly rational when it comes to means, but there is no evidence of her having debated the morality of the various killings—an issue which she brusquely brushes aside when the chorus' raise it (811–19). Here is an agent that can shut out all external influence. But in the present scene Medea's maternal instincts well up with unpredictable spontaneity, creating a division in her mind between them and her vengeful determination. As these feelings emerge, she reflects that she will be deprived of the joys of seeing her children grow up (1021–39) and that her wilfulness or αὐθαδία (1028), a term already applied to her by Jason (631), has created this miserable prospect. This is not a belated moral rejection of the filicide; she is doing no more than coming to realize and regret its emotional cost, as Sophocles' *Electra* regrets the moral necessity of being nasty to her mother. But then suddenly, as she looks at the children, she loses her nerve because their bodily expression poignantly engages her maternal affection (1040–3):

> τί προσδέρκεσθέ μ' ὄμμασιν, τέκνα;
> τί προσγελᾶτε τὸν πανύστατον γέλων;
> αἰαῖ. τί δράσω; καρδία γὰρ οἴχεται,
> γυναῖκες, ὄμμα φαιδρὸν ὡς εἶδον τέκνων.

(Why do you look at me with your eyes, children? Why do you smile on me your last smile? What shall I do? I lost my nerve seeing the children's bright eyes.)

The influence of bodily expression is a feature of Euripidean tragedy which brings a further dimension to the characters' otherwise abstract deliberations. At this point Medea makes an unscheduled and entirely emotionally inspired decision not to proceed with the filicide (1044–5): 'Farewell, previous plans (χαιρέτω βουλεύματα τὰ πρόσθεν); I'll take my children away with me.' (She is planning to escape to Athens.) She reinforces this decision not with a moral argument but with a rational appeal to self-interest: she would suffer twice as much as Jason if she were to go ahead with the deed (1046–7). She then reiterates her decision in almost the same terms: 'Farewell, plans' (χαιρέτω βουλεύματα, 1048). The ring composition gives a deceptive sense of closure.

But now, threatened with frustration, Medea rebels, reminding herself of the consequence of the scorn of her enemies and perversely dismissing her genuine maternal instincts as cowardice and therefore as morally wrong (1049–52):[19]

---

[18] See Lattimore (1964) 37–8.

[19] On Medea's rejection of her feminine self in favour of the male heroic code see Foley (2001) 264–5 who argues that '[a] normal Greek woman had accessible no model of full social and ethical autonomy available to herself. The decision to avenge her wrongs presents no problems for Medea; she borrows heroic masculine ethical standards to articulate her choice and stereotypically feminine duplicity and magic permit her to achieve her goals': ibid. 243. Kovacs (1993) 59, however, asks: 'What could possess a woman, even one of heroic mettle, to destroy her own children? The answer the play seems to suggest is "Zeus." Aegeus' errand to Delphi intersects with Medea's desire for a place of refuge for the furtherance of her revenge. Medea is allowed to suggest pointedly that this intersection is the work of Zeus. The one incidental result, the furthering of Medea's design, seems to be part of Zeus's intention. The same can reasonably be concluded of the other, the change in her plan of revenge. There is reason to think that it is Zeus's will that she should murder her children. Jason's punishment is the perfect one for an oath-breaker. . . . But the agent of divine vengeance will be punished in her turn. That is the way Zeus works.'

$$\kappa\alpha\acute{\iota}\tau\omicron\iota\ \tau\acute{\iota}\ \pi\acute{\alpha}\sigma\chi\omega;\ \beta\omicron\acute{\upsilon}\lambda\omicron\mu\alpha\iota\ \gamma\acute{\epsilon}\lambda\omega\tau'\ \mathring{\omicron}\phi\lambda\epsilon\hat{\iota}\nu$$
$$\mathring{\epsilon}\chi\theta\rho\omicron\grave{\upsilon}\varsigma\ \mu\epsilon\theta\epsilon\hat{\iota}\sigma\alpha\ \tau\omicron\grave{\upsilon}\varsigma\ \mathring{\epsilon}\mu\omicron\grave{\upsilon}\varsigma\ \mathring{\alpha}\zeta\eta\mu\acute{\iota}\omicron\upsilon\varsigma;$$
$$\tau\omicron\lambda\mu\eta\tau\acute{\epsilon}\omicron\nu\ \tau\acute{\alpha}\delta'.\ \mathring{\alpha}\lambda\lambda\grave{\alpha}\ \tau\hat{\eta}\varsigma\ \mathring{\epsilon}\mu\hat{\eta}\varsigma\ \kappa\acute{\alpha}\kappa\eta\varsigma,$$
$$\tau\grave{\omicron}\ \kappa\alpha\grave{\iota}\ \pi\rho\omicron\sigma\acute{\epsilon}\sigma\theta\alpha\iota\ \mu\alpha\lambda\theta\alpha\kappa\omicron\grave{\upsilon}\varsigma\ \lambda\acute{\omicron}\gamma\omicron\upsilon\varsigma\ \phi\rho\epsilon\nu\acute{\iota}.$$

(What's the matter with me? Do I want to let my enemies off scot-free to laugh at me? I must find the nerve to do this thing. What a coward I am, letting thoughts of weakening get into my mind!)

But her maternal feelings now rebel again and she reverts to the idea of escaping with the children (1056–8). However, at this point the so-called *anankē*-motif begins to operate as she realizes the impracticality of escape (1059–66), and so she returns to her resolve to kill them (1067–8), now presumably reinforced by the *anankē* (overwhelming pressure). She continues in this resolve as she embraces the children, but then their bodily presence distresses her even more (1074–5), so she sends them inside, able to look at them no longer and overcome by the whole distressing situation (κακοῖς, 1077) created by her revenge plans. She knows what *kaka* (1078) she will do, but her *thumos* (wrathful heart) is 'greater than' (κρείσσων), that is 'in control of' her [revenge] plans (τῶν ἐμῶν βουλευμάτων) (1078–80). The minimal sense of *kaka* here (at 1078) must be 'actions distressing to myself and to the children'. But she goes on to say that the *thumos* is the cause of mortals' 'greatest *kaka*' (1080). Again the reference may be confined to (amoral) sufferings. On the other hand, the *thumos* with which Medea has hitherto for the most part identified as the source of her morally admirable courage is here condemned. It is at least conceivable that she is at once lamenting the sufferings caused by the *thumos* and morally approving of it (as one might do in the case of one's conscience), but it seems more likely that at this climactic point it has at last dawned on her that the filicide is evil. But even if this realization is barely more than subliminal and more emotionally than rationally based, it is certainly clear to her at this point that she is no longer actively deciding to proceed with her revenge. This passivity implies that she cannot be a moral agent, quite apart from the morality or otherwise of what her *thumos* will drive her to do. She simply recognizes fatalistically what she will do now that her vengeful will has gained the support of the *anankē* arising from the involvement of the children in the palace murders.[20] This sets her radically apart from the Sophoclean heroes whose moral commitment to what they do is unswerving and unequivocal.

Medea's *thumos* is the author of her revenge. The word itself has a long history and frustratingly wide semantic range from Homer down, so that its meaning, as Foley observes, should not be restricted to anger:[21]

Galis (1992) 78 believes that Medea requires 'not merely heroic but supernatural powers' to cross 'the boundary between feminine and masculine *aretē*'.

[20] Schlesinger (1968) 72 maintains that the *anankē* is simply the inner necessity of the revenge: 'Medea is determined to act; she has not merely thought of it, nor has she struggled to the decision. In a sense the revenge is imposed on her by her own nature. She must will it of necessity, and this she knows very well. Even before the great monologue the revenge is a closed matter, and so is the murder of her children, for *this* is the essence of her revenge. But it is very important that she herself come to grips with this fact. The force within Medea that reacts to this necessity is not an opposing will, but rather a simple longing for happiness struggling against a destiny that has forced her to perform deeds of superhuman proportion.' But is Medea to be identified with her *thumos*?

[21] Foley (2001) 254. On *thumos* in Homer and Euripides see ibid. 253.

it is better to characterise *thumos* in the monologue not as 'irrational passion' or 'rage' but as a capacity located in Medea that directs her to act, a 'heart' that can (or at least pretends to itself that it can) choose to side either with the arguments of the revenger or the arguments of the mother (although it is predisposed to the former).[22]

Mastronarde also associates Medea's *thumos* partly with her maternal feelings:

> If we import anachronistically the Platonic division of the soul, we may say that the emotional and spirited part of her soul is engaged on both sides of the struggle: on the one side, her maternal love, pity; on the other, her sense of heroic self and 'face', her wounded pride at sexual rejection, her anger at injustice and betrayal of oaths, her desire to make her enemies suffer as much as or more than she has or will.[23]

The Platonic *thumos*, though indeed an anachronism, is a useful concept here, but it should be restricted, as Plato himself restricts it, to the 'part' of the psyche associated with self-esteem, pride, and the expression of a righteous indignation that stems from self-esteem and pride, as in the examples which the philosopher himself gives. To include in it feelings such as pity and love deprives the concept of its clarity and explanatory power. As Foley observes, 'In Medea's case, the *thumos* that rules her plans, if we read it in the context of the motives for her revenge offered throughout the play, unites jealousy, anger, and courage with justice and a rational principle of heroic action that has consistently operated for Medea: that of harming enemies and helping friends.'[24] (In what sense, if any, such a principle should be termed 'rational' we shall presently consider.)

The Homeric *thumos* is similarly an 'organ' that can swell with a vindictive wrath like that of Medea, and Plato in the *Republic* discusses the passage in the *Odyssey* in which the hero's *thumos*, protesting at the misconduct of the unfaithful maids, must be subjected to the control of reason lest it induce him to attempt an immediate, unscheduled, and no doubt abortive revenge. Plato has divided the *psuchē* into three 'parts': reason (*logistikon*) which concerns itself with the long-term interests of the agent, appetite (*epithumia*), and *thumos* (or *thumoeides*) which is the part that responds in a 'spirited' fashion, particularly to humiliation.[25] Each of these parts is imagined, problematically, as a kind of conscious entity that can engage in means-end reasoning, so that appetite, for example, can reason its way to the food which it desires, though, presumably, it lacks the desire or the capacity to argue (when, that is, it usurps the function of the *logistikon*) that satisfaction of a physical appetite should at all times be the supreme goal of the agent.

It is, curiously, the *Platonic* rather than the Homeric *thumos* (a term to which the philosopher here gives an almost technical and much more restricted sense) that naturally prompts the vengeful responses of Homeric heroes, and the reactions of the Homeric Odysseus in this passage and of Euripides' Medea could be

---

[22] Rickert (1987) 101 cites Lloyd-Jones (1980) 54: 'as often in tragedy the *thumos* is not merely one of several more or less vague terms for the seat of the intelligence but connotes pride, spirit, anger, something like what Plato means by *thumoeides*'. Burnett (1998) 277 also rightly argues against equating *thumos* simply with anger, but she is less convincing in relating it to motherly love at 1079. For a refutation of this idea and in particular for the consequential difficulties in interpreting *kaka* in 1077, 1078, and 1080, see Foley (2001) 252 n. 39.

[23] Mastronarde (2002) 22.   [24] Foley (2001) 256.   [25] See *Rep.* 439d ff.

seen to originate in this Platonic organ. Plato, however, omits to indicate that the Homeric *thumos*, while coinciding somewhat with his own conception in the case he selects, is actually a broader and perhaps vaguer or more fluid entity—and this applies likewise to the Euripidean *thumos*.[26] But because of the correspondence in the particular cases, the Platonic idea is suggestive, for if Plato might have seen Medea's revenge as a product of the *thumos* as he conceived it, he could also have observed that the *thumos* had usurped the function of the *logistikon* and that Medea was implicitly aware of that at the end of the monologue where she virtually admits to herself that her *thumos* is acting not only against her maternal interests but against her overall interests as a person. Medea, in other words, is momentarily aware, in effect, though not explicitly, of the tyranny of the heroic code, and that what she earlier attempted to justify rationally is, at least in the final analysis, an irrational obsession with revenge.

Foley is impressed with the 'inseparable combination of rationality and irrationality, passion and intelligence, in Medea's determination for revenge', citing Gill's comment on the rationality that 'deliberately intensifies, by arguments and exhortation, her own desire to carry out her revenge.'[27] This rationality, however, is spurious, proceeding as it does from a Platonic *thumos* that has usurped the function of the *logistikon*. Medea can defend the 'rationality' of the filicide as the best way to destroy her husband, but she never explains why the original plan to kill him is now to be deemed inadequate. Certainly the filicide will be the *best* way to inflict the *maximum* pain upon him (and the Platonic *thumos* can appropriately engage in such means–end reasoning), but that constitutes less a moral argument than the exaggerated malice of a humiliated victim—in other words the reflex of a Platonic *thumos* that is performing the function of the *logistikon*, and performing it badly.[28] It is not the sheer punishment of Jason that is morally problematical, but the nature and severity of the punishment which Medea designs and the evil it entails for her children, for the Corinthian royal family, and for herself.

Plato does not reach the point of criticizing the heroic code. He does not say that Odysseus' revenge is wrong in principle (nor is it so in the world-view of the poem), only that his *thumos* is impatient. More subversive would have been a case in which the goal of the *thumos* was totally rejected by the *logistikon*. Such cases are more likely to arise in tragedy. While there is nothing wrong with a concern for one's honour, its claims are not absolute, and characters such as Ajax and Medea go too far—Ajax in attempting to kill his peers, Medea in killing her children. The *logistikon*, being conditioned by the circumambient culture, might have sanctioned some kind of revenge, though just about any revenge that Medea, a woman, might have undertaken would have been conventionally illegitimate.

---

[26] On the Homeric *thumos* in relation to this passage see Halliwell (1990) 38–41.

[27] Foley (2001) 257 and n. 49; Gill (1983) 142.

[28] Mastronarde (2002) 22 sees the problem more as a function of the situation than of a failure of reason in the protagonist herself: 'Medea uses her reasoning ability to weigh alternatives, develop plans, adjust her rhetoric to each situation, and perform a calculus of gains and losses, pleasures and pains. In the end, it is not a simple defeat of reason by emotion, but a display of the insufficiency of intellectual qualities to ensure a good outcome in the complex moral crises of human life.' Complex Medea's moral crisis may be, but hardly such as to render filicide an eligible option!

A critique of Medea's morality and of the heroic code that underpins it is implicit in Euripides' play.[29] Discursive argument, the mode of philosophy, might have articulated such a critique quite explicitly, though, as far as we are aware, the Greek philosophers never did so. Tragedy, however, and indeed literature in general, merely provide the materials for the spectator's reflection. This produces discomfort without providing the means of resolving it, and one of the many subjective modern views of the tragic asserts that it entails precisely a negative and unresolvable element. In this play, unease is created about heroic morality through its association with a barbarian female and the revenge to which it leads, but the audience is left to think discursively about the wider issues, if they so wish, and to draw their own conclusions.

In Platonic terms, Medea's *logistikon* has all but ceased to perform its proper function. Reason, of course, in the form of Medea's habitual *sophia* continues to operate, and most effectively, but on the level of means rather than ends, as embodied in her plans (*bouleumata*). Reason as *logistikon* comes briefly and feebly to the aid of Medea's maternal instincts, arguing that the filicide will bring twice as much suffering to her as to Jason. Otherwise it can only reflect passively on the dominance of the *thumos* in the final three verses (1078–80) of the monologue. Medea herself, however, at least at this point, sees her situation 'akratically', as is clear from the pointed antithesis of 1079–80: she knows what she is going to do but she disapproves. This is an unusual case of *akrasia* in that Medea's rational faculty has all along been suborned to support the desires of her vindictive *thumos*, for she has argued, quite legitimately, that Jason has wronged her and the gods (through his perjury) and ought to be punished for it. Moreover, she encountered no inner resistance to her intended revenge in its earlier form (the projected murder of Jason, Creon, and the princess). Within her heroic morality then reason had nothing to protest against. But naturally once her own (maternal) interests came into conflict with the revenge plans, the *logistikon* with its wider concerns began to resist. Still, through most of the Great Monologue, the *thumos* is in the ascendant intellectually as well as emotionally. At the end, however, the *logistikon* assumes intellectual supremacy, but, akratically, it is unable to assume cognitive and affective control over the whole person.

Indeed, to speak of akrasia in Medea's case we really need to know to what she is committed at any given moment. Akrasia occurs when a rational desire and resolve are frustrated by an irrational desire. With Medea, the desire and resolve of the *thumos* are, at bottom, irrational, so akrasia can only occur when the reasonable and legitimate resolve to spare the children predominates. But this occurs only very briefly.[30]

---

[29] Harris (2001) 168 characterizes Medea's revenge as 'disproportionate', but thinks that it would be 'very hypothetical to suggest that he [Euripides] intended a more general lesson about revenge. And if we look forward to what the tragedians said later about revenge, we find that the accepted beliefs had changed little if at all since the time of the *Oresteia*.' Certainly, nothing as specific as a 'lesson' is at issue here.

[30] One might look at the matter subjectively from the point of view of the agent: it is possible to have what one misguidedly thinks is a rational resolve to embark on a particular course of action but to be prevented by what one, again misguidedly, considers to be an irrational desire. In the view of Rickert (1987) 116, Medea is not akratic; she recognizes the evil she is going to do but would consider it worse evil to let her revenge go.

We have noted that the Platonic *logistikon* is the rational part of the soul that is devoted to the overall and long-term interests of the agent, and that in Medea it continues to function, albeit feebly. Here it is interesting to note that Medea's *logistikon* is subject to precisely the limitations of the Platonic organ which render it problematical as a guide to moral action in the just person of the *Republic*. Plato understands what is morally right (*dikaiosunē*) not as a principle of conduct but as a psychological state of harmony of the three parts of the mind (*psuchē*) with the *logistikon* in control. But it is quite unclear why such a harmonious mental state should issue in spontaneous moral action (or even the intention to act morally) rather than merely in a rational pursuit of self-interest, as the *logistikon* guides the judgement of the agent; and Medea at no stage until the very end of the mono-logue clearly considers any of her revenge plans to be morally problematical except in terms of her supposed (heroic) moral obligations to herself; she fears only (through the medium of her *logistikon*, we might say) that they are contrary to her own wider interests.

In the emotional dialectic of the Great Monologue, Euripides brings out how feelings and thoughts simply arise in the mind rather than being summoned there, and how the idea of rational control is something of an artificial construct. Through its mode of direct dramatization in the context of a fictional life, tragedy brings out more subtly, because less schematically, the elusive psychological contours of the agent's mental conflict.

It is clear enough that the Monologue is designed to enlist profound sympathy for Medea but balanced by profound horror. Sympathy is maintained through the impression that Medea is a victim of a part of herself or of an attitude that has become obsessively fixed in her mind and alienated from the rest of her conscious being. Sympathy and moral judgement are essentially different modes of response, so that we cannot engage in both absolutely simultaneously. We sympathize with people *qua* victims and judge them *qua* responsible agents. We respond to Medea as agent and as victim but not at precisely the same time. At this point in the play our strongly adverse moral judgement may override our sympathy and induce us to 'disown' Medea. We could sympathize with her grief and even with a more limited vengefulness, and to that extent she is 'like us', but we might well deny all kinship with a being that can criticize herself for not being brave enough to murder her own children.

Is this a legitimate response to the play? Extreme and self-destructive vengeful-ness is a feature of adherents of the heroic code, and characters such as Achilles and Ajax behave very badly without being dismissed as evil. Medea, though, is a woman, and the act itself is both 'unnatural' and unsanctioned by the context of war. On the other hand, Euripides works against these negatives by his strongly sympathetic portrayal of his protagonist. Having once felt that she is 'like us', it is harder to detach ourselves from her. Nor, after the victory of her *thumos*, does Euripides begin to deny her human feelings. Certainly we are repelled by her ghoulish *schadenfreude* in anticipation of the report of the palace murders (1133–5), but one must remember that once we sanction harming enemies it would seem perverse not to enjoy doing so—though her attitude and the accom-panying messenger's report work strongly against the whole principle.

As she gears herself up to commit filicide Medea struggles again with her maternal feelings, concentrated now in her reluctant hand (1244–5), and we cannot forget her final private and therefore sincere statement on the deed: 'For this short day forget your children and mourn hereafter!' (κἄπειτα θρήνει, 1249).[31] Thus the impression at this point is not of a dehumanized woman, but of a woman victimized by an aspect of her own temperament. Medea remains in a way split; the ancient audience can perhaps 'disown' the *pathological* dominance of her vengefulness (that is deny its relevance to their own psychologies), but they cannot deny some kinship with anger and vengefulness, while of course they would quite happily see the suffering mother as 'like themselves'. It is then the pathological extremity that perhaps sets the audience apart from her—but only perhaps, because, as she tells the chorus, they, like the audience, are not in her shoes and so do not really understand. Otherwise she is indeed like the audience, and the facile moral dismissal of her as a bad woman *totally* alien from the human race becomes impossible.

MEDEA *EX MACHINA*

But there is still the controversial epilogue in which Medea has appeared, to some modern critics at least, as indeed dehumanized. This impression is partly a function of her role as Euripidean *deus*. It has seemed suggestive that the role regularly assumed by a god is here taken on by Medea herself as if she had, at least figuratively, lost her humanity to become a sort of *theos*[32]—though other Euripidean characters with less power and authority than Medea (for example, Eurystheus in *Heracleidae* and Polymestor in *Hecuba*) assume a similar role. The rigidity of such *deus* figures seems to be a function of their role rather than of their characters.[33] Their formulaic implacability, however, suits Medea in that her purpose all along has been to triumph over Jason, and this she does, without denying her maternal feelings (1361–2), though those feelings cannot dominate without ruining her revenge. We have already established that the revenge is successful and will be emotionally satisfying, though it has been bought at a terrible cost.[34] Something similar can be said of Sophocles' Electra whose loving emotions are in eclipse at the end of the play as she consummates her revenge on her enemies.

---

[31] On Medea's perpetual mourning see Boedeker (1991) 107, 112.

[32] See e.g. Barlow (1989) 167; Rehm (1989) 113. On Medea as a *theos* see Cunningham (1954) *passim*; Knox (1977) 206–8. The 'energy she had wasted on Jason was tempered to a deadly instrument to destroy him. It became a *theos*, a relentless, merciless force, the unspeakable violence of the oppressed and betrayed which, because it has been so long pent up, carries everything before it to destruction, even if it destroys what it loves most': ibid. 225. On the problem of Medea's relevance and universality as a dramatic figure and for a review of earlier views of the relationship between the Medea of the epilogue and the earlier Medea see Rohdich (1968) 44–6.

[33] Cunningham (1954) 152.

[34] For Cunningham, ibid. 159–60, the appearance *ex machina* shows that Medea 'has received not reward but some awful and terrible retribution. . . . It forces the audience to realize the effect upon Medea of what she has done, and it emphasizes the point that she could do what she would and get away with it.'

However, it is not merely Medea's enactment of the *deus* role that has given the impression of a loss of humanity, for she performs that role in a magic chariot where she remains inviolable (and this always was the condition of a full and satisfying revenge), as if she were indeed some kind of *theos*. That she is not a god is clear from the fact that she is about to fly to Athens and resume a mortal existence (or so she originally intended and we continue to presume), but her escape is effected with the full support of Helios, the great-grandfather of her victims. We might dismiss the chariot as a merely dramaturgical device analogous to Poseidon's mechanical intervention in the *Hippolytus*, did not Euripides twice (1251–60, 1323–8) direct our attention to the anomaly that the sun, who is traditionally outraged by wrongdoing and pollution, is in this case, it would appear, condoning the deed and aiding the escape of the perpetrator.[35] On the other hand, Helios' action has been justified by pointing to his role as a punisher of perjury.[36] Nevertheless, the anomaly remains, and the text directs us to it. This makes it seem that Euripides intends a kind of metaphysical statement to the effect that Medea's *thumos* shares its irrationality with the daimonic forces of the universe, that it is not merely a non-rational function that is yet amenable to reason in a mind defined by the philosophers as essentially rational.

In this play we find a rather different emphasis than we discovered, for example, in the *Seven* where gods intervene psychologically in the deliberations of the protagonist. Here the boundary between the human and the divine is blurred: Medea the mother is the victim of what we might call the 'daimonic' element, but that element is fused with her own *thumos*. While the Erinys entered into Eteocles' mind, she did not corrupt his judgement as to the course of action necessitated by divine malevolence. The divine universe of Euripides' play betrays no hint as to what, if anything, it requires Medea to do, and yet it seems to be in some sort of sinister harmony with the impulses of her *thumos* and thus to be hostile to human interests.

Whether or not Euripides believed in 'daimonic' forces, an impression remains of a window through the human psyche into a dangerous and at best amoral universe.[37] It suggests that the barrier between virtue and vice is more porous than we might like to imagine, since the irrational can descend easily upon any of us.

---

[35] On the idea that Helios condones the filicide see Kitto (1961) 201 and Collinge (1962) 172.

[36] Foley (2001) 248.

[37] Some critics go further, claiming that divine forces are literally active in the play. Kovacs (1993) *passim* backs Zeus; Burnett (1998) 216 thinks that Medea in forming her own revenge plans is acting out the will of a divine avenger, somewhat like Clytemnestra does in Aeschylus, and that she realizes this after the report of the palace murders: 'In a sense the messenger's speech has done for Medea what Pylades' words did for Orestes in the Aeschylean play, for it has reminded her of her otherworldly allies. What is more, the palace horror has shown her the nature of the power that inhabits her hand: it is fierce and undeniable . . .' (Burnett, however, adduces no evidence for any such realization on Medea's part.) 'However one may ultimately feel about the morality of Medea's conduct, she is a woman who transcends the confines of human powerlessness and takes the rightful, and from a divine standpoint necessary, project of revenge into her own hands. Medea both is authentically herself and at the same time obeys a divine command, punishing where the gods would punish, and with the same superhuman harshness which ultimately deforms her humanity': Wildberg (1999–2000) 240. 'As Medea realizes the magnitude of Jason's offense, she gradually, and not without hesitation, assumes the responsibility for his punishment herself. It is not malice or the inability to control her anger which guides her action, but the punitive sanction from above that is triggered by Jason's perjury, and it is

What then are we to think of Medea as a moral agent, if we can disregard for a moment the total emotional effect of her depiction?[38] We have considered her disturbing relationship to the universe. This leaves us with the immediate context of moral action in tragedy: the *oikos* and the *polis*. Medea, however, is a barbarian who deserted her culture, state, and family. While Euripides does not present her as thinking like a barbarian or even as the Greeks would have imagined barbarians thought,[39] she herself and Jason remind us that she is not culturally a Greek. She is rather an exile in a most precarious position, and, having burnt her bridges, she has no cultural or political loyalties. Indeed for Emily McDermott,

Euripides' introduction into the myth of the mother's purposeful slaying of the children may be appreciated as the perfect culmination of the story as he has chosen to present it. She has despoiled other parents of their children, other children of their parents. She has destroyed her own father. All that is left is for her to turn her deadly hand on her children

and the filicide 'becomes emblematic of the ultimate breakdown in human order'.[40] Medea's consuming loyalty was to Jason, and under the influence of her passion for him she acted with complete immorality. The ultimate source of whatever sense of moral responsibility remains to her is her wounded honour, but then the most depraved persons feel at least a caricature of moral outrage in respect of injustices done to *them*. Admittedly, victims may respond partly out of a more disinterested sense of justice, and this seems to be the case with Medea (and, as we shall see, with Hecuba). But her own moral hypocrisy more than cancels this positive factor.

But right from the heroic age the Greeks put a strong (to our minds too strong) ethical emphasis on being true to one's nature and vindicating one's honour—which is fine so long as it is one's nature to behave virtuously, which brings one's treatment of others into the equation. But Medea is concerned with something much more basic—with the regaining of respect for herself which she sees in terms of retribution or revenge for the humiliation she has received. This self-respect relates to her self-concept which is based in turn on her noble and even divine ancestry.[41] In this she adheres to the Greek heroic code, at least in its

---

precisely Jason's behavior *qua* perjury that arouses her fiercest anger': ibid. 241. See also Rickert (1987) 108–12.

[38] Gellie (1988) 22 believes that 'anything like an ethical judgement is ruled out' because Medea is not a 'unitary personality' (ibid. 17). Indeed, the dramatist, according to this critic, has not succeeded in uniting the heroic Medea the woman, the 'wailing wife' with the 'crafty schemer' or the fiend with the mother. The reasons for these switches are, according to Gellie, 'to be found in the organization of the surface processes of the play'. Medea 'goes on being clever and mad, cruel and soft, perfectly controlled and ungovernable by turns' (ibid. 15–18). But extreme contradictions are by no means infrequent in human nature. It is easy enough to imagine a move from distress and passivity to vindictive murderousness, the coexistence of cunning and emotionalism in a single person, and so on.

[39] See Page (1938) pp. xviii–xxi and, *contra*, Easterling (1977) 180.

[40] McDermott (1989) 108. On Medea's attack on families and no fewer than four cities in her 'ruthless pursuit of her own ends' see ibid. 109.

[41] The nurse observes that she is a princess and so accustomed to indulge her angry moods since no one is allowed to restrain them (119–21). (An Aristotelian would here see the foundations being laid of a vicious and perhaps tyrannical character.) But this will seem scarcely a sufficient explanation of Medea's later crimes. Whether the nurse's comment implies that members of royal families also inherit their difficult and frightening temperaments (δεινὰ λήματα) is not clear.

concern to harm enemies, though she claims, rather speciously, as it turns out, that she is also devoted to helping or being loyal to *philoi*.[42] (The wider and more other-regarding aspects of heroic morality as they appear for example in the *Iliad* are irrelevant here.) The selfish quality of heroic 'morality' (at least when interpreted very narrowly) is brought out starkly in her treatment of innocents, including her own children. And what is this limited and egoistic form of heroic morality but a rationalization of the Platonic *thumos* out of control?

Medea's commitment to revenge in general and to this particular revenge is not a product of decisions or reasoning as such. When she introduces the idea of the filicide to the chorus, she speaks of it as a sort of unnegotiable and inevitable resolve (791–7, 811–19), and in this she resembles the Sophoclean hero. That is not to say, however, that her anger is not rationally justified or justifiable; she has every reason to feel aggrieved and to want Jason punished. Gill has argued that Medea's vengeful attitude is 'more firmly grounded on reflectively-based deliberation'[43] than are her maternal instincts, but perhaps the truth is rather that it *could* be so based or even that Medea, like Electra, is capable of reflecting on and justifying to other people a course of action that she has resolved upon without initial deliberation. But even though Medea intends the filicide partly as an 'exemplary gesture' to force on Jason an awareness of his 'breach of the fundamental principles of *philia*, and the more standard claims on her *philia* represented by the children'[44] (and in this there is a genuinely moral element), the price of the gesture is morally unacceptable, while the gesture itself is vitiated by Medea's ruthlessly self-regarding moral hypocrisy. This is moreover true for an ancient audience, for it can hardly be claimed that anyone else in the play supports the filicide. (A similar moral objection can be brought against the Homeric Achilles' exemplary gesture of withdrawal from the Trojan conflict, at least after his rejection of the compensation.[45])

We have seen how the tragedian by enlisting sympathy for Medea facilitates a complex moral response. Medea is not simply an evil woman whose tragedy leaves us appalled but unmoved to question our shared human nature.[46] If the pressure upon Medea to kill her children can be traced back to her common human nature, we can hardly regard ourselves as free of such impulses and their moral consequences. I am not suggesting here that the spectator explicitly formulates such moral questions as a result of seeing the play, for many of the issues raised more or less implicitly in literature are apt to remain subliminal in the mind. And yet this

---

[42] On the role of *philia* in the play and of Medea's manipulation of the relationship see Schein (1990) *passim*. 'Throughout the play, Medea speaks sincerely and passionately of *philia* as a compact by which two people commit their faith and themselves by sworn oaths, yet at the same time she uses *philia* to destroy, and to justify destroying, those she hates. On the one hand, she is a victim; on the other hand, given the pervasive instrumentality in the play of relationships of *philia*, she is no different from Jason, Creon, or even Aegeus—only more effective': ibid. 68.

[43] Gill (1996) 221.

[44] Ibid. 217.

[45] Achilles' gesture is intended 'to dramatize the extent to which Agamemnon's behaviour has undermined the basis of co-operative *philia*': ibid. 199.

[46] For McDermott (1989) 111, Medea's 'chilling effect is rendered complete by the care the playwright takes . . . to insinuate that all her nihilistic and chaotic urges are not hers alone, but that the seeds of the disorder she embodies are in everyone . . .'. See also ibid. 115.

kind of emotional engagement draws us into what may prove psychologically threatening territory beyond the detached, rational, articulate, and systematic discourse of ethical philosophy and the fully conscious engagement of the rational mind which it requires. What Medea does she does not simply because she is a barbarian or through conformity to the stereotype of the bad woman. Rather she thinks like a humiliated Greek (or indeed like a humiliated human being in general) so that her sense of personal insult stirs her to action in the manner of a Homeric hero, and the code that sanctions such action is thus at least called into question.

CONCLUSION

Medea does not deliberate over the filicide. Once the idea has occurred to her she is completely committed to it until, during the Great Monologue, her maternal feelings brook no further suppression and set up a dialectic with her *thumos*. Medea defines herself as a princess descended from Helios with heroic moral obligations to herself and to *philoi* and enemies. She sees both the filicide and the palace murders as just retribution, and is quite untroubled by the morality of such actions. Medea does not really act in accordance with her stated morality of being kind to friends and hard on enemies, since she neglects the first half of this ethic. The full emotional implications of the filicide dawn on her during the Great Monologue, but she proceeds anyway because by now she is absolutely under the control of her angry *thumos*. She fails therefore to integrate her emotions into her moral stance, since her maternal feelings disrupt her 'moral' commitment to Jason's destruction. Indeed, these feelings bring her to a crisis in which she comes to understand more clearly the source of her 'morality' which is itself nothing more than a rationalization of her vindictive feelings.

12

Euripides: *Hecuba*

HECUBA THE VICTIM OF CIRCUMSTANCES

While Medea's filicide was explained partly by her circumstances, but more significantly by her moral character, Hecuba is overwhelmingly defined, by herself and everyone else in the play, by her circumstances—as the victim par excellence who has lost her husband, most of her children, her material power and prosperity, her youth, and her freedom, and is now barely surviving 'in a temporary military camp at the edge of a non-Greek continent'.[1] In the prologos, the ghost of Polydorus informs us that his mother will in the course of the play see the corpses of her two children, his own and that of Polyxena (45–6), and that his own desire is for burial (49–50). The point of the information is to prepare the audience for what Hecuba will have to face; there is no demand for revenge, and that leaves her free to respond entirely independently. The ghost's monologue ends with the first of a number of references in the play to Hecuba's extreme peripeteia (55–8)— apparently an unspecified divinity's act of compensation for her prosperity.

Hecuba now enters, a decrepit old slave, supported by a stick, and tormented by fears for her remaining children and in particular anxious about the report that Achilles' ghost has demanded a human sacrifice. The chorus soon confirm this report, adding that specifically Polyxena is required (98 ff.) and they urge Hecuba to supplicate (144). The former queen herself laments her old age and her enslaved, husbandless, stateless, almost childless condition (168). Thus she is defined by her many social and personal disabilities contrasted with her former material prosperity.

So far then no moral dimension to Hecuba's character has emerged. She is the pure and extreme victim who has said nothing about a need for stoical acceptance or any attitude required by *eugeneia*. (In this she obviously contrasts with the Sophoclean hero, with Medea, and, it will emerge, with her own daughter, Polyxena.) Nor has any other character so much as intimated that Hecuba's circumstances should elicit any other response than self-pitying lamentation, and even Polyxena is more distressed on her mother's behalf than on her own (197–215).

---

[1] Burnett (1998) 157.

HECUBA AND ODYSSEUS

When Odysseus enters to announce the official resolve to sacrifice Polyxena, he stresses Hecuba's helplessness and her need to submit (225 ff.). But Hecuba at this point abandons passivity in favour of a spirited attempt to dissuade Odysseus from the sacrifice.[2] Here it is important to be clear that the pressure that Achilles' ghost is exerting on his former companions is purely moral; he is not physically preventing them from sailing off. Thus the case for the sacrifice must be based entirely on what is owed to him and to dead patriots in general. The situation is therefore essentially different from that confronted, for example, by Agamemnon in Sophocles' *Electra* where the constraint was such that the Greeks were physically unable to leave Aulis without sacrificing Iphigenia.

Hecuba's attitude is bleakly pragmatic; she anticipates a difficult *agōn* (230), realizing that her status is now that of a slave to whom Odysseus may not be disposed to listen (234–7). She presents herself as a suppliant and argues that Odysseus owes this slave a *charis* or debt of gratitude (implied by ἀχάριστον, 254) in return for saving his life in Troy (implying too that they are now in consequence *philoi* (φίλους, 256)) when he was effectively her slave (249), and that this *charis* should take the form of saving not her life but that of Polyxena.[3] She argues too, in a way characteristic of Euripidean debates wherein the verbal adversaries throw in any and every argument, that human sacrifice is wrong *and* that Helen would have been a more appropriate victim. Furthermore, since *nomos* restrained the Greeks from killing their captives before, the same *nomos* should apply now in Polyxena's case (289). Hecuba adds a personal plea for pity on the basis that Polyxena is the only support remaining to her (279–81), and begs Odysseus to have compassionate respect (*aidōs*) for her in her sufferings (286).

These appeals all exert moral pressure, either in terms of the obligations which flow from the relationships which Hecuba hopes to persuade Odysseus exist between them (relationships associated with *charis, philia,* and *hiketeia*) or through the arguments that support them, but Hecuba's motivation in defending the life of her child is, understandably and realistically, more instinctive than moral,[4] though she certainly occupies the moral high ground over Odysseus.[5] She is similarly motivated in her later retaliation against Polymestor. But with Odysseus no plan takes shape in her mind. She just acts desperately and

---

[2] For a detailed analysis of the arguments on both sides see Michelini (1987) 145–7; Collard (1991) ad 251–95, 299–331.

[3] On the various competing moral claims arising from *charis* see Gregory (1999) ad 136–7.

[4] 'From the outset her children's welfare is her dominant concern, and she takes a vigorous stand against each instance of violence directed against her family': ibid. p. xxxii.

[5] Kovacs (1987) 88 refers to Odysseus' 'cool, amoral "realism", the refusal to apply moral categories that distinguishes the Greek polity throughout the play'. Corey and Eubanks (2003) 225–8, on the other hand, argue (wrongly, I think) that both Odysseus' and Hecuba's positions are theoretical, the former concerned only with the interests of the state, the latter only with a private morality that functions between individuals. Odysseus, as I see it, is probably to be conceived as a mixture of the unscrupulous demagogue intent on augmenting his own power and the agent of the state, while Hecuba is absorbed with saving her daughter's life, not because she discounts the state's interests in theory, but because such interests are irrelevant to her in her present predicament. The arguments themselves are merely instrumental.

straightforwardly in the only way she can to try to save her daughter. She is quite understandably doing what Odysseus cynically admits to having done in Troy: using all kinds of arguments to save a life (250).

G. R. Stanton sees Odysseus as 'torn between his longstanding *philia* relationship with Hekabe and Akhilleus' *philia* relationship with the Greeks as a whole'.[6] Now Odysseus certainly states that it would be 'shameful' (αἰσχρόν, 311) for the Greeks who regarded Achilles as a *philos* (311) when he was alive to ignore this bond now that he is dead, but this specific case relates less to *philia* ultimately than to Odysseus' general argument that the polis should confer post-mortal recognition on those who have served it well and who are worthy of honour, if only for the prudential reason that it will encourage others to similar service (306–20). Stanton, somewhat inconsistently, goes straight on to say that Odysseus 'chooses to put his own popularity before the *philia* relationship with Hekabe'.[7] This is also Hecuba's view (254–7), but, if it is true, then Odysseus is not really torn between conflicting *philia* claims. In fact, he is not 'torn' at all. In principle, Odysseus is confronted with two potentially competing sets of moral obligations—those arising from the web of relationships between him and Hecuba and those asso-. ciated with his role as a highly influential commander within the Greek army. But in fact he identifies without qualm with his military and political role—that is, if we accept that he acts in harmony with what he genuinely considers to be the interests of the army and the state. But if Hecuba is right, he is no more than a demagogue whose motivation is immoral and self-interested.

Whether Odysseus is motivated out of genuine concern for the army and the state or out of a desire for personal influence (or indeed both) is, strictly speaking, left uncertain, though the emotional engagement with the protagonist which the dramatist has produced in the spectator tilts the balance in favour of Hecuba's interpretation; and, as for the morality of Odysseus' case, in the absence of a specific divine command, human sacrifice is an atrocity which no *philia* claim or appeal to the priority of state interests could remotely justify, unless the very salvation of the state depended on it, as perhaps in the *Phoenissae*. In sum, there is no moral dilemma here.

Odysseus remains unpersuaded, so Hecuba acknowledges that she is wasting her breath and urges Polyxena to plead and supplicate (334–41)—not because she will be able to find more plausible arguments, but because she may inspire pity. Polyxena, however, prefers death to slavery, and Hecuba can only cling to her hysterically (398) until she is forced to let go, whereupon she succumbs to a misery wherein she regards herself as all but dead already (431). She has to be supported so as not to faint (438), so when Talthybius arrives to report on the sacrifice he finds her collapsed on the ground and reluctant to move: surely there is no Zeus that looks down on suffering mortals and all is Tyche (495, cf. 581–2).

Euripides thus plunges Hecuba into ever deeper loss and despair. The only relief has been Polyxena's stoical nobility in opting for a heroic death, thus moving her mother to reflect on (moral) nobility (γενναῖος, 592).[8] While in agriculture all depends on fortune inasmuch as bad soil will yield a good crop in a good season

---

[6] Stanton (1995) 33.   [7] Ibid.

[8] On Polyxena's moral position see Lawrence (2010) *passim*.

and good soil a bad crop in a bad season, when it comes to human beings character is unaffected by circumstances or misfortune (though it may be established in the first place by heredity or upbringing) (592–602). Thus Polyxena's essential nobility remained uncorrupted by her terrible peripeteia, and, although a slave in name, she continued to conduct herself with the nobility of a free princess. Some readers who condemn Hecuba's subsequent revenge on Polymestor have found an unconscious irony here, and the moral corruption which they attribute to her would seem to show that either her theory is wrong or she has in spite of appearances always been corrupt.[9]

The play in the meantime returns to the theme of the extremity of Hecuba's sufferings (619 ff., 658–70), in preparation for the revelation of the corpse of Polydorus (674). When this revelation occurs Hecuba is naturally horrified at the Thracian's wicked injustice and pitilessness (714–20), but, interestingly and perhaps significantly, there is no expression of personal hatred. The play has now taken everything from Hecuba and exposed her to repeated blows inflicted by other human beings in a seemingly godless and perhaps random universe. In *Medea* Euripides explored the reaction of a woman isolated from her own society and suddenly deprived of the emotional sustenance of her marriage. Her reaction was extreme and explained by a combination of character and circumstances. Hecuba's deprivation, however, is much more radical, and it could be that Euripides had decided to explore, as it were, a different mix of character and circumstances, a mix in which circumstances strongly predominate, in order to observe how a morally decent, though unheroically conceived (but for that reason more representative) person might react to the most extreme misery inflicted largely by the wickedness of other people. The entrenched critical view has long been that she loses her soul.

HECUBA AND AGAMEMNON

After some hesitation Hecuba decides to supplicate Agamemnon. Does she want to be free? No, she would happily be a slave forever if only she could punish 'evil people' (τοὺς κακούς) (753–7). Material freedom for Hecuba is now a concept drained of all meaning. We are to understand that nothing remains to her (784, 803–11). We may recall other tragic protagonists (Eteocles, for example, or, in a different way, Philoctetes) to whom nothing (or almost nothing) remained save their own sense of moral identity and their need to be true to it. But Hecuba does not reflect on what is owed to her or what she owes herself as a *eugenēs*, nor does she waste time lamenting the murder or pouring out her hatred for the perpetrator; instead she becomes the very spirit of retribution.

In appealing to Agamemnon, she pleads the justice of her cause: Polymestor disregarded all the gods to commit a most unholy act (ἔργον ἀνοσιώτατον, 792); he killed a *xenos*, acting with premeditation, and denied his victim burial (787–97); and Agamemnon, though morally non-committal in this passage, nevertheless

---

[9] For the contrary view see Mossman (1995) 120–2.

clearly sympathizes with Hecuba (783, 785). In a community of Greek enemies that is less than the polis and in a bleak universe that seems bereft of deities, Hecuba asserts that the gods are powerful, as is Nomos (law) which both has power over those same gods (799–800) and is the basis for distinguishing right from wrong (798–801). And yet equity (ἴσον, 805) among human beings depends on the willingness of those human beings to punish *xenos*-killers, temple-violators and the like (802–5).[10] Now the moral world of this play, such as it is, has already been conceived largely in terms of the requirements of various *nomoi*, as we saw in the Odysseus scene. But that same scene undermined our confidence that human beings would respect such *nomoi*.

From her appeal to Agamemnon it would seem that Hecuba believes that the gods cannot or will not (or at least cannot be relied upon to) vindicate Nomos among humans. Agamemnon, for whatever reasons, seems genuinely benevolent towards Hecuba. He claims at least to be moved on all the grounds upon which she appealed: pity for Polydorus and for herself, her status as a suppliant, a concern for the gods and for justice (850–3). All this sounds morally admirable, but it means nothing because, for fear of alienating the army, Agamemnon has no intention of acting (854–63). The Greek commander-in-chief, unlike Odysseus, *is* torn—not, however, between conflicting *moral* obligations to Hecuba and to the army, but between two feelings: his inclination to help Hecuba (which may admittedly be based in part on sincere moral outrage, though in part also on his lust for Cassandra) and his fear of alienating the mob.[11] Again, as in the Odysseus episode, there is no moral conflict, for there is no serious suggestion that Agamemnon should be debating competing obligations (that is, between those to Hecuba and justice and those to a barbarous ally of the Greeks). Rather our support is firmly enlisted for Hecuba against Polymestor and we are made to feel that the justice she craves takes obvious precedence over any other claims. Moreover, it is never suggested that the army either has or should have a moral commitment to its supposed *philia* for the Thracian; the issue is rather Agamemnon's fear that the rabble will think that his disregard of that *philia* indicates an inappropriate commitment to his concubine over the collective interest.[12]

---

[10] On the meaning of Nomos here (law? tradition?) see Collard (1991) ad 798–801. Kovacs (1987) 101 rightly insists that Hecuba's words are 'not a surrendering of the objective validity of the gods or of right and wrong'. Nussbaum (1986) 400, on the other hand, translates *nomos* as 'convention'. 'Deep human agreements (or practices) concerning value are the ultimate authority for moral norms. If 'convention' is wiped out, there is no higher tribunal to which we can appeal. Even the gods exist only within this human world' (ibid.) 'But Hecuba's human *nomos* can, she concedes, itself suffer "destruction" or "corruption". If one party acts against the common understanding, the agreement that made the convention firm is itself weakened; no rock-hard underlying nature shores it up' (ibid. 403–4). In any case, the enforcement of *nomoi*, according to Hecuba, depends on human beings, and that is critical.

[11] For McHardy (2008) 41, 'Euripides here plays on the association between the "masculine" desire to look out for the common good and reject private revenge as opposed to the "feminine" desire to pursue private interests and seek revenge,' but Agamemnon is the leader whose commitment to the cause of the democratic army is the weakest. He is thus the most likely to be swayed by personal considerations: Kovacs (1987) 102. For Agamemnon's relations with Cassandra see Gibert (1995) 69–70.

[12] On the army's ruthless self-interest as a democratic assembly over which their leaders can prevail only by persuasion see Kovacs (1987) 86.

Hecuba then is obliged to resort to what she sees as a morally less relevant but perhaps more persuasive argument that appeals to the Greek leader's sexual relationship with her daughter Cassandra (824–35). Those who condemn her revenge think the alleged moral decline begins here. Unable to persuade by a legitimate appeal to justice, she descends to a particularly shabby appeal to *charis*.[13] But what choice does she have?

Hecuba now realizes in her enslaved condition that no one is truly free, but all are slaves to money, fortune ($\tau \acute{v}\chi\eta$), the rabble, or the laws (864–7), so that any moral agent or agent of justice in particular will inevitably be corrupt—a deeply depressing insight. Still, we must use whatever agents of justice are available and motivate them as best we can, and it is important here to remember that the political background of these events is a military camp in which Agamemnon is only nominally in control and in which decisions are taken in deference to the military mob rather than with a view to abstract justice. Thus the most Hecuba can hope for from Agamemnon is that he will turn a blind eye if she undertakes the retribution herself (868–75).

HECUBA'S ALLEGED MORAL CORRUPTION

It is pleasing to see how the longstanding idea of Hecuba's dehumanization is now going out of fashion, especially since the pioneering work of Meridor and, more recently, Mossman's sensitive book-length study of the play.[14] Modern sensibilities have, understandably, found the blinding of Polymestor and the slaughter of his children barbarous and inhuman. This retribution has been understood, not in terms of broader cultural values, but as a reflection of the individual psychology of Hecuba herself. Edith Hall, for example, in a recent book claims that the play concentrates on 'the psychological *process* by which a victim turns into an avenger'.[15] Accordingly, the task has been to explain Hecuba's supposed moral corruption. This was originally discovered some sixty years ago in an alleged reaction to the self-seeking cynicism of Odysseus and the moral weakness of Agamemnon. Thus, according to Kirkwood, when Hecuba appeals to Nomos, 'the king of men has no interest in maintaining a principle, and Hecuba, already shaken and confused by the Nomos of Odysseus, now follows the example of Agamemnon and abandons Nomos'.[16] (But 'shaken and confused' is an idea without textual warrant.) The 'failure of Agamemnon to act according to principle provides the impulse needed for Hecuba's complete moral ruin'.[17] And so, 'robbed of her reliance on Nomos and of her belief in it, she yields to a

---

[13] 'Hecuba's plea to Odysseus, like her plea to Agamemnon, progresses from the appeal to *dikē* to the appeal to *charis*... and the main difference is that Odysseus rejects both pleas while Agamemnon is affected by the appeal to *charis*': Lloyd (1992) 96. Hecuba's use of Cassandra is not moral degradation but for the Greeks an appropriate *ad hominem* argument: Mossman (1995) 112–13. Scodel (1998) 137–44 has an interesting discussion of this strange, though hardly immoral, appeal to *charis*.

[14] See also Kovacs (1987) 99, 108–9.

[15] Hall (2010) 256: her emphasis.

[16] Kirkwood (1947) 67.   [17] Ibid.

frenzy of revenge and commits the most revolting atrocities without a trace of moral compunction.'[18]

If this were really so, we could ask if Hecuba was unaware of her demoralization or cynically accepted it. It is not, however, *pace* Kirkwood, Hecuba's belief in Nomos that is destroyed, but her confidence that Agamemnon (or perhaps anyone else) will vindicate it. (One can become quite cynical about actual human behaviour and yet remain a moral idealist.) Certainly, Hecuba remarks on the futility of her own moral arguments and deliberately opts for a more directly persuasive approach (814–20). But there is no need to infer *her* moral corruption from this. On the contrary, there is no evidence that she changes more than her tactics. Her new understanding relates not to her own moral character but to Agamemnon's and to the moral environment in which she finds herself.

There are no countervailing pressures on Hecuba as a moral agent, no conflict between justice and self-interest which in her case, through the erosion of the normal conditions that make life meaningful, totally coincide. Retribution for her son—all that she wants now—is precisely what the situation demands. Nor is this justice to be dismissed as no more than a spurious rationalization of that desire. Like Sophocles' Electra, her whole being—moral, emotional, and intellectual—is focused exclusively on retributive justice. And like Electra's, her justice is pervaded through and through by personal interest. This element of personal involvement cuts both ways. While it threatens the victim's moral objectivity, only the victim can fully experience the enormity of the offence. And there is nothing left in Hecuba's life except this offence.

There is no need then to quarrel with the means Hecuba employs to win Agamemnon's cooperation or with the principle of her taking the law into her own hands. In a world in which what stands for political authority is hopelessly corrupt—a world that the gods would seem to have abandoned—Hecuba must organize her own justice.[19] Thus those critics who condemn her are justified in recognizing that for Hecuba nothing else matters apart from her retribution but err in dismissing this as no more than a barbarous revenge.[20] Mossman, on the other hand, states that 'Hecuba is right to take revenge on Polymestor to the extent that he is the guilty party, and that his crime was inflicted on an innocent and inoffensive victim',[21] and Gregory argues, that the vengeance 'was legally enjoined

---

[18] Ibid. 68. Similarly Luschnig (1976) 227 argues that the corruption which Hecuba witnesses around her infects her own morality. Her suffering and reaction to it 'are understandable within the context of the moral chaos of the world to which she must respond'. She is 'presented in a spiritual state of passivity, open, therefore, to corruption' (ibid. 228). 'It is finally the realization that her words are futile that is the beginning of the change in Hecabe. . . . Hecabe has been taught by Odysseus that generosity and gratitude mean nothing in the face of ambition. From Agamemnon she now learns that freedom and justice are meaningless words' (ibid. 231).

[19] Corey and Eubanks (2003) 243, however, argue that the gods are real for the play and are concerned with justice, as Hecuba asserts, even if they do not always intervene to punish or prevent evil. The argument relies on 898–904 and 1289 (because 'the god' does not grant favourable sailing conditions Agamemnon can grant Hecuba the favour she asks, while after her retribution the wind suddenly rises). See also Kovacs (1987) 105, 110–11. Whether or not the change in the weather is to be explained in such terms, the gods hardly impinge on the play's causation. Justice is entirely a human business.

[20] See e.g. Daitz (1971) 222 and Reckford (1985) 114.

[21] Mossman (1995) 180.

on her as Polydorus' surviving relative (749)',[22] though it would hardly be expected of a woman in Hecuba's extreme circumstances.

A much more serious issue is the nature of the retribution she goes on to mete out to Polymestor. It will be remembered that Sophocles' Electra is driven by an urge for retributive justice based on passionate anger—an extreme form perhaps of righteous indignation—combined with a socially derived sense of what is morally right. Moreover, she is able to balance appropriately her feelings with her moral assessment of the situation and her own required response to it. The act of retribution is thus measured and appropriate. The retaliation of Medea, however, we found to be corrupted by a passionate vindictiveness. What then constitutes a measured retaliation against Polymestor? The important consideration here for us in our era would be to avoid collateral damage, the deaths of innocents. To have killed Polymestor would have been entirely fitting retribution, but instead his two innocent children are killed and he is blinded and left alive, presumably on the same psychological principle that motivated Medea: inflict the maximum rather than the appropriate amount of suffering on the perpetrator. In Medea's case this is explicit, and we are privy to her thoughts and feelings throughout. But Hecuba never explains the rationale of her retribution. Nor does any character enquire into it or criticize it on moral grounds. (Jason and the chorus criticize Medea's filicide, and she herself is horrified by it.) Agamemnon states (sincerely or otherwise) that Polymestor got his just deserts (1250–1), and Polymestor himself stops short at lamenting, rather than morally criticizing, his own fate and those of his children. Mossman argues that 'the element of making the punishment fit the crime . . . is paramount; Hecuba has been deprived of her last child . . . and for the punishment to be commensurate Polymestor must be deprived of his'.[23] Certainly this fitting of the punishment to the crime is reinforced in the language of the criminal himself, for 'the few lines that the maimed man has about their [the children's] fate are strewn with words that inevitably bring Polymestor's own victim horribly to mind'.[24] But it is McHardy who puts the most comprehensive case for the moral precision of the retaliation. Hecuba's revenge

is carefully calculated to achieve equivalence. . . . Just as Hecuba has been deprived of her last son by Polymestor, and is forced to live on knowing that her husband's family has died out, so too he is now deprived of his sons and future. Hecuba's betrayal of her guest-friend Polymestor and murder of his sons while they are guests in her tent replicate Polymestor's betrayal of his guest-friend Priam and the murder of his son Polydorus. . . . her revenge is

---

[22] Gregory (1999) pp. xxii–xxiii. On the legal atmosphere of the punishment and the trial see ibid. 29–31. There is also the fact that Hecuba does not carry out the revenge herself. 'This agrees with the spirit of Attic law which specifically forbade to hand over a convicted murderer to the injured party': Meridor (1978) 30–1.

[23] Mossman (1995) 189. 'Polymestor's own villainy is made to seem responsible [for his sons' deaths]: the boys have been caught up in deserved reprisals for their father's monstrous acts; he is the real cause of their deaths': Gellie (1980) 37. Also the children pay for Polymestor: ibid. 37. Hdt 9. 116 ff. shows the cruelty that typifies the punishment of crimes of sacrilege: Burnett (1998) 169.

[24] Burnett (1998) 170. She cites 1077 vs. 716; 1079 vs. 699, 781; 1084 vs. 772. 'Such a speech inspires awe in a listener, as he wonders at the close response of punishment to crime, but it is manifestly not designed to engender pity. As for the rest of Polymestor's lines, they are filled not with grief but with rage and a hatred that becomes a longing for the taste of human flesh—emotions that are understandable, but not conducive to sympathy' (ibid). Nor are the children's corpses displayed (ibid. n. 105).

very carefully balanced against his original attack....By killing all Polymestor's sons Hecuba does more than take a life for a life. However at the same time she creates equivalence between her own position and Polymestor's position—both have now lost all their sons.[25]

According to this argument justice is served (at least in Hecuba's view) by reducing the original perpetrator to the state to which he reduced the victim. This is certainly not our modern notion of justice since we cannot regard the children as mere appendages of their father. But if Hecuba is to be thought of as having conceived her retribution in the terms McHardy suggests, and that may indeed be implicit in the outcome, then she acts with a kind of moral concern, even if it would not meet with our modern approval.[26] At any rate, it certainly seems that Euripides does not want his audience to see the children's deaths as morally objectionable, an idea strongly supported by the fact that the bodies are not displayed.[27]

Polymestor's blinding, which McHardy regards as 'symbolic castration',[28] may have been more disturbing to the audience, but here a hateful and indeed stereotypical Thracian is being paid back in his own savage coin.[29] His ravings on the stage are doubtless grotesque, but they would not evoke much sympathy. It is easy to imagine an audience (and not only an ancient one) thoroughly enjoying it all, for all the moralistic strictures of modern scholars.[30]

But what are we to make of the trial scene?[31] First of all, we need to register the change of tone from the agonized outbursts of Polymestor to the formal agon which makes it appear that both avenger and victim have settled down and are prepared to discuss the matter rationally. We should, however, reject such a reading. The agon should be seen rather as an artificial means of summarizing the cases on either side. This artificiality, however, largely creates the impression that this is a kind of formal trial, and Burnett remarks that Agamemnon's continued partial involvement makes Hecuba's act of revenge 'strangely formal and public'.[32] But the impression of formality comes from the agon form and the debate is scarcely public since it is conducted apart from the Greek army and presumably without their knowledge since Agamemnon does not want to be seen to support Hecuba against Polymestor. Here we might contrast the trial by the Argive assembly of the protagonist of the *Orestes*. Therefore it is quite wrong to

---

[25] McHardy (2008) 42.

[26] Hall (2010) 256 suggests that Hecuba is avenging both her children, even though Polymestor is not responsible for Polyxena's death. But, if so, this is not justice by any terms, ancient or modern. This interpretation depends entirely on the symmetry: two children's lives in requital for two children's lives. There is nothing explicit in the text to suggest it.

[27] Burnett (1998) 170 n. 105.

[28] McHardy (2008) 43.

[29] On blinding as a punishment see Collard (1991) ad 1035–55 and Mossman (1995) 190. On the Thracian stereotype and Polymestor in particular see Hall (1989) 102–10.

[30] See Gellie (1980) 35–6.

[31] Abrahamson (1952) 127, who considers the trial to be one of the 'weirdest' scenes in Euripides, refers to the 'pseudo-orderly procedure' of Agamemnon's arbitration. 'He had known of Hecuba's plan (though not in all its terrible details) and had given her a free hand. And now he listens, an earnest judge, solemnly to Hecuba's and Polymestor's pleas.'

[32] Burnett (1998) 164.

say that under Agamemnon 'the local community gives formal approval to what Hecuba has done', that 'her revenge is taken under the public aegis when the Greeks add exile to the vengeful retaliation already suffered (1284–85)', and that, '[i]nspired by the old woman's act of violence, the Hellenes thus reestablish a rudimentary criminal process.'[33]

Nothing new emerges from this agon. As we have seen, Agamemnon accepts Polymestor's manifest guilt and his punishment without commenting on the particular form of punishment. When Agamemnon adopted his compromise of effectively condoning whatever retribution against Polymestor Hecuba might choose to organize, he made himself ultimately responsible for an act over which he had no control, an act which he knew was to be performed by women who might appear powerless but who were also a terrifyingly unknown quantity, as the socially disabled can be when they feel driven in their desperation to take extra-legal action—as Hecuba's disquieting parallel of the Lemnian massacre emphasizes (876–88; cf. Aesch. *Cho.* 631–4). Agamemnon left with the hope that all would turn out fine (cf. Aesch. *Ag.* 217) and with a platitude about justice (902–4), though he appeared to see his own involvement in the matter as a *charis* for Hecuba rather than as the vindication of justice (899).

The 'bitchification' of Hecuba has occasioned much scholarly debate. It should be seen in the context of the Euripidean epilogue in which the story rejoins the myth tradition, often without thematic continuity;[34] and, even if one concedes such continuity in this case, it is by no means certain that the bitch is an entirely negative image.[35] Indeed, Gregory associates it with 'maternal protectiveness. . . . Hecuba as avenger is singleminded, implacable, unrepentant. Indeed, her meta-morphosis underscores not only her maternity but also an association with the Erinyes, those doglike creatures whose province is blood-vengeance.'[36]

Hecuba does all she can amid the virtual moral vacuum of the 'society' in which she finds herself, and does so in response to a basic human instinct which is positive in being more than a self-interested and primitive desire to strike back or 'even the score', though that is undeniably part of it. (Of course the more respectable notion of retributive justice incorporates, though it moderates, such 'primitive' feelings.) Although there is no dramatization of deliberation preceding Hecuba's resolve, more than blind instinct is involved because she is clearly able to appeal to a universal principle, apply rationality, and even display a certain

---

[33] Burnett (1998) 166.

[34] 'The two objects of Euripidean epilogues are achieved: Hecuba's mythical biography is com-pleted, and the central figure in the play is tied to a place and a place-name known to Athenians': Gellie (1980) 40. 'The fact that the *agon*, with its extreme rationalism, intervenes between the imagery [of Polymestor's assailants as savage dogs at 1078 and 1173] and the prophecy of the metamorphosis should . . . discourage us from associating it with a dehumanization of Hecuba': Mossman (1995) 197.

[35] On the ambivalence of the dog image see Mossman (1995) 200–1. For Hecuba's transformation and her bestiality see Reckford (1985) 118 and 123; Vickers (1973) 83; Nussbaum (1986) 416; Kirk-wood (1947) 61; Buxton (1982) 183. The *pursa dergmata* (1265) 'are not just eyes inflamed with rage' but indicate 'a signal or a beacon fire. . . . The metaphoric emblem that closes the play is thus not Hecuba as an enraged beast, but Hecuba as a flagrant landmark that saves ships and their crews': Burnett (1998) 175.

[36] Gregory (1999) p. xxv.

precision in the punishment. In these respects she resembles Sophocles' Electra and, like her, she exults in the successful retribution.

In contrast to Aeschylean characters and like Sophocles' Electra or Euripides' Medea, Hecuba faces no moral dilemma or challenge—at least in terms of the expectations of the gods or society. It is rather she who decides to fight back in her extreme weakness. The moral right for which she fights is indeed one readily recognized by Greek society (she argues in terms of violation of *xenia*, *philia*, and failure to reciprocate favours). But the significant difference is that no such society exists in polis form and such gods as Zeus Xenios who are supposed to support and vindicate these moral rules are absent from the play. But not only is there a divine and political vacuum; Hecuba experiences the extreme personal vacuum of deprivation of city and any *philos* who can support her. She has, moreover, absolutely nothing to live for save her delegated acts of retribution in which she must believe even in the absence of the social context in which the morality that enjoined them originated. Polyxena's moral predicament is not dissimilar, in that she continues to adhere to a morality when the context for it has disappeared. Although a slave, she continues to enact the moral role of a free aristocrat, and, like her mother, she has no future.[37]

Freedom (and slavery) is clearly a major theme of the play. Agamemnon is in institutional terms the character that enjoys the greatest freedom as the head of an army and of a state. But although he is the commander-in-chief of the Greek army and therefore absolute ruler, as it were, of the militarized 'society' of the play, morally he is the slave of the military mob. This position is perhaps in part the product of the corruption of the institution itself by such demagogic figures as Odysseus who can and do manipulate the troops in their own interest, and it is an ineffectual army indeed that is organized on such a basis. But Agamemnon himself must take some of the blame, since he clearly goes in fear of the mob, without the backbone to assert his moral autonomy and take control, and Hecuba despises him for it while, as we saw, she effectively disempowers all moral agents by her claim that everyone is a slave to something. Hecuba, in contrast to the king of Mycenae, has no institutional power, but is prepared to demand that moral right prevail and then to act herself to vindicate it when her appeal falls on reluctant ears. But if everyone is a slave, how can Hecuba, who is a slave in the most literal sense, be an effective moral agent? The answer is a nice paradox: those who are literal slaves with no future, like Hecuba and Polyxena, are hugely deprived of physical freedom and material perquisites, but they can still exert enough physical freedom (as do both mother and daughter) to vindicate their moral convictions. Precisely because they are slaves, they have nothing to lose and therefore no vulgar self-interest to corrupt their morality.

CONCLUSION

We have seen that Hecuba is defined by circumstances rather than by moral character. She is also defined by her last remaining role—that of mother, and a

---

[37] Polyxena's idea of the aristocratic life is, however, as much materialistic as moral (see especially 349–66) and Lawrence (2010) 23.

mother's moral obligation is to protect her living children and to avenge them if they are murdered. Thus when she can do no more to guarantee their safety, Hecuba turns to vengeance. The moral implications of the crisis she faces are clear inasmuch as vengeance is ideally required, but the circumstances in which she must act are peculiar: there is no civic justice to which she can effectively apply (since Agamemnon refuses to act on her behalf), nor can she rely on the gods. It is most important to see, though, that she exhausts all civilized avenues of retribution before she takes the law into her own hands. She appeals to Nomos and pleads for its vindication, but then finds herself left to act as best she can. When she does act it is through the other Trojan women who perhaps represent what is left of her society, and after she has acted thus vicariously she owns and defends the punishment in an agon, the most rational medium available in a Greek tragedy. It is then quite wrong to say that Hecuba 'comes to behave like a beast herself when her emotions get out of control'.[38] On the contrary, Hecuba's grief and moral outrage are appropriately integrated to form the motivation for her retribution, as are the same feelings in Sophocles' Electra.

Hecuba acts in harmony with her retributive morality. But does she act in harmony with the implicit morality of the play? We have seen that no other character objects to her treatment of Polymestor (and it would have been easy to make a horrified Agamemnon turn against her), nor indeed to her treatment of the children. Therefore, as nasty as the retribution is, it is much more acceptable to conventional Greek sensibilities than to ours.[39] Even so, acts of revenge in Euripides tend to be morally unsettling, and even an ancient audience is surely meant to find this one so, for all their probable enjoyment of Polymestor's pantomimic ravings. The play does not therefore offer comfortable moral closure. But acts of revenge may be morally disturbing because of the character of the avenger (as in the case of Medea) or because of the nature of the situation, in this case the absence of civic justice or indeed any credible civic infrastructure. Hecuba does what has to be done since no one else will act for her, and she acts out of moral outrage and a sense of utter loss, performing the final significant act in a life that would be thenceforth meaningless.

[38] Hall (2010) 257.
[39] She is hardly 'transformed into as culpable a victim as any of them': ibid. 256.

13

Euripides: *Hippolytus*

HIPPOLYTUS' CHASTITY

We are introduced to Hippolytus paying his devotions to Artemis.[1] He has brought her a garland from

a virgin meadow where no shepherd thinks it right to graze his flock, where no scythe has ever come, but in the spring the bee flies through its virgin greenery. Reverence (*aidōs*) tends it with water from the rivers, so that those for whom *sōphrosunē* in all things has not had its everlasting place assigned by teaching but by nature can pick the flowers there—but it is not proper for base men (τοῖς κακοῖσι) to do so.   (73–81: tr. Morwood)

It is clear from Aphrodite's prologue speech that Hippolytus objects to her on moral grounds. However, his moral attitude is a strange one in the ancient world,[2] and his understanding of *aidōs* and *sōphrosunē* is restricted and distorted.[3] Religious purity is a matter of ritual rather than of morality, and to that extent Hippolytus' notion here of a pure space is reminiscent of a space reserved for a deity, one that should be kept free of mortal contamination (i.e. physical violation). Sexual abstinence is valued only in specific situations; for example, before puberty, to avoid adultery, or when acting as a priestess or other religious intermediary. Therefore Hippolytus' permanent commitment to total sexual abstinence appears (and this is unique among Greek tragic characters) morally idiosyncratic and even socially harmful, in so far as it is the kind of virtue that would be ruinous if everyone practised it, and Hippolytus does indeed appear to

---

[1] On the role of Aphrodite's prologue and her influence on the action see Ch. 2, 'Panoramic intervention'.

[2] For further discussion see Barrett (1964) 172–3.

[3] 'By the time of the *Hippolytus . . . sōphrosunē* had acquired a particular association with the control of *erōs*, both female and male, and consequently in that play it is the subject of almost obsessive comment (especially since good sense and refusing *erōs* might lead in different directions)': Harris (2001) 82–3. Gill (1990*b*) 80 distinguishes four senses of *sōphrosunē*: '(i) (sexual) 'chastity' or 'purity'; (ii) 'virtue' in a slightly larger sense, though one that is sometimes difficult to distinguish sharply from that of 'chastity'; (iii) 'self-control', as shown in controlling desire or anger; and (iv) 'good sense' or practical wisdom, as shown in the successful management of one's life'. On Hippolytus' ethic see also Goldhill (1986) 118–19. Sense (iii) would not appear to apply to Hippolytus who is allegedly *sōphrōn* by nature (rather than merely *enkratēs*), while (iv) is at least problematical. Gregory (1991) 62–3 reminds us that *sōphrosunē* is an aristocratic virtue. 'If Euripides has chosen to endow Hippolytus with the outlook of a young oligarch, then the young man's *hamartia* extends far beyond the rejection of sexuality' to haughtiness and exclusiveness 'in the social and political spheres' (ibid. 63).

imply that it should be a universal rule when he condemns Aphrodite as 'the vilest of deities' (13).[4] Moreover, for this young man any *sōphrosunē* worthy of the name is innate, which, as Mills comments, 'is an aristocratic doctrine which conflicts with contemporary democratic ideals, and indeed with the sophists' claims that virtue is teachable'.[5]

It will be remembered that, in his discussion of the spectator's distinctive responses to 'character' and 'personality', Gill states that the personality viewpoint tends to be 'ethically non-standard or interrogatory in its impact, questioning rather than validating existing cultural assumptions'.[6] The audience will be much exposed to Hippolytus' moral position, and it can certainly be said that, even if that position does not exactly question such cultural assumptions, it at least deviates from them both in specific detail and in intensity of commitment. Hippolytus' unconventional morality, then, one would imagine, would strain audience empathy somewhat, though it is possible to admire the sheer fact of a moral commitment without wholly approving of the morality to which the person is committed. On the other hand, Aphrodite's presumably gloating reference to Hippolytus' ignorance that this is his last day alive (56–7) must strongly enlist audience sympathy for him.

The nature of our emotional commitment to Hippolytus becomes clearer in the next scene. As he concludes his devotions to his favourite goddess, one of his servants gently remonstrates with him over his attitude to Aphrodite. He begins by asking his master if he would be willing 'to accept some good advice' (89). Hippolytus responds agreeably, obviously not too proud to learn from a servant. He agrees that we must hate an attitude that is 'haughty' (σεμνόν) and 'socially exclusive' (μὴ πᾶσιν φίλον) (93) and that 'there is a charm to be found in an easy affability' (95–6: tr. Morwood). But Hippolytus refuses to apply this principle to his relations with the goddess of sex (106, 113). The servant deplores his master's inflexibility but sets it down to 'the spirited vehemence of youth' (ὑφ᾽ ἥβης σπλάγχνον ἔντονον φέρων, 118: tr. Morwood), a view that the spectator is thereby encouraged to accept.[7] Allowances will need to be made. The understanding the youth requires will come naturally with maturity. So the servant asks the goddess to understand and forgive, since 'the gods should be wiser than mortals' (120).

But are we not only to share the servant's compassionate understanding but also to agree with him that Hippolytus' moral position is *completely* misguided? This is unlikely in view of the beauty (often remarked upon) of his devotional address to the invisible goddess (73–87) which we have just heard—a speech surely designed to make us see at least that there is a certain nobility in a position

---

[4] On the importance to the Greeks of preserving the family see Mills (2002) 64. Contrast Dimock (1977) 246: 'Hippolytus' way of life, chastity and all ... the best that man can aspire to in this play's terms.' According to Kovacs (1987) 27, the chastity would not have aroused hostility since it was non-threatening.

[5] Mills (2002) 67.

[6] See Ch.1, 'Characterization and conceptions of the self'.

[7] Hippolytus' misogyny is understandable as 'the drastic morality of the young', as the servant says at 117–20: Dimock (1977) 245. Kovacs (1987) 36, however, supports the value of Hippolytus' ideal: 'It may be proper for the servant to worship Aphrodite, but for Hippolytus it would be the betrayal of everything that gives his life meaning.'

which, more broadly viewed, must still seem misguided.[8] Here we have a fine example of the kind of emotional contradictions that can be produced in an audience by tension between sympathy and judgement. It remains true, however, that Hippolytus' moral position is both invalid as a universal principle and extraordinary in itself. Whereas the moral attitudes of other tragic characters reflect a shared aristocratic ethic supported by an idea of their own intrinsic nobility (*eugeneia*), the ethic of the illegitimate Hippolytus seems to be merely the rationalization of an unusually prudish, austere, and immature temperament.

PHAEDRA'S 'DISEASE'

With the parodos the focus shifts to Phaedra's passion or 'disease' (νόσος), and our sympathies are to be temporarily redirected. The passion has become a disease partly because Phaedra is now into the third day of a policy of deliberate self-starvation which seems to have brought her to a state of delirium.[9] The audience knows the divine source of the passion,[10] and the idea of a divine rather than a natural origin is sustained by the speculations of the chorus (141–4). Phaedra herself is now carried in on a bed, accompanied by her nurse. Euripides presents a realistic impression of the restless irritability of a sick person (188–202).[11] The idea of delirium is reinforced as Phaedra gives expression to a strange desire to be out in the natural world (208–11). The nurse finds this desire embarrassing, presumably because respectable Greek women declared no wish to escape from their cloistered existences, but the audience knows that Phaedra's real wish is to be with Hippolytus in his haunts, and she becomes even more explicit (215–22).[12] This is the beginning of Phaedra's involuntary revelation of her passion.

The nurse can make no sense of her ravings, though she, like the chorus and indeed Phaedra herself, attributes her mistress's condition to the visitation of a deity—naturally enough, given the extraordinary intensity of Phaedra's feelings. Phaedra alternates between madness and sanity, and when sane she feels ashamed of her mad utterances (239–46). Aphrodite told us that Phaedra was concealing the passion from the household (40) and that she would die with her reputation

---

[8] On the contrasting beauty and inadequacy of Hippolytus' morality see Barrett (1964) 172–3. 'It is not possible to stand aside and judge Hippolytos' behavior as folly, once we have been pulled into his world and have seen in it the moral and aesthetic beauty that he sees': Michelini (1987) 291. Gill's 'personality viewpoint' is relevant here.

[9] As McDermott (2000) 247 argues, Phaedra's physical disease is a product of her moral resistance and helps to distinguish her from the traditional 'bad' Phaedra.

[10] 'In Phaedra's sudden delirium we are meant to see the direct action of Aphrodite, the fulfilment of her promise . . . to bring Phaedra's secret to light': Kovacs (1987) 41.

[11] Cf. Eur. *Or.* 219–36.

[12] Dimock (1977) 245 thinks that Phaedra admires the beauty and desirability of Hippolytus' ideal though she cannot herself attain it. Ironically, she loves his chastity. 'Phaedra . . . sees herself as an aspiring, and in the end a failed, version of Hippolytus, as regards their shared objective of being—and being seen to be—*sōphrōn*; and this fact seems to underlie her eventual hatred of him and also, perhaps, her passionate desire for him': Gill (1990*b*) 87.

intact (47). It is now confirmed that her motive for silence is indeed what we presumed; unlike her wanton counterpart of the tradition, she is ashamed of her passion.

The nurse now begins her assault on her mistress's determination to remain silent. She tries to reason with her. Since she is sick, surely she needs to say what is wrong so that she can be helped. And if she is not prepared to say what is ailing her, at least she should answer the nurse's questions (293–9). But Phaedra knows that her best defence is to give nothing away. Like Teiresias in the *Tyrannus*, she is convinced that the knowledge which she alone possesses can cause only harm (327).[13] So the first clue emerges accidentally, it would seem, when Phaedra reacts with strong emotion to the nurse's mention of Hippolytus' name in the course of an argument that Phaedra cannot afford to die because her children will then be disinherited by her husband's bastard (304–12).

The tenacious nurse at once latches onto the hint supplied by this reaction to the naming of Hippolytus, and Phaedra unwisely—and doubtless under the pressure of that part of her mind that wants to yield—abandons her policy of total silence to rule out all the nurse's suggestions as to the possible origin of the 'disease' (313–21). When she stops short of revealing the truth, the nurse approaches her as a suppliant (325–6). Phaedra insists that the knowledge will be 'calamitous' (κακά, 327).

> PHAEDRA. You will be ruined. But as things stand I win honour (τιμήν) by what I do.
> NURSE. Why hide it then, when what I beg is for your good?
> PHAEDRA. I must. I am contriving to win glory (literally, 'good things': ἐσθλά) from my shame (ἐκ τῶν ... αἰσχρῶν).
> NURSE. Surely you will appear the more honourable by speaking of it? (329–32: tr. Morwood)

As Knox explains, Phaedra's code of honour requires that virtuous acts be published to the world. It is not good enough simply to know in one's own heart that one is doing the right thing.[14] In Phaedra's case the best course would be for her to keep her original honour by being thought of as a woman free of illicit passions, but if after all she cannot suppress the truth, she can recover some honour by being seen to fight her passion.[15] That is, provided that people, and especially men, are prepared to think compassionately and rationally about any woman who is subject to such a passion. As Phaedra herself will presently declare:

'I knew that the act and the sickness brought disgrace (δυσκλεᾶ) with them and besides I was well aware that I am a woman—an object of loathing to all men (μίσημα πᾶσιν)' (405–7: tr. Morwood).[16]

---

[13] Soph. *OT* 316–17.

[14] Knox (1979*b*) 210; Winnington-Ingram (1960) 179: 'Phaedra is exposed to a dilemma inherent in her ideal: if honour is everything, what is the point of virtuous action, if it is known to none . . . ?'

[15] Since Phaedra has an emotional need to unburden herself, it is possible to see this whole process of revelation as a 'sophistry of the heart for avoiding responsibility': J. Griffin (1990) 135.

[16] Reckford (1974) 316 speculates that the male prejudice 'that women are morally inferior creatures . . . while apparently strengthening Phaedra's resolve to maintain her good reputation, may at the same time have weakened her moral self-confidence, making her more vulnerable to the assaults of the Nurse and, through her, of Aphrodite.'

Now Euripides' picture of Phaedra has to establish itself in the face of a negative and condemnatory tradition. Aphrodite's prologue has already alerted us to the prospect of a noble Phaedra, and now we watch her nobly resisting her passion, or rather the desire for revelation and consummation that is the expression of her passion. The above reference then to the prevailing misogyny is the dramatist's calculated appeal to his audience to broaden their sympathies and open their hearts to this woman now on the verge of revealing the course of her inner moral struggle.[17] There is conflict here again between moral judgement and empathy. Public morality unreasonably disapproves of the sheer existence of such an involuntary passion (as mental illness was severely stigmatized in modern Western societies until recently), and Phaedra herself regards it as a kind of moral pollution (μίασμά τι, 317);[18] but if moral struggle is to be honoured it must be published to the world. Phaedra herself, in her inability to eradicate the passion completely, would presumably prefer to subscribe to a morality which accepted its involuntary nature, so that she could publish it freely and win honour for resisting it, and it is this morality which the audience is invited to adopt.

The supplication works (perhaps as the straw that breaks the camel's back of Phaedra's resolve) and she proceeds to explain. She begins with her mother Pasiphae and her sister Ariadne, both victims of tragic passions: 'It was from their loves (ἐκεῖθεν), not of recent date, that my troubles began' (343: tr. Morwood). Barrett (1964 ad 342–4) interprets Phaedra to mean 'my trouble is one that the women of my family have in their blood' and comments that Euripides 'may, or may not, have known a story told later by Sosikrates (*F. Gr. Hist.* 461 F. 6 ap. Schol. E. *Hipp.* 47), and accepted by Seneca (*Ph.* 124 ff.), that Aphrodite revenged herself on all the Sun's female descendants . . . for his betrayal of her adultery with Ares'. However, such a motive is absent from the prologue where Aphrodite insists that Phaedra is merely her innocent instrument of Hippolytus' destruction. Perhaps we are to think that Phaedra is hereditarily susceptible to tragic passions and that the goddess is working (as deities frequently do) through such a susceptibility.[19]

There is nothing novel, sophistic, or damaging to traditional Greek religion in invoking heredity as a cause. The whole basis of the traditional aristocratic ethos is that qualities, especially positive moral qualities, are inherited, potentially or actually. Homer's Telemachus, who is on occasion directly inspired by a deity, is clearly conceived as having inherited aspects of his father's character and even physical appearance, and the concept of inherited character (*ēthos*) appears in the lion cub parable of Aeschylus' *Agamemnon* where it is hard to separate it from the related idea of an inherited curse with its divine associations.[20] The dramatic point of Phaedra's reference to the females of her family is the ironical discrepancy which we have seen before between the characters' speculations and what we, the audience, know from the prologue.

---

[17] Michelini (1987) 288 remarks that Phaedra's role 'as representative of social values is calculated to inspire sympathy and even respect, in spite of the improper nature of her dilemma'.

[18] See C. Segal (1970) 281.

[19] The references to her mother and sister imply not inherited guilt but 'inherited sexuality': Winnington-Ingram (1960) 175. See also Reckford (1974) 315.

[20] See Ch. 4, 'The wider context of the decision at Aulis'.

As we have seen, before Phaedra's disclosures none of the characters knows what deity is responsible for her condition, though it is assumed that *some* deity must be responsible. After that, Aphrodite is inferred as the cause, but her motivation remains obscure to the characters. Indeed before Artemis informs him to the contrary, Hippolytus believes that he is being punished unfairly for an ancestral sin (1379–83). It never occurs to him to connect his fate with his haughty rejection of the goddess.

Having disclosed the nature of her illness, Phaedra shares with the chorus her speculations about the ruin of human lives (376). Her ideas arise naturally from her own recent attempts to subdue her passion, but are intended to be of general application.[21] She argues that 'sound judgement' (τὸ εὖ φρονεῖν, 378) is insufficient.

> τὰ χρήστ' ἐπιστάμεσθα καὶ γιγνώσκομεν,
> οὐκ ἐκπονοῦμεν δ', οἳ μὲν ἀργίας ὕπο,
> οἳ δ' ἡδονὴν προθέντες ἀντὶ τοῦ καλοῦ
> ἄλλην τιν'. εἰσὶ δ' ἡδοναὶ πολλαὶ βίου,
> μακραί τε λέσχαι καὶ σχολή, τερπνὸν κακόν,
> αἰδώς τε.

(We understand and recognize what is good, but we do not labour to bring it to fulfilment, some of us out of laziness, some because we put something else, some pleasure, before virtue—and there are many pleasures in life, long conversations and indolence, that pleasing vice—and a sense of shame (*aidōs*).)   (380–5: tr. Morwood)

This is a naturalistic approach to human suffering that focuses on the way in which we ourselves are responsible for our distress, locating the problem in *akrasia*. The pleasures listed here that obstruct the good are such as would tempt an idle queen, so again the male spectator is challenged to enter imaginatively a woman's world and reflect on the moral challenges it poses.[22] It would appear then that Phaedra is supplying a natural 'environmental' explanation for her passion. It was born and nurtured during the course of idle gossip and doubtless the attendant daydreaming.[23] Now while Aphrodite can still be invoked to 'overdetermine' this natural causation, her involvement makes the passion irresistible, unlike a passion that is conceived exclusively in natural terms.[24] This can only enhance our moral respect for Phaedra and of course our tragic pity for her.[25] When Phaedra speaks of attempting to 'overcome Aphrodite', she must be personifying the illness, because there could be no question of thwarting a divinity. It suits the nurse, on the other hand, to attribute her mistress's

---

[21] Kovacs (1987) 47, on the other hand, thinks Phaedra's speech about what ruins people is not looking back at the causation of her love but forward to how she is to deal with it: 'The lines are not about any past failure of Phaedra's, but look toward the future.'

[22] Conacher (1967) 36; Winnington-Ingram (1960) 176–7.

[23] Ovid's narrative of the Byblis myth at *Metamorphoses* 9. 453–665 is a wonderful (and highly amusing) *reductio ad absurdum* of the sort of psychological processes at work here.

[24] As Conacher (1967) 27 observes, 'if we ask why Phaedra has fallen helplessly and hopelessly in love with Hippolytus, we must accept the only answer which is given to us in the play: the mythical answer of the prologue, that Aphrodite has caused this as a means of vengeance on Hippolytus'. That said, Phaedra 'seems to show her own moral responsibility' in 'what she elects to do about it' (ibid. 28).

[25] Virgil's Dido is similarly smitten by a god-inspired and therefore irresistible passion.

infatuation quite literally to the goddess because she wishes to represent Phaedra's resistance as a form of hubris.

Phaedra proceeds to explain that she attempted to control her passion in three ways: first by saying nothing about it; then, when that failed, by 'bearing it easily' through 'self-control' or *sōphrosunē* (τῷ σωφρονεῖν, 399);[26] and finally, when that also failed, by suicide (401). In these attempts at control Phaedra's main concern was (and is) her reputation: 'For I would not wish any noble (καλά) actions of mine to remain unsung or any shameful deeds (αἰσχρά) to have many witnesses' (403–4: tr. Morwood). But she is also concerned, like Sophocles' Deianeira, that there be some substance to that reputation—that it be grounded in genuine virtue.[27] She hates

those women who lay claim to virtue (τὰς σώφρονας μὲν ἐν λόγοις) but in secret dare to commit shameful deeds (τόλμας οὐ καλάς). . . . It is this very thing which is driving me to death, my friends—never may I be found guilty of bringing disgrace (αἰσχύνασ') upon my husband or the children I have borne . . . one thing alone competes in life's contest, the consciousness of a just and righteous mind (γνώμην δικαίαν κἀγαθήν) within one . . .

(413–14, 419–21, 426–7: tr. Morwood)[28]

Phaedra intends to preserve both her virtue, by refusing to consummate or further indulge the passion, and her reputation, by dying without her passion coming to light. It is essential to keep the passion concealed, we remember, because dishonour will result from its sheer existence, if known (405–7).

The nurse, on the other hand, intent only on preventing Phaedra's suicide, argues that she should yield to her passion.

No one can bear the force of Cypris when she comes in spate. The one that yields to her, she pursues with gentleness, but whomsoever she finds arrogant or proud (περισσὸν καὶ φρονοῦνθ' . . . μέγα), she seizes and you cannot think how violently she treats him. Cypris roams in the air, she is in the surge of the sea, all things are born from her. It is she who sows and gives love (ἔρον) and it is through love that every one of us on earth is created.

(443–50: tr. Morwood)

She goes on to give examples of gods who were seized by illicit passion: 'But . . . lay aside this wrong-headedness (κακῶν φρενῶν), lay aside this wilfulness (ὑβρίζους)—for it is nothing other than wilfulness (hubris) to wish to be superior to the gods' (473–5: tr. Morwood). Aphrodite herself would no doubt agree. In the prologue she mentions the geographical extent of her sphere (1–4) and announces her policy of punishing those who are 'arrogant' (φρονοῦσιν . . . μέγα) towards her (6). But here we encounter again a clash of moralities. It will be remembered that there was no religious or ethical act that the Aeschylean Eteocles could have performed that would have placated Apollo or the Erinys who desired only his death. In such circumstances the only possible moral action was personally and politically motivated, as the divine will required a crime against the family.

---

[26] As Gill (1990*b*) 90 maintains, Phaedra is trying to be genuinely *sōphrōn*. She identifies herself with acting properly and externalizes the passion as alien, as Cypris.

[27] See Ch. 7, 'Deianeira'.

[28] As Kovacs (1987) 49 observes, 'these lines [413–18] make clear that Phaedra's decision is motivated not merely by the approval or disapproval of others but by her own sense of what is right'.

Similarly, there is nothing that the polluted Oedipus can do to transcend his pollution, and the Euripidean Heracles (as we shall see) can no longer pray to a goddess whose hatred of him is irrational and unconditional. In the same way, Aphrodite is resolved on the death of Phaedra whose morality is simply irrelevant to her (47–50).[29] Thus Phaedra's resistance to revealing the passion is merely an inconvenience to Aphrodite, a small obstacle to be removed on the way to punishing Hippolytus. In principle any conscious resistance to the will of a deity must be an irreligious act, but when a deity is seen to inspire antisocial behaviour there is an obvious moral dissonance. Phaedra and the chorus, in agreeing that the nurse's arguments are immoral (482–3), focus on the socially disruptive effects of adultery and choose to see sexual desire impersonally so as to sidestep the issue of hubris to a personal deity.

When it suits him Euripides can drive a wedge between the personal and the impersonal 'Aphrodite' to the point of undermining the traditional religion. In the agon of the *Troades*, for example, Hecuba rejects Helen's apologia that pleads Aphrodite's compulsion (an apologia similar to that of the nurse in this play), arguing that her mind 'became Cypris', but only, it would seem, in some undefined metaphorical sense, as Hecuba then goes on tactfully to exonerate the goddess of all involvement.[30] But if sexual passion can arise independently of the goddess, she faces the prospect of redundancy. Euripides, it must be said, does not always push matters so far, and to have rationalized the personal Aphrodite out of the *Hippolytus* would have robbed the play of much tragic power. Consequently, the ambivalence remains: Phaedra is at once the victim of a personal Aphrodite whose purpose is irresistible and of a naturalistically conceived desire.

Phaedra then is shocked by the nurse's idea that the passion should be consummated, and the nurse appears to acquiesce. Still, Phaedra is afraid that with a little more pressure she might give way (503–6). The nurse now offers a 'love charm' (φίλτρα θελκτήρια ἔρωτος),

> ἅ σ᾽ οὔτ᾽ ἐπ᾽ αἰσχροῖς οὔτ᾽ ἐπὶ βλάβῃ φρενῶν
> παύσει νόσου τῆσδ᾽, ἢν σὺ μὴ γένῃ κακή.

(which will bring your sickness to an end, cause you no shame, and give your mind no hurt, if you remain steadfast.)   (511–12: tr. Morwood)

It has been suggested that the nurse's proposal is ambiguous, and that the 'charm' may be an aphrodisiac to cure the disease by consummating the passion, but it is hard to imagine how that could be effected without shame or 'hurt' to the mind.[31] In the event, of course, there is no charm and the nurse approaches Hippolytus directly, proposing consummation. So it seems best simply to convict the nurse of lying to Phaedra who sends her off to prepare the 'charm' with a clear prohibition

---

[29] 'In fact, Phaedra is more than just an innocent victim of the goddess; she has already shown her piety by setting up a shrine in the goddess' honor (29–33). She is depicted as one who both recognizes the goddess' power and strives to adhere to her culturally prescribed role. At the same time, through the Nurse's intervention, she mimics the role played by the women in the *exempla* and meets with ruin': Halleran (1991) 116.

[30] *Tro.* 938–50, 983–90.

[31] But on the ambiguities of the passage see Barrett (1964) ad loc. The 'voicing of her suspicions by Phaedra shows that she . . . is not far from seeing through the Nurse': Michelini (1987) 290.

against informing Hippolytus (520).[32] Still, this prohibition not withstanding, there is a clear enough sense here that Phaedra's will to resist is weakening.

HIPPOLYTUS REACTS

But Hippolytus *is* informed. His indignant rejection of the nurse's overtures (which he believes originated with her mistress) is, as has often been pointed out, the response of any decent person,[33] and such a person, without Hippolytus' fanaticism or indeed his abhorrence of perjury, might well have threatened to divulge all and thus invited Phaedra's false incrimination. It is true, of course, that when in the present circumstances she does resolve on calumniating Hippolytus, she attaches a second and subsidiary motive to the primary one of preserving her reputation—the desire to punish him for his arrogant disdain. But, in view of her overwhelming commitment to her reputation, it seems unlikely that this subsidiary motive was needed.[34] Consequently, so long as the causation is viewed entirely naturalistically, the link between Hippolytus' peculiar morality and Phaedra's response is loosened somewhat.

Now, in all the previous plays we have discussed, the characters analysed have drawn on their basic moral principles when deciding how to react to a crisis. In the case of the martial heroes this has taken the form of being true to their martial *aretē* and thereby vindicating their honour. Hippolytus' morality, however, relates to his fierce honesty and fanatical chastity, neither of which is obviously under threat; in other words there *is* (or should be) no crisis at all. All he needs to do is to reject the nurse's proposition, which is, as we have seen, what any decent person in his position would do. Of course he does reject it, but it is not the rejection as such that destroys him but the extraordinary vehemence of his misogyny and Phaedra's false belief that he will perjure himself (690–2), a belief which arises, naturally enough, from his initial angry declaration that he will indeed break his oath (604, 610, 612). So Hippolytus' morality produces no positive action on his part; his reaction to the nurse is precisely that—a reaction, and an unreflecting reaction at that. But then Phaedra's response—the false incrimination—is only the first step towards the fulfilment of his doom. Theseus has to believe it, and of course he believes it immediately and seals his son's fate with a curse. Hippolytus' subsequent attempt to vindicate himself is therefore without point, though the scene with his father clearly brings to the surface an underlying hostility on Theseus' part towards his son's moral ideals, championing, as they do, a life very different from his own, so that when the slightest evidence appears that

[32] There is no evidence to convict Phaedra of hypocrisy, *pace* Fitzgerald (1973) who thinks that Phaedra must have realized what the nurse really intended (ibid. 25) and finds suspect the postponement of her suicide until after Hippolytus' rejection (ibid. 26). But Phaedra surely postpones her death in the hope that the nurse will present her with an antaphrodisiac.
[33] e.g. Kovacs (1987) 27, 56: 'the horror Hippolytus exhibits is fully explicable without the hypothesis of abnormality'.
[34] Cf. Aeschylus' Clytemnestra, for whom the adultery with Cassandra provided a subsidiary, but again unnecessary motive for her husband's murder. Reckford (1974) 316, detects a suggestion that 'Hippolytus' prejudice plays a significant part in Phaedra's moral deterioration.'

Hippolytus has abandoned those ideals his father jumps at the opportunity to believe it (948–57).[35] Had his son espoused traditional heroic *aretē*, he would have had much less difficulty winning his father's approval,[36] and the problem is aggravated by Hippolytus' sanctimonious style—a style that seems to be part and parcel of a morality of fastidious abstinence and which isolates him from others.[37]

This sanctimonious and uncharitable attitude produced Phaedra's subsidiary motive for the incrimination (727–31). Besieged, it would appear, by two evil women, all the chaste young man's misogynistic prejudices seem confirmed and he launches into a long and blistering tirade against the entire female sex (616–68) which, as Avery has emphasized, attacks the discrepancy between women's outward show and their inner impurity, or lack of the true *sōphrosunē* so important to Hippolytus.[38] On the other hand, misogyny is a traditional topos and Hippolytus' response is, as we have seen, not exclusively that of a fanatically chaste person. Towards the end he retracts his threat to break his oath, though clearly he wishes that he had never sworn it (656–8).[39] And even if he is sworn not to divulge the matter, he will indulge his malice in silence: 'I shall come back when my father comes and I shall watch how you look him in the face—you and your mistress too' (661–2: tr. Morwood).

As Gill acutely observes, for Hippolytus

> it is not enough simply to be *sōphrōn* (by his standards); he has to *dramatize* his *sōphrosunē* by rhetorical self-dissociation from those who lack it and by underlining his stance as a morally superior observer of others' faults . . . but it is important also to note that the speech is marked, among Hippolytus' utterances, by its generalizing crudeness and personal viciousness, and that the context invites us to take it as the passionate, even hysterical, response of a man in a state of shock.[40]

That is to say, we are repelled by the crudeness and viciousness, but make allowances because of the shock. As for the need to dramatize his *sōphrosunē*, this is as close as Hippolytus can get to positive action. While all our preceding protagonists could realize their morality in some kind of brave action, Hippolytus' idiosyncratically defined *sōphrosunē* requires precisely abstention from action and is in fact an internal, psychological condition which is supposed to be admirable in

---

[35] The father is 'the exact antithesis of the son as far as sexual behavior is concerned. He fully embodies the conventional "double standard" of male sexuality (cf. 320). Hence he is the person least likely to believe Hippolytus' defence': C. Segal (1970) 293.

[36] 'It is partly because his ideal is so extraordinary that Theseus does not believe his protests of "purity" and innocence and too easily attributes to him opposite proclivities': ibid. 292.

[37] 'The goddess of sexuality punishes him through this particular manifestation of arrogance [i.e. his attitude to sexuality], but it is more generally his sense of superiority . . . which is ultimately his downfall': Mills (2002) 65. Gregory (1991) 61 argues that 'Aphrodite represents the claims of others upon the self, the force that interdicts human beings from passing through life in purity and isolation.' Perhaps, but her domain is surely *erōs* rather than *philia*.

[38] Avery (1968) 26.

[39] According to Michelini (1987) 296, 'Hippolytos' momentary reconsideration of his oath naturalizes him; and Hippolytos the chaste, who sets rules for himself that have no meaning for other men, is a character particularly in need of humanizing and softening touches.' But surely it is the youth's austere idealism rather than his compassion that is at work here.

[40] Gill (1990*b*) 94.

itself. Paradoxically, this eliminates the element of courage or indeed any kind of effort. This is because Hippolytus has no desire to be unchaste. In Aristotelian terms, he truly possesses the virtue of *sōphrosunē* (in his sense); he is not merely self-controlled (*enkratēs*).

PHAEDRA REACTS

Phaedra, whose self-respect is crushed by the tirade, seems to accept as just, at least for a moment, Hippolytus' portrait of women, reflecting as it does the common male prejudice (672). Her earlier justified belief that her moral integrity was intact so long as she did nothing to indulge the passion is here overwhelmed by the idea prevalent in her society (and which she mentioned before) that merely to experience such a passion is immoral—at least for a woman.[41] (Hippolytus, having no respect or sympathy for people who fight immoral impulses, would go further and condemn the sheer existence of passion in any person, male or female.) And yet Phaedra sees herself as the victim of wrong (clearly that of the nurse) without a god to help her (we think of Aphrodite's callous disregard of her interests) (675–9). She is now convinced that Hippolytus will perjure himself, either because she did not hear him revoke that decision (660) or because she does not believe that his anger will allow him to remain silent (689–92).[42] Accordingly, with the ruthlessness of the goddess that possesses her, she resolves to calumniate Hippolytus in order to save her own and her children's reputations:[43] 'For I shall never disgrace (αἰσχυνῶ) the royal house of Crete or come to look Theseus in the face after these shameful deeds—simply to save one life (οὕνεκα ψυχῆς μιᾶς)' (719–21: tr. Morwood).[44]

As she departs for suicide she sees herself as Aphrodite's chosen victim (725–7), not realizing that the goddess is intent on Hippolytus' destruction, and she appends a secondary motive to the desire to protect her reputation. She will teach the superior (ὑψηλός, 730) Hippolytus to display *sōphrosunē* (σωφρονεῖν, 731) in the face of her sufferings—and *sōphrosunē* in a rather different sense from that in which he understands it. That is, she will teach him to '"control himself" by moderating his feelings of anger and disdain'.[45]

So the passion has been revealed contrary to the noble Phaedra's desire; and not only the passion, but the lie that Phaedra intended it to be consummated. Hippolytus is naturally shocked, but is resolved to abide by his oath to remain silent. Phaedra, however, mistakenly believes that he will divulge what he knows and decides therefore to discredit him in advance. This complex causation

---

[41] *Hipp.* 405–7. The Sophoclean Ajax was similarly caught, between the supposed public view of him as worthless on account of the humiliation of the night massacre and his own view of himself as the greatest surviving warrior at Troy.

[42] Is Phaedra out of earshot? Hippolytus has changed his mind once; why not again?: L. P. E. Parker (2001) 45.

[43] On the parallel motivation of Aphrodite and Phaedra see Luschnig (1980) 92.

[44] But whose life? Her own or that of Hippolytus? See Barrett (1964) ad 721.

[45] Gill (1990*b*) 81.

involving considerable misunderstanding weakens, as we have seen, the link between character and outcome and is necessary to preserve as far as possible the moral innocence of and the spectator's sympathy for both of the main characters.[46] In the traditional version of the story, Phaedra's motive for the false incrimination of Hippolytus was to protect her reputation once she had attempted to seduce him. This motive is partially retained here by having Hippolytus believe that Phaedra has employed the nurse to make such a proposition. But the false incrimination implies the earlier, evil Phaedra. How could a noble Phaedra bring herself to such an act? The key was her concern with her reputation, a concern she would naturally share with the bad Phaedra, and indeed with all respectable Greek wives. This concern with reputation then had to overrule her general moral integrity, a thing which could happen quite convincingly in a shame culture. Thus, and perhaps in the first instance as a by-product of dramaturgical considerations, there emerges a morally more interesting Phaedra whose integrity is finally sacrificed on the altar of sheer reputation.[47] True, Aphrodite has destroyed Phaedra physically, but moral weakness of a type to which members of a shame culture are particularly susceptible has destroyed her morally. Apart from the goddess, then, some of the blame must be attributed to Phaedra, but at least as much to the prevailing morality of the culture.

The false incrimination implies not only an evil Phaedra but also an insensitive one who could destroy an innocent and upright young man. The answer to this problem was a priggish and intolerant Hippolytus. It was not enough that he be shocked by what he thought both Phaedra and the nurse intended, for only a libertine would fail to be shocked. He had to display an extreme and particular intolerance; and this Euripides motivated through his fanatical misogyny. This facilitated the introduction of a secondary motive for Phaedra, the desire to punish the insensitive Hippolytus. In this way Hippolytus' arrogance is connected with his destiny. His original arrogance is directed against Aphrodite, and her reaction sets the events in motion; but these events lead also naturally to his doom, as his arrogance in the face of human suffering is part and parcel of his arrogance towards the goddess.[48] 'That he should be horrified and revolted by the proposals

[46] 'As a number of critics have emphasized, the mutual destruction which occurs in the play is not the result of an open and unambiguous confrontation between figures with radically opposed characters and ethical standpoints. Rather it is one in which various kinds of misunderstanding and miscommunication render the motives and characters of the central figures obscure to each other (and in this sense obscure the connection between character and action or word). In particular, at the heart of the play (and of its tragic quality) is the fact that Hippolytus and Phaedra largely fail to communicate to each other, or to others, the way in which they are both powerfully motivated by (versions of) the ideal of *sōphrosunē*, a failure which contributes crucially towards their destroying each other and themselves': ibid. 84–5.

[47] 'Phaedra's tragedy . . . is that she purchases the temporary appearance of "purity" at the price of the deep, inward "purity" which she envisages at 317': C. Segal (1970) 281. 'Phaedra's concern with society not only contrasts with the individualism, or as one might even call it, the non-conformity of Hippolytus. It also contrasts ironically with that inward "purity" which Phaedra herself asserts against the Nurse's conventional view in 316–17: ibid. 282–3. 'If Phaedra allows too much to the outside world and the externalized *aidōs*, Hippolytus allows too little. His "shame" and "purity" are too far removed from the realities both of nature and society (cf. 616–24)': ibid. 294.

[48] See Luschnig (1980) 91 who draws a close parallel between Hippolytus' attitude to Aphrodite and his attitude to Phaedra.

of the Nurse is both natural and proper, but his tirade against women which Phaedra hears is not only harsh but crude and childish.'[49] In terms of the purely human causation, it is thus his arrogance rather than his aversion to sex that causes his destruction. Doubtless that aversion and his misogyny are to be seen as connected, but a sexual libertine who remained unshocked by the nurse's suggestions might still be a misogynist.

FATHER AND SON

Theseus is now in possession of the false incrimination. He immediately curses his son irrevocably (885–90). Euripides thus chooses to seal Hippolytus' fate again so that what follows, in particular his speech in his own defence, is seen to be not only causally irrelevant, but such as to confirm his arrogance.[50] The effect is perhaps similar to the curse that Oedipus brings down unwittingly on himself: we know that he is already doomed, but now he seems doubly so. Theseus, unsure that the curse will work, also exiles Hippolytus (893–8)—an obvious dramaturgical ploy to get the victim to the traditional site of his death.

Because the chorus are sworn to silence, Hippolytus must defend himself, and to do this he has to claim—awkwardly to modern taste—that there is no man 'more virtuous' (σωφρονέστερος, 995) than he.[51] We have to remember though that self-commendation was more acceptable to the ancients than to us. In his initial appearance, Hippolytus claimed that he was innately virtuous in all matters (ἐν τῇ φύσει τὸ σωφρονεῖν, 79–80), but was clearly thinking of his fanatical chastity. Now he reiterates this characterization of his *sōphrosunē* and extends it somewhat.

First of all I understand how to reverence the gods and to have as my friends those who attempt no wrong but would also hold it shame (*aidōs*) to send evil messages to their companions and to repay them with shameful services; I am not one to mock my fellows, father, but I say the same to my friends, both when they are absent and when near.

(996–1001: tr. Morwood)

Here we find the same emphasis on piety, though of course to the exclusion of Aphrodite, and the same emphasis on sexual purity, but he adds a new idea, honesty and openness of speech—an idea embodied in his refusal to perjure

---

[49] Winnington-Ingram (1960) 187. 'To suppose that Phaedra deliberately plans the destruction of an innocent man merely because of the initial cries she heard at 565–600 (and which the audience did not hear) means attributing to her a level of irresponsible malice wholly out of keeping with her character as so far revealed': L. P. E. Parker (2001) 47.

[50] 'He tells the truth throughout, but, especially at the beginning, he is so cool, affected, and prissily didactic that he is bound to appear offensive, especially to Theseus, who is caught in the throes of sorrow and anger': Avery (1968) 28.

[51] On Hippolytus' attitude and tone in this speech see Lloyd (1992) 47–51. '[W]hatever view one takes of such assertions, they are in accordance with Hippolytus' general attitude in the play': ibid. 49. 'The manner in which Hippolytus expresses himself in his debate with Theseus can be seen either as evidence of his remoteness and inability to communicate, or as an example of how rational behaviour is doomed to failure in an irrational situation. This ambiguity is carefully calculated, and is central to the meaning of the play': ibid. 51.

himself, and it is this that makes him an admirable character rather than his fanatical chastity, although the different kinds of 'purity' are perhaps associated. He still remains, *pace* Dimock, a prig when it comes to dealing with other people's weaknesses.[52] Indeed, he offers another oath in support of his innocence. Hippolytus' innocence and moral goodness are consistently harped on for the remainder of the play, but less his chastity than his other qualities. He leaves the stage asserting again his supreme *sōphrosunē* (1100, cf. 995), he protests it again in the midst of his cruel mutilation (ἄνδρ' ἄριστον, 1242), and the messenger himself concludes his speech with a strong assertion of Hippolytus' goodness (ἐσθλόν, 1254).

When the mangled victim is brought on stage he continues to protest his own innocence and the futility of his unrequited virtue (1362–9, 1379–83). Hippolytus is of course wrong about the divine source of his cruel fate, but like the Euripidean Heracles, he feels acutely the injustice of the gods. In claiming to be supreme in virtue, he means of course his particular virtues, his chastity and his honesty. He speaks of 'reverence towards human beings', but this has not extended as yet to Phaedra nor presumably to others who fall short of his conception of virtue.

ARTEMIS

The arrival of Artemis inevitably reinforces Hippolytus' strongly positive view of himself ('It is the nobility of your spirit (τὸ δ' εὐγενές . . . τῶν φρενῶν) that has destroyed you,' 1390),[53] and the dramatist seems thus to intend us to be lenient in judging him, despite the evidence he has provided for criticism.[54] There was no necessity to introduce Artemis; Aphrodite might have reappeared *ex machina*. But that would have necessitated a negative view of Hippolytus, contested perhaps by the characters who might have criticized the goddess for cruelty (as Cadmus criticizes Dionysus at the end of the *Bacchae*).

Artemis informs Hippolytus that Aphrodite destroyed him on account of his chastity and his failure to honour her (1402). Hippolytus responds with the recognition that he is not the sole victim. Phaedra and Theseus are similarly the pawns of the goddess (1403), and Aphrodite's prologue strongly encourages such a reading. On the other hand, a more balanced view must apportion some blame to the human characters.[55] But the focus on the characters as victims prepares the way for a new and refreshing spirit of forgiveness. Hippolytus extends this first to

---

[52] Dimock (1977) 248.

[53] It is 'the central concept of his whole life and character which destroys him': Knox (1979) 221.

[54] On the vindication of Hippolytus see Rabinowitz (1986) 178–9: 'Although Hippolytos is punished by Aphrodite, he is rewarded by Euripides, who brings him on stage for the promise of Artemis and restoration to his father': ibid. 179. 'Euripides increasingly engages our sympathies [for Hippolytus] as opposed to our intellect. As in the *Bacchae*, the victim of the divinity wins our sympathy, and we are seduced away from judging him as wanting. The very viciousness of the punishment ensures that this will be the case': ibid. 180.

[55] Contrast Kovacs (1987) 31: 'the poet did not intend his audience to regard either Hippolytus or Phaedra with ironic disapproval but rather to see them as heroic figures destroyed by a powerful goddess who uses their very strengths against them'.

his father alone (1404–5) whom he pities more than himself on account of his mistake (ἁμαρτίας, 1409). This is the kind of understanding which he was incapable of extending to Phaedra, except perhaps to admit that 'she displayed *sōphrosunē* without possessing the virtue' (1034).[56] But linked with his burgeoning forgiveness of his fellow mortals is a corresponding hostility towards the gods: 'If only the race of mortal men could prove a curse to them!' (1415: tr. Morwood). In reply to this, Artemis promises revenge on Aphrodite's current favourite— perhaps another innocent victim. She tells Theseus to embrace his son and Hippolytus not to hate his father (1431–6). The young man agrees, 'for I have always obeyed your commands' (1443: tr. Morwood), and, as Segal observes, in proceeding to free his father from pollution (1448–9) Hippolytus' 'narrow, priggish purity of 102 and 654–5 has become something deeper and more serious and at the same time more profoundly in touch with the realities of the human condition.'[57]

But Artemis must take her leave lest she be contaminated by the spectacle of a dying mortal, and Hippolytus comments, perhaps with some bitterness, on the relative ease of her departure (1441). He now proceeds to go beyond the goddess' command not to hate his father, forgiving and freeing him from the pollution and guilt of his death.[58] This makes the emotions of the epilogue seem more genuine than is often the case in Euripides. (One thinks of plays such as the *Orestes* where previous human hostilities are too easily banished by divine fiat.) For all the limitations of Artemis' humane feelings, it is possible to see her as genuinely distressed and perhaps even straining against the boundaries of her divine being.[59]

---

[56] Phaedra could not 'keep her passion continuously subdued' but she did 'perform a single act . . . , her suicide, that subdued it once for all': Barrett (1964) 356, ad 1034–5. 'Hippolytus seems to mean that Phaedra acted virtuously in killing herself, although—or, in a different way, because—she was not a virtuous person, in the sense of having chaste desires. He, on the other hand, is *sōphrōn* because he has chaste desires, and also perhaps because he is showing self-control in not breaking his oath; but he has gained no advantage, and has in fact been disadvantaged, by his possession of this quality': Gill (1990*b*) 81. Hippolytus 'is referring to Phaedra's suicide and contrasting her hard-won victory over her passion with his inability to turn his virtuous qualities to good purpose. Beyond its immediate context, the statement suggests that Hippolytus has been led by harsh experience to revise his previous definition of *sōphrosunē*. He here seems to acknowledge that rectitude is not purely innate and cannot be achieved simply through renunciation': Gregory (1991) 75.

[57] C. Segal (1970) 298. '[I]t is just at this moment when Hippolytus is most fully human. As his "purity" becomes more human, so it moves finally farther from the goddess who was originally its source and its object. . . . Death which would defile the remote Olympian can bring a kind of purity between men. . . . Yet this affirmative movement occurs only through an effort of will amid pain and only through compassion, generosity, and endurance, the *karteria* of 1456–7': ibid. 298.

[58] 'Purity at the end is something which Hippolytus can possess by conferring upon another rather than boastfully claiming for himself. And whatever purity he can give is wrung out of his tortured death: it is freedom from the stain of his own death. In granting it he is almost putting himself deliberately among the dead, outside the pale of living men': ibid. 'At Artemis' instigation and in the last moments of his life, Hippolytus succeeds in modeling an attitude that has been absent from previous representations of the middle way: *syngnomē*, comprehension or forgiveness. It is this quality that makes it possible to bridge the gap separating each individual from his fellows and ensures that individual integrity will not be achieved at the expense of other human beings': Gregory (1991) 76. 'Hippolytus takes his cue from Artemis, but he goes far beyond legal technicalities when he absolves his father of responsibility for his death. His decision is based on a clear understanding of everything his father has said and done (ibid. 77).

[59] Kitto (1961) 209 is less generous: 'we breathe a little more freely when this sub-human goddess has taken herself off, leaving the stage to the reconciliation between father and son'.

If we feel that the play has implicitly though powerfully demonstrated the inadequacy of Hippolytus' understanding of the virtue of *sōphrosunē*, Artemis is not helpful here in sharing his restricted view (1402, 1419), as this prevents his attaining a wider self-knowledge which would involve not only the acceptance of the claims of the divinity that has destroyed him but of a wider reality which requires a wider *sōphrosunē* for its successful negotiation.[60] We are reminded of Ajax, who becomes aware of the nature of the world, but prefers to remain inside his psychological limitations. Euripides seems as intent here on the theme of innocence destroyed as he is in *Heracles* where the quality of the hero's virtue is less debatable. Moreover, Artemis, in assigning much of the blame to Aphrodite, understates the very real responsibility of the human characters.[61]

Thus the play ends, like *Trachiniae* and *Heracles*, with the human characters morally affronted by the divine destruction of a mortal. There is little sense of acquiescence at the end of this play, and, as in *Heracles*, the only comfort comes from the little that mortals can do for each other in a hostile world.[62]

Now the human action of Sophocles' *Tyrannus* is causally incomplete and less than fully intelligible without Apollo's contribution. Aphrodite, on the other hand, could be removed from *Hippolytus* without essentially altering the causation. There are no 'coincidences' of the kind that seem naturalistically implausible and there is no obvious case of direct psychological intervention such as we saw in the form of Oedipus' self-blinding. Aphrodite tells us in the prologue that she will this day destroy Hippolytus, a task that will require little effort (21–3) now that she has inspired Phaedra with her passion. The remaining task is to 'reveal the matter to Theseus' (42), but, as we saw in Ch. 2, this is misleading since what is revealed to him is a lie, the alleged violation of Phaedra by Hippolytus (885–6). The effect of this discrepancy is to undermine Aphrodite's authority as a cause and to emphasize rather her dramaturgical role. There is a somewhat similar discrepancy between prediction and outcome in *Ion*, as Apollo fails to anticipate the course of the drama.

To remove Aphrodite from the action would do much less causal than thematic damage. Her first function is to focus the audience on Hippolytus' temperament as the cause of his destiny, even though in naturalistic terms the link is much less direct than concentration on his relationship with Aphrodite would suggest. This focus tends to confer an artificial unity on the causation and, as we have seen, to

---

[60] According to Knox (1979*b*) 223, this wider reality is the 'process of divine government' wherein Aphrodite and Artemis are 'locked in an eternal war'. But this goes beyond the evidence of the text.

[61] Dimock (1977) 253 thinks that Artemis rightly blames Aphrodite: 'in spite of what Phaedra and his father have done to him, he [Hippolytus] is able, as he should, to transfer the blame to Aphrodite' (1403–4).

[62] The play ends with an act of forgiveness, 'something only possible for human beings, not for gods but for their tragic victims. It is man's noblest declaration of independence, and it is made possible by man's tragic position in the world. Hippolytus' forgiveness of his father is an affirmation of purely human values in an inhuman universe': Knox (1979*b*) 228–9. 'With the reconciliation between them [father and son] a gleam of light irradiates the tragedy. Human beings can at least forgive one another, even if the gods cannot forgive': Winnington-Ingram (1960) 191. Dimock thinks that Hippolytus is comforted to the extent that virtue is its own reward. 'If the beauty of this reconciliation gives us a measure of comfort after the terrible things we have been witnessing, it is Artemis' doing . . . [255] . . . Artemis' approval has done much to lighten Hippolytus' pain; but her approval he has always had. It is his father's absolutely unqualified admiration that makes his death a completely happy one' [256].

suggest that the play is primarily concerned with the punishment of hubris. Aphrodite's second function is to enable Euripides to present the characters, and especially Hippolytus, in an unbalanced fashion, more as innocent victims than they would otherwise appear.[63]

However, it is sometimes claimed that since Aphrodite is also (or for some 'merely') a symbol of sexual love Hippolytus is also a victim of his attitude towards sex.[64] This is true enough in the obvious sense that the intolerance associated with his fanaticism contributes to his doom via Phaedra's false incrimination, but even this is very far from being a sufficient or even natural cause of his destruction. Certainly the *inevitability* disappears once the personal goddess is removed from the equation.

Still less can it be argued that Hippolytus is destroyed by sexual 'repression'.[65] This modern concept is concerned more with adverse psychological consequences than with physical ones. Nor can we say that, because the bull is a symbol of sexual potency, the mutilation of Hippolytus by Poseidon's bull symbolizes his destruction by his alleged repressions. There is no link here to the natural chain of causation,[66] nor could an ancient spectator conceivably have reached such a conclusion. Hippolytus is quite happy with his unusual life until Phaedra impacts upon it with her unpredictable infatuation. But in the rebuttal of the 'psychiatric' interpretation the fundamental point is one of methodology. The scientific validity of Freudian psychology apart, it is one thing to psychoanalyse real people, but quite another to do it to characters who are in part at least the conscious constructs of an author, unless they are constructed deliberately in accordance with a Freudian model, as for example the characters of O'Neill's *Mourning Becomes Electra*. Hippolytus' character is in part a given of the myth, and while his attitude to sex may reasonably be seen as inherited from his mother,[67] it cannot be assumed without proof that that tradition carries with it some profound insight about psychology only later articulated by the Freudians. It is much more likely that Euripides constructed his hero's character in accordance with a desire to elicit pity and indignation on behalf of an innocent man, and for that reason emphasized (perhaps to modern taste and perceptions overemphasized) his hero's extreme moral idealism in the form of permanent chastity (a suspect virtue in a post-Freudian world and a mostly irrelevant one in antiquity). At any rate to apply without qualification a Freudian or indeed any other theory of psychology to a

---

[63] The characters 'are by no means helpless victims of Aphrodite but contribute actively to their own ruin through their principles as well as their actions': Gregory (1991) 54.

[64] Conacher (1967) 29 and Fitzgerald (1973) 27, who sees the early speech addressed to Artemis as the beginning of a 'perceptive, and indeed precocious, study of a neurosis and its bases'. Cf. the alleged anxiety over being a bastard (ibid. 28).

[65] Conacher (1967) 44 finds it 'tempting to see a daring piece of symbolism in the destruction of the chaste Hippolytus by the bolting of his own bull-maddened steeds'. Fitzgerald (1973) 27 considers Hippolytus a study in neurosis and moral ambivalence.

[66] Fitzgerald ibid. 29 finds the scene 'descriptive of an inevitable psychological reaction'—a view that depends on a prior resolve to find Freudian references. '[I]t is clearly not the fact of Hippolytus' death with which Euripides is concerned in the messenger scene, but the symbolic potential of its details to inform the audience about the crucial features of Hippolytus' character and circumstances' (ibid. n. 39). This of course inverts the Aristotelian idea that character is present to explain events rather than vice versa.

[67] Halleran (1991) 119.

fictional character is to ignore the fact that other principles than the strictly psychological are involved in characterization.

Since the Greeks were innocent of the sometimes convoluted logic and intuitive leaps of Freudian psychoanalysis, they would not have been as ready as we are to diagnose a manifestly functioning person as subject to an identifiable psycho-pathological condition. Raving madness of course is another matter and could be attributed to temporary (if recurrent) divine possession. Hippolytus is not according to Greek culture mentally ill, though he is certainly guilty of hubris which is a kind of metaphorical madness when senselessness reaches the level of outright defiance (one thinks of Capaneus in the *Seven* or the Sophoclean *Ajax*).

Hippolytus, though guilty of impiety towards Aphrodite, is innocent in the mortal world of all but insensitivity to human weakness and failure to understand another's moral struggle. This is a function partly of his youthful, self-absorbed intensity and manifests in his distorted understanding of the virtue of *sōphrosunē*. Moreover, his impiety towards one deity is counterbalanced by an exaggerated devotion to another. This devotion 'does not, cannot exist in isolation: it defines itself only in antithesis to his neglect of Aphrodite. Excess in one direction produces deficiency in the other.'[68]

CONCLUSION

Phaedra knew, before the action of the play, that her passion for Hippolytus could not be indulged. The issue was simply morally unnegotiable. Her deliberations therefore were entirely practical: how exactly was she to prevent the passion from being indulged or made public? But she fears that the nurse will undermine her moral resolution (503–6) and then, when the nurse offers a remedy, Phaedra allows her to take control. After the nurse has approached Hippolytus Phaedra is faced with a new crisis, as she sees it: the need to secure her reputation. Phaedra defines herself conventionally as a virtuous and respectable wife. This requires marital fidelity, hence her resolve not to indulge her illicit passion. But once the focus of the crisis shifts to the preservation of her reputation, she is prepared to act immorally to attain that end. She disguises this immorality, however, by representing the death she is contriving for Hippolytus as a legitimate punishment for his haughty disdain (728–31). In none of these deliberations is there any clear indication of divine psychological intervention, although the prologue has encouraged us to feel that Aphrodite is intervening at least 'panoramically'.

Hippolytus defines himself in moral terms as a man of innate *sōphrosunē*. This is not a conventional role. Nor is it a rationally thought out position; it is rather a function of temperament and youth. It is difficult to talk about the responsibilities of such a person, partly because this virtue (in the form Hippolytus conceives it) is not associated with a conventional role such as king or warrior general, but also because innate *sōphrosunē* always expresses itself, one would presume, spontaneously and appropriately. On the other hand, a predisposition and a

---

[68] Gregory (1991) 56.

complete commitment to a moral virtue is insufficient in itself for right action. The agent requires accurate understanding as well. Aristotle comes to mind here. The philosopher wisely argued that, although the potential to acquire the virtues is innate, the virtues themselves are not. Rather they must be cultivated, and for this rational understanding is required. Indeed, one of the conditions of true moral action for Aristotle (*NE* 2. 4) is that the agent must have knowledge.

Thus when Hippolytus hears the nurse's indecent proposal he wrongly believes that it originated with Phaedra. Admittedly, even if he had known the truth, Hippolytus is not, at least at that point in the play, a man disposed to admire a woman for fighting a passion to which the person of innate *sōphrosunē* (the only kind he respects) would never have succumbed in the first place. One might argue that Hippolytus' restricted understanding of *sōphrosunē* predisposes him strongly to the vice of intolerance, or, in ancient terms, failing to show pity. In his apologia to Theseus, though, he mitigates his attitude somewhat in admitting that Phaedra did after all display a kind of *sōphrosunē* without being *sōphrōn* in the true sense (1034). When Hippolytus reacts to the nurse's disclosures, he has no inkling of the implications of his response. As for divine intervention, it would appear that Aphrodite must work through a person susceptible to sexual desire, and so there is no question of her invading his mind.

·

14

Euripides: *Heracles*

INTRODUCTION

While the Apolline reality of the *Tyrannus* remains deeply mysterious to the end, the audience at least are aware throughout of the basic discrepancy between appearance and reality—the overarching dramatic irony of the play. The audience of the *Heracles*, on the other hand, is denied this privilege. As the play unfolds we are as ignorant of what is to come as are the characters themselves, as befits a drama in which seemingly random events play such an important role. At the outset we learn that Heracles is in Hades performing his final Labour, but since Megara and the sons she bore him are still alive, we have to revise what would otherwise be our natural assumption—that the Labours are performed in atonement for the insane murder of this family. In the traditional biography of the hero,[1] the completion of the Labours is a natural climax in Heracles' career and a major break before the final episode of the marriage to Deianeira, the poisoned robe, and his eventual apotheosis, though the Labours may be relevant to this finale, as in *Trachiniae*.

In Euripides' play the Labours, instead of being an atonement, are presented, initially at least, as services to Heracles' family (especially his human father Amphitryon), performed for Eurystheus, and motivated ultimately by Hera or 'necessity' ($\tau o \hat{v} \chi \rho \epsilon \grave{\omega} \nu \mu \acute{\epsilon} \tau a$) (17–21), and the tyrant Lycus' persecution of the hero's supplicating family (Amphitryon, Megara, and the children) is in all probability the playwright's invention. We have therefore no means of predicting the sequel, though we can safely suppose that Heracles will return from Hades and save his *philoi*. But since Lycus is a most unimpressive, and indeed anticlimactic, adversary for the great hero, the audience might well anticipate a dull and predictable outcome. Euripides could hardly incorporate the final, Deianeira episode, and he must have discarded, it would seem, the traditional madness. Thus when the madness impacts unexpectedly on the play out of what was perhaps the traditional sequence and hence with radically transformed significance, the audience is drawn powerfully into the moral and religious questions that the drama raises.

---

[1] See Papadopoulou (2005) 74–5.

AMPHITRYON AND MEGARA

These questions emerge, however, long before the madness strikes. As the suppliants' situation deteriorates towards seemingly inevitable death, Amphitryon
and Megara discuss what attitude to take to their predicament. While Amphitryon
is guardedly optimistic, at least at first, Megara is close to despair. She is impressed
by the instability of human affairs, which she associates, conventionally and rather
unspecifically, with the gods (62), citing her royal father's fate and their own
present predicament (63–79). She looks to her father-in-law for counsel. What
hope of salvation can they conceivably entertain? There is no escape, nor are there
any friends (*philoi*) who can help them. They must surely die (80–6).

Amphitryon can offer no rational rebuttal of Megara's assessment, but only
lamely suggest that they stall for time, since they are too weak to use force, and
meanwhile continue to hope. Megara, on the other hand, sees no point in hoping
for the impossible, to which Amphitryon replies with an unconventional inversion of traditional pessimism about the vicissitudes of fortune. If good fortune is
apt to be reversed, argues the old man, then the opposite is equally possible and
Heracles may return after all (87–97).[2] It is the mark of the best and bravest sort of
man (ἀνὴρ ἄριστος, 105) to rely on hope, while despair (ἀπορεῖν, 106) characterizes the coward. Thus against the background of this initial world-view an
appropriate moral response is suggested.

Whether hopefulness is a virtue or a vice depends, however, on the circumstances. Megara, as we saw, considers Amphitryon's hope to be irrational. Sophocles' Ajax similarly feels nothing but contempt for the man who would cling to life
without reasonable hope of living nobly (*Aj.* 473–80), and in his moral world as he
construes it there *is* no hope, since there is absolutely no way he can win renown
among people he respects, and a life without renown he considers worthless.
Amphitryon and his family, on the other hand, could resume meaningful lives if
help arrived. And help does arrive in the shape of Heracles' seemingly miraculous
return. In the unstable world of Euripides' play, the range of reasonable expectation is much broader than it is for Sophocles' Ajax.

Still, the old man's random universe of possibly positive outcomes is morally
unattractive, and underlying all the uncertainty is a pervasive and disagreeable
fact: evil men such as Lycus prevail, while the good are ineffectual. Heracles'
family are weak through old age, youth, or gender, and the friends to whom the
weak would naturally look in their distress are themselves weak, like the chorus of
old warriors; or absent, perhaps dead, like Heracles; or ungrateful and unreliable,
like the people of Thebes and the wider Greek world. In this play the good
characters judge others and themselves chiefly by their moral performance as
philoi. Heracles and his family feel that his father Zeus (339–47) and the Greeks
have betrayed them despite the bond of *philia* (227–8, 558–61); Heracles judges
himself by his readiness to help his family (575–82), the Labours are services to
philoi (17–21, 1252), and Theseus will require himself to be faithful in *philia*

---

[2] Barlow (1996) ad 105–6 comments that Amphitryon's 'expressed faith in hope is at odds with
much of the pessimism of Greek literature'. For Michelini (1987) 250, hope is 'a principle notoriously
uncertain in Greek tradition, and one that will be crushingly repudiated by the action of this play'. See
also Bond's (1982) detailed note ad 105–6.

(1223–5), as the chorus expect of themselves (266–7, 275–6). In a morally ideal world, evil men (one's enemies) would be punished by the good (one's friends), a situation which has always prevailed around Heracles. That the issue is broader than the suppliants' immediate plight is underscored by a later ode in which the chorus find fault with divine wisdom and understanding for not being as humans conceive them (655–72).

In the meantime Lycus urges the family to abandon sanctuary so that he can kill them without pollution. To persuade them to this apparently irrational course of action he has to eliminate the small vestige of hope that yet remains to them. Heracles, he argues, will not return to save them as he is not really Zeus's son and thus no hero of extraordinary powers (145–50). Barlow sees this as a rationalist's attack on the semi-divine Heracles of myth that anticipates the humanizing of the hero at the end of the play.[3] It is at the very least a radical attack on the family's last shred of optimism about the justice of the world. Lycus tries to establish the impossibility of the hero's return by belittling the Labours for not being accomplished through the traditional and indeed contemporary *aretē* of the warrior fighting at close quarters with a spear. Instead, Heracles used a bow, the weapon of the most cowardly of fighters, since it allows them to escape easily (151–64). Not only is the hero's divine paternity questioned, but his courage would seem to fall well below that of the average Homeric warrior or fifth-century hoplite.

Amphitryon sets about defending the bow, stating at the outset that Zeus must defend *his* share of Heracles (170–1)[4]—presumably by accomplishing his live return from Hades, a feat implying certainly *aretē* more than mortal, though Amphitryon alludes, it would appear, to the immortal part of Heracles in referring to his employment of Zeus's thunder against the Giants (177–80). The defence of the bow then is a defence of the mortal aspect, so to speak, of Heracles, and the 'clever invention' ($\pi \acute{a} \nu \sigma o \phi o \nu \ldots \epsilon \mathring{v} \rho \eta \mu a$, 188) of that weapon goes far towards explaining the human aspect of the hero's achievements. The bow, according to Amphitryon (and we must assume that Heracles holds much the same view) is the weapon of the intelligent warrior who, unlike the hoplite, fights at a distance and is essentially a loner,[5] independent of comrades and their possible cowardice (191–2), and therefore of fortune ($\tau \acute{v} \chi \eta s$, 203), or at least the typical fortunes of the battlefield. Paradoxically, however, the bow is anachronistic in both temporal directions. Mythologically and historically, it is associated with an older form of society that predated the polis, whereas its status as a 'clever invention' makes it seem modern, and indeed it was staging a comeback in contemporary warfare with the increasing tactical significance of light troops. In any case, the emphasis on the bow means that the brutal violence associated more with the club is out of sight (at least for the moment).[6]

---

[3] Barlow (1996) ad 140–69. For the attack on archery in antiquity see ibid. ad 159 ff.

[4] See Bond (1982) ad loc.

[5] Heracles 'has failed to forge a network of personal relationships that might benefit his family in their need': Gregory (1991) 130.

[6] Papadopoulou (2005) 137–51 has an excellent discussion of the bow which she concludes is an ambivalent weapon as far as concerns the hero's *aretē*. But it seems to me that the essential point to make is that it deludes its possessor into a false sense of independence and security.

This vaunted independence of the lone fighter is at odds with the pervasive *philia* theme—that we all need friends, and this need is only more obvious in the case of the weak, such as Heracles' family and the sympathetic but decrepit chorus, whose active *philia* is restricted to the mutual physical support required just to stand up (119–30). Although Heracles' independence is specifically tied to his role as an archer, it is emblematic of his whole career as the lone performer of the Labours. When he is involved with others, they always depend on him. Heracles would seem to resemble his idealized deity (1345–6) in needing nothing from others. This ideal of independence, as Foley has argued, sets Heracles at odds with the hoplite ideal of the democratic Athenian polis and renders this 'epinician' hero an anachronistic and unsuitable model for that society.[7]

Heracles then is accustomed to fighting successfully alone. All obstacles give way before him. Fortune (*tuchē*) in this context is restricted to the potential ineffectuality of others, such as a neighbour in the ranks who runs away or fails in some way to protect you. But fortune can attack in other ways. Heracles may be accustomed to coping with external and tangible physical threats, but he is unused to dealing with attacks from within his own mind, just as his namesake in *Trachiniae* is unused to physical assaults from within his own magnificent body.

We have seen that, in the view of Amphitryon and the chorus, the world should be so arranged that the good enjoy prosperity and the evil suffer misery. So when Lycus represents his murderous intentions as simple practical caution ($\epsilon\dot{\upsilon}\lambda\acute{\alpha}\beta\epsilon\iota\alpha\nu$) or self-defence in the form of a pre-emptive strike against obvious enemies (165–9), Amphitryon adopts a naively moral standpoint: 'Why do you want to kill these children?' he asks Lycus. 'What have they done to you?' (206–7). Lycus has just told him why, but Amphitryon is reluctant to accept that stage (not to mention Platonic) tyrants have little respect for conventional morality. He goes on to tell Lycus that he (Lycus) is wise, being a coward ($\kappa\alpha\kappa\acute{o}\varsigma$), to be afraid of the offspring of the 'noble and brave' ($\check{\alpha}\rho\iota\sigma\tau o\nu$) (207–9), but he at once undermines this optimistic idea when he goes on to complain that Zeus is unjustly allowing the cowardly to kill the noble and brave (209–12). Still, if the supreme deity cannot be relied on to dispense destinies according to deserts, then the wind of god's fortune ($\theta\epsilon o\hat{\upsilon}\ \pi\nu\epsilon\hat{\upsilon}\mu\alpha$) may yet change (216). And it is not only the gods that are unjust. The Greeks in general and Thebes in particular are under an obligation to repay Heracles for his services by helping his family (217–28). But as it is, those who can and should help will not, while those who desperately want to help are physically incapable (228–35). Morally, the world is completely awry, and Lycus is only too ready to rub his victims' noses in the fact (238–9).

Megara, however, the apparent realist, concentrates on how to face what she is convinced is the inevitable.[8] Why make things worse by allowing their already triumphant enemy to add insult to injury by scorning them for cowardice (275–86)? The aristocratic tradition of moral *eugeneia* requires them not to shame their *philoi*, living or dead. In particular, Amphitryon who was once a

---

[7] Foley (1985) 150.

[8] Barlow (1996) ad 275–311 sees Megara's speech as full of clichés or 'rhetorical commonplaces' which 'make it seem as if Megara is making supreme efforts to convince herself of her argument by referring to general principles while knowing that really all she feels is despair which no words can make bearable.'

mighty warrior should not allow himself to die a coward's death. Heracles would not want to preserve his children's lives at the price of their honour, and Megara imagines herself following her husband's moral example (287–94). Amphitryon's hope, she contends, is simply irrational: no one comes back from Hades, and Lycus is impervious to moral argument (295–8). What is needed then is a morality for facing inevitable death and not the spurious courage of a futile and self-deluding optimism (309–11).[9]

Amphitryon is now inclined to agree, explaining that he is not afraid to die but wants to save the children (316–18). He asks Lycus to kill him and Megara first (321–5). Megara for all her pride supplicates for the further *charis* (327) of being allowed to clothe the children for the grave. Thus she can vindicate *eugeneia* to the extent of avoiding a particularly humiliating kind of death (by fire), but she still depends on her seemingly all-powerful enemy for the orchestration of the event. (We might recall here the self-deluding 'free' nobility of the Euripidean Polyxena and Iphigenia.)

At this desperate point Amphitryon rails at Zeus in a withering critique of the god (339–47) who, though Heracles' father and his own wife's 'co-husband', has proved an unreliable *philos*. Thus he, a mortal, surpasses Zeus in *aretē* (here 'moral virtue' rather than more narrowly 'courage'). Zeus is moreover an adulterer, and a god who is either 'insensitive' (ἀμαθής: ignorant and without moral sense?) or not 'righteous' (δίκαιος) (cf. 1115). The old man expects the universe to mirror his human commitment to *philia* morality.

Megara reflects on the vanity of the hopes she entertained for her children's future, rendered void now by *tuchē* (460–82); while Amphitryon, resigned to the inevitability of their dying, gives utterance to the traditional tragic philosophy of living life from day to day as pleasantly as you can (503–5).[10] Time does not know how to preserve our hopes, but vanishes, absorbed with its own concerns (506–7). Fortune (*tuchē*) has made him vanish in one day like a feather; wealth and reputation are transitory (509–12).

Some forty years ago Anne Burnett, in a challenging and provocative discussion of the play, argued that the criticisms of Zeus are unfair because based on a kind of impatience, for the god does (or so it would seem) eventually bring Heracles home. She argued also that the suppliants, in being prepared to abandon sanctuary, throw away their only remotely effective defence.[11] It is not clear though that Zeus *is* responsible for Heracles' return and, even if he is, the moral criticisms of the god and of the universe over which he presides remain valid. After the intervening ode and apparently on the point of death, Amphitryon actually prays to Zeus to save the children, but he does so with little faith in the result (497–501). As his speech ends, Heracles appears. Is Euripides here employing the familiar Sophoclean irony of the god who answers the prayer at once but with a

---

[9] According to Chalk (1962) 9–10, Amphitryon's *aretē* is hope, while Megara's is acceptance. 'These two views of *aretē* introduce the contrast that eventually relates the two main parts of the play as a whole, the contrast between the *aretē* of Herakles the Deliverer, which seeks to mould circumstances to man's intentions, and the *aretē* of the stricken Herakles, which endures whatever happens with acceptance.'

[10] See e.g. *Ba.* 910–11.

[11] Burnett (1971) 159–65.

sting? Sophocles' Jocasta and Clytemnestra pray to Apollo for deliverance and it appears to come until hidden facts emerge that turn their joy to misery. Similarly the children will be saved from Lycus only to be killed by their own father. That this is a deliberate irony is clear enough, but whether it testifies to divine power (not to mention justice) is another matter.

HERACLES RETURNS

Heracles now returns to discover that Megara's father and brothers have been murdered (539), that his own family is on the point of suffering a similar fate, and that their supposed friends have been useless (558–61). He threatens a bloodbath of Lycus and those Thebans who have been disloyal (565–73, but cf. 604–6)—a reaction that seems extreme and even barbarous, though in accord with the Homeric Odysseus' treatment of the suitors. An earlier generation of scholars, looking for the origins of the subsequent madness in the psyche of Heracles, were intent on discovering evidence of mental instability and thought that they had found it in this reaction.[12] The ancients, however, as we have seen, considered madness the function not of a settled personality disorder but of a sudden and often inexplicable divine intervention. Heracles is actually not only perfectly sane but circumspect, as his father urges him to be (585 ff.), and pious (607–9).[13] He is also a surprisingly domestic figure—the understanding father and husband, which the poet stresses by giving him fifteen verses for his reassurance of Megara and the children (622–36), although there are earlier hints of such a conception of the hero.[14] The threats of violence are not a symptom of madness but an expression of the traditional *aretē* of a hero who loves his *philoi* and hates his enemies (585–6) and, no doubt, one for whom violence is the principal problem-solving resource. In any case, Lycus is no special challenge to Heracles, so the hero rises as confidently to the occasion as does Oedipus to the crisis of the plague.

Heracles' reaction is immediate and instinctive; he does not, nor does he need to deliberate in order to know what to do. He does, however, reflect that the Labours, performed for his family, would be meaningless if he failed to protect that family now (574–81); nor could he continue to think of himself or be honoured by others as Heracles of the glorious victories (καλλίνικος, 582).[15]

The chorus now sing a sort of ode to youth (637–54) which they rate above even great wealth and power. They go on to argue, rather fancifully, that if the gods had understanding and wisdom as humans conceive them (or 'in their dealings with humans') (κατ' ἄνδρας, 656), they would reward *aretē* with a second youth in a second life and that this would be a way of distinguishing the good from the evil

---

[12] e.g. Verrall's (1905) chapter on the play *passim*; Blaiklock (1951) 122 ff. *Contra*: Barlow (1996) ad 562 ff. As Bond (1982) ad 562–82 observes, 'Heracles' plans are reasonable by fifth-century, let alone heroic standards.'

[13] On the hero's intelligence and *pronoia* in this episode see Gregory (1991) 132–3.

[14] See Papadopoulou (2005) 77–80.

[15] This adjective is constantly associated with Heracles' victories: see 49, 180, 570, 681, 789, 961, 1046.

(655–72). We are reminded of the earlier complaint that the world is not constructed in order to enable the righteous to prosper. But the situation has changed radically and youth, or rather virile maturity, has returned in the form of Heracles to save his family. Right may be expected to prevail, and Amphitryon can now declare that Lycus who has done evil can anticipate suffering evil in return (727–8 cf. 740–1, 755–6).

Lycus is duly punished[16] and the chorus celebrate what they see as divine justice (738, 772–3, 809–14), implicitly condemning the tyrant as one who despised divine power (757–60). But the chorus have changed their tune about the gods somewhat since Heracles' return, and the adjective 'impious' (δυσσεβής, 760) with which they now brand Lycus might equally be applied to Amphitryon for his earlier diatribe against Zeus (339–47). The idea of *tuchē* resurfaces briefly (765–6) and Amphitryon's earlier optimism now seems vindicated as 'hope was realized beyond expectations' (771). And yet that hope was based on the idea of amoral fluctuations in an effectively random universe. Is Heracles' return then the work of a righteous Zeus as the chorus imply perhaps in their celebration of the co-paternity (798–800), or the fortuitous product of an arbitrary fortune?

IRIS AND LYSSA

Theodicy takes a new turn with the arrival of Iris and Lyssa. If a benign Zeus brought Heracles back to save his family, why does he now allow Hera to have her way? Iris tells us that 'destiny' (τὸ χρή, 828; cf. τοῦ χρεών, 21) and Zeus protected the hero so long as he was performing his Labours. We are familiar from the *Iliad* with the idea of Zeus acting in support of destiny, even against his feelings as in the case of his son Sarpedon (16. 431–61), but there is no suggestion here that Heracles' destiny extended to the madness inflicted at the instigation of Hera. There appears to be no reason then why Zeus should not have continued to protect his son.[17] The chorus too are disturbed by Zeus's apparent indifference towards or even inexplicable hatred of his son (1086–7).

In considering this question, though, we have to remember that we are not reading a theological tract but responding to a work of literature, so that the activities of gods, or equally their inactivity, may well reflect the requirements of the myth or the plot. With respect to the passage from the *Iliad*, we might say that Homer's plot required Sarpedon's death, but the bard enhanced the pathos immeasurably by presenting the event as tragically inevitable, an idea reinforced by Zeus's reluctant acceptance. The 'theology' of Zeus's relationship to destiny was presumably plausible to Homer's audience, but it was not the central issue.

---

[16] Barlow (1996) ad 701–62: The murder of Lycus 'presents the audience with a deed more immediate than that of the Labours, yet less drastic in its human implications than the murder of his children'.

[17] Unless, with Gregory (1991) 137, we invoke 'the Olympian principle that gods must respect one another's spheres of influence'. See also Papadopoulou (2005) 77. The *locus classicus* here is surely Zeus's callous disregard of his faithful worshippers in the interests of peace with Hera at *Iliad* 4. 1–67.

So where does this leave us as far as concerns Zeus in the *Heracles*? The answer
depends on how literally we are to understand the gods of the play, and to
determine *that* we need to consider Heracles' dismissal of the traditional deities
at 1340–5. Certainly on the literal level of anthropomorphic gods Zeus appears in
a bad light unless we can show that the hero's sufferings are somehow deserved or
at least natural. This brings us to a central question of Euripides' play—the reason
for and justification of the madness. We saw that earlier critics were concerned to
find the seeds of the hero's madness in his psyche, and so they looked—though in
vain—for signs of psychological instability. But once we remember that madness
could strike arbitrarily at divine fiat, we will focus more on religious than on
psychological causes. The madness comes ultimately from Hera whose traditional
motivation was sexual jealousy, a motive which would fit naturally into a play that
emphasizes the co-paternity of Heracles.

In her first speech Iris offers no clear explanation or justification for Hera's
initiative with which she entirely sympathizes. She does, however, say, at the end,
that Heracles is to learn of Hera's wrath (χόλος, 840) towards him, appending the
comment that 'if he is not punished', or, less likely, 'if he does not restore the
balance of *dikē* [through his downfall]' (μὴ δόντος δίκην, 842), mortals will be
great and the gods 'nowhere', or of no account. The notion that Heracles is guilty
of some crime for which he must be punished is, however, unsupported by any
delinquency on his part hitherto referred to in the play.[18]

But if we take *dikē* in the broader, almost amoral sense of 'the proper world
order', it is conceivable that the hero has in some way disrupted that order and
that Hera's *cholos* attaches to that rather than to the traditional sexual jealousy.
Grube, for example, remarks: 'In this world governed by powerful, ruthless,
superhuman forces, greatness is dangerous in and by itself, without sin on the
great one's part, except the sin of greatness.'[19] Much the same idea is adopted and
elaborated by Kitto who allegorizes the divine *phthonos* and depersonalizes
somewhat the relationship of Zeus and Hera. The hero's 'genius derives dramatically from Zeus; it follows almost automatically that Hera must wish to destroy
it . . . genius of this order is, it seems, more than Nature can long endure; the gift
from Zeus carries with it the inevitable hatred of Hera . . .'.[20] And 'when the
Labours are finished, his "destiny" ceases to protect him, and Nature destroys
what she has produced and used'.[21] Lucas also focuses on the relationship between
Zeus and Hera, interpreting the goddess as a symbol of 'that factor, whatever we
choose to call it, which delays and obstructs the fulfilment of the good'.[22] (But it is
hard to see Zeus as the embodiment of good in this play.) Similarly, Burnett would
have it that it

[18] Barlow (1996) ad 822–73: 'There is no evidence in the text to suggest overweening arrogance on
his part or any kind of *hubris* which might bring down Hera's wrath with more reason.'

[19] Grube (1961) 255–6.

[20] Kitto (1961) 247.

[21] Ibid 248. Compare Greene (1944) 186 who sees Heracles as being 'under divine protection only
so long as he is engaged in his humanitarian labors, but his value ceases there; under the normal
conditions of peaceful life he is exposed to the enmity of the gods and his very strength becomes
dangerous'.

[22] Lucas (1959) 220.

is not mortal jealousy of a female, but pure anger against a male that the goddess is said to feel, and the word used (*cholos*, 840), has nothing of sexual vindictiveness in it. This is the magnificent, almost personified wrath that sometimes came upon a Homeric warrior from outside himself. . . . Iris explains that Hera's general intention is to defend the grandeur of the gods by defeating an attempt at grandeur on the part of man. (841–2)[23]

But while *cholos* is not particularly associated with sexual hostility, it is hardly incompatible with it. Foley, making a somewhat similar point but from a rather different perspective, sees Hera's wrath as a response to a failure of ritual: 'By sacrificial logic . . . Heracles' ritual fails and he is punished by Hera because in his case the ritual no longer functions to divide the divine from the human.'[24] More recently, Griffiths has arged that Hera is both motivated by sexual jealousy and intent on punishing the hero for the removal of Hades' gatekeeper Cerberus, thus destroying the boundary between mortality and immortality.[25] But if, as Griffiths maintains, Hera, in what is surely an unprecedented concern with public relations, was looking for a pretext to punish Heracles, why did she not order her underling Iris to make a point of announcing it to the world rather than telling Lyssa to mind her own business? What was the point of referring to the punishment of an unspecified offence that might have been specified without embarrassment?

But perhaps the most plausible and suggestive variant of this type of interpretation is that of Silk, according to whom Heracles is a threat to the cosmic order because he is anomalous—neither man nor god. 'Heracles ends the play as a credible man: wretched, special, but credible. He begins it as a wholly incredible combination of man and god.'[26] The effect at any rate of the madness is certainly to bring Heracles down to human size, so that he becomes, symbolically, the son of a mortal rather than of Zeus. Perhaps then, as for the Oedipus of the *Tyrannus*, the point is not moral, not a question of individual guilt or innocence, but simply that Heracles, like Oedipus, must attain that basic and typically tragic self-knowledge of his and all human beings' relative insignificance in the scheme of things.

If Iris is, somewhat obliquely, defending Hera's attack on such impersonal grounds, in the eyes of Lyssa it is nevertheless unjust. Now it would have been easy for Euripides to have eliminated Iris altogether and simply have Lyssa appear and announce that she was there to put Hera's desires into effect and that Hera's purpose (somewhat like Athena's in the prologue of *Ajax*) was to remind us all that Heracles, for all his achievements, was nevertheless no more than a puny mortal. No further explanation would have been necessary. But the introduction of two deities in disagreement is a device for airing the issue of Heracles' guilt, or rather innocence. There is an amusing irony in having the goddess of irrationality

---

[23] Burnett (1971) 176–7.   [24] Foley (1985) 198.

[25] Griffiths (2002) 645 argues that there is a specific offence, or rather 'a supposed crime of Herakles that she [Hera] could respond to, and thus unleash her wrath under the guise of *dikē*'. She sees a parallel between the three-bodied Cerberus and the three bodies of the individual children of Heracles, so that the punishment fits the crime. Griffiths would have it that the interpretation of the play hangs on this (in my opinion) rather recondite parallel, but I agree that the audience might feel that Heracles had disturbed the world order by his katabasis.

[26] Silk (1993) 132.

par excellence mount a spirited and reasoned defence of her victim.[27] Heracles, she argues, is famous on earth and among the gods for civilizing land and sea and restoring 'honour and worship' ($\tau\iota\mu\acute{a}s$, 853) to the gods which had lapsed through human impiety. This point about divine honour is crucial. A man who was, like Prometheus, famous for helping human beings might well stir divine resentment for that very reason, and this was the poet's opportunity to present Heracles as encroaching, though unmaliciously, on divine prerogatives. Iris then might have rejoined that that was precisely the point. But the gods care about nothing more than their honour, so they could hardly object to Heracles' efforts to restore it. If they did nevertheless object, Iris could easily have been made to say so.[28] Her reaction, on the other hand, is to tell Lyssa not to step outside of her defined role as the deity of insanity whose present mission is scarcely to practise *sōphrosunē* (857) of all things! Iris' reply is the sort of feeble ploy adopted by people who know that their position is indefensible. But that will come as no surprise to an audience who will expect Hera's motive to be sexual jealousy. So when Iris spoke of Heracles paying the penalty in order to maintain the status of the gods, she meant that gods cannot afford to appear powerless by failing to gratify their desires, and Hera, out of sexual jealousy and spite, was hostile to Heracles' very existence.

Heracles then is the victim of divine injustice, and this is hardly shocking in the traditional tragic cosmos. But once philosophers started to speculate about the gods, moral requirements began to be applied, and in a fragment of Euripides (292 N^2) a character asserts that when gods do evil they are not gods. Righteousness thus comes to be built into the very definition of deity. These philosophical speculations lie behind those embarrassing moral questions about divine motivation and behaviour which Euripidean characters are notorious for asking, whatever conclusions are to be drawn for specific passages.

Thus the sudden, unexpected peripeteia of the madness provokes us to query the nature of the hero's ethico-religious world. In the earlier suppliant scenes Amphitryon effectively suggested that we live in what might as well be a random universe since Zeus's complete unreliability is clear from his failure to respond to the claims of abstract right or *philia*. With the return of the hero all this was naturally and over-optimistically forgotten and the god seemed vindicated, and yet that return might as easily have been explained as the (fortuitous) 'favouring wind' (95) which Amphitryon hoped would come. Now with the sudden assault of the madness, the idea that the universe is pervaded by arbitrary *tuchē* regains credibility, at least in a certain sense. In the universe of traditional Greek religion *tuchē* in its abstract sense is never absolute, since divine actions are never completely unmotivated. In the *Troades* Poseidon accuses Athena who has just abandoned her support of the Greeks of 'leaping at random from one attitude to another' (*Tro.* 67–8), but this turns out to be unfair: the Greeks have offended her

---

[27] The 'paradoxical characterization of Lyssa' is 'specifically designed to point to the unjust conduct of Hera who is made to show gross vindictiveness towards a distinguished and innocent figure': Barlow (1996) 8.

[28] Heracles is 'entirely good throughout. If we look for *hamartiai*, signs of *hubris* or megalomania we shall dilute the responsibility of Hera and so blur the point of the play. . . . The greatness of Herakles provides the occasion for her attack, but it is not even the motive, far less the cause, and there is no *hubris*': Chalk (1962) 15.

by violating her temples (69). Later in the play Hecuba, commenting on the fall of Troy and the reversal of her fortunes, characterizes events (*tuchai*) as arbitrary like a madman (*Tro.* 1203–6), in imagery that recalls Poseidon's characterization of Athena. From the human perspective events can seem random, so that the madness, though intelligibly motivated as the product of Hera's hate, is nevertheless hardly an event that reflects a tightly and still less a morally ordered universe.[29]

Although the Greeks saw madness as a temporary or recurrent divine invasion of the mind,[30] Heracles may have been rendered more susceptible to such an invasion through his violent career and specifically his recent murder of Lycus, as his father suggests (966–7). Behaviour manifested during divinely imposed madness may or may not be in character. In our era we think of alcoholic intoxication as induced in the mind by a temporary invasion of chemicals, while recognizing that character is thereby usually distorted rather than rendered completely inoperative—though the distortion may be considerable. Heracles when mad behaves with great brutality towards his own children whom he mistakes for those of Eurystheus, and that contradicts his conscious attitude to children (or at least his *own* children) (633–6).[31] On the other hand, the hostility exercised against Eurystheus and his children is such as we might expect him to feel, and he certainly subscribes to the idea of taking a brutal revenge on his enemies—a view endorsed by Amphitryon at the prospect of viewing Lycus' corpse (731–3).

As Shelton remarks, although the madness is produced by 'Hera and the arbitrary will of the gods',[32] Heracles' 'decisions about travelling to Eurystheus' court have a shocking realism which indicates that the murder of Eurystheus would not be unwelcome even to the sane Herakles. The mad Herakles is fulfilling a suppressed desire. His seizure of insanity has not created a new personality, but has revealed the dangerous possibilities which existed in the old personality.'[33] For Barlow, the 'whole progress of the delusion step by step is a hideous parody of his career. . . . Had Heracles been really dealing with Eurystheus, he would have been continuing a career in much the same way as we have already seen previously, but the gods are able to disturb the mechanism of the brain so that his vision and perceptions are altered. He behaves habitually but against the wrong objects.'[34]

For G. J. Fitzgerald, Heracles' vindictive violence is a moral problem inherent in his whole nature and career. That his madness comes from Hera does not, according to Fitzgerald, absolve him of responsibility. Heracles 'does not behave uncharacteristically' when mad. (But surely one cannot be held responsible for one's mad acts, even if one *might* have performed similar acts when sane.) 'The slaughter of what he takes to be Eurystheus' family is thoroughly compatible with his usual modes and practices; not only the history of his accustomed deeds . . . but

---

[29] Chalk (1962) 15–16 goes too far in denying the Olympians of the play any human motives (Hera's motive is all too human) and calling them completely chaotic.

[30] Since we see Madness before she enters Heracles it is clear 'that tragic madness is something external, invading, daemonic, autonomous': Padel (1995) 20.

[31] Gregory (1991) 134 thinks that Heracles' sensitivity to his own children shows that the mad crimes violate his nature, but, as Griffiths (2006) 73 points out, 633–6 may mean that everyone loves children in general or just their own.

[32] Shelton (1979) 105–6.   [33] Ibid.   [34] Barlow (1996) 10.

his manifest apititude for and enjoyment in the slaughter makes that clear. The only trouble for him is that the context here is wrong.' Heracles 'does not need to be "mad" to kill Eurystheus' family—, those deeds carry through to achievement the "moral" propositions inherent in the desire and proclamation to kill Lycus . . . the "morality" involved in the proposed and eventual slaughter of Lycus is really that of pure "amoral vindictiveness" '.[35]

Again, more recently, Papadopoulou has argued that the madness 'uses the hero's modes of activity, familiar from his labours, and reverses them. The violence that he uses is the same violence he would use in another context of fighting against enemies while sane.'[36] By traditional standards, though, what is really distressing about the mad killings is not their sheer brutality but that they were directed in ignorance against the hero's nearest and dearest. Still, it is hard to believe that Euripides did not intend his audience to be revolted by the brutality per se of the mad Heracles. As Barlow has argued, the messenger speech confronts us with the reality rather than the romance of violence for the first time in the play.[37]

While Heracles' vindictive *attitude* is doubtless 'amoral' in the eyes of modern critics, it is completely in accord with the heroic ethic of harming enemies. The problem remains, however, of the *extraordinary* brutality of the mad killings, as was the case also in Sophocles' *Ajax.* That hero's perceptions are distorted by Athena, but the brutality of the killings suggests the exaggerated deeds of madness, involving as it does prolonged and gleeful torture of his 'enemies', rather than the martial spirit of the *Iliad* misdirected absurdly against domestic animals. Ajax's mad behaviour acts out nasty fantasies from which sane vengeance would surely recoil.[38] Similarly, in Heracles' case, it is by no means clear that the madness is limited to perceptual misconceptions and that the sane hero would have acted precisely in the same spirit against Eurystheus' children. On the contrary, there is a manic aspect to his rampage which should make us hesitate to characterize the sane Heracles, without more substantial evidence, as 'a man who is willing to use violence against children'.[39] Moreover, in this play and in *Trachiniae* the traditionally positive violence of the hero against *appropriate* enemies is strongly endorsed, and we have to remember that broad cultural condemnation of violence per se is a very recent phenomenon. Ajax, for all his limitations, remains a great hero, and that on the basis of his martial exploits. Similarly, Heracles' Labours remain his claim to fame throughout the play. If a contrary note is struck, the resulting uneasiness is never allowed to infect the argument. It is not implied, for example, that Heracles should turn his back on his whole career as a complete moral disaster. We shall return to this issue below.

---

[35] Fitzgerald (1991) 91–3. On Greek *schadenfreude* see Bond (1982) ad 731–3.

[36] Papadopoulou (2005) 80.

[37] Barlow (1982) *passim.*

[38] One thinks of the Iliadic Hecuba's fantasy of gratifying her hatred of Achilles by eating his liver raw (24. 212–13), and in our own day we hear otherwise mild-mannered people express the desire (which they would never dream of enacting) to punish particularly violent criminals (especially rapists) in extremely savage ways.

[39] Griffiths (2006) 74.

AFTER THE MADNESS

As the hero regains consciousness his initial experience is an unaccustomed loss of mental and physical control. His mind is confused (1091), his breath hot and unsteady (1092–3), and he is surprised to find himself anchored like a ship, with ropes around his chest and arms (1094–5). The moral and psychological debilitation of Heracles in this final section of the play will be echoed in his physical state, and at the end he will be scarcely able to move, as if grief has deprived him even of his physical prowess (1394–8, 1402–3, 1406, 1423–4). Moreover, he is denuded of his defensive weapons, his bow and arrows (1098–100), and though he does not appear to be back in Hades (1101–4) in his disorientation he needs the assistance of a friend (1106–8).

Once informed by Amphitryon of the details of the madness and the murder of his family, Heracles sees no option but suicide in order to avenge his children and escape ill-fame (δύσκλειαν) (1146–52).[40] As Barlow observes, '[i]t is significant that when confronted with the misuse of his physical strength which kills his wife and children his first instinct is again a physical response, namely to kill himself.'[41] But, unlike Ajax, he does not reflect carefully on how this is to be done. 'He has no lyric outburst of despair nor does he agonise in extended long speeches about his suicide as Sophocles' Ajax does . . . As a man of action he decides instantly what he must do, and this propensity to act quickly is characteristic of what we know of him from the efficient execution of the Labours and the murder of Lycus.'[42]

Moreover, while Ajax was intent on recovering his honour through an appropriate and appropriately orchestrated act of courage (457 ff., especially 479–80), Heracles, like Oedipus with the self-blinding, is concerned merely to obliterate consciousness, and especially consciousness of dishonour. Accordingly, he is casual about the means of suicide: the point is simply to be dead; there is no consideration of being *honourably* dead. And it seems we are to assume that he would have proceeded directly to the act of self-slaughter had he not been interrupted by the arrival of Theseus (1153–4). Heracles remains intent on self-annihilation; his shame will now be keenly felt in the presence of his greatest friend, but, as for Oedipus, his concern extends beyond himself to his *philoi* whom he would not allow to be contaminated by his pollution (1155–62). Accordingly he veils his head.

But Theseus, who at first fails to recognize his mighty but fallen friend (1189), is undeterred (1198–205). He points out that nothing can really conceal the terrible reality (1214–17). It is time for him to repay Heracles' *philia* (1214–25), and he believes that *philia* transcends pollution—as does deity (1231–4). Theseus' view that pollution cannot infect a friend (1231–5),[43] if true, saves Heracles from the

---

[40] Barlow (1996) 13. 'Heracles at once decides to kill himself; realization and decision coincide, as Kroeker (1938) 81–2 remarks . . . Heracles' motives for suicide are well analysed by Adkins, CQ ns 16 (1966), 214 f.: (i) grief, 1147; (ii) the desire for justice, 1150; (iii) fear of a bad reputation, 1152': Bond (1982) ad 1146–52.

[41] Barlow (1996) 13. As Lattimore (1964) 43 remarks, Heracles 'assumes, rather than decides, that he must kill himself'.

[42] Barlow (1996) ad 1146 ff.

[43] On pollution see Bond (1982) ad 1155. 'Theseus' arguments against pollution, although extreme, are plausible and conform to cultural changes that were already on foot; and the traditionalist might

terrible moral void into which Oedipus was thrust, leaving him free to communicate with and receive succour from his friend and to ponder his own guilt or innocence. For the moment, though, Heracles is resolved to die because he has reached the extremity of suffering (1239–47, 1251, 1257). But Theseus insists that this would be wrong for him. Amphitryon feels too that suicide would be a further impiety on top of that of the mad killings and that Heracles' suicidal predisposition is a function of his wild lion's *thumos*—i.e. the passionate warrior spirit now turned against himself (1210–13).

The conditions of the lives of certain Sophoclean characters, such as Jocasta in *OT* or Eurydice in *Antigone*, fall below an acceptable level for various obvious reasons. Deianeira and Ajax feel the same, but their predicaments are defined and compounded by a sense of a loss of personal worth. Deianeira feels that she has lost the most important person in her life by her own moral lapse, while Ajax believes that there is no point in life without the honour which can now be restored to him only by suicide. Similarly, it is easy to see why the Euripidean Heracles would feel that his life is unliveable: he has killed his wife and children for whom his Labours were largely performed, and by means of the very qualities for which he was most admired. (Ajax's *aretē* is similarly turned against him by a goddess, but he continues to embrace his sane intention to kill his human enemies.) Heracles is utterly disgraced. What could conceivably be salvaged from that?

But suicide, Theseus believes, would be the response of the 'ordinary man' (ἐπιτυχόντος ἀνθρώπου, 1248), whereas Heracles is the great endurer (ὁ πολλὰ ... τλὰς Ἡρακλῆς, 1250), the benefactor and mighty friend of mortals (εὐεργέτης βροτοῖσι καὶ μέγας φίλος, 1252). Greece would not endure his dying through ἀμαθία (1254), i.e. through a morally insensitive view of the situation. Heracles, however, argues that he has not misconceived things at all. For him his life is indeed unliveable (ἀβίωτον, 1257). First of all, his origins, mortal and immortal, were dubious, as his mortal father Amphitryon was polluted for having killed Heracles' maternal grandfather, while his divine paternity entailed the hostility of Hera (1258–64). While he was still a baby Hera tried to kill him by putting snakes in his cradle, and when he grew up he had endless Labours to perform (1266–78). Now that he is polluted from having killed his family he cannot continue to live in Thebes, nor will he be welcome elsewhere; even the earth itself will reject him so that his life will be miserable and useless; let Hera celebrate for having destroyed 'the innocent benefactor of Greece' (τοὺς εὐεργέτας Ἑλλάδος ... οὐδὲν ὄντας αἰτίους) (1279–1310). Heracles thus feels shame at his mad acts, but not guilt.[44]

Heracles in this speech has dwelt entirely on the negatives—his subjection to *tychai*, as Theseus interprets his speech (1314)—including experiences which he was previously able to ignore in his success or to interpet more positively. The Labours for example were not meaningless tasks but services to humanity, as he admits himself in protesting against Hera's injustice (1307–10). Ajax never

have little to offer in opposition except instinctive feelings of propriety': Michelini (1987) 273. 'For the Euripidean Theseus, it is morally inconceivable that the universe should, through pollution, set obstacles in the way of friendship, but he is not concerned to deny the need for purification': R. C. T. Parker (1983) 310.

[44] As Shelton (1979) 107 remarks, he does not feel guilt, but he does accept responsibility.

devalues his former achievements in this way, but Heracles' terrible pollution combined with his profound (and justified) disillusion with the gods and loss of belief in a just universe has brought him to despair. (Ajax disapproves of the world in the deception speech, but he stops well short of outright moral condemnation of Athena.) Heracles can hardly define himself as καλλίνικος (cf. 582) over his own slaughtered children or boast of his independence of *tuchē*. But he remains a *philos*—though one who must now, on the basis of his former exploits, receive rather than confer favours—and, above all, a man of endurance, the quality by which he must now chiefly define (or rather redefine) himself.

Theseus argues that, since the gods are subject to such *tychai* (misfortunes), still more must mortals accept them. He proposes to take Heracles to Athens, to cleanse his hands of blood, and to give him a share of his own fortune. When he dies he will be honoured by the Athenians for his services to Greece—all of this in return for his services to Theseus (1322–37). It would appear then that the pollution can be removed and that Athens at least will not reject the mighty hero. (The Colonean Oedipus is unacceptable in Thebes, but his services likewise qualify him to be honoured in Athens by a Sophoclean Theseus.) Perhaps the extent of humanity's debt to Heracles makes the need for repayment in some form prevail over the conventional belief in his pollution. Athens, if no other city, will honour the man as he deserves. Suicide then, though the logical course for Ajax, would not be so for Heracles; it would be a failure of endurance in the great endurer.

This idea of endurance and adaptation to *tuchē* or circumstances, sometimes in the hope of a better future, is characteristically Euripidean. In the bleak world of Euripides' *Troades*, for example, when Andromache continues to define herself as Hector's wife—a moral self-definition because she sees herself as having fulfilled the role in an exemplary way—and is now faced with the prospect of sleeping with (of all people) Neoptolemus, Hecuba advises her to compromise and to try to love her new partner, even though this means betraying her dead husband (*Tro.* 643–705). What makes this case especially interesting is the moral uncertainty that attaches to it. The dramatist does not enlist the audience's sympathies for one view over the other, and it is by no means clear that loyalty to a dead husband is a moral imperative that should trump the advantages to be gained from not alienating Achilles' son.

For Heracles, though, adaptation is indeed the morally appropriate response, and it harmonizes with his character and career. It is thus for this hero a moral end in itself, despite a future that promises to be anticlimactic, rather than the means to some greater moral end. On the other hand, the moral focus of Sophocles' heroic endurers—Electra, Philoctetes, and the Colonean Oedipus—is not the endurance itself. Electra, for example, is focused on avenging her father, and her endurance is a necessary condition of doing that effectively. All three refuse to compromise morally in their endurance, and two of them, at least (Electra and Oedipus), await a morally appropriate consummation and not simply a more pleasant future.

Theseus thinks Heracles should endure, but he does not suggest that his friend will continue to be useful to humanity (except, ironically, through cult after his death) or that his life will be happy, pleasurable, or rewarding. It is simply a question of his conforming to a self-conception, or rather, in this case, to a (true) conception of himself held by others (cf. 1254), and it is as if Heracles owes this to the world as much as to himself. This social or, so to speak, extraverted aspect of the hero's definition and meaning contrasts markedly with the moral isolation of Ajax. It contrasts also with the Sophoclean protagonists' ability to define themselves in the most positive way even in the face of disaster and thus rise to the noblest response. This more vulnerable Euripidean hero needs a friend to remind him of his valid self-definition.[45]

HERACLES' TRULY DIVINE DIVINITY

Heracles, however, rejects Theseus' idea that the gods' alleged toleration of their exposure to the blows of fortune proves that human beings must be similarly tolerant (1340–6), though he goes on at once to accept the need to endure, independently of the argument from what the gods supposedly endure. Theseus' view of the gods though gives Heracles a chance to define his own position, and he offers a view which is notoriously incompatible with his own myth. Critics differ over whether the reference to divine adultery applies outside the gods' own mutual relations and in particular whether it applies to Zeus's relations with Alcmene and thereby undermines the whole Heracles myth, but the requirement that a god if truly god needs nothing (and nobody) (1345–6) logically at least carries us entirely beyond the boundaries of anthropomorphic polytheism.[46]

Let us begin with the contention that the theological critique applies only to the gods' mutual relations, and that Zeus's adultery with the mortal Alcmene—one of the play's basic presuppositions—is not at issue. Grube, for example, would have it that

there are no adulterous relationships *between gods* . . . [Heracles] does not explicitly deny the story of his own birth; the audience, even the poet, may not have been alive to the implications, because in their own day there must have been many who would accept myths about the divine birth of Heracles without a murmur but who would never accept the cruder stories of immorality on Olympus.[47]

In a similar vein, Burnett sees the lines as belonging to 'a recognized class of ancient passages in which a speaker decides not to attack but to select and censor his mythic truths'.[48] Such passages certainly exist, and it would be unreasonable to demand philosophical consistency from a dramatist or his audience, but, as Halleran argues, the observations naturally apply to Heracles:

---

[45] Lattimore (1964) 43 observes, 'a moral point has been established by sound rhetoric, but we lack that effect of dramatic compulsion which comes from the concerted drive of character and circumstance'.

[46] Gregory (1991) 146 thinks that the hero's 'fundamental faith in the gods remains unshaken, and he chooses to condemn the false stories that have been told about the gods rather than the gods themselves'. But this is not compatible with rejecting Hera as an object of worship or requiring a god to be entirely independent. Heracles is effectively rejecting the traditional gods.

[47] Grube (1961) 58: his emphasis.

[48] Burnett (1971) 174. See also Gregory (1977) 273 and (1991) 153 n. 51. Also Bond (1982) ad loc.

Theseus' words reply to and even echo the end of Herakles' speech, his condemnation of Hera in which he refers to this union.... And Herakles' pronouncement does apply to his own case, even if he does not expressly say so. True, he does not refer specifically to his own circumstances, but in replying to Theseus' assertions, he echoes his earlier condemnation of Hera's sexual jealousy, the condemnation that concluded his previous speech. And Hera's anger at Zeus's adultery motivates the entire action of the drama.[49]

But how are we to reconcile the god who has no needs with the notorious activities of the Olympians and, for that matter, with the whole principle of 'well-oiled anthropomorphic polytheism'[50] with its interdependent gods? The tone of the hero's statement strongly suggests contemporary philosophical speculation. Commenting on this passage, Guthrie observes:

> Besides moral probity, self-sufficiency was being demanded as an essential property of deity. Aided perhaps by Xenophanes and Eleatic notions of God as 'unmoved' and 'impassible', the rationalism of the time saw the godhead as 'lacking nothing'. These words of Euripides's Heracles can hardly be unconnected with the pronouncement of Antiphon: 'For this reason he has need of nothing, nor does he expect anything from anybody, but is infinite and all-sufficient.[51]

The theology of the passage is clearly at odds with the gods of the play. Desch therefore suggests that Heracles recognizes the activities of the beings we call the gods but refuses to dignify them with that name.[52] This is an attractive solution; the hero, however, seems to reject not just the idea that the gods figure in unedifying stories, but the stories themselves (1346). Moreover, Heracles soon reverts to traditional concepts, referring to Cerberus (1386) (whose existence presumably implies the corresponding existence of the traditional divine universe), and to how they were all destroyed by a single blow (τύχη, 1393) from Hera.

The only escape therefore from acknowledging a contradiction at the heart of the drama is to claim that the implications of the passage are not to be carried beyond the immediate context,[53] though they may be lifted out of the play to set up an ironic interplay with the literal dramatic action.[54] In the words of Michelini, in 'the plane of the play's mimesis of reality, what Heracles says is patently untrue', but with 'the overt reference to the possibility that the *logoi* of the poets may be false, we are forced to consider that *Herakles* itself ... is also a mere fiction'.[55] This view, though rather at odds with modern notions of literary unity, gains some plausibility when we compare Hecuba's appeal, at *Troades* 884–8, to a philosopher's conception of Zeus that is sublimely irrelevant to the surrounding drama.

---

[49] Halleran (1986) 178–9. Also Heath (1987) 61 n. 42.
[50] The term is Burnett's (1971) 175.
[51] Guthrie (1971) 230.
[52] Ibid. 20–1.
[53] Variations on this theme appear in Halleran (1986) 178–9; Heath (1987) 61.
[54] See Halleran (1986) 179–80; Vickers (1973) 324.
[55] Michelini (1987) 275. See also Rehm (1999–2000) 373: 'By attacking the traditional accounts of the gods, Heracles calls into question the very story that he finds himself in, and from which he cannot escape.... The theater becomes a place to examine the underpinnings of both the given myth of Heracles and Euripides' radical new version.'

To suggest that Heracles is mistaken in the play's terms might seem to have the strange consequence of making the less sophisticated theology the true one. On the other hand, the apparent sophistication of the hero's truly divine deity conceals its irrelevance to the human condition. What we need is not an aloof and independent god, but a just god who intervenes in human affairs to forestall or at least correct or punish the abuses described by Amphitryon and the chorus earlier on.

Certainly the universe of the traditional gods of the play, whether 'gods' is the right name for them, or whatever their ontological status, represents the real conditions of human life much better than does Heracles' god that is truly god,[56] and it is the real conditions of human life which the hero has to accommodate. But what are those conditions in the play's terms? At the outset, in the suppliant scene, the drama is set in the rather vaguely defined but familiar universe of Greek tragedy, but the emphasis is on arbitrary *tuchē*, while the justice of Zeus is called into question. While the existence at least of the traditional gods is taken for granted, greater emphasis is placed on forces or principles such as fortune, necessity, and time—forces which, it must be conceded, may be closely associated with the gods or originate with them. But, with the arrival of Heracles and the slaughter of Lycus, Zeus appears vindicated; and, if an audience has the time and the inclination to reflect on Amphitryon's emphasis on *tuchē* and his criticisms of Zeus, they will conclude that he was in error. In any event, at this point they will have adjusted themselves comfortably back into a world in which the gods are more actively engaged. But the debate between Iris and Lyssa exposes the gods as unjust—not an untraditional view, but calculated here to stir our indignation against them. This feeling is further fuelled by Heracles' anger at his tormentor which comes to a head in his rhetorical question: 'Who would pray to such a goddess?' (1307–8). This idea must have seemed more radical to the ancients who might have rejoined, 'Any one with sense would pray to such a goddess; just look at the fate of Hippolytus!' But Heracles is of course implying that Hera is morally unworthy of the normal divine worship (a consideration that would carry much more weight in our era), and he has already dismissed Zeus as unworthy of the paternal role (1266), thus embracing his own nature as entirely human.[57] The Greeks, unlike Heracles, did not insist on moral perfection from their gods; they prayed to them to gain favours or avoid disasters. Heracles, however, can expect nothing positive from Hera.

So the hero, for all intents and purposes, lives in a secular world, for all that he goes on to refer to *Hera's tuchē*.[58] It does not really matter, in the final analysis,

---

[56] Although in Heracles' reflections on the nature of divinity Mastronarde (1986) 208 sees 'the psychological reflex of a good man defiantly insisting on imposing an ideal order and morality on experience', Heracles' god is as remote as Aristotle's and presumably as uninvolved in human affairs as the gods of Epicurus.

[57] Line 1265 'throws out all the panoply with which Heracles has been celebrated throughout his life. This one line destroys the semi-divine image of his miraculous birth which has sustained the faith of the Chorus. In the end he is rehabilitated not by his divine connections but by his own human friends and relatives': Barlow (1996) 9.

[58] According to Foley (1985) 164–5, 'Heracles' slavery to divine *tyche* . . . seems to imply a continued relation to divinity but no confidence in a divine justice.' If such a relation exists, the breakdown of ritual and worship implied by 1307–8 makes it tenuous indeed. As Kroeker (1938) 124 concludes,

whether or not Heracles or the play's audience believe in the play's gods as literally conceived. The important question concerns how and why Heracles is to go on living in a world of *tuchai* which, whether or not they proceed from gods, may as well be arbitrary. Similarly, in Aeschylus' *Seven*, where, unlike in this play, there is absolutely no doubt about the gods' existence, for the short remaining period of his life Eteocles can dispense with them now that he has accepted the inevitability of his death and they want no more from him. The position of Sophocles' *Ajax*, on the other hand, is rather different in that in his final speech he prays for an easy death and passage to Hades.

HERACLES REDEFINES HIMSELF

Though Heracles rejects Theseus' theology, he accepts his moral position on the question of human suffering and he is apparently encouraged by his friend's generous offer.[59] His change of mind may seem too sudden, though realistic depiction of gradual mind change (and indeed of the passage of time in which such changes occur) is perhaps alien to the compressed genre of tragedy. Heracles has just been speaking of the uselessness of his future life and of his total rejection by human society and the natural realm alike. Certainly Theseus' example proves that not all men will reject him, but is ritual cleansing sufficient to overcome the pollution? In any case, Heracles suddenly decides that cowardice ($\delta\epsilon\iota\lambda\iota\alpha\nu$, 1348) is not an option and that in order to face a man's spear he will need to endure psychological misfortunes as well.[60] His priority then seems to be to retain or recover his self-conception as the brave warrior, and for this reason too he must keep the bow (1382–5).[61]

Hera's divinity is questionable, but not her power. For Arrowsmith (1956) 51 'Hera, who in legend made Heracles mad, passes almost insensibly into a hovering symbol of all those irrational and random necessities which the Greek and the play call *Tyche*.'

[59] 'For the victim... the consequence of his pollution lies not so much in immediate danger as in social stigma. Theseus gives Heracles courage to live on by showing him that he is not, after all, wholly cut off from his fellow men. With infinite delicacy he persuades Heracles to confront the outside world, first passively by sight, then by speech, and finally by actual physical contact with one who is not polluted': R. C. T. Parker (1983) 317. See also ibid. 109: 'it seems [for Heracles here, as for Oedipus at Thebes] that pollution derives not from the wrong to the victim, but from the violation of the order of the family; there is expressed through it universal shock, not the particular anger of the victim and his kin'.

[60] For Zürcher (1947) 90–107 Heracles essentially has always been the endurer; tested by the madness, he weakens momentarily only to develop a deeper, more spiritual endurance. According to Yoshitake (1994) 145, 'It is true that Herakles recognises that suicide is $\delta\epsilon\iota\lambda\iota\alpha$, but it is not this recognition... that actually enables the hero to give up the notion of suicide. We are led to think that Herakles rejects suicide on the one hand because he is freed from the threat of disgrace and despair, and on the other because it is inadmissible in this society for a male to commit suicide by reason of grief and self-reproach. The drama rather implies that even Herakles is not able to endure disgrace and despair.'

[61] The new *aretē* contains the old, and 'understanding, induced by suffering, of the hateful implications of action': Chalk (1962) 14. Heracles does not reject his past but 'he adds to his old *aretē* a new kind involving moral rather than physical courage and this enhances his old reputation and transforms him out of the past into a more modern figure': Barlow (1996) 13–14.

Such a life though is undeniably very bleak. Previously Heracles' *philia* towards
his family motivated his Labours and he could enjoy his reputation as the great
endurer and benefactor of Greece. That reputation remains, though undoubtedly
rendered problematical by his pollution, but it is hard not to feel that his career is
over for all that he speaks of standing up to the spears of men (1349–50). He is in
reality a broken man, a slave to chance (1357), permanently saddened by the
terrible ambivalence of his great capacities as symbolized by the bow that protected and will continue to protect him and yet killed his family. The madness is
an adversary he had no chance of defeating, and is surely the most powerful
symbol imaginable of our complete and permanent subservience to arbitrary
forces beyond our control; the independence of the bow (203) has turned out to
be an illusion. Indeed, although Heracles has resolved to withstand the blows of
fortune, the final impressions are of a man who is not yet coping.[62] He asks
Theseus to accompany him to Argos (with Cerberus) for fear of 'suffering some
misfortune' (presumably a euphemism for suicide)[63] when alone and grieving for
the children' (1388), and he leaves the stage physically supported by Theseus,
'totally destroyed and like a boat under tow' (1424), as dependent on his friend as
his children were on him (cf. 631).[64]

We have seen that in retaining the bow the hero is accepting that his capacities
(as symbolized by that weapon) could result in evil as well as good. But we
encounter here the same limitations of individual self-knowledge that we find in
the case of Oedipus. Oedipus accepts that in some degree and sense he created his
own destiny, but he never recognizes a link between that destiny and traits such as
his violent impulsiveness. In the case of Euripides' hero we might also want to
extend awareness further than Heracles does himself, recognizing that violence by
its very nature contains the seeds of evil, and that there is something strange about
the idea of eliminating 'bad' violence by means of 'good'. But this is perhaps an
anachronistic response, and Heracles does not reject the Labours; nor indeed does
the play. The point is not that the hero's entire career was a mistake, but that
violence can be horrendously self-destructive when normal consciousness and
therefore moral autonomy are in abeyance, and if that is a kind of self-knowledge
it is of the more general kind; it is a truth about human nature as such, though
strikingly exemplified in Heracles.

Euripides' dramatization of that part of the Heracles myth in which the hero is
married to Megara is problematical in that the traditional material provides no
sense of closure. Traditionally, his Labours follow the madness and atone for it,
so that Heracles can make a new start, winning glory and attaining the summit
of his self-definition through the Labours and then proceed to the final tragedy

[62] The final image of Heracles 'is not that of a superman who is ready to endure any ill, but that of an
ordinary human being who struggles and will have to *continue* to struggle against grief and self-
reproach': Yoshitake (1994) 145 (his emphasis). For Lesky (1966*b*) 381, the hero 'is shown in the
second part as the wretched, broken man of sorrows, who now needs his strength only to drag himself
through a life of the deepest misery'.

[63] Chalk (1962) 13–14.

[64] Arrowsmith (1956) 53 is more optimistic in believing that the play 'imposes suffering upon men
as their tragic condition, but it also discovers a courage equal to that necessity, a courage founded on
love . . . a new internal courage . . . with the addition of love and perseverance against an intolerable
necessity'. (But to translate *philia* by the English 'love' imports inappropriate connotations.)

(or apotheosis) in the Deianeira section of the myth. Euripides, however, cannot reconnect his play with the tradition. The glory his Heracles won by the Labours has been tarnished by the subsequent madness, and there would have been little point in suggesting that he went off to marry Deianeira and performed various other exploits followed by his death on the pyre, with the attached problem of what to do about the apotheosis.

The end of *Heracles* comes as close as the myth allows to suggesting virtual death.[65] Heracles speaks of enduring and defeating enemies with the bow (1382–5), but there is no sense that he is about to embark on further exploits; he is to settle down in retirement at Athens and (one imagines) wait, anticlimactically, for death rather than for an apotheosis unsuited to the new secular Heracles in his secular universe. A divine epiphany at the end summarizing the traditional future with an apotheosis would have produced the jarring effect of the epilogue of the *Orestes*. Anticlimax seems very much in keeping with a bleak, demythologized, secular world. After all, the Labours have lost much of their significance: the gods, whatever they are in the final analysis, do not appreciate Heracles' defence of their prerogatives, the hero's benefactions to humanity have met with no gratitude except from Theseus, and the whole idea of civilizing the world by cleansing it of evil has been shown to be illusory since evil is still very much with us and in the mind of the would-be civilizer himself. Papadopoulou argues that the sane and the mad violence of Heracles are closely connected through the revenge ethic which reduces the revenger to the level of savagery of the victim he would punish.[66] Still, the play seems to insist on the protagonist's moral integrity, while intimating (at most) that the ethic which that protagonist espouses and which the play itself apparently accepts is nevertheless more deeply problematical. The only optimistic note is struck in the behaviour of Theseus who perhaps to some degree redeems humanity's ingratitude. Theseus of course represents Athens, so again it is the Athenians who alone seem capable of accommodating and appreciating polluted heroes—men such as Orestes, Oedipus, and now Heracles.

Foley argues that the new Heracles is 'an untraditional, spiritualized hero equal to the mutability of human life and valuable for the Athenian *polis*'.[67] But it is not easy to see precisely in what that usefulness consists beyond providing a model of chastened acceptance. For how exactly can ritual continue to be effective when a constructive relationship with the traditional gods has broken down? The role that Foley suggests for the hero in his new context is one of submission and accommodation, rather than inspiration. The play, she states, 'implicitly demonstrates that the ideal of the archaic hero and his individualistic heroism need not conflict with Athenian political ideals, provided that the hero submits to the city, retains self-control, and remains marginal to its higher political life'.[68] But what on earth would be the point—exemplary or inspirational—of such depressing emasculation of a great hero?

---

[65] See Gibert (1995) 141–3.

[66] Papadopoulou (2001a) *passim*; especially 116, 120.

[67] Foley (1985) 150. See also Gregory (1991) 123: 'In consequence of his suffering he develops a scheme of values consonant with the ideology of the democratic polis. Euripides has succeeded in appropriating the panhellenic hero for Athens.'

[68] Foley (1985) 175.

HERACLES' CHARACTERIZATION

There is something strangely unsatisfying about the characterization of the
Euripidean Heracles. He seems designed to illustrate a thesis and to lack the
flesh and blood of Sophocles' heroes or, for that matter, of the Euripidean Medea.
This is in part, perhaps, because he is introduced late into the play in such a way as
to fit into a pre-arranged causal and thematic nexus. In this respect he resembles
Aeschylus' Agamemnon whose career at Troy, like Heracles' Labours, is already
behind him and interpreted for the audience. In the scenes before his entrance,
Agamemnon takes abstract shape as a man, an Atreid, a general who for those
reasons can be expected to act in certain ways as conveyed in the imagery and
moralizing of the choral odes. Heracles we know is the man who pretends to
independence of *tuchē* through his use of the bow (hardly a personal touch) and
the man of the Labours which are celebrated in the great ode. But, as Barlow has
acutely observed, there is something insubstantial, remote, and romanticized
about the evocation of the Labours, which belong to the pretty and often escapist
world of the Euripidean choral ode, a world whose connection to the rest of the
play is often problematic. The effect, at any rate, is of a contrast between a
romanticized heroic world viewed almost pictorially and without moral piquancy
and the 'real' world of the play. As Barlow suggests, the messenger's description of
the mad slaughter of the family seems much more real, and this is because it has
the brutal realism of a Euripidean messenger speech.[69]

When Heracles returns, we are invited to see him as a sensitive father and
husband, which seems quite at odds with his career,[70] to the point that Kamerbeek
has suggested that the tension between the sensitive 'domestic' Heracles and the
traditional Dorian hero has produced the madness by a massive stress reaction.[71]
The theory is attractive, but, unfortunately, there is insufficient evidence for it in
the text and in any case a causal explanation of that kind is perhaps anachronistic
in suggesting a modern mental illness.[72] Above all, it undermines the *tuchē* theme,
and Heracles himself sees the madness as a *tuchē* in the strong sense of 'random
event'. The domestic Heracles fits, however, the theme of dependence and *philia*.
It is as if Euripides is saying that the 'epinician' Heracles as son of a non-existent
Zeus is really, as Silk argues, an impossibility, so that when he is brought down to

---

[69] 'The stylistic devices used by Euripides to present the first stasimon (348 ff.), and the messenger
speech (922 ff.)' make 'the Labours, great though they are, seem part of a mythical fairytale world and
the murder of the children an act of grim realism': Barlow (1996) 11 and ad 348–441. See also Barlow
(1982) *passim*.

[70] 'The Euripidean Heracles' hugeness is made to coexist with an almost Hellenistic ordinariness:
a coexistence as thought-provoking as it is (in point of theatrical character-portrayal) absurd': Silk
(1993) 128.

[71] Kamerbeek (1966) *passim*. See also Pohlenz (1954) 299–300. Bond (1982) ad 562–82 rightly
demurs: 'We must beware of explaining his heroic behaviour in terms applicable to the mental
afflictions of our modern contemporaries. Amphitryon's suggestion that Heracles was maddened by
blood lust (966 f.) is respectable, for blood lust is heroic. But we must not explain Heracles' eventual
madness as caused by his being deranged by the shock of finding his family on the point of death.'

[72] Barlow (1996) ad 20–1 suggests, equally anachronistically in the implication of modern mental
illness, that the madness can be viewed 'as an impersonal destiny, say, which might include a given
nature, a rationalistic explanation' for which the divine motivation is a kind of 'metaphor for some
inexorable compulsion of the hero's own inner self'.

size by Hera/*tuchē*, it is more significantly the shrinking of an extravagant mythic conception of Heracles.

The suppliant scenes present weak, believably human characters living in an unjust universe dominated by random events. The Heracles of the Labours lives in an artificial world because Zeus will not let ordinary human harm happen to him and because he has superhuman *aretē* in physical strength and prowess and a superhuman moral dimension in that he has worked to help gods as well as mortals. This artificial world is able to withstand the slaughter of Lycus but after that it disintegrates. The madness relegates the hero to the human world in which he disowns the paternity of Zeus. Heracles' challenge is to accept the blows of an unjust fortune and to live on without the prospect of *eudaimonia*. To achieve this he will need a measure of his earthly father's tenuously justified optimism and an even greater portion of his wife's noble acceptance of necessity. Morally, he is required to extend his ability to endure into a wider arena that includes his own despairing thoughts as the desire arises in him to end his life. The Aristotelian moral agent strives for the good life, but after the catastrophe Heracles strives only for the sake of realizing a conception of himself.[73] This motivational basis indicates that he subscribes less to a virtue ethic (like Aristotle's) than to what we might term a 'self-concept ethic'—and in this he continues in the heroic tradition.

CONCLUSION

Like Oedipus, Heracles is faced with two crises, one that represents little challenge and another that requires self-redefinition. Thus Heracles has as little trouble with Lycus as Oedipus has in addressing the problem of the plague; the real test comes later. In responding to the consequences of the madness, Heracles, uniquely among the agents we examine, requires the moral support of a friend. (Certainly the Aeschylean Orestes consults Pylades, but his uncertainty is momentary and not profound. Heracles, on the other hand, is faced with a radical adjustment.) Heracles has always defined himself as a great warrior, independent of *tuchē* through the bow that is also the emblem of his capability, but also as the great endurer and friend of humanity. Now only endurance is left, and he must adapt that quality to a new kind of challenge in a new kind of essentially secular world in which *tuchē* prevails. Indeed, as Papadopoulou well observes, 'The extremity of Heracles' reaction against the gods, which matches the extremity of his suffering, turns out to be a catalyst for his assertion of his wish to live.'[74] This matter of self-redefinition is, typically in the heroic context, a moral issue. Emotionally, Heracles is still weak and remains so until the end of the play, and there is a strong sense that, in his 'retirement' in Athens, he will have to struggle for the rest of his life, not with external adversaries, but with despair.

---

[73] The Oedipus of the *Tyrannus* similarly has no positive expectations, but is guided by a sense of a destiny which he must accept. He too is motivated by a 'self-concept' ethic, though of an appallingly negative kind at the end.

[74] Papadopoulou (2005) 188.

15

Euripides: *Electra*

INTRODUCTION

Euripides' *Electra* (and to an even greater extent his *Orestes*) is a self-consciously theatrical and intertextual play. As Goldhill observes: 'Through the explicit and innovative use of theatrical device, the bold intertextuality with other plays, through the explicit marking and undercutting of the formal elements of tragedy, through the aggressive subversion of expectation and rapid variation of levels of reality, Euripides constantly forces awareness of his theatre as theatre.'[1]

The intertextuality relates certainly to Aeschylus' *Oresteia* with its traditional tragic forms and heroic ambience, and perhaps to Sophocles' own *Electra* and to other poetic or dramatic texts now lost to us. Thus the play's notorious realism, explored in detail by Gellie (1981), should be viewed in its relation to such heroic expectations, as Goldhill (1986) and Michelini (1987) in particular have insisted. We are brought to judge the characters in heroic terms, while they are denied both the heroic *eugeneia* and the heroic milieu required to enact their traditional roles. Electra is committed to the assassination of her father's killers and Orestes has returned for that purpose, but the pressure to act comes to a significant degree from the extra-dramatic mythological tradition as well as from personal commitment (in Electra's case, at least), and the matricide in particular is an atrocity in part because of the realistic milieu in which it must be enacted.

THE MORAL AMBIENCE

The moral ambience of Sophocles' drama is largely defined by the heroic characters that dominate his plays. His Electra, for example, provides the moral filter through which we react to the tyranny in Argos. Behind the individual morality of such characters is a heroic, aristocratic tradition of moral *eugeneia*. This unifying filter is absent from Euripides' *Electra*. The protagonist herself subscribes more or less unreflectingly to the obvious and conventional view that her father's killers are evil people deserving of punishment but appears to hold no view at all as to her own moral obligations in regard to them; she predictably believes that Orestes

---

[1] Goldhill (1986) 252–3. What we might call the self-consciousness of this play is nicely brought out by Pelling (2005) 86: 'The play is full of roles to play, functions to perform, burdens to carry, persons to try to be. And nothing sits easily on anyone.'

should take revenge on them, but, as their victim, she is too caught up in her negative *feelings* about them to think with any moral clarity.

Electra's broader moral context then is not the *eugeneia* tradition; indeed the validity of that tradition is radically undermined. In particular, Orestes himself, with unconscious irony, ponders the source and nature of true manliness or courage (εὐανδρίαν, 367). He is later to be accused of its opposite (ἀνανδρίαν, 982). Heredity, he decides, is no guide, since a noble (γενναίου, 369) father can produce a 'nobody' (τὸ μηδὲν ὄντα, 370), good offspring can result from bad parents, while intelligence and good sense can be found in a poor man, and a dearth of those qualities in a rich one (367–72). He concludes that it is safest to judge people by their characters and by the company they keep (384–5). We are hereby warned not to assume that traditional inherited nobility exists to supply the basis for serious moral commitment, and by the standard of his behaviour the peasant farmer is a noble man. Nevertheless, his moral *eugeneia* must remain largely inoperative, since he can have no influence outside his own narrow domestic sphere. Wealth may be irrelevant to true nobility, but it is essential to effective action in the wider world.

When the familiar Sophoclean adjectives *sōphrōn*, *gennaios*, and *eusebēs* appear in the play (53, 253, 261–2), they refer to the farmer who is poor—though his character (*ēthos*) is not (as we have seen) ignoble (δυσγενές) (363)—rather than to any of the 'noble' characters. Electra's sense of nobility, in so far as it exists, relates almost entirely to the expected concomitant material perquisites, a sure sign of a degenerate aristocracy, and Orestes' democratic reflections on nobility level the characters of the play. As O'Brien points out, the major characters' basic motive is fear, which calls to mind the typically Euripidean focus on victims rather than agents.[2] But the passivity of the characters is not restricted to their psychology and morality; there is a noticeable emphasis on the role of chance (*tuchē*) in the moulding of external circumstances. Orestes returns with no definite plan and is advised to improvise as fortune directs (639, 648).

Agamemnon's killers, in particular, are shown to be motivated by fear. Aegisthus, according to the reliable peasant, was intent upon killing both Orestes and Electra, out of fear rather than sheer malice (22, 25); and Clytemnestra was able to talk her lover out of killing Electra with a scheme that would lay this fear to rest. Her motive in this, however, was neither love nor even pity, but fear of what people would think if she condoned the murder of her own child (30). In contrast to such moral vacuity, Electra's peasant husband has waived his conjugal rights for (conventional) moral reasons (43–6, 253–61). Ironically, in a world in which there is no firm link between moral and literal *eugeneia*, the morally noble farmer considers himself unworthy to be Electra's husband because she comes from a 'prosperous' family (ὀλβίων, 45) and even empathizes with Orestes' anticipated horror at the social class of his sister's husband (47–9). Nevertheless, one has to admire the peasant's sensitivity about his reluctant wife's feelings (64–6, cf. 344), and Electra herself, for all her shrewish qualities, is his staunch defender. She realizes that he has refused to aggravate her situation and she is not too proud to help him in his menial tasks, particularly since this gives her an opportunity to

---

[2] O'Brien (1964) 18.

wallow in her degradation (67–76). Not only then is the peasant ineffectual in society at large; he cannot fully embrace his own inner 'nobility'.

ELECTRA'S SITUATION

Sophocles' Electra is alienated from her rightful place in the royal house without being banished from it. Her continued presence there, albeit as a moral outsider, at least allows her to conduct her campaign of continually confronting her father's killers with their crime. Euripides' Electra has been even more disempowered, and can therefore do no more than vent her feelings to the gods and to the shade of her father. For that reason she carries a pot to fetch water from the spring (54–6). She is not required to perform this menial task, but it does afford her an opportunity to unburden herself out of doors by crying out to her father's spirit and calling the gods to witness Aegisthus' and her mother's hubris (54–63). Her self-pity is not only acceptable in the culture and in the genre of tragedy, but expected. The disempowerment of Agamemnon's children reflects adversely on him and contributes significantly to the total evil of the situation.[3]

Thus Electra makes no unsympathetic impression in this first speech, and her attitude to her peasant husband in the next is admirable. Calling him a *philos* like a god and a 'physician' (ἰατρόν, 70) in her ills, she wishes to make him some return by doing her share of the household tasks (67–76).[4] So, however much she may be smarting under the indignities of her material peripeteia, she has in some measure accepted them. Thus, like the peasant, she too is caught between an inner conviction of nobility and her impoverished outward circumstances that make her ambivalent about her identity. However, unlike the peasant, Electra's sense of the noble relates more to the lifestyle in which she was raised than to a sense of inherent moral rectitude.

In her ensuing monody Electra bewails her hard life (120–1), her father's murder (122–4), and her brother's exile (130–4), praying to Zeus for his return (135–9). She recurs thence, and with heightened passion, to the circumstances of her father's assassination (140–66). We have observed that Electra, because of her expulsion from the royal house, is in no position to pursue the active revenge of her Sophoclean counterpart. The most she can do for her father is to continue to mourn him. However, Electra says nothing about an *obligation* to mourn—about the claims of *eugeneia* so important to the Sophoclean Electra—so we must presume that she continues to mourn because there has been no proper closure in the form of a decent burial, let alone retribution.

In the parodos the chorus invite Electra to a festival of Hera. She replies that in her misery (τάλαιν', 178) she lacks any enthusiasm for fine clothing and festivities. She is instead devoted to tears, and her dirty clothes would be an insult to her dead father (175–89). Now our culture allows (unspecified) time to mourn but admires

---

[3] As Lloyd (1986) 5 observes: 'It is . . . misguided to try to distinguish in a Greek lament between the sorrow of the mourner for the dead person and her pity for herself. . . . There is no evidence that such lamentation is confined to especially self-centered individuals.'

[4] She speaks well of him to Orestes at 252 ff.

those who can in due course lay aside their grief and re-engage in social activities. But it would be quite wrong for Electra, who is only a pseudo-wife in an inappropriate and unconsummated marriage and still mourning her father, to take part in such a festival.[5] She lays herself open to modern disapproval, however, because she does not reply from a strong and explicit moral position like that of Sophocles' Electra who would have argued in the sort of terms she uses in criticism of Chrysothemis. The chorus counter Electra's rejection of their offer with the advice that honouring rather than complaining to the gods would be more effective (193–7), but this argument hardly applies to a woman in mourning, and in any case Electra has dismissed the gods as useless (198–200).

ORESTES' *ANAGNORISIS*

When Orestes meets Electra in disguise he claims that he has been sent to find out about her condition. In postponing the recognition in this way Euripides is undoubtedly teasing his audience. For example, when Orestes declares that there is no one whom he has more right to touch than Electra (224), we are not anticipating the anticlimax, 'I have come with news of your brother' (228). Uncertainty, however, surrounds the reasons for the postponement. Why does Orestes feel a continued need to remain in disguise to the point where finally the revelation is made for him? Does this bespeak reluctance to be placed in an irreversible situation? For once he has been clearly informed of Electra's condition and morale (as he has been[6]) and reassured about the reliability of the chorus, there seems no need to hold back. If he wants further information about his sister's state or the state of his father's grave he can get it without continuing to conceal his identity, especially since some seventy verses elapse before the re-entrance of the peasant whom he might be unwilling to trust. We might argue that Orestes is baulking at the matricide, or stress the realistic need for him to be careful which we can see concerns him in his question about the reliability of the chorus (272). There is also the need to test his sister—a theme familiar from Odysseus' testing of Penelope in Homer.[7] It seems pretty clear, though, that psychology is sacrificed here to intertextual theatricality whereby the delayed recognition relates to the placing of this element of the plot in previous versions and thus to the associated expectations of the audience.

Once Orestes has been fully apprised of his sister's physical circumstances, he moves on to test her attitude to his proposed revenge (274–82). It is equally possible that he is hoping for her support in a deed to which he is completely committed (the 'heroic' assumption) or hoping that she will let him off the hook (the 'realistic' assumption), as a number of modern critics have thought. Certainly

---

[5] Lloyd (1986) 7.

[6] Electra's general condition (238); her emaciated body, wasted with grief (239–40); her shaven head (241); her 'deadly' marriage (247); the hut (252); the character of the peasant (253–62); the hubris of Clytemnestra and Aegisthus (264–71); the state of Agamemnon's grave (288–90).

[7] Lloyd (1986) 12. On the 'complex literary and dramatic motives' of the 'prolonged anonymity' see Cropp (1988) p. xxxiv.

Orestes displays strong reluctance to commit matricide later when he actually sees his mother, but since this is true of Aeschylus' Orestes as well, it is not clear that his reluctance has been present from the start.

The delaying of the recognition gives Electra the opportunity to go into more detail about her state and the hubris of Clytemnestra and Aegisthus, but while the case against the killers is further developed, there is nothing here that is fundamentally new. This provides ammunition for those who think that Electra is unprofitably obsessed, and the delay is stretched out further by the re-entry of the peasant and Orestes' reflections on his nobility and nobility in general.

There is also the question of Agamemnon's grave, which obviously does exist after all (cf. 289). Aegisthus, 'so they say', desecrates it, while no one honours it, not even to the extent of libations or a sprig of myrtle (324–5). One imagines that the likes of Sophocles' Electra or Antigone would not have allowed such a thing to happen, and this Electra is neither confined within the palace nor closely watched—as we know from the fact that her pregnancy story is believed. Moreover, that Orestes himself and the old man are able to put offerings on the grave (precisely the libation and myrtle of which Electra complains it has been deprived) suggests that to do so was neither forbidden nor particularly dangerous (509–17). Obviously Electra felt no obligation to do so, or not enough to override her fear of Aegisthus.

Amid all this delay, the only thing that advances the plot is Electra's idea of sending for the old man who is to bring food to supplement the meal. This man will be the means of effecting the recognition. But that only returns us to Orestes' reluctance to reveal himself. The embarrassment of his continuing in his disguise would seem to vindicate, against Electra's outrage, the old man's implication that Electra's 'brave' ($\epsilon\ddot{v}\theta\alpha\rho\sigma\hat{\eta}$, 526) brother would indeed return in secret. She is obviously mistaken, but this does not prove that Orestes is a coward, only that he is not foolhardy. (Are we to judge by a heroic or a realistic standard?) Every tragic Orestes returns in secret. There is also a further raising of the *eugeneia* question when the old man comments that Orestes and Pylades *look* noble, but appearances can be deceptive (550–1). It seems then (from this and Orestes' earlier reflections) that the audience are to apply the criterion of moral *eugeneia* to Orestes himself. So far the evidence is insufficient for a judgement.

Whatever the reasons for the postponement of the recognition, Orestes is certainly quick to move on to the question of the mechanema to be used in the killing of Aegisthus (596 ff.). That he relies on the old man for advice (consider the stichomythia of 599–646 in which Orestes asks the questions and the old man replies) is not a sign of passivity but reflects the need for 'inside' knowledge. Orestes here focuses on Aegisthus but clearly intends to include the matricide in the plan (640–6) until Electra relieves him of the responsibility.[8] The plan to kill Clytemnestra is then developed by Electra in a corresponding stichomythia with the old man in which *she* takes the initiative. This does not necessarily imply that

---

[8] In the earlier scenes Orestes takes the matricide for granted, 'missing its implications up to the moment when he is faced with the act, and visualising it only in a rather abstract way': Cropp (1988) p. xxxii.

Electra is more proactive than Orestes; rather it suggests that she, like the old man, has the inside knowledge needed to hatch an effective plan.

THE KILLING OF AEGISTHUS

Aegisthus is sacrificing to the Nymphs (785–6) in a ceremony which, like all rituals conducted by Agamemnon's killers, is no more than a travesty in which the celebrant prays to hold onto his ill-gotten gains (805–8). Thus there can be no question of significant sacrilege on the part of Orestes.[9] Nor is there significant violation of hospitality (*xenia*) (779, 787–96, 831), since Orestes' situation is precisely that of Odysseus in respect of the Suitors. In any case, neither the suitors in Homer nor Aegisthus here are legitimate hosts. Certainly Aegisthus seems pleasant enough as (spurious) host, but, as Hamlet knows, one can smile and be a villain.[10] The murder itself is ugly with the vivid realism of a Euripidean messenger narrative, but, as we have seen, Orestes is forced to proceed by stealth, and one can admire the bold ruse by which he asks for a sharper sword after exploiting the *tuchē* of being invited to cut up the carcass. The *xenia* and corrupted sacrifice motifs lend a certain piquancy to the episode, but there is no need to think of them as producing any kind of moral aporia in the minds of the audience. Certainly the ugly realism of the killing undercuts conventional heroic expectations, but that is insufficient to undercut its morality.[11] The matricide is similarly ugly in its realism, but in that case the revulsion it inspires, together with the enormity of the act in whatever circumstances, is sufficient to carry our moral judgement along with it—as we shall see.

This Electra, unlike her counterpart in Sophocles, has had no regular contact with Aegisthus, though she naturally has hated him all along for his original crime against her father, his sustained adultery with her mother, and for his alleged desecration of the grave. When Orestes returns with the body he gives her permission to abuse it. Electra, though a bit reluctant to be criticized for vilifying the dead (902), soon proceeds to do so, saying all the things she was too frightened to say to Aegisthus' face when he was alive. If we expected an impressive diatribe, we are disappointed. When it comes down to it, there is not a lot to be said, and since Aegisthus is past hearing and the revenge upon him is now formally complete, the purpose can only be personal catharsis for Electra.[12] Addressing her remarks to his corpse (or his severed head) she accuses him of depriving herself and Orestes of a father, marrying Clytemnestra shamelessly, and killing

---

[9] Aegisthus is sacrilegious in usurping Agamemnon's position; we are not to be disturbed by Orestes' exploitation of a religious ceremony: Burnett (1998) 233–5.

[10] Critics have found a problem in the allegedly incompatible impressions of Aegisthus offered in the play, but like Shakespeare's Claudius he is a killer, a lout, and a boon companion. The realistic component of the play's characterization accounts for this. See also Lloyd (1992) 57.

[11] On the rightness of the tyrannicide of Aegisthus (for all his geniality), as opposed to the matricide see Cropp (1988) pp. xxxi–xxxii and ad 774–858.

[12] Electra's 'gratuitous' speech against Aegisthus 'begins to show us the true extent of El.'s obsessive hatred, which then emerges more and more clearly and alienates sympathy from the matricide': Cropp (1988) ad 880–1146. On the speech see also Pelling (2005) 87.

Agamemnon. Everything else she says, being morally nugatory, is either astonishingly feeble or beside the point: in marrying Clytemnestra Aegisthus expected to have a faithful wife (but what is the evidence that he was mistaken?); his life with her was 'very painful' (ἄλγιστα, 925)(how?) although it seemed otherwise; he played second fiddle to his wife (931); he thought that being rich made him important (939) (but where is the evidence, and so what?). Electra (and perhaps Euripides) seem to be casting about here desperately for something dramatically relevant to say.[13] And if such 'moral' considerations held some interest for the audience and are important to the realistic world of the play, again the prestige and relevance of the revenge suffers in its unheroic milieu.

MATRICIDE

As for her mother, Electra has reviled her for the murder of Agamemnon and the adultery with Aegisthus (122–4, 264–5, 157 ff., 211) and for throwing her out of the house to please her paramour (60–3). She has commented briefly on her mother's wealth in contrast to her own squalid poverty (314–18), and expressed a readiness to kill her or see her dead (279–81). It is sometimes alleged that she is obsessed with her mother's sexual and material status that so contrasts with her own.[14] At any rate, her jealousy of Clytemnestra emerges briefly but strongly in her two memorable comments, the first when she catches sight of her walking into the trap (965–6) and the second as she escorts her into the hut (1139–40), but it is going too far to claim that this is her real or essential motivation, although, unlike Sophocles' Electra, her own material conditions are of considerable concern to her.

When Aeschylus' Orestes baulks at the matricide (*Cho.* 899) he does so on the grounds of *aidōs*, a kind of instinctive moral reluctance aroused by the display of the maternal breast and by his mother's explicit appeal for *aidōs* with a reference to her nurturing role (*Cho.* 896–8). Similarly, Euripides' Orestes, as his sister interprets it, experiences a surge of pity as he catches sight of his mother and is reminded that she bore and nursed him (967–9). Presumably he too feels something we may describe as *aidōs* when he states that it is not right to kill his mother (973). This Orestes is prepared to impugn the traditional divine wisdom; his Aeschylean counterpart does not go so far, and Pylades in any case confines the

---

[13] Electra's 'bias and the conventions of invective encourage us to see them [her claims] as exaggerated, one-sided and not wholly true. . . . What she gives is a hostile account of a contemptible man, a *woman's* account (hence the concentration on sexual topics), and a victim's': Cropp (1988) ad 907–56.

[14] The matricide is not retribution on behalf of Agamemnon, but 'the primary feminine return of an injury that afflicted not honor but sexual status and that came from a female enemy': Burnett (1998) 237. Cropp (1988) p. xxxvi argues, I think correctly, that the 'claims of Agamemnon and of justice remain relevant as the origin and the justification of her [Electra's] resentment; but the personal grievances come to be seen as an integral element in it, feeding her vengefulness and inducing that single-minded extremity of hatred which leads to matricide'.

issue to divine power, suppressing the question of divine moral authority: 'Make yourself an enemy of all men rather than of the gods' (*Cho.* 902).[15]

Electra, however, ignores the psychological dimension and presents the issue in the narrower terms of supposed physical suffering in store for Orestes if he proceeds (974), and she expects none. Neither she nor Orestes is anticipating any primarily *emotional* harm to themselves, and Orestes answers her on the plane of religious pollution and its material consequences for him: he will be impure and will be forced into exile (975). Electra, presumably in her enthusiasm for the matricide, perversely refuses to see that a dilemma exists at all, insisting that Orestes will be guilty of impiety (to the god and to a parent) if he fails to avenge his father (976, 978). In his anguish Orestes now wonders if it was rather an avenging spirit (*alastōr*, 979) that issued the oracle, presumably since such beings are single-mindedly determined that vengeance be carried out and have no interest in any dilemmas that might emerge for their human agents. But for Electra the *alastōr* is a most unlikely hypothesis, given that the instruction came from the Delphic tripod (980). If that is true, then Orestes still anticipates being left in the lurch by Apollo and firmly asserts that the oracle is not a good one (981). However, Electra is able to prevail against this judgement with an accusation of cowardice (ἀνανδρίαν, 982), implying (unfairly) that her brother is concealing a straightforward failure of nerve behind his various objections. Lady Macbeth is successful with a similar ploy, though neither she nor Electra has, finally, the courage of her convictions.[16]

Electra brings no reflective intelligence to bear upon the morality of the matricide: she just wants her mother killed and she has no doubts that she deserves to die.[17] When Orestes feels pity, Electra can recognize it but not share it. Because of her uncritical emotional commitment to the matricide, she does not explore with Orestes the real dilemma occasioned by his religious obligations to both parents and the tension between the conventional *eusebeia* owed to a mother and Apollo's specific religious command. Orestes recognizes the dilemma, feels *aidōs* and pity for his mother, and is convinced on balance that the oracle is wrong. Still, he is unable to resist because of the combined pressure of his sister and of the god's authority.[18]

One is reminded here of the carpet scene of the *Agamemnon*. In both scenes a dominant woman is able to override the instinctive reluctance of the male. We noticed that in the Aeschylean scene Agamemnon began with a clear, rationally based resolve to shun divine envy, but was distracted from it by the intrusion of red herrings combining with an underlying desire to tread the fabrics. Orestes

---

[15] On parallels and contrasts with *Choephori* see Lloyd (1992) 58–9.

[16] Electra applies the heroic code to Orestes, as Medea does to herself in the Great Monologue: reluctance to slaughter a close relative is just a form of cowardice when vengeance is required (*El.* 982; *Med.* 1051).

[17] Harris (2001) 279 unaccountably believes that Electra's revenge is '*not* the product of violent and unreasoning passion' (his emphasis) and for that reason perhaps is 'acceptable to poet and audience' (!)

[18] As Lloyd (1986) 18 observes: 'In Aeschylus the dilemma is represented as a conflict between opposing sets of values, which are to some extent objectified, and Aeschylus can develop this conflict in the trilogy as a whole. Euripides, on the other hand, concentrates on Orestes' difficulty in doing the deed and on his subsequent remorse. The problem is thus internalised.' He concentrates also of course on Electra's personal motives.

here begins with an instinctive moral resistance, though he is perhaps not absolutely certain. His desire works in the opposite way to that of Agamemnon in Aeschylus: Orestes does not secretly want to kill his mother, so desire and moral intuition are on the same side. On the other side are divine authority (which one might perhaps associate with moral authority) and the strong will of his sister which enlists the god's presumed moral authority. Orestes caves in because of the taunt of cowardice, which would seem to suggest that he is indeed morally uncertain. Orestes' mind is divided between the feeling of compassion and the fear of cowardice, between a moral intuition and a supposed contrary moral authority, and between asserting his own will and yielding to Electra's stronger will.[19]

The morality of Clytemnestra is important in directing our sympathies in the matter of the matricide. In Sophocles, she is both evil and base. Here she is a rather superficial woman caught in anxiety about her reputation. Such a concern was culturally central for Greek women, but there is an instructive contrast with Sophocles' Deianeira who we saw was concerned not only to seem but to be *sōphrōn*—as was Euripides' Phaedra, at least initially. Clytemnestra in this play is motivated *only* by fear of what people will think (27–30). When she arrives at the hut and makes her decorous descent from her wain her moral triviality emerges in her reference to her slaves whom she regards as some sort of compensation (though inadequate) for the life of her daughter Iphigenia (1002–3).

In the agon with Electra, Clytemnestra argues, as did her Sophoclean counterpart, that Agamemnon had wronged her by killing her daughter (1018 ff.).[20] She could, she says, have forgiven him had he done it to save his city or to benefit his house by saving other children at the cost of one, but he did it so that Menelaus could recover a wife whose promiscuity he could not suppress. But even that was not enough to motivate the murder of a husband; Cassandra was the last straw (1030–4). In Sophocles, Electra argues that Agamemnon had no choice but to sacrifice (he could go neither home nor to Troy).[21] No account of Artemis' conditions is given here, so perhaps we are to assume that Agamemnon did have a choice as he seems to have had traditionally, and certainly in Aeschylus. Clytemnestra's argument is based on viewing the war reductively, which may well be how Euripides intends us to see it.

Our natural assumption that Clytemnestra will defend the deed in the agon conditions us to read it with that expectation, but shortly after its conclusion she actually expresses regret (1105–6) and admits that she was carried away by anger against her husband (1109–10). We realize that she is only pleading mitigating circumstances and asking for understanding.[22] Indeed, rather than prefacing her speech with a plea to her daughter to acknowledge the justice of her act, she asks

---

[19] Lloyd (1986) 19 maintains that it is 'mistaken to argue . . . that Orestes is prompted only by Electra's taunts of cowardice (982). What she means is that he should not allow his scruples to prevent him from obeying the god: fear of cowardice is not itself a motive.' But Electra allows his scruples no weight at all, and for an aristocrat to entertain the slightest possibility that his scruples are really a rationalization of ordinary cowardice is enough to rob those scruples of persuasive power.

[20] Soph. *El.* 530–48.

[21] Ibid. 573–4.

[22] But cf. Burnett (1998) 240: 'She killed him [Agamemnon] for the most sordid reasons assigned by the tradition, and she is proud of her crime.'

her only to recognize that she does not deserve to be hated (1015–17).[23] Clytemnestra's reduced plea ought to take some of the wind out of Electra's sails. She does not now have to contend that the deed was wrong; she can only contend that the plea in mitigation was hypocritical. Accordingly, Electra tries to show that her mother was already set on adultery before Iphigenia was sacrificed, but it is hard to know what we are supposed to make of her 'evidence'.[24] Sympathetic characters in Euripidean *agones* sometimes present extremely feeble arguments which ride on the back of the basic sympathy we feel for them.[25] Here Electra argues that the murder of Agamemnon was not a response to the sacrifice of Iphigenia and to his liaison with Cassandra, because her mother was looking for an illicit sexual liaison as soon as her husband's back was turned. This idea is based on an alleged concern for her appearance as evidenced by her preening before the mirror (1069–75). One could object that Homer's Penelope continued to look gorgeous among the Suitors, without subversive intentions. The other piece of evidence seems even feebler: Clytemnestra was the only Greek woman whose eyes were 'clouded' (συννεφοῦσαν ὄμματα, 1078) when she heard news of Greek success at Troy on the rather precarious grounds that this made her husband's return more likely (1079). In a play much concerned with verisimilitude, how does Electra know that she was the only woman to be affected thus, and the inference from clouded eyes to hatred of her husband involves an outrageous leap.[26] One would think that Euripides could have supplied his protagonist with stronger evidence— perhaps that Clytemnestra had already begun her affair with Aegisthus before the news of the sacrifice of Iphigenia was reported back to Argos.[27] Electra concludes with her familiar complaint about her own material circumstances: the murder of Agamemnon aside, why did Clytemnestra not make over the property to her son and daughter? (1086 ff.). Aegisthus of course would never have countenanced that.

It is impossible to gauge whether Euripides intended the audience's basic sympathy for Electra to override a closer scrutiny of her arguments here, and perhaps it is best to go on the overall impression that comes out of the agon— which, I think, is that Clytemnestra should be accorded *some* sympathy: less than she herself desires but enough, if not to lessen her guilt significantly, at least to

---

[23] Clytemnestra's 'attempt at a defence (1011–50) draws attention to the blindness of Electra's hatred—blindness to the possibility of making a mistake and living to regret it (like Clytemnestra herself: 1105–10)': Cropp (1988) p. xxx. 'The dramatic issue is not guilt but the response to guilt; condemnation is tempered by the extenuations Cl. offers, her regrets, her unwitting defencelessness; approval of El. by her gloating vengefulness': ibid. 168 and ad 1102–46. On the conciliatory Clytemnestra see also Lloyd (1992) 69.

[24] 'The queen's expression of her motivation is challenged by Electra's version of the events, which itself seems far from a privileged expression of the truth. With Euripides, the myth and the characters of myth are fractured in a series of competing *logoi*, different readings, different paradigms for behaviour and understanding': Goldhill (1986) 256.

[25] See Heath (1987) 58.

[26] But contrast the interesting observation of Mossman (2001) 381–2: 'Making Clytemnestra's preening in the mirror indicate her faithlessness is not just conventional: it takes us into the boudoir and seems to justify her claim to special knowledge, as does her account of Clytemnestra's reaction to news from Troy.'

[27] Pelling (2005) 88 remarks that 'it may all be true, but by now we have lost confidence in any Electra narrative'.

aggravate our unease about the matricide.[28] The sequel bears this out. Electra then has been deprived of the opportunity of putting a strong case for the matricide, at least in the agon. (There is also the need to deceive her mother, unlike in the corresponding Sophoclean agon which is conducted well before any matricidal plan has been devised.) Her case is more or less traditional. Clytemnestra killed her husband and deprived the children of their patrimony. Naturally she must die. But Electra's prosecution of the matricide is, as is usually observed, clearly based on a high degree of personal hatred which comes out in a number of vicious remarks. It is this blind hatred which drives her into pressuring Orestes with insufficient moral deliberation, when the occasion arises, into matricide.

As Clytemnestra proceeds off the stage to her death, Electra locates the matricide in the context of a corrupted sacrifice, an unnatural wedding and an ironical *charis* (1142–6). The chorus at this point support the deed as just retribution, dwelling on the heinous nature of the original crime, as Agamemnon was killed on his homecoming with an axe by a raging 'lioness'—a figure appropriate enough to Aeschylus' Clytemnestra but strangely at odds with the Clytemnestra we have seen in this play. The conventional shriek is heard from within (1167) and immediately the killers re-enter, 'stained in streams of their mother's blood newly shed' (1172–3; cf. Soph. *El.* 1422–3), but filled with remorse. Their lyric report merges the messenger's account with the conventional mourning over the ekkyklema. (In Sophocles the parallel scene is avoided altogether as the body is used in the mechanema to trap Aegisthus, while in Aeschylus it is transformed into a scene of mourning for Agamemnon, rather than for the most recent victims, and thus of self-justification for Orestes.)

Like the Aeschylean Cassandra's evocations of Agamemnon's murder, the power of the Euripidean evocation of the matricide consists partly in its fragmentation, as Orestes constructs a verbal montage of the matricide in which the images recur to his mind out of their chronological order. He begins with his mother's exposure of her breast (1206–7). In Aeschylus this was a calculated, even rhetorical, gesture, its message all but explicit in the imagery of Clytemnestra's accompanying explanation (*Cho.* 896–8). Orestes was to imagine the pleasures of infantile suckling and of the mother's nurturing role. But here his mother bares her breast during the very act of matricide (1207)—impulsively, instinctively, desperately. Next the sight of his mother's body on the ground (1208–9), and then back to her touching his chin or face in an impulsive gesture of supplication (1214–17). We must relive with Orestes the physical resistance of the victim who, while he is trying to plunge the sword into her throat, hangs on his cheeks in a desperate and messy embrace (no formal supplication) that makes him drop the

---

[28] Clytemnestra is 'a woman who is despicably ordinary as she enjoys the profits of an unspeakable crime': Burnett (1998) 240. O'Brien (1964) 38–9, on the other hand, sees the conventionally sympathetic Electra and Orestes as having become 'moral replicas of their tormentors. The essential sameness of Electra and Clytemnestra, of Orestes and Aegisthus, renders morally irrelevant all the conventional ways of distinguishing good from wicked in this legend. The pervasive theme of canons of judgement makes it clear that there is no sure standard which separates oppressor from oppressed.' This is, I think, an exaggeration, but Euripides has certainly narrowed the gap between the 'good' and the 'evil' characters. The view of Cropp (1988) p. xxxii is, I think, as usual, most apposite: 'Euripides . . . attenuates Clytemnestra's wickedness just enough to allow her murder to be a tragic *pathos*—a just punishment, but morally repugnant in its execution.'

sword (1216–17). (We dare not imagine his mental state as he bent down to
retrieve it.) Then he has to line up the sword with his mother's throat and *plunge*
(1223) it in (no mere slitting) with his face covered to protect him from her dying,
Gorgonesque gaze (1218–24).[29]

Throughout this whole ordeal it is hard not to credit Orestes with a terrible
mental resistance in answer to the physical resistance of the victim, with both
contending against his resolve as he copes somehow with the intimacy of facial
contact in the religiously significant act of supplication. Not only are the bodies in
question evoked for us as seemingly visible to our mind's eye, but the actions
described are such as to draw us into an appallingly vicarious experience of the
nervous and muscular dimension of the act of mother-murder. With all this
Electra is involved at the very least empathically.

The physical details of the matricide are entirely appropriate to the tone and
meaning of the play as a whole. Orestes would distance himself from the act by
calling it a sacrifice, but it has none of the reassuring impersonality of a ritual act
sanctioned by a society and its religion. This is a truth that emerges from a
consideration of the motives of Electra and the *reductio ad absurdum* of Apollo,
but it is also powerfully reflected in the deed itself which is physically, ritually, and
emotionally messy and goes horribly wrong, so that its physical grossness triggers
in the killers and in the audience a sense of revulsion that renders all rationalization superfluous and obscene.

The Euripidean Electra then for all her malicious enthusiasm is revolted by the
deed in a way that her morally superior Sophoclean counterpart is not. This is
because she is confronted with the unexpected: she never realized just how terrible
the physical act of matricide would be. It is as if she has been living in a dream.
Her mother, like Aegisthus, is a convenient human target for her hatred of her
material conditions since she is (with him) the cause of those conditions, but in
her rural isolation Electra has ceased to relate in any way to her mother as she
really is. What her mother had come to mean for her was, as we saw, nicely caught
in her immediate envious reaction to seeing her for the first time after so long:
how fine she looks in her smart clothes and carriage! Burnett refers to 'a new sort
of vengeance, a retaliation built on resentment, a violence that looks to the
improvement of wordly condition rather than to the restoration of honor, and
that takes its most effective inspiration neither from Delphi nor from the under-
world but from a jealous envy of those who have won what the avenger has lost'.[30]

Sophocles' Electra, on the other hand, saw her mother day in and day out,
locked in constant slanging matches with her. She had formed a clear moral
appraisal of Clytemnestra which sanctioned her death. Accordingly, she reassures
her brother that when the time arrives she will have no problem concealing her
reaction to the change of circumstances: she will face her mother with that same
fixed hatred that is etched on her being (Soph. *El.* 1309 ff.). She has long ago
worked through what Clytemnestra is and what she deserves and what that will
entail. And she is present immediately before the deed, describing her mother's

---

[29] For Orestes as a sort of Perseus slaying the 'gorgons' of Aegisthus and his mother see O'Brien
(1964) 17–18, 21. Orestes, through the matricide, is symbolically transformed into a gorgon himself
(1195–7).
[30] Burnett (1998) 242.

actions. She is of course spared the sight of the actual killing, but when she hears her mother shriek, far from being traumatized, she can only think of the *lex talionis*: her mother cries out for pity, but—as Electra shouts back at her—she had none for Orestes (when she thought he was dead) or for her husband when she killed him (1412). And we know that this is true.

The Euripidean Electra's lack of moral integrity or understanding reflects the moral void of the play with the demise of traditional *eugeneia* and its replacement by the bleak materialism of a degenerate aristocracy. The characters are morally asleep; their thinking about the matricide before the deed is conventional; they have no real knowledge of their own feelings, nor have they thought through the morality of the issue.[31] After the deed the reality is obvious enough to them, but the accompanying 'self-knowledge' is of the most basic and elementary kind. Associated with the moral void referred to above is a new emphasis on amoral emotion as a determinant of attitude and action. The matricide is driven essentially by Electra's hatred, but when the hatred evaporates during the matricide there is no moral commitment to motivate the deed. We saw in the Great Monologue of *Medea* how 'moral' commitment to the filicide was in danger of subversion by emotion elicited by a physical sight or experience—that of the children's 'bright eyes' (ὄμμα φαιδρόν, 1043). In *Iphigenia at Aulis*, Menelaus at first strongly supports the sacrifice of his niece, but at the sight of his reluctant brother's tears (*IA* 477–80) he changes his mind (or so he says) and produces a whole series of arguments against killing her (*IA* 481–97).[32] These arguments, though rational enough in themselves, actually originate in a more or less casual feeling elicited by physical sight; they do not express a deep, abiding, and, above all, emotionally stabilizing moral conviction. On the other hand, as soon as Sophocles' Ajax recognizes the feeling of pity in himself, he suppresses it as alien to his true moral nature.

This moral bankruptcy is reflected on the divine level. Apollo's oracle appears a senseless anachronism and even the Dioscuri condemn it as the foolish utterance of a wise god (1245–6). The divine realm is reduced to incoherence. In the words of Gellie, '[i]t is hard to find the metaphysical dimension, the force out there that is cruelly hostile to man's highest resolves. Instead there is only the inner disintegration that results from man's inability to cope with his own emotional processes.'[33] We note too that there has been no hint of divine support during the play— no ironical divine responses to prayers for deliverance and no prophetic dreams. Mossman would have it that 'what is wrong with Electra and Orestes is not that they are not heroic, but that their heroism is horribly misdirected'.[34] But it depends what one means by 'heroic'. Although they would not be ludicrously out of place in the world of the second half of the *Odyssey*, they lack the

---

[31] 'None of Euripides' antagonists...is quite equal to his or her role in the legend': O'Brien (1964) 19.

[32] It is immaterial whether or not Menelaus is speaking the truth here; what is important is that he must consider his explanation psychologically plausible.

[33] Gellie (1981) 9.

[34] Mossman (2001) 377.

larger-than-life qualities of the hero of that epic.[35] Nor are they heroic in the Sophoclean sense of being motivated by moral *eugeneia*. They have, however, been placed in what is nominally a heroic moral framework by the requirement that they enact the myth with its heroic presuppositions about the talio, but Electra in particular has debased that idea by her ordinary subheroic motivation. Still, critics such as Lloyd have forced us to modify the old idea of Electra as hateful to the point of perversion; certainly she is driven by malice, but we retain more sympathy for her than the other view allows. As Lloyd observes, 'If the matricide is shown at the end of the play to have been a mistake, it is no less tragic that such an act should be the responsibility of plausible and sympathetic characters than of the warped and inadequate individuals that Electra and Orestes are often thought to be.'[36]

CONCLUSION

Electra does not define herself in moral terms, and in fact her sense of her identity in general is somewhat confused. A princess married off to a peasant, she does not, however, hold herself entirely aloof from this new life which she resents while being sufficiently immersed in it for it to affect her sense of who she is. Her moral attitude to the two revenge killings is conventional and unreflective, at least in anticipation, so she avoids the moral issues that surround Orestes' dilemma and anticipates neither the devastating emotional consequences of the matricide nor her own moral about-face on the issue. Orestes, similarly, is without explicit moral self-definition, though he has appropriate, if conventional, moral intuitions regarding the matricide. However, he allows his sister to override these intuitions and to force him into matricide.

---

[35] '...*Electra* owes much to the *Odyssey* in complexity and variety, humour and incongruity, sentimentality and domesticity—as if Euripides were leavening tragedy's Iliadic severity with the *Odyssey*'s humane range and moral subtlety': Cropp (1988) p. xxix.

[36] Lloyd (1986) 19. For Burnett (1998) 226–7 Electra is 'not a portrait of a pathological human being, but the representation of a heroic human action in its decadence'.

16

Euripides: *Bacchae*

INTRODUCTION

We have proceeded thus far by investigating the nature of the crisis confronted by a major character and asking, in cases where there is divine involvement, what the god requires of the mortal and the moral implications of the mortal's response. In turning to *Bacchae* we need to bear in mind that Dionysus, like the Aphrodite of *Hippolytus*, is at once an anthropomorphic god who presides over a religious cult with its rituals and, at a more broadly symbolic level, a force of nature. Hippolytus has no quarrel with Aphrodite as a personal deity; rather he rejects her because he detests her sphere of activity. Pentheus' rejection of Dionysus is more radical in that he rejects the sheer existence of the god, but the emotional basis of this rejection turns out to be more significant, as Pentheus does not admit the necessity for what Dionysus' religion offers the celebrant or indeed the need to express the 'Dionysiac' dimension of life. In what follows it will be important to distinguish the cult from the life-force, and the literal from the symbolic.

PROLOGUE

Dionysus appears in the prologue in the form of a personal, anthropomorphic god and informs us that his purpose in coming to Thebes is to establish his cult and manifest himself as a god (21–2). He has begun with Thebes because his mother's sisters, in denying that Zeus mated with Semele, effectively denied his divinity. For this denial he has deranged them and sent them off to Cithaeron as Bacchants (20–38). The aunts' offence, in the brief reference to it here, looks like a simple mistake rather than an act of deliberate impiety. (It is of course possible to violate a religious requirement unwittingly, as Oedipus does at the beginning of the *Coloneus*.)

As for Pentheus, the god describes him as a *theomachos* (a fighter against a god). This 'theomachy' takes the form of excluding Dionysus from worship (i.e. libation and prayer) (45). We have to wait for Pentheus' entrance speech for confirmation that he shares his aunts' denial of Zeus's paternity (242–5), and there is no suggestion at this stage that he hates what Dionysus *represents*, as Hippolytus hates Aphrodite because he hates sex. (Indeed, it is not yet clear exactly what Dionysus does represent.) Unlike Aphrodite, who has, already in the prologue of *Hippolytus*, taken steps to punish her enemy, Dionysus will, more mysteriously, 'show' (ἐνδείξομαι) Pentheus and all of Thebes that he is indeed a god (47).[1] There was nothing for Aphrodite to show Hippolytus, as he had no doubts about the personal existence of the goddess herself or of the reality of the sexual instinct, but Pentheus is effectively denying a whole dimension of life. When Dionysus appears to Pentheus he does so disguised as a Lydian stranger and never requires that he be identified as Dionysus. All he appears to want is the king's consent to the establishment of his religion in Thebes, and when Pentheus resists, the god confronts him with evidence for his own reality in the form of a number of spectacular miracles which raise questions about the nature of perception and reality in general that take us beyond the specific concerns of this new religion. The young king, however, persists in his rejection to the point of an absurd refusal to face facts until eventually the god appears to abandon his case as hopeless and resolves to encompass his destruction.

But what is it to face facts in this play? Here we have to distinguish the various planes on which the play communicates. On the literal level of the dramatic action all the miracles evoked or described must be accepted as really occurring; otherwise Pentheus would be completely vindicated in his denial of Dionysus' divinity and the god's associated ability to perform miracles. To interpret the play in that Verrallian way is to reduce it to incoherence.[2] But besides the strictly religious dimension of Dionysus, there is a wider psychological symbolism grounded in the emotional experience of being a Bacchant, quite apart from whether what one witnesses in the Bacchic state really happens. As I have insisted, it does really happen on the level of the dramatic action, but this is not the central psychological point. Psychologically, we are concerned with an altered state of consciousness in opposition to normal consciousness. In the terms of the literal action, the altered state accompanies and in some cases even seems to make possible the production of miracles, which we might associate with an altered state of reality, or perhaps an alternative reality, corresponding to or correlated with the altered state of consciousness. (Once the Bacchants enter their trance they are able to produce milk, wine, and honey spontaneously from nature.) Outside the play's action, however, we might be inclined to deny that such an alternative reality (i.e. miraculous events) really exists, in which case we would have to speak of people who make such claims as the Bacchants make as deluded. But in the play's terms they are not deluded, so the two competing realities—the ordinary world and the Dionysiac—are, on the level of the dramatic action, irreducible.

A number of secondary antitheses are associated with this primary one between the ordinary and the Dionysiac. Richard Seaford refers to two kinds of power (the temporal power of the state and the Dionysiac), two kinds of perception (the ordinary and the Dionysiac), and pervasive dualities such as Greek and barbarian, man and god, man and woman, human and animal, reality and illusion (this last one correlated with the dual perceptions).[3]

---

[1] As Seaford (1997) suggests ad loc, 'mainly or entirely in the epiphany described at 616–37'.
[2] Verrall (1910) 1–163.
[3] Seaford (1997) 31–2.

PARODOS

How then does the Dionysiac seek to establish its validity, especially in the eyes of Pentheus, as a genuine mode of perception corresponding to a genuine alternate reality? It is important that the cult's adherents are not advocating the total substitution of Bacchic consciousness for the ordinary type; as Teiresias will presently declare, there are two important 'deities' in human life, not only Dionysus, but also Demeter (who here represents everyday life). The parodos of the play presents the audience (though not Pentheus who is yet to appear) with a powerful evocation of the cult's central activity which emphasizes its emotional attractiveness, particularly in that it offers the adherent a rapturous state of consciousness alleged to be mystical communion with the god. This rapturous state culminates in the ritual dismemberment (*sparagmos*) and consumption (*omophagia*) of the raw victim which represents the ingesting of the god. The chorus cannot of course prove to the sceptic that such a communion occurs; they can only hope to persuade their hearers that such a state is desirable and to do this by communicating their own enthusiasm. An unbeliever could dismiss the whole thing as delusion and hysteria and find *sparagmos* and *omophagia* more revolting than attractive and perhaps even a threat to civilized life. (Hallucinogenic drugs provide an obvious enough modern parallel. Some are attracted by them; others are not.)

CADMUS AND TEIRESIAS

If the parodos seeks to recommend the cult on emotional rather than rational grounds, with the entrance of the elderly Cadmus and Teiresias it appears in quite a different light as the old seer turned theologian of the new religion attempts to explain it in something like rational terms. As Teiresias calls him from the house (170), Cadmus describes the prophet as 'wise' in character and utterance (σοφήν, σοφοῦ: 179), though Teiresias' claim to wisdom is traditionally based on his divinely inspired interpretation of the will of Apollo. Although Cadmus apparently knows little about the matter, he is happy to accept Teiresias' direction, especially since exalting the god will at the same time exalt the family (181–3). But he and the seer are very old men, so that their Bacchic regalia is in danger of producing a humorous effect, as Pentheus sees to his angry dismay (248–52). The two old men may claim to have forgotten their age (184–90), but Cadmus at least quickly begins to have doubts. Should they go to Cithaeron by chariot? (191) Will Teiresias take his hand? (197) Will one old man lead another, like a child? (193); and by the end of the scene their energy has all but evaporated and Teiresias is now speaking of 'slavery' to the god (363–6; δουλευτέον, 366). Teiresias' earlier reassurance that Dionysus would take them to the mountain 'without toil' (194) now seems more religiously correct than realistic. The claim then that the old are equally obliged with the young to 'dance' (205) appears ridiculous.[4] Of course it

---

[4] Seaford (1997) ad 170–369 sees the mood as festive rather than comic, pointing to Ar. *Frogs* 345–8 as an instance of Bacchic rejuvenation of old men. (The other passage he cites, Plato, *Laws* 665–6,

was, in the poet's day, quite possible to worship Dionysus with much less exertion, so the seer's claim, if he really does speak for the god, is absurd only in the terms of the primitive ritual at issue in the play. It certainly does not follow that the Dionysiac in its wider sense is irrelevant to the old.

But why did Euripides choose to introduce this note of absurdity? It would have been easy enough to have represented the old men (like Iolaus in *Heracleidae*[5]) as really transformed. Certainly the poet seems to have taken a rather grim pleasure in representing the decrepitude of the aged,[6] but hardly for the sake of realism as an end in itself. At any rate, one effect is that Pentheus' already strong prejudice against the god and his cult is reinforced. It is as if Euripides is raising the familiar obstacles which the sceptic faces when trying to give a fair hearing to religious devotees, though Pentheus is admittedly not a man to give anyone a fair hearing. The religion, as Teiresias interprets it, prescribes a course of action that is repugnant to common sense (very old men engaging in strenuous dancing), so that a wedge is driven between the religion itself and human attempts to explain or justify it. (Surely the claim that the old must 'dance' is false.) The gap will soon widen when we listen to the sophistries that the seer pronounces while actually disparaging sophistries. The problem is perhaps that theology is a more or less rational attempt to talk about the mysterious and the non-rational, and for that reason it is apt to teeter on the brink of nonsense, and this alienates the rationalist even more from an uncongenial mindset. Pentheus is hardly a rationalist, but the principle applies in any case.

Teiresias defends the Dionysiac religion by appealing to ancient traditional wisdom which he claims mere logical ingenuity practised by human beings (200–3) can never overthrow.[7] What is the relevance of ancient wisdom when Dionysus is a new god? Here again we are reminded that there is a symbolic dimension to Dionysus. The specific god and religion are new in the era in which the action is set, but they represent the broader Dionysiac dimension which is as old as nature itself. The point about logical ingenuity is perhaps that clever sophistries tend to impede openness and susceptibility to religious piety. At any

---

actually concerns singing rather than Bacchic dancing.) This is the orthodox religious position, and presumably some temporary 'rejuvenation' might have been experienced at the state festivals, but these are milder forms of revel than in *Bacchae*, and the fact remains that Euripides goes out of his way to show that the men are not in fact rejuvenated. Seidensticker (1978) 314 attributes the comedy to a need to retain our sympathy for Pentheus at this stage. If the old men had really been rejuvenated and noble, we might have been alienated from him. 'The emotional intensity and fascinating ambivalence of the *Bacchae* derives in no small part from the fact that our sympathy shifts back and forth between Pentheus and the god' (ibid.). As Gregory (1985) 28 points out, Pentheus presumably thinks that the old men are bent on sex orgies since that is what he conceives the cult to be all about.

[5] Eur. *Hcld.* 851–63.

[6] e.g. the chorus and Amphitryon in *Heracles*, Peleus in *Andromache*, and Teiresias in *Phoenissae*.

[7] The lines are corrupt. See the discussion in Seaford (1997) ad 199–203. According to Seaford ibid., 'the new god is in fact ancient' and Teiresias' later thigh theory is not designed to overthrow the myths but to find 'an inner meaning in them'. See also Dodds (1960) ad 201–3. Conacher (1967) 62–3 is similarly positive: 'even as he [Teiresias] deprecates the overconfident rationalism which would reject this mysterious force, he allows the King (and us) to look at Dionysianism in something like the light of reason. In so doing, it is inevitable (considering his poet and the times) that he should blend the mythical tradition, in which "dramatically" he speaks, with the language of fifth century sophistic thought.'

rate, the seer's antithesis of the rational with the traditional signals an ongoing debate in the play as to the nature of *sophia* (wisdom, cleverness), or indeed as to the 'true' reality and the right morality in light of it, an issue which will be discussed in detail below. But then, as has often been remarked, Teiresias' explanation of the Dionysiac is itself imbued with sophistic thought.[8] Certainly the seer does not dismiss rational argument per se as invalid; he merely claims that no argument could invalidate tradition. (One is reminded perhaps of the claim that theology must fall silent in the presence of revealed mysteries such as the Christian Trinity.)

CADMUS, TEIRESIAS, AND PENTHEUS

A flustered (ἐπτόηται, 214[9]) and irate Pentheus now arrives and explains his rejection of Dionysus. Although one might (perhaps naively) have expected the god's opponent to have been characterized by a calm rationality to set against the emotional enthusiasm of the cult, Pentheus is consistently presented as in some kind of disturbed emotional state, so that a common critical view holds (correctly, I think) that the obviously irrational aspects of Pentheus are essentially Dionysiac. (The recurrence of *ptoēsis* at 1268 in the person of Agave supports this view.) In this respect he is more subtly conceived than Hippolytus who is certainly not betrayed by an Aphrodite within. Interestingly enough, Sophocles' Ajax provides a closer parallel to Pentheus' psychic condition than does Hippolytus, as we shall see below.

On the face of it, Pentheus rejects the god because, like his aunts, he does not believe that he is a god at all. There is a contrast here with Hippolytus who fully acknowledges Aphrodite's reality but hates the sphere of life over which she presides. In denial of the god's divinity Pentheus rejects the story of his birth, insisting that Semele's child was a mere mortal (242–7). But it soon becomes clear that he also objects to Dionysus' sphere of activity, or at least to what he wrongly conceives to be his sphere of activity, and this is the significant rejection. He refers to 'fake' (πλασταῖσι, 218) Bacchic revels (without the implication that there are contrasting genuine ones) and to 'this new god, whoever he may be' (218–19). Thus Euripides supports the king's rejection of the birth story with a temperamental (or perhaps even a cultural) suspicion of anything new. To be dramatically significant, his objection to the cult must be more profound than a casual error of fact.

Pentheus considers the revels no more than a cover for unseemly sexual and alcoholic indulgence (221–5), but at the same time he would appear to demonstrate a prurient interest in these alleged activities, as suggested by the vivid imagery of πτώσσουσαν ('slinking off', 223; 233–8). This is confirmed by a number of his later reactions. Also, it is a topic to which he recurs at the end of his opening

---

[8] On the sophistic anachronism see Dodds ibid.; Winnington-Ingram (1948) 41–3; Conacher (1967) 76.

[9] According to Seaford (1997) ad 214, *ptoesis* or 'fluttering nervous excitement' is characteristic of mystic initiands.

speech (260–2). Since Pentheus is regularly (and anachronistically) regarded by modern interpreters as mentally ill,[10] it should be stated here that prurient interest in what one finds morally offensive is normal enough and not even hypocritical so long as one admits to a contradiction between one's morality and other mental functions less than completely under control and from which one wishes to dissociate oneself. To cite an amusing ancient example, Plato's Leontius in the *Republic* (439e–440a) is pruriently attracted to corpses, much to the disgust of his own self-respect as embodied in the spirited, but ultimately ineffectual protest on the part of his *thumos*. Prurient fascination is doubtless unattractive, but it is not indicative of psychological illness in the ancient context, nor particularly in ours— though in our day some people regard absorption in pornography as an addiction and for that reason primarily a therapeutic rather than a moral issue. If Pentheus' extremely 'soft core' prurience were a form of mental illness, there would be few sane people among us and no *raison d'être* for the tabloid press.[11] In any case, prurience is rife among males in societies that repress women, particularly in forms apt to increase curiosity about them. Pentheus, it will be argued, is not mentally ill, though his prurience is an important factor in his downfall.

Thus far then Dionysus' opponents are guilty of misconceptions rather than of deliberate impiety or immorality: Pentheus is wrong about the god's divinity and wrong about his rituals and their significance. What evidence then do the god and the god's self-appointed representative Teiresias offer Pentheus which ought to change his mind on these two matters?

TEIRESIAS ON DIONYSUS

Teiresias now begins his extended apologia for the new religion, though the audience is more likely to give him a fair hearing than is the irate Pentheus who has already made up his mind. The seer begins by criticizing Pentheus in terms that would suggest that the young king is an irresponsible sophistic demagogue given to deploying glib arguments without substance (266–71). Indeed, Rohdich argues that the play (together with other Euripidean tragedies) is designed as a kind of refutation of sophistic rationalism and its allegedly untragic world view.[12] Although the clever sophist might seem the god's ideal antagonist, the label does not apply very well to Pentheus who has not offered a clever argument but merely voiced a prejudiced reaction based on some unreliable reports (215–25). More-over, Teiresias proceeds to offer some pretty sophistical arguments himself.[13] He claims first that two things are foremost in human life: Demeter associated with the 'dry' element, or at least with basic sustenance; and Dionysus associated with

[10] For a refreshing exception see Rosenmeyer (1968) 370.

[11] To suggest a modern parallel, would one seriously describe as mentally ill a young happily married man who disapproved of group sex but was curious enough about it to want to look at a photograph? Or who found it sexually titillating without either wanting to engage in it or approving of people who did?

[12] See e.g. Rohdich (1968) 131.

[13] For a satirical view of Teiresias see Deichgräber (1935) *passim*.

wine and the relief of suffering that inebriation brings (274–83).[14] No Greek would have thought that these deities were the two most important in the pantheon, so their significance must be in what they represent, and the seer himself remarks that the names do not really matter (276). Clearly Teiresias is recommending Dionysus' sphere of activity which he sees as altered states of consciousness and the relief from daily cares which such states offer. The argument here is essentially the same as the implicit argument of the parodos: the Dionysiac religion is commended as a celebration of an important reality in human affairs.[15]

Euripides pushes the symbolic argument to absurdity when Teiresias says that a god (i.e. Dionysus as wine) is poured out to a god (Dionysus as anthropomorphic deity), which has the effect of highlighting the uneasy dichotomy in ancient religion between the god and his sphere. Euripides shows us, in the absurdities about thighs and pledges, that ancient myths struggle to survive rationalization. The unfortunate consequence, however, is likely to be the ejection of the baby with the bath water: the theology and the mythology of the religion may well be absurd, but they are nevertheless an attempt to point to an important truth. It will be remembered that in *Heracles* Euripides undermines the literal reality of the Olympians while retaining something like their symbolic import, as the arbitrary and unjust behaviour of Zeus and Hera continues to reflect the realities of the protagonist's world even after a more exalted conception of divinity has been introduced. Similarly here, though less jarringly, Dionysus and his myths and miracles remain valid for the action, even if outside of it the audience are encouraged to interpret them symbolically and psychologically.

Pentheus is in no state to listen to such arguments as Teiresias offers, nor would he be intellectually capable of responding to them. If he were in any state to listen, he might reply, if he could free himself from his basic misconception about the Bacchants, that he despised the sphere of life that this so-called god represents (as Hippolytus understood but despised Aphrodite), in which case he would be effectively rejecting a fundamental need common to all human beings. Euripides, however, did not, as a modern writer would probably do, suggest that Hippolytus was denying a manifest need to express his sexual nature. Therefore Sophocles' *Ajax* offers a closer parallel to Pentheus since, in rejecting Athena's assistance, he failed to acknowledge an important human reality which eventually destroyed him. But the rejection of the reality of even the anthropomorphic Dionysus complicates Pentheus' position. Theoretically, he could say, as we might, that Dionysus the god is non-existent, but that, as a fiction, he symbolizes an important aspect of human life and especially of the human psyche.

But this escape is not available in a Greek tragedy where the gods undeniably exist for the literal action. Still, this would leave him with the option of following the Euripidean Heracles who acknowledges the power of *tuchē* while effectively disempowering Hera who, by the end, has roughly become a symbol of

---

[14] On this passage see Dodds (1960) ad 274–85.

[15] 'The Stranger proclaims and propagates the myth, whereas Teiresias substitutes a rational explanation for it. Also, while Teiresias confines the function of the Dionysiac cult within the civic context, the Stranger shifts the focus away from the polis, to the supernatural events on the mountain, which are reported by the two Messengers': Papadopolou (2001*b*) 29.

it. But if Euripides is uninterested here in discrediting the literal gods and is content to let them stand as symbols, Pentheus would have to forget that he disbelieved in the traditional story of the god's birth and unobtrusively shift the focus to the god's sphere and symbolic significance. In any case, Teiresias' arguments are, as we saw, really concerned with the necessity of what the god represents rather than with the literal reality of the god himself. As has often been remarked, the matter is complicated by the fact that what the god represents is a permanent factor in human life whereas the god himself is new on the scene. The newness is important because it is accompanied by the 'new' and untraditional behaviour of the women which elicits Pentheus' hostility, but the deeper truth is that the women are really expressing something eternal.

Teiresias' rationalization of the story of Dionysus' birth is just the sort of thing to confirm atheists in their atheism. Not that Pentheus is an out-and-out atheist, of course, but he is atheistical in respect of one god and perhaps in respect to religious awe in general. The seer attempts to make an absurd mythological tale credible by an obviously partial and inadequate rationalization and goes on to associate the god with a couple of familiar mad or inspired states. He offers one significant observation: that *sōphrosunē* (i.e. sexual purity) in women is a matter of *phusis* and therefore cannot be corrupted in the course of the Bacchic revels (and later the *sōphrosunē* of the women is indeed emphasized). This is reminiscent of Hippolytus' view that the only *sōphrosunē* worthy of the name is innate. Teiresias seems to be arguing that there is no point in controlling women to stop them becoming unchaste, because they are either chaste or unchaste by nature. Pentheus might reply that he does not really care how they are chaste, by nature or by constraint, as long as they are. Even so, Teiresias has certainly offered no evidence for his assertion.

The seer completes his case by accusing Pentheus of madness. At the outset he had accused him of lacking sense (268, 271); now he repeats that Pentheus' judgement is 'sick' (311). This charge is now upgraded to an accusation of actual and severe madness (326). This is not a reference to mental illness in the modern sense, but a statement of the inevitable mental condition of a *theomachos*, a kind of terrifying and partly wilful blindness and ignorance that we associate also with the hubrist. This is a bit unfair to Pentheus at this stage, at least. The hubris of a Capaneus, for example, is obviously crazy in that the wrath of Zeus and his punitive use of the thunderbolt are universally accepted truths in the culture. But Dionysus is a new god and Pentheus' rejection has not yet been shown to be based on a kind of wilful defiance. Euripides continues to make Pentheus' position seem reasonable (though tragically misguided) when Cadmus suggests that he should at least pretend to believe in the god in the interests of family glory.

Pentheus has now been driven more deeply into his wrath (and madness, at least according to the seer: 358–9), and his response to Teiresias (ordering the desecration of his place of augury) is that of a tyrant. Before we lose sympathy for him, however, we should remember that Oedipus, another angry and deluded king, in the *Tyrannus* resolves to execute Creon on absolutely no evidence. Pentheus at least has still heard nothing to persuade him that he is wrong, and in this he contrasts with the Creon of *Antigone* who for a long time stubbornly adheres to his position in spite of clear evidence to the contrary.

PENTHEUS AND DIONYSUS

With the arrest of the women Pentheus is confronted with the first miracle, their escape with the help of the Stranger. At this point his inadequacies begin to bite. He simply ignores the miracle, as he will ignore later and greater miracles, remaining obsessively committed to his prejudiced view. This seemingly wilful ignorance at last consigns him to the company of crazy hubrists. Pentheus is more interested in the Stranger's appearance (453–9), though we have seen that this does not necessarily entail an 'unhealthy' fixation. Commentators have pointed to Pentheus' evocative description of the seductive Stranger as the first indication of an unhealthy sexual fascination with his enemy,[16] but it seems safer to see the passage as a further indication of Pentheus' firm prejudice about the sexual nature of the cult. In fact his evocation of the god is hardly wide of the mark, and to be able to recognize someone's lewd appeal to a given class of people hardly proves that one is attracted oneself. Unless we are politically correct, we can all recognize the garb of the typical prostitute and its erotic intention without finding it attractive.

Pentheus begins his interrogation of the Stranger, an exercise which is complicated by the fact that the god neither intends to reveal his true identity nor (it would seem) requires Pentheus to discover it since he refers to Dionysus as a separate person who inspired him to bring his rites to Greece (465–6). Surely no one who rejected the literal existence of an anthropomorphic god could be brought to believe in that god unless the god appeared to him *in propria persona* (and since Dionysus is a new god he will not have as yet any recognized anthropomorphic embodiment) and accompanied by an obvious display of divine power. Dionysus here actively discourages Pentheus from recognizing him as the god, though he brings with him a display of his characteristic power.

Pentheus' interrogation of the Stranger concerning the cult highlights the king's unimaginative literal-mindedness. His questions are certainly not typical of a sophistic rationalist. For example, he is interested to know if the god inspired the Stranger by night or in the light of day (469). This is perhaps connected with the plain man's suspicion of anything that would conceal itself, and when Pentheus asks for a description of the rites Dionysus refuses on the grounds that the uninitiated are not entitled to know (472). This is religiously correct, but it naturally alienates Pentheus who is already convinced that the cult is a cover for illicit activities. He goes on to ask what advantage (ὄνησιν, 473) the worshippers derive from the cult, and it is hard to imagine that here he envisages any spiritual advantage, since what we call spirituality is pretty alien to traditional Greek religion. Again on religious grounds Dionysus refuses to answer (474). Pentheus now asks what the god looked like when the Stranger met him (477), but he is told that he took any form he wanted (478). Pentheus considers this an evasion (479), but the point is that Dionysus has no fixed shape, being a god of transformations and impersonations—that is to say, he can transform himself and the consciousness of the perceiver. Later Pentheus will mistake a bull and a phantom for the

---

[16] See in particular the detailed discussion in Barlow (1971) 89–92. See also Winnington-Ingram (1948) 46, ('unrealised sexual preoccupation') 47, 74; Conacher (1967) 62.

Stranger (618, 630), just as now the god is standing near but Pentheus cannot see him (500–2). In the same literal vein, the un-postmodern Pentheus cannot accept cultural relativity (483–4): he can only ignorantly criticize foreign customs as inferior (483) and return to his obsession about the corruption of women (487).[17]

Pentheus' ignorance is nicely encapsulated towards the end of the scene. Dionysus, says the Stranger, is standing near now and can see how Pentheus is abusing him, but Pentheus cannot see the god because he is impious (502). Believers sometimes dismiss atheism as a kind of wilful refusal to open the heart to God—a refusal masquerading (it is alleged) as honest, open-minded intellectual rejection. The implication seems to be that reason is an inadequate tool for judging these matters or that reason is invoked to conceal a temperamental aversion to religious commitment and the loss of personal autonomy it is presumed to entail. Such a wilfully irreligious person might be characterized, as the god characterizes Pentheus here, as impious rather than merely in error. As far as objective evidence goes, it remains true that Pentheus has not exactly been presented with proof of Dionysus' existence; all he has seen is a stranger who seems to have some admittedly impressive supernatural powers. This should be enough to shake his confidence in his settled view. But in characterizing him as impious Dionysus is perhaps accusing Pentheus of having a closed mind, of not accepting that there is more in heaven and earth than is dreamt of in his philosophy. If so, it would seem that Pentheus' alleged moral failing (impiety or *asebeia*) is a kind of temperamental blindness, in which case we might be inclined to say that it only becomes a specifically moral failing when the blindness is wilful. But since moral awareness is compromised by ignorance of the facts of a morally relevant situation, it cannot be divorced from breadth of understanding, which in some matters is partly a function of temperament. We saw that Ajax's moral awareness is compromised by his temperamental inability or at least reluctance to admit the extent to which he is dependent on forces outside his conscious mind; and, in Dionysus' words, Pentheus 'does not know what sort of life he is living, what he is doing or who he is' (506).[18]

Dionysus has just accused Pentheus of a lack of self-knowledge. Now the Greek god of self-knowledge is Apollo, and the self-knowledge he enjoins is a clear realization of the implications of being human and mortal rather than divine. Self-knowledge of this kind may come, however, via a more personal realization, as Oedipus discovers that he has committed parricide and incest. But that terrible understanding only reinforces the underlying truth regarding human insignificance in general. Dionysus, on the other hand, is a god associated with the transgression of boundaries to the point that the celebrant at the climax of the ritual becomes united with the god. But this temporary mystical communion is only a heightening or intensification of one's permanent relationship with Dionysus as the god within. Figuratively, one becomes an initiate simply by spontaneously acknowledging the Dionysiac aspect of one's nature. Pentheus' ignorance is of the universal need to express the Dionysiac.

---

[17] In the fashionable jargon, women and barbarians are for Pentheus 'the Other'.
[18] Seaford (1997) translates, 'what your life is'. See his note ad 506.

THE PALACE MIRACLES

Pentheus' refusal to acknowledge patent fact reaches the height of absurdity with the palace miracles when he ignores the collapse of at least his stables in his obsession with catching the god.[19] The symbolism of the miracles has been much discussed so it will be enough here to remark that Pentheus' essential error about the cult, that Dionysus equals Aphrodite, is here extended into the realm of delusion, and a deluded person is obviously bereft of moral awareness. Pentheus' adversary is immeasurably beyond his capacity to understand or control.

THE FIRST MESSENGER

The emphasis up till now has been upon the more ecstatic, stimulating, and indeed violent aspects of the Dionysiac religion, but with the first messenger's report the focus shifts to the tranquil aspects of the cult with the violence presented as a distortion brought about by outside interference. This is not a retraction or correction of the previous view; Euripides is not telling us that the cult is violent only when there is interference, because the violent *sparagmos* and *omophagia* evoked in the parodos are central to the mystic communion with the god and therefore at the very heart of this religion. Nevertheless, a kind of *sōphrosunē* is integral even to Dionysus, and the calm and self-assured god associates wisdom (*sophia*) with measure and self-control (σώφρον' εὐοργησίαν, 641–2). But increasingly the destructive violence is linked with resistance to Dionysus as Pentheus contemplates bloodier retaliations.

Pentheus' refusal to accept the divinity of Dionysus makes him underestimate the threat posed by the violent women and believe that he can control them by military force. His intractable inflexibility might seem hard to explain in view of the overwhelming evidence with which he is confronted. Like Creon in *Antigone*, Pentheus is carried away by the sheer momentum of his own stubbornness, but Creon's resistance suddenly collapses under the weight of evidence. Pentheus therefore fits the pattern of the incorrigible *theomachos*, and so it remains only for Dionysus to punish him. If we urge in mitigation that Pentheus is young, prejudiced, and literal-minded, this is irrelevant to a god who must avenge the dishonour he has sustained.

---

[19] See Winnington-Ingram (1948) 82–4. See also Fisher (1992) 88: '[T]he palace miracles, while real for the audience as dramatic events, are also symbolic in the sense of being representations of the god's nature. Dionysus is the god who liberates the instinctive life in man, and his escape from prison symbolizes this part of his nature. But it is only a symbol in so far as all myth is a representation of the nature of divinity; and all tragedy is a representation of the ways of gods to men.' As far as dramatic representation goes, '[t]he audience sees not a miracle, but a chorus enacting the experience of a miracle, or presenting a theatrical illusion': Foley (1985) 221. C. Segal in Burian (1985) 159 comments: 'Even if there was some visual representation of the destruction of the palace, the discrepancy between what could probably be shown on the stage and the stranger/god's remark at 633 . . . forces us to recognize the symbolic nature of what is shown onstage. The very contradiction self-consciously calls attention to the symbolic dimension of the dramatic action.'

THE 'BEWITCHING' OF PENTHEUS

The god now attracts Pentheus' attention with an inarticulate cry (810).[20] He asks him whether he would like to see the Bacchants, and Pentheus is surprisingly eager, so eager in fact that one commentator remarks that 'the question has touched a hidden spring in Pentheus' mind, and his self-mastery vanishes.'[21] It is almost as if the Stranger has caught Pentheus' eye and begun to hypnotize him. Certainly he begins to speak not exactly out of character but at least as if inebriated.[22] By the 'logic' of overdetermination this is of course compatible with simultaneous psychic invasion by Dionysus. He is, however, quick to censor his enthusiastic outburst by stating that he would be distressed to see the women drunk, but Dionysus, like a kind of Socrates,[23] highlights the contradiction: Pentheus would enjoy seeing what distresses him (815).

Is Pentheus therefore here finally unmasked as the prurient puritan—prurient in his desire to see the women and puritanical in his censure of them?[24] I have argued that, although Pentheus displays some prurient interest in Dionysus and the women, there is nothing unnatural about this. Moreover, as Gregory observes, 'neither his assumptions about the women's activities, nor his outrage, is abnormal for his culture'.[25] His transgression is rather an eagerness 'to see what he should not see' (912), that is to see what an uninitiated person such as he is should not see.[26] As for the alleged puritanism, Pentheus expresses no Hippolytean distaste for sex as such, but like most of the males in the audience he has rather a low opinion of women and believes in keeping them under strict control.[27]

So why then is he so keen to see the bacchants? In all probability his lewd interest in them has been magnified by his possession by the god, a possession, as remarked above, very like inebriation.[28] Gregory sees his curiosity as 'one aspect of his fundamental *hamartia*: the application of secular criteria to a religious phenomenon'.[29] This is to see Pentheus' fundamental transgression as religious, and naturally Dionysus will view it in these terms.

---

[20] See Dodds (1960) ad 810–12.   [21] Ibid.

[22] For the similarity of Pentheus' bewitched state to inebriation see Grube (1961) 415; Winnington-Ingram (1948) 117.

[23] Rohdich (1968) 149–50.

[24] Grube (1961) 403; Winnington-Ingram (1948) 58; Conacher (1967) 59. Rosenmeyer (1968) 164, on the other hand, insists that Pentheus 'is a whole man, with none of his vitality curtailed or held in check. But he is also a king, a perfect representative of the humanistic Greek ideal of the ordered life, a political being rather than a lawless beast.' Accordingly, he sees the change in Pentheus, consequent on the bewitching, as 'not a transition from one phase of life to another, much less a lapse into sickness or perversion, but quite simply death' (ibid. 167).

[25] Gregory (1985) 27.

[26] Ibid. 25.

[27] Some readers claim that Pentheus hates women. I see no cogent evidence for this, and I cannot see that it would be of great psychological significance since it is possible to hate women while desiring them sexually, and it is suppressed sexual desire rather than 'romantic' love that is at issue here. The culture too was notoriously misogynistic. Admittedly, Pentheus is unmarried, but he is still young.

[28] According to Conacher (1967) 67–8, 'Dionysus makes use of tendencies already present in the psyche of Pentheus', and for Dodds (1960) 172 'the poet shows us the supernatural attacking the victim's personality at its weakest point—working upon and through nature, not against it'.

[29] Gregory (1985) 29.

On the other hand, Pentheus' unshakeable misconception about the cult may be the main reason for his eagerness to see them misbehaving, as Diller suggested more than half a century ago. Pentheus is keen to confirm his prejudices and so discredit the Stranger: he wants to see the Bacchants in order to convict them of debauchery. 'It would expose the hated enemy and annihilate him morally.'[30] This motive harmonizes nicely with his attitude throughout and does not require us to invoke anachronistic psychology. It is an attitude that stays with him almost to the end (see e.g. 957, 1062).

Foley, however, looks at the matter psychologically in terms of her metatheatrical interpretation of the play. 'Pentheus is sacrificed because he cannot understand and incorporate truth in the symbolic form that festival and theater offer to the adherent, the spectator, and the *polis*.'[31] This view is based on her argument that Dionysus is staging a play within a play which 'implicates the audience in the drama and calls attention to its own art as reality. That is, theatrical illusion demonstrates the reality of the god, and illusion and symbol are the only modes of access to a god who can take whatever form he wishes.'[32] But it would seem to me that it is the audience, and especially a modern audience, rather than Pentheus who must be able to respond to the play's symbolism. That is, the spectator must be able to see that, whatever one believes about the literal Dionysus and his religion, deeper psychological, not to say epistemological, truths are at issue. Pentheus, on the other hand, within the terms of his culture, is required to accept that the god literally exists and that the religion he has introduced must be recognized and practised. But, as we have seen, in order to come to that acceptance he would need not only to acknowledge the miracles as miracles and therefore as substantial (though not conclusive) evidence for the god's reality but also to open his heart and mind to what was for the Greeks an unconventional mode of religious experience.

An important reason the conception of Pentheus' basic character carries conviction is because he fits the pattern of the fate of the *theomachos* and specifically the *theomachos* of Dionysiac myth. (One thinks here of the fates of Lycurgus, the Proetids, the Minyads, or the pirates.) In other words, Pentheus persists with his resistance because that is what *theomachoi* against this god traditionally do. On the other hand, so far am I from wishing to disparage psychological explanations that I am about to offer one myself.

There is an acquiescent submissiveness about Pentheus while he is possessed by the god. The strange accord between hostile deity and mortal is reminiscent of the mad Ajax's temporarily harmonious relations with Athena, discussed in Ch. 6.[33] In both cases the deities are intent on humiliating their victims and preparing the way for their deaths, but more than the rejection of an anthropomorphic deity is at issue. Both Ajax and Pentheus reject their full humanity. Neither can accept those parts of his nature (and of the world which forms the context for the human condition) that are outside his conscious control. One might say that they cannot

---

[30] Diller (1983) 365. See also Seaford who, commenting on 957–8, observes that the lines 'may indicate prurience on P.'s part, but not necessarily. He may, as the next line suggests (and despite 686–8, 940), be eager to be vindicated in his earlier conviction (221–5) by catching the maenads *in flagrante delicto.*'

[31] Foley (1985) 207.   [32] Ibid. 220.   [33] See Ch. 6, 'Ajax and Athena'.

accept that the self is greater than the ego. Ajax displays this tendency in his rejection of any outside help; he wants his achievements to be wholly his (and he defines himself too narrowly), on the assumption that he could control all the contingencies of life. Pentheus cannot accept irrational disorder. In this he is not exclusively the individual since his kingly role makes him, at least in principle, the representative and custodian of the ordered life of the polis, so that his attitude to women apparently out of control is by no means idiosyncratic. But the irrational disorder is not entirely outside Pentheus' own psyche, as his own violent and indeed irrational reactions demonstrate. Critics then are right to argue that there is a Dionysiac element suppressed and unacknowledged in him.

Such talk of the ego and the self is of course unthinkable without the influence of Freud and 'depth psychology', but these two terms help us articulate the psychological conditions of Ajax and Pentheus tolerably well without our venturing further into the complex and controversial dynamics of psychoanalysis. In my opening remarks in Ch. 2, I argue that we can distinguish in both cultures, our own and the ancient, (1) the conscious mind characterized by deliberation and regulation of mental events; and (2) all mental events that fall outside it, whether we want to include these in the self or attribute them to a divine being.[34] In madness, then, the irrational invades the conscious minds of Ajax and Pentheus forcing a kind of acceptance on them, as symbolized in their apparently friendly relations with the deity involved. But because they are mad this acceptance can only be destructive; both men remain trapped in their misconceptions: Ajax believes that he has more or less subdued Athena to his will, confining her to the subsidiary and inferior role of 'ally', and Pentheus thinks that Dionysus is obligingly helping him to prove what he has believed all along. Indeed, the highly disputed quality of *sophia* (824) Pentheus now attributes admiringly to the Stranger, but it is the practical *sophia* required to facilitate his spying.

There are then major similarities between the mad episodes of Ajax and Pentheus. In each case an important psychological truth is thrown into sharper focus, but the settled mental conditions of the two men are not, in ancient terms, a form of mental illness, an anachronistic concept, as we have seen.[35] On the other hand, in answer to the objection to the application of 'psychoanalytic concepts such as unconscious desire and repression to Pentheus', on the grounds that 'he has no existence beyond the drama', Seaford argues that 'the power of the representation of a character may reside precisely in its concentration on a coherent set of symptoms (*as if* the character had an unconscious formed over time)'.[36] But this 'as if' is a feature of characterization in general, since, psychoanalysis apart, the reader or spectator may be invited to postulate a psychological history for a character on the basis of present behaviour (not to say 'symptoms'). But the pertinent issue here is whether it is legitimate to apply an anachronistic theory of personality to a fictional character—or, more broadly, a theory of personality that is alien to the culture of the fictional work in question. As I argued in Ch. 1, there is nothing wrong with bringing our own terms of reference

---

[34] See Ch. 2, 'Introduction'.
[35] See Ch. 3, 'The curse and Eteocles' mental state'.
[36] Seaford (1997) 33.

to the interpretation of ancient texts. In fact, we can scarcely avoid doing so. But, as I stated there, we have to take care to observe the distinction between a 'primary' interpretation that respects the ancient concepts and perceptions and the 'secondary' analyses that come from our culture. Otherwise we might say, quite wrongly, that Hippolytus is repressed, simply because we cannot believe that anyone with his attitude to sex could fail to be repressed. It is important to be clear, however, that this distinction does not apply when the subjects are real people. It is clearly legitimate, for example, to use modern Western medicine to diagnose the cause of the deaths of dead people from another era, provided of course that there is sufficient evidence for the diagnosis. Therefore, if Hippolytus were a real ancient person and we had the evidence about his character which we have about the fictional Hippolytus, we might be justified in saying that he was repressed. But Pentheus, as a character in an ancient fictional work, is not and cannot be a repressed neurotic, since he was conceived and exists within a culture to which the concept of repression is alien, though to us he may resemble neurotics in various respects. Moreover, by the same principle, we cannot overrule a positive interpretation offered in the work. We cannot, for example, deny that Pentheus is bewitched by Dionysus on the grounds that no such god exists.

The 'testing' of Pentheus can seem like a game of cat and mouse because the man is obviously incorrigible and the god seems to enjoy his easy ascendancy over him.[37] Throughout these scenes we have a certain limited sympathy for Pentheus as the victim of something beyond his power and comprehension, but also some for Dionysus who is calm and patient with him. This sympathy for the god is limited by his obvious pleasure in teasing Pentheus and by the fact that he is a god for whom one's sympathy could never be profound since a god cannot really suffer or be victimized. Once Dionysus starts to punish Pentheus he becomes horribly vindictive, and our sympathy for the man grows, but only because he is a helpless victim, and even this sympathy is qualified by a measure of disgust at what Pentheus has become. After the catastrophe our sympathy is substantially redirected at Agave.[38] It ought to be qualified perhaps by the fact that she too was a *theomachos*, but this point is not stressed and the theomachy was based only on her disbelief in the story of the god's birth. At the end we agree with Cadmus that the punishment was too severe (1348), not only on Pentheus but on Cadmus himself and on Agave. Traditionally, this is the way of Greek gods and it is pointless to complain, but Euripides, against the background of sophistic religious scepticism, invites us to judge the god by human moral standards. Our attitude to Dionysus has moved thus from a certain limited sympathy to loathing qualified by the fact that he is a god and that traditionally we have not been used to judging him.[39]

---

[37] See e.g. Diller (1983) 365.

[38] On our detachment from Pentheus see Winnington-Ingram (1948) 161.

[39] 'For Cadmus too [as well as for Agave] the god's revelation of his true power and legitimacy in Thebes comes not as a religious experience but as a reflection on the destructive vengeance of the god and as a protest, futile though it is, against his excessive cruelty and injustice … All the hopes for rebirth and renewal that initiation brings are dashed to the ground, not only in Pentheus' horrible death as a pseudo-maenad but also in the mood of dispersion and despair in the closing scene': C. Segal (1999–2000) 289–90.

PENTHEUS' MORAL INADEQUACIES

What then is Pentheus' moral failing and to what extent does it depend on a lack of moral awareness? First there is the question of self-definition. Sophoclean heroes define themselves by their *eugeneia* which provides them with a moral basis for their responses to the crises they face. Euripidean heroes, on the other hand, are apt to seem passive victims. This is true even of the 'transitional' case of Medea who starts out like a Sophoclean hero apparently in control of her moral responses and sure about what they should be but ends up as much the victim of her own *thumos*. Hecuba faces a situation of moral evil where the correct course (punishment of the guilty party) is clear without appeal to an inherent moral nature and the problem is the practical one of how to achieve it. Hippolytus is largely passive because he does not understand that he faces a crisis, but he has a strong and to some extent perverse moral commitment which actually destroys him. But Pentheus is defined almost entirely negatively: he has ordinary views and prejudices rather than strong positive moral commitments that would regulate his own behaviour in a demanding way and he is irascible and so inclined to tyrannous reactions.[40] Thus he is far from representing the ideal king.[41] Because his adversary is throughout a god and that god is on stage with him, he inevitably appears a pathetic and deluded victim, as would the Sophoclean Ajax if the whole play were taken up with the madness scene.

Pentheus' moral inadequacies are well summarized by Winnington-Ingram.[42]

[U]pon his crude assumptions he [Pentheus] is prepared to punish without adequate evidence. He allows his public action to be dictated by his private character and thereby puts himself in the wrong. . . . [He] has none of the self-knowledge that is necessary for self-control; he cannot recognise the springs of his own actions and, in particular, that element of irrationality and violence in himself which he shares with those he is persecuting. It is these things that will betray him, and that deprive his claim to authority of any real foundation.

Pentheus fails then (like the Creon of *Antigone*) in his moral obligations to himself, to the individuals around him, to the gods, and of course to the state. As Seaford argues, 'nowhere in the text is Pentheus, or his hostility to the new cult, associated with the order or the interests of the polis'.[43] Moreover, it is clearly in the interests of the polis that the new religion be accepted, since there is no question of the Dionysiac consciousness supplanting the ordinary civic type.

---

[40] See also Diller (1983) 363 for whom Pentheus 'lacks sufficient means to face the new movement, having merely the will to assert himself. He orients himself mentally by applying the most obviously banal concepts, his knowledge of the effect of sex and alcohol, family gossip and national prejudices.'

[41] *Pace* Rosenmeyer (1968) 384–5. Contrast C. Segal (1999–2000) 285: 'The "fear" that Pentheus inspires in the city [in his defence of Cadmus against insult: 1316–22] only reflects ironically on his failures as a king. Far from solidifying and stabilizing the civic order, it operates only within the narrow limits of his own household, alienates the citizens, and works against the harmonious relation of divine and human realms in which the healthy polis flourishes.'

[42] Winnington-Ingram (1948) 76–7.

[43] Seaford (1997) 43. The Creon of *Antigone* at least thought he was defending the state's interests (Soph. *Ant.* 178–91). On Pentheus' conventionally tyrannical qualities see Seaford ibid.

Dionysus represents no threat whatever to ordered life, as the celebration of the cult is to be integrated into the city's communal life and confined to the relevant festivals. It is never suggested that ordinary civic life is to be replaced by indiscriminate Bacchic orgies on Cithaeron. Luckily for the Thebans, the god chooses to make an example of their king, while not only preserving the city but also ensuring their acceptance of himself, if to a great extent on the basis of the terror he inspires.

Historically, accepting Dionysus never spelt the end of civilized and civic life as the Greeks knew it. But Pentheus could not have known what the immediate or long-term consequences would have been. Not that he ever formulates the problem as the Dionysiac threat to civilized life. He cannot do that because he never understands the true nature of this new religion. He does not argue either that the cult as he misconceives it constitutes such a threat, though perhaps his prejudice implies that he assumes something of the kind. His response is a knee-jerk reaction rather than intelligently considered. We can say though that obviously he should have retained an open mind or at least corrected his prejudices as the evidence became overwhelming.

PENTHEUS AND MORAL AWARENESS

Let us then briefly review Pentheus' moral awareness in light of our list of questions. First of all, he does not define himself in any terms, moral or otherwise, nor particularly as a king with a set of obligations, though presumably we are to imagine that he acts on such an assumption. He reacts, as we have seen, quite unreflectingly out of a set of prejudices. Nor is he aware of the specifically moral implications of the crisis. How could he be when he misreads it so radically? He does act of course in harmony with his moral beliefs, but again unreflectingly. His morality is therefore inappropriate in the play's terms. (What might constitute an appropriate moral response we shall presently consider.) Pentheus obviously completely misunderstands the facts of the situation and the probable consequences of his projected actions (he thinks that military force will solve the problem). As far as concerns the integration of his emotions into his deliberations, it has to be said that he reacts rather than deliberates and that his emotions (especially anger, hostility, and anxiety) largely determine those reactions. Finally, his reactions (since we cannot really call them deliberations) are free until the bewitching scene, after which there is divine intervention, though this takes the form of distorting rather than replacing his normal thinking. This puts it in my second category of psychological intervention.[44] Pentheus then is deluded in that he does not realize that Dionysus is distorting his thinking. Ajax's situation is similar.

---

[44] See pp. 33–4.

THE MORAL CHALLENGE OF THE DIONYSIAC

Let us leave Pentheus' deplorable inadequacies and turn to a broader consideration of the moral challenge of the Dionysiac, both the religion and the psychological phenomenon. First of all we need to ask what it means exactly, in the play's
terms, to accept the Dionysiac religion, and what *is* the Dionysiac philosophy of
life as enunciated in the play? I alluded in my introductory remarks to this chapter
to two competing and irreducible realities—the ordinary world and the Dionysiac.
Naturally, these worlds have their own moralities. Greek ethical philosophy
proceeds from the question 'How can I acquire *eudaimonia*?' In the Archaic
period it was generally assumed that *eudaimonia*, although not entirely divorced
from mental attitude and morality, consisted to a considerable degree in what the
philosophers called 'external goods' (health, wealth, thriving children, and so on)
and that these advantages were overwhelmingly a matter of luck or divine
dispensation.[45] The focus on *eudaimonia* as a state of mind is much more a
feature of later ethical philosophy. The 'righteous' (*dikaios*) person of Plato's
Republic has clearly attained *eudaimonia* through an inner, psychological harmony among the three 'elements' of the mind (*psyche*). External goods scarcely enter
the picture. Similarly, the focus of the Bacchants' philosophy, enunciated initially
in the parodos, is *eudaimonia* (μάκαρ, εὐδαίμων: 72) conceived as a mental state
achieved by joining one's mind to the *thiasos* (the sacred band) (θιασεύεται ψυχάν,
75–6). Then, in the first stasimon, the chorus take up Teiresias' contrast between
true and false *sophia* (traditional ancestral wisdom as opposed to superficially
clever sophistries), referring to Pentheus' 'unbridled tongue' (387) and identifying
true *sophia* with the traditional injunction to 'think mortal thoughts' (395–6).
Since life is short it is madness to 'chase big ideas' (398) rather than living in the
present, that is, presumably, living life like the masses (416–32). Again the
assumption seems to be that Pentheus is some kind of deluded sophistical hubrist,
and perhaps that is the sort of character Euripides needed him to represent, at
least on some occasions, though this, as we have seen, hardly catches the character
as he is actually conceived. The Dionysiac consciousness too is broadened here
from ecstatic mystical irrationalism to include the kind of unreflective, unintellec-
tual life of simple people who live for the moment. So there is much more at issue
here than a specific ecstatic religion. This celebration of the unexamined life is
notably anti-Socratic, and the religious communion advocated is completely
antithetical to the rational communion with the divine exalted, for example, by
Aristotle and the Stoics.

The chorus recur to the theme of *eudaimonia* in the third stasimon, which,
following the bewitching, comes at a point when we may well feel strongly
alienated from the god. *eudaimonia* is represented here chiefly as release from
danger or toils (the fawn simile (866–76), entering harbour to shelter from a storm
at sea (902–3), getting on top of one's troubles (904–5)). But, most significantly,
the Archaic idea that *eudaimonia* refers to the overall quality of an entire life ('call
no man happy until he is dead') is rejected in favour of focusing on each day as it

---

[45] See e.g. Hdt. 1. 30–3.

comes and being *eudaimōn* or indeed 'blessed' (μακαρίζω, 912) on a daily basis.[46] This makes sense in the Bacchic context since the Bacchic state, viewed psychologically, is temporary, and if one lives for the day and does not think of the future then why not find *eudaimonia* within the single day, the apparently eternal present, as it were? On the other hand, if the matter is viewed from a religious perspective, initiates into the Dionysiac religion are in a sense permanently blessed, even if the Bacchic state of mind does not permeate every minute of their lives. In the epilogue Dionysus claims that the Theban royal family would have enjoyed *eudaimonia* if they had accepted him as their ally (ηὐδαιμονεῖτ' ἄν, 1343), which presumably means that individuals would have enjoyed the blessings of initiation, and the polis the protection of the god. Of course for the Theban royal house the *eudaimonia* of the cult is horribly perverted. Agave is *eudaimōn* as a huntress (1258) until she returns to normal consciousness, and she believes that Cadmus is 'blessed' (μακάριος, 1242–3) in her success. Cadmus himself has a rather different view of the matter (ὄψιν οὐκ εὐδαίμονα, 1232). But twice sandwiched into this ode that celebrates the joys of escape is an ugly delight in taking revenge (877–81 = 897–901).

> τί τὸ σοφόν; ἢ τι κάλλιον
> παρὰ θεῶν γέρας ἐν βροτοῖς
> ἢ χεῖρ' ὑπὲρ κορυφᾶς
> τῶν ἐχθρῶν κρείσσω κατέχειν;
> ὅ τι καλὸν φίλον αἰεί.

(What is wisdom? Or what is a fairer gift from the gods found among mortals than to hold a conquering hand over the crest of enemies? What is fair is always dear.'[47])

In the words of Winnington-Ingram, 'The effort of thought and criticism is eliminated; the individual transcends his own weakness in the acceptance of a tradition, which at the same time enables him to gratify his simplest and strongest impulses. For is the tradition ultimately anything but the codification of these impulses?'[48]

---

[46] The idea of focusing on the day is traditional, though not identified with *eudaimonia*. See e.g. Eur. *Hec.* 627–8, *Her.* 503–5.

[47] Seaford disputes the traditional reading, setting a question mark after βροτοῖς and translating: 'What is the wise (gift), or what is the finer gift from the gods among mortals? Is it to hold the hand powerful over the head of your enemies? (No, for) What is fine is dear always.' (He takes 'fine' to refer to the state of the Dionysiac initiate.) But why should the chorus, apparently apropos of nothing, mention the (admittedly traditional) pleasure of taking revenge in this context only to reject it immediately? On Seaford's reading (though not on the traditional one) they could hardly be referring to the god's forthcoming punishment of Pentheus, because they are all in favour of it. Moreover, the resulting ellipsis which Seaford fills with '(No, for)' is very awkward indeed, not to mention the fact that the chorus cannot now be telling us specifically what they consider to be 'fine'. If we retain the traditional reading, the Bacchants advocate conventional wisdom, and enjoying harming enemies is part of that.

[48] Winnington-Ingram (1948) 111. Foley (1985) 222 remarks that '[t]he Asian women . . . do not occupy the same position, emotionally, intellectually, or perceptually, between the royal family and the audience as the chorus in other tragedies. Though voicing uncannily familiar Greek ethical sentiments, they are ultimately a voice alien to the community and use the language of *sōphrosunē* (self-control and moderation) and *hēsuchia* (apolitical quiet) to serve their passionate desire for revenge.' See also Winnington-Ingram (1948) 111, 113: . . . It is the laws which the herd accepts and dictates which the Bacchanals recognise as eternal and as having an unchallengeable basis in nature' [113]. See also

Not only do the Bacchants have their own understanding of *eudaimonia*; they also reinterpret the virtues that lead to its attainment. *sophia* then is conventional wisdom as contrasted with sophistries and it relates to following the traditional customs (*nomoi*) (31, 890–6), including taking revenge on enemies (877–91). Pentheus, by contrast, is 'godless' (ἄθεον), 'lawless' (ἄνομον), and 'unjust' (ἄδικον) (995). Related to the acceptance of tradition is thinking thoughts appropriate to mere human beings (395–6, 427–32). *sōphrosunē*, on the other hand, is associated in the play mostly with a proper restraint in word or deed. Dionysus warns Pentheus to be *sōphrōn* and not bind him (504). Finally, there is the paradoxical and chaste *sōphrosunē* of the Bacchants until they are disturbed (σωφρόνως, 686; εὐκοσμίας, 693).[49]

We see then that, although there is considerable overlap between traditional wisdom and Bacchic philosophy, familiar concepts are given an unusual twist through being refracted through this ecstatic religion. The rather unfair and exaggerated effect of this refraction is to make the collected wisdom of the ages appear the product of a benighted and dangerous irrationalism, particularly since the poet seems to focus on the worst aspects of tradition—its rejection of any innovative thought that might subvert it and its celebration of the sadistic delights of harming enemies.

What would it mean to be morally aware in terms of this philosophy? It could only mean to be aware of and subscribe to the traditional wisdom and in particular the tenets of the Dionysiac religion. In the Greek context we think of morality as regulating our relations with the self, other individuals (especially *philoi*), the state, and the gods, but during Bacchic communion all rational thought is suspended and the god, as it were, takes over. The ritual proceeds in a certain order and virtues like the chaste *sōphrosunē* of the Bacchants express themselves spontaneously. But all this depends on the temporary nature of the Dionysiac which cannot supply a morality for ordinary civic life.

Pentheus' position is a difficult one since, as a king, he is charged with maintaining security and traditional moral standards. No other character in Greek tragedy is confronted with the need to admit and integrate such an alien cultural practice, and one that could seem immoral. What is required here is an intelligent and committed tolerance based on a proper understanding (but not necessarily unqualified approval) of manifestations of the Dionysiac, both narrowly religious and more broadly psychological. Pentheus could and should have corrected his false idea that the women were guilty of sexual misconduct, but their behaviour nevertheless appeared frighteningly disordered and untraditional. To admit the Dionysiac in the widest sense of the word (that is, not just the specific religion but the irrational element in life however it might manifest) is to acknowledge not only that humans (and indeed the universe) are not entirely rational but that they

---

C. Segal (1982) 28: 'The paradox of traditional gnomic wisdom in the mouths of figures who are extraneous, if not actually hostile, to the polis throws us off balance and leaves us without a secure ethical center, a single clear focus of values.'

[49] For *eukosmia* in the play see Gold (1977) *passim*.

cannot be compelled to be so, and that tactical concessions to irrationality have to be made.[50]

It seems paradoxical that the morally correct course could be to accept the irrational without trying to resist or control it, particularly since much of Greek ethical theory is based on suppressing or controlling irrational impulses and obeying reason. In a context such as this the moral dimension becomes problematic in the way that it is in, for example, Freudian psychology—that is, as a rational element functioning (or attempting to function) within the broader dynamics of a psychological entity that is fundamentally irrational.[51] The task then is not to choose the ('good') rational and reject the ('bad') irrational, but to carve out a place for the rational within this larger non-rational dynamic of the psyche which has, the play insists, its own validity and its own heterodox 'order', though also its own horrors. And this kind of inscrutable and impenetrable order is, after all, characteristic also of the outer, 'divine' world which the Greeks encountered and which is so marvellously embodied in Sophocles' *Oedipus Tyrannus*. There is then a strong, and rather disturbingly 'postmodern' sense of competing realities in *Bacchae*.[52] The required moral response is, paradoxically, to transcend an exclusively moral response and recognize the need to give way before a force that cannot be contained by moral rigidity. This would remain a moral response because it would aim at the good of the community and of everyone in it.[53]

The challenge of Dionysus then is not one that can be met in the currency of conventional morality, heroic or other. Other heroes face hostile gods, but they are still able to respond in a morally conventional way, often in order to save their honour, but a king in Pentheus' position could not, like a Sophoclean hero, draw on his *eugeneia*, or, like an Aeschylean hero, on his role in order to combat a threat from an enemy that must be subdued, for neither a god nor a psychological reality can be subdued. Indeed, Pentheus' knee-jerk military response would have proved disastrous. The unique challenge presented to Pentheus is precisely to relax his moral attitudes, to allow his people, especially the women, licence to behave for a time in what seems (but is not really) a completely undisciplined way.

The limited indulgence of the irrational which I am suggesting as an appropriate moral response is no guarantee of safety. The cult in this play represents, finally, more than the tamed Dionysiac religion of the fifth century. It represents the irrational contents of the mind, including an urge to revenge and to bestial violence. The costs of suppression are clear enough in both messenger speeches

[50] Similarly, in our own day, the efforts of militant atheists to destroy religion, if successful, would only result in the substitution of disorganized for (what they conceive to be) organized superstition.

[51] 'The recognition of Dionysus is . . . partly a recognition that the god's mysterious divinity and power is finally beyond the control of human knowledge': Goldhill (1986) 260. '. . . the possibility of directly perceiving Dionysus in an adequate manner with human eyes is challenged throughout the action of the play from the disguised god's entrance to his final, ambivalent epiphany': ibid. 276.

[52] Gregory (1985) 30, who examines the motif of seeing in *Bacchae*, comments: 'The play itself provides the best demonstration that nothing is absolute: the motif of seeing is just one means whereby a drama which seems to justify the authority of traditional religion reveals itself as simultaneously imbued with a sophistic spirit of relativism.'

[53] 'Just as Teiresias tells us that man cannot live by bread alone, so Euripides tells us that man cannot survive by reason alone. Only in his recognition of this fact, only in his saving of the intellectual life by admitting its proper limitations, can Euripides be labelled an irrationalist': Conacher (1967) 72.

where the ritual *sparagmos* is perverted by outside interference and with calamitous results. Still, although the horrors that end the play are in part the consequences of resisting the cult, they are so revolting that one tends to forget the fact of resistance and turn against the god altogether. Euripides presumably counted on such a response. He wanted to leave us on a note of pessimism.[54]

The gods in earlier tragedy, Euripidean and other, could thwart human moral aspirations, but for Euripides the individual's self-definition in overwhelmingly moral terms, with the emotional element supporting the moral (like the Platonic *thumos* performing its proper function), is a delusion. The divisive irrational elements in the psyche are too powerful. In this, Euripides' most insightful play, a single god is used to symbolize these irrational elements as a whole,[55] but in such a way as to suggest strongly that they are necessary and that they need not be entirely destructive. While in *Hippolytus* Aphrodite is seen acting only destructively, in the *Bacchae* there is a countervailing emphasis on the joys and creative possibilities of Dionysus, though admittedly, '[t]he joyful, exuberant side of Dionysiac worship described in the odes of the first half of the play . . . keeps retreating further into the background as the play goes on.'[56]

---

[54] 'Euripides may be asking his audience to see clearly, like Agave, the reality, the consequences, and the horror of the Dionysiac religion. Significantly, it is this last impression of the destructive elements of Dionysiac worship and of the total rejection of such a religion with which Euripides chooses to leave his audience as the *Bacchae* ends': Kalke (1985) 425–6. Contrast Burnett (1970) 27 and McGinty (1978) 89, who sees the violence of the cult entirely as a response to resistance. The myths concerned with resistance to the god 'stand as an implicit curb against destructive action on the part of the devotees. Lycurgus, the daughters of Cadmos, of Minyas and of Proitos all cause or directly inflict death, but only because they stand under the condemnation of the god. The myths, hence, associate anti-social action with improper rather than proper divine–human relations and, despite their violence, indirectly celebrate a harmonious world.' Winnington-Ingram (1948) 28 maintains that Euripides feels distaste for both the personal Dionysus and the negative aspects of his religion.

[55] With a somewhat different emphasis, Rohdich (1968) 138 sees the cult as a symbol of all that opposed to what he calls the Socratic and the sophistic.

[56] C. Segal (1999–2000) 291.

17

Conclusion

MORAL AUTONOMY AND DIVINE INTERVENTION

Moral awareness in an agent presupposes a sense of moral responsibility which, however conceived, is in turn predicated on a corresponding conception of moral autonomy. To be clear about autonomy we need a conception of the self, and we saw in the second chapter that both we and the ancients could postulate a conscious part of the mind that can regulate at least some of its mental events as opposed to an unconscious part from which 'alien' mental events irrupt unbidden into consciousness. We have defined moral autonomy as existing when the conscious mind is free of external intervention. In ancient tragedy, such intervention, when it occurs, tends to originate with the gods. We have seen that the gods' intervention in human affairs takes two forms, the panoramic and the psychological. In the first form a god (or gods) oversees and manipulates an episode or segment of a mortal's life. The god may construct material events, anticipate and thus factor in human psychological events, or engage in direct psychological intervention which can seem logically implied even if it is not specified. The gods are almost always latent forces in the background of Greek tragedy and for that reason represent a constant threat to human autonomy. However, for the most part this threat remains unrealized, and the human characters are presented as the source of their own thoughts, feelings, and actions and are judged accordingly by their fellow characters.

The Fury and Apollo cooperate to fulfil the destiny of Oedipus' sons in the *Seven* by mysterious immanent panoramic intervention of such a kind that Eteocles will be faced with his brother at the seventh gate. We cannot know to what extent, if any, these deities influence, rather than merely anticipate, Eteocles' individual decisions at each of the gates, but there is undoubtedly direct psychological intervention at the point when Eteocles feels himself subject to a powerful urge to fight. Eteocles' judgement, however, is unaffected, though the god-inspired emotion hurries him on to meet the doom he rationally knows to be inevitable. Divine panoramic involvement is present throughout *Oresteia* too, from the contrivance of the dilemma at Aulis to the trial in the Areopagus court. Throughout this process the question of psychological intervention arises crucially at two points: in the state of mind (*parakopa*) that overtakes Agamemnon during or immediately after his decision and in the form of the *alastōr* that overdetermines Clytemnestra's crime. In neither case, however, is autonomy compromised because the decisions of both human agents proceed from their settled characters.

Although Athena maddens Sophocles' Ajax, later, when he deliberates, his consciousness is quite free of outside intervention. The goddess prepares the way 'panoramically' for the suicide by creating, through the madness, a situation to which she (presumably) knows Ajax will respond in the way that he does. In *Trachiniae*, the divine intervention is more elusive; the oracles seem by their very existence to imply some kind of ordered world, and Heracles' strange intuition about his destiny in the shape of his two instructions to his son seems to confirm this sense of order. The gods, and Zeus in particular, hold themselves aloof leaving Heracles and Deianeira to deliberate independently. (Cypris in the play acts with no intelligible purpose and is barely more than a personification of erotic desire.) In the *Tyrannus*, Apollo's predictions call forth from the human agents reactions which the god foresees and factors in to his purpose, which is the fulfilment and revelation of Oedipus' destiny. He contrives also the 'coincidences' of the play and, merging mysteriously with Oedipus' *daimōn*, he overdetermines, but at the same time gives focus and direction to Oedipus' paradoxically autonomous purpose in the self-blinding scene. Thus the panoramic and psychological intervention in the play operates very much as in the *Seven*. In the Sophoclean *Electra*, on the other hand, Apollo's involvement is less obtrusive. There is the ironical answer to Clytemnestra's prayer, which recalls a similar irony in respect to Jocasta's in the *Tyrannus*, but the oracle merely confirms Orestes' pre-existing purpose, so that the characters are autonomous throughout. Even less obtrusive is the divine involvement in *Philoctetes*, wherein the divine purpose is realized as the culmination of the human interaction (the friendly union of the hero and Neoptolemus, the frustration of Odysseus' scheme, though not of his ultimate purpose) with a gentle push from the superhuman Heracles.

In the *Medea*, as regularly in Euripidean tragedy, there is little or no sense of divine immanence, for all that Medea calls on Zeus. Medea's plans are hatched without divine interference or direction, and by the time of her controversial appearance on the chariot her deliberations and her revenge are complete. The divine associations of her 'epiphany' then are purely symbolic. Similarly, in *Hippolytus*, despite Aphrodite's declared purpose in the prologue, we do not feel her presence in the action. Artemis, on the other hand, makes no claims to intervene psychologically; she provides rather an object for Hippolytus' devotion. In *Heracles*, Hera operates through Lyssa, but complete autonomy returns to Heracles for his subsequent deliberations. In the Euripidean *Electra* Apollo's oracle merely issues a command. In *Bacchae*, Pentheus is temporarily possessed by Dionysus, but this has no significant effect on any moral deliberations as his pre-existing attitudes remain.

SELF-DEFINITION

In Aeschylus the issues are, as it were, logically prior and the characters are then conceived in order to work the issues out in dramatic terms; Sophocles, on the other hand, starts with strongly self-defined characters who know what they believe in and want and are self-united in getting it. Thus they recognize moral crises and are free to respond to them or ignore them, though to ignore them would contradict their fundamental natures. On the other hand, Euripides' characters, even those that have a moral self-concept, tend to be undermined (like Medea and Phaedra) by emotions they can neither integrate nor control, and in some of the later plays (as in *Electra* and *IA*) the changing emotions largely control the characters' correspondingly changing beliefs.

A number of our agents—exceptions are Euripides' Hecuba, Electra, Pentheus, and Agamemnon (in the *IA*)—define themselves either explicitly or implicitly and in moral terms. The military leaders or warriors among them see themselves as such and are aware of and accept some at least of the corresponding conventional moral obligations that attach to the role. Certainly Eteocles and almost certainly Agamemnon accept that they have obligations to those that they lead, and all these warriors feel obliged to behave virtuously and to vindicate their honour. This is true also of Philoctetes in his isolation, though he has come to emphasize the gentler heroic virtue of *philophrosunē* (to use the Homeric term), and of the young Neoptolemus, though his initial self-definition is rather restricted. Among the women, Deianeira and Phaedra see themselves as 'good' in the special sense that Greek males applied the term to their sex, whereas Sophocles' Electra and Euripides' Medea define themselves morally but unconventionally. Electra ignores the societal constraints of her gender and looks to her *eugeneia* which, in her view, requires her not only to vindicate her father by doing all she can to punish his killers, but, more remarkably, to vindicate abstract right. Medea, on the other hand, recognizes that her gender is significant, that it entails huge social disabilities. Nevertheless, like the Sophoclean Electra, Medea defines herself by her *eugeneia*, and in particular her descent from Helios, which, she is convinced, obliges her to take revenge on her enemies. Thus, although these women adopt morally unconventional roles which entail morally unconventional responses, the morality to which they subscribe is, paradoxically, thoroughly conventional. Oedipus defines himself in part conventionally as a compassionate and responsible ruler (and he accepts the responsibilities attached to that role), but also as a solver of riddles in the public interest. Hippolytus defines himself idiosyncratically in terms of his own conception of innate *sōphrosunē*, and since such a blessed moral condition is its own guarantee of moral action there is no need for him to concern himself with specific responsibilities.

Hecuba and the Euripidean Electra do not define themselves in such terms. Hecuba sees herself at first as an aged slave who was once a queen and, after the deaths of Polyxena and Polydorus, more radically, as all but non-existent. She is, after all, a woman without a state or a family or meaningful human context, and without a future. Her revenge on Polymestor does not spring from a moral self-conception; she does not speak of owing it to herself as a particular kind of person. The revenge is all that she has left, and her consuming desire for it is in part a product of the familiar Euripidean 'revenge reflex' (though the phenomenon is by no means restricted to that dramatist), that is, it is characteristic of human nature to desire revenge when injured, an attitude supported by the ethic of harming enemies. But her revenge is also a product of a morally valid desire for retributive justice, a desire that seems in a way more impressive to the extent that it is almost impersonal since it proceeds from a person who no longer has any other need.

Euripides' Electra's desire for the matricide, on the other hand, in no way proceeds from an abstract desire for justice. In the absence of moral self-definition, Electra is driven by unreflecting hatred and, after the deed, by remorse. This is in a play much interested in the problematical question of moral *eugeneia*, a quality which Electra and her brother clearly lack. This lack of moral nobility is a feature of the *IA* too wherein the characters are driven primarily by a haphazard succession of emotions.

Why is it then that so many characters define themselves, at least implicitly, in moral terms? This feature of tragedy is to a great extent a function of the heroic moral ambience of the plays. For these characters honour is of supreme importance, though it must be based on genuine virtue. It is natural enough to define oneself to a considerable extent in terms of one's function in society and therefore to be dedicated to performing that function well. Moreover, we tend to find in Greek culture an underlying assumption that the happy life, in so far as it is possible, is closely associated with the moral life. This is obviously true of ancient ethical philosophy which is an investigation of the nature of *eudaimonia*—an investigation which soon finds itself obliged to focus on ethical considerations. (It never occurred to serious thinkers to divorce happiness from virtue, though moral action in tragedy may entail much inescapable unhappiness.[1])

But, even before the era of the ethical philosophers, when *eudaimonia* was considered even more precarious and a matter to be adjudicated only after the alleged possessor's death, the closest one could get to a settled happiness was to be secure in one's honour, and that could always be vindicated and so virtually guaranteed by a (possibly fatal) act of exemplary courage. (The Hector of the *Iliad* is here the obvious case in point. He can scarcely bear to think about his family's probable future, but he can secure his honour in perpetuity by facing Achilles, and his honour trumps even his love for his family.) The characters of tragedy therefore are given to moral self-definition because self-interest and the naturally eudaimonistic morality of Greek culture tend to converge for them. A moment's reflection will reveal that none of those that define themselves in moral terms, with the exception of Medea, would have seen any advantage in acting other than according to their morality. The only alternative for Eteocles, for example, is the dishonour of a *cowardly* fratricide; Sophocles' Electra makes her life even more unpleasant than it already is, but she could not have endured to live like her sister; and Hippolytus could not have abandoned his honesty merely to save his life. Medea, on the other hand, reluctantly fulfils her original 'moral' purpose, though she comes to realize that it has been hijacked by her *thumos*. Morality for the majority of these tragic agents, then, relates to being true to themselves. This may of course entail behaving well towards others, so that the self-orientation of this sort of morality does not lead inevitably to exclusive concern with oneself, which is, of course, antithetical to what we understand today by morality.

---

[1] The Thrasymachus of the first book of Plato's *Republic* maintains that injustice frequently pays, but he is not a serious thinker.

SELF-REDEFINITION

Some of our agents face the prospect of partial self-redefinition, though not in Aeschylus. Ajax, for example, in his deception speech realizes that he has been 'feminized' by Tecmessa's appeal to the point that he actually pities her, and he knows that this presents a threat to his resolve. He has come to understand too that he lives in an undesirably unstable world in which friends and enemies can change places unpredictably and in which he too could change. Since self-definition relates closely to the way one sees the world, the threat that the world is not as one supposed entails a corresponding threat to one's self-view as one is faced with redefining one's place in it, and Ajax's self-view has already been challenged and clearly shaken by the Judgement of Arms which honoured a man very much more at home in the world as it really is. Ajax of course avoids redefining himself. The Sophoclean Heracles, on the other hand, does adapt. Faced with the disintegration of the body that made possible all the achievements by which he defined himself, only courage in the face of what promises to be a painful death is left to him. So he salvages this virtue and adapts it. But Oedipus' redefinition is the most traumatic and radical. He has to accept that his pollution has given him a kind of negative worth and that all that is left is precisely that acceptance. Neoptolemus, however, is an interesting case. Consciously, he returns to his original moral self-definition, but his actual moral life has in fact moved far beyond it under the influence of Philoctetes.

Medea has defined herself by her commitment to heroic values, underrating her maternal role, but although she does not exactly redefine herself, she comes to realize the extent to which her *thumos* is controlling her. The Euripidean Heracles has to abandon his sense of independence of *tuchē* and accept the need for friends. He also has to see his bow and thus his famous ability and achievements in a morally more ambivalent light. He holds onto his endurance and reapplies it to a potentially disempowered and inglorious future.

INTUITIVE MORAL RESPONSE

Many of the characters are in tune with the moral world of their play (though with varying degrees of understanding, as we shall see below) and with their own self-concept based on noble birth or role which provides them with a conventional morality implicitly validated (sometimes with reservations) by the plays. Thus it is not particularly surprising that they tend to see instantly and intuitively what is required, without deliberation, provided, that is, that they do not confront a moral dilemma.

Some of the characters who respond intuitively without the need to deliberate nevertheless justify their positions to other characters or to the chorus. Thus Aeschylus' Eteocles explains to the chorus that the gods hate his family and desire only his death, that he must meet that death bravely and that delay is pointless. Sophocles' Ajax in the deception speech, struck by sudden pity and the understanding that the world is changeable, appears to be, if not exactly deliberating, then rehearsing aloud and in that way perhaps working through and coming to

terms with his new insights while confirming his intuition about their implications for himself. (The intuition is of course that he will not adapt.) Oedipus
justifies the apparently impulsive self-blinding to the chorus after the event, and
Sophocles' Electra discusses her position from various perspectives with her sister,
mother and chorus. In doing so she speaks as one who has already considered
fully the implications of her stand. Euripides' Phaedra has clearly deliberated
before the action; not about what basic moral attitude she is to adopt towards the
passion—which is obvious—but about the means to be employed to prevent any
morally undesirable consequences.

Medea comes intuitively to her decision to kill the children and then refuses to
discuss it, since it is clearly the most powerful means of punishing Jason. Later,
though, in the Great Monologue, she has second thoughts in a way that is new
among our tragic agents. She even changes her mind. The dialectic of this speech
is not, as we have seen, that of intellectual deliberation: it is rather an emotional
dialectic energized by the alternate incursion and retreat of her maternal feelings
so that 'rational' arguments attach temporarily to both sides in alternation until
she finally realizes that her *thumos* will dictate the outcome.

DELIBERATIVE MORAL RESPONSE

Of those characters who deliberate, the Aeschylean Agamemnon at Aulis is the
most famous, perhaps because the issues seem, for a while at least, more evenly
balanced for him so that he appears to confront, in the most representative way, a
genuine moral dilemma. In *Choephori*, Orestes deliberates only briefly as *aidōs*
arises in him at the immediate prospect of matricide and then returns to a position
he has strongly endorsed throughout the play up until that point. Among Sophoclean agents Ajax quickly decides to vindicate his honour and then deliberates
about the means; Deianeira deliberates in a muddled way over the moral and
practical appropriateness of using the salve. She proceeds when advised to do so
on practical grounds. Moral clarity returns only after the event. Neoptolemus, at
the prospect of practising an unnatural deceit, engages in what we might perhaps
call deliberations—or at least he allows Odysseus' arguments and general influence to sway him. But his moral concern at this point is corrupted by his powerful
desire for glory. Later in the same play, Philoctetes is involved in purely moral
deliberations as to whether he should accept his new friend's well-meaning advice
or stick to his ethic of avoiding enemies.

The Euripidean Heracles deliberates under the stimulus of Theseus' exhortations that he remember his former self-concept as the great endurer and friend of
man, but he moves on to consider the moral implications of returning to but also
modifying such a self-definition, especially the need to keep the bow and the
importance of friendship. The Orestes of Euripides' *Electra* is forced to consider
the issues as his mother arrives and his sister insists on the matricide. He begins
with a strong moral intuition that the deed is wrong, but he yields to Electra's
pressure and her irrelevant charge of cowardice. Like Aeschylus' Agamemnon in
the carpet scene, he allows another person to undermine his moral autonomy and

induce him to yield to the force of her personality rather than to a moral argument.

The agent's response to a crisis is intuitive when he or she sees at once that there is no competing moral claim to be taken into account. Thus for Eteocles the alternatives are brave or cowardly fratricide, for Ajax a brave death or cowardly and dishonourable survival, for the Sophoclean Heracles again a brave death or a cowardly one, for Oedipus the truth that will save the city or a despicable ignorance, and for the Sophoclean Electra noble resistance or cowardly submission to evil. In the cases of the deliberators, on the other hand, there are serious moral alternatives. So the difference—intuitive or deliberative response—is a function of situation rather than character. Deianeira, though, is an interesting case because of her lack of moral clarity. She wants to be a virtuous, honoured, and loved wife, but the salve, the means of guaranteeing this state, should appear morally dubious to her.

INTEGRATION OF EMOTIONS

The agents' emotions generally support their morality. Eteocles' passionate Fury-inspired desire to meet his brother and Oedipus' *daimōn*-supported overwrought condition harmonize with what they resolve to do, and Agamemnon's decision at Aulis is supported by a strange mental state (his *parakopa*) whereby he shuts his mind to pity. In each of these cases emotional autonomy might be said to be impaired, but not to the point of subverting a rational moral position. (As we have observed, the emotional autonomy of an inebriated agent may be obviously impaired, while his or her judgement remains unaffected because the amount of alcohol drunk is below the threshold of significant distortion of rational thought. In such a state, alcohol-fuelled enthusiasm might well hasten the performance of a rationally determined action.)

Aeschylus' Orestes, despite his momentary *aidōs*, is grimly determined to kill his mother; indeed, all his motivation combines to that end. Heracles is utterly set on Hyllus' fulfilment of his instructions as his angry anticipation of disobedience shows. Oedipus is similarly concentrated first on how to find Laius' killer and then on how to respond to the revelation, so there is no room for contrary feelings. (He loses heart for a while after the discussion of the road rage incident.) Sophocles' Electra is a fine case of properly integrated emotions. Her moral view combines with her feelings of grief for her father and outrage at his murder and at the evil situation that prevails in Argos.

Ajax, on the other hand, has to resist his inchoate pity, though otherwise he is grimly sure that the world is out of joint and he is therefore determined to leave it. Neoptolemus, in contrast, recovers his morality under the dual pressure of an appropriate pity for Philoctetes and a profound and increasingly unbearable sense of moral unease occasioned by his deception of the hero. Disharmony, though, is more typical of Euripidean moral agents, though the Sophoclean Deianeira is ruled at first by feeling rather than morality. (We have seen that, unlike our other Sophoclean moral agents, she does not confront her predicament in an essentially moral way.) For Phaedra, an overwhelming and undesirable emotion is precisely the occasion for the application of her moral principles and the object is not to integrate the emotion but to eradicate it. Throughout the early scenes of the play we feel the peremptory pressure of Phaedra's passion pressing her hard to involuntary revelation countered by a kind of anxious horror which is the emotion that supports her morality. Medea, in contrast, identifies with her angry and vengeful feelings unequivocally until the Great Monologue during which a new feeling, maternal sorrow, irrupts into her consciousness. This feeling she naturally cannot integrate with her morality of vengeance which requires the filicide, and although she dismisses it as immoral cowardice it finally brings her to intuit that her irrational *thumos* is driving her revenge. Thus she fails to integrate her contrary emotions; instead her maternal feelings impact on her against her will and undermine her 'moral' conviction, though she proceeds with the filicide itself since this is now beyond her integrated control, driven as she is by what is almost a rogue part of her, the *thumos*, a part with which, paradoxically, she almost identified herself, at least before this scene. The predominant emotion of the Euripidean Heracles at the time of his final resolve is despair at his own polluted state and at the moral condition of the universe that allowed an innocent man to be struck down. This despair corrupts his self-concept and is thus not to be integrated but overcome, and it is Theseus' role to facilitate this. Euripides' Electra is, as we have seen, motivated throughout by a vindictiveness which has generated her supposedly moral desire for matricide.

THE INFLUENCE OF OTHERS

Clytemnestra's contribution to Agamemnon's resolve in the carpet scene is negative and malicious as she works to undermine her husband's entirely proper resolve to avoid the fabrics. Similarly, Euripides' Electra undermines Orestes' reluctance to kill his mother by an irrelevant accusation of cowardice. The chorus of the *Seven* try to dissuade Eteocles from fratricide, whereas the Orestes of *Choephori* actively solicits Pylades' advice and proceeds to act on it at once. Ajax unceremoniously rejects Tecmessa's plea, but it nevertheless has its effect. Deianeira consults the chorus with disastrous results. Sophocles' Electra explains herself sympathetically to her chorus, but is not influenced by them. The chorus of the *Tyrannus* offer Oedipus unsolicited advice about the self-blinding after the event, which he peremptorily rejects. Philoctetes and Neoptolemus, on the other hand, are positively influenced by one another—especially Neoptolemus whose whole moral vision is enriched by his contact with the older man. Phaedra is undermined by the unsolicited counsel of the nurse, but while she loses her authority she does not actually yield morally. Her subsequent moral corruption is all her own work. The Euripidean Heracles relies on Theseus to initiate his reconsideration of the meaning of his life.

THE AGENT'S MORALITY AND THE IMPLICIT MORALITY OF THE PLAY

As we have seen, the characters' morality is directed to self, family, state, and gods. If a specific agent satisfies the claims of all these entities in the best way possible in the circumstances, he or she is in harmony with the play's implicit morality unless conventional standards are undermined. (For example, in the case of *Orestes* we cannot flatly assert that the protagonist was right to kill his mother in accordance with the standards of the heroic world of *Choephori*, since Tyndareus argues that he should have prosecuted his mother in a court of law. Whether Tyndareus' objection is reasonable is another matter, but its existence complicates the question of the play's implicit morality.)

Aeschylus' Eteocles correctly discharges his moral responsibilities in the best way possible in all these areas. He is true to his self-conception as a brave warrior; the curse and his brother's behaviour prevent him from displaying conventional fraternal piety; he discharges his duty to the state in each of the seven appointments and his control of the chorus's panic; and, finally, there is nothing he can do to appease the gods. We can say then that he is in tune with the implicit morality of the play. Otherwise, we should have to endorse an alternative course of action. This is not to deny the appalling nature of fratricide; rather it is to recognize its unavoidability.

Agamemnon's case is not so clear-cut. The play seems to blame him, through the chorus, for killing his daughter while suggesting that he was (regardless of conscious intention) nevertheless fulfilling the will of Zeus. Orestes' declared motives show that he acts for himself, for the family (apart from its delinquent member, his mother), for the state, and for the Olympian gods, at least, whose moral and judicial dispensations triumphantly conclude the trilogy. Orestes operates in a morally and juridically imperfect world in which moral dilemmas such as his can arise, but this situation is finally corrected through the civic justice inaugurated in the final play.

Ajax exists not in a state, but in a heroic community in which the hierarchy of authority is none too clearly defined.[2] Nevertheless, his attitude to his peers whom he has made his enemies is antisocial and morally wrong. Odysseus, however, insists that Ajax be honoured for his former glorious services to this heroic community, even though he later turned against it. The play raises the issue of how great but uncontrollable and self-legislating men are to be incorporated into the state. Ajax neglects his immediate *philoi* in looking exclusively to the vindication of his own honour. Moreover, his arrogant independence offends the gods, but once he has been punished by Athena his relationship with her is at an end, though by his suicide it would seem that he unconsciously fulfils her desire for him. Ajax then is decidedly out of harmony with the moral world of the play, but he does much to redeem himself by leaving it, and after his death he is honoured in spite of everything.

The Heracles of *Trachiniae* is another great man who strongly resists integration into civilized society, though, paradoxically, his mighty services have

---

[2] Consider the different views of Menelaus and Teucer (*Aj.* 1052–104).

prepared the way for such societies. His Labours are overshadowed in the play by the escapade at Oechalia in which his barbarous and especially vindictive and lustful qualities are unpleasantly emphasized. Once we see the hero in person in a morally significant situation, his moral options are, like those of Aeschylus' Eteocles, reduced to one: whether to accept a situation bravely or otherwise. The gods appear to require nothing of him and there is no significant state or even community to provide a context for his death. We might be inclined to criticize his treatment of Hyllus (not to mention the innocent Lichas), but his unyielding demands of his son might appear justified when viewed in the light of their mysterious 'historical' purpose. At the end he remains, like Ajax, a great hero, though an exceedingly unattractive one. His wife Deianeira, on the other hand, subscribes to a completely conventional morality to which she returns after a short, but disastrous lapse.

Oedipus acts with the best possible moral will in all the relevant contexts—self, family, state, and gods—and he does all that could conceivably be required of him before and after the revelation. (His high-handed treatment of Teiresias and Creon leads to no serious consequences.) His predicament, however, is complicated by his existential status as a polluted wretch. In the eyes of the gods he is hateful and less than worthless simply because of his identity, but we, the audience, are invited to admire his fine qualities, particularly at the end.

The Sophoclean Electra in her persecution of her mother and Aegisthus acts in her own interest, in that of the state, and in harmony at least with Apollo's purpose even if the god is concerned with Orestes rather than with her. While Electra's campaign against her mother is undeniably unattractive, her moral commitment to it is never seriously questioned by any other character, and the gods are presented as coming out in support of Orestes' revenge. In contrast, Philoctetes' heroic morality of implacable hostility to enemies is clearly shown, by the arguments of Neoptolemus and Heracles, to be inadequate in the play's terms.

Medea's 'morality' is of course implicitly condemned by the play. No other character approves of the palace murders or the filicide (though some might have approved of Jason being punished in another way), and Medea herself comes to realize that she is driven by her irrational *thumos*.

Hecuba's punishment of Polymestor is prefaced by her appeal to Agamemnon for official justice in harmony with universal Nomos. But because there is no normal state and Agamemnon is not the man to risk his own position in order to vindicate a principle, Hecuba has to proceed in her own way, and the result, though undeniably ugly, is preferable, in ancient eyes at least, to leaving the miscreant unpunished.

Hippolytus is, as we have seen, a morally unusual case. Since he credits himself with innate *sōphrosunē*, which he understands as chastity, honesty, and simplicity, he is convinced that his dealings with others must be unfailingly righteous. He does not realize that his prudery produces an undesirable lack of compassion, though he corrects this insensitivity to some degree after the catastrophe in his limited pity for Phaedra and his forgiveness of his father. The play, through the medium of the other characters, seems basically to approve of him, though more than his depiction rationally allows. Phaedra intends to be a conventionally good woman, but the god-sent passion is too much for her and she descends to the calumniation of her stepson, of which the play obviously disapproves. There is no significant political dimension.

Heracles' Labours evince his strong commitment to the human race, and more particularly to the Greeks, the Thebans, and his own family. He overthrows a tyrant, Lycus, but that is only incidentally a political act since his primary purpose is to save his family. He is also at first committed to the gods in upholding their worship and honour (Eur. *Her.* 853). Later Zeus deserts him and allows Hera to attack. Heracles therefore rejects the gods and sees himself as living more or less under the rule of Tyche. The play encourages this view since Theseus does not dispute his friend's new theology and it takes up a theme introduced in the suppliant scene by Amphitryon. Conventional *philia* morality, an important theme, is strongly reinforced when Heracles' rehabilitation so clearly depends on the ministrations of Theseus.

Conventional morality generally goes unquestioned in tragedy with the exception of the injunction to harm enemies, though even that is presented as morally necessary in some contexts (e.g. in *Choephori* and Sophocles' *Electra*). The agents, however, often encounter very unconventional situations, but their strong self-concepts (where these apply) combined with their passionate adherence to conventional morality ensure a clear way through. (Even Sophocles' Electra's stance is, as we have seen, morally conventional, though not for a woman.) Except for some obvious cases, the plays for the most part implicitly approve of the agents' choices, but this does not guarantee a happy ending, and doing the right thing may only mitigate suffering because the conditions of life (as embodied in the divine will) are unfair: Eteocles, Orestes, and Oedipus, for example, all act correctly, but within constricted circumstances in which suffering is unavoidable.

MORAL AWARENESS

Moral awareness relates to the sophistication of the situation to be understood and to the often corresponding sophistication of the characters. First prize here must go, somewhat controversially, to Sophocles' Electra. Her situation is the most sophisticatedly conceived of any in the plays. There is no externally imposed crisis and no dilemma calling for a decision which reveals a simple role-defined character trait. Electra recognizes a moral requirement that is not role-defined. In fact her sister argues that her role requires her to remain morally quiescent. Her position is, moreover, complicated by several strands of feeling. First of all, though she is prey to no moral doubts about her campaign, she is emotionally uncomfortable with it because it involves harming someone (her mother) who should in normal circumstances be a friend/relative, and she realizes that harming enemies who were once friends, though morally required in this case, is emotionally (though not morally) destructive of the person doing the harm. This infects her feelings about herself. She knows that her behaviour is unattractive and violates conventional morality, or would do so in a normal situation. But she is clearly aware too that all this is morally irrelevant. Still her emotions are not entirely at odds with her morality. She loved her father and continues to mourn for him, and she hates his killers. Thus her moral feelings are fuelled, but not corrupted by, a deeply instinctive love (as she sees it) and her passionate wrath. This synergy of love, anger, and morality is, in the Greek world, altogether appropriate. Finally, Electra is the one character in these plays who is prepared to examine her own motives in public to the point of admitting their problematic aspects. She does not of course alter her convictions, but, unlike the unconciliatory Antigone, she does go so far as to ask the chorus to try to understand her.

Ajax also reflects on his moral convictions and betrays a certain uneasiness with them. But this uneasiness is born of external pressure, the emotional appeal and arguments of Tecmessa. At first he recognizes a moral responsibility to himself to restore his honour, and his thoughts are at that time directed to the manner of this restoration. All other moral responsibilities are simply ignored, and at the conclusion of Tecmessa's speech Ajax states bluntly that she should mind her own business. Later, however, in the deception speech he comes, if not to recognize, at least to feel the emotional force of her claims. His response to this is not to open up the whole moral issue for reconsideration, but to hurry to the business of restoring his honour by suicide. He begins to realize that he has misunderstood the social and indeed the cosmic context in which his moral deliberations have taken place, but he opts to ignore the world order rather than abandon his morality, which of course his suicide enables him to do. The perspective afforded us by the post-suicide scenes makes the moral inadequacy of Ajax clear, though the sophistication of the treatment remains in the form of a character who to some extent revisits his earlier moral thinking and finds himself on the brink of a major revision should he continue to live.

Neoptolemus begins the play with a limited moral awareness which is a function of his self-definition in terms of two of his father's famous qualities. He allows this awareness to become submerged, but it eventually forces itself back into his consciousness. His implicit morality all the while develops through the influence of Philoctetes, even if he never actually redefines himself morally.

Sophocles' Deianeira provides another case of moral reflection and development. At first she is not even primarily concerned to act morally. Ultimately, her moral integrity is of supreme importance to her, but initially her concern is to recover Heracles' love (as she understands it) and her honourable position as his wife. While she is not unconcerned about the moral implications of using the salve, morality is not in the forefront of her mind. Instead she hopes that the moral issues can be safely glossed over, and in this she surrenders her judgement for a while to the chorus who, she hopes, will tell her what she wants to hear—that employing the salve would be morally acceptable and practically safe. Deianeira would hate to be branded an evil, interfering wife, but she thinks the risk is worth taking if the salve is likely to work. In short, we see a subtle form of self-deception. Once the truth emerges, though, the moral fog entirely dissipates.

Phaedra, by contrast, proceeds morally in the opposite direction. We know that Aphrodite is bent on her destruction, but by a cruel irony Phaedra has also undermined her own moral resistance by one of her moral strategies (starving herself to death). Her concern with honour is her undoing. The nurse persuades her to reveal the nature of the *nosos* on the ground that the resistance she is putting up can only be admired if people know precisely in what it consists. Once the truth is out Phaedra becomes even more vulnerable to the Nurse, but when the latter precipitates the catastrophe by her distorted disclosures to Hippolytus,

Phaedra's preoccupation with sheer reputation induces her to represent her lethal incrimination of the young man as teaching him a lesson.

Among our moral agents the women are of particular interest because they eschew conventionally feminine responses, and that forces them to innovate. Many of the men are warriors whose morality is a simple adherence to the harsher aspects of the heroic code. Ajax is a partial exception in that he is prepared to acknowledge the influence of a woman's interpretation of heroic morality—one that emphasizes the gentler virtues. Deianeira, as we have seen, puts herself at odds with conventional female morality, but her act is still wrong by much wider moral standards. Sophocles' Electra, on the other hand, chooses to forge her own morality, and she does this to some extent, but not entirely, on the basis of male heroic values. Her situation is distinctly feminine; she cannot at first envisage killing her victims herself, hence her prolonged and emotionally self-destructive campaign. Morally, this is unknown territory, and it facilitates her complex analysis of her feelings.

Euripides' Medea displays a moral complexity of a different kind. She too decides that there exists a morally and emotionally unendurable situation in which she is morally obliged to act—though in her case solely in her own interests. We are encouraged initially to expect nothing moral, but rather some barbarous act motivated by emotional overreaction. But as Medea becomes more rational (indeed impressively so) we begin to see her situation more in moral terms. We never lose entirely though a sense of her utter ruthlessness, and the hypocrisy of moral posturing on the part of a woman who has already killed out of immoral self-interest and misplaced erotic devotion. On embracing the filicide as the ultimate revenge, Medea claims to be espousing the principles of the heroic code—loyalty to friends, harm to enemies. But this is grotesquely incompatible with filicide, so that her 'morality' collapses into a rationalization of sheer vengefulness on the part of a generally immoral woman. In the Great Monologue at first the emotional (but not the moral) implications of filicide take hold of Medea, while she remains 'morally' (as she sees it) committed to it. By the end she is bleakly aware that her *thumos*, with or without moral justification, is driving her revenge contrary to her overall interests. A similar realization, albeit after the act, comes to Euripides' Electra who, like Medea and unlike her Sophoclean counterpart, has not properly distinguished her vengeful feelings from her moral responsibilities. This is why her own emotional reaction to the matricide takes her completely by surprise.

Eteocles, Agamemnon, and Orestes are all Aeschylean characters but their degrees of awareness differ considerably. How does this happen in the context of Aeschylus' universe in which the individual is largely defined by membership in a family and thus by the theology of inherited roles and situations? One answer is that their situations produce different possibilities. Eteocles is essentially aware of the curse and its implications throughout the play, though it is not always in the forefront of his mind. His full awareness comes with Polyneices at the seventh gate. Agamemnon, on the other hand, is not presented as conscious of the workings of a family curse. Indeed, the curse plays a less prominent role in this play, so that there is nothing specific for Agamemnon to anticipate as a result of sacrificing or failing to sacrifice his daughter. (Of course, he can and does generally anticipate disaster either way.) He might conceivably anticipate trouble from Clytemnestra, but it is not obvious that she would resort to murdering him. He knows that Artemis has made the sacrifice a prerequisite for the voyage to Troy, and he should know that Zeus Xenios might reasonably desire the sack of that city, but he can have none of the justified certainty which Eteocles possesses. Awareness here then is inevitably impeded by the uncertainties inherent in the situation. The audience can foresee Agamemnon's murder because they know the myth, but they could not reliably or infallibly foresee it purely on the basis of the theology of the play conveyed obliquely through the odes and the accompanying imagery (that the gods are watchful of mass killers and of those who 'trample', or that lion cubs grow up like their parents).

However, the obliqueness of the theology is not enough to excuse Agamemnon. While Eteocles' orientation is always specifically moral, as is strikingly conveyed to us throughout the shield scene, Agamemnon is more influenced by other considerations. At Aulis the terms of his debate involve moral considerations but they are not formally moral. To be sure, Agamemnon has a choice, which again complicates his situation. But he does not apply any standard of selection; he cannot *contemplate* desertion, and that is all. Above all, he ends the debate with a pathetic hope that all will be well, as if he is knowingly suppressing the truth. This tendency to suppression re-emerges more strikingly in the carpet scene where he allows a moral conviction to be overridden by a desire. It is not that he is fully aware but chooses to walk on the fabrics; rather he suppresses his awareness almost wilfully.

Orestes' awareness is very much a function of his role and situation by which he is overwhelmingly defined. In a nutshell, he is required to do Apollo's will, so the best attitude for him to adopt is complete conformity, as Pylades reminds him. As it happens, there is much to be said for the god's position. It chimes well with Orestes' morally legitimate, though role-determined, motives. Orestes would seem though to be insensitive to the implications of matricide through the earlier scenes. But this is less 'psychological' than dramaturgical. Aeschylus wants all the forces of the play and its characters to be behind Orestes, and he manipulates our sympathies accordingly. At the crisis Orestes is morally aware of the *aidōs* required of a son, but he is saved the need to think through the relative moral claims by his *amoral* awareness that he cannot disobey Apollo. Thus situation and role together reduce the need for moral awareness. The extent to which he has been a vehicle of Olympian designs emerges clearly in the final play of the trilogy.

While Aeschylus' characters are defined almost exclusively by role and situa-tion, Sophoclean characters are more individually conceived. Ajax defines himself not only as a warrior (which is his role), but as the greatest surviving warrior at Troy. But this self-definition turns out to involve a major misconception about his relationship with the divine. Thus Sophoclean characters are up against the universe more generally and as individuals. Moreover, instead of facing a dilemma with two prescribed options they face a situation which they choose to interpret as presenting a moral challenge. They intuit immediately what they see as morally required though they may have to debate the practicalities. (Deianeira is an exception. Her response is not essentially moral, though her partly suppressed moral feelings eventually assert themselves.) Their moral intuitions are then, however, exposed to criticism from others, but they can debate and defend their positions with varying degrees of validity. They may also be exposed to resistance from their own emotions, but they always remain morally on track, whether or not their moral judgements are correct in the play's terms. Of the Sophoclean characters analysed, Heracles shows the least awareness. He does not see the link between his character and his *nosos*, nor does he apply his moral virtue (courage) in a morally complex situation or receive any input from other characters. Indeed, his predicament unavoidably so confines him that his simple courage is really his only option. At the other extreme is Electra who responds morally to a situation that others, such as her sister, would ignore. She intuits an appropriate course of action, defends it against both sympathetic and hostile disagreement, is herself aware of the emotional tensions it produces, and admits that there is a price to be paid. Oedipus' situation, on the other hand, is unique in that he is revealed as a being for whom normal, rational moral responses seem impossible or irrelevant.

References

ABRAHAMSON, E. L. (1952), 'Euripides' Tragedy of Hecuba', *TAPA* 83: 120–9.

ADAMSON, J., FREADMAN, R., and PARKER, D. (1998), *Renegotiating Ethics in Literature, Philosophy, and Theory* (Cambridge).

ADKINS, A. W. H. (1966), 'Basic Greek Values in Euripides' *Hecuba* and *Hercules Furens*', *CQ* NS 16: 192–219.

——(1982), 'Values, Goals, and Emotions in the *Iliad*' *CP* 77: 292–326.

ARROWSMITH, W. (1956), 'Introduction to *Heracles*', in D. Grene and R. Lattimore (eds.), *The Complete Greek Tragedies. Euripides II* (Chicago) 44–59.

AVERY, H. C. (1965), 'Heracles, Philoctetes, Neoptolemus', *Hermes* 93: 279–97.

——(1968), 'My tongue swore, but my mind is unsworn', *TAPA* 99: 19–35.

BAIN, D. (1993), 'A Misunderstood Scene in Sophokles, *Oidipous* (*O.T.* 300–462)', in McAuslan and Walcot, 81–92.

BARLOW, S. (1971), *The Imagery of Euripides* (London).

——(1981), 'Sophocles' Ajax and Euripides' Heracles', *Ramus* 10: 112–28.

——(1982), 'Structure and Dramatic Realism in Euripides' *Heracles*', *G&R* 29: 115–25.

——(1989), 'Stereotype and Reversal in Euripides' *Medea*', *G&R* 36: 158–71.

——(ed.) (1996), *Euripides: Heracles* (Warminster).

BARRETT, W. S. (1964), *Euripides: Hippolytos* (Oxford).

BELFIORE, E. (1993–4), '*Xenia* in Sophocles' *Philoctetes*', *CJ* 89: 113–29.

——(2000), *Murder Among Friends: Violation of* Philia *in Greek Tragedy* (Oxford).

BEYE, C. R. (1970), 'Sophocles' *Philoctetes* and the Homeric Embassy', *TAPA* 101: 63–75.

BIGGS, P. (1966), 'The Disease Theme in Sophocles' *Ajax, Philoctetes* and *Trachiniae*', *CP* 61: 223–35.

BLAIKLOCK, E. M. (1952), *The Male Characters of Euripides* (Wellington).

BLOMQVIST, J. (1982), 'Human and Divine Action in Euripides' *Hippolytus*', *Hermes* 110: 398–414.

BLONDELL, R. (1999), 'Introduction to *Medea*', in R. Blondell, M.-K. Gamel, N. S. Rabinowitz, and B. Zweig (eds.), *Women on the Edge: Four Plays by Euripides* (New York), 149–68.

BLOOM, H. (ed.) (1988), *Sophocles'* Oedipus Rex (New York).

BLUNDELL, M. W. (1988), 'The *phusis* of Neoptolemus in Sophocles' *Philoctetes*' *GR* 35: 137–48.

——(1989), *Helping Friends and Harming Enemies* (Cambridge).

BOEDEKER, D. (1991), 'Euripides' Medea and the Vanity of *Logoi*', *CP* 86: 95–112.

BOND, G. W. (1982), *Euripides: Heracles* (Oxford).

BOSTOCK, D. (2000), *Aristotle's Ethics* (London).

BRADSHAW, D. J. (1991), 'The Ajax Myth and the Polis: Old Values and New', in Pozzi and Wickersham, 99–125.

BROADIE, S., and ROWE, C. (2002), *Aristotle: Nicomachean Ethics* (Oxford).

BROWN, A. L. (1977), 'Eteocles and the Chorus in the *Seven against Thebes*', *Phoenix* 31: 300–17.

BURIAN, P. (ed.) (1985), *Directions in Euripidean Criticism* (Duke, NC).

BURNETT, A. P. (1970), 'Pentheus and Dionysus: Host and Guest', *CP* 65: 15–29.

——(1971), *Catastrophe Survived: Euripides' Plays of Mixed Reversal* (Oxford).

——(1998), *Revenge in Attic and Later Tragedy* (Berkeley and Los Angeles).

BUTTREY, T. V. (1958), 'Accident and Design in Euripides' *Medea*', *AJP* 79: 1–17.

BUXTON, R. G. A. (1982), *Persuasion in Greek Tragedy: A Study of* Peitho (Cambridge).

BUXTON, R. G. A. (1996), 'What Can you Rely on in *Oedipus Rex*', in Silk, 38–48.

CAIRNS, D. L. (1991), 'Shaming Friends: Sophocles' *Electra*', *Prudentia* 23: 19–30.

—— (1993), AIDOS: *The Psychology and Ethics of Honour and Shame in Ancient Greek Literature* (Oxford).

—— (2005), 'Values', in Gregory, 305–20.

—— (forthcoming), 'Divine and Human Action in the *Oedipus Tyrannus*', in Cairns and Lurie.

—— and LURIE, M. (forthcoming), *Tragedy and Archaic Greek Thought* (Swansea).

CARAWAN, E. (2000), 'Deianira's Guilt', *TAPA* 130: 189–237.

CHALK, H. H. O. (1962), '*Arete* and *Bia* in Euripides' *Herakles*', *JHS* 82: 7–18.

COHEN, D. (1993), 'The Theodicy of Aeschylus: Justice and Tyranny in the *Oresteia*', in McAuslan and Walcot, 45–57.

COLLARD, C. (1991), *Euripides:* Hecuba (Warminster).

COLLINGE, N. E. (1962), 'Medea *ex machina*', *CP* 57: 170–2.

CONACHER, D. J. (1967), *Euripidean Drama* (London).

—— (1987), *Aeschylus'* Oresteia: *A Literary Commentary* (Toronto).

—— (1997), 'Sophocles' *Trachiniae*: Some Observations', *AJP* 118: 21–34.

COREY, D., and EUBANKS, C. (2003), 'Private and Public Virtue in Euripides' *Hecuba*', *Interpretation* 30: 223–49.

CRANE, G. (1990), 'Ajax, the Unexpected, and the Deception Speech', *CP* 85: 89–101.

CROPP, M. J. (ed.) (1988), *Euripides:* Electra (Warminster).

—— FANTHAM, E., and SCULLY, S. (eds.) (1986), *Greek Tragedy and its Legacy: Essays Presented to D. J. Conacher* (Calgary).

CUNNINGHAM, M. P. (1954), 'Medea *apo mechanes*', *CP* 49: 151–60.

DAITZ, S. G. (1971), 'Concepts of Freedom and Slavery in Euripides' *Hecuba*', *Hermes* 99: 217–26.

DAVIDSON, J. F. (1985), 'Sophoclean Dramaturgy and the Ajax Burial Debates', *Ramus* 14: 16–29.

DEICHGRÄBER, K. (1935), 'Die Kadmos-Teiresiasszene in Euripides' *Bakchen*', *Hermes* 70: 322–49.

DENNISTON, J. D., and PAGE, D. L. (1957), *Aeschylus:* Agamemnon (Oxford).

DESCH, W. (1986), 'Die Herakles des Euripides und die Götter', *Philologus* 130: 8–23.

DILLER, H. (1966), 'thumos de kreisson ton emon bouleumaton' [Gk], *Hermes* 94: 267–75.

—— (1983), 'Euripides' Final Phase: the *Bacchae*', in E. Segal (ed.), 357–69, 447–9. (Translated from 'Die Bakchen und ihre Stellung im Spätwerk des Euripides', *Akad. Mainz* 5 (1955), 453–71.

DIMOCK, G. E. (1977), 'Euripides' *Hippolytus*, or virtue rewarded', *YClS* 25: 239–58.

DODDS, E. R. (1929), 'Euripides the Irrationalist', *CR* 43: 97–104.

—— (1950), *The Greeks and the Irrational* (Berkeley).

—— (1960), *Euripides*: Bacchae. 2nd edn. (Oxford).

—— (1988), 'On Misunderstanding the *Oedipus Rex*', in Bloom, 35–47.

DOVER, K. J. (1973), 'Some Neglected Aspects of Agamemnon's Dilemma', *JHS* 93: 58–69.

—— (1974), *Greek Popular Morality in the Time of Plato and Aristotle* (Oxford).

EASTERLING, P. E. (1973), 'Presentation of Character in Aeschylus', *G&R* 20: 3–19.

—— (1977), 'The Infanticide in Euripides' *Medea*', *YCS* 25: 177–91.

—— (ed.) (1982), *Sophocles:* Trachiniae (Cambridge).

—— (1997), 'Constructing the Heroic', in Pelling, 21–37.

ERBSE, H. (1993), 'Sophokles über die geistliche Blindheit der Menschen', *ICS* 28: 57–71.

EUBEN, J. P. (ed.) (1986), *Greek Tragedy and Political Theory* (Berkeley and Los Angeles).

EWANS, M. (1975), 'Agamemnon at Aulis: A Study in the *Oresteia*', *Ramus* 4: 17–32.

FAGLES, R. (1984), *Sophocles: The Three Theban Plays* (Harmondsworth).

FARAONE, C. A. (1994), 'Deianira's Mistake and the Demise of Heracles: Erotic Magic in Sophocles' *Trachiniae*', *Helios* 21: 115–35.

FINKELBERG, M. (1998), '*Timē* and *Aretē* in Homer', *CQ* 48: 14–28.

FISCHER, J. M., and RAVIZZA, M. (eds.) (1993), *Perspectives on Moral Responsibility* (Ithaca, NY).

FISHER, R. K. (1992), 'The "Palace Miracles" in Euripides' *Bacchae*. A Reconsideration', *AJP* 113: 179–88.

FITZGERALD, G. J. (1973), 'Misconception, Hypocrisy, and the Structure of Euripides' *Hippolytus*', *Ramus* 2: 20–40.

——(1991), 'The Euripidean Heracles: an Intellectual and a Coward?' *Mnemosyne* 44: 85–95.

FOLEY, H. P. (1985), *Ritual Irony: Poetry and Sacrifice in Euripides* (Ithaca, NY).

——(2001), *Female Acts in Greek Tragedy* (Princeton, NJ).

FRAENKEL, E. (1950), *Aeschylus*: Agamemnon. 3 vols. (Oxford).

GAGARIN, M. (1976), *Aeschylean Drama* (Berkeley, Calif.).

——(1987), 'Morality in Homer', *CP* 82: 285–306.

GALIS, L. (1992), 'Medea's Metamorphosis', *Eranos* 90: 65–81.

GANTZ, T. (1982), 'Inherited Guilt in Aeschylus', *CJ* 78: 1–23.

GARTON, C. (1972), *Personal Aspects of the Roman Theatre* (Toronto).

GARVIE, A. F. (ed.) (1986), *Aeschylus*: Choephori (Oxford).

——(1998) (ed.), *Sophocles*: Ajax (Warminster).

GELLIE, G. H. (1972), *Sophocles: A Reading* (Melbourne).

——(1980), '*Hecuba* and Tragedy', *Antichthon* 14: 30–44.

——(1981), 'Tragedy and Euripides' *Electra*', *BICS* 28: 1–12.

——(1988), 'The Character of Medea', *BICS* 35: 15–22.

GELLRICH, M. W. (1984), 'Aristotle's *Poetics* and the Problem of Tragic Conflict', *Ramus* 13: 155–69.

GERT, B. (1998), *Morality: Its Nature and Justification* (New York).

GIBERT, J. (1995), *Change of Mind in Greek Tragedy*. Hypomnemata 108 (Göttingen).

——(1997), 'Euripides' *Hippolytus* Plays: Which Came First?' *CQ* 47: 85–97.

GILL, C. (1980), 'Bow, Oracle, and Epiphany in Sophocles' *Philoctetes*' *GR* 27: 137–46.

——(1983), 'Did Chrysippus understand Medea?', *Phronesis* 28: 136–49.

——(1990*a*), 'The Character–Personality Distinction', in Pelling, 1–31.

——(1990*b*), 'The Articulation of the Self in Euripides' *Hippolytus*', in Powell, 76–107.

——(1996), *Personality in Greek Epic, Tragedy, and Philosophy* (Oxford).

GLANNON, W. (2002), *The Mental Basis of Responsibility* (Aldershot).

GOLD, B. K. (1977), '*Eukosmia* in Euripides' *Bacchae*', *AJP* 98: 3–15.

GOLDBERG, S. L. (1993), *Agents and Lives. Moral Thinking in Literature* (Cambridge).

GOLDHILL, S. D. (1986), *Reading Greek Tragedy* (Cambridge).

——(1990), 'Character and Action, Representation and Reading: Greek Tragedy and its Critics', in Pelling, 100–127.

——(2000), 'Civic Ideology and the Problem of Difference: The Politics of Aeschylean Tragedy, Once Again', *JHS* 120: 34–56.

GOULD, J. (2001), *Myth, Ritual, Memory, and Exchange: Essays in Greek Literature and Culture* (Oxford).

GREENE, W. C. (1944), *Moira: Fate, Good and Evil in Greek Thought* (Cambridge, Mass.).

GREENWOOD, L. H. G. (1953), *Aspects of Euripidean Tragedy* (Cambridge).

GREGORY, J. (1977), 'Euripides' *Heracles*', in *YClS* 25: 259–75.

——(1985), 'Some Aspects of Seeing in Euripides' *Bacchae*', *GR* 32: 23–31.

——(1991), *Euripides and the Instruction of the Athenians* (Ann Arbor, Mich.).

——(1995), 'The Encounter at the Crossroads in Sophocles' *Oedipus Tyrannus*', *JHS* 115: 141–6.

GREGORY, J. (1999), *Euripides:* Hecuba (Atlanta).

—— (2005), (ed.) *A Companion to Greek Tragedy* (London).

GRIFFIN, D. R. (1983), 'Relativism, Divine Causation, and Biblical Theology', in Thomas 117–36.

GRIFFIN, J. (1990), 'Characterization in Euripides: *Hippolytus* and *Iphigenia in Aulis*', in Pelling, 128–49.

GRIFFITH, M. (2005), 'Authority Figures', in Gregory, 333–51.

—— and MASTRONARDE, D. J. (eds.) (1990), *The Cabinet of the Muses: Essays on Classical and Comparative Literature in Honor of Thomas J. Rosenmeyer* (Atlanta).

GRIFFITH, R. D. (1992), 'Asserting Eternal Providence: Theodicy in Sophocles' *Oedipus the King'*, *ICS* 17: 193–211.

GRIFFITHS, E. M. (2002), 'Euripides' *Herakles* and the Pursuit of Immortality', *Mnemosyne* 55: 641–56.

—— (2006), *Euripides:* Heracles (London).

GRUBE, G. M. A. (1961), *The Drama of Euripides.* 2nd edn. (London).

GUTHRIE, W. K. C. (1971), *The Sophists* (Cambridge).

HALL, E. (1989), *Inventing the Barbarian: Greek Self-Definition through Tragedy* (Oxford).

—— (2010), *Greek Tragedy. Suffering under the Sun* (Oxford).

—— and HARROP, S. (eds.) (2010), *Theorising Performance: Greek Drama, Cultural History and Critical Practice* (London).

HALLERAN, M. R. (1986), 'Rhetoric, Irony and the Ending of Euripides' *Herakles'*, *CA* 5: 171–81.

—— (1991), '*Gamos* and Destruction in Euripides' *Hippolytus'*, *TAPA* 121: 109–21.

HALLIWELL, S. (1986), *Aristotle's* Poetics (London).

—— (1990), 'Traditional Greek Conceptions of Character', in Pelling, 32–59.

—— (ed. and tr.) (1995), Aristotle: *Poetics* (Cambridge Mass.).

Hammond, N .G. L. (1965), 'Personal Freedom and its Limitations in the *Oresteia'*, *JHS* 85: 42–55.

HARRIS, W. V. (2001), *Restraining Rage: The Ideology of Anger Control in Classical Antiquity* (Cambridge, Mass.).

HAWKINS, A. H. (1999), 'Ethical Tragedy and Sophocles' *Philoctetes'* *CW* 92: 337–57.

HEATH, M. (1987), *The Poetics of Greek Tragedy* (London).

HELM, J. J. (2004), 'Aeschylus' Genealogy of Morals', *TAPA* 134: 23–54.

HERINGTON, J. (1986), *Aeschylus* (New Haven, Conn.).

HESTER, D. A. (1979), 'The Heroic Distemper', *Prometheus* 5: 241–55.

HORSLEY, G. H. R. (1980), 'Apollo in Sophocles' *Electra'*, *Antichthon* 14: 18–29.

HUBBARD, T. K. (2003), 'The Architecture of Sophocles' *Ajax'*, *Hermes* 131: 158–71.

HUTCHINSON, G. O. (ed.) (1985), *Aeschylus:* Septem contra Thebas (Oxford).

IRWIN, T. H. (1988), 'Socrates and the Tragic Hero', in Pucci, 55–83.

JACKSON, E. (1988), 'The Argument of *Septem contra Thebas*, *Phoenix* 42: 287–303.

JOHNSON, P (2004), *Moral Philosophers and the Novel* (Basingstoke).

JONES. J. (1962), *On Aristotle and Greek Tragedy* (London).

KALKE, C. M. (1985), 'The Making of a Thyrsus: The Transformation of Pentheus in Euripides' *Bacchae'*, *AJP* 106: 23–31.

KAMERBEEK, J. C. (1966), 'Unity and Meaning of Euripides' *Heracles'*, *Mnemosyne* 19: 1–16.

—— (1970), *The Plays of Sophocles: Commentaries*, ii. The Trachiniae (Leiden).

KANE, R. L. (1975), 'Prophecy and Perception in the *Oedipus Rex'*, *TAPA* 105: 189–208.

—— (1988), 'The Structure of Sophocles' *Trachiniae*: "Diptych" or "Trilogy"?', *Phoenix* 42: 198–211.

KELLS, J. H. (ed.) (1973), *Sophocles:* Electra (Cambridge).

KIRKPATRICK, F. G. (1983), 'Understanding an Act of God', in Thomas, 163–80.

KIRKWOOD, G. M. (1947), 'Hecuba and *Nomos*', *TAPA* 78: 61–8.
——(1958), *A Study of Sophoclean Drama* (Ithaca, NY).
——(1969), 'Eteocles *oiakostrophos*', *Phoenix* 23: 9–25.
——(1994), 'Persuasion and Allusion in Sophocles' *Philoctetes*', *Hermes* 122: 425–36.
KITTO, H. D. F. (1956), *Form and Meaning in Drama* (London).
——(1958), *Sophocles: Dramatist and Philosopher* (Oxford).
——(1961), *Greek Tragedy: A Literary Study*. 2nd edn. (London).
KITZINGER, R. (1991), 'Why Mourning Becomes Elektra', *ClassAnt* 10: 298–327.
KNOX, B. M. W. (1957), *Oedipus at Thebes* (New Haven, Conn.).
——(1966), *The Heroic Temper: Studies in Sophoclean Tragedy* (Berkeley and Los Angeles).
——(1977), 'The *Medea* of Euripides', *YCS* 25: 193–225.
——(1979a), 'The *Ajax* of Sophocles', in *Word and Action: Essays on the Ancient Theatre* (Baltimore), 125–60. (Repr. from *HSCP* 65 (1961).)
——(1979b), 'The *Hippolytus* of Euripides', in *Word and Action: Essays on the Ancient Theatre* (Baltimore), 205–30. (Repr. from *YCS* 13 (1952).)
——(1984), 'Introduction' (to *Oedipus the King*) in Fagles, 131–51.
KÖHNKEN, A. (1972), 'Götterrahmen und menschliches Handeln in Euripides' *Hippolytos*', *Hermes* 100: 179–90.
KONSTAN, D. (1999), 'The Tragic Emotions', *Comparative Drama* 33: 1–21.
KOVACS, D. (1986), 'On Medea's Great Monologue', *CQ* 36: 343–52.
——(1987), *The Heroic Muse: Studies in the* Hippolytus *and the* Hecuba *of Euripides* (Baltimore).
——(1993), 'Zeus in Euripides' *Medea*', 114: 45–70.
KROEKER, E. (1938), 'Der Herakles des Euripides' (Diss. Leipzig).
KUPPERMAN, J. (1991), *Character* (New York).
LANDFESTER, M. (1990), 'Über Sinn und Sinnlosigkeit menschlichen Leids in den Tragödien Sophokles', *A&A* 36: 53–66.
LATTIMORE, R. (1964), *Story Patterns in Greek Tragedy* (London).
LAWRENCE, S. E. (1976), 'Artemis in the *Agamemnon*', *AJP* 97: 97–110.
——(1978), 'The Dramatic Epistemology of Sophocles' *Trachiniae*', *Phoenix* 32: 288–304.
——(2003), 'Moral Decisions in Homer', *Scholia*, NS 12: 27–33.
——(2008), 'Apollo and his Purpose in Sophocles' *OT*', *Studia Humaniora Tartuensia* 9.A.2: 1–18.
——(2010), 'Stoic Morality and Polyxena's 'Free' Death in Euripides' *Hecuba*', *AC* 53: 21–32.
LEBECK, A. (1971), *The Oresteia* (Cambridge, Mass.).
LESKY, A. (1961), 'Eteokles in den *Sieben gegen Theben*', *WS* 74: 5–17.
——(1965), *Greek Tragedy*, tr. H. A. Frankfort (London).
——(1966a), 'Decision and Responsibility in the Tragedy of Aeschylus', *JHS* 86: 78–85.
——(1966b), *A History of Greek Literature*, tr. J. Willis and C. de Heer (London).
LETTERS, F. J. H. (1953), *The Life and Work of Sophocles* (London).
LLOYD, M. (1986), 'Realism and Character in Euripides' *Electra*', *Phoenix* 40: 1–19.
——(1992), *The Agon in Euripides* (Oxford).
——(2005), *Sophocles: Electra* (London).
LLOYD-JONES, H. (1962), 'The Guilt of Agamemnon', *CQ* 12: 187–99.
——(1980), 'Euripides, *Medea* 1056–80', *Wue Jbb* NS 6: 51–9.
——(1994) *Sophocles*. 2 vols. (Cambridge, Mass.).
LUCAS, D. W. (1959), *The Greek Tragic Poets*. 3rd edn. (London).
LUSCHNIG, C. A. E. (1976), 'Euripides' *Hecabe*: The Time is out of Joint', *CJ* 71: 227–34.
——(1980), 'Men and Gods in Euripides' *Hippolytus*', *Ramus* 9: 89–100.
MCAUSLAN, I., and WALCOT, P. (eds.) (1993), *Greek Tragedy*. Greece and Rome Studies 2 (Oxford).

McCall, M. (1972), 'The *Trachiniae*: Structure, Focus, and Heracles', *AJP* 93: 142–63.

McConnell, T. C. (1996), 'Moral Residues and Dilemmas', in Mason, 36–47.

McDermott, E. A. (1989), *Euripides' Medea. The Incarnation of Disorder* (University Park, Pa.).

—— (2000), 'Euripides' Second Thoughts', *TAPA* 130: 231–59.

McGinty, P. (1978), 'Dionysos's Revenge and the Validation of the Hellenic World-View', *Harvard Theological Review* 71: 77–94.

McHardy (2008), *Revenge in Athenian Culture* (London).

MacLeod, L. (2001), *Dolos and Dike in Sophokles' Elektra* (Boston).

March, J. R. (1991–3), 'Sophocles' *Ajax*: The Death and Burial of a Hero', *BICS* 38: 1–36.

—— (ed.) (2001), *Sophocles:* Electra (Warminster).

Mason, H. E. (ed.) (1996), *Moral Dilemmas and Moral Theory* (New York).

Mastronarde, D. J. (1986), 'The Optimistic Rationalist in Euripides: Theseus, Jocasta, Oedipus', in Cropp, Fantham, and Scully.

—— (ed.) (2002), *Euripides:* Medea (Cambridge).

—— (1999–2000), 'Euripidean Tragedy and Genre: The Terminology and its Problems', *ICS* 24–5: 23–39.

—— (2005), 'The Gods', in Gregory, 321–32.

Meier, C. (1993), *The Political Art of Greek Tragedy*, trans. A. Webber (Cambridge).

Meridor, R. (1978), 'Hecuba's Revenge', *AJP* 99: 28–35.

Michelini, A. N. (1987), *Euripides and the Tragic Tradition* (Madison, Wis.).

—— (1999–2000), 'The Expansion of Myth in Late Euripides', *ICS* 24–5: 41–57.

Mikalson, J. D. (1983), *Athenian Popular Religion* (Chapel Hill, NC).

Mills, S. (2002), Euripides: *Hippolytus* (London).

Minadeo, R. (1967), 'Plot, Theme and Meaning in Sophocles' *Electra*', *Class. et Med.* 28: 114–42.

Morwood, J. (ed. and trans.) (1998), *Euripides:* Medea *and Other Plays* (Oxford).

Mossman, J. M. (1995), *Wild Justice: A Study of Euripides'* Hecuba (Oxford).

—— (2001), 'Women's Speech in Greek Tragedy: The Case of Electra and Clytemnestra in Euripides' *Electra*', *CQ* 51: 374–84.

Nappa, C. (1994), '*Agamemnon* 717–36: The Parable of the Lion Cub', *Mnemosyne* 47: 82–7.

Nielsen, R. M. (1978), 'Sophocles' *Ajax*: A Matter of Judgment', *Antichthon* 12: 18–27.

North, H. (1966), *Sophrosyne. Self-Knowledge and Self-Restraint in Greek Literature* (Ithaca, NY).

Nussbaum, M. C. (1986), *The Fragility of Goodness* (Cambridge).

O'Brien, M. J. (1964), 'Orestes and the Gorgon: Euripides' *Electra*', *AJP* 85: 17–18.

Otis, B. (1960), 'The Unity of the *Seven against Thebes*', *GRBS* 3: 153–74.

Padel, R. (1981), 'Madness in Fifth-Century Athenian Tragedy', in P. Heelas and A. Lock (eds.), *Indigenous Psychologies: The Anthropology of the Self* (London), pp. 105–31.

—— (1992), *In and Out of the Mind. Greek Images of the Tragic Self* (Princeton).

—— (1995), *Whom Gods Destroy: Elements of Greek and Tragic Madness* (Princeton, NJ).

Page, D. L. (1938), *Euripides:* Medea (Oxford).

Papadopoulou, T. (2001*a*), 'Revenge in Euripides' *Heracles*', in F. Budelmann and P. Michelakis (eds.), *Homer, Tragedy and Beyond* (London), 113–28.

—— (2001*b*), 'The Prophetic Figure in Euripides' *Phoenissae* and *Bacchae*', *Hermes* 129: 21–31.

Parker, L. P. E. (2001), 'Where is Phaedra?' *GR* 48: 45–52.

—— (2005), Heracles *and Euripidean Tragedy* (Cambridge).

Parker, R. C. T. (1983), *Miasma: Pollution and Purification in Early Greek Religion* (Oxford).

—— (1997), 'Gods Cruel and Kind: Tragic and Civic Theology', in Pelling, 143–60.

PELLING, C. B. R. (1990) (ed.), *Characterization and Individuality in Greek Literature* (Oxford).

—— (1997) (ed.), *Greek Tragedy and the Historian* (Oxford).

—— (2005), 'Tragedy, Rhetoric, and Performance Culture', in Gregory (2005), 83–102.

PERADOTTO, J. J. (1969), 'The Omen of the Eagles and the *ethos* of Agamemnon', *Phoenix* 23: 237–63.

PODLECKI, A. J. (1964), 'The Character of Eteocles in Aeschylus' *Septem*', *TAPA* 95: 283–99.

POHLENZ, M. (1954), *Die Griechische Tragödie* (Göttingen).

POWELL, A. (1990), *Euripides, Women, and Sexuality* (London).

POZZI, D. C., and WICKERSHAM, J. M. (eds.) (1991), *Myth and the Polis* (Ithaca, NY).

PUCCI, P. (1988), *Language and the Tragic Hero: Essays on Greek Tragedy in Honor of Gordon M. Kirkwood* (Atlanta).

RABINOWITZ, N. S. (1986), 'Aphrodite and the Audience: Engendering the Reader', *Arethusa* 19: 171–83.

RECKFORD, K. J. (1974), 'Phaedra and Pasiphae: The Pull Backward,' *TAPA* 104: 307–28.

—— (1985), 'Concepts of Demoralization in the *Hecuba*', in Burian, 112–28.

REHM, R. (1989), '*Medea* and the Logos of the Heroic', *Eranos* 87: 97–115.

—— (1999–2000), 'The Play of Space: Before, Behind, and Beyond in Euripides' *Heracles*', *ICS* 24–5: 363–75.

REINHARDT, K. (1979), *Sophocles*, tr. H. and D. Harvey (Oxford).

REVERDIN, O. (ed.) (1960). *Euripide*. Entretiens sur l'antiquité classique 6 (Vandœuvres-Geneva).

RICKERT, G. A. (1987), 'Akrasia and Euripides' *Medea*', *HSCP* 91: 91–117.

RINGER, M. (1998), *Electra and the Empty Urn: Metatheater and Role Playing in Sophocles* (Chapel Hill, NC).

ROBERTS, D. H. (1988), 'Sophoclean Endings: Another Story', *Arethusa* 21: 177–94.

—— (1989), 'Different Stories: Sophoclean Narrative(s) in the *Philoctetes*' *TAPA* 119: 161–76.

ROHDICH, H. (1968), *Die Euripideische Tragödie* (Heidelberg).

ROISMAN, H. M. (1988), 'Oedipus' Curse in Aeschylus' *Septem*', *Eranos* 86: 77–84.

RORTY, A. O. (ed.) (1992a), *Essays on Aristotle's Poetics* (Princeton, NJ).

—— (1992b), 'The Psychology of Aristotelian Tragedy', in Rorty (1992a) 1–22.

ROSE, A. R. (1982), 'The Significance of the Nurse's Speech in Aeschylus's *Choephoroe*', *CB* 58: 49–50.

ROSENMEYER, T. G. (1968), '*Tragedy and Religion: The* Bacchae', in E. Segal, 370–89.

—— (1982), *The Art of Aeschylus* (Berkeley and Los Angeles).

SCHEIN, S. (1990), '*Philia* in Euripides' *Medea*', in Griffith and Mastronarde, 57–73.

SCHLESINGER, E. (1968), 'On Euripides' *Medea*', in E. Segal, (ed.), 70–89.

SCHWARTZ, J. D. (1986), 'Human Action and Political Action in *Oedipus Tyrannos*', in Euben; 183–209.

SCODEL, R. (1984), *Sophocles* (Boston).

—— (1998), 'The Captive's Dilemma: Sexual Acquiescence in Euripides' *Hecuba* and *Troades*', *HSCP* 98: 137–54.

SCOTT, M. (1979), 'Pity and Pathos in Homer' *AC* 22: 1–14.

SEAFORD, R. (1997), *Euripides*: Bacchae (Warminster).

SEALE, D. (1982), *Vision and Stagecraft in Sophocles* (London).

SEGAL, C. (1966), 'The *Electra* of Sophocles', *TAPA* 97: 473–545.

—— (1970), 'Shame and Purity in Euripides' *Hippolytus*', *Hermes* 98: 278–99.

—— (1977), 'Philoctetes and the Imperishable Piety', *Hermes* 105: 133–58.

—— (1981), *Tragedy and Civilization: An Interpretation of Sophocles* (Cambridge, Mass.).

—— (1982), *Dionysiac Poetics and Euripides'* Bacchae (Princeton, NJ).

—— (1985), 'The Bacchae as Metatragedy', in Burian, 156–73.

SEGAL, C. (1988), 'The Music of the Sphinx: The Problem of Language in *Oedipus Tyrannus*', in Bloom, 127–42.

——(1999–2000), 'Lament and Recognition: A Reconsideration of the Ending of the *Bacchae*', *ICS* 24–5: 273–91.

——(2001), Oedipus Tyrannus: *Tragic Heroism and the Limits of Knowledge* (2nd edn.) (New York).

SEGAL, E. (ed.) (1968), *Euripides: A Collection of Critical Essays* (Englewood Cliffs, NJ).

——(1983), *Oxford Readings in Greek Tragedy* (Oxford).

SEIDENSTICKER, B. (1978), 'Comic Elements in Euripides' *Bacchae*', *AJP* 99: 303–20.

SEWELL-RUTTER, N. J. (2007), *Guilt by Descent: Moral Inheritance and Decision Making in Greek Tragedy* (Oxford).

SHELTON, J.-A. (1979), 'Structural Unity and Meaning of Euripides' *Herakles*', *Eranos* 77: 101–10.

SHEPPARD, J. T. (1927), '*Electra*: A Defence of Sophocles', *CR* 41: 2–9.

SHERMAN, S. (1992), '*Hamartia* and Virtue', in Rorty (1992*a*) 177–96.

SIEGEL, H. (1981), 'Agamemnon in Euripides' *Iphigenia at Aulis*', *Hermes* 109: 257–65.

SILK, M. S. (1993), 'Heracles and Greek Tragedy', in McAuslan and Walcot, 116–37.

——(ed.) (1996), *Tragedy and the Tragic: Greek Theatre and Beyond* (Oxford).

SIMPSON, M. (1969), 'Sophocles' Ajax: His Madness and Transformation', *Arethusa* 2: 88–103.

——(1971), 'Why Does Agamemnon Yield?', *Parola del Passato* 137: 94–101.

SINNOT-ARMSTRONG, W. (1996), 'Moral Dilemmas and Rights', in Mason, 48–65.

SNELL, B. (1928), *Aischylos und das Handeln im Drama* (Leipzig).

——(1953), *The Discovery of the Mind*, tr. T. G. Rosenmeyer (Cambridge, Mass.).

SOLMSEN, F. (1937), 'The Erinys in Aischylos' *Septem*', *TAPA* 68: 197–220.

SOMMERSTEIN, A. H. (1980), 'Artemis in *Agamemnon*: A Postscript', *AJP* 101: 165–9.

——(1989), *Aeschylean Tragedy* (Bari).

——(1997), 'Alternative Scenarios in Sophocles' *Electra*', *Prometheus* 23: 193–214.

——(2008), *Aeschylus*, 3 vols. (Cambridge, Mass.).

——(forthcoming), '*Ate* in Aeschylus'.

SORUM, C. E. (1986), 'Sophocles' *Ajax* in Context', *CW* 79: 361–77.

STANFORD, W. B. (ed.) (1963), *Sophocles*: Ajax (London).

STANTON, G. R. (1987), 'The End of Medea's Monologue: Euripides, *Medea* 1078–80', *RhM* 130: 97–106.

——(1995), 'Aristocratic Obligation in Euripides' *Hekabe*', *Mnemosyne* 48: 11–33.

STEPHENS, J. C. (1995), 'The Wound of Philoctetes', *Mnemosyne* 48: 153–68.

STEVENS, P. T. (1978), 'Sophocles: *Electra*, Doom or Triumph?', *G&R* 25: 111–20.

STINTON, T. C. W. (1975), '*Hamartia* in Aristotle and Greek Tragedy', *CQ* 25: 221–54. (Repr. (1990), in *Collected Papers on Greek Tragedy* (Oxford).)

SZLEZAK, T. A. (1981), 'Sophokles' *Elektra* und das Problem des ironischen Dramas', *Museum Helveticum* 38: 1–21.

TAPLIN, O. (1978), *Greek Tragedy in Action* (London).

TESSITORE, A. (2003), 'Justice, Politics and Piety in Sophocles' *Philoctetes*', *Review of Politics* 65: 61–88.

THOMAS, O. C. (ed.) (1983), *God's Activity in the World: The Contemporary Problem* (Chico, Calif.).

TYLER, J. (1974), 'Sophocles' *Ajax* and Sophoclean Plot Construction', *AJP* 95: 24–42.

VELLACOTT, P. (1979–80), 'Aeschylus' *Seven Against Thebes*', *CW* 73: 211–19.

——(1984), 'Aeschylus' Orestes', *CW* 77: 145–57.

VELLEMAN, J. D. (1992), 'What Happens When Someone Acts?', *Mind* 101: 461–81.

VERNANT, J-P., and VIDAL-NAQUET, P. (1981), *Tragedy and Myth in Ancient Greece* (Brighton).

References 329

—— (1988), 'Ambiguity and Reversal: On the Enigmatic Structure of *Oedipus Rex*', in Bloom, 103–26.

VERRALL, A. W. (1895), *Euripides the Rationalist* (Cambridge).

—— (1905), *Essays on Four Plays of Euripides* (Cambridge).

—— (1910), *The Bacchants of Euripides and Other Essays* (1910).

VICKERS, B. (1973), *Towards Greek Tragedy* (London).

WHITMAN, C. H. (1951), *Sophocles: A Study of Heroic Humanism* (Cambridge, Mass.).

WILDBERG, D. (1999–2000), 'Piety as Service, Epiphany as Reciprocity: Two Observations on the Religious Meaning of the Gods in Euripides', *ICS* 24–5: 235–56.

WILLIAMS, B. (1993), *Shame and Necessity* (Berkeley).

WINKLER, J. J., and ZEITLIN, F. I. (eds.) (1990), *Nothing to do with Dionysos: Athenian Drama in its Social Context* (Princeton NJ).

WINNINGTON-INGRAM, R. P. (1948), *Euripides and Dionysus* (Cambridge).

—— (1960), 'Hippolytus: A Study in Causation', in Reverdin, 169–97.

—— (1980), *Sophocles: An Interpretation* (Cambridge).

—— (1983), *Studies in Aeschylus* (Cambridge).

WOLFF, C. (1965), 'The Design and Myth in Euripides' *Ion*', *HSCPh* 69: 169–94.

WOODARD, T. (ed.) (1966), *Sophocles* (Englewood Cliffs, NJ).

YOSHITAKE, S. (1994), 'Disgrace, Grief and Other Ills: Herakles' Rejection of Suicide', *JHS* 114: 135–53.

ZANKER, G. (1992), 'Sophocles' *Ajax* and the Heroic Values of the *Iliad*', *CQ* 42: 20–5.

—— (1994), *The Heart of Achilles: Characterization and Personal Ethics in the* Iliad (Ann Arbor).

ZEITLIN, F. I. (1965), 'The Motif of the Corrupted Sacrifice in Aeschylus' *Oresteia*', *TAPA* 96: 463–508.

ZÜRCHER, W. (1947), *Die Darstellung des Menschen im Drama des Euripides* (Basle).

Index